GLOBALISATION AND GOVERNANCE
IN THE PACIFIC ISLANDS

GLOBALISATION AND GOVERNANCE
IN THE PACIFIC ISLANDS

Editor: STEWART FIRTH

State, Society and Governance in Melanesia Program
Studies in State and Society in the Pacific, No. 1

E PRESS

Published by ANU E Press
The Australian National University
Canberra ACT 0200, Australia
Email: anuepress@anu.edu.au
Web: http://epress.anu.edu.au

National Library of Australia
Cataloguing-in-Publication entry

Globalisation and governance in the Pacific Islands.

Bibliography.
ISBN 1 920942 97 1 (pbk)
ISBN 1 920942 98 X (online)

1. Globalization - Oceania - Congresses. 2. Oceania - Politics and government - Congresses. I. Firth, Stewart, 1944- . II. State Society and Governance in Melanesia Project.

320.995

All rights reserved. No part of this publication may be reproduced, stored in a retrieval system or transmitted in any form or by any means, electronic, mechanical, photocopying or otherwise, without the prior permission of the publisher.

Cover design by Teresa Prowse

This edition © 2006 ANU E Press

Table of Contents

Acknowledgements	vii
Introduction	1
1. Keynote Address — From Neo-Liberalism to the New Medievalism *John Rapley*	7
2. Treading Water in Rapids? Non-Governmental Organisations and Resistance to Neo-Liberalism in Pacific Island States *Claire Slatter*	23
3. Regionalism and Cultural Identity: Putting the Pacific back into the plan *Elise Huffer*	43

LABOUR MIGRATION

4. Migration, Dependency and Inequality in the Pacific: Old Wine in Bigger Bottles? (Part 1) *John Connell*	59
5. Migration, Dependency and Inequality in the Pacific: Old Wine in Bigger Bottles? (Part 2) *John Connell*	81
6. Globalisation, New Labour Migration and Development in Fiji *Manoranjan Mohanty*	107
7. 'Tonga Only Wants Our Money': The children of Tongan migrants *Helen Lee*	121
8. Labour Mobility in the Pacific: Creating seasonal work programs in Australia *Nic Maclellan and Peter Mares*	137
9. Contemporary Migration Within the Pacific Islands: The case of Fijian skilled workers in Kiribati and Marshall Islands *Avelina Rokoduru*	173

SUGAR AND GARMENTS

10. Fiji: Sugar and sweatshirts, migrants and remittances *Kate Hannan*	189
11. End of the Line? Globalisation and Fiji's Garment Industry *Donovan Storey*	217

CORPORATE AND STATE GOVERNANCE IN MINING AND FORESTRY

12. Global Capital and Local Ownership in Solomon Islands' Forestry Industry *Tarcisius Tara Kabutaulaka*	239
13. Mining, Social Change and Corporate Social Responsibility: Drawing lines in the Papua New Guinea mud *Glenn Banks*	259
14. The 'Resource Curse' and Governance: A Papua New Guinean perspective *Mel Togolo*	275

TRADITION, CULTURE AND POLITICS

15. Keynote Address — Governance in Fiji: The interplay between indigenous tradition, culture and politics *Ratu Joni Madraiwiwi* — 289

16. The State of the State in Fiji: Some failings in the periphery *Vijay Naidu* — 297

17. Power Sharing in Fiji and New Caledonia *Jon Fraenkel* — 317

18. More Than 20 Years of Political Stability in Samoa under the Human Rights Protection Party *Asofou So'o* — 349

19. Matai Titles and Modern Corruption in Samoa: Costs, expectations and consequences for families and society *A. Morgan Tuimaleali'ifano* — 363

MEDIA, CIVIL SOCIETY AND DEMOCRACY

20. Keynote Address — Keeping the Information Flow Open: A key condition for good government in Micronesia *Father Francis X. Hezel* — 375

21. Governance, Globalisation and the PNG Media: A survival dilemma *Joe R. Kanekane* — 385

22. Democracy in Papua New Guinea: Challenges from a rights-based approach *Orovu Sepoe* — 399

23. Governance and Livelihood Realities in Solomon Islands *Morgan Wairiu* — 409

LIST OF CONTRIBUTORS — 417

INDEX — 423

Acknowledgements

Editing a collection of conference papers is a joint endeavour. I would like to extend my sincere thanks to the following people for their valued assistance: David Hegarty of the State, Society and Governance in Melanesia Project at the ANU invited me to organise the conference on which this book is based and gave me the opportunity to edit the papers. Hank Nelson and Peter King offered excellent critical advice. Jan Borrie copy-edited with a keen eye. Sue Rider, with endless efficiency, supported the project administratively. Ben Marwick gave vital technical assistance and Duncan Beard arranged final design and publication by ANU E Press. Like all editors, I owe most to the contributors who wrote the chapters and whose book it truly is.

Introduction

Stewart Firth

The State, Society and Governance in Melanesia Project at the Australian National University organised a conference on globalisation and governance in the Pacific Islands in October 2005, and this volume brings together the papers delivered by the participants, who came from Papua New Guinea (PNG), Solomon Islands, Fiji, Samoa, the Federated States of Micronesia (FSM), Hawai'i, New Zealand and Jamaica as well as from within Australia. The conference, held in Old Canberra House over three days, was generously supported by funding from the Australian Government through AusAID.

The aim of the conference was twofold.

First, we sought to explore the impact of globalising processes in the South Pacific on regional economies and political systems. We wanted to know more about the effect of free trade on industries such as sugar and garments in Fiji, the consequences of ever-increasing labour migration from Samoa, Tonga, Fiji and other Island countries and the continuing repercussions of mining and forestry in PNG and Solomon Islands. As the Hon. Tuilaepa Aiono Sailele Malielegaoi, Prime Minister of Samoa, has said, 'We now live in a so-called globalised world and our efforts to reduce or adapt to its negative impacts will continue to test our resilience. What is clear is that globalisation, even if it does deal an unfair hand to small island economies, is here to stay' (AusAID, *Pacific 2020: Challenges and Opportunities for Growth*, Canberra 2006: 60). Given the political conversation in the Pacific Islands about globalisation, we want to hear all voices on the issue, critical and otherwise.

Second, we wanted to revisit key issues in the debate about good governance, such as the role of culture and tradition in Pacific politics and the importance of a free media. And we sought to examine the state of play in governance in different parts of the region, in particular PNG, Solomon Islands, the FSM, Fiji and Samoa.

Our first theme, then, is globalisation.

In one sense globalisation is not new and has affected the Pacific Islands since outsiders first ventured there over two centuries ago. Globalisation in another sense is a phenomenon of the past quarter-century or so. The new globalisation can be described as accelerated incorporation into the global economy under neo-liberal conditions, a process characterised by constantly intensifying economic exchanges across national borders, a communications revolution that continues to shrink the globe, and the worldwide shift by governments to neo-liberal economic policies intended to make this globalising process possible.

In the modern context, then, globalisation has become synonymous with neo-liberalism in economics.

Pacific Island governments and regional institutions have embraced the conventional wisdom that economic reform and globalisation are good for the region. Heavily dependent on globalising aid donors, they could hardly do otherwise. From 1997 the governments of the Pacific Islands Forum, which brings together the independent countries of the region, began sending representatives to annual meetings of economic ministers — the so-called Forum Economic Ministers' Meetings (FEMM) — who committed themselves to deregulating economic life, minimising subsidies, privatising government enterprises, assisting foreign investment, improving public accountability, reducing tariffs and moving towards complete free trade. The economic policies favoured by the Asian Development Bank (ADB), the World Bank, the World Trade Organisation (WTO) and the International Monetary Fund (IMF) became those now enunciated by Pacific Island countries whether they were directly connected to those institutions or not. Like much 'policy' that emanates from island governments, this commitment to reform was frequently rhetorical, designed to reassure donors that the region should continue to receive aid, and did not always lead to immediate change. But a process of gradual reform was set in train and has continued ever since.

Our second theme is governance.

There seems to be no argument against good governance. Who cannot be in favour of accountable, efficient, transparent and responsive government and public administration apart from those who benefit from the opposite? Yet we should remember that good governance is part of a wider globalising message preached by aid donors and international institutions, who see good governance as the best way to implement globalisation and the free market, and who rather like to place the blame for failure not on global institutions but on national shortcomings in the developing countries. And we should also reflect on the extent to which good governance depends on Western assumptions about individual interests and responsibilities and the virtues of democracy. That said, few Pacific Islanders would not want their leaders to be more honest and efficient, their services more reliable and their life chances more assured.

Before we proceed, we should remember that the life chances and economic opportunities of Pacific Islanders differ markedly from one part of the region to another for a number of reasons that go beyond globalisation and governance to culture and history.

One reason is political status. Territorial status and free association protect a minority of Pacific Islanders from the need to survive economically by themselves. The inhabitants of territories of metropolitan states such as Guam, the Northern Marianas and American Samoa (for the United States) and New

Caledonia, French Polynesia and Wallis and Futuna (for France) have easily the highest standards of living in the Pacific. Incorporated in one way or another into the advanced world, they are subsidised by foreign economies that have benefited from globalisation. People who live in countries that are freely associated with metropolitan states (Palau, the FSM and the Marshall Islands with the USA and the Cook Islands and Niue with New Zealand) also benefit from their connection with the rich world, above all by having the right to migrate to it, an opportunity that many have taken. The majority of Pacific Islanders who live in the nine independent Pacific Island countries (Fiji, Kiribati, Nauru, PNG, Samoa, Solomon Islands, Tonga, Tuvalu and Vanuatu) are on their own, with much lower standards of living and much less freedom to benefit from globalisation.

A second, related reason is differential access by citizens of independent Pacific states to labour markets outside the Pacific. Samoa and Tonga have been remittance economies since the early 1990s, and Fiji is increasingly becoming one, as their citizens migrate to New Zealand, Australia, Canada and the USA and spend time as foreign workers elsewhere in the Pacific and in the Middle East. Access to labour markets overseas is also available to people from Kiribati and Tuvalu, especially to men employed in the merchant marine, but is denied to all but a tiny proportion of people in the Melanesian west of the region that confronts the most serious economic problems.

A third set of reasons are historical, cultural and demographic. Solomon Islands, Vanuatu and PNG, which lie in the Melanesian culture area, rank considerably lower on the United Nations Human Development Index than Fiji and the Polynesian countries to the east. The outside world reached them later than their eastern neighbours — the PNG Highlands, for example, did not encounter modernity in any sustained way until after World War II — and they consist of hundreds of different identity groups thrown together by the experience of colonial rule but with little else to foster a sense of common national destiny. In Fiji, Samoa, Tonga, Tuvalu and Kiribati, by contrast, the modern nation-state is home to a majority population of Pacific Islanders speaking a single language, possessing a common sense of national identity and bound together by a culture of chieftainship and hierarchy that has adapted more readily to the demands of modern government than have the more egalitarian political cultures to the west. At the same time, population growth is significantly greater in Solomon Islands, Vanuatu and PNG than in Fiji, Samoa and Tonga. Where half the population has not reached adulthood, as is the case in Solomon Islands, Vanuatu and PNG, the challenge of increasing GDP per capita is correspondingly greater.

The book begins with globalisation, and with the global and regional context of economic policy. To place the Pacific Islands experience in the widest frame of reference, we invited John Rapley from the University of the West Indies in

Jamaica to open the conference. In the first of three keynote addresses, he offers an explanation of why, since the 1970s, neo-liberal economic doctrine favouring growth at the expense of equality has replaced Keynesianism as the policy fashion, and suggests where the rise in inequality might now lead us. Claire Slatter follows by placing the global movement against globalisation in its regional context, and arguing that civil society in the Pacific Islands needs to do more to influence the present direction of economic and trade policy. Her chapter is a critique of neo-liberal policy and non-governmental organisations. Elise Huffer focuses on the Pacific Plan adopted by the Pacific Islands Forum in 2005 as a route to regional integration. 'People are protected from the destructuring or disintegrating effects of the market in large part,' she argues, 'by their cultural values and practices, including emphasis on solidarity and reciprocity, attachment to land, and focus on obligations and duties to others.' She wants these values to be in the plan as originally promised.

Six chapters on labour migration follow. The first two, by John Connell, offer a detailed and comprehensive analysis of the state of migration in the Pacific Islands. Connell argues that remittances continue to have positive effects on island economies: MIRAB (Migration, Remittances, Aid and Bureaucracy) still works and is even being emulated, as in Fiji. Migration has 'deferred and mitigated, but not resolved' the region's problems of poverty and development, he believes, and the long term for migration might be less positive than the short term. Manoranjan Mohanty focuses on Fiji and its recent emergence as an economy benefiting considerably from remittances. Helen Lee examines Tonga, a classic MIRAB state, and contends that second-generation Tongans in Australia, with a diminishing sense of connection to the homeland, are far less likely than their parents to send money back to relatives. The one hope, she suggests, would be a change of Australian policy enabling Tongans to undertake seasonal work in Australia. Nic Maclellan and Peter Mares subject the whole issue of a seasonal work scheme for Pacific Islanders to detailed and careful scrutiny, comparing it with a Canadian scheme for the Caribbean and Mexico showing how it could work decisively in favour of Pacific Islanders and Australians. And Avelina Rokoduru alerts us to migration within the Pacific Islands, following Fijians who have found work in the Marshall Islands, and finding the reasons why they have gone there.

In the next section, on sugar and garments, Kate Hannan points to tough times ahead for Fiji's sugar and garment industries as they contend with the loss of special arrangements and the coming of free trade. Urbanisation in the Suva-Nausori corridor will intensify, she argues, and government will need to recognise and support the informal sector as people from the rural areas seek to survive in the city. At the same time, the new migration of labour from Fiji to the Middle East and elsewhere has pitfalls of its own, not least proposals to regulate, control and tax remittance income. Donovan Storey concentrates on

Fiji's garment industry in the wake of the end of the Multi Fibre Arrangement in 2005; he describes its history under more favourable arrangements, and predicts an uncertain future for this experiment in Pacific Islands' industrialisation.

Tarcisius Tara Kabutaulaka opens the discussion of corporate and state governance in the resource sector with a study of the interactions between global capital and local communities in the case of forestry in Solomon Islands. Solomon Islanders, he suggests, are not mere passive victims of logging companies, but are strategising and negotiating in order to benefit most from what is on offer. Glenn Banks develops the theme of interaction in his analysis of relations between the Porgera Joint Venture mine in the PNG Highlands and local communities, both landholders within the special mining lease and those beyond who also want benefits and rewards. His theme is the fine line that the company must walk to sustain the mine and the community at the same time. Mel Togolo argues against the 'resource curse' thesis in the case of PNG. The problem, he says, is not that companies are extracting minerals and petroleum but that governments are not maintaining good governance and sound national economic management.

The book then shifts gear from the economic to the political and from globalisation to governance, beginning with five chapters on the interaction of tradition, culture and politics.

Fiji's Vice-President, Ratu Joni Madraiwiwi, in the second keynote address to the conference, reminds us of the ineluctable facts of his country's history: 'Colonial rule, entrenchment of Fijian chiefly structures and the Indo-Fijian presence resulted in the evolution of communal politics grounded in notions of Fijian identity. In the transition to independence and subsequently, there was little recognition or understanding by Fijians of the full implications of democracy. The commitments made by Fijian decision-makers, in political settlements with other communities, were not necessarily shared by their people.' Fijian leaders, he says, need to develop a vision of their country that is 'inclusive and truly multicultural' if Fiji's potential is to be realised. Vijay Naidu subjects the State in Fiji to unsparing scrutiny, emphasising the deleterious effects of race politics, the domination of the Fijian chiefly class and the growth of poverty and inequality since 1987. Jon Fraenkel charts the unhappy history of the rigid power-sharing provisions of Fiji's 1997 Constitution and compares them with more flexible and successful arrangements in the French territory of New Caledonia. Asofou So'o asks why Samoa has been so stable politically for the past two decades, and finds the answer not only in Samoa's thoughtful blending of Western and indigenous political institutions, but in intelligent leadership in times of crisis and the pervasive influence of kin loyalties and the *fa'a Samoa* (the Samoan way). Morgan Tuimaleali'ifano, less positive about his country, recounts the case of a title installation ceremony in Samoa corrupted by money and greed.

In the third keynote address, Francis Hezel draws on 40 years' experience of living in Micronesia to introduce the topic of media, civil society and governance. Good governance, he points out, depends on people knowing what their governments are doing and therefore on an active free press. But traditions in Micronesia, as elsewhere in the Pacific, too often block the flow of information. People hoard knowledge as a possession and do not want it to damage the good personal relations on which small communities depend. Joe Kanekane shows that the PNG media has endeavoured to alert citizens to their rights and describes the PNG Media Council's war against corruption, but he concedes that the media is constrained, above all, by the need to make money. Orovu Sepoe calls for a rights-based approach to democracy in PNG, and sees potential for a better future in properly implementing the *Organic Law on the Integrity of Political Parties and Candidates* and limited preferential voting. Finally, Morgan Wairiu finds ordinary people to be marginalised by the modern system of government in Solomon Islands, and calls on his compatriots to seize the opportunity offered by the Regional Assistance Mission to Solomon Islands to construct governance that is more inclusive and that underpins people's livelihoods.

1. Keynote Address — From Neo-Liberalism to the New Medievalism

John Rapley

In the autumn of 1950, a young man, the son of refugees from Nazi Germany, enrolled in the economics program at the University of Chicago. Chicago's department of economics was an unusual place in those days. Ever since the publication of John Maynard Keynes' *General Theory* in 1936, Keynesian economics — with its stress on the use of state intervention to manage economic development — had become more or less orthodoxy. Chicago stood against this trend, becoming something of a refuge for neoclassical economists. Neoclassical economics, with its faith in free markets, minimalist government and the ability of mathematical models to explain human behaviour, ran against the then-dominant consensus in Western economics, which believed that state management could ensure an economic growth rate that benefited owners and workers alike. Neoclassical theory tended to take a less sunny view of economic management, believing that there were costs in economic efficiency to redistribution. Among its most famous exponents, a fierce critic of Keynes who would go on to win the Nobel Prize in economics, was Milton Friedman.

Professor Friedman did not take well to his new student, whose name was Andre Gunder Frank. The feeling, by all accounts, was mutual. Professor Friedman's belief in free markets and respect for individual liberty, initiative and responsibility was evangelical. Frank, though, found Friedman's economics odious, especially since it tolerated and even justified inequality. The rebellious young doctoral candidate called for an economics that privileged equity over efficiency. So tense were Frank's relations with his mentors that he was asked to leave the department, though he returned quietly in 1957 to finish his dissertation.

Friedman developed much warmer ties to a set of Frank's classmates. In the 1950s, the University of Chicago and Chile's Catholic University signed an exchange agreement, funded by the Ford and Rockefeller Foundations and USAID, which was designed to facilitate the process of what was called 'ideological transfer'. Under this agreement, Chicago economists flew to Santiago to teach, while Chilean graduates received fellowships to study at Chicago. There, many of them gravitated towards the so-called money workshop put on by Professor Friedman. They came to hold him in much greater esteem than Frank had ever managed. Back in Chile, they came to be known as the 'Chicago Boys', libertarian economists in a time when Chile was moving ever further into a state-led and ultimately socialist economy.

Frank's juxtaposition of equity and efficiency was, in fact, a fitting metaphor for the Cold War that was then being fought on many battlefields, Chile being but one. Arguably, from its earliest days at the start of the industrial age, what defined socialism had been its elevation of equality as a primary goal of human society. Not satisfied with the equality of rights that liberal theorists celebrated, socialists had always dreamed of creating a more equitable society in the allocation of resources. For economists, this created a difficult dilemma. It was long believed that inequality spurred savings and innovation, and gave people the restless appetite that drove work and accumulation. But if inequality was good for the economy, the lessons of 19th-century Europe showed that it could be bad for the polity. And an unstable political system, riven by conflicts between owners and workers, would eventually be bad for the economy.

For a while, Keynesian economics appeared to navigate a middle path between these two competing objectives — economic liberty and equality. Keynes had no particular love of socialism, and on the face of it did not concern himself with the matter of equity. Rather, his goal was to find a way to make capitalism more efficient. As it happened, though, that goal had the happy consequence of augmenting equity at the same time. Unlike the neoclassical economics that was still dominant in the Great Depression, Professor Keynes tended to see the operations of the demand side of economic equilibrium as most amenable to policy interventions. Thus, government policies that regulated demand could be used to manage the business cycle. In particular, fiscal policy, by redistributing wealth, could raise levels of demand and thereby prevent economies from sinking into recession.

The widespread adoption of Keynesian economic strategies in the West coincided with a rebound in economic growth that took hold about 1948, when the economic collapse occasioned by World War II bottomed out, and stability returned to Europe. The next quarter-century would see more or less continued economic expansion. So successful did Keynesianism seem to be that even conservative parties jettisoned their free-market thinking and warmed to the doctrine. Coinciding with the spread of demand management was the rapid expansion of welfare states in the West. In consequence, the age of the Keynesian welfare state did see income inequalities decline in the West. By the 1960s, the resultant perception — namely, that everyone was now a stakeholder in this system — led some scholars to speak of the end of ideology. Economists said recessions had been banished forever.

While income inequality declined in the industrial democracies, however, it remained greater than in the socialist economies. By 1948, of course, the socialist bloc had expanded quite dramatically from its early days after the Russian Revolution. Having liberated six East European countries from the Nazis, Moscow installed client regimes. In two other neighbouring countries — Albania and

Yugoslavia — indigenous rebellions against Nazi occupation had brought communists to power. China had been swept by revolution. Korea would soon follow. Vietnam was seething.

While each of these countries would tinker with the model of socialist development, fundamentally, they all built their experiments on the same core principles. Markets, seen as the field on which exploitation occurred, were more or less abolished. Central planners were to allocate resources according to a rational design that met political goals. In short, politics would rule economics: the economy was to operate according to rational design, and reoriented to meet human needs. Or so it was supposed. The long and short of it was that prices, and wages, were fixed by the government. In consequence, large — immense, in the Soviet case — and centralised bureaucracies were built to allocate resources.

Despite the intellectual fashion today, which is to dismiss the socialist experiments as failed deviants, they did make accomplishments. Scientific development, particularly in the Soviet Union, reached heights that belied the largely undeveloped status of the underlying economies. At least in the earlier decades, growth rates were strong, even spectacular, as was the case for Russia in the 1930s. China, meanwhile, performed favourably compared with India. Of course, some of this can be attributed to a forcible raising of the savings rate, which required harsh, and at times even brutal, tactics.

Perhaps the most significant achievement of the socialist economies was to make marked strides towards reducing inequality. The Marxist dream of building a classless society never came to pass. Nevertheless, the measures of income distribution like the Gini Coefficient indicated that socialist states generally created more equitable societies than did their capitalist counterparts. The administrative fixing of salaries and wages, and the regulation of prices, ensured that a society's output could be distributed in such a way as to maximise the gains for those on the lower rungs of the economic ladder.

This equality did not come without a price. Efficiency was sacrificed on the egalitarian altar. Bureaucratically dictated prices did not always reflect true conditions of demand and supply. Surpluses and scarcities coexisted. When goods were cheaply available, what typically resulted were excesses of demand. What then followed was rationing or — that ubiquitous feature of the Soviet economy — queueing. Importantly, while central planning was generally up to the task of managing any resource-allocation that could be measured quantitatively, it struggled badly when it came to qualitative transformations. Bureaucrats could, for example, determine how many shoes should be produced in any given year, and mobilise the resources necessary to the task. But when it came to improving the quality of those shoes, it was an entirely different matter. The popular fascination with the West that came to characterise Russian culture by the 1980s apparently had less to do with a love of democracy than a desire for fashionable clothing, catchy music and cameras that didn't require more than one person to operate.

It is not that socialism was technologically backwards; far from it. The Soviet Union was remarkable in having built a powerful military-scientific complex atop what was, in large measure, still a resource-dependent Third-World economy. But if they could produce scientists and engineers as innovative as the Americans or Japanese, why could they not produce a more dynamic economy? The genius of American triumph in the Cold War indeed seemed to lie in the market economy. When the Pentagon wanted new military technology, it bought from private contractors, whose interest was in gaining the sale by raising their product quality. Once the product was developed, they could maximise their returns by privatising the technology. This served the Pentagon well, because to the extent that the firm recouped its costs through private sales, the price to the military dropped. Much of the technology we take for granted in our daily lives began its existence on the drawing boards of US defence contractors. In the Soviet Union, by contrast, control of information by the military prevented much technology being turned to civilian uses. The result was that the Soviet Union's military-scientific complex ended up bankrupting the economy. By the 1980s, the country's economy was going nowhere, at the very time that citizen demands were beginning to multiply.

Chile provided a vivid illustration of these advantages and disadvantages of socialism. Its income distribution on the eve of Salvador Allende's overthrow provided evidence of the egalitarianism of the socialist experiment. But its economy was beset by inefficiencies that sank it into crisis. Income distribution bought by printing money led to runaway inflation. Low returns on capital inhibited investment. This further exacerbated supply shortages, thereby worsening inflation. Restive workers, dissatisfied with the pace of change in Chile, repeatedly shut down plants, worsening productivity. By 1973, the economy was struggling badly. With or without US intervention, covert sabotage and a corporate campaign to end the socialist experiment, the Chilean economy was almost certainly doomed to continued crisis. The military intervention succeeded in no small measure because it was toppling an edifice that had already been teetering for some time.

Did the Chilean experiment in socialism fail? The answer really depends on whom you ask. One of Allende's economic advisers was in fact Frank, who joined the legion of leftist intellectuals flocking into Chile at its time of euphoria. Given that he had called for an economics of equity over efficiency, he could rightly point to the Chilean experiment as a success in social justice that was undone by capitalist intransigence and foreign meddling.

But Frank was now a refugee once again, wandering the world looking for a new home. And the new wave of intellectuals flying into Chile took a different view. The Chicago Boys, many of whom stayed in exile during the Allende years, eagerly returned home. Once there, they quickly wormed their way into the junta that had been cobbled together to govern Chile. They then invited their old mentor, none other than Friedman, to fly in and lend his authority to their campaign to turn Chile from a socialist utopia into a neo-liberal one.

So radical a break with Chile's recent past did the Chicago Boys propose that Friedman, in a famous speech in Santiago, called it 'shock therapy'. The term would become almost mythical in the popular lexicon of the neo-liberal age. Friedman convinced his audience that a gradual approach to reforming the Chilean economy might well fail. The country had to make a radical break with its socialist past. Friedman so persuaded his audience, at the head of which sat the President, Augusto Pinochet, that within weeks his former students — the Chicago Boys — had taken over all the important economic ministries, as well as the Central Bank. Soon after Friedman flew back home to Chicago, the finance minister announced that the country would indeed begin its shock therapy.

From the late 1960s, governments had been experimenting with neoclassical policy remedies in various spheres of their economies. What made the Chilean experiment so bold was that it was, arguably, the first thoroughgoing neo-liberal transformation of a society. From top to bottom — via budget cuts, privatisations, mass lay-offs, deregulation, import liberalisation and the like — Chile reversed its socialist revolution. It was no simple task. Socialism had sunk deep roots in the country, and the junta decided to dig them right up and exterminate them. The process was brutal. And the economy struggled at first. But, by the 1980s, the painful restructuring had put the country back on a growth path.

One of Pinochet's earliest supporters had been a then little-known British politician named Margaret Thatcher. Recently elected as leader of Britain's Conservative Party, she heralded a whole new direction for Britain. Many wrote her off as hopelessly outside the mainstream of British politics. The traditional Toryism of her party accepted noblesse oblige as the price of a stratified society, and gradual decline as the inevitable future of a nation whose glories lay mostly in the past. Thatcher's commitment to individual liberty, responsibility and the entrepreneurial spirit made her an ideal neo-liberal. As she would always say, she gravitated to the thinking of Friedman, but only because his theories confirmed her deep-seated convictions.

About the same time Friedman was giving his Chilean lecture tour, Thatcher received a visit from an American. They had both heard of one another, but no more than that. When he paid his courtesy-call on his European tour, however, Ronald Reagan so engaged Thatcher that they struck up a friendship that would last the rest of his life.

Within four years, of course, just as Chile was turning its economic corner, Thatcher was moving into Downing Street. The next year, she was toasting Reagan's victory in the US presidential election. The neo-liberal age, sown in a Chilean revolution, was now going into full bloom. Britain went through its own shock therapy of union-busting, fiscal austerity and monetary tightening. And just as Thatcher took on the coal miners, President Reagan signalled his determination to end union power when he crushed a strike by American air traffic controllers.

The years that followed saw one Western country after another turn towards neo-liberalism. Most often, this was done without electoral shock waves. Sometimes, right-wing governments moved further right. Everywhere, left-wing parties began to leave behind their socialist heritage as they opted for a 'third way' or 'new middle'. Arguably, the last stand of Keynesianism in the developed world took place in France. The French had bucked the Thatcher-Reagan tide by electing an old-fashioned socialist, François Mitterrand, to the presidency in 1981. France, like Britain and the USA, was wrestling with a deep recession. But while the British and Americans were trying neo-liberal therapy, France opted for an old-fashioned treatment: a Keynesian reflation strategy based on a program of heavy government spending. It produced a tremendous fillip ... to German industry. The situation in France failed to improve and, in 1983, the French socialists threw up their hands and caved in to the neo-liberal revolution. It was, in the industrial world, the last great stand of Keynesian economics.

That same recession was, in all likelihood, the turning point across the world. Having been put on the agenda of the industrial democracies by disgruntled voters who had lost faith in Keynesian politicians, neo-liberalism would now be placed on the global agenda by the global economic slowdown. Why?

To understand, we need to back up a few years. In the same year that Allende was overthrown in Chile, 1973, the modern world experienced its first oil shock. Incidentally, this shock, by inducing a major recession in the industrial countries, brought an end to the 'golden age' of growth that had until then made Keynesianism seem so triumphant. The failure of governing elites to find a lasting response to the resultant economic crisis is what brought on the crisis of confidence in Keynesianism. In this context, neo-liberal politicians such as Thatcher found a receptive audience with their promise of new solutions to what was, apparently, a new problem.

Be that as it may, the effect of the oil shock was to flood the bank accounts of Persian Gulf governments with dollars (the currency used to settle oil contracts on world markets). This money was recirculated through the Western banking system, which meant the world's major banks now had more money than they knew what to do with. But because they were paying interest on those deposits, they had to find someone to borrow the money in a hurry. They found receptive clients in Third-World governments, who faced the opportunity of obtaining credit at bargain-basement prices. If, instead of locking into long-term rates, they opted for variable-rate loans, they could bring their real rates of interest down to zero. The lure was irresistible.

On the face of it, it was perfectly sensible. Problems arose only in 1979, when the Iranian Revolution sent the Shah into exile and withdrew Iranian oil from the world market. Prices again surged. Once more, the Western economies went into recession. But this time, rather than try to reflate their economies with Keynesian stimulus packages, Western governments opted for a different approach. After all, as evidenced by the British and American elections, they were starting to come under new management. Rather than tackle the slump in demand, they chose to target the surge of inflation. Choking off demand with tight monetary policies — which in practice meant high interest rates — became the order of the day.

Here, then, was the situation: the world economy was in recession as a result of the oil shock. Demand for primary exports suffered particularly badly, driving down commodity prices. Obviously, Third World countries suffered the most. But it got worse: having run up their debts after the first oil shock, they now had to pay them back at surging rates of interest. It got still worse: the high interest rates in the USA drove up demand for the dollar, as foreigners chased the high returns on US savings accounts. And since the loans had to be repaid in dollars, Third-World governments had to set aside even more of their own earnings to buy loans. It was a perfect storm: developing countries saw their revenues plunge just as their expenditures soared. The bank was going to bust.

That is why Third-World governments had no choice but to turn to the IMF and World Bank to beg assistance. And assistance came with strings attached. The IMF has always been a neo-liberal institution; that is its mandate. But the World Bank had only recently come under the influence of neo-liberalism, and that was because Reagan had placed one of his allies in its presidency when he came to office. The long and short of it is that, during the 1980s, governments across Africa and Latin America found themselves moving inexorably, reluctantly onto the neo-liberal road.

But the real high-water mark of neo-liberalism came, arguably, in the 1990s. That is when most of the Middle East began to adopt neo-liberal strategies. Very importantly, India, after a decade of piecemeal and largely symbolic reforms, shifted determinedly towards neo-liberalism. Democratisation in Latin America consolidated the neo-liberal drift. And importantly — very importantly — socialism fell.

In fact, socialism had been falling for a good while. In China, it had been doing so quietly since the mid-1970s. In the autumn of 1973, shortly after the overthrow of Allende, the Chinese Communist Party, following its own logic, rehabilitated

Deng Xiaoping after his exile of the Cultural Revolution. Deng embodied the pragmatism of the faction in the party that was concerned that mainland China was falling behind Taiwan and Hong Kong in the development race. If there was to be any hope of Beijing one day retaking control of her renegade province, she had to do better economically. Within a couple of years, economic reform was on Beijing's agenda. By the end of the decade — as it happened, about the same time that Thatcher came to office — China began her long, transformative experience with economic reform.

Elsewhere, socialism was struggling badly by the 1980s. Despite the occasional revolution here or there, socialism's apparent global advance had stalled. Nowhere were socialist economies particularly healthy, for the reasons discussed earlier. The Soviet Union tried its hand at reform in the 1980s, but the inept handling of the process did not provide a new impetus, as happened in China. Instead, the economy all but collapsed. In the process, Moscow signalled to her east European allies that she could no longer subsidise them. There followed the dramatic autumn of 1989, where one East European government after another collapsed. The message to the Soviet Union's remaining client states in the Third World was clear: you are on your own. Some, such as Vietnam, Mozambique and, eventually, Angola, pragmatically reformed. Others, such as Ethiopia, broke up, as abandoned old friends fled into exile.

Thus, by the 1990s, as US-trained economists flew into Warsaw and Moscow to advise governments on how to implement their own brands of shock therapy, neo-liberalism was pretty much the only game in town. First-World countries no longer had to fight communism. Now, they tailored their aid policies to push reluctant governments towards free markets. In the Pacific region, neo-liberalism made its first appearance, arguably, after the 1987 Fiji coup. As Stewart Firth has shown, however, policy changes in Australia (in 1994) and the European Union (in 1996) prodded governments to adopt neo-liberal reform packages if they wished to continue benefiting from aid arrangements. The last hold-outs to neo-liberalism were the East and South-East Asian countries. There, capitalist economies had been managed by interventionist states, a model dismissed by American policy-makers as 'crony capitalism'. But when this model went into crisis in 1997-98, a new set of governments found themselves having to approach the IMF for rescue packages. And the IMF, which at that moment depended on the US Treasury for its financing, ended up passing on the recommendations of the Treasury Department in its aid stipulations. And, despite the pro-poor rhetoric of the Clinton Administration, the Treasury Department at that time was pursuing an aggressive neo-liberal agenda. By the end of the 20th century, therefore, in a dramatic quarter-century, most of the world's countries had shifted from state-led development to free markets.

That is a whirlwind tour of the neo-liberal age. But why speak of it in the past tense? Is the neo-liberal age finished? Surely, to judge from the ubiquity of neo-liberalism, reports of its death would seem greatly exaggerated.

This is where the debate gets really interesting. On one side, neo-liberal triumphalists tell us that the world is flat and that neo-liberal globalisation is a force of nature that only Luddites dare resist. But, on the other hand, each time people of their ilk try to get together to celebrate their victory, they are dogged by thousands of protesters who say globalisation is dead. Who is right?

The correct answer probably lies somewhere in between. We have not entered a new age. We have, however, exited the old one, making this something of an interregnum. And I would suggest that the symbolic date on which the neo-liberal age ended was September 11, 2001, the date the command structure of history's most powerful empire was temporarily decapitated by a handful of men armed with box-cutters — conveniently, as it happens, also 28 years *to the day* after the overthrow of Salvador Allende.

To explain this cut-off point for the neo-liberal age, we need first to draw up a balance sheet of this period in history. The range of experience is vast, the issues complex, the data highly variable, mixed and often difficult to compare. Nevertheless, broadly speaking, one can arguably sum up the historical record by saying that, as a very general rule, neo-liberalism ushered in an age of faster growth, but rising inequality. Growth manifested itself most strongly in the 1990s, at least until the Asian Crisis of 1997-98. Obviously, not all countries benefited equally from neo-liberal reforms, but defenders of neo-liberalism can often fairly say that where reforms yielded sub-optimal results, it might have been because they were inadequately or improperly applied. Equally, critics of neo-liberalism often fail to give adequate attention to the problem of the counterfactual. Simply pointing to poor economic performance that coexists with neo-liberal reforms does not in itself indict neo-liberalism very strongly. In many countries, a plausible case can be made that economic performance was going to be bad, owing to pre-existing factors (themselves often the legacy of the sort of statist development policies sometimes held up as an alternative to neo-liberalism), and that what neo-liberal reforms succeeded in doing was arresting or at least mitigating contraction.

Arguably, therefore, the aggregate data acquit neo-liberalism on the count of failing to deliver growth. It is in translating that growth into an equitable distribution that neo-liberalism comes off badly. Once again, in painting on such a broad canvas, the perils of generalisation must be acknowledged. But there is now a good pool of anecdotal evidence, which appears to be corroborated by statistical surveys of the developed countries, which, taken together, make it reasonable to conclude that more often than not, neo-liberal reform has led to a widening of the income gap.

So, Friedman was right: the attempt to create egalitarian societies was bad for growth. But then, Frank was right as well: neo-liberalism's singleminded focus on growth was bad for equality. Which one matters more?

Again, the answer depends on whom you ask. Neo-liberals, who see individuals as essentially asocial and rational utility-maximisers, reckon that people use themselves as reference points. If that's the case, it follows that if we are richer this year than the last, we must therefore be happier. And since the aggregate data suggest that most of the planet's citizens are, in fact, richer than they were a generation ago, why all this apparent unhappiness with the neo-liberal age?

The answer might lie, at least in part, in social psychology. Humans, after all, are social animals. As a result, they are more likely to use not themselves, but their peer groups, as reference points. If you and your neighbour no longer need to ride the bus, but own your own cars, you might still not feel better off if your friend is driving a Lexus while you are stuck with a Corolla. Inequality thus matters. Indeed, while the subject remains controversial, there is a good body of evidence that suggests that in a situation of rising inequality, political instability will augment *even when* incomes are rising across the board.

But there is more to it than just that. This rise in inequality has occurred at the same time that the State has — so to speak — retreated. In truth, there are but a few countries where the State has actually reduced its share of total economic expenditure. In a couple of countries — Somalia comes readily to mind, as does Afghanistan — there is, for all intents and purposes, no longer a central government. But, by and large, reports of the death of the State have proved greatly exaggerated. The difficulty is that a stationary state is, in relative terms, a slowly retreating one. Nowhere is this more the case than in the Third World.

This is because of a phenomenon so tectonic, we scarcely notice it: urbanisation. In the history of humankind, few revolutions can match it in scale and impact. After spending millennia close to the land that provided them with their sustenance, humans began a massive migration to the cities. It started two centuries ago, and picked up speed in the 20th century when Third-World cities began growing at unprecedented rates. In the next generation, for the first time in history, more humans will live in cities than rural areas. The nation-state, which was built atop urban economies, expanded to provide the wide range of cities people once provided in their own communities. So, where public expenditure fails to keep up with the growth of cities, problems can arise as citizens begin to look for new political patrons.

One of the first warning signs of this came back in the 1970s. Iran's oil-rich economy was booming in the wake of the first oil shock. As it did so, Tehran exploded, going from what had once been a provincial backwater to a major world city. But despite its immense resources, the Government could not keep up with the basic demands of all these citizens for water, housing, roads and security. Into this breach stepped Islamist organisations, raising funds from charitable donations and creating a virtual state within a state. This provided the basis of operations for the very movements that would later bring down the Shah.

Today, in much of the Third World, we are seeing similar developments. The competition for resources is played out on a field whose traditional arbiter — the State — lacks the largesse needed to buy the loyalty of an ever-increasing number of players. As a result, on the sidelines, and sometimes even in the centre of the field, new huddles form as those who can 'deliver the goods' buy supporters.

Sometimes, as happened in Iran, this starts with legitimate groups. Islamic charities have played an important role in several Middle Eastern countries. Groups with less benign agendas, however, can often penetrate the networks established for legitimate purposes in order to pursue their own goals. An instance of this can be found in al Qaeda, the metonym for the amorphous global network of terrorist organisations that operates through legitimate channels of communication throughout the Muslim world.

Other times, the goals have illegitimate purposes from the start. Transnational criminal organisations have taken advantage of the explosion in demand for their services — drugs, money laundering, human trafficking. They have operated along the legitimate vectors of communication established in the global age, which thus made it easy to escape detection. They have sometimes formed opportunistic alliances with transnational terrorist organisations. And, in many cases, they have built up vast pools of resources. They have then used some of these to create virtual states within states in many Third-World cities (and sometimes in rural areas as well).

Where the State can no longer provide employment, build houses, pave roads or police the streets, or where the police are so woefully underpaid that they supplement their incomes from corruption, sometimes turning on the very citizens they are meant to protect, in such cases, private armies and mini-states might fill the vacuum left behind by a retreating state. A former senior officer in Jamaica's police force once said it well, when he lamented that the war on drugs that the USA wanted him to fight — and for which purpose it had then loaned him some helicopters — was 'unwinnable'. For in whole stretches of downtown Kingston, the children were being fed, clothed and schooled by drug money, and nobody was going to bite the hand that fed them. He knew who the gang members were, could arrest them all tonight and bring them before judges in the morning. But nobody would testify against them.

Indeed, in some Kingston communities, the Jamaican State is all but absent. Gunmen patrol the streets. There is a legal system, replete with 'courts' and even, in some cases, 'defence attorneys'. There is a rudimentary welfare system.

And it all works fairly well. So it goes in other Third-World cities, from Rio de Janeiro to Lagos.

The State has not, however, disappeared. State retreat is not the same as state failure. Ineffectual though they might have become at times, these countries still maintain armies, police forces, bureaucracies and court systems. When they have to, governments can send their troops in with force majeure, as Nigeria does periodically to discipline wayward regional movements. What results is a struggle over turf, one that sometimes becomes quite violent. And state agents end up having to cooperate with private agents, whether it is policemen negotiating with gunmen or politicians meeting with criminal leaders to try to work out peace deals.

So, we have neither a strong state nor anarchy. Instead, what is emerging in many Third World countries is a phenomenon sometimes called the new medievalism. This emergent form of political system is so-called because it is characterised by overlapping and multiple authorities. Sovereignty is now, at best, negotiated. Rather than mere decentralisation, what we are seeing is the emergence of autonomous political agents, equipped with their own resource bases, which make them resistant to a reimposition of centralised control, giving them the power they need to interpenetrate with the state.

With one or two possible exceptions — highly decentralised federations such as Canada and Belgium could conceivably slide into neo-medievalism at some point in the future, though neither scenario seems very likely — the new medievalism is essentially confined to the developing world. It is rural and urban. Large stretches of the Andes, of the tropical rainforest in the Democratic Republic of Congo, of the borderlands separating Pakistan from Afghanistan, and of Afghanistan itself, could be seen to be governed within neo-medieval frameworks. Perhaps the future of neo-medievalism lies within the burgeoning cities of the Third World; those which, as nodes integrated into the global economy, standing often in the vanguard of global trends, are most likely to intensify the thrust towards the new medievalism. Cities such as Rio de Janeiro, Kingston, Lagos, and Mexican cities on the US border — these and many others arguably have portions that have seceded from the nation-state without constituting themselves as independent entities.

These communities are more than just states within states. They represent a new kind of state. Moreover, given their implication in the global economy, and their linkages to global cities in the First World that serve as access points to the markets their criminal enterprises serve, they are injecting manifestations of their organisation into the rich countries. Thus, for instance, gang warfare or apparently random murders in Toronto or London that seem senseless and anarchic within the context of those societies take on a new, brutally rational meaning when analysed within the context of the activities of gangs back in

Jamaica or Nigeria (or Russia, or Albania, or a host of other countries). We might not be seeing the new medievalism in the developed countries. The transnationalisation of crime is not new. Nor are backward linkages to homelands that generate the criminal organisations. But what might be novel is the increasing difficulty of prosecuting criminals — whether they be terrorists or criminals — who can find shelter in communities that have constituted themselves as largely autonomous entities.

Because it is not quite anarchy, some have taken a rather sanguine attitude to the new medievalism. Perhaps, they say, it might even be a new form of politics; a postmodern politics, in which traditionally oppressed groups have liberated themselves from oppressive states — as in Iraq, where the possible future break-up of a country might be bad for the nationalist project, but good for historically oppressed Shi'ites and Kurds. Moreover, in some places, the new medievalism might be quite benign. In much of sub-Saharan Africa, the reassertion of autonomy by sub-national agents in the face of state retreat reveals just how limited the penetration of the nation-state was in these societies. A new medievalism might, in some places, be a political system more appropriate to the needs of these societies. In short, it is possible to imagine a new medievalism that is not all bad.

Nevertheless, as many of us know all too well, neo-medievalist tendencies can also herald more troubling scenarios. There is always the danger that the process of reconfiguration might not end at the Middle Ages. It might go further back, to a sort of Dark Ages, as happened in Rwanda during its genocide, or the former Yugoslavia in its civil war, or — dare one say it? — the Solomon Islands. There is a subtext to the new medievalism: just as the original medievalism was built atop the triumph of German tribes over the Roman Empire, the new medievalism can itself degenerate into a cold, ruthless struggle for resources. This, of course, is happening in a context where abundance has never been greater, but relative scarcities never more acute.

Does all this mean that we face an inevitable future of declining states, a resurgent barbarism and a clash of civilisations? Not necessarily. The future will undoubtedly be challenging. But, as every economics freshman realises, risks and returns vary in equal proportions. In this case, the dangers and opportunities lie side by side.

The global economic landscape has been transformed by China's dramatic reinsertion into the global economy, and its likely return to the centre of the global political economy (at least in terms of gross output). We are only just beginning to feel the effects of this change, and they are already profound. Her booming industries are flooding world markets with finished goods. Her ravenous appetite for inputs has driven up demand for primary commodities. With prices on manufactured goods declining, and those on primary goods rising, we have entered an unusual conjuncture, the type of which the world economy has not seen in a very long time: the terms of trade have shifted, if only temporarily, in favour of developing countries.

Add to this the likelihood that the bias in global capital flows will favour developing countries in the next few years. After the Asian Crisis, four-fifths of the planet's savings pool flowed into one country, the USA. There, it inflated bubbles in stock, then bonds, then property markets. As each of these reached their limits, the direction of investment began to gradually move back in favour of developing countries. Barring major exogenous shocks, or a sharp downward correction in US financial markets as financial capital gradually moves in a new direction — if any of these eventualities occurred, they would quickly reverberate around the world — there are grounds for cautious optimism that the premium on investment in the Third World will decline, making capital more readily available.

Conceivably, therefore, big opportunities lie ahead. But all is not rosy. China's relatively vast labour reserve has so depressed global wages that the conventional path to Third-World development — proceeding through labour-intensive manufacturing, to skilled manufacturing, and then to services — the sort of route Singapore or South Korea followed, is probably now an extinct option. Likely trends in future trade deals are likely to confirm this. And, as the experience of Pacific Islands can attest, being forced to compete with China in the assembly of low-end products — textiles come rapidly to mind — is a prescription for economic failure.

Therefore, we truly have entered a new age. Future development models will have to draw on new blueprints, which in some cases will probably require a frog-leap over the industrial age and into an information-based one. But the capital expenditure needed for this sort of transition will probably demand a capital transfer on a scale even greater than private markets, despite their new-found optimism over 'emerging markets', might be able to mobilise. Global challenges will require global solutions. Are we up to it?

It is a lot to hope for. Still, it might not be an impossible dream. One of the things September 11 drove home was that the new medievalism would — as surely as the old medievalism defeated Rome — bring an end to any present-day 'empires'. Nodes in the world economy are intimately linked by formal vectors of communication. Pockets of opulence live beside seas of poverty. Geographical distance has been annihilated. When you can log onto the Internet and easily see — and practically experience — how the 'other half lives', the notion that worlds are really apart begins to tumble. Resentment grows. It festers. And it can move along those very vectors of communication, to deliver drugs, dirty money, bombs, or indeed the bodies that will carry them.

The metaphor of my policeman is apt. It will not be enough for anyone to fight a war on terror. It will have no more chance of success than did his war on drugs. Until the children are fed, clothed and schooled on money earned in the formal economy, at levels that give the citizens of this planet a reason to 'buy into' the system, and to pay taxes to the State that will provide them with decent security, the war will remain unwinnable. Slowly, that reality seems to be seeping into the world's consciousness: that, like it or not, we will either rise together, or sink back as one into a new Middle Ages. There is no assurance of either eventuality. But it is certain that we do live in a fascinating age.

2. Treading Water in Rapids? Non-Governmental Organisations and Resistance to Neo-Liberalism in Pacific Island States

Claire Slatter

> Today we are so mesmerized by globalisation and the World Trade Organisation that development has become a very technical pursuit. It's no longer a question of creative thinking, or of having a vision and trying to pursue that vision (never mind about its practicalities) which I think was the spirit of the 1960s and 1970s. There was no limitation on visions then.
>
> — Amelia Rokotuivuna, Pacific activist for peace and justice, February 2005

Introduction

In the current new world order of neo-liberalism, civil society organisations have emerged as an important countervailing force to the power of multilateral institutions and transnational corporations, and as watchdogs on states. The global movement against neo-liberalism and its manifestation in economic and trade liberalisation is an unprecedented international resistance movement comprising a broad range of civil society organisations, social movements, development NGOs and public interest groups opposed to the ideological, economic and political forces that have been reshaping the world in the past 16 or so years with devastating impacts on the lives of millions of people, and the environment. The movement is in many respects a post-Cold War sociopolitical formation in which old hierarchies, ideological divisions and dogmas have no place and are strongly contested by contemporary definitions and understandings of human rights, insistence on transparent, democratic practice and participatory leadership, respect for diversity, and opposition to extremism and fundamentalism of all kinds. Transcending nation-states in its mobilisation of citizens of the globe, it's also a distinctly 21st-century movement, whose organisation has been made possible by the forces of globalisation itself. Its vision, expressed in the World Social Forum slogan 'Another World *is* Possible', underscores its unequivocal rejection of the 'there-is-no-alternative' dictum and affirms a belief in and commitment to alternatives.

As realities in the Pacific region have begun to change in the past decade as a consequence of the impacts of economic globalisation and the implementation of neo-liberal policies by Pacific Island governments, a handful of NGOs and civil society organisations in the region have begun to critically analyse economic and trade policy, to link with organisations and movements working on the same issues in other regions or globally, and to challenge governments over 'reforms' being implemented on the direction or advice of multilateral and bilateral donors. In comparison with the far larger number of organisations and individuals in the region engaged in advocacy and defence of democracy and human rights, however, this fledgling 'movement' against neo-liberalism and economic and trade liberalisation lacks a critical mass, as well as a clear agenda and the resources to pursue it.

This paper contexualises the emergence of 'resistance' to mainstream economic thinking in the Pacific region against the backdrop of the global movement against neo-liberalism, on the one hand, and a region-wide program of economic 'reform' on the other. It advances reasons for the sporadic nature of resistance to current economic orthodoxy in Pacific Island countries, highlighting recent challenges made by regional NGOs and some of the difficulties NGOs have playing a watchdog role in relation to economic and trade policy in Pacific Island states. It suggests that civil society organisations need to equip themselves to play a much stronger advocacy role in influencing economic and trade policy, but in order to be able to do this effectively they first need to sharpen their understanding of the present global political economy and the forces that are shaping it, and develop a clear vision of the kind of future they want Pacific people to enjoy. With Pacific governments rapidly committing themselves to liberalisation agreements that have not been debated publicly, intermittent or half-hearted resistance by NGOs is meaningless and tantamount to trying to tread water in rapids.

Global civil society challenges to neo-liberalism

A philosophy that hinges on a belief in individualism, free enterprise, lowered taxes, deregulated economies and labour markets, and small government, neo-liberalism idealises free markets and the market-friendly State and privileges the 'private sector' or corporate interests at the expense of public interests and welfare. For the past two decades, aided by the so-called Third-World debt crisis since the early 1980s and the collapse of socialism from 1989, neo-liberal economic policies have been successfully imposed or peddled in countries across the developing world by the IMF, the World Bank and its regional derivatives and donor agencies alike. The progressive liberalisation of markets since 1995 through negotiated trade rules among member states of the WTO has effectively enshrined neo-liberal ideas within a new, albeit strongly contested, framework of international law, while neo-liberal discourses on 'growth', 'efficiency', 'reform' and 'governance' emerging from World Development Reports [1] have come to dominate development thinking.

The movement against economic globalisation and neo-liberalism emerged in response to mounting concerns about the serious social and economic crises and extreme inequalities resulting from the implementation of restructuring and liberalisation policies across the developing world, the injustice of Third-World debt, and the growing power of international financial institutions, the WTO, and transnational corporations. The unprecedented facility for global organisation made possible by the Internet was a key factor in mobilising the movement and continues to be critical to its organisation, growth and effectiveness. Equally or perhaps more significant in spawning this movement was the series of UN development conferences in the 1990s that engaged thousands of NGOs from the First and the Third World in its processes and saw the emergence of new frameworks for global policy-making (particularly the rights-based approach) as a result of understandings and agreements achieved through negotiations that took place within them (*UN System and Civil Society* 2003).

Considered one of the key drivers of increased civil society engagement in global policy-making and the shaping of world public opinion, the UN conferences and their preparatory and review processes gave unprecedented opportunities to NGOs and civil society groups to not only influence, and indeed set, global policy agendas, but to meet and share information and analyses among themselves, build alliances, networks and campaigns, and strategise.[2] Although splits and tensions among the NGOs certainly emerged, replacing the 'single global cleavage of the Cold War … by multiple fault lines' (ibid.), the conferences contributed to the elaboration of what might be considered a global civil society agenda, in which reforms in global governance institutions, including the UN itself, became a key goal.[3] More importantly, the plans of action that emerged from conference negotiations provided NGOs with considerable leverage to hold national governments and multilateral institutions to account on commitments made at the conferences. This marked a turning point for many NGOs and, undoubtedly, one of the most significant outcomes of the UN conferences of the 1990s was the empowering of NGOs and the metamorphosis of many of them into effective lobbying organisations, equipped with a keen understanding of global political economy, an unequivocal human rights framework, and the necessary research and analytical capacity to play an advocacy and a watchdog role in global, regional and national policy arenas.

Outside the UN, civil society organisations and NGOs targeted WTO Ministerial Conferences in Seattle, Doha and Cancun, protesting against the WTO's undemocratic processes, unfair trade rules, privileging of corporate interests and devastation of livelihoods. A successful global campaign by civil society organisations had, in 1998, torpedoed an EU-proposed multilateral agreement on investment under the WTO, which would have given multinational corporations far-reaching rights, including the right to sue states. The campaign was triggered by the leaking of details of the proposed agreement to a Canadian NGO. In 1999 and 2003, this global 'movement' for economic justice and fair trade, drawing support from a broad cross-section of global civil society, including feminists, environmentalists, human rights activists, indigenous, labour and farmers' movements, contributed to derailing WTO ministerial talks in Seattle and Cancun. Indeed, by 2003, civil society campaigns dealing with debt, fair trade and development, health before patents and profits, and corporate social responsibility had begun to show effect, testifying to the collective power of global civil society as a countervailing force against the growing power of multilateral institutions and corporations, and as a watchdog on states.

As amorphous as the movement against neo-liberalism and economic globalisation is, its diverse 'membership' does cohere around an unequivocal renunciation of neo-liberal orthodoxy and the new world order being constructed on this blueprint. This is evident in the already cited slogan of the World Social Forum (WSF). An 'impressive General Assembly of civil society' (*UN System and Civil Society* 2003: 16), which began to convene annually in Porto Alegre, Brazil, from January 2001 as a developing-world counter to the World Economic Forum in Davos, Switzerland, the WSF represents an annual gathering of forces of an unprecedented global protest movement.[4] Latin American sociologist Boaventura de Sousa Santos, in a detailed political analysis of WSF, explains its significance in simply 'claiming the *existence of alternatives* to neo-liberal globalisation'. The WSF, he points out, holds 'no clearly defined ideology either in defining what it rejects or what it asserts'; yet, in a context in which 'the conservative utopia prevails absolutely', to '*affirm the possibility* of alternatives' is better than to define them (Boaventura 2003). In Boaventura's view, the WSF is an entirely 'new social and political phenomenon' that is non-hierarchical and even leaderless, in that no one person or group can assume leadership or speak in its name. In their book on the second WSF, Fisher and Ponniah, in a similar vein, claim that the WSF represents 'a new democratic cosmopolitanism, a new anti-capitalist transnationalism, a new intellectual nomadism, a great movement of the multitude' (Fisher and Ponniah 2003: xvi).

Certainly the WSF's political and moral force lies as much in the diversity and multiplicity of resistant voices that emerge strong and clear from within it, albeit with some discordant notes,[5] to challenge hegemonic globalisation and insist on alternatives, as it does in the open, participatory processes put in place and implemented by organisations and groups which comprise the WSF's International Council. The numbers of people attending the WSF have also grown exponentially since 2001, increasing fivefold from 20,000 participants in 2001 to 100,000 in 2003, with the number of workshops and countries represented rising from 420 to 1,286, and 117 to 156, respectively, in the same period. Yet

NGOs are the organisational forms through which social movements function in today's world. And it is the sustained and dedicated work of a large number of NGOs concerned about the current world order that succeeds in convening thousands of civil society opponents of economic globalisation at the WSF each year. Most of these NGOs play an active watchdog role in relation to multilateral institutions, OECD states, regional and other groupings of states in the First and Third World, and keep a watching brief on the various global and regional policy-making fora.

Only a handful of Pacific NGOs have sent representatives to the WSF but several more have engaged in other events organised by global Thirld-World networks working on globalisation and trade liberalisation, or have otherwise become linked to regional and global networks involved in advocacy for global economic justice. Yet very few NGOs in the region have engaged in research, advocacy or activism on these issues at home, much less organised in a sustained way at the regional level to influence the processes of regional economic and trade policy-making that have been in evidence since the mid-1990s. The rest of this paper explores why this is so, against the backgrounds of neo-liberal influence and a region-wide and donor-driven program of 'reform' in the Pacific, and the issues currently occupying NGOs in the region. It is suggested that the primary challenges to regional and national NGOs in the Pacific are to firstly equip themselves to engage critically in debates on economic and trade policy, and secondly to find and use their critical voice.

Neo-liberal reform and civil society resistance in the Pacific region

Consensus among multilateral and bilateral donors in the region on the Pacific Island states' best economic policy options saw the prioritisation of economic restructuring in donor aid programming from the mid-1990s.[6] Inspired by two World Bank reports on economies in the region (World Bank 1991, 1993), the urgings of neo-liberal policy advocates in Australian and New Zealand academia,[7] and the restructuring experience of New Zealand, 'economic reform' (as it's euphemistically termed in the Pacific) has been underwritten primarily by the ADB through a program of lending that is now being strongly criticised for having saddled Pacific Island states with burdensome debts.[8]

The Pacific Islands Forum, formerly the South Pacific Forum, has played a key role in regional economic restructuring, functioning as a channel for the diffusion of neo-liberal economic ideas and thinking among Pacific Island leaders, and as the principal implementing agency in the externally driven program of 'reforms'.[9] From 1999, the work of the Pacific Islands Forum Secretariat began to focus increasingly on trade liberalisation and compliance with WTO principles and trade rules — two regional trade agreements, the Pacific Island Countries Trade

Agreement (PICTA) and the Pacific Agreement on Closer Economic Relations (with Australia and New Zealand; PACER), emerged from Secretariat processes. After the signing of the Cotonou Agreement between African, Caribbean and Pacific (ACP) countries and the EU in 2000, and the inclusion of six more Pacific Island states in the ACP group, the Secretariat also assumed responsibility for coordinating negotiations between Pacific ACP countries and the EU on a Regional Economic Partnership Agreement, and subsidiary agreements. Meanwhile, with Tonga successfully completing its WTO accession requirements in November 2005, Vanuatu requesting a reopening of the WTO accession package it agreed to and then shelved in 2001 (with a view to renegotiating the terms on which it joins the WTO), and Samoa preparing to accede, Pacific states are moving rapidly down the path of liberalisation.

Although discordant notes have been heard within the Pacific Islands Forum [10] and Pacific Island leaders were vexed about Australia and New Zealand's manipulations to secure PACER,[11] and although Vanuatu officials have expressed strong criticisms of ADB-designed reform programs (Gay and Joy n.d.), the Forum Secretariat remains committed to pushing economic 'reform' and trade liberalisation in the region, national governments appear to still be firmly on board for the rest of the regional reform voyage, and 'reform-speak' has become the dominant discourse in the region, within and outside government.

Publications of substantial critiques of current economic policy are rare. Mainstream academia in the Pacific has largely taken no issue with 'reform' policies or their economic rationale. The process of economic restructuring in the region has indeed been facilitated by the virtual absence of contrary academic opinion.[12] Not only have most regional economists failed to debate, much less critique, the neo-liberal economic arguments of economic 'reform' advocates within governments and intergovernmental institutions, several have been active advocates of these policies. The recent restructuring and marketing of programs and jobs at the University of the South Pacific has made many academics beneficiaries of market-based 'reforms', introducing new inequalities through non-transparent processes of private negotiation on individual employment contracts that would have been considered unfair in a previous era.

There is a general dearth of information in the public domain on the origins, objectives and implications of structural adjustment policies, little if any coverage in the mainstream media of the negative impacts of such policies or of trade liberalisation elsewhere in the developing world, and next to no informed debate on these issues in national parliaments. The finding by researchers who produced the *USP Report on Strengthening Regional Cooperation through Enhanced Engagement with NGOs* that 59 per cent of participants in the consultations they held knew 'little/nothing about trade' is not surprising; nor is the finding that

63 per cent knew 'little/nothing about what the Forum Secretariat does' (Sutherland et al. 2005).

Organised civil society opposition to 'reform' in Pacific Island countries has tended to be sporadic, confined largely to national contexts, and occurring at different times, over different issues and involving different protagonists, such that solidarity from civil society organisations in other parts of the region has most often been limited if not completely absent. Moreover, in most Pacific Island countries, pressing national issues have often taken precedence over programs of 'reform', claiming the attention and energy of NGOs. Even where broad coalitions of NGOs have emerged, such as in Fiji with the NGO Coalition on Human Rights and the Human Rights and Democracy Movement in Tonga, challenging economic and trade policy has not really been part of their remit. Ironically, precisely because the strongest NGOs are preoccupied in pro-democracy, anti-corruption struggles, so-called economic 'reform' has been able to proceed largely unchallenged. Even more ironically, these movements often cite political conditionality and good governance discourses in support of their causes, without fully appreciating their neo-liberal nuances, association with deregulation/liberalisation policies and their implications.

The earliest resistance to 'reform' policies in Fiji occurred immediately after the military coups in 1987 and came from the trade union movement, which challenged the repressive labour laws imposed by decree and tax-free factories, two of the earliest elements in the post-coup government's deregulation program, and subsequently opposed other dimensions of structural adjustment, including taxation 'reforms', corporatisation and privatisation of state entities, and public sector 'reform'. In addition to soliciting solidarity action against the labour decrees, the Fiji Trades Union Congress published statements in the press, and when permits could be obtained organised public protests, all of which were usually portrayed as oppositional 'political action' because of the Congress's close links with the Fiji Labour Party, which had been deposed in the coup.

The leading and most persistent critic of economic restructuring from within the churches in the Pacific has been Fiji-based Father Kevin Barr, whose prolific writings, on behalf of the Fiji Council of Churches' Research Group, the Peace, Justice and Integrity of Creation project of the Catholic Church, and, more recently, the Ecumenical Centre for Research, Education and Advocacy (ECREA), combine a strong critique of economic globalisation based on Christian social theology with evidence-based analysis of growing poverty in Fiji and the region. Largely due to the publications and advocacy work of Fr Barr and those with whom he works, church-based organisations can be credited with tracking and critiquing current economic policy and its impacts in the region. This work has not been uncontested, however, and the metamorphosis of the Fiji Council of

Churches' Research Group into ECREA gave Fr Barr and others in the Church working on economic justice issues a far freer hand.

Violent opposition to economic restructuring occurred in PNG in 1995 when massive protests were staged against an IMF/World Bank-proposed Land Mobilisation Program aimed at 'freeing up' land and providing security of tenure or property rights. Six years later, in 2001, 13 days of rioting and protests over government plans to retrench one-third of the PNG Army on the advice of a Commonwealth Eminent Persons Group, funded by Australia and led by a former New Zealand Secretary of Defence (Standish 2001), saw four students shot and killed. [13]

In October 2002, after pressure from various official quarters, the private sector and civil society, and the realisation that it had 'given away too much' (Kelsey 2004a), the Vanuatu Government shelved a completed WTO accession package. The accession negotiations, which began after Vanuatu applied to join the WTO in 1995, had subjected Vanuatu to a range of WTO-plus demands from the WTO Working Party, including demands for radical liberalisation of services. [14] In Oxfam New Zealand's view, acceding under the terms agreed to by Vanuatu would have exposed the country to 'the worst kind of corporate cream-skimming in the education and hospital sectors' (Oxfam NZ 2005). Vanuatu's supposedly publicly endorsed Comprehensive Reform Program, which began in 1997 and was underwritten by an ADB loan approved in 1998, had in large part been aimed at preparing Vanuatu for WTO accession, as indicated by the tariff reductions and value-added tax put in place by the Vanuatu Government as part of ADB conditionality (Oxfam NZ 2005: 10).

The most recent civil society challenges to reform and trade liberalisation have occurred in Tonga. A massive strike by civil servants in 2005 was triggered by the impacts of public sector reforms, which had introduced large remuneration increases for very senior public servants. The success of the strike, together with the growing strength of Tonga's Democracy Movement and public disenchantment with the impacts of a consumption tax (introduced to offset expected revenue losses from tariff reduction once Tonga joined the WTO), encouraged a broad coalition of NGOs, trade unions and church organisations to convene a workshop in late October on the implications of Tonga's accession to the WTO under terms agreed to during WTO Working Party negotiations, and subsequently to organise a public campaign to try to stop the Tongan Government from proceeding with the accession plans. Though the campaign did not succeed in halting the accession process, it raised public understanding of Tonga's WTO obligations and their social and economic implications.

Organised opposition to neo-liberalism and 'reform' at the regional level has until recently been largely absent, intermittent expressions of concern notwithstanding. Although an annual NGO Parallel Forum, convened since 1995, at the same time and in the same location as the Pacific Islands Forum, provided an opportunity to regional NGOs to closely monitor and track the work of the Forum Secretariat in driving the regional reform agenda, and to advance policy critiques and an alternative vision, participating organisations seemed to be preoccupied with their own work programs, which did not include keeping a watching brief on regional economic policy commitments and their implementation at the national level. Criticisms of the 'reform' agenda made at Parallel Forums were therefore not sustained by any substantial research, analysis and advocacy work carried out regionally, or even nationally, by way of follow up. From 2001, a number of initiatives saw a stepping up of regional-level responses to 'reform' and trade liberalisation. In 2001, after a regional consultation convened by the World Council of Churches in Geneva, Pacific churches adopted a collectively authored platform document to which Fr Barr contributed, critiquing economic globalisation and the neo-liberal ideas and values that fuel it. Titled *'Island of Hope' — The Pacific Churches' Response on Alternatives to Economic Globalisation*, the document asserted Pacific economic values of redistribution or resource-sharing and communal 'ownership' and social values of sharing responsibility for the welfare of kin, and investing in social solidarity. The same year, a Regional Consultation on Globalisation, Trade, Investment and Debt, organised by ECREA and held in Nadave, Fiji, brought together regional NGOs working on development and rights, and triggered the creation of the Pacific Network on Globalisation (PANG) with the objective of conducting research, analysis and advocacy on economic and trade policy issues.

Recent NGO challenges to Pacific governments and the Pacific Islands Forum Secretariat

The formation of PANG as a regional network tasked by its Steering Committee with raising public debate with a view to influencing decisions made at the regional level in relation to economic and trade policy, saw the beginning of substantial criticism from civil society of Pacific Island leaders and the Pacific Islands Forum Secretariat. PANG began by challenging the Pacific Islands Forum Secretariat (PANG 2002) on its misrepresentation of PICTA and PACER, and the less than independent social impact study of PICTA it had commissioned and accepted from two University of the South Pacific professors who underplayed its negative impacts (Forsyth and Plange 2001). The network subsequently engaged Auckland University law professor Jane Kelsey, New Zealand's leading critic of structural adjustment and the WTO, to undertake a critical analysis of PACER and its likely impacts on Pacific Island states.

Two hard-hitting reports on PACER were produced for PANG that year by Kelsey (Kelsey 2004a, 2004b) after 'extensive interviews with politicians, diplomats, trade officials, consultants, business people and NGOs, as well as published and unpublished reports and files at the NZ Ministry of Foreign

Affairs' (PANG Media Advisory 2004). They were delivered to Pacific Island governments (several of whom quietly expressed appreciation to PANG for the work and alternative perspective), and disseminated widely among NGOs in the region with the aim of empowering 'people of the Pacific region to engage in critical decisions on trade and economic agreements that will decide their future' (ibid.). The next year Kelsey was hired by the World Council of Churches' new Pacific Office in Suva to produce a 'People's Guide to the Pacific's Economic Partnership Agreement Negotiations with the European Union', and the resulting publication was similarly publicised and disseminated widely throughout the region (Kelsey 2005a). Since losing its very able and dynamic coordinator, Stanley Simpson, to the UN Development Program (UNDP) at the end of 2004, PANG's work has lost some of its momentum, although its substantial contribution to raising public awareness of regional economic policy and trade agreements and encouraging debate, critique and civil society resistance, is still being realised.

In the past two years, and largely to comply with obligations under the Cotonou Agreement to consult with civil society, the Forum Secretariat has been including selected NGO representatives in stakeholder consultations and in some advisory or reference groups in relation to the Economic Partnership Agreement process. At the same time, however, a process emanating largely from outside the Pacific Islands, involving consultations by an Eminent Persons' Group, largely left out civil society and inspired a controversial 'Pacific Plan' that drew strong objections from regional NGOs, which organised themselves for an unprecedented confrontation with Pacific governments and the Forum Secretariat. The plan, adopted by the Pacific Islands Forum Meeting in Port Moresby in October 2005, is a 'road map' for further trade liberalisation in the region under PICTA, PACER and the Economic Partnership Agreement with the EU.

Presented as if it had originated from Forum Island leaders themselves, and marketed actively through a series of national consultations intended to secure maximum public ownership, the Pacific Plan's authorship was later revealed to reside in the Australian Department of Foreign Affairs and Trade. [15] Pacific regional NGOs reacted vehemently to the Pacific Plan, issuing a statement endorsed by a large number of organisations [16] calling for a two-year moratorium on the plan to enable 'a more comprehensive and genuine consultation process' to take place and 'informed consent' to be obtained from Pacific people (*Pacific Magazine* 2005). The NGO statement criticised the plan for claiming to 'treasure the diversity of the Pacific' and to seek a future in which 'its cultures, traditions and religious beliefs are valued, honoured and developed' while completely disregarding these. It also slammed the processes through which the Pacific Plan emerged, public support was being mobilised, and the haste with which it was being pushed through. Greenpeace Oceans campaigner Lagi Toribau summarised the NGO's substantial critique well with her comment after the Port Moresby meeting that despite considerable rhetoric about security in the plan, it failed to deliver 'true security for Pacific Island communities, such as health, food and real energy security' (Hamed 2005). What was missing from the NGO statement was a more substantial critique of the Pacific Plan and how it linked with the 'reform' and liberalisation agendas; and the statement was the weaker for the absence of a substantial critique of what the plan was really about.

A parallel Civil Society Forum held in Port Moresby before the official forum meeting saw regional and national civil society leaders repeat their longstanding request for a formal arrangement through which to channel their concerns to Pacific leaders at the forum meeting each year. NGOs do not have observer status at any sessions of the official forum meetings, although some of them, such as the Pacific Concerns Resource Centre, have been able to gain access as accredited 'journalists' for their own newsletter. Nor are NGOs consulted regularly by governments in the region. With national policy being set increasingly through agreements and commitments made by governments at regional intergovernmental meetings, and most often without reference to national parliaments, some regular form of civil society consultation at the regional level is called for, as is a system of accrediting NGOs to observe at least some sessions of the official meeting, with the opportunity to try to influence debates and decision making. Until now, NGOs have had to content themselves with the arrangement, followed at the 2005 forum meeting, of formally presenting their concerns and statements to a representative of the Forum Secretariat (in 2005, to Secretary-General, Greg Irwin), who relays them to heads of governments at the official meeting. They have been immensely grateful for the attention paid to them by New Zealand Prime Minister, Helen Clark, who has, since the 2003 Pacific Islands Forum, taken the time to pay the Parallel Forum a visit. The goodwill that this has engendered among regional NGOs towards the New Zealand Prime Minister is evident, and has softened criticisms that might otherwise be directed at New Zealand for its role in pushing the Pacific Plan.

The exclusion of Pacific NGOs from observing at intergovernmental meetings of the Pacific Islands Forum stands in stark contrast with the access and representation NGOs have come to enjoy, and expect, in UN processes. At the same time, securing representation or an avenue for regular consultation with governments at Forum meetings without making the necessary investment in collective research and analysis of economic and trade policy issues — to ensure that access to the forum meetings was utilised effectively to influence meeting outcomes — would be a wasteful and meaningless exercise.

NGO constraints and challenges

NGOs in the Pacific operate under a number of constraints. Questioning of their legitimacy (Who do they represent? To whom are they accountable?) has become a familiar theme and clearly stems from discomfort or wariness on the part of governments about NGOs playing an advocacy, even worse a watchdog, role.

Latent tensions that exist between those who see themselves as the legitimate (i.e., elected) leaders of Pacific people and those who are seen, at best, as self-appointed guardians of the public interest are not helped by NGO-bashing. The savage attack made by Professor Ron Crocombe on regional NGOs behind the Pacific Plan statement no doubt provided welcome grist for the mills of those Pacific leaders who might have little regard, much less respect, for NGOs. [17]

While such attitudes might suggest a strict demarcation between the spheres of government and civil society in Pacific states, this is not necessarily the case. Many Pacific governments have had in the past, and still have, close working relations with selected national NGOs and/or NGO umbrella bodies. In some cases, NGOs are aligned so closely to a government they are effectively 'subcontracted' to carry out work it would otherwise do, as in the case of the Soqosoqo Vakamarama in Fiji and Women's Interest Officers. Conservative NGOs overwhelmingly predominate in the Pacific. Mostly charities or apolitical providers of services, they do not present any challenges to the political leadership and usually enjoy an easy relationship with governments.

In the past decade or so, some NGOs in the Pacific assumed strong advocacy roles in support of women's rights, democracy and human rights, peace and development, media freedom, good governance and the rule of law. They have also worked to try to ensure that states meet their obligations in respect of international conventions they have signed onto, or commitments they have agreed to through UN conferences. Women's NGOs in Fiji and Samoa, for instance, played key roles in shadow-reporting on their countries' performance in relation to their obligations to the Convention on the Elimination of all Forms of Discrimination Against Women, while the NGO Coalition on Human Rights in Fiji produced a shadow report on Fiji's Convention on the Elimination of Racial Discrimination obligations.

As organised pressure groups, some of these NGOs came to acquire the kind of negative image once reserved for trade unions, and became the bane of governments. This is especially so for high-profile, outspoken NGOs which regularly use the media to criticise or challenge governments, and/or resort to using the courts if necessary in pursuit of their objectives. If their stance concurs with that of an opposition party or movement they might be branded 'political'. In extreme circumstances, governments might go as far as stripping them of their legal standing, using the conveniently available colonial-era legislation under which NGOs are required to register, which narrowly circumscribes the activities they are legally authorised to undertake. The deregistration of Fiji's Citizens' Constitutional Forum served as a stern lesson to NGOs not to take their watchdog role too far. If the stated commitments to civil society consultations in the Cotonou Agreement and other such treaties are to have any real meaning, however, new legislation that provides proper protection to the diverse range of civil society organisations that exist today is urgently required. After the deregistration of the Fijian Forum, the Pacific Concerns Resource Centre commissioned the University of the South Pacific's Institute for Justice and Applied Legal Studies to undertake a review of legislative and regulatory frameworks under which civil society organisations register in ACP member states in the region (Lakshman 2001), but existing legislation, based on the idea of NGOs as 'charities', remains in place. Until they are repealed, NGOs which take on governments remain vulnerable.

Kinship and friendship ties between people in small Pacific Island states, as well as the prevailing 'customs of respect', can make it difficult or uncomfortable for NGOs to confront governments. This is not helped by the revolving door between NGOs and government in some countries and, while it might be defended by many NGOs as an effective 'inside-outside' strategy, it can have the effect of moderating positions taken by NGOs, weakening their ability to hold governments or regional bodies to account. Criticising government tends to bring charges of being 'anti-government', or siding with an opposition party, or 'being political', which NGOs that have a place at the table, so to speak, are not expected to be, although strong NGO leaders retain their autonomy and are not in any way compromised by engaging with governments and intergovernmental bodies.

The resource constraints of small island states are often theorised. These constraints extend to human resources and, among the region's people, the numbers of those with the capacity, critical perspective and inclination to be activists are in short supply. Becoming an activist is a heart and soul thing — it comes from an understanding of, and deep concern about, injustice and a dedication to working to change it. In a small society it takes courage to remain an activist, and it often carries considerable personal costs. In today's world of professionalised NGOs, activists are a dying breed. And the Pacific has recently lost some of its leading public intellectuals and activists — Amelia Rokotuivuna and Grace Molisa among them. Some critics and activists have also, sadly, been lost to better paying international organisations within the region or abroad in what some might describe as cooptation. This is particularly the case where critical minds have been lost to institutions involved in reform implementation, where they might take on the agenda of reform out of an honest concern to turn the region around, and address problems that really exist but for which they are no longer exploring alternative 'solutions' to the ones being put before them by the drivers of economic liberalisation.

NGOs have also been adversely affected by funding constraints and over-dependence on donor support. Competition among NGOs for limited grant funds, the influence of donor priorities on NGO agendas, the burden that donor reporting places on NGOs, and the resultant professionalisation of NGOs, have all had the effect of changing the nature of Pacific NGOs. While they are better resourced today than ever before, and are encouraged to take on wider social responsibilities as states are urged to narrow theirs, understanding how and why they have come to be so apparently favoured is important. In a Greenpeace report on aid, published in 2002, Teresia Teaiwa wrote, 'In the Pacific, aid surrounds us like the ocean. We are implicated in it and by it' (Teaiwa et al. 2002). A sobering statement, to be sure, but the bottom line surely is that no amount of funding or aid should buy NGO silence.

Challenging economic 'reform' and trade liberalisation requires having a critical perspective on development. There is almost no one today asking questions that used to be asked in the 1970s — the decade of independence for some Pacific Island states — such as 'Development for whom?' and 'Who decides?'. Contrary to the claims of a recent ADB report on poverty (Abbott and Pollard 2004), which commented on the obstacle to 'reform' presented by University of the South Pacific academics who were teaching outmoded development studies at odds with current policies, there are precious few critics of neo-liberalism within academia, at the University of the South Pacific and elsewhere. As such, it's a sad indictment of the ADB authors, and of the ADB, that they should want no dissenting voices or alternative perspectives to be heard in academia. The reality is that critical development theory is slipping off the curriculum, supposedly invalidated by the prevailing 'wisdom' of neo-liberalism. Few who emerge from regional universities are equipped with a critical perspective, nor have they had any experience of working voluntarily with NGOs on issues of concern while they were students. Global issues have tended not to interest or concern students outside of the classroom; student politics in Fiji has been largely corrupted by ethnic and national politics, and 'sitting allowances' paid to students for attending their own council meetings condition them to expect to be remunerated for any involvement in civic affairs. Outside university, with the exception of what feminist organisations are providing, there are no training or mentoring programs for activists interested in broader development issues or public policy.

Despite the constraints on NGO advocacy and activism discussed above, NGOs in the Pacific have unprecedented resources for effective advocacy today. They have the means of accessing information and analyses produced by their counterparts abroad, are able to connect via email to a vast global network of NGOs to seek solidarity support for national campaigns, as well as to the media, intergovernmental bodies, and even political leaders of other states. Indeed, the primary blocks to Pacific NGOs working effectively to counter the forces of neo-liberalism in the region are, firstly, the low priority they individually and collectively give to research and analysis of economic and trade issues — not least because they have yet to acquire understanding and expertise in these issues — and, secondly, the absence of an alternative vision for the future of the Pacific. If they are well-organised, inspired by a clear vision of the kind of future they want to build in the Pacific, and equipped with a clear understanding of the political economy of globalisation and neo-liberalism and with the capacity to be effective advocates and watchdogs, civil society organisations in the Pacific region can become a force to be reckoned with. But unless they give priority to working collectively on economic and trade issues — and there is an urgent need to do so as things are moving rapidly in respect to trade liberalisation in the region — NGOs will lose the opportunity to effect any real change in present developments. It is imperative that we reclaim what Amelia Rokotuivuna referred to as the 'spirit of the 1960s and 1970s', when deciding development options meant thinking creatively and deciding for ourselves what kind of society we wanted to build.

References

Abbott, David and Steve Pollard. 2004. *Hardship and Poverty in the Pacific.* Asian Development Bank.

Alley, Roderic. 2000. *The Domestic Politics of International Relations; Cases from Australia, New Zealand and Oceania.* Aldershot, UK, and Burlington, VT: Ashgate.

Cardoso, Fernando Henrique. 2003. 'Civil Society and Global Governance.' Contextual paper prepared by the panel's chairman. High Level Panel on UN-Civil Society.

Choudry, Aziz. 2002. 'The ADB — "Governing" The Pacific?' Paper produced for Focus on the Global South, April.

Boaventura de Sousa Santos, Início. 2003. *The World Social Forum: Toward A Counter-Hegemonic Globalization.* Presentation at the XXIV International Congress of the Latin American Studies Association, Dallas, March 27-29, http://www.ces.uc.pt/bss/fsm.php

Field, Michael. 2005. 'Pacific Rumblings.' *The Dominion Post.* Tuesday, October 11, 2005.

Firth, Stewart. 2000. 'The Pacific Islands and the Globalization Agenda.' *The Contemporary Pacific*, 12, 1. pp. 178–92.

Fisher, William F. and Thomas Ponniah. 2003. *Another World is Possible: Popular Alternatives to Globalisation at the World Social Forum.* Nova Scotia: Zed Books, Fernwood Publishing Ltd, and London and New York: Zed Books.

Forsyth, David and Nii-K Plange. 2001. *Social Impact Assessment of Membership of the Pacific Free Trade Area.* Suva: University of the South Pacific.

Fry, Greg. 1997. 'Australia and the South Pacific: the Rationalist Ascendancy.' In J. Ravenhill and J. Cotton (eds), *Seeking Asian Engagement: Australia* in *World Affairs 1991-95,* Melbourne: Oxford University Press. Pp. 314–34.

Fry, Greg. 2006. 'Whose Oceania? Contending conceptions of community in Pacific region-building.' In Michael Powles (ed.), *Pacific Futures — Towards A Pacific Community?*, Canberra: Pandanus Books.

Gay, Daniel and Roy Mickey Joy. n.d. *Vanuatu*. Port Vila: Overseas Development Institute and Vanuatu Department of Trade, Industry and Investment and Bangkok: ESCAP. http://www.unescap.org/tid/publication/t&ipub2278_van.pdf

Hamed, Omar. 2005. 'Neo-Colonialism Ratified At Pacific Islands Forum.' In *Just Focus — Youth Focus for a Just World*, http://www.justfocus.org.nz/articles/2005/11/04/neo-colonialism-ratified-at-pacific-islands-forum/

Hughes, Helen. 2003. 'Aid Has Failed the Pacific.' Centre for Independent Studies, *Issue Analysis*, No. 33, May 7.

Kelsey, Jane. 2004a. *Big Brothers Behaving Badly: The Implications for the Pacific Islands of the Pacific Agreement on Closer Economic Relations (PACER)*. Pacific Network on Globalisation (PANG), Interim Report.

Kelsey, Jane. 2004b. *A People's Guide to PACER — The Implications for the Pacific Islands of the Pacific Agreement on Closer Economic Relations (PACER)*. Suva: Pacific Network on Globalisation (PANG).

Kelsey, Jane. 2004c. 'Acceding Countries As Pawns In A Power Play: A Case Study Of The Pacific Islands.' Focus on the Global South, August 23, 2004, http://www.focusweb.org/content/view/442/36/

Kelsey, Jane. 2005a. *A People's Guide To The Pacific's Economic Partnership Agreement, Negotiations between the Pacific Islands and the European Union pursuant to the Cotonou Agreement 2000*. Suva: World Council of Churches Office in the Pacific. http://www.arena.org.nz/REPA.pdf

Kelsey, Jane. 2005b. 'Reflections on Strengthening Regional Cooperation Through Enhanced Engagement with Civil Society', PIAS-DG, USP.

Lakshman, C. 2001. *Review of Legislative and Regulations Framework Governing the Establishment and Legal Status of the Civil Society Sector in the Pacific Member States of the ACP*. Suva: IJALS, University of the South Pacific and Pacific Concerns Resource Centre.

Murray, Warwick. 1998a. 'The Price of Putting All Your Pumpkins in One basket: The Tongan Squash Export Boom.' Suva: *Te Amokura*, Development Studies Centre, University of the South Pacific.

Murray, Warwick. 1998b. 'The Global Agro-Food Complex, Neo-Liberalism and Small Farmers in Chile: Lessons for the Pacific Islands?' *The Journal of Pacific Studies*, 22, 1&2. pp 27-60.

Oxfam New Zealand. 2004. Annex to the Submission by Oxfam New Zealand to the Foreign Affairs, Defence and Trade Committee on the Inquiry into New Zealand's Relationship with Tonga. September.

Oxfam New Zealand. 2005. *Make Extortion History*.

Pacific Magazine Online. 'Moratorium Call for Pacific Plan.' Thursday September 15, 2005, http://www.pacificislands.cc/pina/pinadefault2.php?urlpinaid=16889

Pacific Network on Globalisation PANG. 2002. 'What's in it for the Pacific? A critical response to PICTA, PACER and the Pacific Islands Forum's Social Impact Assessment.' *Fiji Sun*, February 18.

Pacific Region NGOs. 2005. Civil Society Statement on Pacific Plan. September.

Slatter, Claire. 1989. 'Anti-Unionism in Fiji.' *Social Alternatives*, 8 (2).

Slatter, Claire. 1991. 'Economic Recovery on the Backs of Women Workers: Women and tax free enterprises in Fiji.' *Review* (Suva: School of Social and Economic Development, University of the South Pacific), 12 (19).

Slatter, Claire. 1994. 'Banking on the Growth Model? The World Bank and Market Policies in the Pacific.' In 'Atu Emberson-Bain (ed.), *Sustainable Development or Malignant Growth? Perspectives of Pacific Island Women*, Suva: Marama Publications. pp. 17-36.

Slatter, Claire. 1996. 'None of our Business? Women and Political and Economic Issues in the 1990s.' *The Pacific Journal of Theology*, Series II, No. 15. pp. 64-72.

Slatter, Claire. 2001. 'Economic restructuring in the Pacific: external agendas, internal impacts and growing dissent.' *Tok Blong Pasifik*.

Slatter, Claire. 2003. 'A Commentary on Helen Hughes'"Aid Has Failed the Pacific" (Centre for Independent Studies, *Issue Analysis*, No. 33, 7 May 2003).' *USP Beat,* Vol. 3, Issue 10, July 29, 2003. http://www.dev-zone.org/kcdocs/5938slatter.html

Slatter, Claire. 2006. 'Neo-liberalism and the disciplining of Pacific Island States — the dual challenges of a global economic creed and a changed geo-political order.' In Michael Powles (ed.), *Pacific Futures*, Canberra: Pandanus Books.

Standish, Bill. 2001. 'Papua New Guinea in 1999-2000.' *Journal of Pacific History,* 36 (3). pp. 285-98.

Stromquist, Nelly, P. n.d. 'The Impact of Globalization on Education and Gender: An Emergent Cross-National Balance'. Rossier School of Education, University of Southern California. http://www.edu.unp.ac.za/kenton/programme/papers/Impact_of_Globalization.htm

Submission of Oxfam New Zealand to the Foreign Affairs, Defence and Trade Committee on the Inquiry into New Zealand's Relationship with Tonga, April 2, 2004.

Sutherland, William. 2000. 'Global Imperatives and Economic Reform in the Pacific Island States.' *Development and Change,* 31 (2). pp. 459-80.

Sutherland, William with Robbie Robertson, Malakai Koloamatangi and Tarcisius Kabutaulaka. 2005. *Strengthening Regional Cooperation Through Enhanced Engagement with Civil Society*. Suva: Pacific Institute for Advanced Studies in Development and Governance, USP.

Tate, Belinda. 2005. *The NGO Environment in Samoa: A case study of the socio-political environment's impact on local NGOs*. MA thesis, Development Studies, School of Earth Sciences, Victoria University, Wellington.

Taylor, Viviene. 2000. *Marketisation of Governance: Critical Feminist Perspectives from the South*. A Development Alternatives with Women for a New Era (DAWN) publication. Cape Town: SADEP, University of Cape Town.

Teaiwa, Teresia K., Sandra Tarte, Nic Maclellan and Maureen Penjueli. 2002. *Turning the Tide: Towards a Pacific solution to conditional aid*. Suva and Sydney, Greenpeace Australia Pacific.

United Nations. 2003. *The UN System and Civil Society — An Inventory and Analysis of Practices*. Background Paper for the Secretary-General's Panel of Eminent Persons on United Nations Relations with Civil Society, May.

World Bank. 1991. *Towards Higher Growth in the Pacific Island Economies: Lessons from the 1980s, Vol. 1: Regional Overview; Vol. 2: Country Surveys*.

World Bank. 1993. *Pacific Island Economies: Toward Efficient and Sustainable Growth. Vol 1: Overview*. Report No. 11351-EAP. March 8, 1993.

World Bank. 1995. *Pacific Island Economies: Building a Resilient Economic Base for the Twenty-First Century*. Report No. 13803-EAP. February.

World Bank. 2002. *Embarking on a Global Voyage: Trade Liberalisation and Complementary Reforms in the Pacific*. Pacific Islands Regional Economic Report, No. 24417-EAP. Poverty Reduction and Economic Management Unit, East Asia and Pacific Region.

World Council of Churches. 2001. *Island of Hope — The Pacific Churches' Response On Alternatives To Economic Globalisation*.

ENDNOTES

[1] The World Bank first introduced a concern with the issue of 'governance' in a 1989 report on sub-Saharan Africa (*Sub-Saharan Africa: From Crisis to Sustainable Growth*), a concern which, after the publication of its World Development Report in 1997, entitled *The State in a Changing World*, would come to dominate World Bank reports on the economies of developing regions and spark a major discourse on governance in academic and development circles in the 1990s.

[2] See *The UN System and Civil Society* (2003) for a concise but comprehensive history and analysis of NGO involvement in UN processes. It records how major NGO campaigns, such as those against apartheid, for an international code of conduct for the marketing of breast-milk substitutes, for increased official development aid, and to minimise the negative social impacts of structural adjustment, earned them respect within the UN system, and highlights the September 1994 statement by then UN Secretary-General, Boutros Boutros-Ghali, that NGOs were 'a basic form of popular participation in the present-day world. Their participation in international organizations is, in a way, a guarantee of [their] political legitimacy', and that the UN was no longer a forum for sovereign states alone — that 'NGOs are now considered full participants in international life'. See also Edwards, M. and A. Fowler (eds), 2002, *The Earth Scan Reader on NGO Management*, London: Earthscan, which records how, by the 1990s, European and North American thinking on civil society and its contribution to social and economic development had begun to penetrate donor organisations and multilateral institutions including the World Bank (see Tate 2005).

[3] The demand for reform of global governance institutions was linked to a curious convergence of discourses from the left and the right on the need for institutional reform of the State (see Taylor 2000).

[4] The WSF brings together representatives of social movements which waged historic struggles for political equality and self-determination, peace and justice in the last century (e.g., the labour movement, independence and sovereignty movements, civil and political rights movements, movements against racism and apartheid, peace, disarmament and environmental movements and women's and indigenous peoples' movements) and those of more recent vintage (e.g., minority rights movements, movements for the cancellation of Third-World Debt and controls on finance capital, campaigns to end militarism, violence against women and trafficking, human rights movements and movements against fascist or fundamentalist extremism). The presence of some left-wing parties and political liberation movements primarily from Latin America in the WSF, and also of some reactionary political elements, raised questions and met with some resistance within the WSF, although the WSF's determination to remain open to all groups means that a wide spectrum of interests can be expected to find a place within it.

[5] Blindness among the WSF's otherwise progressive (left-wing) organisers to the assault on women's rights from rising neo-conservatism, virulent religious and cultural fundamentalism and aggressive militarism led feminists within the WSF to caucus, strategise and, from 2004, organise a separate event before the WSF, the International Feminist Dialogues, which draws representatives from most of the leading international and regional feminist networks.

[6] In 1998, 11 donor agencies were funding or had assisted public sector reform projects in one or more of the following seven countries of the region: Cook Islands, FSM, Fiji, Republic of the Marshall Islands, Vanuatu, Samoa and Tonga. These included the IMF, the Pacific Financial Technical Advisory Centre, WHO, UNDP, the EU, AusAID, the New Zealand Ministry of Foreign Affairs and Trade, the Japanese Development Agency, French aid agencies, USAID and other US agencies and ESCAP Pacific Operations Centre.

[7] In the past 15 years, free market advocates within Australian and New Zealand academia have been producing analyses of Pacific Island economies and states, some of them commissioned or otherwise supported by their governments, or written for multilateral institutions such as the World Bank and the ADB. (See Fry 1997.) A recent series of hardline analyses of Pacific Island economies and states, written by former Director of The Australian National University's National Centre for Development Studies (NCDS), Helen Hughes, has been published by the Sydney-based, right-wing policy think tank, the Centre for International Studies. See Hughes (2003), and Slatter (2003, 2004) for a critique.

[8] See Gay and Joy (n.d.) for a critical perspective on Vanuatu's ADB-funded Comprehensive Reform Program (CRP) through which Vanuatu's external debt grew to 31.2 per cent of GDP by 2002. Misgivings about ADB's structural adjustment lending to Pacific Island states were also expressed privately to the author by a former ADB consultant who disclosed that the ADB had saddled the island states with huge debts, that it was now having difficulty placing loans funds allocated for the Pacific as Pacific Island states were wary, and PNG and Solomon Islands had already announced that they did not want any more ADB loans.

[9] See Sutherland (2000) and Slatter (2004) for further discussion of the role of the Forum Secretariat.

[10] Sutherland (2000) documents critical statements made by the FSM President, Jacob Nena, when opening the 29th South Pacific Forum in Pohnpei in 1998, and Roderic Alley (2000) records Marshall Islands Finance Minister de Brum's publicly expressed irritation at the heavy hand of the ADB; while Choudry (2002) records the Prime Minister of Niue, Sani Lakatani's, pointed statements about the Pacific Islands' loss of sovereignty in an emerging 'new order of colonialism'. The most vociferous and bitter criticism has come from the PNG Prime Minister, Michael Somare.

[11] See Kelsey (2004a) for an exposé of how Australia and New Zealand bullied their way into securing PACER.

[12] Among University of the South Pacific academics at the time, only the published work of Firth (2000), Murray (1998a, 1998b) and Slatter (1989, 1991, 1994, 1996, 2001) took a critical perspective of economic globalisation.

[13] The planned retrenchment of 2,000 soldiers would have cost 70 million kina in compensation payments. The plans, which included the disbanding of the civil engineering battalion and sale of Murray Barracks and the naval establishment in Lombrum in Manus, had not involved any consultation or explanation for those affected, according to Bernard Narakobi.

[14] According to Kelsey (2004c), Vanuatu made commitments to liberalise professional services, basic and value-added telecommunications services, environmental, wholesale, retail, insurance, banking services, hotels and restaurants, primary, secondary, higher, adult and other education services, and sewerage, refuse disposal, sanitation and general construction services.

[15] See Michael Field (2005) and Elise Huffer's critique in this volume.

[16] Pacific regional NGOs which signed the statement were: Council of Pacific Education, Disabled People's International, Fiji Women's Crisis Centre, Pacific Women's Network Against Violence Against Women, Foundation of the People's of the South Pacific International, Greenpeace Pacific, South Pacific Oceanic Council of Trade Unions, Pacific Concerns Resource Centre, Pacific Conference of Churches, Pacific Foundation for the Advancement of Women, Pacific Islands Broadcasting Association, Pacific Islands Association of Non-Government Organisations, World Council of Churches — Pacific, and the World Wide Fund for Nature. Of these organisations, only one, the Fiji Women's Crisis Centre, is a national organisation.

[17] Crocombe disparaged the NGOs as being Suva-based and therefore not 'regional' and accused them of capturing massive resources for themselves from donors abroad by misrepresenting themselves as regional, and of purporting to represent people in the region.

3. Regionalism and Cultural Identity: Putting the Pacific back into the plan

Elise Huffer

> We treasure the diversity of the Pacific and seek a future in which its cultures, traditions and religious beliefs are valued, honoured and developed.
>
> — Forum Leaders' vision, expressed in the *Auckland Declaration* of April 2004

In April 2004, the Pacific Islands Forum leaders issued the *Auckland Declaration*, paving the way for the design of a Pacific Plan for Strengthening Regional Cooperation and Integration. The plan is part of a process of reform officially launched through the endorsement at the 2003 Forum Leaders' meeting of New Zealand Prime Minister, Helen Clark's, request, as chair of the forum, to review the 'forum's role, functions and Secretariat'. An Eminent Persons' Group (EPG) was set up and, after region-wide consultations, it drafted a review, entitled *Pacific Cooperation: Views of the Region*, in which it recommended the endorsement by Pacific leaders of a Pacific Plan 'to create stronger and deeper links between the countries of the region' (EPG 2004: 21).

The plan was thus envisioned as a way to strengthen the region and particularly to help it adapt to encroaching global conditions, in accordance with the EPG's stern assessment that: 'The bottom line is that future inter-country relationships will need to be closer and more mutually supportive if the region is to avoid decline and international marginalisation.' Leaders in the region are no doubt concerned about the problems their countries are facing, such as growing unemployment, poverty, crime, lack of resources to provide basic services and opportunities to their peoples, as well as tensions between national and local governance norms and institutions. There is a genuine conviction that the region is having difficulty coping with global pressures and changes. As the EPG review states, 'Modernisation and globalisation have brought wonders to our shores but they have also exposed the vulnerability of our small island developing states. They have threatened our family and community bonds and values, weakened our ability to live off the land and sea, and upset our harmony with the natural environment. Nevertheless we shall stand strong to preserve our region, our heritage and the best aspects of our traditions, and enhance them for the benefit of future generations.'

The plan was conceptualised by the EPG as the tool that would ensure that the leaders' Pacific vision could be translated into reality via intensified regional cooperation. But in its understanding of the purpose of regionalism the EPG emphasised the need for a 'focus on people'. In particular, it affirmed that '[t]ogether we shall work to ensure that this is a region where people matter more than anything else, and where every person feels loved, needed and able to enjoy a free, responsible and worthwhile life'. As a guide to ensuring that this focus on people was upheld, the EPG noted a series of areas that it considered required 'immediate attention' at the regional level. The first area listed was 'cultural identity'.

One of the fundamental aspects of contemporary Pacific culture and cultural identity is its ideal of a focus on people, relationships, on caring and sharing networks, and on working together for the betterment of all. Furthermore, cultural identity is a bond that brings Pacific Island countries and peoples together. As the EPG states, 'Our cultures link us with other Pacific peoples, and with our sea, land and ancestors.' Unfortunately, at present, the plan endorsed by the Forum Leaders in 2005 has little to say about culture. Cultural issues are viewed only as strategic objectives under two of the four goals of the plan, namely, sustainable development and good governance, but not as the foundation for further regional integration.

This paper argues that Pacific Island countries have traditionally sought to make cultural identity the foundation of regionalism and that it is in their best interest to continue to build on this approach if regionalism is to have any meaning for the peoples of the Pacific Islands and if it is to become an effective tool for the betterment of governance and development in the Pacific. The paper begins with a brief overview of the current draft plan, its process, main objectives, and its inadequacy in addressing cultural identity. It then discusses the past role of culture in establishing a foundation for regionalism and the difficulties of integrating culture in regionalism, before suggesting ways in which cultural identity can be promoted as a platform for furthering regionalism.

The plan

The Pacific Plan is a blueprint for paving the way from the existing form of regional cooperation towards other more integrated forms of regionalism. The authors of the plan are known as the Task Force. They were supported by the Forum Secretariat and based their approach on an ADB report written by Roman Grynberg and others. They identified three 'quite different concepts' of regionalism: regional cooperation, regional provision of public goods and services, and regional integration. They suggested that even though there were costs and benefits attached to moving from regional cooperation to either of the other two forms of regionalism, 'In the Pacific, regional approaches to overcoming capacity limitations in service delivery at a national level, and increasing economic opportunities through market integration are expected to provide the highest gains' (Final Draft 2005: 5). In order to fulfil this regional shift, the plan 'identifies a wide range of regional initiatives', which are listed under four key areas: economic growth, sustainable development, good governance and regional security. The plan puts forward 15 strategic objectives, which range from free trade to enhanced policing to the development of national sustainable development plans and a regional ombudsman's office. But before looking briefly at the content of the plan and its treatment of cultural identity in the strategic objectives and accompanying initiatives, it is useful to say a few words about the plan process.

The process

It should first be noted that there has not been extensive debate about the purpose, range and forms regionalism should take in the future in spite of the plan's consultation process. The EPG review consultations that were carried out in 2003 focused primarily on re-examining the role of the forum. The specific outcomes of the EPG review, as stated in its terms of reference, were 'a refreshed mandate and vision for the Pacific Islands Forum and an improved capacity within the Forum that allows it to provide leadership to the region on regional cooperation and integration' (EPG 2004: 58). While the idea of a Pacific Plan for greater regional cooperation grew out of that review, the process of consultation for the review did not focus on what sort or the extent of regionalism the peoples of the region aspire to. In addition, even though the EPG did consult with a variety of groups and institutions, the process was rushed, with the review team having less than a month to meet people face to face.

The initial draft Pacific Plan, dated December 2004 and put together by the Plan Task Force, was made available for national and regional consultations held in all countries of the region. But because the draft itself made assumptions about the benefits of regionalism (initiatives were presented under three time lines: early practical, medium-term and longer-term benefits), it might have pre-empted a debate about the benefits and costs of moving from one form of regionalism to another. Understandably, the authors of the draft were keen to set a framework for discussions, but, as a result, questions such as who currently benefits from regionalism, in what ways, whose interests regionalism serves, what sort of regionalism would benefit which countries (according to size, population, resources, etc.), and what sort of region is envisaged in 10 years and 20 years, were not widely asked, far less answered. Yet they *were* to some extent raised in the *Toward a New Pacific Regionalism* report that the Task Force used in framing the various drafts. Unfortunately, the way the drafts were designed and the way the plan now stands are not conducive to asking or answering these fundamental questions before moving on to practical initiatives. The plan process should have provided an opportunity for a thorough stocktake of regionalism and allowed for the development of a clear vision through a longer and more widespread consultation process.

These important questions about the raison d'être and finality of regionalism as well as its possible forms tie in directly to the question of cultural identity at the regional level. This was recognised in the terms of reference of the Task Force, which stated that one of the issues the Task Force should consider was: 'A practical definition of a Pacific regional approach (i.e., a definition of "regionality") noting Leaders' declaration on the importance of maintaining and strengthening Pacific cultural identity.' However, defining 'regionality' with a strong focus on cultural identity was eschewed by the Task Force. This, in combination with the lack of widespread consultation during the drafting phase of the plan, has led to questions about the plan's suitability for the region, an aspect that is discussed in some of the plan submissions by regional civil society organisations.

The content of the plan and culture

The successive drafts of the plan have addressed culture essentially as a technical issue to be addressed through initiatives proposed under two of the four areas of economic growth, sustainable development, good governance and security. In the first draft, written in December 2004, culture appeared only as a component of sustainable development (in the medium-term benefit column) under the enigmatic description: 'Development of a regional plan to maintain and strengthen Pacific cultural identity through regional agencies, including relevant studies.' The draft gave no place to culture in the other priority areas. It was not mentioned as an asset either under economic growth or security. Under the good governance goal, reference to culture was made only indirectly in the proposed 'development of a regional approach to, and training in alternative dispute/conflict resolution as a cost effective alternative to the adversarial system'.

The plan identifies the strategic objective 'Recognise and protect cultural values, identities and traditional knowledge' under the sustainable development goal and proposes two specific initiatives for the first three years (2006–08): 1) 'Develop a strategy to maintain and strengthen Pacific cultural identity' (which appears under the 'agree in principle' category), and 2) 'Create an institution to advocate for and protect traditional knowledge and intellectual property rights' (under the 'further analysis' category). It also lists the following initiative under the good governance goal: 'Enhance governance mechanisms, including in resource management, and in the harmonization of traditional and modern values and structures.' This is listed in the implementation phase and the activity consists of 'support [for] the close coordination of existing initiatives including the USP's Pacific Institute of Advanced Studies in Development and Governance' (Final Draft 2005: 17).

According to an Issues Paper on 'Culture and the Pacific Plan' drafted by the Pacific Plan Office at the Forum Secretariat, culture is also earmarked to be considered in other plan initiatives, including in the assessment of the impacts of PACER and Free Trade Agreements for the region; support for the private sector; formulation and implementation of National Sustainable Development Strategies; upgrading of statistical information systems and databases; and implementation of a regional tourism marketing and investment plan.

Although this might appear to address the 'issue' of culture, it does not answer the question of formulating a 'practical definition of a Pacific regional approach'. The plan does not say what a *Pacific* regional approach is; it merely suggests what different forms of regionalism are possible (cooperation, regional provision of public goods and services and integration) and presents a list of initiatives to achieve further integration. In other words, it does not say anything about what is 'Pacific' about the plan other than its geographic focus.

Making culture central to the plan: building on the past

Is culture really important to regionalism in the Pacific? The track record of regional cooperation suggests that it is. In its review, the EPG wrote that the Pacific Way, 'however much it evolves to meet the demands of a changing world … will have at its core one unchanging truth: regional interconnectedness, the idea that there is a Pacific way of doing things that is open to, but different from, the way Americans or Europeans or Asians might do things' (EPG 2004: 14).

The Pacific Way was at the heart of the Pacific Islands' initial engagement in regionalism, even though that engagement was driven mainly by the security concerns of the metropolitan powers in the aftermath of World War II. For many years, the concept of the 'Pacific Way' was used by Pacific Island states to define and differentiate themselves from other developing countries and regions of the world. Coined at the UN in 1970 by Ratu Sir Kamisese Mara, the then Prime Minister of Fiji, it came to symbolise a way of doing things specific to the Pacific: a way that emphasised moderation, respect, consensual dialogue, inclusiveness, as well as 'preparedness to negotiate, flexibility, adaptation and compromise'. It reflected a constructed regional consciousness as well as a gradual approach to modernisation and development. And for island leaders it symbolised a new start based on the assertion of a pan-Pacific ideal. The Pacific Way ideology therefore became a tool for continued cooperation with metropolitan powers and a diplomatic device for maintaining Pacific protocol and approaches (based on harmony and pragmatism) in regional and international affairs. And its general message was that Pacific Island countries were willing to work together with metropolitan countries but that the latter should respect them and not confuse them with Africa or other developing regions.

Today the idea of the Pacific Way is in need of a facelift. As the EPG admits: 'The Pacific Way is one of the region's greatest assets, but the concept must evolve and be reasserted if it is to remain relevant.' As an ideal, the Pacific Way has been damaged by political changes and, in some cases, crises, which have taken place in many of the Pacific Island countries (Fiji's coups in 1987 and 2000 have no doubt caused damage to the concept). It also has not been given sufficient substance even though the EPG tries to do so: 'In our view, this concept or style — which is often mentioned but seldom defined — implies honesty, mutual respect and tolerance. It is based on recognition and acceptance of differences, but with an underlying awareness of the need to find unity and consensus. The Pacific Way is guided by a sense of justice, compassion, tolerance and understanding. It is about working together' (EPG 2004: 20).

Now might be a good time to build on the Pacific Way as defined above and used by Pacific leaders for some 20 years, with the objective of defining a Pacific 'regionality' in which Pacific values, concepts and practices become the foundation for further cooperation. This approach is substantially different from including culture and cultural identity as mere token gestures. As Ron Crocombe warns with reference to the current plan process, it is no use highlighting culture only to undermine it through contradictory measures: 'The leaders emphasize the value they place on the strengthening of Pacific Islands languages and cultures. There are however, potential conflicts between some parts of the documents and others. Double-talk helps no one in the long run. Pacific cultures and languages are to be "strengthened", traditions and cultures are to be "honoured and developed". But many other aspects of the documents ensure they will be weakened and marginalized' (Crocombe 2005: 300).

This paper advocates placing Pacific values at the core of regionalism and building on cultural identity to give regionalism meaning and coherence. As Crocombe reminds us, there are 'two main bases to effective regional organizations anywhere in the world':

1. Material interactions: trade, investment, free movement of people, etc. For the Pacific Island region, these are very low, and account for only a small proportion of the total for almost any country.
2. Identity factors. It is in this area that Pacific Island regionalism has greater strengths — including feelings of common origins and historical experiences, common elements in value systems, cultural patterns and symbolic representation.

He goes on to explain that the identity factors are particularly important in the region:

> In most of the world's regional organizations both material and identity factors are strong. In the Pacific Islands, however, it is unlikely that the material factors will grow significantly. If regional cooperation is to be promoted, therefore, more emphasis needs to be given to the identity factors. (Crocombe 2004: 300).

At present, the plan misses the points made by Crocombe and the EPG review, namely that cultural identity is what links Pacific peoples, is an all-encompassing feature of life in the Pacific and is what peoples throughout the region have in common. Culture is viewed as an asset; it is a 'renewed source of wealth', of confidence and sustenance, even if it does pose many challenges and is complex to grasp. Addressing culture within the Plan by cutting it up into compartmentalised categories such as good governance and sustainable development rather than making it the foundation of the plan is a mismatched approach.

The difficulties of integrating culture

There are three interrelated reasons why it has been so difficult to make cultural identity an integral part of regional governance (beyond the rhetorical level) and the Pacific Plan: lack of political will and leadership, and pressure; lack of available conceptual tools to integrate culture into practical economic and political measures; and lack of understanding of what kinds of benefits could result from integrating cultural identity into a formal high-level regional plan of action.

Although Pacific Island leaders have spoken consistently about the need to better incorporate cultural values and norms in development and governance in the region, they have not made it a priority when it comes to implementation. One reason for this might be domination of the forum by countries or leaders who do not see Pacific culture, with its emphasis on solidarity and networks rather than competition and individual pursuit, as viable or beneficial for the region's development. Another is the lack of political leadership in regional affairs in the past 10 to 15 years, a period during which, as reported by the EPG, decisions have been formulated increasingly by officials rather than leaders, with the expectation that leaders will simply approve.

In addition to the lack of political direction, there is no doubt a lack of conceptual tools for integrating culture into existing political and economic frameworks (as well as a lack of will to develop them). There has been little research or strategic thinking about how to devise ways for the formal economy and political institutions to work hand in hand with communal structures and resource ownership, and to take advantage of community 'networking'.

There has been little effort in the region to understand how communities can utilise their human and cultural resources to enhance livelihoods while participating in the market economy. Advocates of the market economy assume that it will provide answers and that people will adapt to it — they do not envision another more appropriate solution, which is that the market should adapt itself to the social and cultural context. This is a more difficult task and involves some rethinking away from market and globalisation dogma, which asserts that globalisation is inescapable and that it is up to society to adapt to economic integration while conceding cultural, political and social disintegration. In its response to globalization, the region has thus far been reluctant (or has found it difficult) to go beyond declarations about the importance of people and culture into developing strategies for implementation.

Culture and regionalism: a strategy

There are three interrelated levels through which culture can be made central to the Pacific Plan. The first level is that of guiding principles; the second is that of a governance framework for the region and the plan; and the third level is that of strategic objectives or practical initiatives.

As Crocombe points out, 'basic to any culture is its value system'. He adds, however, that value systems vary within Pacific cultures (Crocombe 2005: 302). It is undeniable that there is real cultural diversity in the Pacific, but there are also many common values and similar practices. This is what Pacific leaders have been alluding to for many years in their references to the Pacific Way and to Pacific values. Although it is the role of the leaders and peoples of the region to agree on the predominant values together, we could suggest here, based on research already conducted by regional scholars and thinkers, that common values in the Pacific revolve around concepts of solidarity and reciprocity; the fostering and maintenance of kinship networks and relationships; attachment to land and sea; respect and care for others; the upholding of human dignity; and consultation and shared leadership.

These values (and perhaps others yet to be defined) should be made the basis for the guiding principles of regionalism: in other words, all initiatives and processes should be measured against these values. Guiding principles/norms would therefore seek to ensure that Pacific values were enhanced or promoted by regional initiatives. This is a step beyond framing a vision, which, although it provides an indication of how the region views itself (or what it aspires to), does not imply any commitment. A set of guiding principles, on the other hand, would clearly outline the values that the region seeks to uphold. It would be the responsibility of all those involved in regional decision-making to assess whether regional initiatives respect the guiding principles.

In order to facilitate this, culture should be incorporated at a second level, through the rethinking of a governance framework, or, as Grynberg and his co-authors refer to it, through the development of a 'political track' for the region (ADB 2005: xxvi). A political track that is cognisant of culture would seek not to create new 'mega-institutions', which further bureaucratise and centralise regional decision-making, but rather provide the means for enhancing dialogue between communities and the region (understood as regional institutions and regional leadership), and bringing regionalism to local communities.

How to do this was one of the questions raised in a report by William Sutherland and others entitled *Strengthening Regional Cooperation through Enhanced Engagement with Civil Society*. This report was based on a project that aimed to 'seek community views on whether and how regional co-operation could be strengthened through enhanced community engagement', in which two-day community dialogues were held in Suva, Lautoka, Apia and Honiara (Sutherland 2005: 6). Participants were asked to find strategies to increase community engagement in regionalism. Four forms of engagement were suggested: 'direct engagement' where 'community representatives ... engage directly with regional organizations'; 'engagement through Regional Representatives', that is, 'through representatives of national associations of community groups or through regional umbrella organizations'; 'engagement through Regional Liaison Units, i.e., 'the formation of "regional liaison units" through which the community could work'; and 'engagement through a Pacific parliament' (Sutherland 2005: 26–7).

Although our focus here is not on strengthening regional cooperation but on encouraging the region and its institutions to better integrate cultural norms and practices, the suggestions listed above provide some ideas about implementing a 'political track'. Which of these would be most likely to promote the valuing of cultural identity at the regional level? The simple answer for present purposes is: all or any of the above.

This is because the main objective would be that, whatever form of engagement is put forward, community voices, rather than solely those that are representative of the State, are heard directly. Any of the above suggestions can most likely help to achieve this if implemented with that objective in mind. If the purpose of regionalism is to enhance the lives of people, it must have the means to understand and connect directly with those people. In the Pacific, communities rather than the State are the regulatory agents of society. People are protected from the destructuring or disintegrating effects of the market in large part by their cultural values and practices, including emphasis on solidarity and reciprocity, attachment to land, and focus on obligations and duties to others. In many countries of the Pacific, the State has limited capacity to regulate the impact of globalisation and the market as well as limited legitimacy. The community is in large part responsible for making sure that economic imperatives do not overwhelm society, rather that they are framed within a social structure that moderates them. (This is not to deny that it is becoming increasingly difficult for communities to do this as demands for consumerism grow.)

Regionalism should also focus on developing state capacity. But if we agree that it is important for regionalism to promote cultural identity as well as a 'focus on people', as the EPG advocated, it is logical for regional institutions and processes to work directly with those who practice or live cultural identity. Regionalism should seek to work closely with the institutions that hold the most political legitimacy — and these are generally local communities. This concurs with one of the key findings in Sutherland's report that 'the community clearly wants regional organizations to be more engaged with them and not just through governments', and might also address the real and perceived inequalities in the spread of the benefits of regionalism. As Crocombe states: 'Despite a rhetoric of priority for the poor, and verbal commitment to the Millennium Development Goals, it appears that the benefits of regional activity have gone disproportionately to the urban privileged' (2005: 299).

The suggestion for liaison offices reasserts the idea that a 'physical presence' is important for the effectiveness of regionalism and the 'distribution of benefits'. It also ensures that regional institutions are more attuned to the range of contexts in the region. In Crocombe's words, 'A danger of too much centralization is that staff of regional organizations spend more time interacting with each other and less with people throughout the region they are intended to serve' (2005: 299).

The recommendations put forward in the Sutherland report address the logistical aspects of improved interaction between communities and the region, including regionalism: 'accord[ing] the community the same recognition given [to] the private sector'; 'help[ing] communities to form regional associations'; 'explor[ing] the establishment of Regional Liaison Units based in Forum Islands Countries'; and 'work[ing] towards a Pacific Parliament with direct community representation' (2005: 4). It remains to be seen which would be cost-effective in providing consistent and beneficial interaction between the 'people' and regionalism.

Apart from the 'logistics' of interaction there is also the question of modes of interaction. How regionalism engages with people at all levels is as important as the structures that are created. This concern was raised at the forum leaders' level in their expressed desire to spend more time in discussion and 'less in "ticking-off" large volumes of paperwork provided by ministers and officials'. As the EPG commented (based on experience), '[I]mpossibly long meeting agendas and an overload of paperwork militate against good decision-making' (EPG 2004: 11). Not only should 'the Pacific Islands Forum … continue its tradition of decisions through consensus based on a fluid agenda of discussion' (Powell [2005] argues that 'because this process is consistent with the cultural norms of Islanders, the execution of decisions by the Forum [carries] a needed level of legitimacy'), but regionalism should extend this mode of interaction to other levels. This relates directly to the concept of *talanoa* that Sitiveni Halapua has theorised about and advocated. Halapua organised a series of high-level *talanoa* dialogues between political leaders in Fiji after the 2000 coup, applying principles of reconciliation, inclusion and respect for cultural traditions. Even though it is important to be able to come to decisions so that actions are implemented, it is imperative for leaders and people, including bureaucrats, to have the opportunity to reflect on the purpose of regional action. It is not enough to leave this to academics. In addition, as pointed out by Powell, Halapua and others, *talanoa* is a process suited to reflection and decision-making in the region.

The third level at which cultural identity could be promoted is through regional initiatives or 'strategic objectives'. Among the 15 strategic objectives listed in the final draft of the Pacific Plan, only one deals specifically with cultural identity: Strategic Objective 11 (under sustainable development), which is to '[r]ecognise and Protect cultural values, identities and traditional knowledge' (Final Draft 2005: 16). The associated initiatives and milestones are not very clear so it is difficult to judge their potential efficacy at this point. But clearly the importance of preventing bio-piracy and protecting indigenous knowledge are urgent.

Another initiative to favour cultural identity (in this case, fomenting a greater appreciation and sharing of pan-Pacific cultural identity) is to foster greater exchanges between people of the region. The FSM emphasised this aspect in its national consultation plan submission under a section entitled 'Building a regional identity'. In it, the FSM advocates free skilled labour movement in the region as well as the 'establishment of a system of short-term secondment and exchange of officials' among Pacific nations. Crocombe makes a similar suggestion: 'If regional integration is to succeed in the long term, more attention needs to be given to human mobility.' He goes on to make concrete suggestions about how to make this possible, including a 'regional identity card', 'professional mobility', 'dual citizenship', 'teacher, student and media exchanges', as well as a 'Pacific volunteer service'. As Crocombe points out, in the case of exchanges, most of these occur 'between countries of the Forum region and countries outside it, but do not exist [in the case of teacher, student and media exchanges] … within the Forum Islands region'. The plan lists including 'temporary movement of labour' in the Pacific Island Countries Trade Agreement but this appears as a purely economic growth measure rather than as a wider initiative to foster cultural exchange, understanding and development.

Another area that requires more attention is acknowledgment of the role of cultural and social capital. The point here is not to instrumentalise culture but to consider it as a key component in the development of economic policy. In other words, the region should seriously consider how to adapt economic practices to cultural contexts rather than the reverse. The Pacific Plan Office briefly addresses this question in its *Culture and the Pacific Plan* Issues Paper, but it is difficult to understand what it is advocating:

In an environment focused on economic growth and trade, those interested in conserving culture attempt to justify support for the issue through analysis of the economic value it contributes to the economy. However, its real value may lie in the loss Pacific Islanders will face after it is gone, as the tangible aspects of culture that contribute to the economy [are] only a small part of the whole. On the other hand, the lack of concerted effort in the field of culture also means that commercialization and exploitation of traditional knowledge, flora and fauna is a missed opportunity to share in the income that can be derived from it.

Does this mean that addressing culture in economic terms should be limited to the area of 'commercialisation and exploitation of traditional knowledge, flora and fauna'? To view the 'tangible aspects of culture that contribute to the economy as *only a small part of the whole*' is somewhat perplexing. Culture *is* a whole, it is civilisation embodied in thought and action; the economy is but a part of culture and of life. At least that is how it is viewed in the Pacific (and by many people throughout the world, including leading economists such as Amartya Sen).

Putting the economy at the service of culture and of life and society perhaps requires a shift in thinking, and it might be difficult to list this as a 'strategic objective'. But an objective of the Pacific Plan should be to consider it as an all-encompassing, core issue, one that is at the heart and not the margins of governance, economic growth, sustainable development and security.

Conclusion

In conclusion, we might want to ask ourselves again: what is the final aim of Pacific regionalism? Should it be an expression of values or an expression of interests? The sensible answer is that it is about both, and yet in the Pacific Plan now adopted by the forum, interests clearly trump values. The interests the plan seeks to promote are those that serve primarily economic integration without considering the values of the people it represents.

This is in spite of the fact that leaders have traditionally viewed regionalism in a humane way, with the Pacific Way preserving a particular outlook on society and the world. The EPG reiterated this outlook in its assertion that 'the real strength of the region lies in the character of its people, who have demonstrated throughout their history a high level of resourcefulness and resilience'. This positive outlook on the capacity of the peoples of the region to find the solutions to their problems is indicated by the additional statement that '[w]e are well used to surviving, and eventually prospering, in the face of hardship, invasions and natural disasters' (EPG 2004: 18). The point here is not to advocate complacency but to indicate that regionalism plans must build on these strengths not attempt to replace or contravene them.

Pacific cultural values such as solidarity and reciprocity and respect for kinship networks need to become the guiding principles of Pacific regionalism; communities need to be given a direct voice in regional institutions, and human mobility among island states needs to be encouraged not only for economic reasons but as part of a project to enhance a sense of regional identity. Above all, moves towards regional economic integration need to be tested constantly against the criterion of whether or not they reflect Pacific cultural values, and whether they enhance community.

References

ADB. 2005. 'Towards a New Pacific Regionalism.' *Pacific Studies Series*. An Asian Development Bank–Commonwealth Secretariat Joint Report to the Pacific Islands Forum Secretariat.

Crocombe, R. 2005. *International context and lessons from other regions*. Report posted on the Pacific Plan web site, September.

EPG. 2004. *Pacific Cooperation: Voices of the Region, The Eminent Persons' Group Review of the Pacific Islands Forum*, April.

Lind, Christopher. 2001. 'Integration and Disintegration — Ethics, Economic Globalisation and the Island of Hope.' In World Council of Churches, *Island of Hope: A Pacific Alternative to Economic Globalisation, Report of the Churches' Conference on Economic Globalisation — Island of Hope, Nadi, Fiji, August 12–18 2001*. pp. 63–82.

Pacific Islands Forum Secretariat. 2005. *Final Draft: A Pacific Plan for Strengthening Regional Cooperation and Integration*. Pacific Islands Forum Secretariat, September.

Powell, P. T. 2005. '"Too Young to Marry": economic convergence and the case against the integration of Pacific states.' In Satish Chand (ed.), *Pacific Island Regional Integration and Governance*, Canberra: Asia Pacific Press. Downloadable from ANU E-Press.

Ratuva, S. 2005. *Social Security in Fiji, Kiribati, Samoa, Solomon Islands and Vanuatu: Traditional Social Protection Systems in the Pacific — culture, customs and safety nets*. August 2005. Suva, Fiji: International Labour Office.

Raulston Saul, John. 2005. *The Collapse of Globalism and the Reinvention of the World*. Viking.

Sutherland, W. with R. Robertson, M. Koloamatangi and T. Kabutaulaka. 2005. *Strengthening Regional Cooperation through Enhanced Engagement with Civil Society*. Suva: PIAS-DG, USP.

Labour Migration

4. Migration, Dependency and Inequality in the Pacific: Old Wine in Bigger Bottles? (Part 1)

John Connell

A quarter of a century ago, I wrote a paper whose title was the first part of that above (Connell 1980), which sought to provide an overview of the complex relationship between migration, remittances and rural development in the region, and largely concluded that this had been negative for the sending regions. The conclusion stated that 'remittances on the smaller islands tend to foster dependence rather than inequality; on the largest islands they generate inequality rather than dependence. But both trends are ubiquitous' (1980: 51). Such sweeping conclusions, centred on dependency theory, were not without criticism (e.g., Hayes 1991). Given the present extraordinary global and regional interest in migration issues, and the substantial increase in most forms of migration in the region in the past quarter of a century, it is timely to revisit these conclusions in the light of more recent data and trends. Moreover, there has now been about half a century of international migration from several parts of the Pacific, and especially from Polynesian states, hence it is useful to review their experiences. Almost all post-World War II international migration from the island Pacific has occurred since the 1960s. Since then there has been continued migration from 'mature migration' economies, mostly in Polynesia, and a rise in migration from all other island states.

As emigration continues, small and vulnerable South Pacific states have become irrevocably a peripheral and dependent part of a wider world. Contemporary patterns of migration have diversified, and have become more selective and skilled, demographic structures have changed, and the restructuring of global and island economic landscapes present different development contexts. The life courses of island people, present or absent, are embedded increasingly in international ties, and island states have sought out new migration opportunities. Island states, individuals and various international agencies have attached new and increased significance to migration, remittance flows, return migration and the role of the diaspora, in contexts where 'conventional' developments strategies have achieved limited success.

An economic context

The variety of reasons put forward to explain migration in the South Pacific sometimes seems interminable and the problems of generalisation considerable.

Apart from migration as a result of natural hazards, migration is largely a response to real and perceived inequalities in socioeconomic opportunities, within and between states. Social influences are important, especially in terms of access to education and health services, and are in turn often a function of economic issues. Migration remains, in different forms, a strategy of moving from a poorer area to a richer one in search of social and economic mobility abroad or at home. It is related to the economic aspirations of migrant households and to development in island states, hence it is useful to set migration within the context of economic change in the region.

Major influences on migration have been rising expectations of what constitutes a satisfactory standard of living, a desirable occupation and a suitable mix of accessible services and amenities. In parallel with changing aspirations and the increased necessity to earn cash, agricultural work throughout the Pacific has lost prestige and the declining participation of young men in the agricultural economy is ubiquitous, despite rising levels of unemployment. There is a widening gap between rising expectations and the reality of limited domestic employment and incomes. Changes in values, following increased educational opportunities and the expansion of bureaucratic (largely urban) employment within the region from the 1970s, have further oriented migration streams outwards, as local employment opportunities have not kept pace with population growth.

The islands and island states of the Pacific, with the exception of PNG, are small and vulnerable. Many states are isolated and fragmented, with numerous populated islands and, in Melanesia, with many distinct language and cultural groups. Prospects for economic growth are limited, especially in Polynesia and Micronesia, where no island state has a population of more than 250,000. Five island states are officially classified as least-developed countries. Although the region does not suffer from the absolute depths of poverty experienced in some parts of the developing world, it does have social and economic problems (Abbott and Pollard 2004). Generally, growing populations have intensified pressure on lands and seas. Economic growth has been disappointing since independence, usually about 30 years ago, though mining and tourism offer solid prospects in a few places. This has resulted in a series of imposed attempts at restructuring, including structural adjustment programs in various countries, urged by institutions such as the World Bank and the ADB.

Most countries, other than the large Melanesian states, have benefited substantially from aid and from remittances from overseas migrants, enabling them to run big current account deficits, maintain substantial bureaucracies and undertake relatively large public investment programs of a kind that could not otherwise be financed. The Pacific Islands are the most heavily aid-assisted part of the world on a per capita basis. The public sector increasingly dominates formal economic activity almost everywhere, despite efforts at restructuring.

Economic growth in the region has been limited with one important consequence: in every state formal sector jobs are being created more slowly than school leavers are emerging from the education system. The consequences are rising unemployment, the growth of the informal sector and visible signs of poverty within urban areas. Although poverty is not a welcome word in most parts of the region, and few countries officially admit that it exists, there is growing evidence that it is widespread, though disguised by words such as 'hardship' (Abbott and Pollard 2004). Much poverty is also hidden in outer islands and on remote mountain sides, where there is a poverty of opportunity and minimal access to crucial educational and health resources, alongside employment opportunities. One consequence of this is sustained rural-urban migration; hence a major task for most states is to create employment and provide services for outer islands and remote places that would stimulate development and reduce migration and thus unmanageable urban growth.

Until quite recently, there was a widespread belief that poverty did not exist in the Pacific, because of the existence of urban and rural 'safety nets', where extended families could and would support those who for whatever reason experienced temporary problems. There is now good evidence that both of these are breaking down and it is no longer possible, if it ever was, for urban people simply to return and be supported by rural kin (Connell 2003a: 68–70). Absolute poverty is not generally apparent in the Pacific; however, some households are poor in the sense that they do not have enough food, clean water or access to adequate housing or a basic education (Bryant 1993); and poverty is significantly worse in Melanesia and Micronesia than in Polynesia (Abbott and Pollard 2004: 20). Indeed in PNG relatively recent data suggest that in 1996 as many as 41 per cent of rural people and 16 per cent of urban people were living below the poverty line (Allen et al. 2005). In Fiji, firstly, the extent of poverty grew significantly between 1975 and 1991 when the Fijian economy was growing relatively rapidly. In other words, no effective trickle-down effect was occurring, which meant that inequalities were simultaneously increasing. Secondly, Fiji has achieved greater levels of economic growth than other island states, hence the extent of poverty and inequality is probably greater in other places, notably in Melanesia and Micronesia (Connell 2003a).

In every state urban areas are growing faster than the rate of population growth. Consequently, informal settlements are growing particularly quickly, as the supply of land and formal housing is inadequate to meet the needs of new migrants (or even established residents). In the two largest cities in the region, Port Moresby and Suva, settlements house more than half the urban population. In Suva, the expansion of settlements is a result of rural-urban migration precipitated by the demand for services (especially education), the expiry of land leases and the breakdown of extended families. Similar rationales exist elsewhere.

Many urban poor live in settlements, and socioeconomic inequalities are most evident in urban areas. Those who are poorest are those with little support from the rural economy and no opportunity to move away from town when poverty, rising unemployment, old age or social disorder make life difficult. In settlements such as Blacksands, Vila (Vanuatu), insecurity over land tenure and employment ensured that migrants often contemplated return migration but usually chose to remain for their children's sake. Most households in Blacksands had incomes below the national average and at least a quarter had problems meeting school fees, paying rent and providing food. Most supplemented their cash incomes from subsistence food gardens (Mecartney 2001), an option not always open to settlement residents, especially in Port Moresby. Low incomes and a lack of support during illness or unemployment give a sense of biding time, waiting for unforeseen and uncertain opportunities and sometimes securing multiple jobs, maintaining strict budgets and abandoning some 'traditional' obligations, simply to get by. Many urban residents survive rather than prosper in the city.

One consequence of urban growth exceeding urban job creation is the steady emergence of the informal sector, with particularly rapid growth in prostitution and the rise of crime. In the two main cities, and elsewhere, the rise of urban poverty and the informal sector has been marked by new repressions of the poor and marginalised, in new forms of anti-urban policies, as they are forced out of urban areas, most dramatically by the bulldozing of settlements, and by attempts to devolve solutions to the churches from the State, rather than by concerted attempts to devise welfare and employment policies that might reduce such problems (Connell 2003d; Koczberski et al. 2001). Anti-urbanism is not matched by pro-ruralism. Even urban markets and market vendors have been opposed by urban and national governments, despite their ability to provide substantial employment for youths and women. Social disorganisation and crime are functions of substantial inequalities in access to land, housing and other services. Port Moresby has been declared the most unlivable city in the world, because of the extent of crime and violence, much of it fuelled by lack of access to urban resources.

Unemployment is essentially an urban phenomenon, and rising unemployment occurs in all urban areas, though there are rarely adequate measures of its extent. Where there are more or less reliable measurements, urban unemployment is never below 10 per cent and might well be higher in many cases. Unemployment is particularly high among youths (Bryant 1993: 46; Abbott and Pollard 2004), and there is growing recognition of the existence of significant numbers of unemployed and marginalised youth in most urban centres, such as Port Vila

(Mitchell 2004); and inadequate access to employment, land and credit have led to increased levels of unemployment in the small Vava'u town of Neiafu and in Nuku'alofa (Gailey 1992b). This, in turn, has stimulated emigration. Broadly similar conditions occur throughout the region, but are much less evident and undocumented in the smaller states (Abbott and Pollard 2004). They are seedbeds of discontent and incentives to migration, but those affected are among the least able to achieve, or gain from, it.

Urban poverty bears some relationship to internal migration since it is evident at least in PNG, but almost certainly elsewhere, that the urban poor are often those who have migrated from the most impoverished rural areas (such as remote areas on the fringes of the Highlands). People are thus moving away from rural poverty, in the sense of inadequate access to employment and income-earning activities, and towards services; yet migration tends to transfer poverty to urban areas. It is in this very broad context, which takes minimal note of either substantial or subtle regional variations, that migration is embedded.

A population context?

All states within the region are going through the demographic transition: hence the 'doomsday syndrome', which was prevalent a decade ago as the Pacific, and especially traced to Melanesia, then seemingly facing explosive growth rates, is now a thing of the past. (Fry 1997: 333–4; Chappell 2005: 295; cf. Bedford 2003). Nonetheless, population growth rates remain high in some states. While the average population growth rate is about 2.2 per cent, in Vanuatu and Solomon Islands it is about 2.6 per cent, though in both states it is now falling. In several states, such as Fiji, Tonga and Samoa, growth rates are less than 1 per cent, partly because of high levels of out-migration. Here, as elsewhere in the region, there are very great differences.

Throughout the region life expectancies have risen in the past quarter of a century, but remain lowest in the Melanesian states. Infant mortality rates are also highest in Melanesia, with PNG and Kiribati (at 88 per thousand) being the worst of the region. In PNG there is evidence that the infant mortality rates are increasing largely because of the inadequate, and declining, provision of health services to rural areas. Some of the worst health and mortality problems are experienced in the growing urban settlements, especially in Port Moresby and those urban areas established on coral atolls (Connell and Lea 1992).

Although prolonged rural-urban migration, increasing pressure on rural land and urban services, rising youth unemployment, social discontent and high levels of maternal mortality all contributed to a more favourable climate for establishing population policies, as in PNG (McMurray 1992: 13), developing and implementing population policies has proved difficult. The factors that are most conducive to successful population policies — integration of population and development policies, improved rural development and communications to spread new values and reduce the economic significance of children, formal sector employment opportunities for women of increasing age of marriage — are usually absent. The outcome of high population growth rates has been that in most states there is a preponderance of young adults in the population, a situation that has placed strains on land resources, but also on employment markets, education and social organisation. A critical development issue throughout the Pacific is that of maintaining, let alone improving, present standards of living in the face of continued population increase.

In certain localised contexts, population pressure on resources is perceived as a growing problem. This is true in parts of the Highlands of PNG, and also in some coral atolls where, at least in Kiribati and Tuvalu, a 'Malthusian crisis' was recognised as early as the 1880s (Munro and Bedford 1980), and Islanders were being resettled in the 1940s. There are many local areas where population pressure on resources has created tensions, where land is not freely available, but is zealously guarded by its traditional owners. In Solomon Islands recent conflicts around Honiara were partly a consequence of Malaitans leaving their own densely populated island and settling on the land of the local Guadalcanal population, who resented the loss of their resources (and the greater competition for scarce urban jobs). More broadly, it has recently been argued that there is a possible correlation between recent political tensions in the Melanesian region (Fiji, Vanuatu and the Solomon Islands), where migration is said to be limited or non-existent, and Polynesian and Micronesian states, where migration has been considerable and political stability much greater (Ware 2005). The argument no longer holds true for Fiji, and in any case there are other crucial differences and indications of tensions elsewhere (most recently in Tonga), which suggest that the relationship between migration, population pressure on resources and political tensions is much more complex.

Internal migration

International movements (see below) are paralleled by intensified migration within particular countries. This migration has been characterised by movement away from remote islands and isolated rural areas to more accessible coastal locations and particularly to urban areas, which have usually grown steadily in recent years. Thus national populations have become increasingly concentrated on the more central urbanised islands, accentuating problems of service delivery in remote areas. This situation has in turn accentuated and accounted for further movement away from isolated areas.

The depopulation of small islands and remote mountainous areas is widespread. Employment opportunities and services are concentrated in the urban centres and on small island states; where manpower and capital are often limited, centralisation is inevitable at some scale. The more educated have tended to migrate first and migrants have left many rural areas to take advantage of superior urban educational and employment opportunities. In Blacksands settlement (Port Vila) some 7 per cent of families had moved there for better education for their children (Mecartney 2001). In other parts of Melanesia, migrants have moved away from inadequate rural opportunities, not because of the perceived superiority of urban opportunities, but out of increasing rural poverty.

In most Pacific countries, earning power is concentrated increasingly among urban bureaucracies while the absence of developed state mechanisms (such as progressive taxation, unemployment benefits and pension schemes) for affecting transfers of income minimises redistribution towards rural areas other than through personal remittances. Yet ultimately an economic rationale, real or latent, underlies most migration moves. Simply stated, in Port Vila, one of the most important reasons was *'long winem smal vatu from no gat rod long winim vatu long aelan'* (to earn a little money since there's no way to earn money on the home island) (Mitchell 2000: 172). For many that is reason enough. Growing inequalities, coupled with rising expectations, are the concomitants of increased migration.

Within the Melanesian states especially, remittances from urban to rural areas continue to play an important role, especially where migration is from small islands, such as Ponam or Ware in PNG. Otherwise they are of lesser economic significance, though they might be of considerable social significance (Mecartney 2001). Even for remote parts of large islands such as Tanna, Vanuatu, however, remittances from urban migrants are the single largest source of income in several villages (Winthorpe 2004).

Expectations are rising steadily but, at the same time, employment crises in many urban areas, growing populations, inflation, static (or even falling) commodity prices and the declining availability of land in some areas, slowly increase the gap between expectation and reality, at the same time as it becomes more visible. This increasing gap is a critical problem. Experiences and perceptions of the wider world, its values and its material rewards further underlie the migratory experience.

The existence of kin in urban areas is a major influence and support. Not only do they provide demonstrations, or create images, of an impressive lifestyle, they might also provide remittances (the visible monetary symbols of success), fares and accommodation for new migrants to the city. Indeed, migration is often best seen 'as an almost inevitable decision that they [villagers] will have to make sooner or later and once this view is accepted a sort of migration momentum develops' (Walsh 1982: 7). The spreading taste for commodities has influenced work habits and, for many in the Pacific, the largest cities and the metropolitan countries exercise a powerful allure, offer a sense of future and simply validate migration. In urban areas, especially in Melanesia and Micronesia, growing differentiation has occurred between those permanent urban residents who are relatively poor (including some long-established urban villagers and the migrants from poor rural areas) and others who are well off. The particularly disadvantaged had little or no support from the rural economy and no opportunity to move away from town when poverty, rising unemployment, old age or social disorder made urban life difficult, at least for those who were, in one way or another, 'trapped' in town. In Blacksands, insecurity over land tenure and employment ensured that migrants contemplated return, but most realistically believed they would remain in town for their children's sake (Mecartney 2001: 80). As in many international contexts (see below) return migration is constantly deferred ('until children leave school', 'until enough money is saved', 'until retirement', etc.) until the point where it becomes implausible. The combination of growing urban permanency, high unemployment and increased expectations has put considerable pressure on urban services.

Until relatively recently, urbanisation in the Pacific was viewed positively, but since independence attitudes to urbanisation have hardened, through prejudice against squatter settlements. In PNG especially opposition to urbanisation has continued, from urban authorities and influential leaders (Connell and Lea 2002; Goddard 2001; Koczberski et al. 2001) in the guise of achieving order and cleanliness, reducing crime and unemployment, freeing land for business development and demonstrating that the State was not weak. Pervasive opposition to urbanisation has delayed and discouraged the development of coordinated plans for urban management, and hence the reduction of urban development problems. Ironically there is no evidence that it has slowed rural-urban migration.

International migration

Since the 1960s there has been accelerated migration from the Pacific region, as Islanders begin to seek employment and access to services in the metropolitan states on the fringes of the region: mainly New Zealand, Australia and the USA. International migration remains primarily a Polynesian phenomenon, and a phenomenon of the past half-century. Many people from Niue, the Cook Islands, American Samoa, Tonga and Samoa have moved either to New Zealand (whence some have gone on to Australia) or, increasingly, as the New Zealand economy has stagnated and immigration restrictions have become tighter, to the USA (Connell 1987a) — legally or illegally. For the smallest states, including the Cook Islands, Niue, Tokelau and Pitcairn, migration has been particularly dramatic since a majority of the ethnic population live overseas. Niue, Tokelau and the Cook Islands have experienced declining populations in the past quarter of a century, while it has long been forecast that the smallest state, Pitcairn, might simply disappear as its population falls below what is sustainable (Connell 1988b). Niue too is presently seeking immigration from Tuvalu as its population has declined sharply in the recent context of Cyclone Heta and a long-term 'culture of migration' (Connell 2006). Larger states, such as Samoa and Tonga, have experienced very limited population growth as emigration has become something of a 'safety valve' for high population growth rates (cf. Ware 2005), but more obviously for, at best, slowly growing economies.

In the larger countries of Melanesia, economies have perhaps been more viable, political ties less effective and emigration conspicuous by its absence, though there has been significant emigration from Fiji, especially of Indo-Fijians. This dramatically accelerated after the 1987 and 2000 coups, with migration to Australia, New Zealand and also Canada. Quite new patterns of skilled migration have taken nurses from Fiji to a diversity of destinations from the Marshall Islands and Palau to New Zealand and the United Arab Emirates (e.g., Rokoduru 2002; Connell 2004b), and took rugby players beyond the 'traditional' destinations of New Zealand and Australia to Japan and the United Kingdom. Even newer patterns of emigration have become particularly important in the past couple of years with a new structure of migration to the Middle East, emphasising the manner in which new and highly paid overseas employment opportunities are being grasped firmly, even in a threatening security and social context.

In mid-2005, some 134 Fijian soldiers were deployed in Iraq, and the Government was contemplating sending another 90 to join the peacekeeping forces, continuing a long-existing policy of Fijian soldiers working for the UN, for example, in Lebanon. A second group of Fijian soldiers was in Iraq as members of the British Army, with one estimate putting this number as high as 1,000 (Pareti 2005a). Others were peacekeepers in the Solomon Islands (as they had earlier been in Bougainville). Many former Fijian soldiers were employed as security guards for private companies in the major Iraqi cities, and other Fijians were employed in support roles in Kuwait, covering engineering, mechanical and IT roles.

Estimates of the numbers recruited to the Middle East from Fiji are variable but have gone as high as 20,000, within little more than two years (Pareti 2005b), though this figure relates to the numbers recruited, who had paid fees of more than $F150 (emphasising the demand), rather than those who had actually migrated, which might be about 2,500. Recruitment has covered all regions of Fiji, appears to have focused entirely on ethnic Fijians, and recruitment companies have allocated quotas to churches.

Recruitment drives have touched on circuits of the Methodist Church to the extent of job quotas for specific church circuits. On farmlands in Baulevu, beside the Rewa River, groups of men wait and hope they will be included in the 150 quota given to the Kasavu Methodist Church. In Raiwaqa in Suva, and Nadera, the Methodist Church has offered to use church funds to pay for application fees for members hoping for a job in Kuwait if they agree to repay the money.

In Dreketi Tikina, in Macuata, a village used its development fund to pay for application fees. Similar stories have been heard from Koro Island and other villages around the country (Pareti 2005a).

Such a village basis for migration, and support for and selection of migrants, is reminiscent of earlier labour migration schemes to New Zealand (see below). There are, however, real disadvantages, in terms of the loss of skills to Fiji (Pareti 2005b) and circumstances where more than a dozen workers have been killed in the Middle East.

So substantial has this migration become that a recent study of migration and remittances in Fiji (and Tonga) revealed that as many as one-third of all households in Fiji had at least one overseas migrant, and remitter (compared with 60 per cent in Tonga), and 43 per cent of households received remittances (compared with 90 per cent in Tonga). In circumstances where households might be the migrant unit (especially for Indo-Fijians), this is a remarkably high percentage, after a relatively short period of engagement in international labour migration, and already reflects the substantial presence of Fijians in the security industry in the Middle East (Brown et al. 2006). Moreover, Indo-Fijian households were also remittance recipients, contrary to earlier beliefs that few received remittances. It has been stated that the earnings of 250 Fijian soldiers working in Iraq for a UK security company totalled nearly $F5 million in a six-month period in 2004–05, with all that pay being sent back to bank accounts in Fiji (*Pacific Islands Report*, April 14, 2005). Recent estimates have suggested that remittances to Fiji were about $A269 million in 2005 (Brown et al. 2006) or would reach about $F350 million in 2005 (Pareti 2005b), well up from the $A71 million in 2002, and substantially more than transfers from Fiji (Gani 2005). These recent events in Fiji emphasise and dramatise the 'outward urge' that has become so powerful in the region.

The former US territories of Micronesia — Palau, the FSM and particularly the Marshall Islands — have increasingly exhibited similar trends (Ahlburg and Levin, 1990; Hezel and Levin 1996; Hezel and Lightfoot 2005), with an equally substantial growth in recent migration flows. In the past 20 years, emigration accelerated from the FSM and the Marshall Islands, as the signing of the Compacts of Free Association guaranteed migration rights in the USA and its territories. Between 1990 and 2004, more than 13,000 people left the Marshall Islands for the USA, especially after government jobs were lost in public sector reforms (a situation that has also been true of the Cook Islands), so that one in five Marshallese now lives in the USA (*Fiji Times*, September 7, 2005). FSM is following a similar course. The migration process in Micronesia is becoming increasingly similar to that in other parts of the South Pacific: a steady outflow, the growth of relatively permanent urban communities overseas (beyond student groups), the return flow of remittances and growing interest in migration.

Kiribati and Tuvalu have been characterised by migration for even longer, dating back into the 19th century, but of contract labour — mainly to Nauru (for employment in the phosphate mining industry) or to work in the international shipping industry (for which both countries have training schools) — hence return migration is normal, and the impact on national population change much less significant. In the past decade, Tuvalu has experienced accelerated migration, and has requested new opportunities in metropolitan states, while the Tuvalu community in New Zealand is growing steadily. Nowhere does the demand for migration appear to be decelerating.

Interest in migration has long been such that in Samoa, when prospects for emigration were particularly poor at the start of the 1980s, the 'broken dreams' of potential migrants contributed to a significant rise in youth suicide (Macpherson and Macpherson 1987). At a national level the economic future of several states hinges partly on the continued flow of remittances, and hence on some continuity of migration (Ahlburg 1991; Connell and Brown 1995). The possibility of blocked migration in the future, a situation ever present in public debate (Macpherson 1992; Shankman 1993), emphasises the potential problem of a high rate of natural increase in case emigration is substantially reduced, especially since there is now a 'culture of migration' where emigration is normal, expected and anticipated, and an important element in household and national social and economic systems.

In recent years migration opportunities in metropolitan states have tended to decline, and are increasingly targeted towards skilled migrants rather than family reunions. Thus migration flows from the Pacific are increasingly likely to be of skilled migrants from various sectors including health (Connell 2004a, 2004b) and education (Voigt-Graf 2003), as the overall number of migrants from the independent states has tended to fall. Structural changes within metropolitan states have meant that certain sectors, notably health, are short of skilled workers. Pacific Island nurses, usually entering the bottom levels of the 'global health care chain', have migrated much greater distances, to the United Arab Emirates and beyond, as demand intensifies. Before the early 1980s, male migration had preceded female or family migration throughout the South Pacific, but there is now minimal gender bias in the numbers of Pacific Islanders migrating to the Pacific Rim; however, preferences are shifting towards women. In many cases, families migrate as units either as skilled migrants on the basis of one of the spouse's qualifications or as family migrants. There are, however, flows of specific occupational categories, which are either male or female dominated. For instance, Fijian women have migrated as nurses, domestic helpers and care-givers, while Fijian men have moved overseas as soldiers, tourism workers and employees of private security companies (Voigt-Graf and Connell 2005).

Thus in recent years migration has become more complex, globalisation has extended the number of destinations and brought longer migration chains, migration has become more selective, and part of that selectivity has favoured the migration of women. The more remote and rural parts of the island states are even less likely to be perceived as favourable places of residence. This has been matched with continued urbanisation throughout the island region. Although the largest concentrations of Pacific Islanders are in overseas destinations, such as Auckland and Honolulu, urbanisation now characterises the Pacific (Connell and Lea 2002), especially where international migration remains largely absent.

A rationale

Migration decisions are usually shaped within a family context, as migrants leave to meet certain family expectations, the key one of which is usually financial support for kin. Migration has rarely been an individual decision to meet individual goals, nor has it been dictated by national interests (except perhaps in the case of Kiribati and Tuvalu). Migration is directed at improving the living standards of those who remain at home and the lifestyle and income of the migrants. In Tonga, 'there are few opportunities for socioeconomic advancement … and migration is perceived as the only solution' (Lee 2004: 135). In Samoa, the reason for migration was simply 'to seek wealth for all' (Muliaina 2001: 25). Consequently, 'families deliberate carefully about which members would be most likely to do well overseas and be reliable in sending remittances' (Gailey 1992b: 465; Cowling 1990). Through this process, extended households, as in Tonga, have transformed themselves into 'transnational corporations of kin', which strategically allocate family labour to local and overseas destinations to maximise income opportunities, minimise risk and benefit from resultant remittance flows (Marcus 1981). To an even greater extent, therefore, than for internal migration (where health, education and social reasons explain some part of migration), international migration is more evidently an economic phenomenon, though other factors are necessarily involved.

Developing this notion, Bertram (1986: 820) has suggested that migrant extended households are characterised 'by remittance transfers among various component parts of the "transnational corporations of kin" which direct the allocation of each island's family labour around the regional economy', and in so doing not only help to maintain these family and communal networks but even enlarge their social fields of interaction, incorporating them into multi-local networks of support and empowerment. Similarly, for households in Samoa, 'having young wage earners abroad diversified families' earnings streams and reduced their dependence on high-risk activities. Having family members in several locations abroad diversified earning sources and reduced risk levels still further' (Macpherson 2004: 168). Moreover, Macpherson went on to argue that families 'using intelligence from migrants abroad, periodically surveyed risks and returns in various enclaves and encouraged others abroad to relocate in places in which returns were found to be higher and risks lower'.

In this way Samoans were, for example, encouraged to join the US military because jobs were assured, wages were higher and education could be obtained without loss of earnings. 'If this analysis depicts Samoans as calculative and instrumental, it is because in relation to risk and return they are necessarily so … [as] risks and returns available in various places were formally canvassed and modeled by families' (ibid.). While this form of household consensus certainly occurs, and demonstrates the significance of access to the migration-remittances nexus, it has been argued that applying the same kind of model in Tonga tends to portray families as being in agreement about their economic aims and functions, whereas there are often conflicts and tensions within them (Lee 2004: 136). In Kiribati and Tuvalu, where seafarers are away from their wives and parents and send remittances to both, there are frequent disagreements about their allocation and use (Dennis 2003: 35). There are household uncertainties about outcomes in various places. Moreover, more than a decade ago, James argued that in many Tongan villages remittances were becoming individualised and the idea of a transnational community of kin was becoming increasingly invalid (James 1993b: 361; Lee 2003: 31). The extent of greater individualisation is impossible to determine, but such conflicts over use emphasise, rather than downplay, the role of remittances.

Political factors have also been significant influences on migration in various contexts, notably in the migration from Fiji that followed the 1987 and 2000 coups, and in the skilled migration from Bougainville and the Solomon Islands during the recent crises. In Fiji, migration was not only of ethnic Indians, arguably most affected by the coups, but of Fijians, emphasising how migration could be seen as 'a barometer of fear' of further conflict (Narayan and Smyth 2003). Environmental factors have similarly influenced migration. There has been recent movement from such places as the Carteret Islands in PNG, where localised sea-level rise posed particular problems, and even more recently from Manam (PNG) and the northern islands of the Marianas, after volcanic eruptions. Cyclone Heta, which devastated Niue in January 2004, destroying almost one-quarter of the houses on the island, even prompted some thoughts about the permanent abandonment of the island (with the remaining 1,500 people following so many of their kin to New Zealand). Global warming poses a future threat to the islands, and especially to more than 100 populated coral atolls, should sea-level rise occur. In Tuvalu, fears are such that emigration has already occurred in anticipation of new difficulties (Connell 2003d). Island states are in no position financially, geographically or politically to defend themselves against such potential threats, but if — perhaps when — the worst does occur, Islanders might become a new stream of environmental refugees to metropolitan states.

Remittances

Remittances play an increasingly important role, especially in the smaller island states. In many countries remittances form a significant part of disposable income, hence the smaller island states (specifically initially Kiribati, Tokelau, Cook Islands and Tuvalu) have long been conceptualised as MIRAB states, where Migration, Remittances, Aid and the resultant largely urban Bureaucracy are central to the socioeconomic system (Bertram and Watters 1985). The notion of MIRAB is applicable also in rather larger states such as Samoa and Tonga, where remittances constitute some of the highest proportions of GNP of any country in the world. While this acronym is disliked in the Pacific, for cultural reasons and because of its implication of a 'handout mentality', it nonetheless suggests the centrality of migration and remittances in the island states, and has been largely unchallenged for two decades (Bertram 1999). It spawned other acronyms such as MURAB, which places extra and appropriate emphasis on the attendant urbanisation within island states such as Tuvalu (Munro 1990), and even MIAB, where migration did not initially stimulate a significant flow of remittances, as in some parts of Micronesia (Ogden 1994; Karakita 1997), though there is now a shift in this direction (Grieco 2003; Connell and Brown 2005).

Because of the continued and increasing significance of remittances, the sustainability of remittance-dependent development is particularly important — and necessarily uncertain — especially if, in the countries of origin, the need for remittances grows faster than its supply (Macpherson 1992), or if the number and flow of migrants dwindle. The rate of growth of migration to major destinations, namely New Zealand, Australia and the USA, has declined in recent years due to the restructuring of migration controls; return migration has also sometimes been considerable (Maron 2001), and migration has become increasingly more selective towards those with skills (Liki 2001; Brown and Connell 2004). Even with continued migration, however, an anticipated imbalance is assumed to occur because of the dynamics of settlement migration. With family reunification and with greater integration of migrants in the host communities, their ability and willingness to remit have been expected to decline over time (e.g., Macpherson 1994). If that were so, without other sources of income, the future of the economies of remittance-dependent Pacific countries would be uncertain.

Only recently have second and third generations of Pacific Islanders grown up outside their island 'homes'; hence the extent to which they will remit to the island Pacific (and even whether they can be described as 'Islanders' or 'migrants') is not well known. There is some evidence that the links between second-generation Samoans in New Zealand and Tongans in Australia with Samoans in Samoa and Tongans in Tonga respectively are declining, though, at least in the latter case, links are maintained with other migrant Tongans elsewhere

(Muliaina 2001; Lee 2003, 2004a). Similarly, these new generations are more likely to act as individuals rather than perceive themselves as members of wider transnational social groupings. Anecdotal evidence points to the growing individualism of overseas migrants, but especially to the increasing numbers of second-generation Islanders born overseas, and the reduced likelihood of such people sending remittances to their 'home' countries, especially if they take up host country citizenship. Thus one migrant Tongan has observed of the Australian context: 'People who were born here [Tonga] or went to school here send remittances. People born there? No way!' (quoted by James 1997: 20). Many Tongans in Melbourne have lost interest in continued financial support of their overseas kin, as their sense of *kavenga* (obligations) has declined over time (Lee 2004). Similarly skilled Tongan migrants in Sydney are increasingly stating that they no longer remit (Fusitu'a 2000). Though data on Tongan and Samoan nurses in Australia indicate that even skilled migrants sustain remittances at high levels and over long periods, those data date from the mid-1990s (Brown and Connell 2004, 2005), though circumstances might not have changed.

Remittances are particularly important in the smaller states of Polynesia and Micronesia, and in the more remote islands in those states. Thus for the tiny coral atoll of Manihiki (Cook Islands), migration and the resultant remittances have been seen as so crucial that they constitute nothing less than a socioeconomic strategy for collective survival (Underhill 1989). In Nanumea, in Tuvalu, remittances grew from being about half of the island income in the 1970s and 1980s to some 75 per cent in the 1990s, in large part because of the collapse of copra marketing as world prices slumped (Chambers and Chambers 2001: 156). In Kiribati, the 2000 census recorded that overseas remittances, primarily from seamen, were the primary source of income for as many as 30 per cent of households in the urban centre of South Tarawa, and, in 2002, some 35 per cent of all households in Tuvalu received remittances. In both countries this was usually the main source of income in the outer islands (Abbott and Pollard 2004; Borovnik 2003). Similar situations occur in other small islands and island states, and there is mounting evidence that the northern Micronesian states are now following this pattern (Connell and Brown 2005: 6).

Conventional wisdom suggests that remittances are used overwhelmingly for consumption objectives and inadequate amounts are directed towards investment. There are, however, alternative perceptions of the use of remittances and issues of fungibility (where the specific use of remittances cannot easily be distinguished from other spending patterns and might distort them) (Connell and Brown 2005). After debt repayment, remittances are used for housing and for community goals (such as water tanks and churches), airfares and education (an investment in social capital). They are also used for various forms of investment, sometimes in the agricultural sector but more frequently in the service sector, and especially in stores and transport businesses. In Samoa and elsewhere, remittance money has constituted the start-up funds for many shopkeepers and other small business entrepreneurs. Half of all market vendors in Apia (Samoa), all of whom received remittances, claimed that some had been used as capital for the purchase of seeds, fertiliser and tools to engage in food production for sale (Muliaina 2001: 28). Even on a small outer island such as Falahola (Tonga), remittances have been used for economic ventures, ranging from agriculture to tourism, though remoteness has limited their success (James 1991: 18–20). Throughout Tonga the increased use of remittances for investment purposes, in fishing, agriculture, stores and transport businesses, attests to the shift from consumption to investment (Faeamani 1995; Walker and Brown 1995), which has occurred in part as consumption goals have been satisfied. This transition has also occurred in Pakistan (Helweg 1983), parts of rural PNG (Boyd 1990) and in similar small-island environments in several parts of the eastern Caribbean (Connell and Conway 2000). While the transition might benefit economic development, at least one anthropologist (Small 1997: 134, 195, 199) has raised concerns that it might also further emphasise intra-village (and country) economic inequalities and hamper social development.

Remittances have also contributed to urban investments of various kinds. The expansion of the Nuku'alofa flea market in Tonga since the mid-1980s demonstrated the manner in which many households used remittances as an investment in their market stalls, and later economic diversification (Brown and Connell 1993). Moreover, as James has noted, 'It has been argued that remittances take away the motivation of locals to produce, but the facts of local entrepreneurship seem to contradict this since large consignments of local products ... are sent to relatives overseas for sale among the Polynesian population' (1991: 2). Even in the most difficult circumstances, remittance recipients make efforts to invest where they can. In the outer islands of Kiribati, where most remittances went into providing basic needs, and the custom of *bubuti* (a request that cannot be refused) makes savings let alone business almost impossible, all recipients nevertheless sought to retain some income to invest in land purchase, doughnut bakeries, stores or even in sewing material for blouses that might later be sold (Borovnik 2004). Here, as elsewhere, there is no evidence that any part of the economy is abandoned or neglected but that remittances enable some limited diversification. Where there are opportunities, and where consumption goals have been satisfied, remittances are used for investment, to stimulate entrepreneurial and trading activity, increase the extent of formal sector employment and produce multiplier effects.

Even so, it has often been argued that remittances (and aid) are not conducive to private sector development, broadly what Ahlburg (1995: 42) has called the 'disincentive effect'. Indeed, the MIRAB model implies that there is a strong bureaucratic outcome, which might stifle, rather than enable, increased productivity. This perspective was stressed by a series of authors in the 1990s, in overt or subtle attacks on the perceived stultifying role of aid in the region and the consequent necessity to stimulate the private sector (e.g., MacMaster 1993; Browne 1995; Duncan 1994; Pollard 1995; La Plagne et al. 2001). In the case of Tonga, Sturton argued that '[t]he Tongan economy displays all the characteristic markings of the "Dutch disease" where a dominant export activity attracts a disproportionate command over resources, pushes up domestic production costs, and reduces international competitiveness. In the Tongan case the "booming" sector has become development assistance and migrants' remittances' (1992: 3). Similarly, Faeamani has argued that, through the combination of the loss of young adults and an inflow of cash in the form of remittances and goods, 'there is a consequent reduction in garden size and production' (1995: 140; see Fairbairn 1993). More generally, several authors have stressed the wide-ranging notions of dependency that remittances appear to create.

It is implausible that remittances have no disincentive effects, but there is remarkably little direct evidence of this. MacMaster has suggested that in the Cook Islands, Tonga and Samoa remittances are 'a mixed blessing as they undermine the incentive to work and are rarely spent on productive investment. They are normally used for unproductive ceremonial purposes or on imported luxury consumption items' (1993: 279). These and other similar statements and conclusions (e.g., Ahlburg 1991: 39; Finau 1994: 308; World Bank 1990: 4) have suggested overall that 'it is not clear that the net effect of remittances and aid is conducive to long-term economic viability and prosperity' (Cuthbertson and Cole 1995: xiv). Few of these studies present data that justify these assumptions and conclusions.

It is all too often assumed that there is no desire to maximise (or even improve) incomes, hence Islanders become perceived as somewhat irrational or even lazy. Indeed, as Muliaina has observed, even second-generation Samoans in New Zealand assume that their relatives in Samoa are failing to take proper economic advantage of obvious land and marine resources (2001: 33). A similar situation appears to be more broadly true in the Pacific:

The growing flows of remittances into some countries (Kiribati, Samoa, Tonga, Tuvalu and increasingly Fiji Islands) are giving rise to what many [Islander] respondents termed laziness or over-dependence on others. This 'easy money' was perceived by many respondents to be a disincentive for young people to actively look for work. (Abbott and Pollard 2004: 61)

It is at least as likely that actively looking for work might well have been a waste of time. Moreover, subsistence activity is only exceptionally abandoned or reduced, despite remittances and attitudes in opposition to it. Where conditions are appropriate to adequate income generation, even where remittances have reached high levels, the private sector might flourish and be stimulated by remittances.

The 'crowding out' argument was prominent in the initial formulation of the MIRAB model by Bertram and Watters, who argued that, with additional sources of income from remittances (and indirectly from aid), people 'can be expected to evaluate the return on [agricultural] investments relative to the alternatives. On this basis it would be expected that as the alternatives to commercially oriented agriculture would improve, so a reallocation of household effort away from agriculture would take place' (1985: 511). Despite Faeamani's (1995) observations on declining production in Tongan villages, this might be exceptional, and indeed might be more likely to be a function of labour shortages (Evans 1996, 2001). Even so, as agricultural decline does occur, as has partly happened in the Cook Islands and Niue (Connell and Brown 2005), it is 'what is required for efficient economic behaviour: that the family allocates its resources to the highest productive use, even if it happens that this particular use is not "productive" in the "domestic" economy, but rather in a "foreign" economy' (Poirine 1998: 77).

Most studies of remittances have observed that a significant proportion of remittances support 'traditional' customs and obligations. This is at least in part because economic opportunities are few, so investing in custom avoids what would amount to 'intensive self-exploitation in agricultural activity' and gives villagers respect and autonomy (Evans 2001: 17–18). Similarly, sellers in the Nuku'alofa flea market, most of whose goods arrived as remittances — and who might be seen as involved in trade and investment, the fetishisation of cash, sales rather than gifts, thus epitomising the rise of market capitalism — preferred to see themselves as located within complex, reciprocal exchange systems that 'maintained the social integrity of Tongan society despite diasporic fragmentation' (Besnier 2004: 19). It is simply more appropriate to engage in exchange and gift-giving rather than sale and purchase, hence commercial practices are downplayed in favour of social obligations. The social and the economic cannot be disentangled.

Successful development of small businesses provides some incentive for those who have sent remittances to return home and manage those businesses. In overseas Polynesian households that include nurses, the greatest propensity to return comes from those with business investments at home (Brown and Connell 2004). International migration has provided new opportunities for women, including those in remote areas and outer islands, as in Tonga, where the production of traditional textiles (*koloa*) for the ceremonial economy is a prime example (Horan 2002). Overseas Tongan women lack access to the required raw materials and often also to time, instead importing these textiles from Tonga. Their reciprocal contribution of remittances further exemplifies how remittances are constituted through a process that might be seen simultaneously as social exchange and trade.

The MIRAB model has been largely unchallenged for two decades (Bertram 1999), and continues to be recognised in new contexts. It has, however, been appropriately observed that the model appears to largely deny any real semblance of agency to Pacific Islanders, other than as migrants, though this has been evident, for example, in a range of autonomous agricultural and other activities, such as the 1990s' boom in squash cultivation in Tonga (van der Grijp 1999; cf. Hooper 1993), and in the above example of *koloa* production. Moreover, it is evident that

> Islanders in their homelands are not the parasites on their relatives abroad that misinterpreters of 'remittances' would have us believe. Economists do not take account of the social centrality of the ancient practice of reciprocity. … They overlook the fact that for everything homeland relatives receive they reciprocate with goods they themselves produce, by maintaining ancestral roots and lands for everyone. … This is not dependence but interdependence. (Hau'ofa 1994: 157; van der Grijp 2004)

At the very least, remittances have complex and important social and economic dimensions.

The use and structure of remittances have changed over time, with significant intergenerational shifts in their structure. Initially remittances are sent to parents — as is so clearly happens in the majority of Pacific cases — and in an economic sense can be seen as repayment for their past investment in the human capital of the migrant; in a social sense this is usually expressed as duty, loyalty and maintenance of family ties. A second wave of remittances is subsequently more likely to be dominated by brothers and sisters and by children; this phase might also correspond with a decline in the volume of remittances. Decline after the death of parents seems ubiquitous (e.g., Muliaina 2001: 25). That phase can be seen as an investment in the human capital of the next generation (Brown and Poirine 2005). The third and final phase represents payments to spouses — and indirectly (via investment) to the remitters themselves, as return migration and/or retirement are approached. Some shifts in the destination of remittances are universal, sometimes paralleled by a decline in volumes, but both trends point to a structure that increasingly favours the interests of the senders.

The limited available evidence on the remittance patterns of the second generation indicates that, as Lee (2003, 2004a, 2004b) and Muliaina (2001) have emphasised, they respond only indirectly through the urgings of their parents and their sense of family, and they therefore contribute very limited sums. This is particularly significant as migration opportunities decline and the number of overseas-born

'Islanders' becomes the majority. Thus overseas-born Tongans (or 'Tongans') in New Zealand, as also in Melbourne (Lee 2004b), alongside Cook Islanders, Niueans and others in New Zealand, are now a majority rather than a minority. Not only does this probably mean that for all these groups their remittances are limited, but their social and economic ties are likely to increasingly be with each other rather than with 'home', so accentuating this trend. Lee (2004b: 10–11) has thus concluded that

> [u]nless there are profound changes in the relationship of the younger generations with the Tongan 'homeland' and in their sense of 'belonging', the prospect of maintaining current levels of remittances is remote, which gives serious concern for Tonga's economic situation.

She further warned against the complacency of many people in Tonga, and institutions outside, towards the notion that remittances would continue into the indefinite future (ibid.). As overseas generations lose language and cultural skills, or 'marry out', their sense of belonging must decline. Moreover, there is no certainty that migrants' economic status will always improve.

Overall, remittances have contributed substantially to welfare in most states, especially improved housing, and to raised levels of consumption. Despite widespread concerns that remittances are spent rather than invested and constitute a 'moral hazard' by reducing the incentive of recipients to work (Wheatley 2003), there is limited evidence in support of this in the Pacific. Remittances are invested where this is feasible and opportunities exist and, as in other parts of the world, there has been a shift in the use of remittances from consumption to investment (Connell and Brown 2005). Remittances have contributed to employment (especially in the service and construction sectors) and eased balance of payments problems, despite contributing to inflation. Moreover, remittances have been sustained to a higher level and over longer periods than has been predicted, or has occurred in other parts of the world. This has often entailed some sacrifices by senders, to the extent that this might have hampered their own futures; thus, in a recent article lamenting the educational and economic success of Pacific Islanders in Australia, a Tongan lawyer stated, 'If the kids are not doing too well at school, they could spend $30 on tutoring. Rather than send away $1,000 to the folks back home that $30 investment will pay off in the long term' (quoted in Tora 2005: 5). That shift towards prioritising the nuclear family is occurring only slowly.

There is no consensus on whether remittances improve or worsen income distribution. This is unsurprising given diverse contexts. Until relatively recently, the dominant view was that remittances tended to reinforce income inequality, by enhancing the capacity of recipient households to invest in additional migration, education and other income-generating assets (Connell 1980; Shankman 1976). Some village-level studies have demonstrated considerable income inequality (Hardaker et al. 1987) and suggested that this is partly a result of remittance flows (Gailey 1992a; Small 1997: 134, 195). It is certainly a widespread perception; Marcus thus suggested, almost a decade ago, that 'the capacity to call on international resources has become a crucial factor in influencing a family's local economic conditions. The lowest stratum in contemporary Tonga are those totally dependent on the nation-state framework, and the limited resources it embodies, without any overseas options at all' (Marcus 1993: 29–30). Indeed, it is increasingly argued, as in Tonga, that 'every family needs to have someone overseas. Otherwise the family is to be pitied' (quoted in Small 1997: 152). Hence, in contrast with Western societies, it is often the single-female-headed households that survive most effectively (Gailey 1992a). More recent empirical studies, however, based on survey data have tended to challenge this view, and some macro-economic data suggest that remittances have not led to increased inter-household income inequality, at least within Tonga (Ahlburg 1991). Ahlburg (1991, 1995) and Brown (1995) found that the distribution of household income with remittances was less skewed than the distribution without remittances, while other recent studies indicated that inequality was a function of many factors, of which the migration-remittance nexus might have been an unimportant part (Evans 2001; Muliaina 2001; Halatuituia 2001). The most recent studies of migration and remittances in Tonga and Fiji have shown that those households with migrants were more likely to have a higher income, independent of remittances, but the direction of causality was unclear (Brown et al. 2006). A consensus in very diverse circumstances is improbable.

A number of conclusions on remittances are, however, possible. Firstly, there has been a consistently substantial and growing volume of remittances especially in the Polynesian states (making up a significant part of national income, in excess of the value of exports and aid). Secondly, the use of these remittances has gone through a partial transition from consumption to investment, as many consumption goals have been met, at least in part. Thirdly, remittances have been particularly important in the most remote islands where development needs are less well met (and probably therefore reduce inequality). Fourthly, remittances contribute to valuable objectives such as human resource development, and are a means of maintaining social networks and creating social capital (Grieco 2003). In several contexts, especially in smaller islands, education is highly valued, in a general sense and for the development of specific skills (for example, in health provision), in order to create human capital for potential migration. Overall remittances are positive and satisfying for households but insufficient in and of themselves to influence national development goals. Fifthly, households seek to increase incomes by migration and remittance strategies, even by fostering obligations and 'implicit contracts'. Even with imperfect knowledge, households are consciously making decisions in favour of the quantity and quality of education of children that boost their chances for migration and thus the supply of remittances (Brown and Connell 2004). Migration and remittances thus stem from and contribute directly and indirectly to human capital formation.

5. Migration, Dependency and Inequality in the Pacific: Old Wine in Bigger Bottles? (Part 2)

John Connell

The proportion of skilled and highly skilled Pacific Islanders among all migrants is increasing, as a result of shortages in the receiving countries, some of which — as in New Zealand and the USA — have led to private sector recruitment in the Pacific Islands. Low remuneration, poor promotion opportunities, limited training and further educational opportunities, poor working and living conditions, particularly in remote regions, are push factors for skilled migrants. The growing shortage of skilled workers has also contributed to increased intra-Pacific migration, with workers migrating to countries offering better work conditions and salaries, such as Fijian nurses and teachers migrating to the Marshall Islands and Palau, and tourism workers moving to the Cook Islands.

Selectivity and skilled migration

As metropolitan states have made migration more difficult and sought skilled migrants, illegal migration (and overstaying) and the growing dominance of skilled migration have occurred. Fiji and other island states are now seen in Australia as 'high-risk' states because of the extent of overstaying, and there are many illegal Fijian and other overstayers in the USA (e.g., Scott 2003) and New Zealand. Skilled migrants, and particularly skilled health workers, but also teachers (Voigt-Graf 2003) and football players, have made up growing proportions of migrants, especially from Tonga, Samoa and, in the wake of the 1987 and 2000 coups, Fiji. This brain-drain has become critical in some small states.

Skilled workers in general, and medical workers in particular, represent a high proportion of immigrants from island states to metropolitan states because of the increased focus on skilled migration (within declining immigration numbers) in most destinations, and the continued (and increasing) demand for health workers there (see below). Each of the principal destinations for skilled migrants — the USA, Canada, Australia and New Zealand — has the acquisition of permanent skilled migrants as one of the objectives of its immigration policies. Ironically, many of those migrants become part of a 'brain loss' or 'brain-waste' because their qualifications, despite contributing to gaining them entry, are unrecognised in the destination.

Emigration rates of skilled people have increased steadily in Pacific Island countries, particularly as overseas recruitment occurs, and especially for health workers. As a result, there is a shortage of skilled health practitioners in almost all island states. Doctors are twice as likely to migrate as nurses because wage differentials are greater, and because most nurses are women and men are often the primary decision-makers regarding migration (Brown and Connell 2004). Female Fijian nurses, however, frequently took the decision to migrate autonomously, often leaving their husbands and children behind, mainly for higher wages, but also to escape marriage problems and customary obligations (Rokoduru 2002). The recent migration of teachers and nurses to Kiribati and the Marshall Islands indicates the significance of skilled labour migration within the Pacific region, usually to countries with better working conditions and higher salaries (Rokoduru 2002: 44). Skilled migration is unlikely to decrease, given the significance of skilled worker shortages in each of the 'standard' destinations, and increased shortages in newer, more distant markets.

Outcome of skill loss

The loss of skilled labour has been a serious issue for several island states, but perhaps especially for some of the smallest, which need, but have few, skilled workers. In larger states such as Fiji, the loss is significant and problematic. Of the 8,669 professionals who left Fiji between 1987 and 2001, 2,728 were teachers, 1,774 architects and engineers, 1,410 accountants, 1,137 medical professionals and 1,620 were other professionals (Voigt-Graf 2003). Even these figures might well underestimate the true numbers due to the unreliability of data sources, overstaying, and so on, and Fiji has also lost airline pilots, army personnel and sportsmen. A survey in 2000 of the Fiji Nurses' Association found that 88 per cent of nurses migrated for higher wages; and across the region at least two-thirds of migrant workers sought higher wages (Connell 2004a). Between May 2001 and 2002, 32 doctors emigrated and the Ministry of Health has had to recruit 56 doctors from the Philippines and the Indian subcontinent to fill the gaps (Chandra 2003: 194–5). This has raised concerns about the costs and the cultural differences between patients and health workers. In some smaller states the brain drain has been equally excessive; the Cook Islands, for example, lost more than half its vocationally qualified population in the single decade from 1966 to 1976 (Connell 2005a) and much the same happened again in the mid-1990s when the national economy collapsed.

Return migration has not solved labour shortage problems and, as in Fiji and other states, the Cook Islands has turned towards Asian labour markets for replacements (Connell 2005a). In the case of the migration of Tongans and Samoans to the USA alone, 'Emigration results in the permanent loss of young educated skilled labour from the Pacific Island nations. Skilled labour is in short supply and emigration probably hinders development' (Ahlburg and Levin

1990: 84). This is certainly true more generally in the health sector, where more costly (and sometimes less skilled) replacements have sometimes been required, and in the movement of sportsmen. The combination of changing aspirations and the migration of the more educated young contributes to the brain and skill drain from national peripheries and from small states, perhaps ultimately worsening the welfare and bargaining position of those places (Connell 2004a). In small island states, it is unusually difficult to replace skilled migrants, because of the duration of training that is required and the very small demand for particular skills.

The outcome in the health sector is that basic needs are less well satisfied, especially in more remote areas, and there is a loss of morale among those who have remained, as working conditions deteriorate. Wards are closed, waiting lists and times lengthen, examinations are more cursory, or complicated by cultural differences (Connell 2004a). Large proportions of budgets are directed to referrals to distant places, and the Millennium Development Goals recede into the distance. It is equally evident that, because of the necessity for appropriate skills training, it is more difficult to substitute for (or transfer from elsewhere in the public service) absent skills in the health workforce.

Given the global demand for skilled health workers, and active recruiting by New Zealand and other states in the region (especially Fiji) there is no easy solution (Connell 2004a, 2004b). Recent work, however, has shown that nurses at least send very high levels of remittances, sustained over long periods, to the extent that their remittances are almost certainly substantially above the training costs (Brown and Connell 2004). At the same time, more nurses are joining the profession because it provides migration opportunities, hence some of the Pacific states are moving towards the situation in the Philippines, where nurses are effectively trained to be migrants. This does suggest that the economic costs of skilled migration are not as great as has been feared and might not even be negative, even if training is in the public sector and remittances are private, and it is impossible to accurately cost the health disadvantages of high levels of emigration.

Helen Ware has argued that the problems of 'brain-drain' are overstated and having an excess of professionals is not a bad thing if they have the chance to work overseas, while emigration frees up the job market at home (Sharp 2005). These are, however, two quite different contexts and job markets that have become conflated. There is a surplus of teachers in Fiji, at the same time as there is a deficit of doctors, measured by unfilled vacancies and declining service provision. While other skilled migration losses, outside the health sector, might not now be either generally significant or have negative implications, such demand-driven migration is likely to have negative consequences in the future.

There are hints that this might already be so in the context of the migration of sportsmen and military personnel.

Return migration

At no time during the past quarter of a century has there been substantial return migration, due at least partly to the great differences in income levels between the island Pacific and the metropolitan periphery, and to a host of social factors. Return migration appears to be primarily of unskilled workers (and retirees), though skilled migrants do return, despite the discrepancy in wages and working conditions (Liki 2001; Brown and Connell 2004a), so that there is return migration across a wide range of categories and age groups (Maron 2001). For the Cook Islands, many skilled, qualified and experienced people have returned and have been able to use their skills in a range of occupations, not merely in the public service (Hooker and Varcoe 1999: 96), though the Cook Islands is unusual since wages and salaries in the islands are more comparable with those in the destination. Limited return is a function of the situation in which the children of migrants are educated in the destination country and have lost some degree of contact with 'home' societies, even to the extent that they have lost critical linguistic and other skills. This is also linked to a gradual shift in the demographic balance, especially in the Polynesian states, from those states to the metropolitan fringe; relatives are increasingly likely to be found in destinations and thus there is reduced incentive to return to what is less likely to be seen as 'home'. This has obvious implications for the migration of skilled labour.

A policy context?

Within countries there is some ambivalence towards migration. In Melanesia there are major concerns about perceptions of excess migration to urban centres and often draconian policies directed to reversing migration flows, notably in PNG but also in Vanuatu and the Solomon Islands (Connell and Lea 2002; Connell 2003a). Since such practices address the symptoms of largely rural development problems, rather than their causes, they have failed to slow migration. Policies that focus on decentralisation and regional development are largely things of the past (Connell 1987c) as states exercise a more limited role in policy formation. Broadly based rural and regional development policies are unlikely to be implemented.

No country has sought to discourage international migration in recent years though several have expressed particular concerns, mainly attached to the loss of skilled labour (including nurses and army personnel), the breaching of bonds by scholarship holders or, in the case of Niue, particularly extensive migration. Early Development Plans in Samoa and Tonga did express limited concern, but there was no attempt to translate these concerns into policies that might discourage migration (especially where bureaucrats themselves were sometimes the prime beneficiaries of international migration). For the past quarter of a century, governments have neither sought to intervene in emigration nor tried to curb the loss of skilled and unskilled workers. They are unlikely to do so in the future.

Fiji is one country where there have been serious concerns about some impacts of recent migration, frequent high-level discussions of its consequences, but no policy formation to discourage it. Concerns have been expressed in Fiji within the Ministry of Health, by military leaders and by the Fiji Employers' Federation and the Ministry for Employment Opportunities (e.g., *Fiji Times*, April 2, 2004). Bonding of students who study on government scholarships has been the only policy directed at (temporarily) retaining qualified people (although most countries have sought to provide in-country tertiary training, thus discouraging international migration at formative ages). The Fiji Government, however, once tended to regard emigrants as 'traitors' and some policies effectively punished return migrants, for example, where migrant nurses had to start on a lower salary on re-employment in Fiji compared with before migration (Rokoduru 2002). While this policy discourages the temporary migration of nurses in the first place, it also discourages return migration in a sector where there are acute shortages.

More recently, however, Fiji has sought overseas migration opportunities, partly as a legacy of earlier perceptions. In 1977, the Fiji Minister of Labour argued that the provision of overseas employment was 'the greatest form of overseas aid any government can offer' (quoted in *The Fiji Times*, December 19, 1977). A quarter of a century later, in 2004, after the Minister of Labour, Kenneth Zinck, had finalised contracts for migrant workers to go to Kuwait, he commented that '[w]e need to look for overseas companies to employ locals to combat poverty and unemployment. [We are] already holding talks about sending workers to either Australia or New Zealand to [work on] apple farms. This should be finalized soon' (*Fiji Sun*, December 20, 2004). Zinck has also argued that the USA could assist by legalising the status of Fijians who now work illegally as care-givers there (Scott 2003), which would enable them to provide more support for relatives in Fiji:

For a country like Fiji, it will be good if they can give an amnesty to our people there because these people are actually sending money home to feed their families. All I'm asking the government of the United States is to give our people amnesty at least, now that [the] WTO has ordered the United States to scrap the garment export quota it usually offers us. (Quoted in Pareti 2005b: 46)

Such notions of a form of reciprocity were exactly what Tuvalu had long been arguing for with respect to the greenhouse effect, and have economic parallels in Nauru.

Several countries have trained workers for overseas employment, notably in the Marine Training Schools of Tuvalu and Kiribati, and there has been recent discussion in the region of the possibilities of adopting a 'Philippines model': expanding and developing the Tuvalu and Kiribati models to include skilled workers such as nurses, for whom there is global demand, centred on the dual assumptions that many such skilled workers will migrate anyway and that their remittances will be greater than the cost of the training, hence there will be a net benefit to the sending countries. The Commonwealth Secretariat, alongside the Pacific Islands Forum Secretariat, has recently commissioned a study of the potential for a regional training program for nurses (Duncan 2005). Kiribati has sought to extend the seaman program to cover nurses, and Tonga and Samoa would like to train more professionals than can be employed locally (Ware 2005: 445, 446), and benefit from presumably superior remittance flows. This shift to the deliberate export of skilled workers has major potential ramifications for development.

At various times and in various contexts island states have sought greater migration opportunities elsewhere. During the nickel boom in New Caledonia in the 1970s, leaders from Tonga, the then Gilbert and Ellice Islands (Kiribati and Tuvalu) and Fiji all requested opportunities for their citizens to work in New Caledonia but all were rejected, with the French territory preferring to bring workers from the two other French Pacific territories, less because of language issues than because they would be 'docile labour and reliable voters' (Connell 1987b: 217). There is a curious contemporary echo of this in the decision of New Caledonia to import as many as 4,000 Filipino workers for the Goro nickel mine rather than hire local workers, despite union demands, or bring workers from regional sources (*Oceania Flash*, September 6, 2005). In the three decades since the 1970s many countries, notably Tuvalu, have sought more migration opportunities for their citizens, on economic and environmental grounds.

On several occasions, Tuvalu has drawn attention to the particular difficulties of sustaining populations in a small, densely populated island state, with few resources, alongside the problems of absorbing return migrants, while threatened by climate change (Connell 2003e: 94–5). Such requests fell on stony ground in Australia, though New Zealand provided a migration quota of 50 households per year. In the context of the emerging Pacific Plan, the President of Kiribati observed that 'mobility of labour is the big issue' (quoted in *Islands Business*, April 2005: 5). PNG has also requested guest worker positions for agricultural workers in Australia, while the PNG academic John Ngongorr has argued that young Papua New Guineans would benefit from agricultural work in Australia, and might also gain additional social skills (Sharp 2005).

While New Zealand has established quotas for migration from the Pacific, favouring its former colony of Samoa, neither Australia nor the USA has developed particular policies for the island states. Apart from Niueans, Tokelauans and Cook Islanders, with free access to New Zealand, most Tongans, Fijians and others have migrated to New Zealand under the family migration and the general skills categories. In 2002, New Zealand introduced the 'Pacific Access Category' under which an annual quota of 250 Tongans, 75 Tuvaluans and 50 i-Kiribati were granted entry to New Zealand ('Esau and Hirai 2002: 22), thus making more widely available specific provisions for more of the Pacific region.

At different times, in Australia at least, specific policies enabling greater migration from the Pacific have been suggested, but never implemented, despite a long history of policy consideration (Connell 1988b). The *Report of the Committee to Review the Australian Overseas Aid Program* (the Jackson Report) argued in 1984 for two of the smaller countries in the region that '[t]heir long-term development prospects are discouraging. In view of structural problems which are beyond their control and beyond the reach of aid. Australia should make available limited opportunities for immigration from Kiribati and Tuvalu' (Australian Government 1984: 8), and thus go beyond traditional ideas of aid to provide special immigration quotas for the two countries, with which Australia had hitherto had few formal ties (Australian Government 1984: 181). Two decades ago this then radical idea was wholly ignored, from concern that if Tuvalu and Kiribati were accorded special consideration this would become the thin end of the wedge for other countries to follow.

A 1989 review of Australia's relations with the region called for Australia to introduce a work experience program for Islanders, but it too was rejected. The review also noted that 'the issue of migration has the potential to damage Australia–South Pacific relations, particularly as population pressures in the region increase' (Australian Government 1989: 123). Nonetheless, academics and others regularly touted similar possibilities. In 1990, Rowan Callick echoed the Fijian Minister's comments: 'In terms of relations with island nations, there are few levers more practical, helpful and yet of course sensitive than immigration.' He went on to recommend that the Australian Government play a role in taxing such overseas workers, thus ensuring a steady and reliable flow of remittances that would not only be highly beneficial to the island states, and would more directly assist households than overseas aid, but 'could prove an interesting alternative to the prospect of endlessly propping up micro-economies through aid' (Callick 1990: 15). Not all have favoured more expanded migration opportunities (as opposed to labour migration), arguing that they might lead to higher birth rates in sending countries and/or welfare ghettoes in destinations (Cuthbertson and Cole 1995; Hughes 2003), though there appears to be little support for such prognostications. A review of aid policy in 1997 returned to the issue of migration and made what had become a now almost familiar statement that granting Pacific Islanders the right to live and work in Australia 'may prove to be more cost-effective than continuing high levels of aid in perpetuity' and again met an equally familiar rejection.

Dobell (2003) has similarly suggested that Australia should move towards special short-term migration provisions, rather than aid, for island states, a view further supported in the Australian Senate review of Australia's relations with the region, which again argued in favour of special migration schemes to fill labour shortages in Australia, especially in seasonal agricultural work, and argued that risks of overstaying would be lessened if workers knew that they could return each year (as happens in Canada) and/or if the schemes were managed in the home country (which might, however, produce a different outcome). In familiar vein, however, the Australian Immigration Department argued against such 'low-skill migration schemes', emphasising how the idea of Pacific guest workers had become the 'great taboo' of Australia's Pacific policy.

Most recently, Helen Ware has argued that whereas in other parts of the world the slogan 'trade not aid' makes sense, in the Pacific, where trade options are limited, it should be 'migration rights for the poor not handouts for the rich', to avoid continuous aid delivery. She has further argued that because numbers are small (other than in PNG), Australia and New Zealand could 'readily take all those who wish to come in from the Pacific (especially if short-term migrant worker schemes are accepted)' (Ware 2005: 451–2), and that they could be employed in jobs such as fruit picking and working in nursing homes. Since various nationalities are allowed to enter Australia on working holiday visas, and the supposedly non-discriminatory migration policy treats New Zealand differently, '[i]t is simple racism not to allow our Pacific neighbours the same access to work in Australia. Australia is all for free trade in goods — where we are the ones who benefit. Why not free trade in people where the benefit is equal on both sides? The Pacific Islanders supply the labour and earn money to take home, and Australia gets the work done and forms closer bonds with its neighbours. As sea levels rise we will have to take them in any case' (quoted in Anon. 2005). Ware has also argued that 'it is a humane and cheap way of keeping the region secure' (quoted in Sharp 2005: 30). Stewart Firth has taken an apparently similar perspective in arguing that Australia might play the same role for Melanesia that New Zealand does for Polynesia, by enabling Melanesians to come as guest workers and generate millions of dollars of remittances (*Pacbeat*, September 15, 2005), though many of those who send remittances from New Zealand are settlers rather than short-term migrant workers. There is therefore a growing consensus that relaxation of migration restrictions and the introduction of a guest worker policy might benefit island states.

After Nauru's economic crisis, Australia has quite remarkably examined the possibility of developing a migration-remittance economy that might benefit Nauru in the absence of other obvious alternatives, which presumably would be centred in Australia where there is already a tiny migrant Nauruan community. Australia has, however, rejected a request from PNG to allow Papua New Guineans to undertake seasonal work in Australia, with the Minister for Immigration observing that 'there are issues of people overstaying and that would bring into question the credibility of such a program and obviously issues of other countries then saying we'd like the same opportunity' (*Pacific Islands Report*, December 16, 2004). By August 2005, the Government was again examining the possibility of guest worker migration with the Parliamentary Secretary for Foreign Affairs, Bruce Billson, stating somewhat blandly that '[t]here's a lot of work to be done. We are not closed off to the idea. It's [a] work in progress' (ABC, August 11, 2005), but later observing that there should be reciprocal rights for Australian workers. Similarly, in response to the National Farmers' Federation's demand for labour migrants, a Department of Immigration spokesperson stated that there were no plans to change policy (ABC Radio, September 21, 2005: see below), and opponents of guest work continue to argue that it would be hard to regulate, it could take jobs from Australians and guest workers might be vulnerable to exploitation (*Pacbeat*, September 22, 2005). The Australian Workers' Union has argued that '[g]uest workers are vulnerable to exploitation, depress local wages for Australian workers and could form an illegal immigrant underclass' (quoted in *Australian Financial Review*, November 21, 2005).

In 2005, Australia also considered the possibility of recruiting as many as 2,000 soldiers from Pacific Island states to serve in the Australian Defence Force, where there are similar labour shortages. This has raised familiar questions about 'the culture' of the Australian Defence Force, the extent to which this would add quality and the value of such personnel in regional missions (*Pacbeat*, August 26, September 14, 2005). Were this to be implemented it is probable that many recruits would be from Fiji, they would be trainees rather than existing military, and they would be considered skilled migrants rather than guest workers.

Australia presently experiences almost full employment and there are repeated demands, sometimes from unexpected quarters, for more open labour migration to Australia. There are particularly evident shortages of unskilled workers in the agricultural sector and of skilled health workers, and Australia as a whole, and states such as NSW, have recently become even more interested in attracting greater numbers of migrant health (and other) workers. Most recently, the National Farmers' Federation and the ALP have argued for the introduction of a guest worker scheme that would draw agricultural workers from Pacific Rim-aid recipient countries (National Farmers' Federation 2006; Sercombe 2005).

It is readily evident that refugees have been highly efficient workers in rural and regional contexts (Stilwell 2003), and that rural labour migration policies — effectively a 'guest worker' scheme — in New Zealand were of considerable value to New Zealand and Fiji, ending only when New Zealand imposed political sanctions on Fiji (Levick and Bedford 1988). In Canada and the USA, there have been several seemingly successful short-term employment programs, taking Caribbean health and agricultural workers to the southern states, which might also be models. Given these precedents, similar schemes in Australia might work well. Though some Islanders are notorious overstayers, this has been at no obvious cost to Australia and the greatest enthusiasm for such schemes has come mainly from those farmers who are the present beneficiaries of Pacific Islander employment. There is no question that the Melanesian states are the more impoverished in the region (alongside the atoll states) and would therefore be best placed to benefit from a guest worker scheme, yet fewer Melanesians are English speakers and — despite 19th-century blackbirding (which provides an intriguing precedent) — there is minimal tradition of migration to Australia or elsewhere. It is not therefore surprising that Bedford has commented that '[a]rguably the most contentious issue confronting Australia and New Zealand in the Pacific during the next half century will be how to cope with pressure for an emigration outlet from Melanesia' (Bedford 2003: 37). Space, and the current rapidity of change, preclude more detailed consideration.

Many migrants from the Pacific have been employed in the secondary labour sector, working in unregulated, non-unionised employment and being paid low and irregular wages (Khoo et al. 2006). This has been particularly true for Micronesians, who have migrated to the USA relatively recently, and for workers in the unregulated nursing home sector where there has been a considerable degree of exploitation of women. Similarly, there has been reported ill-treatment and exploitation of Fijians working in the Cook Islands (*Fiji Times*, August 30, 2004), where some 200 work, mostly in hotels and other service industries without being protected legally. Some have no work contracts at all while the contracts of others have been breached by their employers (Khoo et al. 2006). Tongans have exploited other Tongans in Hawai'i and elsewhere in the USA and cases of human trafficking have come to court (*Fiji Times*, September 8, 2005). In some contexts, notably the last example, such illegalities emphasise the demand for migration opportunities, and the need for there to be regulation of migration and labour contracts.

It is possible to be concerned that once a culture of migration is established short-term workers will prove to be long-term residents (as in Europe, where the 'Polish plumber syndrome' is a major contemporary discourse), as the antithesis of flexible labour markets. This poses complex questions about the relationships between employment and society, the needs of rural and regional Australia, multiculturalism and even of 'Australian values', which cannot be discussed here.

Conclusion: the outward urge

In this century alone there has been a spectacular increase in overseas migration from the Pacific, and in unmet demand for it, from individuals, whose dreams might turn to dust, and from governments, who have put increased pressure on countries such as Australia to relax what are perceived to be overly restrictive and even unethical migration policies. After about 30 years of independence, and disappointment over the challenges and fruits of development, there is a new outward urge that is beginning to spill over into Melanesia. That urge parallels labour demands in destinations such as the USA, Australia and the Middle East, especially in the agricultural, security and health sectors, and a slight possibility that metropolitan migration policies might be relaxed in favour of Pacific Islanders. Migration, already changing fast, might be on the verge of taking quite new forms.

The extent of international migration, and growing demands for migration opportunities, well evident in Fiji, are indicative of a region where the best economic opportunities are seen by many households to be overseas rather than in the islands themselves. For even relatively large states such as Samoa and Tonga there are now as many ethnic Samoans and Tongans overseas as there are at home. The future — a diasporic future — is perceived to be elsewhere. While the continuity of Pitcairn emphasises that the Pacific will not become the 'earth's empty quarter' (Ward 1989), it will be increasingly dependent on migration opportunities in other parts of the world. Indeed, there is a growing belief that '[s]ustainable development in the 21st century, as in New Zealand and Australia, will depend heavily on opportunities for young people to travel overseas for training and employment' (Bedford 2003: 37). For small island states that dependence is both positive and negative.

Within countries, migration occurs primarily out of a context of poverty of income and opportunities and unemployment, yet this nexus is itself also one outcome of internal migration, and is concentrated in the largest towns of Melanesia. The most visible and quantifiable existence of deprivation occurs in island states which have potential national development prospects, yet almost no international migration. In Melanesia colonial partition and regulation have lessened wider connections, and even reduced the extent of older forms of circulation. By contrast, in Polynesia and Micronesia, where local development opportunities are few, international migration — rarely in contexts of poverty and unemployment — has intensified and created extensive diasporic communities.

In the short term, a number of distinct benefits accrue to individual migrants and their families and to the sending societies. Migration has reduced the level of open and disguised unemployment, although it has also contributed to a loss of skilled human resources in the 'modern' sector. In the case of migration of

Tongans and Samoans to the USA alone, '[e]migration results in the permanent loss of young educated skilled labour from the Pacific Island nations. Skilled labour is in short supply and emigration probably hinders development' (Ahlburg and Levin 1990: 84). This is certainly true more generally in the health sector where more costly replacements have been required (Brown and Connell 2004a; Connell 2004a); it is true of the government sector in Samoa (Liki 1994), and certainly also true elsewhere. Exceptions occur where wages and salary levels are more comparable with those in the main migrant destinations, as in several politically dependent territories, such as the Cook Islands (Hooker and Varcoe 1999), though the Cook Islands and Guam have struggled to achieve the return migration of health workers (*Pacbeat*, September 15, 2005).

Remittances compensate for skill losses, though they flow largely to the private sector and only incidentally support the public sector where most skills are generated. Moreover, remittances are maintained for very long periods — beyond what has hitherto been recorded in most other world regions — and in quite new socioeconomic contexts (Morton 1998, 1999: 237). The most striking conclusion of the most detailed studies is that remittances do not decline over time, emphasising that migrants are ultimately motivated by factors other than altruistic family support, such as asset accumulation and investment at 'home', as the intergenerational flow of remittances takes on a more individualistic element (Brown 1997, 1998). Despite an abundance of predictions that remittances will fade over time, as migrants find new commitments elsewhere, they have resolutely failed to do so in quite different contexts (Brown et al. 2006; Simati and Gibson 2001). As long as there are needy kin in the islands, remittances will reach them. This also reflects the pervasiveness of island social mores, and perhaps some discrimination in destinations that increases the desire to maintain island social ties. For whatever combination of reasons, there is room for some degree of optimism that remittance flows will not decline significantly in the near future, but alongside pessimism that this will not continue indefinitely, especially for non-migrant generations. Thus far at least, MIRAB has proved sustainable, and in Melanesia even worthy of emulation.

That conclusion depends in large part on the continuity of migration flows. Ordinarily it might be expected that this would continue where possible in circumstances where there have been structural reforms that reduce public sector employment, wages and salaries remain low and unequal, working conditions are sometimes difficult and hierarchical, commodity prices stagnate and there are many kin overseas. Moreover, for some skilled groups such as nurses, there is now international recruitment. But if opportunities decline and, as Muliaina has argued, if there is a continued tightening of immigration policies in major Samoan destinations, for whatever reason, 'the standard of living of rural Samoans, as opposed to urban dwellers, may be expected to decline in the next decade' (Muliaina 2001: 20). If that is true of Samoa it is true of all other Pacific states where there is presently a significant dependence on remittances. Moreover, Muliaina reached that conclusion primarily for a Samoan village about 12 kilometres from the capital where there were several business ventures and commuting to urban employment. Remote locations would face greater difficulties.

While international migration has had positive and negative effects in the Pacific, the significance of the positive effects (particularly increased standards of living) must be contrasted with the limited development potential of many states and their failure to achieve significant economic growth or sustainable development. In most of the South Pacific, the greater self-sufficiency that would follow a decline of migration and remittances would be difficult and painful (Connell 1980). A quarter of a century later these statements can be re-emphasised in a wider context. Demand for migration and remittances is likely to be sustained, alongside rising expectations, in conditions of limited national economic growth. The voices of those who urge more self-reliant development strategies have been stilled. This new diaspora has remarkably quickly come to characterise contemporary Pacific Island states. In this context the need to maximise the benefits from migration and remittances becomes ever more pressing.

Despite the immediate benefits of international migration, long-term international migration of skilled workers might impose considerable costs. Governments have not controlled or directed the use of remittances (and nor have they sought to do so) while the rising material consumption levels following migration tend to generate increased demand for consumer goods. Expectations never decline. This demand can usually be satisfied only by further migration, as long as other sources of national income prove difficult to develop. Inequalities might increase, and the establishment of population (and migration) policies might be delayed further.

It is now a commonplace that about as many Tongans and Samoans are overseas as are at 'home', while in the smallest Polynesian states the balance has shifted overwhelmingly overseas (and especially to New Zealand). Notions of home thus change, provoking anxious and partisan debates over the extent to which cultures are retained or transformed, and become hybrid or syncretic, resulting in new phrases such as 'rooted cosmopolitanism' (Clifford 2001) to reflect the clash or combination of new residences, roots and routes. Traditions become reconstructed, articulated in ever changing forms and evident across now deterritorialised nations, islands and cultures. While identities might be hybrid and hyphenated, they might also, as in the case of Samoans in New Zealand, represent successful cosmopolitans 'at ease in multiple worlds, rather than natives of place torn by new and multiple allegiances' (Yi-Fu Tuan, quoted in Western 1992: 269; Connell 1995; Anae 2001). While cultures shift, citizenship changes and new loyalties emerge, economic ties to home have remained remarkably resilient.

Migrants and their children remain 'migrants' though their identities have changed. New technology has made connectivity more fashionable and more feasible, as the Pacific, fully one-third of the Earth's surface, has experienced a new 'cartography of compression' (Kempf 1999), where telephones, email and chat pages have created 'cyber-Polys' (Morton 1999). Home nations and islands remain powerful unifying symbols for migrants and their children. Hence in these new transnational meta-societies, and

[i]n an uncertain global political economy, even the most cosmopolitan Samoan must ensure that Samoa is not merely a nostalgic fantasy, but a potentially real destination. … Migration is rarely absolute, unambivalent or final; it is not a cause and consequence of a definite break with a cultural life that is part of history, but a partial and conditional state, characterised by ambiguity and indeterminacy. A fixed status presupposes that the future can be foretold. Uncertainty defines the experience of migration, even in second generations. (Connell 1995: 277)

Contraction and compression of the world through migration and electronics, and their consequences, from remittances to inter-regional kinship, have widened international ties, yet ultimately, in a wide variety of contexts, from the Melanesian island of Kairiru to the Polynesian atolls of Tokelau, those migrants who are regarded as successful are often those who have contributed most to the village (Smith 1994: 227; Huntsman and Hooper 1996: 324). These are 'the conquerors of the outside world' (Godelier 1986), in new guises.

However the impact of migration might be judged and debated, in terms of diverse migration streams, and ideologies from economic growth to dependency (van Fossen 2005), it is evident that alongside growing numbers of potential migrants there is growing interest in migration in island governments. Those who are most involved are those who have assessed migration most positively and 'voted with their feet' — or would like to do so. There might be greater inequalities in some sending contexts, at village or national levels, but there is little doubt that migration has provided new and welcome development opportunities. Pragmatism has overwhelmed intellectual doubts; short-term need has triumphed over long-term planning. Opportunities are eagerly sought. While many migrants are indeed within the disadvantaged secondary sector of metropolitan labour markets, and they and others have been deskilled during migration, they have accepted outcomes that, however disappointing, might well be superior to what has been left behind. Especially in circumstances where there appear to be possibilities for new forms of migration, and especially to Australia, migration will continue.

Migration has become an even more conscious household strategy, because of its crucial role in generating remittances, and there is growing evidence that island households are encouraging training and employment in careers with scope for migration. It is not yet evident that states themselves are training such highly skilled individuals for migration, but there are precedents in Kiribati and Tuvalu, where seamen are trained for the international labour market, and there is definite interest. Indeed, from the northern Pacific, the 'Philippines model' of training an excess of health workers for the 'global care chain' provides a possibility for smaller island states. While it might be expected that national development policies should encourage return migration, and such policies exist (Connell 2004a), alongside the recruitment, training and retention of those with skills, it now seems unlikely that policies will be developed and implemented to discourage or prevent further skilled migration, especially of women, but rather that skilled migration might be encouraged.

At a very different scale, international agencies, undoubtedly in a context of gathering aid fatigue, are increasingly stressing the role of diasporas and return migration in national development — an unreasonable focus on the potential role of emigrants, not least because their remittances support households, rather than the nations they have moved away from. Such a new form of 'international self-reliance' is inherently problematic.

The narrow yet open economies of the region are influenced increasingly by transitions in the international economic system, and particularly the superior growth of Pacific Rim nations, which has enabled migration. Foreign investment, tourism, new communications and intensified trade have drawn the Pacific Islands more comprehensively into the global system. In rather different ways, the futures of each of the Polynesian and Micronesian states (except perhaps Guam and French Polynesia) are bound up with the present and future of international migration and the ability of these countries to seek out new potential destinations overseas. All have retained interests in overseas employment opportunities. Tuvalu and Kiribati have experienced resettlement overseas, and Tonga has leased agricultural land in Asia. Tuvalu's Prime Minister has stressed that his country is continuing to seek employment and migration opportunities in Australia and that Tuvalu 'would not take no for an answer' on the provision of either employment or education opportunities, regarded as necessary for economic survival and even more critical in the face of future sea-level rise (Connell 1999, 2003d). Rising material consumption levels following migration have generated increased demand for consumer goods, a demand that can be satisfied only by further migration, as migrants bypass the small towns of the Pacific to seek superior living conditions beyond.

The shift from a more broadly based structure of migration towards more skilled migration has created a new dimension of inequality. No longer are the poor so easily able to move (though that was never easy, at least from independent states, and that might change if guest worker schemes are [re]introduced), whereas the relatively rich (or at least those who have acquired training and marketable skills) are actively courted and recruited. There is growing international competition not just for 'the creative class' (Florida 2005) but for a wide range of skilled workers. This inequality also has national dimensions, most affecting the relatively poor Melanesian countries, where access to training opportunities is inferior to that in other parts of the region (though the loss of skilled workers might be unsustainable). New wine varieties are filling old bottles.

Uneven development is unlikely to decrease, but while poverty is evident in several states, few governments recognise its existence, and even fewer have sought policy solutions. The rhetoric of self-reliance, at national and household levels, has disguised a situation in which there has been a growing dependence on external sources of funding, whether from aid, remittances or investment. This has, in part, contributed to new forms of socioeconomic inequality in cities, and incipient class formation, though ethnic and regional divisions and traditional power structures are of pervasive importance. International migration has deferred and mitigated, but not resolved, issues of poverty but also of development. The combination of weak economies, overburdened bureaucracies, urban unemployment, fractured social networks and uneven development challenge notions of sustainable development. Most Pacific Island states are likely to remain weak for the foreseeable future, become increasingly dependent on the wider world and require new forms of external support and intervention.International migration constitutes one increasingly less hesitant solution: an expanding and unsatisfied outward urge, a necessary bottom-up globalisation that will always be uneven and somewhat unsatisfying.

References (Parts 1 and 2)

Abbott, D. and S. Pollard.2004. *Hardship and Poverty in the Pacific*. Manila: Asian Development Bank.

Ahlburg, D. 1991. 'Remittances and Their Impact: A Study of Tonga and Western Samoa.' *Pacific Policy Papers*, No. 7. Canberra: National Centre for Development Studies.

Ahlburg, D. 1995. 'Migration, Remittances and the Distribution of Income: evidence from the Pacific.' *Asian and Pacific Migration Journal*, 4. pp. 157–68.

Ahlburg, D. and R. Brown. 1998. 'Migrants' Intentions to Return Home and Capital Transfers: A Study of Tongans and Samoans in Australia.' *The Journal of Development Studies*, 35. pp. 125–51.

Ahlburg, D. and M. Levin. 1990. *The North East Passage: A Study of Pacific Islander Migration to American Samoa and the United States.* Canberra: National Centre for Development Studies.

Allen, B., R. M. Bourke and J. Gibson. 2005. 'Poor Places in Papua New Guinea.' *Asia Pacific Viewpoint*, 46.

Anae, M. .2001. 'The New "Vikings of the Sunrise": New Zealand-Borns in the Information Age.' In C. Macpherson, P. Spoonley and M. Anae (eds), *Tangata O Te Moana Nui. The Evolving Identities of Pacific Peoples in Aotearoa/New Zealand.* Palmerston North: Dunmore Press. pp. 101–21.

Anon. 2005. 'Islanders should come as paid, working "guests" says academic.' *UNE News and Events*, June 16, 2005.

Australian Government. 1984. *Report of the Committee to Review the Australian Aid Program.* Canberra: AGPS.

Australian Government. 1989. *Australia's Relations with the South Pacific.* Canberra: AGPS.

Australian Government. 2003. *A Pacific engaged — Australia's relations with Papua New Guinea and the island states of the south-west Pacific.* Canberra: Foreign Affairs, Defence and Trade References Committee, Parliament of Australia.

Bedford, R. 2003. 'Doomsday revisited: A perspective on Pacific populations in the early twenty-first century.' *Development Bulletin*, 62 (August). pp. 34–8.

Bertram, G. 1986. 'Sustainable Development in South Pacific Micro-economies.' *World Development*, 14. pp. 809-22.

Bertram, G. 1999. 'The MIRAB Model Twelve Years On.' *The Contemporary Pacific*, 11. pp. 105–38.

Bertram, G. and R. F. Watters. 1985. 'The MIRAB Economy in South Pacific Microstates.' *Pacific Viewpoint*, 26. pp. 497–520.

Besnier, N. 2004. 'Consumption and Cosmopolitanism: Practising Modernity at the Second-Hand Marketplace in Nuku'alofa, Tonga.' *Anthropological Quarterly*, 77. pp. 7–45.

Borovnik, M. 2003. *Seafarers in Kiribati — Consequences of International Labour Circulation.* Unpublished PhD thesis, University of Canterbury, Christchurch.

Borovnik, M. 2004. 'Seafarer remittances to Kiribati: where do the benefits fall?' Unpublished paper presented at 'Beyond MIRAB: the Political Economy of Small Islands in the 21st Century', Victoria University, Wellington.

Boyd, D. 1990. 'New Wealth and Old Power: Circulation, Remittances and the Control of Inequality in an Eastern Highlands community, Papua New Guinea.' In J. Connell (ed.), *Migration and Development in the South Pacific,* NCDS Pacific Research Monograph No. 24, Canberra: The Australian National University. pp. 97–106.

Brown, R. 1998. 'Do Pacific Island Migrants' Remittances Decline Over Time? Evidence from Tongans and Western Samoans in Australia.' *The Contemporary Pacific*, 10. pp. 107–51.

Brown, R. and J. Connell. 1993. 'The Global Flea Market: Migration, Remittances and the Informal Economy in Tonga.' *Development and Change*, 24. pp. 611–47.

Brown, R. and J. Connell. 2004. 'The Migration of Doctors and Nurses from South Pacific Island Nations.' *Social Science and Medicine*, 58. pp. 2193–210.

Brown, R. P. C. and B. Poirine. 2005. 'A Model of Migrants' Remittances with Human Capital Investment and Intrafamilial Transfers.' *International Migration Review*, 39. pp. 407–38.

Brown, R., J. Connell, E. Jimenez and G. Leeves. 2006. *A Household Survey of Migrants' Remittances and their Uses in the Pacific Islands: Fiji and Tonga*. University of Queensland, School of Economics.

Browne, C. 1995. *Pacific Island IMF Member Countries: Recent Economic Development and Medium-Term Prospects*. Washington: IMF.

Bryant, J. 1993. *Urban Poverty and the Environment in the South Pacific*. Armidale: University of New England.

Callick, R. 1990. 'There's plenty of room at Australia's inn.' *Australian Financial Review*, December 14, 1990, p. 15.

Chambers, K. and A. Chambers. 2001. *Unity of Heart. Culture and Change in a Polynesian Atoll Society*. Prospect Heights: Waveland Press.

Chandra, D. 2003. 'International Migration from Fiji: Gender and Human Development Issues.' *Asian and Pacific Migration Journal*, 13. pp. 179–204.

Chappell, D. 2005. '"Africanization" in the Pacific: Blaming Others for Disorder in the Periphery?' *Comparative Studies in Society and History*, 47. pp. 286–317.

Clark, P. 2004. *The economic impact of contracted labour upon the livelihoods of small Pacific Island States: An examination of the expenditure patterns of I-Kiribati and Tuvaluan seafarers and their dependents*. Unpublished

Masters of Social Planning and Development thesis, University of Queensland.

Clifford, J. 2001. 'Indigenous Articulations.' *The Contemporary Pacific*, 13. pp. 468–90.

Cobb-Clark, D. M. and Connolly. 1997. 'A Worldwide Market for Skilled Migrants: Can Australia Compete?' *International Migration Review*, 31. pp. 670–93.

Connell, J. 1980. 'Remittances and Rural Development: Migration, Dependency and Inequality in the South Pacific.' *National Centre for Development Studies Occasional Paper*, No. 22. Canberra: The Australian National University.

Connell, J. 1987a. 'Paradise Left? Pacific Island Voyagers in the Modern World.' In J. Fawcett and B. Carino (eds), *Pacific Bridges. The New Immigration from Asia and the Pacific Islands*, New York: Center for Migration Studies. pp. 375–404.

Connell, J. 1987b. 'New Caledonia or Kanaky? The political history of a French colony.' *National Centre for Development Studies Pacific Research Monograph*, No. 18. Canberra: The Australian National University.

Connell, J. 1987c. 'Migration, Rural Development and Policy Formation in the South Pacific.' *Journal of Rural Studies*, 3. pp. 105–21.

Connell, J. 1988a. 'Sovereignty and Survival: Island Microstates in the Third World.' *Research Monograph*, No. 3. University of Sydney: Department of Geography.

Connell, J. 1988b. 'The End Ever Nigh: Contemporary Population Changes on Pitcairn Island.' *GeoJournal*, 16. pp. 193–200.

Connell, J. 1988c. 'Emigration from the South Pacific: An Australian Perspective.' In Australia Government, *Immigration. A Commitment to Australia*, Volume 3, Canberra: AGPS. pp. 1–22.

Connell, J. 1995. 'In Samoan Worlds. Culture, Migration, Identity and Albert Wendt.' In R. King, J. Connell and P. White (eds), *Writing Across Worlds. Literature and Migration*, London: Routledge. pp. 263–79.

Connell, J. 1997a. *Papua New Guinea. The Struggle for Development*. London: Routledge.

Connell, J. 1997b. 'Health in Papua New Guinea: A decline in development.' *Australian Geographical Studies*, 35. pp. 271–93.

Connell, J. 1999. 'Environmental Change, Economic Development and Emigration in Tuvalu.' *Pacific Studies*, 22. pp. 1–20.

Connell, J. 2003a. 'An Ocean of Discontent? Contemporary Migration and Deprivation in the South Pacific.' In R. Iredale (ed.), *Migration in the Asia Pacific*, London: Edward Elgar. pp. 55–78.

Connell, J. 2003c. 'New Caledonia: An Infinite Pause in Decolonization?' *The Round Table*, 368. pp. 125–43.

Connell, J. 2003d. 'Regulation of space in the contemporary postcolonial Pacific city: Port Moresby and Suva.' *Asia Pacific Viewpoint*, 44. pp. 243–58.

Connell, J. 2003e. 'Losing Ground? Tuvalu, the Greenhouse Effect and the Garbage Can.' *Asia Pacific Viewpoint*, 44. pp. 89–107.

Connell, J. 2004a. *The Migration of Skilled Health Personnel in the Pacific Region*. Manila: WHO.

Connell, J. 2004b. 'The Migration of Skilled Health Workers: From the Pacific islands to the World.' *Asian and Pacific Migration Journal*, 13. pp. 155–77.

Connell, J. 2005a. 'A Nation in Decline? Migration and Emigration from the Cook Islands.' *Asian and Pacific Migration Journal*, 14. pp. 327–50.

Connell, J. 2006. 'Niue: Embracing a Culture of Migration.' *Journal of Ethnic and Migration Studies*, in press.

Connell, J. and R. Brown. 1995. 'Migration and Remittances in the South Pacific: Toward new perspectives.' *Asian and Pacific Migration Journal*, 4. pp. 1–33.

Connell, J. and R. Brown. 2004. 'The Remittances of Migrant Tongan and Samoan Nurses in Australia.' *Human Resources for Health*, 2 (2).

Connell, J. and R. Brown. 2005. *Remittances in the Pacific. An Overview*. Manila: Asian Development Bank.

Connell, J. and D. Conway. 2000. 'Migration and Remittances in Island Microstates: A comparative perspective on the South Pacific and the Caribbean.' *International Journal of Urban and Regional Research*, 24. pp. 52–78.

Connell, J. and J. Lea. 2002. *Urbanisation in the Island Pacific*. London: Routledge.

Cowling, W. 1990. 'Motivations for Contemporary Tongan Migration.' In P. Herda, J. Terrell and N. Gunson (eds), *Tongan Culture and History*, Canberra: ANU. pp. 187–205.

Crocombe, R. 2001. *The South Pacific*. Suva: Institute of Pacific Studies, USP.

Curson, P. 1979. 'Migration, remittances and social networks among Cook Islanders.' *Pacific Viewpoint*, 20. pp. 185–98.

Cuthbertson, S. and R. Cole. 2003. *Population Growth in the South Pacific Island States*. Canberra: AGPS.

Dennis, J. 2003. *Pacific Island Seafarers. A study of the economic and social implications of seafaring on dependants and communities*. Suva: Secretariat of the Pacific Community.

Dobell, G. 2003. 'The Reluctant Pacific Nation: Policy Taboos, Popular Amnesia and Political Failure.' *Quadrant*, 396 (May). pp. 16–23.

Duncan, R. 1994. 'On Achieving Sound and Stable Economic Policies in the Pacific Islands.' *Pacific Economic Bulletin*, 9 (1). pp. 21–5.

Duncan, R. 2005. *Benefit-Cost Analysis of a Pacific Regional Nurse Training Facility*. Suva: USP (mimeo).

'Esau, R. and H. Shogo. 2002. 'Contemporary migration research in Tonga, trends, issues and the future.' In K. Lyon and C. Voigt-Graf (eds), *5th International APMRN Conference, Fiji 2002: Selected Papers, APMRN Working Paper*, No. 12, Wollongong: APMRN. pp. 21–6.

Evans, M. 2001. *Persistence of the Gift. Tongan Tradition in Transnational Context*. Waterloo: Wilfred Laurier University Press.

Faeamani, S. 1995. 'The Impact of Remittances on Rural Development in Tongan Villages.' *Asian and Pacific Migration Journal*, 4. pp. 139–56.

Fairbairn, T. 1993. 'Remittance Income. Its Importance for some Pacific Island Countries and Implications for Production.' In G. McCall and J. Connell (eds), *A World Perspective on Pacific Islander Migration, UNSW Centre for South Pacific Studies, Monograph*, No. 6, Sydney. pp. 311–18.

Florida, R. 2005. *The Flight of the Creative Class. The New Global Competition for Talent*. New York: Harper.

Fry, G. 1997. 'Framing the Islands: Knowledge and Power in Changing Australian Images of the South Pacific.' *The Contemporary Pacific*, 9. pp. 305–44.

Fusitu'a, P. 2000. Personal comment, November 11.

Gailey, C. W. 1992a. 'A Good Man is Hard to Find.' *Critique of Anthropology*, 12. pp. 47–74.

Gailey, C. W. 1992b. 'State Formation, Development and Social Change in Tonga.' In A. Robillard (ed.), *Social Change in the Pacific Islands*, London: Kegan Paul International. pp. 322–45.

Gani, A. 2005. Fiji's emigrant transfers and potential macroeconomic effects. *Pacific Economic Bulletin*. 20, 2.

Goddard, M. 2001. 'From rolling thunder to reggae: Imagining squatter settlements in Papua New Guinea.' *The Contemporary Pacific*, 13. pp. 1–32.

Godelier, M. 1986. *The Making of Great Men*. Cambridge: Cambridge University Press.

Grieco, E. 2003. *The Remittance Behavior of Immigrant Households: Micronesians in Hawaii and Guam*. New York: LFB Scholarly Publishing LLC.

Halatuituia, S. 2001. *Tonga's Contemporary Land Tenure System: Reality and Rhetoric*. Unpublished Ph.D thesis, University of Sydney, Sydney.

Hau'ofa, E. 1994. 'Our Sea of Islands.' *The Contemporary Pacific*, 6. pp. 147–61.

Hayes, G. 1991. 'Migration, Metascience and Development Policy in Island Polynesia.' *The Contemporary Pacific*, 3. pp. 1–58.

Helweg, W. H. 1983. 'Emigrant Remittances: Their Nature and Impact on a Punjab Community.' *New Community*, 10. pp. 435–43.

Hezel, F. and M. Levin. 1996. 'New Trends in Micronesian Migration: FSM Migration to Guam and the Marianas.' *Pacific Studies*, 19. pp. 91–114.

Hezel, F. and C. Lightfoot. 2005. 'Myths of the FSM Economy.' *Micronesian Counselor*, No. 59.

Hooker, K. and J. Varcoe. 1999. 'Migration and the Cook Islands.' In J. Overton and R. Scheyvens (eds), *Strategies for Sustainable Development. Experiences from the Pacific*, Sydney: UNSW Press. pp. 91–9.

Hooper, A. 1993. 'The MIRAB Transition in Fakaofo.' *Pacific Viewpoint*, 34. pp. 241–64.

Horan, J. 2002. 'Indigenous wealth and development: Micro-credit schemes in Tonga.' *Asia Pacific Viewpoint*, 43. pp. 205–21.

Hughes, H. 2003. 'Aid Has Failed The Pacific.' *Issue Analysis*, No. 33. Sydney: Centre for Independent Studies.

Huntsman, J. and A. Hooper. 1996. *Tokelau. A Historical Ethnography*. Auckland: Auckland University Press.

Jackson, R. T. 1976. *An Introduction to the Urban Geography of Papua New Guinea*. Port Moresby: UPNG.

James, K. E. 1991. 'Migration and Remittances: A Tongan Village Perspective.' *Pacific Viewpoint*, 32. pp. 1–23.

James, K. 1993a. 'The Rhetoric and Reality of Change and Development in Small Pacific Communities.' *Pacific Viewpoint*, 34. pp. 135–52.

James, K. 1993b. 'Cash and Kin. Aspects of Migration and Remittance from the Perspective of a Fishing Village in Vava'u, Tonga.' In G. McCall and J.

Connell (eds), *A World Perspective on Pacific Islander Migration*, *UNSW Centre for South Pacific Studies Monograph*, No. 6, Sydney. pp. 359–74.

James, K. 1997. 'Reading the Leaves: The Role of Tongan Women's Traditional Wealth and Other "Contraflows" in the Processes of Modern Migration and Remittance.' *Pacific Studies*, 20. pp. 1–27.

Karakita, Y. 1997. 'Prior to MIRAB?: Remittances and Inter-Island Relations in Woleai Atoll, Yap State, Federated States of Micronesia.' In K. Sudo and S. Yoshida (eds), *Contemporary Migration in Oceania: Diaspora and Network*, Osaka: Japan Centre for Area Studies. pp. 11–24.

Kempf, W. 1999. 'Cosmologies, Cities and Cultural Constructions of Space: Oceanic Enlargements of the World.' *Pacific Studies*, 22. pp. 97–114.

Khoo, S.-E., E. Ho and C. Voigt-Graf. 2006. 'Gendered Migration, Livelihood and Entitlements in Australia, New Zealand and the Pacific Islands.' In N. Piper (ed.), *UNRISD Policy Report on Gender and Development*, Geneva: UNRISD (in press).

Koczberski, G., G. Curry and J. Connell. 2001. 'Full circle or spiralling out of control? State violence and the control of urbanisation in Papua New Guinea.' *Urban Studies*, 38. pp. 2017–36.

La Plagne, P., M. Treadgold and J. Baldry. 2001. 'A Model of Aid Impact in some South Pacific Microstates.' *World Development*, 29. pp. 365–83.

Lee, H. 2003. *Tongans Overseas. Between Two Shores*. Honolulu: University of Hawai'i Press.

Lee, H. 2004a. 'All Tongans Are Connected: Tongan Transnationalism.' In V. Lockwood (ed.), *Globalization and Culture Change in the Pacific Islands*, New Jersey: Pearson. pp. 133–48.

Lee, H. 2004b. '"Second generation" Tongan transnationalism: hope for the future.' Unpublished paper presented at 'Beyond MIRAB: The Political Economy of Small Islands in the 21st Century', Victoria University, Wellington.

Levick, W. and R. Bedford. 1988. 'Fiji Labour Migration to New Zealand in the 1980s.' *New Zealand Geographer*, 44. pp. 14–21.

Liki, A. 1994. *E Tele A'a o le Tagata: Career Choices of Samoan Professionals within and beyond their Nu'u Moni*. Unpublished MA thesis, University of the South Pacific, Suva.

MacMaster, J. 1993. 'Strategies to Stimulate Private Sector Development in the Pacific Island Economies.' In R. Cole and S. Tambunlertchai (eds), *The Future of Asia-Pacific Economies*, Canberra: NCDS. pp. 275–313.

McMurray, C. 1992. 'Issues in population planning: The case of Papua New Guinea.' *Development Bulletin*, 24. pp. 13–16.

Macpherson, C. 1992. 'Economic and Political Restructuring and the Sustainability of Migrant Remittances: The Case of Western Samoa.' *The Contemporary Pacific*, 4. pp. 109–36.

Macpherson, C. 1994. 'Changing Patterns of Commitment to Island Homelands: A case study of Western Samoa.' *Pacific Viewpoint*, 17. pp. 83–116.

Macpherson, C. 2004. 'Transnationalism and Transformation in Samoan Society.' In V. Lockwood (ed.), *Globalization and Culture Change in the Pacific Islands*, New Jersey: Pearson. pp. 165–81.

Macpherson, C. and L. Macpherson. 1987. 'Toward an explanation of recent trends in suicide in Western Samoa.' *Man*, 22. pp. 305–30.

Marcus, G. E. 1981. 'Power on the Extreme Periphery: The Perspective of Tongan Elites in the Modern World System.' *Pacific Viewpoint*, 22. pp. 48–64.

Marcus, G. E. 1993. 'Tonga's Contemporary Globalizing Strategies: Trading on Sovereignty Amidst International Migration.' In T. Harding and B. Wallace (eds), *Contemporary Pacific Societies*, Englewood Cliffs: Prentice Hall. pp. 21–33.

Maron, N. 2001. *Return to Nukunuku. Identity, Culture and Return Migration in Tonga*. BA thesis, School of Geosciences, University of Sydney.

Mecartney, S. 2001. *Blacksands Settlement: Towards Urban Permanence in Vanuatu*. Unpublished MA thesis, University of Sydney.

Mitchell, J. 2004. '"Killing Time" in a Postcolonial Town: Young People and Settlements in Port Vila, Vanuatu.' In V. Lockwood (ed.), *Globalization and Culture Change in the Pacific Islands*, New Jersey: Pearson. pp. 358–76.

Morton, H. 1998. 'Creating Their Own Culture: Diasporic Tongans.' *The Contemporary Pacific*, 10. pp. 1–30.

Morton, H. 1999. 'Islanders in Space: Tongans Online.' In R. King and J. Connell (eds), *Small Worlds, Global Lives. Islands and Migration*, London: Pinter. pp. 235–53.

Muliaina, T. 2001. 'Remittances, the Social System and Development in Samoa.' In V. Naidu, E. Vasta and C. Hawksley (eds), *Current Trends in South Pacific Migration, Asia Pacific Migration Research Network Working Paper*, No. 7, Wollongong: Centre for Asia Pacific Social Transformation Studies. pp. 20–40.

Munro, D. 1990. 'Transnational corporations of kin and the MIRAB system: The case of Tuvalu.' *Pacific Viewpoint*, 31. pp. 63–6.

Munro, D. and R. Bedford. 1980. 'Historical backgrounds.' In *A Report on the Results of the Census of Tuvalu*, Funafuti: Government of Tuvalu. pp. 1–13.

Narayan, P. and R. Smyth. 2003. 'The Determinants of Emigration from Fiji to New Zealand.' *International Migration*, 41. pp. 33–58.

National Farmers' Federation. 2005. *Labour Shortage Action Plan*. Canberra: NFF.

Ogden, M. 1994. 'MIRAB and the Republic of the Marshall Islands.' *Isla*, 2. pp. 237–72.

Pareti, S. 2005a. 'Fiji's Long, Risky Road to Kuwait.' *Island Business* (April).

Pareti, S. 2005b. 'Human Labour: Lucrative Export.' *Islands Business* (May). pp. 45–6.

Poirine, B. 1998. 'Should We Hate or Love MIRAB?' *The Contemporary Pacific*, 10. pp. 65–105.

Pollard, S. 1995. 'Pacific Economic Policy: To Invest or to Protect?' *Pacific Islands Development Program Working Paper*, No. 11. Honolulu: East West Center.

Rokoduru, A. 2002. 'The contemporary migration of skilled labour from Fiji to Pacific Island Countries (PICs).' In K. Lyon and C. Voigt-Graf (eds), *5th International APMRN Conference, Fiji 2002: Selected Papers*, APMRN Working Paper, No. 12, Wollongong: APMRN. pp. 43–8.

Scott, G. G. 2003. 'Situating Fijian Transmigrants: Towards Racialised Transnational Social Spaces of the Undocumented.' *International Journal of Population Geography*, 9. pp. 181–98.

Sercombe, B. 2005. *Towards a Pacific Community*. Canberra: ALP.

Shankman, P. 1993. 'The Samoan Exodus.' In V. Lockwood et al. (eds), *Contemporary Pacific Societies*, Englewood Cliffs: Prentice Hall. pp. 156–70.

Sharp, S. 2005. 'Opening Oz's Doors.' *Pacific Magazine*, 30 (August).

Simati, A. M. and J. Gibson. 2001. 'Do Remittances Decay? Evidence from Tuvaluan Migrants in New Zealand.' *Pacific Economic Bulletin*, 16 (1). pp. 55–63.

Small, C. 1997. *Voyages: From Tongan Villages to American Suburbs*. Ithaca: Cornell University Press.

Smith, M. F. 1994. *Hard Times on Kairiru Island. Poverty, Development and Morality in a Papua New Guinea Village*. Honolulu: University of Hawai'i Press.

Stilwell, F. 2003. 'Refugees in a Region: Afghans in Young, NSW.' *Urban Policy and Research*, 21. pp. 235–48.

Sturton, M. 1992. 'Tonga: Development Through Agricultural Exports.' *Pacific Islands Development Program Economic Report*, No. 4. Honolulu.

Tora, I. 2005. 'Greener Pastures. Are Migrant Islanders Failing Their Kids?' *Pacific*, 30 (9), September. p. 5.

Underhill, Y. 1989. *Population mobility as a household strategy: The case of Manihiki Atoll, Cook Islands.*' Unpublished MA thesis, University of Hawai'i, Honolulu.

van der Grijp, P. 2004. *Identity and Development. Tongan Culture, Agriculture and the Perenniality of the Gift*. Leiden: KITLV Press.

van Fossen, A. 2005. *South Pacific Futures. Oceania Towards 2050*. Brisbane: Foundation for Development Cooperation.

Voigt-Graf, C. 2003. 'Fijian teachers on the move: Causes, implications and policies.' *Asia Pacific Viewpoint*, 44. pp. 163–74.

Voigt-Graf, C. and J. Connell. 2005. 'Towards Autonomy? Gendered Migration in Pacific Island countries.' *Novara* (in press).

Walker, A. and R. P. C. Brown. 1995. 'From Consumption to Savings? Interpreting Tongan and Western Samoan Sample Survey Data on Remittances.' *Asian and Pacific Migration Journal*, 4. pp. 89–116.

Walsh, A. C. 1982. *Migration Urbanisation and Development in South Pacific Countries*. Bangkok: ESCAP.

Ward, R. G. 1989. 'Earth's Empty Quarter? The Pacific Islands in a Pacific Century.' *Geographical Journal*, 155. pp. 235–46.

Ware, H. 2005. 'Demography, Migration and Conflict in the Pacific.' *Journal of Peace Research*, 42. pp. 435–54.

Western, J. 1992. *A Passage to England. Barbadian Londoners Speak of Home*. London: UCL Press.

Wheatley, A. 2003. 'Remittances: An economic lifeline or a liability?' *Yahoo! India News*, December 18.

Winthorpe, M. 2004. *Words from Whitesands: Reef Management in Tanna, Vanuatu*. Unpublished B.Sc. Hons thesis, University of Sydney.

World Bank. 1991. *Towards Higher Growth in Pacific Island Economies*. Washington: World Bank.

6. Globalisation, New Labour Migration and Development in Fiji

Manoranjan Mohanty

Introduction

Globalisation and migration are the two predominant and intertwined phenomena in the world today. Human mobility has become an integral part of the global economy. Since the early 1990s, the world has been witnessing a rapid process of internationalisation of capital, technology and economic activities. Global corporate activities through multinational and transnational corporations have grown rapidly. Trade and financial liberalisation is increasingly pronounced. The growth of mass media along with the development in transport and communication technologies and the free flow of information are leading to a rapidly 'shrinking world'. It is now an interconnected 'one world', whose economies, societies and cultures are more closely intertwined in what is commonly referred to as a 'global village'.

There has been increasing interaction and integration of national economic systems through the growth in international trade, investment and capital flows. Societies, economies and polities are now more interconnected, interdependent and affected by global changes.

Globalisation is now characterised by shrinking space and time and by vanishing borders, and globalising processes are dismantling obstacles to movement. As a result, there has been an increasing flow of people, goods, services, ideas, technologies and information across international borders. In simple terms, globalisation is defined as a 'process that widens the extent and form of cross-border transactions among peoples, assets, goods and services and that deepens the economic interdependence between and among globalising entities, which may be private or public institutions or governments' (Lubbers 2000). Globalisation is not new but the present era of globalisation is characterised by new markets (e.g., foreign exchanges operating 24 hours a day); by new tools (e.g., Internet links, cellular phones); by new actors (e.g., the WTO); and by new rules (e.g., multilateral agreements on trade).

Globalising processes have far-reaching social, demographic, economic, political and environmental consequences. For example, the growing demand for labour in the international market and advancing transport and communication technologies have resulted in mass movements of people across national borders. The impact of such globalisation is, however, uneven and varies from country to country.

This chapter explores the interlinkages between globalisation, international migration and development. It examines the emerging trends and contributing factors for labour migration in Oceania with special reference to the Fiji Islands. It also explores the impact of globalising processes on labour migration, trends in the flow of remittances and the overall impact of migration on development in the Fiji Islands.

Globalisation and transnational migration

Contemporary international migration is a systemic element in the process of globalisation and globalising processes are likely to increase migration pressures. The international migration system is now more integrated and has become more transnational in nature than ever before. According to a study by the International Labour Organisation (ILO), globalisation is expected to intensify international migration in the 21st century as 'the free flow of goods and capital worsens income inequalities and shakes up traditional [labour] markets' (Stalker 2000). The study says this is not because of 'a liberalisation of immigration controls but because of growing [labour] supply pressures, rising income inequalities within and across nations brought about by globalisation itself and the revolution in information and communication technologies' (Stalker 2000).

Globalisation as a social and economic process prompts a 'proliferation of cross-border flows and transnational social networks' (Castles 2001) that connects migrants across transnational space. In a rapidly globalised world, the patterns of migration and the migrants' social relationships are changing fast. The migrants move in what are called 'transnational social spaces', which are the preconditions for and also the products of globalising processes (Faist 2000).

Globalisation has provided migrants with powerful tools such as Internet communication, mobile phones and email for close interaction with their homelands. As a result, transnational global networks have been established which in turn prompt more cross-border migration. The process of globalisation makes cultural and social capital available to migrants. While cultural capital refers to knowledge of other societies as well as information about migration and job opportunities, social capital encompasses migration networks that help further movements. Within transnational social spaces, most migrants prefer to move to places where their own communities have already settled. As a result, a 'chain migratory system' is being established.

Dimensions of international migration

International migration is a dynamic and fast-growing phenomenon. It is increasing not only in scale and speed, but is characterised by wide diversities in terms of people and countries involved (Global Commission on International Migration 2005: 42). The volume of migrants has increased dramatically and is expected to continue to rise in the future. According to the report by the Global

Commission on International Migration (2005: 83), the number of international migrants has increased from 82 million in 1970 to nearly 200 million in 2005 — or more than double in a span of 35 years. Of all international migrants, almost half were women and migrant populations represented 3 per cent of the total world population, which is equivalent to the population of Brazil, the fifth-largest country in the world. Another emerging migratory trend due largely to the globalising process is that some traditional emigrant countries have become countries of immigrants (for example, Ireland), and, similarly, many immigrant countries now have large emigrant flows, e.g., Australia, New Zealand and the UK (International Organisation of Migration 2005).

The Global Commission on International Migration's report (2005: 83) said that the immigrants' share of the total population was highest in Australia (Oceania; 18.7 per cent) followed by North America (12.9 per cent), Western Europe (7.7 per cent), Africa (2 per cent), Asia (1.4 per cent) and Latin America (1.1 per cent). The report also said that major global markets for migrants were the USA (20 per cent) followed by the Russian Federation (13.3 per cent), Germany (7.3 per cent), Ukraine (4 per cent) and India (3.6 per cent).

International migration and development

Labour migration is one of the key forces of socioeconomic development. Relationships between migration and development are complex and multidimensional. Migration of people endowed with high levels of 'human capital' is beneficial and it helps the economic growth and development of many countries in the developing world such as Bangladesh, China, India and the Philippines. The emigration in labour surplus in developing countries provides a 'safety valve' for unemployed youth and relieves pressure on the labour market. Migration is also seen as one of the major contributors to population changes, which have significant impact on the process of development.

Globalising processes have prompted a 'brain drain' through large-scale emigration and also a 'brain gain' through returned skilled migrants. Some Asian countries, such as China, India and the Philippines, for example, see a shift from 'brain drain' to 'brain gain' as a result of their proactive policies to attract back emigrants with acquired skills and education (International Organisation of Migration 2005: 19). Hugo et al. (2001: 9) also found that countries such as China, India and Korea were witnessing 'hyper mobility involving remigration and return'. The outflow of human capital resources is seen to be beneficial to some developing countries due to the foreign exchange earnings generated through remittances. In many developing countries, remittances constitute a more important source of income than the Official Development Assistance (ODA) and Foreign Direct Investment (FDI) (Global Commission on International Migration 2005: 85).

Globally, the formal transfers of remittances were about $A202 billion in 2004 and another $A404 billion were transferred informally (Global Commission on International Migration 2005: 85). Remitters use informal channels because they are cheaper and better suited to transferring funds to remote areas where formal channels do not operate (Ratha 2004). The formal transfers of remittances almost tripled the value of ODA and were the second largest source of external funding for developing countries after FDI (Global Commission on International Migration 2005: 85). According to the report of the Global Commission on International Migration, the three leading remittance-receiving countries in 2004 were Mexico ($A21.5 billion a year), India ($A13.4 billion) and the Philippines ($A12 billion).

Remittances, Internet communication and access to travel, together with the support of migrant communities within the diaspora and hometown associations all provide the conditions for the transnational migrants to reside abroad and maintain ties with their country of origin, and are creating powerful tools for development (International Organisation of Migration 2005: 15). The role of remittances in economic growth and development is debatable, but many agree that remittances can help alleviate poverty and play a critical role in economic growth and development.

Migration trends in Oceania

Migration in Oceania is significant, with almost six million international migrants in the region in 2000. It shows the highest percentage per regional population globally and one of the highest rates of migration, growing at a rate of 2.1 per cent annually (International Organisation of Migration 2005). As seen elsewhere, there are more female than male international migrants in the Oceania region (Global Commission on International Migration 2005: 83).

The immigrant countries of Oceania, such as Australia and New Zealand, have experienced large emigrant flows in recent years. For example, during 2002–03, 50,463 people left Australia permanently, with most going to the UK, the USA and Asia. Similarly, New Zealand had a permanent emigration of 62,300 people during 2003–04 (International Organisation of Migration 2005: 130). Australasia (Australia and New Zealand), however, remains one of the major labour markets in Oceania, attracting more skilled immigrants worldwide including from Fiji and the other Pacific Island countries. In 2000, there were 5.8 million migrants in Australia alone (Global Commission on International Migration 2005).

Many small island countries in the Pacific region, such as Tonga and Samoa, have gained from the outflow of human capital resources largely to the Pacific Rim metropolitan countries, through the generation of foreign exchange from remittances sent by emigrants. According to Small and Dixon (2004), in the case of Tonga, 'it is migration, along with remittances of cash and goods from [those] who live and work overseas, that keeps the Tongan economy afloat'. Remittances are its major source of foreign exchange, accounting for about 50 per cent of GDP in 2002. About 75 per cent of all Tongan households reported receiving remittances from overseas and in some villages, remittances accounted for as much as 50 per cent of all household income. The inflow has helped in economic growth and development in the Pacific MIRAB economies (Bertram and Watters 1985).

The changing nature of labour migration in Fiji

Fiji is no exception. Globalisation has impacted on Fiji's labour migration directly and indirectly. Fiji has become a country of origin, transit and destination for migrants. In order to understand thoroughly the influences of globalising processes on labour migration in the Fiji Islands, an analysis of outward and inward movements of people is essential. There have been changing trends in labour migration in Fiji as a result of global changes and changing political, economic and developmental priorities in Fiji. Broadly, labour migration in the Fiji Islands can be identified in three phases as: mass immigration (1879–1919 and 1920–36); permanent labour migration (1970 onwards); temporary labour migration and contemporary immigration (since the early 1990s).

1. Mass immigration phase (1879–1920 and 1920–36)

As a product of the British indentured labour system, Indian immigrants, called *'girmitiyas'*, came to Fiji in 1879 to work in sugarcane plantations. Indians succeeded Melanesians as plantation labourers (Connell 1985: 45). Between 1879 and 1916, 60,000 Indian migrants arrived in Fiji and their work helped create the foundations of Fiji's sugar-based economy (Lal 2003). The system of indentured labour ended officially on January 1, 1920. By that time, there was a sizeable free Indian population in Fiji and they were mostly farmers from Punjab, and traders and merchants from Gujarat (Lal 2003). The Gujarati population in Fiji increased from 324 in 1921 to 2,500 by 1936 (Ali and Crocombe 1981). Their arrival prompted the rapid growth of trade and business in the Fiji Islands. The majority of Asians, particularly the Chinese, immigrated to Pacific countries and to Fiji under two systems. Some came under an indentured labour system and others as 'free emigrants' on a credit system (Willson, Moore and Munro 1990: 80). The first Chinese settlement was recorded in Levuka, the old capital of Fiji, in the 1870s, its occupants being gold miners from Australia who came to Fiji when the Australian mines were depleted (Yee 1974: 300).

2. Permanent labour migration phase (since 1970)

A process of permanent emigration started during and after independence in 1970 and it has been a continuing process since then. Fiji witnessed 'great waves' of outflow of skilled human resources during the 1980s and 1990s and again after May 2000 (Mohanty 2001, 2002). The total official outflow from Fiji was more than 91,000 between 1987 and 2004 (Table 1). Unofficial independent sources, however, estimate the figure to be more than 100,000 (Bedford 1989). Between 2000 and 2004, 27,000 citizens emigrated from Fiji. The permanent emigration process is dominated by the Indo-Fijians (88–9 per cent). The annual average rate of migration showed a varied pattern over the years. Before the 1987 coups, the annual average migration rate was 2,300 migrants a year, which increased to 4,900 during 1987–99, and to 5,800 migrants a year during 2000–03 (Mohanty 2001). Fiji has lost more than 3,800 professionals, technical and related workers since the coup in 2000 (Table 1). This represents more than half of Fiji's stock of middle- to high-level workers (Government of Fiji 2002: 41). Teachers are the single most dominant professional group that Fiji has been losing.

Table 1: Emigration of Fijian citizens by ethnic group and professional workers, 1987–2004

Year	Fijians	Indo-Fijians	Others	Total	Annual average emigration rate	Professionals**	
						Total	Annual average
1987–99	3,926	57,159	3,124	64,209	4,939	6,869	528
2000–04*	2,373	23,585	1,126	27,084	5,413	3,826	765
1987–2004*	6,299	80,744	4,250	91,293	5,070	10,695	594

* The figure for 2004 is from January to September.
** Includes professional, technical and related workers.
Source: Fiji Bureau of Statistics, 1987–2004, Tourism and Migration Statistics and Statistical News.

New Zealand, Australia, the USA and Canada are the four major traditional destination countries of Fiji's migrants. In 1980, about two-thirds of Fiji's emigrants entered Canada and the USA and another 29 per cent went to Australasia (Mohanty 2001: 63). Since 1987, this trend has been reversed. This reversal is attributed to many factors, such as geographic proximity, skilled labour demand, family reunion and the changing immigration policies of the receiving countries.

Push and pull factors are at work in the international migration process in Fiji. While factors such as land insecurities, unemployment (5–7 per cent during 1980–2001) and political upheavals were the main contributing push factors for emigration, the higher pay and standard of living, better economic opportunities, better health facilities and educational prospects for children in the metropolitan countries are some of the pull factors that greatly influenced migration decisions. The Reserve Bank of Fiji *Quarterly Review* said, '[I]t is quite clear that the political instability generated by [the] events of 1987 and 2000 gave greater impetus to the emigration process' (Government of Fiji 2002b: 40). Fiji lost more through the outflow of human capital resources than it gained through remittances. According to one estimate, the country lost directly and indirectly about $F45 million annually through its human capital loss (Reddy, Mohanty and Naidu

2004). Forsyth (1991: 37–44) in his study also found that there were large net negative flows of remittances in 1990.

3. Temporary labour migration phase (since the early 1990s)

From the 1970s to the 1990s, Fiji remained a labour emigrant country in Oceania. Partly under the influences of globalising processes, there has been a shift in trends in international migration in Fiji in the recent period. In addition to the continuing permanent Indo-Fijian emigration from the country, Fiji has been witnessing new trends in temporary migration, mostly indigenous Fijians, including peacekeeping forces, security personnel, nurses, sportspeople and students. Most of the indigenous Fijian migrants are moving to non-traditional areas such as the Middle East. For example, 'more than 1,000 former Fiji military and police officers are employed in Iraq' (*Fiji Times* 2005b). Under the influence of globalising processes, geographic proximity is no longer the primary driver of Fiji's current international migration. The Indo-Fijian and Fijian transmigrant populations created over the years maintain close ties with the homeland and remain actively involved in the social, cultural, economic and political life of Fiji. As Lal (2003: 5) says, '[A]lthough they live abroad, they maintain active contact with Fiji through a variety of means: the internet, telephone, video, periodic re-visits and remitting money and goods to Fiji.' The transnational overseas social networks also prompt more migration from Fiji.

Fiji's international peacekeeping

One of the major trends in recent years is the intensification of the temporary movement of peacekeeping forces from Fiji to distant parts of the world. Fiji gives high priority to participation in the UN's international peacekeeping processes, which dates from the late 1970s with the dispatch of the first troops to Lebanon in 1978 under the UN Interim Force in Lebanon (UNIFIL), and intensified in the 1990s. Fiji's international peacekeeping forces have been posted to global flashpoints under various missions, mostly under the UN but sometimes not, as in the case of the Sinai, Bougainville and Solomon Islands. Apart from joining the British Army, Fiji's soldiers have been playing a prominent role in international peace and security and in the process of nation-building in conflict-laden countries such as Afghanistan, Angola, PNG (Bougainville), Croatia, East Timor, Iraq, Kosovo, Kuwait, Lebanon, Namibia, Zimbabwe, Rwanda, Egypt (the Sinai), Solomon Islands, Somalia and, recently, Sudan. In addition, the number of Fijians working for private security companies as guards, escorts and other security personnel, especially in the Middle East, is significant. The movement of peacekeeping forces and security personnel overseas has generated substantial personal remittances (Table 2).

Student mobility is another type of temporary migration from Fiji. There have been an increasing number of students on overseas scholarship programs. The number of overseas scholarships awarded to students from Fiji was more than 530 during 1991–2000 (Fiji Public Service Commission 2002). In addition, Indo-Fijian cultural and social associations overseas are sponsoring Indo-Fijian students from Fiji (Lal 2003: 5).

Nurses from Fiji have been migrating to other Pacific countries and the UK. Rokoduru (2002) in her research finds that nurses have been migrating from Fiji to the Marshall Islands since 1995. She found 11 nurses from Fiji (29 per cent of the total) were working in Ebeye's Health Centre in 2002 and they were predominantly single males. A step-wise migration process is also at work as more than half of the Fijian nurses wanted to migrate to the USA after a stay of five years in the Marshall Islands.

A notable trend in Fiji's migratory stream is that the proportion of Indo-Fijian emigrants has been declining and, in contrast, the proportion of indigenous Fijians has been on the rise. The proportion of indigenous Fijian migrants to total emigration has doubled from 5 per cent in 1991 to 10 per cent in 2003 (Fiji Bureau of Statistics 1991–2003). Correspondingly, the proportion of Indo-Fijian emigrants has declined from 90 per cent to 86 per cent during the same period. This changing trend might be attributed more to the impact of globalising processes and to exogenous factors rather than endogenous ones. Although the number of indigenous Fijians in the total emigration stream remains relatively small, the progressive increase in proportion of indigenous Fijian emigration and skilled categories is of great concern. As Robertson (2005) says, the 'recent desire by as many as 15,000 mainly Fijians to work in West Asia has generated domestic racial fears'.

There are marked differences between the 'old' and 'new' contemporary labour migratory trends in Fiji. While the former was predominantly a permanent and partly involuntary type consisting largely of Indo-Fijians, and attributed primarily to endogenous factors, the latter is a temporary, voluntary type consisting of indigenous Fijians under internal as well as external or global influences. Another difference is that while the former stream was towards traditional areas such as Australia, Canada, New Zealand and the USA, the latter is towards new areas, especially the Middle East and Pacific countries. Moreover, while the former type of migration contributed insignificantly to the generation of remittances, the new migration is primarily a remittance-generating and development-driven process.

4. Contemporary immigration

Large-scale skilled emigration from Fiji has been accompanied by increased immigration in recent decades. In 2000, Asian immigrants accounted for about half of the total immigrants in Fiji. Chinese immigrants are the oldest and the largest Asian migrant groups in Fiji. They accounted for a little less than one-third of the total immigrants to Fiji and slightly less than two-thirds of the transnational Asian immigrants in the country in 2000 (Government of Fiji 2001). Other immigrants to Fiji came from Australia (16 per cent), the EU (9 per cent), New Zealand (9 per cent), the USA (6 per cent), the UK (4 per cent) and the Pacific Islands (4 per cent).

Remittances in Fiji

Fiji, traditionally a non-remittance country, is now becoming a remittance economy with thousands of citizens heading to work overseas. The country has joined other Pacific remittance economies such as Samoa and Tonga.

Until the late 1990s, the volume of remittances in Fiji due to the old (permanent) migration was insignificant. For example, it was only about $F36 million in 1993, mainly in the form of gifts and maintenances. Since the late 1990s, Fiji has been generating remittances mainly through personal receipts from new labour migrants, especially peacekeeping forces. Personal remittances accounted for about 97 per cent of the total remittances to the country in 2004. Personal remittances involve three categories of receipts: gifts and maintenance received by individuals, funds brought into the country by the immigrants, including legacies, and salaries and allowances of expatriates and pensions for retirees. While personal receipts through salary and allowances constituted little more than two-thirds of the total remittances, receipts in the form of gifts and maintenance received by individuals accounted for a little less than one-third in 2004 (Reserve Bank of Fiji 2005). The remittances through immigrant transfers constituted insignificant proportions of the total personal remittances (0.3 per cent).

The volume of remittances in Fiji has increased since 2000. Between 1993 and 1999, the growth of remittances was slow, only 38 per cent with an average figure of $F49 million a year. It increased more than 218 per cent during 2000–04, with an average amount of $F205 million a year (Table 2). The flow of total personal remittances accounted for more than $F1 billion during the period 2000–04. This dramatic rise was due mainly to the remittances generated through the salaries and allowances of peacekeeping forces and private security personnel abroad.

Table 2: Trends in personal remittances in Fiji, 1993–2004

Period	Total personal remittances ($F million)	Annual average rate ($F million)	Change %
1993–99	344.32	49.2	+38.4
2000–04	1,023.50	204.7	+218.3
1993–2004	1,367.82	114.0	726.2

Source: Reserve Bank of Fiji, 2005.

The volume of formally transferred remittances has increased from about $F36 million in 1993 to $F297 million in 2004, a growth of more than 720 per cent between 1993 and 2004 (Table 2). Beside the formal transfer, a substantial volume of personal remittances is transferred to Fiji informally and remains officially unrecorded (*Fiji Times* 2005a). The total volume of remittances from formal and informal transfers to Fiji can be estimated at $F450–500 million. This accounts for about 7 per cent of the GDP of the country.

As Table 3 shows, the income generated through personal remittances in Fiji is now next to the foreign exchange earnings through tourism. In 2004, personal remittances were worth more than earnings from garments, textiles and footwear and were also worth more than sugar, gold, fish and mineral water export earnings combined (Table 3).

Table 3: Sectoral foreign exchange earnings and remittances in Fiji, 1999–2004

Item	Foreign exchange earnings ($F million) 1999	Foreign exchange earnings ($F million) 2004	Growth % 1999–2004
Tourism	559.0	727.0	+30.0
Garments, textiles and footwear	365.9	291.0	-20.5
Sugar and molasses	275.6	188.4	-31.6
Gold	76.4	88.5	+15.8
Fish	57.5	85.0	+47.8
Mineral water	5.9	53.0	+798.3
Personal remittances	49.8	297.4	+497.2

Source: Government of Fiji, Reserve Bank of Fiji and Trade Release, 2005.

Migration and development in Fiji

Labour migration helps economic growth and development in many countries of the world. The migration-development relationships are, however, critical in small Pacific Island states such as Fiji, where a limited human resource stock exists and the demand for skilled human resources exceeds supply. While the outflow of skilled migrants is seen as conducive to the development of the larger countries of Asia, in smaller states such as Fiji it is regarded mostly as detrimental to sustainable development.

Migration and development relationships can be understood through labour demand and supply relations, demographic changes and remittance-development linkages. The large-scale emigration from Fiji is not only changing Fiji's population dynamics, it is influencing its political dynamics. Permanent emigration from Fiji has created serious shortages of skilled manpower in the economy. There are 'some critical areas, such as the medical profession, teaching and other specialized services, where labour shortages were most acute and still exist today' (Government of Fiji 2002: 42). This has greatly impacted on productivity, thus jeopardising the long-term development process. Due to skilled emigration, the quality of services and the overall human development of the country have been affected to a large extent. This is evidenced in the current UNDP *Human Development Report* (2005), which shows that Fiji's Human Development Index rank fell to 92 in 2005 from its previous rank of 66 in 2000. Yet migration also has positive impacts on development, for example, expanding export opportunities for local businesses and increasing traffic for the national airlines. Emigration in Fiji is also seen as a 'safety valve' in a situation when the supply of formal jobs has fallen short of the demand of fresh entrants to the labour force.

The growing remittances generated through temporary labour migration from Fiji in recent years might play a significant role in the context of low foreign investment and declining sugar and garment export earnings. Whether remittances are used for 'consumption or buying houses, or for other investments, they stimulate demand for goods and services in the economy' and 'enable a country to pay for imports, repay foreign debt and improve creditworthiness' (International Organisation of Migration 2005: 269). They also help alleviate poverty. As studies show, personal remittances derived through nurses' migration from Fiji, for example, have helped family members 'to pay for general family subsistence, for the welfare of their children and ... other traditional obligations in Fiji' (Rokoduru 2002).

Conclusion

Fiji is at the crossroads. International labour migration from Fiji has always been of concern primarily because of the drain of human and financial capital from the country. The draining of labour and financial capital from its system might inhibit economic growth and jeopardise the process of development. A small island developing state such as Fiji, with its limited human resource stock, cannot afford to lose human capital, the basic foundation for achieving sustainable development; however, the international migration trends, especially for Indo-Fijians, are likely to change in the future.

In the quest for alternative development strategies in the wake of declines in the sugar and garment sectors, the new trends of Fijian labour migration to distant locations might be seen as a viable development option provided the remittances are invested productively. The temporary new migration might also counter the loss of financial capital incurred through skilled emigration.

Migration, development and international relations are closely linked. With the signing of diplomatic ties and the growth of good bilateral relations with countries such as China, India, Japan and Kuwait in recent times, there exists a potential for improvement in trade and investment in Fiji. Positive international ties and globalising processes might accelerate new labour mobility in Fiji and a consequent growth of remittances and economic growth in the future.

References

Ali, A. and R. Crocombe. 1981. *Pacific Indians*. Suva: Institute of Pacific Studies, University of the South Pacific.

Bedford, R. D. 1989. 'Out of Fiji … A perspective on migration after the coups.' *Pacific Viewpoint*, 30 (2). pp. 142–53.

Beine, M. et al. 1999. *Brain Drain and Economic Growth: Theory and Evidence*. University de Versailles, http://www.cybercable.tm.fr/-jarmah/public_html/HRRapoport11.htm

Bertram, I. G. and R. F. Watters. 1985. 'The MIRAB economy in South Pacific microstates.' *Pacific Viewpoint*, 26. pp. 498–519.

Castles, S. 2001. 'Migration and community formation under conditions of globalization.' Paper presented at conference on *Reinventing Society in the New Economy*, March 9–10, University of Toronto, Canada.

Connell, J. 1985. 'Migration, Employment and Development in the South Pacific.' *Country Report*, No. 4. Noumea: South Pacific Commission.

Faist, T. 2000. 'Transnationalisation in international migration; implications for the study of citizenship and culture.' *Ethnic and Racial Studies*, 23 (2). pp. 189-222.

Fiji Bureau of Statistics. 1987–2004. *Tourism and Migration Statistics and Statistical News*. Suva: Fiji Bureau of Statistics.

Fiji Times. 2005a. 'State to study second largest foreign exchange earner.' November 11. p. 8.

Fiji Times. 2005b. 'Fijians sing carols in Iraq.' December 22. p. 10.

Fiji Public Service Commission. 1991–95. *Annual Reports*. Suva: Fiji Public Service Commission.

Fiji Public Service Commission. 2002. *Fiji Government Scholarship Awards*. Public Service Commission, http://www.fijichris.gov.fj/

Forsyth, D. J. C. 1991. *Migration and Remittance in the South Pacific Forum Island Countries*. Unpublished report prepared for the South Pacific Forum Secretariat, Suva, Fiji.

Global Commission on International Migration. 2005. *Migration in an interconnected World: New directions for action.* A report of the Global Commission on International Migration, Geneva, Switzerland, October.

Government of Fiji, Fiji Islands Bureau of Statistics. 1998. *Fiji 1996 Census of Population and Housing: General Tables.* Suva: Fiji Islands Bureau of Statistics.

Government of Fiji. 2002a. *Annual Reports — 2000 and 2001.* Suva: Immigration Department.

Government of Fiji. 2002b. 'Impact of brain drain in Fiji.' *RBF Quarterly Review* (December). pp. 40–5.

Hugo, G. with D. Rudd and K. Harris. 2001. 'Emigration from Australia: Economic implications.' *Committee for the Economic Development of Australia Information Paper*, No. 77, June.

International Organisation of Migration. 2005. *World Migration Report: Costs and Benefits of International Migration*, Vol. 3. Geneva, Switzerland.

Lal, B. V. 2003. *Fiji Islands: From immigration to emigration.* Canberra: The Australian National University.
http://www.migrationinformation.org/profiles/display.cfm?ID=110

Lubbers, R. 2000. *Trends in economic and social globalisation: Challenges and obstacles.* Cambridge, Mass.: Harvard University. http://globalize.kub.nl/

Mohanty, M. 2001. 'Contemporary emigration from Fiji: Some trends and issues in the post-Independence era.' In V. Naidu, E. Vasta and C. Hawksley (eds), *Current Trends in South Pacific Migration, Working Paper* No. 7, APMRN Secretariat, University of Wollongong. pp. 54–73.

Mohanty, M. 2002. 'Human capital resource outflow and development in Fiji islands.' In S. M. Lee and S. Chongsithiphol (eds), *E-Globalisation in the Pacific Age, Proceedings of Pan-Pacific Conference XIX,* May 29–31, 2002, Bangkok. pp. 363–5.

Ratha, D. 2004. *Understanding the importance of remittances.* Washington: Migration Policy Institute, World Bank.
http://www.migrationinformation.org/Feature/display.cfm?ID=256

Reddy, M., M. Mohanty and V. Naidu. 2004. 'Economic cost of human capital loss from Fiji: Implications for sustainable development.' *International Migration Review*, 38 (4). pp. 1447–62.

Reserve Bank of Fiji. 2005. 'Statistics on personal remittances.' Personal communication, Economics Department, Reserve Bank of Fiji, Suva, Fiji.

Robertson, R. 2005. 'From multiculturalism to trans-culturalism: Moving beyond post colonialism in Fiji.' Paper presented at a seminar in the Pacific

> Institute of Advanced Studies in Development and Governance, University of the South Pacific, Suva, Fiji.

Rokoduru, A. 2002. 'The contemporary migration of skilled labour from Fiji to Pacific Island countries (PICS).' In R. Bedford (ed.), *5th International APMRN Conference, Fiji 2002: Selected Papers, Working Paper* No. 12, APMRN Secretariat, University of Wollongong. pp. 43–8.

Small, C. A. and D. L. Dixon. 2004. *Tonga: Migration and the homeland*. February. http://www.migration.org/feature/print.cfm?ID=198

Stalker, P. 2000. *Workers Without Frontiers — The Impact of Globalisation on International Migration*. Geneva: ILO.

Taylor, J. E. 1999. 'The new economics of labour migration and the role of remittances in migration process.' *Journal of International Migration*, 37 (1). pp. 63–88.

UNDP. 2005. *Human Development Report*. New York: Oxford University Press.

Willson, M., C. Moore and D. Munro. 1990. 'Asian workers in the Pacific.' In C. Moore, J. Leckie and D. Munro (eds), *Labour in the South Pacific*, Townsville: James Cook University.

Yee, S. J. 1974. *The Chinese in the Pacific*. Suva, Fiji: theSouth Pacific Social Sciences in association with the UNDP.

7. 'Tonga Only Wants Our Money': The children of Tongan migrants

Helen Lee

> We simply just want to survive. We cannot survive while trying to sustain our respective Tongan community, if we are expected to subsidize Tonga's frail economy. It is not our responsibility. That is the responsibility of Tonga's government ... We do not want to perpetuate the financial blunders of generations past and give, give, give our way to the unemployment line, the welfare line, to government housing or homelessness ... As for the issue of identity, let me ask you this: why should we sustain the economy of a country that hasn't made an effort to embrace our generation? ... Tonga only wants our money, but not us.
>
> — Richard Wolfgramm, email posted on *Pacific Beat* online, Radio Australia, February 18, 2005

This statement, from a member of the second generation of Tongans in the USA, eloquently captures the key issues to be addressed in this chapter. Richard Wolfgramm is the publisher of a bimonthly English-language magazine for Tongans, *Ano Masima News*, based in Salt Lake City, Utah. Although he has been relatively successful, he readily admits that he does not send remittances to Tonga, partly because he has no family there whom he feels obligated to support, but also because the demands of participating in his local Tongan community are high. His statement reflects the views of many second-generation Tongans in the diaspora: he does not feel responsible for supporting Tonga's economy, he resents the burden such support placed on his parents' generation, and he believes Tonga welcomes his financial contribution yet does not accept him as truly 'Tongan'.

The reluctance of second-generation Tongans to shoulder the burden their parents have borne raises some serious questions about Tonga's future economic situation that are only just beginning to be considered. Since they began migrating in significant numbers in the 1970s, Tongan migrants have bolstered Tonga's economy, generating about half of its GDP each year. In 2002–03, for example, official remittances were about $T150 million (DFAT 2003: 2), or about $A114 million. This figure could be less than half of the actual total received in that year, because it does not include money and goods sent through informal channels (Brown and Foster 1995).

Tonga is among the Pacific nations that have been identified since the 1980s as MIRAB economies, based on Migration, Remittances, Aid and Bureaucracy. The acronym was developed originally by Bertram and Watters (1985) in relation to Pacific states linked to New Zealand and expanded to include other Pacific nations with similar economic situations (see also Bertram 1986; Bertram and Watters 1986). The MIRAB model posits that 'transnational corporations of kin' operate to maximise support from migrants to kin in the homeland, and that a continuing flow of new migrants contributes to the sustainability of remittance levels.

Like other MIRAB states, Tonga is a resource-poor nation unable to find sustainable alternative sources of income to remittances. While some members of the ruling elite in Tonga have managed to amass considerable wealth, the majority of the population survives on low wages, some subsistence production and the money and goods sent by family overseas. A range of factors such as transport costs, high tariffs, environmental factors and fluctuating markets have all contributed to the failure of many income-generating ventures attempted over the years. Even tourism, one of the mainstays of many small economies, has never been successful in Tonga, in part because of the close proximity of Fiji, a far cheaper and more tourist-oriented alternative. Aid is a significant income source, yet the amount received is dwarfed by the remittances sent by Tongans overseas.

The future of these remittances is the focus of this paper and of the research I am currently conducting into second-generation Tongan transnationalism. Here I argue that only a low level of economic support for Tonga is likely to be provided by the second and subsequent generations of Tongans in the diaspora, and that this has worrying implications for Tonga's future economic and social stability.

The sustainability of remittances

There is now a substantial literature debating the MIRAB model (for recent discussions, see Bertram 1999; and Poirine 1998), and much of this work addresses the claim made by Bertram and Watters that aid and remittances 'appear capable of continuous reproduction at least until the turn of the century' (1985: 501). Some studies have supported this claim, citing sustained high levels of remittances while others have supported the 'remittance decay hypothesis', which posits that the longer migrants remain overseas the lower the level of their remittances (Brown and Foster 1995: 38). Thus far, the sustainability debate has centred almost entirely on first-generation migrants.

There also has been a focus on how remittances are being used, with a continuing debate about whether this is primarily for consumption or investment. This debate is concerned with whether remittances help or hinder economic development, and in recent years has included consideration of the changing nature of remittances, such as goods for resale at flea markets, for example (Brown and Connell 1993). In some cases, remittances are being replaced by informal trade, as with Tongans overseas sending goods for Tongan businesses, and receiving in return agricultural products to sell to niche markets of Islander communities. Again, the focus of such work has been on migrants rather than their children.

Closely tied to the issue of what uses are made of remittances is the question of *why* remittances are sent, and it is simplistic to assume that they are just altruistic gifts to kin and country. Remittances are also sent for personal investment, to maintain land rights, and to prepare for retirement, although in the latter case few elderly Tongans do in fact return to Tonga because their children and grandchildren are based overseas. If we look at these migrants' reasons for remitting, it is obvious that few members of the second generation overseas are likely to have similar motives, so why *would* they remit?

Warnings that remittances and other ties to Tonga are likely to decline have been made since the mid-1980s, although they have been paid little heed. Professor Futa Helu, a Tongan academic, argued that overseas-born Tongans would not have 'the same sentiments, the same attachment to the homefolks as their parents had', and asserted that remittances would 'dry up sooner or later' (1985: 3). He concluded that 'all in all, we can say that the Tongan economy is facing a bleak future. We cannot continue to put our faith in remittances and transfers from Tongans abroad' (1985: 6; see also Finau 1993). This bleak future was outlined in detail by Campbell (1992: 71), who suggested that

> [a]ny lessening in the level of remittances will cause an abrupt fall in Tongan imports rather than a further widening of the trade deficit. A reduced import level would have a seriously adverse effect on government revenue directly and lead to further losses from the consequential contraction of other activity, especially in construction. A reverse multiplier effect would cause many bankruptcies in the retail sector, the contraction of government services, and a declining standard of living that would force many people back into the subsistence economy, with increased pressure on land and kinship relationships. Political upheaval could be a further downstream effect.

Such warnings have been ignored by the Tongan Government, and by many outside analysts; for example, the ADB's recent overview of Tonga's economy stated simply that the medium-term trend would be that 'remittances are expected to increase and to underpin private consumption as source economies grow' (2005: 227). This ignores the very real possibility that those remittances will decline in the longer term and that this could constitute a substantial threat to Tonga's economic future.

Investigating second-generation transnationalism

The lack of attention being paid to the potential impact of a decline in remittances on Tonga's long-term economic security is of concern, and has inspired the research I am conducting, with funding from the Australian Research Council. This research involves investigating the transnational practices of second-generation Tongans, particularly those in Australia, in order to discover the form and extent of their ties to their parents' homeland. Transnational ties are taken to be all forms of connection between a homeland and its population overseas, from phone calls and emails to remittances of money and goods and informal trade links. My use of 'transnational' also takes into account the multidirectional nature of such connections: Tongans in the islands also send goods to family members in the diaspora, and Tongans in different parts of the diaspora maintain complex networks of connections that can be quite distinct from ties to Tonga itself. Indeed, one of the questions the project addresses is whether the increasing ties *across* the diaspora are having any impact on ties to the islands: do they 'dilute' the strength of connections to Tonga?

Very little research has been carried out on second-generation transnationalism worldwide, and what little there is strongly suggests that transnational ties differ markedly between the first and second generation. In a collected volume on transnational families in Europe, several authors 'stress that points of contact weaken substantially in the transition from the first to second generation of immigrant populations' (Bryceson and Vuorela 2002). For example, Kane's contribution looks at immigrants from three West African countries in France, who developed strong links with their countries of origin through community development work in the home villages. However, 'second generation youth do not feel obliged to take part in the village association ... the migrants' children do not feel they owe anything to the village. The strong emotional ties between the migrant and his native land ... [are] not replicated in the second generation' (Kane 2002: 261).

Similar findings are reported in Levitt and Waters (2002), the first collection of papers to focus entirely on second-generation transnationalism. Most of the authors conclude that transnationalism declines with the second generation, and Rumbaut's paper in this collection, a study of Asian, Mexican and Latin American migrants in the USA, found that overall only a tiny proportion (2.4 per cent) had visited their parents' country of origin and remitted at least once a year (2002). Although Rumbaut does not quantify their remittances, their low level of engagement with the home countries is likely to be reflected in low levels of remittances. Other studies have shown similar results: Menjivar, for example, claims that for Guatemalan immigrants in the USA, second-generation transnationalism is 'marginal at best, and sometimes seemingly forced' (2002:

14). Menjivar concludes that most are unlikely to sustain long-term ties with Guatemala.

Vertovec points out that it is not really known what kinds of links members of the second generation in any migrant group will maintain. 'Processes and patterns conditioning the intergenerational succession and reproduction of transnational ties remain largely under-researched and under-theorised' (Vertovec 2001: 577). So little is known of second-generation transnationalism that it is unclear what factors influence the likelihood of transnational practices being maintained, how these fluctuate at different stages of the life cycle and what they mean to people. As Jones-Correa (2002: 238) has observed, remittances can be a chore to one person and a political statement to another. He also points to the difficulties of predicting the future decisions and life trajectories of members of the second generation.

This problem of future uncertainties has struck me in my continuing research with Tongans overseas. If we look at some of the Tongan youth in cities such as Sydney, Salt Lake City and Los Angeles, who are caught up in gang violence and substance abuse, how can we possibly predict their life trajectories? If they eventually 'settle down' and move into mainstream jobs and domesticity, is this any guarantee that they will suddenly establish ties to Tonga and begin sending remittances? Will other young people, struggling against the poverty their families have faced since they migrated, find a way to help support Tonga's economy? Even those who have 'made it' in their host nation might be unwilling to provide the level of financial support their parents gave to Tonga since this would mean sacrificing some of the material and other benefits of their success. There are complex issues here, including the resentment of many young people of their parents' funnelling of family income to churches and Tonga, and the pressure placed on them to be evidence of the success of the migration process. Migration was not just about helping kin in Tonga, but to increase the opportunities for migrants' children, and where those children have been able to achieve some upward social mobility, they need to demonstrate this through their lifestyles. Further complicating the picture is the point made by Wolfgramm in the quotation above: that participation in the local community can also absorb considerable resources.

Second-generation Tongans do not necessarily lack any sense of moral obligation to kin, but they are likely to enact this in relation to their immediate family members, who are also overseas, rather than to more distant kin in Tonga. As the first-generation migrants age, responsibility for their care will fall increasingly on their children, whose resources will be stretched even further and will be less likely to be directed to Tonga. And, while they feel a moral obligation to kin, they are less likely to be involved in the status-building in Tonga that also has been an inherent aspect of their parents' transnational ties.

Wolfgramm has claimed that for the second generation, '[W]e bear a lot of responsibilities here in our overseas communities to ourselves and to our families and it's really a burden that's taken a lot of our time and a lot of our energies, and it's hard for us to carry that burden and at the same time be expected to subsidise — and I use the word subsidise — Tonga's economy by sending remittances back to Tonga' (*Pacific Beat* online, Radio Australia, March 10, 2005). Another Tongan involved in *Ano Masima News*, 'Anapesi Ka'ili, also spoke on the *Pacific Beat* program and argued that many young Tongans in the USA were holding onto their Tongan identity, yet were 'redefining what it means to be Tongan, and how they choose to identify that. And for many of them remittances is not one of the ways in which they're seeing it play out in their Tonganness … remittances have been something that many of them have really shied away from and [they] don't really see it as something that they would like to continue' (online March 10, 2005). She adds that many of the younger Tongans overseas do want to keep up their connection with Tonga, but through phone calls, return visits and other ties, not through remittances. This creates intergenerational tensions, with some of the older Tongans insisting that 'the only way you can identify as being Tongan is by the remittances being sent home'; however, she notes that even some of the older generation are resisting this pressure. In a response posted on the *Pacific Beat* web site after these interviews, one contributor commented that she sends money only because her elderly father is still alive in Tonga, adding 'our children will not do what we're doing now' (online February 24, 2005). Even within Tonga younger people are beginning to look for ways to lighten the burden of kinship and other obligations and to focus more on their own immediate family (James 2002: 286).

Elsewhere (Lee 2003, 2004) I have outlined the obstacles to young diasporic Tongans' maintenance of ties to Tonga, such as their lack of language and cultural skills and therefore absence of a secure identity as 'Tongan'; the economic and social problems within the diaspora; and young people's disapproval of many of the practices of their parents' generation, such as the time and resources devoted to the churches, and the funnelling of substantial amounts of family income sent as remittances. The high rate of intermarriage in Tongan populations overseas also tends to reduce the likelihood of remitting for Tongan spouses, let alone the children of these unions. Many young Tongans overseas tend to lack any strong sense of connection to Tonga, making it unlikely that they would feel any obligation to remit. Visits to Tonga can encourage this sense of connection, and can lead to more contact between migrants' descendants and kin in the homeland, yet there is no guarantee that economic support is forthcoming, at least not to the extent needed to sustain current levels. It can also be a strategy that can backfire and for many young Tongans, visiting Tonga can be confronting and seriously challenge their identification as 'Tongan' (Lee 2003).

For Tongans and other Pacific Islanders, there is a growing literature focusing on identity issues for members of the second generation, and their experiences in the host countries, but little on their remittance practices, and very little on their other ties to the islands. Where their parents' homelands are discussed, it tends to be in terms of emotional ties rather than actual connections and economic involvement. My own previous work on the Tongan diaspora shared these concerns, and the ties of the second-generation Tongans to Tonga were addressed primarily in terms of their impact on young people's negotiations of identity (Lee 2003).

Other work on the Tongan diaspora, even that which deals specifically with transnationalism, tends to avoid the question of second-generation transnationalism. In the only monograph to focus on Tongan transnationalism, Evans states in his conclusion simply that he has relatively little to add to the question of whether transnational ties are sustainable, and adds: 'At some level the long term continuity of both ideology and practice is an empirical question which must await answers' (2001: 160). While disappointing, his lack of consideration of second-generation transnationalism is understandable, given that his book focuses on the transnational practices of Tongans in Tonga, rather than the overseas population. Small's study (1997), which does focus on Tongan migrants' transnationalism, does not address the question of second-generation transnationalism in any detail; however, she argues that remittances will inevitably decline as the number of overseas-born Tongans outnumber the Tongan-born.

Piloting the 'Tongan ties' project

My own research into second-generation Tongan transnationalism began in 2005 and entails the collection of qualitative and quantitative data, primarily from second-generation Tongans in Australia aged between 18 and 30. This includes in-depth interviews, which will be conducted with participants from six different locations in Australia, and email surveys repeated weekly for a total of four months to track participants' transnational connections practices. In addition, an email discussion list has been established to encourage a continuing dialogue among participants about the issues associated with transnationalism. The project will also entail several short periods of fieldwork in Tonga, to interview 18- to 30-year-olds who remain in the islands.

A pilot of the interviews and email surveys has recently been completed with a sample of 10 participants from Melbourne, aged between 20 and 29, with six females and four males. The sample is varied in terms of religious affiliation, occupation, assets and financial obligations, and household configurations, yet some clear patterns can be seen in the transnational practices and attitudes of this small but diverse group.

Overall, the participants have a low level of involvement with Tonga, maintaining contact with just a few family members, and three have no contact with anyone in Tonga. There is a slightly higher level of involvement with other Tongans in the diaspora, beyond Melbourne. This limited contact with family and friends in Tonga and elsewhere is mostly by phone and email and varies in frequency from daily to yearly. For some, their contact with relatives elsewhere in the diaspora also involves sending gifts occasionally, but none sends money and in one case a young man was the recipient of money from family overseas. Most of the participants attend churches with predominantly Tongan congregations but have no involvement in other Tongan organisations in Melbourne. The churches held fundraising events every two or three months, which most attended, and while most of the participants said they donated amounts between $20⁵ and $100 on these occasions, not all events were to raise funds to send to Tonga.

The participants' direct ties to Tonga are limited, although most have visited the islands either for holidays or for church events. They have a low level of interest in Tongan politics, but keep up with current events in Tonga through Tongan newspapers, Internet sites and radio programs, and by word of mouth. Most say they have little or no sense of obligation or responsibility to the Church in Tonga, to the royal family, or to the country itself; where they do feel any obligation it is only to family. However, only three of the 10 send money to family directly and the remainder send either clothing or gifts occasionally, or give money to their parents when asked, to be forwarded to family in Tonga, or they contribute nothing at all. The pattern of remitting found in this group supports the argument made by James (1993: 360) that the 'transnational corporations of kin' central to the MIRAB model no longer operate for Tongans, with people tending to remit on an individual basis or as a nuclear family.

An interesting pattern that emerged in the pilot interviews was that some young women from the diaspora were developing relationships with men in Tonga while on holidays or church-related visits. Two of the six women interviewed had previously had a boyfriend in Tonga and two were currently in such a relationship; in all cases, their main connection to Tonga during the relationship was with their boyfriends rather than family. They reported sending these men gifts of clothing, DVDs and CDs, rather than money, with their main expenditure being on phone calls to Tonga. Although the males interviewed did not mention similar relationships, one woman claimed as many males as females were involved with partners in Tonga. Another woman suggested that for men this was more likely to be 'a fling or whatever and [they] come back and [do] not feel any connection to the person in Tonga', while another said the young men 'mainly go there to sow their wild oats' whereas women 'are looking more for the whole marriage thing'.

When asked about their sense of responsibility to family in Tonga, the participants' responses were mixed. One woman (27, single) replied: 'I've never felt that. You know, my parents, if there has been any responsibilities or obligations to family, it has usually been my parents and my uncles and my aunties, but it's normally stopped there too, it's never really come down to the kids.' Nevertheless, she estimated that she had sent about $1,000 to Tonga in the past year, as well as clothing and gifts. Two other women said their parents had not encouraged them to have any connection to Tonga, and while one (single, 26) felt no responsibility to anyone there and sent no remittances, the other (single, 28) explained that she did feel a sense of obligation, 'because they don't have what we have here'. She estimated that she had sent about $600 in the past year, as well as some gifts, to the three relatives in Tonga with whom she maintained contact. Two men who at present have no direct contact with family in Tonga had different reasons for this: one (single, 20) had previously sent money but felt it was more than he wanted to give, and said: 'I see sometimes … them using that as an excuse or as a gate to open any time they need anything.' The other (married, 29) explained: 'I guess one day we're going to end up like our parents, supporting family back in Tonga. I won't do it yet, but I know one day I'm going to and I guess my kids will take over that role one day.' For now, he gives money only through his parents, when they ask him.

All of the participants readily acknowledged that without remittances Tongans in the islands would suffer. All predicted that the standard of living would decline, and some made comments such as 'They would probably starve', or 'I think they might kill themselves!', or asked 'How are they going to live if their family from overseas aren't going to lend a hand?' Most felt, however, that even now, with high levels of remittances, Tonga was struggling. One woman (single, 27) commented: 'I don't like going back to Tonga and seeing people suffer and then it makes me feel worse when I come back to Australia … Whenever I'm there visiting I feel that the poor are getting poorer and the rich are just getting richer and it just builds my anger and makes me feel frustrated for the people that live there … the whole political system, I think, is corrupt and I just feel sorry for the people that live in Tonga.'

Almost all participants commented on Tonga's political problems, with one woman (single, 25) saying, 'Oh, Tonga! Everybody's got problems there! There's [sic] money problems, there's politics, there's parliament, there's [sic] quite a few.' Another woman (single, 26) said, 'All I hear about Tonga: everything's corrupt.' These problems appear to be putting them off being more involved with Tonga, or taking more interest in Tongan news. As one young woman (single, 28) observed about Tongan politics, 'Stuff I found out kind of put me off wanting to know.'

The six-week Tongan Public Service strike that ended in September 2005 put a tremendous strain on the resources of strikers and their families. Tongans overseas rallied to provide support through donations of money and food. They also voiced their concerns about the situation in Tonga, and in Auckland a street march and protest meeting were held in support of the strikers. This support was not surprising, as Tongan migrants have not only provided remittances but have exerted political influence in Tonga for decades. In the 1980s, for example, they brought their influence to bear during a strike by nurses and when legislation relating to land owned by Tongans overseas was being considered (see Helu 1985). They have also been vocal in their support of the pro-democracy movement that emerged in Tonga in the 1980s, and expressed their concerns about the many political scandals that have erupted in Tonga in the intervening years. As Hau'ofa noted in 1994, '[F]rom their bases abroad they are exerting significant influences on their homeland' (p. 423).

The extent to which members of the second generation were involved in supporting the recent strike is unclear, but the attitudes of those interviewed towards Tongan politics suggests they would be less likely than their parents to actively engage in political struggle from the diaspora. During the strike, Sefita Ha'ouli, news director at an Auckland radio station, commented that in New Zealand, there was 'a little group of young Tongans growing up ... [whose] understanding of the issue in Tonga is such that they're turned off by it. They're saying we don't want a bar of it. They are supportive of what is being done, but they don't want to be engaged. And I think this may be a trend that we'll see as things progress' (*Pacific Beat* online, Radio Australia, August 2, 2005).

In another interview during the strike, Dr Malakai Koloamatangi, a Tongan political scientist at Canterbury University in New Zealand, said the Tongan Government needed to realise 'that a lot of what is going on depends to a great extent on how Tongans overseas provide support for Tonga. I mean, in just the simple matter of government expenditure, if Tongans overseas were to cut their remittances drastically, it would affect the government's ability ... to stay above water, so it's that simple' (*Pacific Beat* online, Radio Australia, August 26, 2005).

The issue of remittances cannot be separated from the broader connections between Tonga and its population in the diaspora, particularly the emotional ties and sense of belonging to the island nation that are shared by many Tongan migrants. Clearly, if this sense of belonging and other feelings of connection to Tonga are not as strong for their children, the likelihood is that they will be less willing to send remittances. If this is so, it raises the question of Tonga's future as a viable state: what alternatives are there to redress this likely drop in remittance income?

More migration as a solution?

Tonga's economic future is precarious, and heavily reliant on the expectation of continued high levels of remittances. If the second generation does not maintain these remittances at these high levels, and alternative sources of income are unlikely to be found, the obvious solution would appear to be an increased flow of new migrants. This solution is impossible without changes to the immigration policies of the main host nations — the USA, New Zealand and Australia — which have tightened in recent years and made it more difficult for Tongans to migrate.

In Australia, there has been an overall downward trend in migration from Tonga in the past two decades; numbers have fluctuated annually from a high of 287 in 1997 to 83 in 2001, and have not reached more than 200 since 1998 (Australian Bureau of Statistics 2003). The most recent figures available are from 2002-3, during which period 92 Tongan-born migrants arrived in Australia from Tonga, and a further 116 who were Tongan-born citizens of New Zealand (DIMIA, online 2003a). Only three of the 92 were in the skilled migrant category; the remainder were family migrants and thus could include migrants of any age, such as elderly relatives of previous migrants or young children. Of course, as more family members join those already living overseas, migrants' networks of relatives in Tonga shrink and remittances are likely to decline as a consequence. During that same period, 103 Tongans left Australia permanently; 47 had been in Australia for more than 10 years (DIMIA, online 2003b). Net migration for that period was thus 105. Of the new migrants, any adults arriving from New Zealand are likely to have already established any remitting practices they intended to maintain, so only those from Tonga can be considered potential 'new remitters', so in effect it could be argued that there was a net drop in potential new remitters in Australia for that year.

Whether or not this pattern is also found in New Zealand and the USA needs further research, however, compiling accurate migration statistics is extremely difficult. Tonga does not maintain adequate statistical records of migrant departures, each host nation has its own methods of data collection and classification, and there are a number of 'overstayers' in each host nation who are not recorded. If it can be shown that migration is in fact declining, it can be predicted that the MIRAB model will begin to unravel for countries such as Tonga, where the migration-remittance nexus has been so crucial for sustaining their economies.

There is some faint hope that Australia will review its migration policies for Pacific Islanders, in the wake of the Australian Senate report, *A Pacific Engaged* (Foreign Affairs, Defence and Trade References Committee 2003). Much of the evidence to the committee concerned special migration access for Pacific Islanders, to 'learn new skills and earn money that could be remitted back to the home country to support family networks and contribute to their economies' (p. 69). Labour migration schemes have been considered since the early 1980s, and in 1997 the report of the Committee of Review of Australia's aid policy stated that special migration programs for Islanders 'may prove to be more cost-effective than continuing high levels of aid in perpetuity. Limited access to Australia, either on a temporary or a permanent basis, has been argued for as an effective way to assist the very small states whose only export is labour services' (cited p. 70). The Senate Committee concluded that a guest worker scheme would support 'Australia's national interest in so far as it would contribute to the sustainable economic and social development of the region, contributing to stability' (p. 75).

Australian governments have, however, long resisted the introduction of such schemes, arguing that there is a high rate of unemployment for 'low-skill[ed] people in Australia' and that there is a risk of workers being exploited, or overstaying their visas (pp. 73–4). This resistance was again evident at the Pacific Islands Forum meeting in October 2005, when the Australian Government rejected recommendations in the forum's Pacific Plan to initiate temporary labour mobility programs. Nevertheless, the issue continues to be debated and is likely to be revisited as Pacific nations' economic woes continue to worsen.

Conclusion

The possibility of Australia opening its doors to guest workers is one of the few rays of hope Tonga has for counteracting the serious threat posed by the potential loss of remittances as many members of the second generation overseas reject the burden of responsibility for Tonga's economic wellbeing shouldered for so long by their parents. In the past few years, Tonga has faced increasing internal unrest as its citizens express their discontent with the many effects of poor governance. The expectations of the population have risen more rapidly than their standard of living, culminating in the 2005 Public Service strike in which wage rises of up to 80 per cent were demanded. While the strikers were victorious and massive wage rises have been promised, the Tongan Government has claimed that 73 per cent of all government expenditure now will be on wages (*Pacific Beat* online, Radio Australia, September 7, 2005). In January 2006, Tonga's Minister of Labour, Commerce and Industries, Feleti Sevele, admitted that Tonga was facing financial disaster (*Pacific Magazine* 2006). More than ever before, Tonga needs the income generated by remittances, and the very real possibility that they will decline before too long needs to be addressed urgently not only within Tonga but by the governments of host nations, in whose immigration policies a possible solution could be found.

References

Asian Development Bank. 2005. *Asian Development Outlook 2005 (Tonga)*.
    http://www.adb.org/Documents/Books/ADO/2005/ton.asp

Australian Bureau of Statistics. 2003. 'Year of arrival by most common birthplaces of individuals for persons of Tongan ancestry.' *2001 Census of population and housing*. Table supplied by ABS.

Australian Department of Foreign Affairs and Trade. 2003. *Kingdom of Tonga: Country brief, August 2003*.
    http://www.dfat.gov.au/geo/tonga/tonga_brief.html

Bertram, G. 1986. '"Sustainable development" in Pacific micro-economies.' *World Development*, 14, 7. pp. 809–22.

Bertram, G. 1999. 'The MIRAB model twelve years on.' *The Contemporary Pacific*, 11, 1. pp. 105–38.

Bertram, G. and R. Watters. 1985. 'The MIRAB economy in South Pacific microstates.' *Pacific Viewpoint*, 26, 3. pp. 497–519.

Bertram, G. and R. Watters. 1986. 'The MIRAB process: Earlier analyses in context.' *Pacific Viewpoint*, 27, 1. pp. 47–59.

Brown, R. 1995. 'Hidden foreign exchange flows: Estimating unofficial remittances to Tonga and Western Samoa.' *Asian and Pacific Migration Journal* 4, 1. pp. 35–54.

Brown, R. and J. Connell. 1993. 'The global flea market: Migration, remittances and the informal economy in Tonga.' *Development and Change*, 24. pp. 611–47.

Brown, R. and J. Foster. 1995. 'Some common fallacies about migrants' remittances in the South Pacific: Lessons from Tongan and West Samoan research.' *Pacific Viewpoint*, 36, 1. pp. 29–45.

Bryceson, D. and U. Vuorela. 2002. 'Transnational families in the twenty-first century.' In D. Bryceson and U. Vuorela (eds), *The transnational family: New European frontiers and global networks*, Oxford: Berg.

Campbell, I. 1992. 'A historical perspective on aid and dependency: The example of Tonga.' *Pacific Studies*, 15, 3. pp. 59–75.

Department of Immigration and Multicultural and Indigenous Affairs. Online 2003a. *Settler Arrivals: Selected Countries of Birth by Migration Stream, for the Financial Year 2002–03*.
    Http://www.immi.gov.au/statistics/stat_info/oad/settlers/setdatb.htm

Department of Immigration and Multicultural and Indigenous Affairs. Online 2003b. *Permanent Departures by Selected Country of Birth by Length of*

Stay, 2002–03.
Http://www.immi.gov.au/statistics/stat_info/oad/perm_dep/permdep.htm

Evans, M. 2003. *Persistence of the Gift: Tongan tradition in transnational context*. Waterloo: Wilfred Laurier Press.

Finau, P. P. 1993. 'How immigration affects the home country.' In G. McCall and J. Connell (eds), *A world perspective on Pacific Islander migration: Australia, New Zealand and the USA*, Pacific Studies Monograph No. 6, Sydney: University of New South Wales. pp. 307–10.

Foreign Affairs, Defence and Trade References Committee. 2003. *A Pacific Engaged: Australia's relations with Papua New Guinea and the island states of the south-west Pacific*. Report tabled on August 12 in the Senate of the Parliament of Australia.
http://www.aph.gov.au/Senate/committee/fadt_ctte/reports/index.htm

Hau'ofa, E. 1994. 'Thy kingdom come: The democratization of aristocratic Tonga.' *The Contemporary Pacific*, 6 (2). pp. 414–27.

Helu, F. 1985. 'Tonga in the 1990s.' Address delivered to New Zealand Institute of Foreign Affairs and Ministry of Foreign Affairs, Wellington.

James, K. 1993. 'Cash and kin. Aspects of migration and remittance from the perspective of a fishing village in Vava'u, Tonga.' In G. McCall and J. Connell (eds), *A world perspective on Pacific Islander migration: Australia, New Zealand and the USA*, Pacific Studies Monograph No. 6, Sydney: University of New South Wales. pp. 359–74.

Jones-Correa, M. 2002. 'The study of transnationalism among the children of immigrants: Where we are and where we should be headed.' In P. Levitt and M. Waters (eds), *The Changing Face of Home: The transnational lives of the second generation*, New York: Russell Sage Foundation. pp. 221–41.

Kane, A. 2002. 'Senegal's village diaspora and the people left ahead.' In D. Bryceson and U. Vuorela (eds), *The Transnational Family: New European frontiers and global networks*, Oxford: Berg.

Lee, H. 2003. *Tongans Overseas: Between two shores*. Honolulu: University of Hawai'i Press.

Lee, H. 2004. '"Second generation" Tongan transnationalism: Hope for the future?' *Asia Pacific Viewpoint*, 45, 2. pp. 235–54.

Levitt, P. and M. Waters (eds) 2002. *The Changing Face of Home: The transnational lives of the second generation*. New York: Russell Sage Foundation.

Menjivar, C. 2002. 'Living in two worlds? Guatemalan-origin children in the United States and emerging transnationalism.' *Journal of Ethnic and Migration Studies*, 28, 3. pp. 531–55.

Pacific Magazine online. 2006. 'Tonga: Economy hits rock bottom, Commerce Minister says.' January 11.

Poirine, B. 1998. 'Should we hate or love MIRAB?' *The Contemporary Pacific*, 10, 1. pp. 65–105.

Rumbaut, R. G. 2002. 'Severed or sustained attachments? Language, identity, and imagined communities in the post-immigrant generation.' in P. Levitt and M. Waters (eds), *The Changing Face of Home: The transnational lives of the second generation*, New York: Russell Sage Foundation. pp. 43–95.

Small, C. 1997. *Voyages: From Tongan villages to American suburbs*. Ithaca: Cornell University Press.

Vertovec, S. 2001. 'Transnationalism and identity.' *Journal of Ethnic and Migration Studies,* 27, 4. pp. 573–82.

8. Labour Mobility in the Pacific: Creating seasonal work programs in Australia

Nic Maclellan and Peter Mares

Introduction

Australia has long benefited from the labour of working people from the Pacific Islands, from the Kanakas who helped build the Queensland sugar industry in the 19th century, to women today, sewing Country Road shirts for a dollar an hour in a Fiji garment factory.

Pacific workers today are international and mobile: i-Kiribati and Tuvaluan seafarers staff the global shipping trade; Samoan and Tongan labourers work in factories and building sites in Sydney and Auckland or pick fruit in Australia's Murray Valley (often as 'illegal' or undocumented workers); more than 1,000 Fijians work in Iraq and Kuwait as security guards, truck drivers and labourers, while Fijian soldiers and police officers serve in peacekeeping operations around the globe. Meanwhile, Indo-Fijian and Tongan computer technicians, nurses, accountants and teachers migrate to find a better life, in the face of political turmoil and limited career opportunities in their homeland.

This movement of people has had a massive impact on the Pacific. In the colonial era, plantations of sugar in Fiji and pineapples in Hawai'i were built largely on migrant and indentured labour on alienated indigenous land. 'Blackbirding' in Melanesia robbed many islands of their young men between 1860 and 1900 and helped build the sugar industry in Queensland. [1]

Today, there is extensive domestic migration to Pacific towns and cities from rural areas and outlying islands. This internal population movement is often the precursor to international migration, either to other Pacific Island nations or to industrialised countries. It can also be 'circular' migration, with people returning to their home areas after fulfilling their desire for earnings, education or career advancement. Large numbers of people in the Pacific Islands migrate in search of the three Es: education, employment and enjoyment. Often they end up instead with the three Ds — jobs that are dirty, difficult and dangerous — and governments are left to deal with the social consequences of the three Ms: mobile men with money.

A high percentage of Polynesian and Micronesian Islanders now live overseas, especially in Pacific Rim countries such as Australia, Aotearoa/New Zealand, Canada and the USA. Some freely associated states and territories have migration rights to their former colonial power. In smaller islands such as Niue, Cook Islands, Rotuma and Wallis and Futuna, the number of people living overseas is greater than the numbers who remain. More Cook Islanders live in New Zealand than in the Cook Islands, more American Samoans in the USA than in their home islands. The geographer Gerard Ward (1999) suggests that the Polynesian triangle needs to be extended to incorporate Los Angeles, Sydney and Auckland.

Migration has become an outlet for the population pressures evident in many island nations and remittances sent home play a vital part in the economy of countries such as Tonga, Samoa, Niue, Tuvalu, Kiribati, the Cook Islands, Wallis and Futuna and Fiji. In turn, there is concern in Fiji, Tonga and Micronesia about the importation of Asian labour as domestic workers, sex workers and garment industry labourers. [2]

These patterns of migration provide benefits such as the transfer of remittances, the repatriation of skills and education, the promotion of tourism and the seeding of funds for small business development (Brown and Walker 1995). However, migration also has social costs. The immigration policies of developed nations favour those with skills and high levels of education, and there is an extensive literature on the 'brain drain' from the Pacific as rugby players, teachers, nurses, accountants and other professionals and tradespeople move to jobs offshore that offer better pay or career advancement.

In this way, Pacific Island nations are robbed of the skilled workers who are most needed, while low or semi-skilled workers who most need jobs are left behind and remain unemployed, with limited job opportunities in the formal wage sector. Labour force and population data from the Secretariat of the Pacific Community show that the youth bulge in most island nations will mean that employment generation will become increasingly urgent in the Pacific in coming decades, and there is growing discussion about the potential to address it through greater international labour mobility. [3]

The pressing need to find jobs for Pacific Island workers coincides with the emergence of gaps in the labour force of developed nations. In countries such as Australia, lower birth rates, the ageing demographic profile, increased personal wealth, the provision of social welfare, sustained economic growth, low unemployment and higher levels of education have combined to reduce the supply of workers who are available (or willing) to undertake physically demanding labour for relatively low pay. This has opened up debate about the potential for temporary employment schemes for Pacific Islanders to work in overseas labour markets, particularly in seasonal pursuits in agriculture.

This issue of labour migration and seasonal work is on the agenda of Pacific island governments and donor agencies:

- a 2003 inquiry by Australia's Senate Foreign Affairs, Defence and Trade References Committee (2003: 69-75) on Australia's relations with the Pacific recommended that the Australian Government support civil society and private sector organisations to develop a pilot program for seasonal workers to come to Australia from the Pacific.
- the Forum Secretariat hosted a Remittances Roundtable in March 2005, studying the link between remittances, migration and labour market flexibility in current regional trade negotiations (Pacific Islands Forum Secretariat 2005).
- the ADB has published an overview of the role of remittances in Pacific Island economies, in the context of research on poverty and hardship in island countries (Connell and Brown 2005).
- the World Bank is currently conducting research on labour mobility and market access, investigating ways of improving migration opportunities so that Pacific labour can move to where the jobs are found in the region. [4]
- the Australian Agency for International Development (AusAID) is developing 'Pacific 2020' scenarios that look at demography and development projections for the next 15 years. [5]

At the October 2005 meeting of the Pacific Islands Forum, held in PNG, the issue of labour mobility was a key topic as Forum members discussed increasing regional integration. Pacific Island community, academic and government leaders widely express the belief that increased labour market access, especially for unskilled workers, is a central component of regional economic integration under the Pacific Plan adopted at the 2005 Forum. PNG's Foreign Minister, Sir Rabbie Namaliu, has stated: 'We believe that permitting increased labour mobility should be part of Australia's and New Zealand's commitment to implementing the Pacific Plan. It is one way to demonstrate to our leaders that they are serious about assisting island countries to develop their capacity and their economies' (*Australian Financial Review*, October 26, 2005, p. 8).

At the Forum meeting, however, Australia's Prime Minister, John Howard, firmly expressed his opposition to proposals to create temporary work schemes in Australia. [6] In a December 2005 statement issued to the regional media, Australia's Foreign Minister, Alexander Downer, reiterated government policy against temporary work schemes, stating that the 'answer to the Pacific's large and growing unemployment problems does not lie in a few hundred unskilled young people coming to Australia to pick fruit for a few months of the year'. [7]

In spite of Prime Minister Howard's firm 'no' to seasonal work programs at the 2005 Forum leaders' meeting, the issue *is* still being debated in Australia and there is continuing lobbying by business leaders and farmers' organisations. [8] The Australian Senate Employment, Workplace Relations and Education Committee began a further inquiry into Pacific Region Seasonal Labour Programs in December 2005, to examine whether a seasonal work program could meet labour shortages in rural Australia and advance the economic development of Pacific nations. [9]

As part of a wider research project conducted with the Institute for Social Research of Swinburne University, [10] this chapter will briefly discuss the role of remittances in Pacific economies and development, before outlining a proposal for a pilot program of seasonal work for Islanders in Australia's horticulture industry. It will discuss Canada's Seasonal Agricultural Workers' Program (CSAWP) as a model for seasonal work programs, but will look at a range of issues — concerning regulation, labour rights and social impacts — that would need to be addressed if seasonal work schemes were to operate without evoking memories of blackbirding.

Remittances and Pacific development

Labour mobility and trade negotiations

Pacific Island governments have made gaining greater access to the labour markets of Australia and New Zealand an explicit policy goal. They see it as a crucial element in long-term job creation and social development. As a result, the issue of labour mobility has emerged as a key element in regional trade negotiations. The starting point of these various negotiations focused on trade in goods, but trade in services and labour mobility have become increasingly central to the discussions. There are three main strands to the trade negotiations involving Pacific Island nations: PICTA, the Pacific Island Countries Trade Agreement, covers trade in goods for the 14 Forum island countries *excluding* Australia and New Zealand. PICTA was endorsed at the Forum Heads of Government meeting in Nauru in August 2001 and provides for the phased elimination of tariffs between island countries. The larger island economies should have abolished most tariffs by 2009 and the smaller ones by 2011. The phasing in of the agreement over this period is to be accompanied by strategies to help governments adopt alternative taxes and economic reform measures to compensate for the revenue they will lose from tariff reductions. PACER, the Pacific Agreement on Closer Economic Relations, was also endorsed at the Forum meeting in Nauru in 2001. It sets out a broader umbrella agreement for all Forum members *including* Australia and New Zealand. [11] An Economic Partnership Agreement (EPA) is being negotiated between the EU and Pacific members of the African, Caribbean and Pacific grouping (ACP), under the Cotonou Agreement. A deal should be finalised by December 2007.

These three strands of trade negotiations are interlinked. For example, PACER requires that Australia and New Zealand be treated at least on the same negotiating basis as the EU. Hence, any provisions agreed to by Pacific Island nations under the EPA will have a flow-on effect on trade agreements with their more immediate neighbours. This is important since Pacific Island negotiations towards an EPA with the EU include discussions on labour mobility. As such they open the door to similar negotiations under PACER, a forum seen as far more crucial to Pacific Island governments given the much greater significance of the Australian and New Zealand labour markets as a potential source of future employment for Pacific Islanders. [12]

The issue of greater labour mobility is a sensitive topic for Forum member governments, as the pace and manner of structural readjustment and trade liberalisation are being debated widely in the Pacific. The Asian Development Bank (1999) acknowledges that the Forum Economic Ministers' Meeting Action Plan is based on 'market friendly policies widely accepted as economically sensible, albeit politically difficult to implement'. But many NGOs and church organisations are critical of the process, arguing that trade agreements are finalised without parliamentary debate or extensive community consultation; that there has not been enough research and analysis of the social and cultural impacts of economic and trade reform; that economic models proposed for developing nations in Africa, Asia and Latin America are not appropriate for small island developing states; and that there are severe imbalances in island countries' political and economic weight compared with Australia, New Zealand and Europe, making the rhetoric of 'level-playing-field' negotiations a joke. [13]

The 'temporary movement of natural persons' (known as 'Mode 4') forms part of negotiations under the General Agreement on Trade in Services (GATS), however, the focus of Mode 4 discussions is on skilled workers, even though the lower-skilled services workforce is not excluded. Currently, the movement of labour from the Pacific to Australia focuses mainly on skilled trades and professional staff — nurses, teachers, rugby players, accountants and tradespeople — who have the necessary points for immigration and residency requirements. As well as permanent migration, there is already an increasing trend towards temporary entry for employment of skilled migrants in Australia — but discussion about temporary entry for unskilled workers is only just beginning (Riley 2005).

The loss of skilled workers is causing significant problems for island nations, but another concern is the growing pool of unskilled and semi-skilled workers who cannot find employment in the formal sector of island economies, especially as 40 per cent of island populations are aged under 20 years. [14] For example, the Fiji Government estimates that there are about 17,000 new job seekers each year in Fiji (school leavers and late entrants to the job market), but only about 9,700 job opportunities in the formal sector (Fiji 2002: 42).

It is here that politics trumps economics and we see a shift from the language of 'trade' to the language of 'migration' in regional negotiations. As Professor Jane Kelsey (2005) of Auckland University notes in her study of the EPA negotiations,

'Richer countries fear an influx of workers from poor countries, so they treat this as a trade issue when it involves skilled workers from those countries that fuel the "brain drain", but it reverts to an immigration issue when it involves low-skilled workers.'

The growing importance of remittances

Traditionally, smaller Polynesian states such as Tonga, Samoa, Tuvalu, Wallis and Futuna, Niue and the Cook Islands have been reliant on remittances from migrants or seasonal workers to complement Official Development Assistance (ODA) and very limited access to Foreign Direct Investment (FDI). There is currently renewed investigation of the ways in which remittances contribute to social and economic development in the Pacific, as part of a global academic debate about the role of remittances in investment as well as consumption (World Bank 2006). But it's clear that more Pacific workers are seeking employment in Pacific Rim countries and that remittances continue to play a central role in island economies for many Forum member countries.

For example, a crucial source of revenue for Tuvalu and Kiribati are the remittances of seafarers who crew vessels for international shipping companies from North America and Europe. The number of i-Kiribati seafarers has risen from 788 (in 1989) to 1,366 (in 1999) and the number of Tuvaluan seafarers from 67 (in 1996) to 241 (in 1999). Maria Borovnik's (2006) study of seafarers' remittances in Kiribati estimates that 57 per cent of funds remitted to wives are spent on basic needs, 30 per cent saved for investment and 13 per cent spent on school fees. For the seafarers themselves, 36 per cent don't save, 20 per cent have bought a house and land while 44 per cent are saving for a house and land. Because of the i-Kiribati tradition of *bubuti* (a request by a family member that cannot be refused), cash and goods coming into the community spread through the extended family, rather than remaining with one individual.

For its overseas exchange transactions, Tonga has seen a steady increase of private receipts through remittances in the past four years, from 105 million pa'anga (2001) to P184 million (2004). By comparison, in 2003–04, trade in merchandise raised just P28.3 million and services P52.7 million (National Reserve Bank of Tonga 2004: 6).

Even one of the Pacific's largest countries, Fiji, is increasingly reliant on overseas remittances, which are playing a crucial role in Fiji's foreign exchange earnings. The country has historically relied on sugar and gold mining, and more recently tourism and garment manufacture, but in the past decade, the amount of remittances has increased to a level where they earn more foreign exchange than other sectors except tourism (see Table 1).

Table 1: Increase in foreign exchange earnings for Fiji, 1994–2004

Year	Tourism	Remittances	Textile, clothing and footwear	Sugar and molasses	Gold	Fish	Mineral water
1994	393	56	163	266	63	64	–
2004	682	306	291	188	88	85	53

Source: Reserve Bank of Fiji — figures in $F million.

Of more than $F306 million of remittances earned in 2004, $F200 million came from the salaries and allowances of Fiji citizens working overseas. Given that significant amounts of remittances are transmitted directly within the family, such as cash carried by hand, these Reserve Bank figures underestimate the real amount. Fiji's Reserve Bank Governor, Savenaca Narube, notes, 'We are only capturing remittances that flow through the financial system. There are other kinds that are carried in person and sent through the ordinary mail. There are also those remittances in kind. One estimate puts these unrecorded remittances at over $150 million, lifting total remittances above retained tourist receipts.' [15] The inflow of remittances in recent years is doubly important, given the significant outflow of funds through emigrant transfers. Fiji faces significant problems as skilled workers move offshore seeking better career paths, training and job opportunities. Many left Fiji after the 1987 and 2000 coups, including teachers, nurses, doctors and other professional staff. Since the 1987 coups, an estimated $A696.9 million has left Fiji in the form of emigrants' transfers, with more than 5,000 people migrating from Fiji every year (Azmat 2005).

But many lesser skilled workers are going overseas too. Fijian women travel as domestic workers, aged carers and nannies to the USA or other Pacific countries, while Fijian men are increasingly recruited in military-related roles. As the US and British armed forces fail to meet their recruitment targets, they have been expanding their recruitment overseas. There are currently more than 2,000 Fijian soldiers in the British Army, and the UK Government is expanding recruitment in its former colony (*BBC News Online*, 9 November, 2004). Large numbers of Fijian men are also being recruited by private companies to work as soldiers, security guards, truck drivers and labourers to work in or near the conflict zone of Iraq.

Case study: Iraq

In January 2005, Fiji's Minister for Labour, Kenneth Zinck, announced that 'the Government knows that more men are leaving for Kuwait and Iraq and it is a good thing because it is providing employment for the unemployed. This is one solution to the increasing unemployment rate in the country today' (*Fiji Times*, 19 January, 2005). By mid-2005, there were more than 1,000 Fijians working in Iraq and Kuwait. They were employed by local subsidiaries of US and British security corporations, such as Global Risk Strategies, Homeland Security Limited,

ArmorGroup, Sabre International Fiji, Triple Canopy and Meridian Services Agency.

More people are signing up for work in the Middle East, despite growing public concern at the number of casualties in Iraq, and even though returning troops have complained about the failure to obtain the promised benefits and welfare payments to families.[16] Eighty Fijians recruited by Meridian Services as drivers in Iraq claimed in July 2005 that they had not been paid for the past three months. The men said that PWC Logistics had not met the promised pay rates and conditions set out in contracts signed in Fiji, with 100 men either terminated or simply walking off the job. One driver said:

> Out of the 350 officers that are left here, we have quite a few who have been terminated, some have just left the job because they are not being paid and only those that have been paid buy food for the whole group. Some of us who could not stand this kind of living have returned to Fiji but the rest are here because we need the money to support our families (*Fiji Times*, 7 July 2005).

Returning personnel called for Meridian's local coordinator, Timoci Lolohea, to be investigated by Fiji's Labour Ministry and police, but, by January 2006, the issue had not been referred to police by the Labour Ministry (*Fiji TV National News*, 30 December, 2005). Some 20,000 people in Fiji have paid a registration fee of at least $F150 to Meridian, in order to be listed for work in Kuwait, even though there were only 2,000 jobs on offer. Fijian journalist Samisoni Pareti (2005) has reported that villages have used their development funds to pay for application fees and that Meridian's recruitment drives have touched on Methodist Church networks, using church funds to pay for application fees, with the money repaid if a job is found in Kuwait.

The experience of recruitment of former soldiers and unskilled workers in Iraq and Kuwait raises some pertinent issues for any proposed recruitment for temporary work in Australia. Obviously, the security hazards and pay rates are different, but the boom of recruiting for Iraq and Kuwait has raised many issues for the Government of Fiji: the unregulated role of private recruitment contractors, the social impact on family life, and the capacity of government to support workers with pay disputes or post-deployment health problems. The Iraq/Kuwait experience also raises another set of questions about the social impact of labour migration on the family and community life of those left at home.

Social impacts

The 'paradise' image of Pacific life promoted by the tourist industry belies the significant changes in social structures in the Pacific, with changing patterns of work, urbanisation and gender roles. A number of people interviewed for this research stressed that traditional economies of rural villages were under challenge, and that seasonal worker schemes could exacerbate some trends. [17] Current deployments of Fijian men as UN peacekeepers, British soldiers or private security guards in Iraq have provided evidence of psychological stress on children and negative impacts on educational standards. Church leaders reported a number of cases of family break-up, infidelity and new relationships forming, as one spouse worked overseas for lengthy periods. There are a number of anecdotal reports of Pacific men who had married in Australia to obtain residency rights, even though they had a wife and family at home. Community leaders are worried about how increased amounts of migrant work will affect gender roles in rural villages. There are concerns about the loss of male role models, and the potential impact that departing young workers will have on the traditional gendered allocation of jobs. An ageing population in rural areas, as young people migrate to urban centres or overseas, might impact on agricultural production and add burdens on already stressed health services. And there are particular burdens on ageing women. Women who have not worked in the formal sector do not have superannuation such as the Fiji National Provident Fund, and are reliant on financial support from working children. There is often an added burden of unpaid childcare for older women, as their daughters enter the workforce.

Women's groups such as the Fiji Women's Rights Movement (FWRM) and the Catholic Women's League of Tonga have reaffirmed concerns over a range of impacts on overseas workers: on women, on family life and on children. FWRM has conducted research surveys on sexual harassment in the workplace, and these problems could be exacerbated if women were working overseas as seasonal agricultural workers, unless there was close regulation and support to stop workplace harassment and bullying (Fiji Women's Right Movement 1998, 2002).

A growing concern is a pattern of suicide among Pacific youth in Fiji, Samoa, the FSM, the Marshall Islands, Palau and Guam, with the Pacific having the highest youth suicide rates in the world (UNICEF Pacific 1998). For Indo-Fijians and in Samoa, suicide rates among young women exceed those for young men, which is unusual for almost all populations in the world (Booth 2000). This youth crisis is in part connected to the absence of parents and relatives: researchers such as the Micronesian Seminar's Father Francis Hezel (1985, 1989) have highlighted the effects of globalisation as one of the many elements contributing to youth suicide, as customary and family mechanisms for conflict resolution have been shattered by migration. While extended families often used tight authority systems, they also provided older relatives with whom young men and women could talk about their problems. With family members working overseas, traditional family reconciliation mechanisms are not working as effectively.

Pacific regional organisations have undertaken studies of the actions of overseas workers that have negative as well as positive impacts on the social and economic circumstances of dependants and communities. One interesting case study was conducted by the Secretariat of the Pacific Community on Tuvaluan and i-Kiribati seafarers' remittance spending and the economic and social implications of seafaring for community development (Dennis 2003). Although the type of work, recruitment and skill levels for sailors and length of absence are different to seasonal agricultural work, the study provides important pointers on social issues that would be useful in designing pilot programs for temporary agricultural work in Australia.

- The seafarers' wages were the basis of economic support for many people within the home community, ranging from one to 30 people. The report estimates that 4,200 people in Tuvalu (population 10,000) and 10,200 people in Kiribati (population 85,000) were directly dependent on the seafarers' incomes.
- Loss of employment by seafarers due to illness or injury had 'catastrophic' effects on the economic circumstances of some families.
- Wives and partners of seafarers reported difficulties maintaining contact with overseas workers, causing stress and depression. This was exacerbated because depression is not considered a real health problem in many Pacific cultures.
- Some seafarers engaged in unsafe sexual activity while overseas, often under the influence of alcohol. There is an increased risk of HIV/AIDS and STDs for these workers, but also for wives/partners who find it difficult to refuse unprotected sex when their husbands return from overseas, and face violence if they refuse.
- An increase in violence against spouses was also related to alcohol abuse, with returning sailors engaging in drinking sessions with their mates. Women were reluctant to report domestic violence to police in this case because 70-80 per cent were dependent on their spouse/partner's income.
- The majority of wives/partners and children reported difficulties resuming relationships with returning seafarers.
- There are complex gender and childhood development issues when parents communicate largely with their spouse rather than their children while overseas. Children also reported anger or annoyance at their father on his return, for disrupting household routines, ignoring their personal development, or diverting their mother's attention to caring for her spouse rather than her children.
- There is some internal migration from outer islands to Tarawa, as seafarers' families move to the capital to avail themselves of more time with their spouse/parent between voyages.

Remittances and development

There has been a long debate among Pacific academics over economies based on the MIRAB model and the role of remittances in national development (Bertram and Watters 1985, Bertram 1999).

Many research studies around the world argue that remittances from second- and third-generation migrants will decline over time, due to family reunification in the overseas country or greater integration of the migrant into the host community. This suggests that it is dangerous for governments to base economic strategy on a continuing stream of remittances, which will ebb and flow according to a range of factors (e.g., migration policies, economic recession in receiving countries, or the adoption over time of individualistic values that clash with communalist village traditions). However, the ADB's March 2005 overview of remittances in the Pacific questions the generalisation of the unsustainability of remittance flows (Connell and Brown 2005). Although there is a need for further research, there are already Pacific case studies that indicate continuing financial support to family members at home from long-term migrants (Brown 1998, Somati and Gibson 2001). There are a growing number of case studies on the impact of remittances in the Pacific Islands. Researchers such as Richard Brown, John Connell (Connell and Brown 2005) and Avelina Rokoduru (2004) are looking at issues such as savings, investment, consumption and social impacts on women and family life. This research contributes to a global debate about the role of remittances in investment (World Bank 2006).

The World Bank, the Forum Secretariat and Pacific universities are engaged in new research programs to update data on remittance flows, and key questions are:

- Do some people remit more than others? (E.g., nurses are generally excellent remitters and seasonal workers returning home after temporary employment are also likely to remit a large proportion of income.)
- Significant amounts of remittances are used for consumption support rather than investment and savings, but there is a changing trend with evidence of investment in human and physical capital (e.g., children in households with family members overseas sending remittances appear to have higher education levels than those without). Beyond this, an increase in consumption is not necessarily a negative — it can have positive benefits for family welfare, if it results in improved housing, better sanitation and better nutrition (e.g., the replacement of wood-burning stoves with gas stoves in kitchens can dramatically improve women's health).
- What levels of funds are remitted to households without a family member overseas? (Continuing research by Professor Richard Brown of the University of Queensland shows that households in Tonga and Fiji receive remittances even if they don't have a family member overseas and that overseas migrants

remit to organisations and their own business/superannuation funds, as well as to family members.)
- Not all remittances are in cash and significant amounts go back through informal means rather than the formal banking system (with people carrying cash by hand, transmitting funds through Western Union, or purchasing and carrying goods and other in-kind contributions). Can finance services be developed to assist cheap and efficient transfers of funds?
- Some people are more likely than others to invest (older and returning migrants; people with small businesses in the home country; occupational groups who remit generously). Can policies be tailored to encourage them to invest in community/cooperative/small business schemes?

A central issue is whether Forum member countries can develop options for seasonal and temporary work, rather than permanent migration, to allow new opportunities for work and remittances.

Pacific Islands Forum Secretary-General, Greg Urwin, notes that one major stumbling block to negotiating increased labour market access is the issue of reciprocity — whether Pacific Island countries will have to open their labour market to Australian and New Zealand workers in return for access for unskilled workers in the larger economies. [18] Australia's Parliamentary Secretary for Foreign Affairs, Bruce Billson (2005a), stressed that opening the Australian labour market would be a two-way process. The opposition Australian Labor Party (ALP) supports increased labour mobility as part of a broader regional Pacific community. But the ALP's 2005 policy paper *Towards a Pacific Community* also says that, in return, there must be increased economic and administrative reform in island countries (Sercombe 2005). For the Government, Billson (2005b) also stated that the issue of labour market access would be negotiated as part of a package of trade issues, rather than as a separate treaty. But presenting the issue of labour market access as a trade issue removes the development focus of the whole process, and downplays many of the adverse social impacts — an issue of concern to Pacific Island governments, which see labour market access as primarily a development issue and one that should not require reciprocal rights of access for Australia and New Zealand. [19] Iosefa Maiava, Deputy Secretary-General of the Pacific Islands Forum Secretariat, notes that 'if there is to be reciprocity, it should be as equitable as possible recognising the different scales and different needs of Forum member countries'. [20]

Pacific economists see an increase of remittances as an important source of boosting foreign reserves and addressing the severe balance of payments gap between Australia, New Zealand and Pacific island neighbours — a gap that is likely to only worsen if tariff protections are dismantled under PACER and imports replace domestic production. [21] As University of the South Pacific economist Professor Wadan Narsey points out, in a future era of 'free' trade, remittances from temporary or seasonal labour schemes could replace key agricultural industries such as sugar as a source of revenue:

> PACER will almost certainly add to the already substantial pool of unemployed labour, so remittances from the export of unskilled labour to Australia and [New Zealand] may turn out to be an important counterbalancing flow which reduces the size of the deficit, even if it is unlikely to completely eliminate it, and relieve pressure on the high rates of unemployment in Fiji. It may be emphasised that what needs to be investigated is not free and permanent access for [Fijian] unskilled labour, but temporary worker schemes for specific periods of time, in specific industries where Australia and [New Zealand] face labour shortages (Narsey 2004).

Modelling seasonal work schemes in Australia

Seasonal work and horticulture — Australia and the world

At the October 2005 Pacific Islands Forum, Prime Minister John Howard (2005) stated, 'We always have a preference for permanent settlement for migration. … I think you either invite someone to come to your country to stay as a permanent citizen or you don't.'

Australia does already allow temporary entry, but only for full-fee paying overseas students and skilled workers. The business sector has increasing access to short-term visas — known as 'Business (Long-Stay)' or '457' visas — to bring in workers to cover skill shortages. Originally this category was used exclusively to bring in professionals such as IT specialists and medical staff but in recent years the catchment has broadened to include more traditional tradespeople such as welders (Robinson 2004). The number of temporary visas issued to skilled workers has jumped dramatically during the life of the Howard Government: there were 40,124 business long-stay visas granted in the 2003–04 financial year, up from just 9,600 in 1996–97 (Department of Immigration, Migrants and Multicultural Affairs 2005: 67-9, Moran 2004). The growth of this component of the migration program reflects an international trend towards micro- or niche migration schemes designed to overcome labour shortages in particular industries at particular times.

In other countries such schemes also extend to low or semi-skilled workers, particularly in agriculture. There has been 'a generally steady upward trend in inflows of seasonal workers since the beginning of the 1990s' and each year half a million seasonal workers from non-EU countries are employed in EU agriculture, especially in Germany, which issued 260,000 seasonal work permits in 2001 (United Nations Department of Economic and Social Affairs 2004, Ratha 2004). In fact, Australia and New Zealand might be the only developed nations that do not import seasonal labour for agriculture (Pickering and Barnes 2005).

Currently primary producers in Australia's agriculture and horticulture sectors rely on documented ('legal') and undocumented ('illegal') workers to meet seasonal labour market needs. The documented workforce includes itinerant farm labourers, family members, local casual workers, students, grey nomads (retirees travelling around Australia) and backpackers on the Working Holiday Maker Scheme (Harding and Webster 2002). The undocumented workforce consists of unauthorised residents (primarily from Pacific Island, South-East Asian and Chinese backgrounds), overseas students working in excess of permitted hours, Australians working while in receipt of benefits and foreign travellers working without authorisation.

The rural sector is one of the four major areas of employment for undocumented workers in Australia. [22] Union officials claim that 'a significant proportion' of Victoria's fresh fruit crop is picked by undocumented workers who are highly vulnerable to exploitation and in some cases are offered wages as low as $A3 an hour (Hughes and Schwartz 2004). Meanwhile primary producers are vulnerable to immigration raids that can have a devastating effect on output during highly time-sensitive harvest periods.

The gross value of horticultural production in Australia in 2002 was estimated by the industry to be $A9.65 billion, and by the Australian Bureau of Statistics to be $A6.75 billion (Horticulture Australia Limited 2004). After rapid growth in the late 1990s, however, the fruit and vegetable industry currently faces significant challenges. Internationally, the high dollar has made Australian fruit and vegetables more expensive in markets where they must compete with subsidised European and North American produce and with produce from lower-wage countries such as China, South Africa and Chile. Domestically, the supermarket duopoly, increasing concentration in the food-processing sector, cheap imports of canned and frozen food and rising input costs (such as water, fuel and fertiliser) have growers in the grip of a cost-price squeeze. As a result of these pressures, traditional family farms are increasingly giving way to industrial-scale agriculture that can produce more efficiently through economies of scale (the number of farms in Australia declined by 25 per cent in 20 years to 2002–03 and average farm size increased from 2,720 hectares to 3,340 hectares) (Productivity Commission 2005: 31). The romantic image of Australian family farmers struggling to scratch a living from their own block of land is increasingly giving way to a more prosaic reality of professional farm managers and low-paid farm workers whose only connection to the land is that it supplies them with a job (Productivity Commission 2005: 99). [23] Agricultural workers are the lowest paid workers in the economy and their jobs are more likely to be casual or part-time than in most other sectors (Productivity Commission 2005: 106-7). Combined with the process of rural flight, this has led to growing labour shortages that are often temporary and seasonal in nature.

In response to pressure from the farm lobby, Immigration Minister, Amanda Vanstone, has created additional incentives for young travellers to take up agricultural work by allowing 'working holiday-makers' who do three months of 'seasonal harvest work in regional Australia' to apply for an additional 12-month visa. But the changes do not guarantee that backpackers will undertake a second stint of agricultural work and primary producers complain that backpackers' travel plans often take priority over working.

Canada's Seasonal Agricultural Workers' Program

Of the existing seasonal agricultural workers' schemes overseas, the one operating in Canada appears to provide the most useful lessons for Australia and the Pacific — not because it offers a perfect model that could be translated to Australian conditions, rather because it has been subject to extensive study and critique.

Canada's Seasonal Agricultural Workers' Program (CSAWP) has operated to bring temporary workers from the Caribbean since 1966 and from Mexico since 1974. In 2002, the program brought 19,000 workers to Canada (85 per cent of them to the province of Ontario) for an average of four months' employment. (The maximum stay allowable under the scheme is eight months.) Farmers need approval from local employment centres to certify that no Canadian workers are available to fill the jobs (though after the first year of involvement in the scheme such approval is largely perfunctory).

Farmers must provide the migrant workers with free housing (including meals or cooking facilities) and must guarantee them a minimum of 240 hours' work over six weeks at or above prevailing minimum-wage rates. Employers must take out workers' compensation insurance to cover the migrants in the case of industrial accidents, and must pay the cost of the migrants' international airfare, which can be partially recouped (to about 50 per cent). While working in Canada, the migrants pay local taxes and are covered by Canada's universal health care system.

A major study of CSAWP as a 'model of best practice and migrant worker participation in the benefits of economic globalisation' was undertaken by the North South Institute in Canada (Preibisch 2004, Griffith 2004, Downes and Odle-Worrell 2004). This research suggests that CSAWP has benefits at a number of levels.

For Canadian growers and Canadian rural communities:

- CSAWP increases labour reliability at times of peak demand, and enables growers to plan production increases with greater confidence.
- seasonal employment of foreign workers maintains and expands employment in higher skilled jobs, through the expansion of associated rural industries (e.g., transport services, construction, food processing).

- local spending by seasonal migrant workers provides an economic boost to Canadian country towns and helps to sustain local businesses (e.g., shops) and services (e.g., banks, post offices) that might otherwise be in danger of closing.
- the scheme offers a legal route to farm jobs that would probably otherwise be filled by undocumented workers. Growers need not fear being in breach of the law or suffering the disruption of immigration raids.

For migrant workers:

- CSAWP provides opportunities for un- or underemployed Mexican and Caribbean workers to earn income at pay rates well above those on offer in their home countries.
- workers return home each year and use their savings and remittances to improve housing, nutrition, clothing and health care for their families. Workers and their families enjoy greater income security and increased access to consumer goods.
- the scheme has long-term development outcomes in source countries; in particular, the children of migrant labourers are likely to stay longer in school. (Jamaican workers were found to spend up to 35 per cent of remittances on children's education and there was a positive correlation between the number of years workers were employed in CSAWP and their children's school leaving age [Verduzco and Lozano 2004]) This finding is consistent with other surveys on the high proportion of migrant workers' remittances used to fund spending on children's education (United Nations Department of Economic and Social Affairs 2004).
- workers are spared the smugglers' fees and risky journeys required to enter North America without the appropriate papers, and can live free of the corrosive fear that they might be discovered working illegally. Unlike undocumented workers, they return home regularly and are not forced to endure long years of separation from loved ones.
- the scheme is more accessible to the very poor in the source countries, those who do not have the financial resources to pay the guides or bribes required to engage in cross-border travel as undocumented migrants. Greater equity is achievable, because recruitment of seasonal workers can be targeted at impoverished regions, the unemployed and the landless.
- the scheme creates mechanisms (at least on paper) to protect the rights of foreign workers in terms of wages, health and safety and regulated work hours — protections that are denied to undocumented workers.

The Canadian scheme is not, however, without its problems. The United Food and Commercial Workers' (UFCW) Union in Canada says the exploitation of migrant workers under CSAWP is a 'shameful little secret' (United Food and Commercial Workers' Union 2002: 21). There have been occasional protests and strikes by migrant workers, cases of abuse and exploitation, examples of substandard or overcrowded accommodation, and industrial accidents due to insufficient training, inadequate safety equipment or overlong working hours (Martin 2003, Basok 2003, Ferguson 2004). In Ontario, where most migrants are employed, agricultural workers are effectively prevented from organising in trade unions (although this is currently subject to legal challenge) and are not covered by workplace health and safety legislation (although provincial occupational health and safety laws will be extended to agriculture in June 2006).

One of the strengths of the Canadian scheme is that it operates under an umbrella of bilateral (government-to-government) agreements, which provide for an annual review. This means that problems and inadequacies in the scheme can be addressed, and contracts and regulations updated. The agreements also provide a formal mechanism (consular liaison officers) for workers to raise grievances through their diplomatic mission. There is, however, also a downside here: the consular liaison officers are seen to be too remote from the workers and to suffer from a conflict of interest (maintaining good relations with Canada and the smooth operation of the scheme versus taking up the fight on behalf of individual workers). Government officials in Canada and Mexico express frustration at the large amount of bureaucratic activity generated by a scheme that employs relatively small numbers of people.

Another positive feature of the Canadian scheme is that it provides continuity. Growers can request the same workers back each year, which means that they retain the skills that workers have built up and do not need to invest constantly in retraining. This can also be a plus for the migrant workers as they become familiar with their employer, their work, the local community and each other. Again, however, this strength of the scheme can also be a weakness. Workers are essentially 'bonded' to a particular employer for the duration of their stay in Canada, and the employer has an almost absolute power to send them home before their contracts expire, on the basis of 'non-compliance, refusal to work, *or any other sufficient reason*' (United Food and Commercial Workers' Union 2003: 14). Workers can thus be trapped in exploitative or abusive situations and have very little power to refuse unreasonable demands such as working excessive hours or in unsafe conditions.

Labour mobility from the Pacific

There is growing pressure for Australia to establish seasonal work schemes for the Pacific. Forum island governments are lobbying Canberra on the issue and the Melanesian Spearhead Group has argued for temporary access for workers with qualifications below tertiary level, including seasonal agricultural workers.[24]

In its 2003 inquiry on Australia's relations with the region, the Senate Foreign Affairs, Defence and Trade Committee received numerous submissions suggesting schemes to bring workers from the Pacific and recommended 'a pilot program to allow for labour to be sourced from the region for seasonal work in Australia.' (Senate Foreign Affairs 2003). In its formal reply to the Senate report, however, the Australian Government simply 'noted' the recommendation for a pilot study, adding a one-line response: 'Australia has traditionally not supported programs to bring low skilled seasonal workers to Australia.' [25] The obstacles to such a scheme are political and bureaucratic.

Firstly, there is a popular antipathy to 'cheap foreign labour' from Asia and the Pacific that has historical roots stretching back at least as far as the Victorian gold rush. Memories of 'blackbirding' also raise concern over the wages and working conditions for foreign workers.

Secondly, there is an entrenched orthodoxy within government that sees only highly skilled or capital-rich migrants as being of value to Australia. The bias against low-skilled migrants was formalised by the Fitzgerald Report into Australia's immigration program in 1988 and intensified further after 1996, as the Howard Government decisively shifted the emphasis of the migration program to favour skilled and business migrants at the expense of family reunion (Jupp 2003: 145-6).

Thirdly, despite the increase in temporary skilled migration, there remains a bias towards permanent, rather than short-term, migration. Australia's Department of Immigration, Multicultural and Indigenous Affairs (DIMIA) believes that temporary migrant labour schemes 'fail to provide long-term benefits for either sending or receiving countries'. [26] Prime Minister John Howard responded to the idea of using overseas workers to pick fruit by saying on ABC Regional Radio that 'for a long period of time we have put our face against a guest worker approach', which could result in '[losing] control of a significant part of our immigration program' (Bedford 2004), while Treasurer Peter Costello has voiced the view that visas for short-stay 'guest workers' would be 'against the national ethos' (Colman 2005).

Fourthly, importing labour is problematic for the Australian labour movement. The national leadership of the Australian Council of Trade Unions (ACTU) has expressed some sympathy for the idea of a Pacific Island labour program with a developmental component and has even been involved in discussions about a proposed pilot program to bring workers from Fiji to Shepparton in central Victoria. But in the context of sweeping government changes that will weaken the role of unions in Australia's industrial relations system, the ACTU has firmed its opposition to 'circular' labour programs, arguing that international labour agreements should give Pacific workers the right to permanent residency. [27] There has been vocal opposition from specific unions to the idea of bringing in 'cheap' labour. Bill Shorten, President of the Australian Workers' Union (AWU), says, '[G]uest work arrangements are exploitative of the guest and exploitative of unemployed Australians.' (Metherell 2005). Australian unions have stressed that they would only support schemes that involved government and union regulation of wages and conditions and respected union membership.

A common argument for opposing temporary labour programs from the Pacific is that they would be discriminatory under Australia's immigration policy. There are, however, precedents for country-specific programs, such as the Working Holiday Maker Scheme in Australia, which provides travellers aged 18 to 30 with a 12-month visa that entitles them to work in Australia for up to three months at a time with any single employer. This scheme, based on bilateral agreements with 18 states or territories, does not take in any Pacific Island nations. [28] Other countries have quotas restricted to Forum member countries, such as New Zealand's Pacific Access programs or the European agreement for a quota of i-Kiribati and Tuvaluan seafarers in the EU offshore shipping fleet.

Another frequent objection to the idea of seasonal labour programs in Australia is the fear that temporary workers will overstay their visas and 'disappear' into the community (adding to the stock of undocumented migrants). The Canadian experience suggests that this fear is greatly exaggerated. Of the 15,123 workers who entered Ontario under CSAWP in 2004, only 221 (or less than 1.5 per cent) were listed as going absent from their jobs without leave and some of these would have returned to their homeland early. All workers were reported to have left Canada and returned home by the end of the year (Foreign Agricultural Management Service 2004). Initially, the low overstay rate in the Canadian scheme was engineered through recruitment criteria that were skewed to select those seasonal workers deemed most likely to return to their homeland — that is, male workers who were married with children still at home (Basok 2000). Recently, however, the scheme has also been opened up to single men and to women.

The most important factor in the low overstay rates in the Canadian scheme appears to be that workers can return to their homeland with the expectation that they will be re-engaged to work in Canada under CSAWP the next year. This 'partly explains the lower number of overstayers compared with those in other similar programs' in other countries (United Nations Department of Economic and Social Affairs 2004). For example, a scheme in the UK to allow final-year university students from non-EU Eastern European countries to work in agriculture has an estimated overstay rate of 10 per cent (United Kingdom Home Office 2002). In the UK case, the seasonal migrants know that the opportunity to work in the UK is a one-off so the incentive to overstay is greater.

Requirements for effective seasonal workers' schemes

Government officials and community leaders interviewed in the Pacific for this research all welcomed the idea of developing seasonal work schemes to allow Pacific Islanders greater access to the Australian labour market. However, church and NGO leaders all raised a range of issues about social impacts — on labour rights, family life and development outcomes for women — that would need to be addressed if such schemes were to function effectively.[29] Global trends and the appealing symmetry of a scheme to allow foreign workers to fill seasonal gaps in Australia's rural labour market should not blind us to potential obstacles and dangers. The problems experienced with the Canadian scheme — despite its 'world's best practice' status — underline the need for careful design and implementation. The following sections outline some issues that need to be addressed in creating pilot seasonal work schemes.

Labour rights and working conditions

In Australia, trade union leaders stress that any seasonal work scheme must not be used to undercut wages and conditions for Australian workers, and must adhere to core labour conventions and standards.[30] The International Labour Organisation (ILO) has a range of conventions covering core labour standards. The ILO also has specific conventions (97 and 143) covering migrant workers, yet these have not been ratified by Australia or by any Pacific Island governments.[31] The Pacific Conference of Churches (PCC) has also called on Pacific governments to sign, ratify and implement the provisions of the Convention on Protection of the Rights of All Migrant Workers and Members of Their Families (Migrant Workers' Convention).[32] The convention came into force in July 2003, but thus far has not been signed or ratified by Australia, New Zealand or any other member of the Pacific Islands Forum.

The experience in Canada suggests that problems will arise when migrant workers are tied to a specific employer, especially if there is no ability for them to organise collectively. Any seasonal labour scheme in Australia needs to have safeguards built in to protect workers' rights and guarantee freedom of association. There should also be a mechanism of independent dispute resolution to manage conflicts when they arise. Together with sectors such as construction and mining, farming and agricultural work are among the most hazardous industries for workers and compliance with occupational health and safety laws will be essential — there could be complex legal and practical issues for workers to claim treatment and compensation for workplace injuries after they return home. There is also a need to develop training programs for health and safety issues such as use of pesticides (which could have positive spin-offs for farm safety when the worker returns to farming and fishing in the Pacific).

Recruitment and government regulation

The 2003 Senate Committee into Australia's relations with the region recommends a pilot scheme, but says that 'the model developed [should] provide for management and organisational arrangements to be the responsibility of the source country and adequate mechanisms be put in place for training and transfer of skills' (Senate Foreign Affairs 2003).

Such a proposal, however, places the burden on small island states, while the Australian Government and private sector reduce or avoid their responsibility for the costs as well as the benefits of seasonal work schemes. A more realistic approach would involve some government-to-government framework or treaty, as in Canada's CSAWP, outlining the responsibilities of both governments. Pacific governments will need extra resources to effectively manage the scheme, and in our view its operation should be integrated with the official aid program to ensure maximum development outcomes. There is a problem seeing these programs as simply an issue of 'trade in services', instead of a component of the social and economic development of Australia's nearest neighbours.

Unions believe that any seasonal workers' scheme must involve more than monitoring of conditions for temporary workers. The scheme must be regulated by government, and there must be a system of sanctions for breaches of those regulations. Australian and Pacific unions, through the ACTU and the South Pacific Council of Trade Unions, would seek collaboration with and involvement in any institutions created to regulate the scheme. [33]

The need for targeted and ethical recruitment of seasonal workers takes on particular importance given the disparities in wage levels between Australia and most island countries. There is anecdotal information on skilled workers travelling to Australia for fruit picking and unskilled labouring work, because they could earn more than their own trade or profession (e.g., schoolteachers who travel to Australia on a tourist visa during the long summer break, and go fruit picking for a couple of months after briefly visiting relatives). It is our view that recruitment schemes should be targeting the unskilled, rather than taking skilled trades and professional staff away from the workforce.

One pitfall for a more regulated scheme is that many rural villagers from the Pacific would have less comfort with a complex bureaucratic scheme, especially where the only High Commission is located in the capital city. Given low levels of literacy in Melanesian countries such as PNG, Vanuatu and Solomon Islands, and 'a cultural aversion to lots of paperwork' [34] from many Islanders, there might be costs and delays in regulation and recruitment procedures. Experience in Canada suggests that complexity can result in migrant workers missing out on their entitlements — for example, tax returns or worker's compensation — because they do not have the skills to negotiate bureaucratic systems. Similarly, horticultural producers do not have time to deal with complex paperwork at the height of the harvest — so while a scheme must be regulated it also needs to be user friendly for workers and employers. There is also a need to develop 'a culture of saving', to encourage investment of remittances.

There is also a question of where employment contracts are signed, as this has some implications for labour rights: for example, under Fiji's *Employment Act*, signing a contract in Fiji allows provisions of the act to apply, while signing a contract overseas does not. This has implications if an employee wants the Ministry of Labour to follow up breaches of contract, unpaid or delayed wages, long-term occupational health problems, and so on.

Similarly, any seasonal labour program will need to take account of taxation agreements (or the lack of them) between Australia and the Pacific. Currently non-residents who perform harvest labour in Australia (working holiday-makers) are taxed at a higher rate than resident workers (29 per cent rather than 13 per cent) and do not benefit from the tax-free threshold (Australian National Audit Office 2005: 95-6). Unless this provision is altered, Pacific Islanders performing seasonal work could find themselves subject to double taxation.

There will be political issues relating to undocumented workers from Pacific Island countries, currently living or working in Australia and New Zealand in breach of their visa conditions. The creation of a regulated temporary work program could be accompanied by an amnesty, which would give time for undocumented workers to regularise their position, either as permanent migrants or as temporary workers. The issue of residency rights for workers is of crucial concern for Australian unions and Pacific communities in Australia, and migration policy would need to be coordinated with the introduction of seasonal work programs.[35]

Addressing social impacts on families

Emele Duituturaga, Chief Executive Officer of Fiji's Ministry of Women, Social Welfare and Poverty Alleviation, states that the Government of Fiji 'would support a regulated, managed scheme for seasonal workers. We have few jobs and a limited industry and manufacturing base, with a young and growing population.'[36] Duituturaga stresses, however, that there are significant social impacts from migrant worker schemes — the benefits of increased income for the family and community must be weighed against the social costs, especially for women and children. There are also questions of how many benefits from remittances go directly to families, while the costs and burdens of welfare and social adjustment are carried by government, at a time when many Pacific governments are often stretched to capacity in providing basic services. In response to these social impacts, the Secretariat of the Pacific Community's Regional Maritime Program has developed social responsibility modules for training seafarers — it would be worth further study to see whether elements of these pre-departure training programs (e.g., on HIV/AIDS) could be adapted for use in pilot programs for seasonal agricultural workers. It is also worth considering whether a maximum length of absence should be imposed on the scheme to ensure that workers are not separated from their families for extended periods of time — for example, visas to work in Australia could be capped at six months within any 12-month period so that workers would be sure to spend at least half the year in their home communities.

Information and community support

There is a need for pre-departure training and information sessions for seasonal workers as a crucial element of any scheme. Informants stressed the importance of providing accurate and timely information to prospective seasonal workers before they joined schemes or travelled. Such information could cover a spectrum of issues, including wage rates, labour conditions (hours, meal breaks, occupational health and safety), cultural issues, visa and consular advice, banking and remittance procedures, etc. There could also be discussion of social issues that might face bored, isolated workers, including substance abuse, gambling and the risk of HIV/AIDS (Rokoduru 2004).

Local communities could discuss collectively issues of the increase of funds into the community, with advice on family budgeting or allocation of savings, planning family business ventures or investing in local community projects.

Our proposal suggests that pre-departure recruitment, training and orientation should involve a range of participants, representing governments of the sending and host nations, growers/employers, unions and church leaders. Such orientation programs could be funded by a levy on employers and applicants, or with government subsidy. Employers and governments could assist with communication between seasonal workers and their families/communities at home. Employers could provide telephones and computer terminals with Internet and email access in church or community centres in Australia, while sending governments, NGOs and aid donors could assist with computer-training programs for families at home. There is also the potential for Pacific Island communities and churches in Australia to play a support role for seasonal workers.

Creating incentives to avoid overstaying

As discussed above, a key concern with temporary labour programs is that workers will fail to return home when their seasonal work is ended. There is the potential for positive and negative incentives to reduce overstaying, which would involve governments developing policy that could assist seasonal workers to return to their home country.

Under its 'risk factor list' for assessing visa applications, the Australian Department of Immigration and Indigenous Affairs (DIMIA) already has strict requirements for visitors from Fiji, Tonga and other Pacific countries because of people overstaying in the past. DIMIA told the 2003 Senate inquiry into Australia's relations with the region that without 'very strong enforcement', the non-return of seasonal workers would incur significant expenses for government: 'Overstay issues associated with low-skilled guest worker schemes also cannot be underestimated, given the experience in other places. It is certainly true that overstay rates, non-return rates and the rates of protection visa applications from visitors from the South Pacific are quite high. They would be amongst the factors that we would need to take into account in considering any guest worker scheme.' (Senate Foreign Affairs 2003). However, Reverend Jason Kioa, President of the Tonga Australia Association, stresses that 'most overstayers are homesick — they really want to go back home, but are restricted by the potential legal and financial costs of being caught by Immigration'. [37]

The dilemma for all undocumented workers is that they must stay below the radar for as long as possible in order to maximise their earnings in Australia: they know that once they are caught or decide to leave the country voluntarily, there will be no possibility of future return. Pacific church leaders in Australia are often involved in supporting parishioners in times of crisis (e.g., when a family member dies at home, but the overstayer cannot return home because of visa restrictions). Reverend Kioa believes that a scheme that would allow people to travel back and forth between Australia and Tonga would help reduce overstaying and the stresses on family life, and the breakdown of families by the extended absence of undocumented or migrant workers.

After the 2005 Pacific Islands Forum, Fiji's Prime Minister, Laisenia Qarase, stated: 'To me the most disappointing thing about this Forum is Australia's reluctance to start such a scheme. In my point of view, demand for seasonal or temporary labour always exists in those two countries and we know visitors to those countries have been employed illegally. Australia and New Zealand's concern [that] the scheme will increase illegal immigrants is not fair. This is a suggestion to put it on a proper arrangement, legally recognized with rules, regulations and a management system in place' (*Fiji Times*, 27 October 2005). Pacific Islands Forum Secretary-General, Greg Urwin, has also noted that seasonal migration to Australia by Pacific Islanders is different from past waves of postwar migration from southern Europe, in that many Islanders are landowners, maintain connections with extended family groups and have a continuing status in their home country. [38] There is an extensive literature discussing this 'transnational network of kin' in the Pacific. [39] Narsey has suggested: 'An essential part of the scheme could be the payment of a large proportion of the wages into trust funds for each worker, which are released in Fiji upon the satisfactory completion of the labour contract and return of the worker. This would not only ensure that Fiji enjoys the remittance benefits, but there is also an incentive for workers to abide by the rules and return after the end of the labour contract.' (Narsey 2004).

There is an important reservation to make in response to Dr Narsey's suggestion: if compulsory savings are to be deducted from the workers' wages, then it is imperative that at least some of this money is immediately available to family members in the home country for necessary living expenses. There are existing schemes where employers transmit funds home on a regular basis on behalf of the seasonal worker, such as the i-Kiribati and Tuvaluan seafarers' program (Dennis 2003).

There are other ways to maximise the likelihood of return. For example, it could be a requirement that workers return home before they can claim a refund for taxes paid in Australia, or before they can access superannuation contributions made by them or on their behalf. As in Canada, the recruitment criteria of seasonal workers could be skewed to select migrants deemed most likely to return to their homeland — that is, workers who are married with children still at home. There is a significant trade-off here, however, since such a selection bias requires the extended separation of a parent from his or her children. Selection criteria of this nature also discriminate against young, unmarried workers (such as school leavers), who might be those most urgently in need of a job.

It is our contention that the most powerful factor in ensuring that workers return home at the end of the season will be the secure knowledge that they can be re-engaged to work in Australia for a similar amount of time in subsequent years.

Government policy to support migrant workers

As well as developing disincentives, there is a need for Pacific governments to develop positive policies that encourage remittances and legal return. At present, few Pacific governments have comprehensive legislation or regulations to assist migrant workers with the rollover of any superannuation or pension rights; reduced freight costs to bring home goods; tax benefits for repatriated funds; and maintenance of seniority and leave entitlements for former government workers. Another problem is that costs of transferring remittances are relatively high, and sometimes insecure. Governments find it difficult to accurately account for the transfer of personal remittances, as people returning from overseas often carry cash or goods and hand it directly to family members, without any record in financial institutions.

Western Union is a major means of transferring funds from overseas, even though the rates are relatively expensive. The attraction of sending money through Western Union is the ease of access, especially in rural areas and outer islands where there are few commercial banks — an estimated 300,000 people in Fiji, out of a population of 870,000, do not have a bank account (ANZ 2004). With the increase in overseas remittances, commercial banks are looking to develop new products to tap the market of overseas migrants and seasonal workers in Australia, New Zealand and the USA.

The March 2005 Forum Secretariat Remittance Roundtable recognised a number of steps that governments could take to enable increased remittance flows (Pacific Islands Forum Secretariat, 2005):

- revising visa criteria to open up international labour markets to Pacific Island workers, particularly the unskilled;
- developing and promoting innovative and appropriate savings and investment instruments for overseas migrants and seasonal workers, encouraging workers to invest their pensions, bonuses and personal savings in the home country;
- developing more affordable and secure remittance systems (simplifying paperwork, and regulating and reducing costs for transferring money);
- adjusting tax policies for remitted funds, which are derived mainly from wages and salaries and have already been taxed overseas;
- developing government, NGO and church programs to look after the needs of migrant workers (information, social, consular assistance, human rights, etc.) and of family members left behind;
- improving financial literacy with advisory and training schemes to encourage returning seasonal workers to invest their earnings (e.g., business set-up advisory programs, micro-credit schemes, investment matching funds);
- adapting the educational, vocational and training curricula to reflect the fact that many workers are contributing to an international rather than domestic labour market.

Sharing the costs

As the above discussion makes clear, any seasonal labour scheme for Pacific Islanders to work in Australia will involve costs — the bureaucratic costs of regulation, administration and oversight, and the practical costs of airfares, visas, medical checks and accommodation. A key question in the design of the scheme will be how those costs are to be shared between growers, workers and governments without sacrificing equity or efficiency. As Philip Martin has noted, there has been a decline in the role of no-fee public sector employment services, and a rise in the role of for-profit private sector recruitment agencies. As a result, 'the general trend in the migrant recruiting business has been for costs to be shifted from employers to workers' (Martin 2005). In an unregulated environment, the disparity in wealth and opportunity between First- and Third-World countries creates conditions in which recruitment agencies can extract exorbitant 'application fees' from would-be migrant workers who are hungry for jobs, and then drive down the conditions and pay under which they are expected to work. As Martin comments, 'In most cases, migrants who have incurred debts to go abroad wind up being forced to make the adjustments from the promises to the realities, not employers' (Martin 2005: 3). This trend is objectionable for obvious reasons — it imposes the greatest costs on the most disadvantaged actors.

It is our view that employers should share the costs of any seasonal workers' scheme in Australia. Equity is only one consideration here; another is that there should be a monetary incentive for employers to look first to the local labour market to secure workers.

While Canada's scheme has been tailored much more heavily to the needs of employers than workers, it does provide a reasonable model of cost sharing. As noted above, growers must provide free accommodation in addition to wages. They also pay a non-recoverable fee of $35 per worker to the Foreign Agricultural Resource Management Service (FARMS), an employer-run, non-profit, federally incorporated agency that is authorised by the Canadian Government to coordinate and organise the scheme. Workers' travel is organised through CanAg travel services, which is a subsidiary of FARMS. Farmers pay the cost of all transport within Canada, and must advance the cost of international travel with approximately half of this cost later recouped via deductions from workers' wages. Farmers must also pay the visa fee of $CND150 up front, although this amount can be recouped fully through wage deductions. In recovering costs from workers, however, farmers can deduct a maximum of five per cent of gross earnings per pay period (in the case of Mexican workers) or $3.50 a day (for Caribbean workers).

Conclusion — beyond trade and economics

If Australia is to introduce a seasonal employment scheme and open up its labour market to Pacific Island workers, the starting point should be a series of small-scale pilot projects. The scheme should not be conceived purely in terms of economic exchange, or as a bargaining chip in trade negotiations intended to further liberalise Pacific Island economies. Rather, it should be regarded as a development opportunity: a mechanism to advance, however modestly, sustainable economic and social development in the communities from which the workers come, and to encourage the expansion of 'people-to-people' contacts between Australia and the Pacific.

A model for this approach can be found in 'Agricultores Solidarios' (Farmers for Solidarity) in Spain. The Farmers' Union of Catalonia, the Livestock and Produce Farmers of Valencia and the Farmers' Union of Majorca have set up a program to meet their need for additional seasonal labour while also encouraging 'human, economic and social development in less favoured agrarian societies' (Peix nd). Under the program, seasonal migrant workers are recruited from Colombia,

Morocco and Romania. There is a strong emphasis on training and on encouraging positive interaction between the migrant workers and their host communities in Spain. Program coordinator Maria Peix (2004) describes it as 'a two-way exchange that involves civil society', with the temporary workers becoming 'development agents that boost new processes led by themselves in their countries of origin'.

In Australia, we envisage building on the model of 'sister city' relationships that exists between some regional municipalities and localities in the Pacific. Under this scenario, a particular region (for example, Weather Coast in Solomon Islands) might be twinned with an area in country Victoria (such as the Swan Hill region). In addition to recruiting seasonal workers from a region of the Solomon Islands to work in horticulture, associated educational activities could be devised for schools in Swan Hill and community organisations (perhaps Pacific church groups) could take a lead role in organising social events and cultural activities to welcome the workers into the community. Volunteer programs (Australian Volunteers International and Australian Business Volunteers), service clubs (Rotary, Lions, etc.) and other NGOs could coordinate development activities with targeted communities. Workers would be engaged in some level of formal training — for example, in first aid, chemical safety and handling — to ensure that they go home with useful skills as well as money in their pockets. Community-based organisations in both countries could cooperate to develop ways for remittances to contribute to general development activities, through micro-finance schemes, small business programs and the education of young women.

Seasonal employment programs for Pacific Islanders to work in Australian horticulture are not a panacea for the challenges of unemployment and underemployment in Forum member countries. Nor will such schemes transform the economic development prospects of small island states or solve the challenges faced by Australian family farmers squeezed by rising prices, cheap overseas imports and an all-powerful supermarket duopoly. Nevertheless, a seasonal labour program does have the potential to make a material difference to the wellbeing of significant numbers of Pacific Island workers and their families — especially those living in rural areas and outer islands. It also has the potential to significantly ease the seasonal labour shortages that hold back Australia's horticultural industry.

There are currently organisations seeking to initiate seasonal work programs, and regional bodies such as the Pacific Islands Forum should facilitate government-to-government discussions to create a framework for pilot projects — a contribution to the education, employment and enjoyment sought by many people in the Pacific.

References

ANZ 2004. *ANZ Coconut Wireless*, Issue 3, November 2004.

Asian Development Bank, 1999. 'Pursuing Economic Reform in the Pacific', *Pacific Studies Series* No. 18, Manila: ADB.

Australian National Audit Office 2005. *Audit Report* No. 47 2004–05 Commonwealth of Australia, Canberra.

Azmat Gani 2005. 'Fiji emigrant transfers and potential macro-economic effects', *Pacific Economic Bulletin* 20(2): 117–28.

Basok, Tanya 2003. *Tortillas and Tomatoes: Transmigrant Mexican Harvesters in Canada*, Montreal and Kingston: McGill–Queens University Press.

Basok, Tanya 2000. 'He came, he saw, he … stayed. Guest worker programs and the issue of non-return', *International Migration*, 38(2): 215–36.

Bedford, Kathy 2004. 'Interview with John Howard', Radio Broadcast *ABC Regional Victoria*, 20 April, Retrieved 6 October 2006 from http://www.pm.gov.au/news/interviews/Interview805.html

Bertram, Geoffrey 1999. 'The MIRAB model 12 years on', *The Contemporary Pacific* 1: 105–38.

Bertram Geoffrey and Ray Watters 1985. 'The MIRAB economy in Pacific Microstates', *Pacific Viewpoint* 26(3): 497–519

Billson, Bruce 2005a. 'Australia to consider movement of labour around the Pacific', Radio broadcast, *Pacific Beat*, Radio Australia, 12 August.

Billson, Bruce 2005b. 'Forum countries consider regional trade framework', Radio broadcast, *Pacific Beat*, Radio Australia, 1 June.

Booth, Heather 2000. 'Suicide in the Pacific Islands', in Brij V. Lal and Kate Fortune (eds), *The Pacific Islands: An Encyclopedia,* Honolulu: University of Hawai'i Press, p. 439-440.

Borovnik, M. 2006. 'Working overseas: Seafarers' remittances and their distribution in Kiribati.' *Asia Pacific Viewpoint* 47(1), 151-161.

Brown, Richard 1998. 'Do migrants' remittances decline over time? Evidence from Tongans and Western Samoans in Australia' *The Contemporary Pacific* 10(1): 107–51

Brown, Richard and Adrian Walker, 1995. 'Migrants and their remittances', *Pacific Studies Monograph* No.17, Centre for Pacific Studies, Armidale: University of New South Wales.

Cole, Rodney (ed.), 1993. *Pacific 2010: Challenging the future,* Pacific Policy Paper 9, Canberra: National Centre for Development Studies.

Colman, Elizabeth 2005. '"Guest" workers prop up economy', *The Weekend Australian,* 5–6 March, p. 1.

Connell, John and Richard Brown, 2005. *Remittances in the Pacific — An overview,* Manila: Asian Development Bank, March.

Dennis, Jennifer 2003. *Pacific Island seafarers — a study of the economic and social implications of seafaring on dependants and communities*, Suva: Pacific Seafarers Training Program, Regional Maritime Program, Secretariat of the Pacific Community.

Department of Immigration, Migrants and Multicultural Affairs 2005. *Population Flows: Immigration Aspects 2003-04 Edition*. Retrieved 6 October 2006 from http://www.immi.gov.au/media/publications/statistics/popflows2003-4/index.htm

Downes, Andrew and Cyrilene Odle-Worrell, 2004. *Canadian migrant agricultural workers' program research project — the Caribbean component*, executive summary, North South Institute, Retrieved 6 October 2006 from http://www.nsi-ins.ca/english/pdf/exec_sum_downes.pdf

Ferguson, Sue 2004. 'Hard Time in Canadian fields' *Macleans,* 11October. Retrieved 6 October 2006 from http://www.macleans.ca/topstories/canada/article.jsp?content=20041011_90409_90409

Fiji. 2002. *Rebuilding confidence for stability and growth for a peaceful, prosperous Fiji*, Strategic Development Plan 2003-2005, Parliamentary Paper No. 72, Fiji.

Fiji Women's Rights Movement, 2002. *Sexual harassment in the workplace — the Fijian perspective,* Suva: FWRM.

Fiji Women's Rights Movement, 1998. *Labouring Under the Law*, Suva: FWRM.

Foreign Agricultural Management Service 2004 *Regional Report — Caribbean/Mexican Seasonal Agricultural Workers Programs as of 31/12/2004.* Canada.

Griffith, David 2004. *The Canadian and United States migrant agricultural workers programs: Parallels and divergence between two North American seasonal migrant agricultural labour markets with respect to "best practices"*, executive summary. North South Institute. Retrieved 6 October 2006 from http://www.nsi-ins.ca/english/pdf/exec_sum_griffith.pdf

Harding, Glenys and Elizabeth Webster, 2002. *The Working Holiday Maker Scheme and the Australian Labour Market,* Melbourne Institute of Applied Economic and Social Research, University of Melbourne, Retrieved 6 October 2006 from http://www.immi.gov.au/media/publications/pdf/whm_pt1.pdf

Hezel, F. X. 1989. 'Suicide and the Micronesian Family', *The Contemporary Pacific* 1(1): 43–74

Hezel, F. X et al. (eds), 1985. *Culture, Youth and Suicide in the Pacific: Papers from an East-West Center Conference, Working Papers Series*, Pacific Islands Studies Program, Honolulu: University of Hawai'i.

Horticulture Australia Limited, 2004. *The Australian Horticulture Statistics Handbook 2004*

Howard, John 2005. *Australian Financial Review*, October 26.

Hughes, Gary and Larry Schwartz 2004. 'Outlaw labour, rorts and all', *Sunday Age,* 28 March

Jupp, James 2003, *From White Australia to Woomera: The story of Australian immigration,* Cambridge: Cambridge University Press.

Kelsey, Jane 2005. *A People's Guide to the Pacific's Economic Partnership Agreement*, Suva: WCC, March.

Kelsey, Jane 2004. *Big Brothers Behaving Badly — the implications for the Pacific Islands of the Pacific Agreement on Closer Economic Relations,* Suva: PANG

Lee, Helen 2003. *Tongans Overseas — between two shores* Honolulu: University of Hawai'i Press.

Martin, Philip L. 2005. 'Merchants of labour: Agents of the evolving migration infrastructure', *International Institute of Labour Studies' Decent Work Research Program, Discussion Paper* DP/158/2005, International Institute for Labour Studies, Geneva

Martin, Phillip L. 2003. *Managing Labour Migration: Temporary Worker Programs for the 21st Century*, International Institute for Labour Studies, Geneva

Metherell, Mark 2005. 'Labour-starved nation flirts with overseas recruits', *Sydney Morning Herald,* 24 February,.

Ministry of Labour 2005. *Occupational Health and Safety on Farms*, Backgrounder05-83, Ministry of Labour and Ministry of Agriculture and Food, Canada, Ontario. Retrieved 6 October 2006 from http://www.labour.gov.on.ca/english/news/pdf/2005/05-83b.pdf

Moore, C. 1985. *Kanaka — a history of Melanesian Mackay,* Port Moresby: UPNG.

Moran, Susannah 2004. 'Temporary visas plug skills gap', *Australian Financial Review,* 24 September.

Narsey, Wadan, 2004. *PIC development: Remittances and other alternatives to regional integration,* paper presented at the FDC workshop on

'Remittances, Microfinance and Technology: Leveraging development impact for Pacific States', Brisbane, June 10–11.

National Reserve Bank of Tonga 2004. Overseas Exchange Transactions' *Annual Report 2003–04*.Tonga.

Pacific Islands Forum Secretariat, 2005. *Summary record — remittances roundtable 21 March 2005,* Forum paper, March 29

Pareti, Samisoni 2005. 'Fiji's long, risky road to Kuwait', *Pacific Islands Report*, 22 April 2005. Retrieved 6 October 2006 from http://archives.pireport.org/archive/2005/April/04-22-ft.htm

Peix, Andreu no date. 'Farmers for Solidarity', *Dossier Migrations et Développement*. French Ministry of Foreign Affairs.

Peix, Maria 2004. *'Agricultores Solidarios' (Farmers for Solidarity) promote regular migration flows between temporary workers' countries of origin and of destination.* Press release, Forum Barcelona, 4 September.

Pickering, Sue and Helen Barnes 2005. 'Towards a sustainable workforce across horticulture', *The Orchardist* (New Zealand), May, pp. 30–4

Preibisch, Kerry 2004. *Social relations between agricultural workers, their employers, and the residents of rural Ontario*, executive summary. North South Institute, Retrieved 6 October 2006 from http://www.nsi-ins.ca/english/pdf/exec_sum_preibisch.pdf

Productivity Commission 2005. *Trends in Australian Agriculture*, Commission Research Paper. Australian Government Productivity Commission, Canberra.

Ratha, Dilip 2004. 'Understanding the importance of remittances', *Migration Information Source*, Retrieved 6 October 2006 from http://www.migrationinformation.org/Feature/display.cfm?id=256

Riley, James 2005. 'Temporary visa jobs coming and going', *The Weekend Australian*, March 5–6.

Robinson, Paul 2004. 'Workers flown in from China', *The Age,* 21 December.

Rokoduru, Avelina 2005. 'Remittances, the case of Fiji's skilled migrant workers in the Republics of Kiribati and the Marshall Islands', presentation to Forum Secretariat Remittances Roundtable, 21 March.

Rokoduru, Avelina 2004. 'Fiji's women migrants and human rights — the case of nurses and teachers in the Republic of Marshall Islands', *Journal of Pacific Studies* 27(2): 205–227.

Russell, Roy 2004. *Jamaican workers' participation in CSAWP and development consequences in the workers' rural home communities,* executive summary,

North South Institute, Retrieved 6 October 2006 from http://www.nsi-ins.ca/english/pdf/exec_sum_russell.pdf

Senate Foreign Affairs 2003. *A Pacific Engaged — Australia's relations with Papua New Guinea and the islands of the south west Pacific,* Canberra, Defence and Trade References Committee

Sercombe, Bob 2005. *Towards a Pacific Community.* Canberra, ALP Pacific Policy Discussion Paper.

Shanahan, Dennis, 2005. 'Howard, Clark shut out seasonal workers', *The Australian*, October 26

Simati, Aunese Makoi and John Gibson 2001. 'Do remittances decay? Evidence from Tuvaluan migrants in New Zealand', *Pacific Economic Bulletin* 16(1):55–63

United Nations Department of Economic and Social Affairs 2004. *World Economic and Social Survey 2004, Part II, International Migration*, New York: United Nations. http://www.un.org/esa/policy/wess/wess2004files/part2web/part2web.pdf

UNICEF Pacific 1998. *State of Pacific Youth Report 1998*, Suva: UNICEF Pacific.

United Food and Commercial Workers' Union 2003. *National report: The status of migrant farm workers in Canada, December 2003.* Canada: UFCW Canada and theCanadian Labour Congress. Retrieved 6 October 2006 from Retrieved 6 October 2006 from http://www.ufcw.ca/Theme/UFCW/files/ag2003e.pdf

United Food and Commercial Workers' Union 2002. *National report: The status of migrant farm workers in Canada, December 2002.* Canada: UFCW Canada and the Canadian Labour Congress. Retrieved 6 October 2006 from http://www.ufcw.ca/Theme/UFCW/files/National%20ReportENG.pdf

United Kingdom Home Office, 2002. *Review of the Seasonal Agricultural Workers' Scheme 2002 Work Permits UK*, May, Retrieved 6 October 2006 from http://www.homeoffice.gov.uk/documents/cons-2002-saws

Verduzco, Gustavo and Maria Lozano, 2004. *Mexican farm workers' participation in Canada's seasonal agricultural labour market and development consequences in their rural home communities*, executive summary, North South Institute, Retrieved 6 October 2006 from http://www.nsi-ins.ca/english/pdf/exec_sum_verduzco.pdf

Ward, R. Gerard 1999. 'Widening Worlds, Shrinking Worlds? The Reshaping of Oceania', Pacific Distinguished Lecture, Centre for the Contemporary Pacific, ANU, Canberra.

World Bank 2006. *Global Economic Prospects 2006: The Economic Implications of Remittances and Migration,* Washington: World Bank.

World Council of Churches Pacific Office, 2001. *Islands of Hope — a Pacific alternative to Economic Globalisation,* Geneva :WCC

ENDNOTES

[1] For discussion, see the special editions on 'Migration and labour' of the *Journal of Pacific Studies*, Vol. 18, 1994–95, and Vol. 27, 2, November 2004 and Moore (1985)

[2] See, for example, the special edition of *The Contemporary Pacific*, 'Asia in the Pacific — migrant labour and tourism in the Republic of Palau', Vol. 12, No. 2, Fall 2000.

[3] Labour force data from the Secretariat of the Pacific Community PRISM project at http://www.spc.int/prism/social/lab_force.html

[4] The authors have contributed a chapter to the World Bank study *At Home and Away: Expanding Job Opportunities for Pacific Islanders through Labour Mobility*, 2006, on 'Improving Development Outcomes in the Pacific Through Labour Mobility'.

[5] A decade ago, Australian academics and journalists contributed to the ideological push for economic policy change in the Pacific, through the Pacific 2010 Project, See Cole (1993).

[6] For examples of regional media coverage, see Shanahan (2005); 'Fiji prime minister miffed over Pacific work permits', *Fiji Times*, October 27, 2005; 'Aussie, Kiwi leaders cool to Pacific work permits', *PNG Post-Courier*, October 26, 2005; Cynthia Banham, 'Seasonal worker entry not on — PM', *Sydney Morning Herald*, October 27, 2005.

[7] Alexander Downer, 'Downer responds to allegations', *Fiji Daily Post*, December 2, 2005; 'Aussies against work schemes', *Fiji Times,* December 2, 2005. See also transcript of interview on Downer's web site, September 30, 2005: http://www.foreignminister.gov.au/transcripts/2005/050930_abc.html

[8] See, for example, interviews with Bob Lyon (Vice-President of the Australia–PNG Business Council and immediate past President of the Australia–Pacific Islands Business Council), 'More calls for Australian labour mobility scheme', *Pacific Beat*, Radio Australia, 15 December, 2005; Duncan Fraser of the National Farmers' Federation, 'Farmers support call to allow Pacific seasonal workers', *Pacific Beat*, Radio Australia, 27 October, 2005; Professor Robbie Robertson, Director of Development Studies, University of the South Pacific, 'Academic rejects labour mobility concerns', *Pacific Beat*, Radio Australia, 7 December, 2005.

[9] The inquiry is due to report in August 2006. See: 'http://www.aph.gov.au/Senate/committee/eet_ctte/contract_labour/index.htm'

[10] Peter Mares and Nic Maclellan work as journalists and are research fellows at the Institute for Social Research at Swinburne University in Melbourne, Australia. This paper draws on their continuing research for the 'Pacific Labour and Australian Horticulture' project, funded through the Australian Research Council Industry Linkage scheme. Their industry partners are Oxfam Australia, Swan Hill Rural City Council and the Sunraysia Mallee Economic Development Board.

[11] PACER came into force in October 2002 and PICTA came into force in April 2003 after six countries ratified it. The text of the two agreements can be found on the Pacific Islands Forum Secretariat web site at www.forumsec.org.fj

[12] Interview with Forum Secretary-General, Greg Urwin, Suva, June 2005. See also Narsey (2004).

[13] For church and NGO critiques, see World Council of Churches Pacific Office (2001), Kelsey (2004) and (2005).

[14] Population data and demographic trends for island nations are detailed by the Secretariat of the Pacific Community Demography/Population Program: http://www.spc.int/demog/

[15] Savenaca Narube, Governor of the Reserve Bank of Fiji, transcript of speech to the Fiji Australia Business Forum, 17 October, 2005: http://www.bis.org/review/r051019c.pdf

[16] 'Fijians survive bloody shoot-out', *Fiji Sun*, December 23, 2003; 'Iraq guards sent home in disgrace', *Fiji Times*, 26 December, 2003; 'Iraq guards come home to pay battle', *Fiji Times,* 20 January, 2004.

[17] Interviews with Prof. Ron Duncan (PIAS-DG, USP), Seema Naidu (FWRM), Avelina Rokodoru (USP), Tupou Vere (PCRC), Suva, June 2005; Betty Blake (Catholic Women's League of Tonga), June 2005.

[18] Interview with Forum Secretary-General, Greg Urwin, Suva, June 2005.

[19] Interview with Sanjesh Naidu, Ministry of Finance and Planning, Government of Fiji, Suva, June 2005.

[20] Iosefa Maiava, Deputy Secretary-General of the Pacific Islands Forum Secretariat, World Bank seminar on remittances and labour mobility, Suva, November 2005.

[21] Interview with Resina Katafono, Senior Economist, Reserve Bank of Fiji, Suva, June 2005.

[22] The other main sectors being hospitality, the sex industry and factories.

[23] Over the 20 years to 2003–04, the proportion of employees in the agricultural workforce has increased from 33 per cent to 51 per cent, while the combined share of employers' own account and contributing family workers has fallen from 67 per cent to 49 per cent.

[24] Interviews with Greg Urwin (Forum Secretariat), Emele Duituturaga (Fiji), Sanjesh Naidu (Fiji), Akilisi Pohiva (Tonga), June 2005.

[25] Government response to *A Pacific Engaged*, Canberra, April 2005. This formal response to the August 2003 Senate report was dated April 5, 2005, but was issued only on June 24, 2005, the day after Parliament broke for its winter recess.

[26] Submission to 2003 Senate inquiry. See Senate Foreign Affairs (2003)

[27] 'Unions support Senate report on labour mobility', interview with ACTU President, Sharan Burrow, *Pacific Beat*, Radio Australia, August 13, 2003. Interviews with Alison Tate, International Officer, Australian Council of Trade Unions (ACTU), Melbourne, June 2005; Alan Matheson, former ACTU International Officer, Melbourne, May 2005.

[28] Australia's current reciprocal working holiday arrangements are all with the developed states or territories that the Immigration Department regards as posing a 'low immigration risk', namely Belgium, Canada, Cyprus, Denmark, Finland, France, Germany, Hong Kong, Ireland, Italy, Japan, Korea, Malta, Netherlands, Norway, Sweden, Taiwan and the UK. NSW MLC Charlie Lynn has called for the working holiday scheme to be extended to PNG. 'It's time to dump our "unofficial" White Australia policy against black Melanesians', media release, February 23, 2005.

[29] Interviews with Reverend Jason Kioa (Tongan Australia Association), Melbourne, May 2005; Father Kevin Barr (Ecumenical Centre for Research, Education and Advocacy [ECREA]), Suva, June 2005; Betty Blake, Catholic Women's League of Tonga, Nuku'alofa, June 2005; Revered Simote Vea, Tonga National Council of Churches, Nuku'alofa, June 2005; Reverend Leva Kila Pat, Pacific Conference of Churches, Suva, June 2005; Feiloakitau Kaho Tevi, World Council of Churches Pacific Office, Suva, June 2005.

[30] Interview with Rajeshwar Singh, President, South Pacific Council of Trade Unions, Suva, June 2005; interview with Tate, Matheson, op. cit.

[31] ILO C. 97 *Migration for Employment Convention (Revised), 1949,* and ILO C. 143 *Migrant Workers (Supplementary Provisions) Convention, 1975.*

[32] Interviews with Tevi, Kila Pat and Vea, op. cit.

[33] Interviews with Tate, Matheson, Singh, op. cit.

[34] Interview with Reverend Jason Kioa, May 2005. The issue was also raised by Avelina Rokoduru, interview, Suva, June 2005.

[35] Interview with executive of Tongan Australia Association, Melbourne, November 2005.

[36] Interview with Emele Duituturaga, Suva, June 2005.

[37] Interview with Reverend Jason Kioa, May 2005.

[38] Interview with Forum Secretary-General, Greg Urwin, Suva, June 2005.

[39] For the example of Tonga, see Lee (2003)

9. Contemporary Migration Within the Pacific Islands: The case of Fijian skilled workers in Kiribati and Marshall Islands

Avelina Rokoduru

Contemporary skilled migration from Fiji to other Pacific Island countries began in the early 1980s and has continued since. There are Fijian citizens who work as domestic help as well as in the hotel industry in Cook Islands, and there are nurses, teachers, doctors, lawyers, pilots, mechanics, electricians and technicians in the Federated States of Micronesia, Guam, Kiribati, Marshall Islands and Vanuatu. With the coming of the Regional Assistance Mission to Solomon Islands in 2003, we have seen policemen and women moving to Solomon Islands. What is more, the trend is likely to continue if the Pacific Plan, which envisages greater labour mobility among Pacific Islands Forum countries, becomes reality. This paper provides a detailed discussion of the Fijian migrants in the Marshall Islands and Kiribati to illustrate this new phenomenon of intra-regional skilled migration from Fiji.

A profile of the Fijian migrants

There were 49 Fijian labour migrants who were interviewed in the Marshalls and Kiribati. Of these, 37 per cent were males and 63 per cent were females. By ethnic division, 77 per cent were native Fijians, 15 per cent were Indo-Fijians, 4 per cent were Rotumans and the remaining 4 per cent included Rabians (Fiji-born Gilbertese) and a naturalised Filipino resident. The Fijian migrants in this study have lived a minimum of one to a maximum of 37 years in their Pacific Island destination. The ages of the migrants ranged from 22 to 65 years with 22 per cent of the migrants in their 20s, 32 per cent in their thirties, 28 per cent in their forties and about 18 per cent in their fifties and sixties. The average age was 26 years; therefore, the majority of the migrants were well within the active working-age group of 20 to 50. Finally, their religious affiliation varied between Christian denominations (92 per cent), Hinduism (6 per cent), and the remaining two per cent were Buddhists.

The number of years of work experience for the Fijian migrants in the Marshall Islands ranged from three to 40 years in Fiji before their departure. On the other hand, the Fijian workers on Tarawa, Kiribati, had accumulated one to 19 years of work experience in Fiji before their migration. On the whole, the Fijian migrants are indeed experienced and skilled in their various professions.

The migrants worked in various occupational categories ranging from civil servants in Kiribati to government physicians in the Marshalls. Other types of jobs taken up by Fijian migrants included bartender, dental therapist, dentist, domestic worker, hotel worker, kindergarten teacher, lawyer, physician and shipping officer. The majority of these job categories required a specific level of academic competence, which was fulfilled by the migrants in this study.

Table 1: Occupational categories for Fijian migrants by sex in Kiribati and Marshall Islands, 2002.

Occupational category	Marshall Islands (%) (No.)		Kiribati (%) (No.)		Total (%) (No.)
	Males	Females	Males	Females	
Hotel workers	2	4	0	0	6
Mechanics	2	0	4	0	6
Nurses	2	31	0	2	35
Kindergarten teachers	0	2	0	0	2
Primary teachers	6	8	0	0	14
Secondary teachers	12	12	2	0	27
Lawyers	2	0	0	0	2
Dentists and therapists	0	2	0	2	4
Civil servants	0	0	0	2	2
Others	0	2	0	0	2
Total	27 (13)	61 (30)	6 (3)	6 (3)	100 (49)

Note: The Fijian migrants worked at various places in their host countries. The percentages are calculated to the nearest whole number.
Source: Fieldwork data from Kiribati and Marshall Islands, June–August, 2002.

About 90 per cent of the migrants indicated tertiary education as the highest level of education they had attained, and worked in the civil service, or as bartenders, kindergarten teachers, primary and secondary schoolteachers, nurses, doctors and dental therapists, lawyers and shipping officers. The remaining 10 per cent of the workers stated reaching only secondary school-level education. These migrants worked as mechanics and hotel workers in Kiribati and Marshall Islands, respectively.

Table 2: Academic qualifications of Fijian skilled migrants in Kiribati and Marshall Islands, 2002.

Academic qualification achieved	Marshall Islands (%) (No.)	Kiribati (%) (No.)
Certificate	30	33
Diploma	47	50
Degree	21	17
Postgraduate diploma	2	0
Total	100 (43)	100 (6)

Note: Only the highest academic qualification was considered for this question.
Source: Fieldwork data, Kiribati and Marshall Islands. June–August 2002.

This group of Fijian labour migrants to Kiribati and the Marshalls was mostly female, mostly ethnic Fijians, young, skilled and experienced in their fields of occupation.

Push factors for mobility out of Fiji

There were various socioeconomic factors that motivated the migrants to travel to other Pacific Island countries for employment. These push factors have been tabled with the most important preceding the others.

Table 3: Reasons for departing from Fiji by order of importance.

Reasons	Kiribati (%) (No.)	Marshall Islands (%) (No.)	Total (%) (No.)
Inadequate pay/salary in Fiji	17	55	72
Work conditions in Fiji not good	0	21	21
A desire for a new living and working environment	17	2	19
Travel and adventure	17	0	17
Political instability	17	0	17
Other reasons	50	26	76
Total	118 (7)	104 (45)	222(52)

Note: This is a multiple response question and percentage totals might be more than 100.
Source: Fieldwork data from Kiribati and Marshall Islands, June–August 2002.

The most important motivation for the Fijian migrants was that pay offered locally was inadequate compared with what they were being offered in their host countries. For instance, a Fijian graduate secondary schoolteacher working regular hours between 8.30am and 4.30pm was being paid $F13,000. The same teacher could earn $A20,000 ($F34,000) at a secondary school in the Marshall Islands.

Other reasons for leaving Fiji were to accompany a spouse or relatives, that there was more need for their skill in the host country, that it was a divine calling to serve, to move out of the country because of retirement, to facilitate immigration to metropolitan countries, to avoid the racial discrimination experienced in Fiji, because chances for promotion in Fiji were slim, as well as the opportunity to be near parents. These results reflect the work of Leweniqila and others (2000: 7), who noted that 'the nightingales' were leaving Fiji for other countries, including other Pacific Island countries, to work, due to poor work conditions, a very low salary scale and poor management of those in the nursing profession.

On the other hand, except for one response noting racial discrimination as a push factor in this study, the results generally depart from the conclusions reached by Mohanty (2001: 58). He argues that the key push factors for Indo-Fijian migration are social and economic insecurities arising from land tenure problems; fear of political uncertainty and insecurity; discrimination; rural terrorism and problems of law and order; and the continuing political and constitutional crises. The racial profiles of the two studies explain much of this difference in motivating factors for labour migration. Indo-Fijians leave Fiji for different reasons than Fijians.

Contracts

The labour contract, a formal agreement between employer and employee over critical labour and living conditions, provides the framework around which everything else that concerns that relationship revolves. In this study, the contracts and terms of conditions were very important because 72 per cent of the respondents indicated that these had influenced their decision to find employment in Kiribati and the Marshall Islands. Employment contracts for the nurses and teachers in both countries generally varied between two- to three-year terms, which were renewable annually after the successful completion of the first term, or contracts were reviewed annually and renewed as negotiated by the employers and the Fijian migrant. For instance, for teachers in the Marshalls, employment begins with a probationary period, which lasts for the first 12 months of the two-year contract. Wages are paid fortnightly in 26 pay periods a year, for which 10 months are basically for teaching work. The remaining two months are allocated for national holidays, including a spring and semester break.

The Marshall Islands is an independent republic which was under American occupation and subsequent administration from 1943 to 1979. The Marshalls became self-governing in 1979 and independent in 1986, entering into a Compact of Free Association with the USA, which retains long-term control over the Marshalls' defence and economy. The compact has recently been renewed. Given that history, the Marshalls' currency is the US dollar and is generally twice as strong as the Fijian dollar. This currency differential is an added bonus for the Fijian migrants.

For instance, registered nurses in Fiji generally start at the salary level of a staff nurse at $F10,920, which increases gradually to $F15,409 by the time they have worked for at least 12 years in the service (FNA 2002: 62 [1]) and at least 87 per cent of Fiji's nurses fall into this salary category. In this study, 90 per cent of the nurses who moved to Kiribati and the Marshalls were qualified staff nurses from Fiji. On arrival in the Marshall Islands, the salary scale of the Fijian nurses began at $US18,000 ($A24,000), an equivalent of about $F40,000. This represented a huge increase for women who were still working as staff nurses. It meant that staff nurses working in the Marshalls were receiving the equivalent of the salary of the Principal of the Fiji Nursing School, or more. Indeed, the salary differentials in this case were too overwhelming to resist.

Table 4: Fijian nurses — salary levels by ranges by percentage of nursing positions, 2002.

Fijian nursing positions and percentage of nurses in workforce in Fiji	Fijian salary range $F (approximate)	Marshall Islands salary range $US ($F equivalent)
Principal, Fiji School of Nursing (FSN) — 0.01%	32,802–42,424	–
Senior matron and Vice-Principal (FSN) —0.02%	24,939–32,266	–
Senior nursing tutors — 1%	19,166–24,813	–
Senior sisters and nursing practitioners — 8.9%	16,260–19,639	–
Sisters — 3%	13,920–16,917	–
Staff nurses — 87%	10,920–15,409	18,000–25,000 (40,659–56,471)

Note: Conversions based on May 2002 exchange rates.
Source: Fiji Nursing Association 45th Annual General Meeting Report, March, 2002, p. 62.

In the case of teachers in Fiji, the starting salaries of graduate teachers began at $F17,283 and increased gradually to $F39,516 for principals (PSC 2003). Yet, the Fijian teachers in the Marshall Islands generally started at about $US16,380 ($A22,072), the equivalent of about $F37,000. Therefore, the starting salary of an assistant secondary schoolteacher in the Marshalls was equivalent to that of a principal at a secondary school in Fiji. The issue of yearly increases and bonuses for the teachers in the Marshalls has not been factored into the salaries considered above. In this case, the salary differentials again were too good to resist for the Fijian migrant teachers in this study. Consequently, about 51 per cent of the total migrants indicated their salary differentials as a distinct advantage of their migration.

Table 5: Fiji/Marshall Islands teachers — salary levels by position, 2003.

Teaching position	Fiji salary level and ranges $F (approximate)	Marshall Islands salary level and range $US (equivalent to $F net — approximate)
Principals (secondary)	28,293–39,516	–
Vice-Principals (secondary)	25,937–32,562	–
Assistant principals (secondary)	21,397–30,415	–
Heads of departments (secondary)	21,397–25,103	–
Assistant teachers (secondary) University graduates with teaching certificates	17,283–20,006	16,380–19,000 (37,000–42,918)
Assistant teachers (secondary) Fiji College of Advanced Education Diplomas	15,126–19,010	–
Head teachers (primary school)	24,971–33,996	33,800 (76,349)
Assistant teachers (primary school) B.Ed. university graduates with teaching certificates	17,283–19,056	11,960–14,000 (27,016–31,624)
Assistant teachers (primary school) Diplomas with teaching certificates	12,990–15,126	7,280–11,960 (16,444–27,016)
Kindergarten teachers	14,000	18,000 (40,659)

Note: July 2002 exchange rates.
Source: Public Service Commission, 2004, 2003 Civil List — Making A Difference, Suva: PSC.

All the Fijian women in this study were paid on a fortnightly basis according to their contracts. About 18 per cent of them were able to graduate to a higher scale of pay (apart from the regular increments), while 82 per cent remained on the initial salary scale they had been hired at. The main reason for the stagnation of the women's salary scale was that the women had just started working in their host country. Most of the women who had received salary increases had received them only once at the time of this research with the exception of a woman who had received three increases, in 1994, 1995 and in 2002. She was working as a nurse at the time of this study. As well, about 53 per cent of the women also received the 13th salary (a mandatory annual year-end additional monthly salary [2]) even though it was not specifically stated in their contract, while 47 per cent could not say whether they received this salary as they were not aware of the concept. The 53rd-week salary (which applied only to people paid weekly and only for times when the work year had 53 weeks), did not apply to the migrant women as they were receiving fortnightly pay.

The majority of the migrants enjoyed medical benefits. For instance, about 83 per cent of the Fijian women received free or subsidised medical coverage depending on the seriousness of each medical case. The nurses in the Marshalls indicated receiving free medical treatment was part of their package, excluding illnesses that needed special medical attention. The latter medical needs are met by their employers and subsidised by the health insurance scheme the nurses are affiliated to. On the other hand, 12 per cent of the women workers indicated not being included in any medical coverage (hotel workers and a maid) and 5 per cent of the women were not aware of this benefit being granted them.

All the teachers in the Marshalls are included in the Group Health Insurance scheme for civil servants, receive sick leave and personal leave, and can be awarded compensation for on-the-job injuries. They are also eligible for medical care at 7 per cent of their gross earnings — a sum divided equally between the employer and the migrant teacher.

The employers also provided either a housing allowance or accommodation for the duration of the contract, as well as return transportation costs for the migrant and his/her family and possessions from the point of hire to the Marshalls and Kiribati at the successful completion of a contract. The teachers at the University of the South Pacific–Republic of the Marshall Islands Joint Project were provided free daily transport to and from work. On the other hand, the teachers working at Church of God High School in Tarawa, Kiribati, lived in the school compound and did not need transport, though this was provided for medical trips to the hospital. Meanwhile, nurses living on Kwajalein (a US military base) were provided with daily ferry and taxi tickets to and from the Ebeye Hospital where they worked, whereas the nurses living on Majuro were provided with subsidised transport to and from the hospital. Travel and meal allowances were paid out during night shifts, which also involved a special pay rate, and about 82 per cent of the Fijian women migrants were given transport to and from work, the majority of whom (59 per cent) enjoyed subsidised transportation paid for by their employers.

Case study one: Fijian migrants' salaries at Ebeye Health Clinic, Marshall Islands, 2002

In Fiji, a staff nurse receives an average monthly income of $F312.20, compared with $US660 ($A889) in the Marshall Islands, which is the equivalent of some $F1,490 a month. The Fijian and Marshall Islands nurses' salaries were paid fortnightly and the difference in amounts was substantial. Case study one: Salaries for Fijian migrant health workers, Ebeye Health Clinic, 2002 (from fieldwork data, July–August 2002.) Occupation at Ebeye Health Clinic Monthly net ($US) Equivalent ($F)

Case study one: Salaries for Fijian migrant health workers, Ebeye Health Clinic, 2002.

Occupation at Ebeye Health Clinic	Monthly net ($US)	Equivalent ($F)
Staff nurse	660	1,490
Staff nurse	684	1,545
Staff nurse	800	1,807
Staff nurse	1,067	2,410
Staff nurse	1,200	2,710
Staff nurse	1,170	2,642
Dental officer	4,000	9,035
Staff physician	6,044	13,652

Note: The medical personnel from Fiji received attractive packages from the Health Administration in Ebeye.
Source: Fieldwork data, July–August 2002.

Where housing or allowances were provided, additional costs for house renovations and furniture needs and maintenance were fully met by the employer. Other costs such as domestic bills including compound upkeep, water, electricity, gas and telephone were either subsidised or fully met by the employer.

> I live with my employers in the basement of the hotel and they are generous to me. I am provided accommodation, and free electricity, water, phone and house furnishings. So I just buy food and clothes.
> (Hotel worker, interview, August 2002)

About 94 per cent of the Fijian migrants enjoyed paid annual leave ranging from two weeks to two months for teachers, with the exception of the people who worked as missionaries. On the other hand, about 87 per cent of the women stated that they were entitled to paid annual leave while 2 per cent indicated otherwise. The remaining 11 per cent were not aware whether they had this benefit. This group included the women working at a local hotel and in the mission field in the Marshalls.

For those women who enjoyed paid annual leave, leave lengths ranged from two to six weeks a year. Meanwhile, about 24 per cent of the women migrants were given maternity leave by their employers as a benefit. A further 35 per cent stated they were not awarded this benefit, while 12 per cent were not aware of this benefit. The remaining 29 per cent did not state whether this benefit was included in their contracts.

> We came on the understanding to come and work, not to come and get pregnant. We are not expected to get pregnant while working here. (Nurse 12, interview, July 2002)

The superannuation schemes considered in this study included provident and pensions funds for the migrants. All the migrants deducted funds from their salaries for these schemes but only a few have enjoyed their benefits. The Fijian workers in Kiribati received superannuation at the end of their contracts, whereas only those migrants who had turned 55 years of age received their benefits in the Marshalls. The latter had fulfilled the conditions that dictated that migrant workers could receive their provident and/or pension refunds only upon the age of 55 and must be physically present in Majuro to receive their refund cheques.

Therefore, for the Fijian women in the Marshalls, only 41 per cent indicated the provident fund as a benefit, while 59 per cent said it was not a benefit at all. They thought the schemes were counterproductive as they had no intention of working in the Marshalls until the age of 55. Therefore, they were being denied funds they had rightfully earned and would most likely lose because the total expenses involved in returning to receive a cheque would be much higher than the refund itself. This response was another indication that this form of migration was only temporary and short-term for most of the migrants.

A mere 6 per cent of the women had enjoyed a promotion at their workplace. The subjects had received their promotion in 1999 and 2000 respectively. Further, the majority of the women did not know the prospects for promotion at their workplaces if they worked for a period of five years. It can be concluded that job promotions depended on the status of the migration (in this case, it was temporary) and the availability of local skilled labour in the host country.

Remittances

Generally, migrant remittances refer to any form of goods sent from the migrants to a receiving country. Remittances are usually perceived to be a one-way flow from the migrant to recipients but this is not so for this study, as will be discussed in this section.

Most Fijian migrants in Kiribati and the Marshalls sent something home to Fiji. 92 per cent sent money, 63 per cent also sent gifts of clothes, and food (6 per cent). Many of the migrants sent money home regularly (54 per cent), while 21 per cent sent home money only on request. Regular remitters sent money to Fiji every fortnight when they received their salaries. A further 17 per cent sent money home only for special occasions, for example, birthdays, and to assist on the death of a family member. Eight per cent of the respondents chose not to answer this question. The amount of cash remittances sent home ranged from $A134 to $A1,644 fortnightly — for the 71 per cent of the respondents who chose to answer this. There was an isolated case of a respondent sending home $A3,234 to assist the family after the death of a relative.

Table 6: Fortnightly monetary remittances sent by Fijian migrants by host country, 2002.

Amount of money sent fortnightly	Marshall Islands % (No.)	Kiribati % (No.)	Total % (No.)
$0–100	53	66	55
$101–200	3	0	2
$201–300	6	0	5
$301–400	8	17	11
$401–500	6	0	5
$501–600	8	0	7
$601–700	3	0	2
$701–800	3	0	2
$801–900	6	0	5
$1,000–1,200	0	17	2
$1,201–1,300	3	0	2
$2,400	3	0	2
Total of respondents	100 (36)	100 (6)	100 (42)

Note: Remittances were sent fortnightly to family members, friends, academic and financial institutions.
Soucre: Fieldwork data from Kiribati and Marshall Islands, June–August 2002.

Up to 23 per cent of the respondents sent monetary remittances to their children while 19 per cent sent remittances to their spouses. The majority (27 per cent) sent remittances to their parents because they were looking after the children of the migrants in Fiji, and another 6 per cent sent monetary remittances to the Housing Authority of Fiji and home finance providers for housing properties they had invested in. A few respondents made direct payments to educational institutions for school fees, settled car loans, paid for life insurance schemes and paid domestic bills for electricity and telephone services. Sisters and other relatives (17 per cent) also received monetary remittances from the migrants.

There was an active exchange of goods and money between the migrants in their host countries and their families and friends back home in Fiji. The majority (80 per cent) of the Fijian subjects asked for things that were not available in their host destinations to be sent from home. These were mostly for their personal consumption.

Table 7: Money and other items received from Fiji.

Kiribati	Marshall Islands
Curry powder, chillies, spices, tinned tuna, baked taro and cassava, kava, baby products, traditional artefacts (mats, *tapa*, *salusalu*), Fijian scented oils, Fijian and Hindi music and other language entertainment audiotapes and other entertainment audio, CDs, videos and DVDs, money	Clothes, kava, snacks, cosmetics, kitchenware, crochet string, custard powder, root crops, curry powder, chillies, spices, pocket-*sulus*, yams, cassava, taro, baby products, tea, traditional artefacts (mats, *tapa*, *salusalu*), Fijian scented oils, sandals, Fijian music and other entertainment audiotapes, CDs, videos and DVDs, money

Note: There were regular two-way exchanges of money and items between the migrants and their families and friends in Fiji.
Source: Fieldwork data, 2002.

Most of the items were sent by postal courier or taken by people passing through Kiribati and the Marshall Islands. The migrants would send money and related instructions for particular expensive items such as kava and scented oil, while the other items were either sent across at regular intervals or packaged and taken across by Fijian travellers to those Pacific Island countries. The networks were well established between the migrants, their relatives, friends and co-workers and especially with the contact points (Fijian citizens), who regularly travelled the region working for regional institutions, private businesses or NGOs. These contact points became messengers and couriers between the migrants and Fiji.

Case study two: Remittances of Fijian nurses in Ebeye, Marshall Islands

The nurses sent money, clothes and other gift items to Fiji. In monetary terms, the seven nurses who answered this survey remitted between $US266 ($A358) and $US890 ($A1,199) to Fiji in a fortnight from the local Western Union office. This would be the equivalent of $F600 to $2,010 a fortnight. The money was sent to families, friends and institutions.

Table 8: Cash remittances sent by Fijian nurses, Ebeye Health Clinic, 2002.

Approximates $US	Fijian equivalent $F	No. of nurses
266	600	2
267	603	1
356	804	3
444	1,002	1
890	2,010	1
Total: 2223	5019	8

Source: Fieldwork data, July–August 2002.

These remittances were sent to parents and/or spouses in order to pay for general family subsistence, for the welfare of their children and to meet telephone, water, electricity and gas bills, home, car and other property loans, school and medical fees and other traditional obligations in Fiji

Legal aspects of work and travel

There is a need to establish the legal status of the Fijian migrants in this section. Kassim (in Toh Thian Ser 1998: 68),[3] while discussing contemporary migration within and from South-East Asia, has classified immigrant workers into two categories: they are either *legal* or *illegal*. But the line demarcating the two can be very blurred and the two categories can become interchangeable. At the same time, an alien might enter a country legally but work there illegally, without a work permit.

While Kassim also elaborated on what illegal workers were, this paper will focus mainly on his definition of a legal alien as it closely identifies with the labour migrant situation being discussed here. Therefore, according to Kassim,[4] alien workers are regarded as legal when they conform to the immigration and labour laws of the host country. Further, they can be recruited in two ways: 1) they might have been recruited directly from the sending countries, brought in through authorised ports of entry and given temporary work permits; or 2) they might have arrived illegally and worked without employment permits but were later regularised through an amnesty exercise.

In the context of this research, most of the Fijian labour migrants (89 per cent) were recruited in Fiji by recruiting agents or government officials for various government ministries of the host countries (50 per cent), private schools and tertiary institutions (21 per cent), businesses (12 per cent), and churches (6 per cent), and were taken into the host countries through authorised ports of entry. They were also granted temporary work permits or contracts of various lengths, from a minimum of two years up to indefinite periods. On the basis of Kassim's work, the labour migrants from Fiji represented in this study are *legal alien workers*. The remaining workers (11 per cent) had accompanied their spouses and were later recruited to work. They too were offered temporary work permits and contracts to allow them to work in Kiribati and the Marshall Islands.

Approximately 98 per cent of the skilled migrants were issued with work permits and these were granted either while still in Fiji (therefore, they signed on as expatriates with a different set of work conditions and salary scales) or on entry into their destination country. The latter were hired on a local contract basis, for example, some as teachers and government officials in Kiribati and some as nurses and teachers in the Marshalls:

> I'm a civil servant. I just applied for the job, went on six months' probation and started work and I'm still here. (Dental therapist 33, interview, August 2002)

The length and validity of employment contracts varied from one year (8 per cent of the respondents), to two years (68 per cent), three years (6 per cent) or for even longer periods (18 per cent). Most of the nurses and teachers worked for two- or three-year terms before renewal (43 per cent) or are intending to return to Fiji (57 per cent) at the end of their current contract. The high percentages for renewals and the intention to return support the argument that Fijian labour migration to other parts of the Pacific is temporary and might be circular migration. This can be determined only by further studies.

Finally, 96 per cent of the respondents indicated that they did not pay a bond deposit to immigration officials at their entry point to destination countries. There has been a prevailing general attitude of acceptance of Fijian nationals entering other Pacific Islands on the strength of their Fijian passports alone. Therefore, Fijian nationals may enter certain Pacific Island countries without a formal visa if the length of their stay is less than a month. With current and future socioeconomic and political developments taking place in Fiji and within the region, this state of affairs might change. Indeed, the absence of a bond deposit and a month's visa-free visit for Fijian citizens encourages temporary migration to some Pacific Island countries and creates employment opportunities for those who are so inclined.

Conclusion

Skilled labour migration from Fiji to other Pacific Island countries is a new trend of migration whose future is yet to be mapped. While the main reasons for labour migration from Fiji to other metropolitan countries were based on economic and/or political insecurities, the main reasons for migration in this study were more economic and social in nature. While international migration (and labour migration at that) for Fiji is dominated by Indo-Fijians and is permanent or long term in nature, this study shows an opposite effect, where intra-regional skilled labour migration is dominated by ethnic Fijians and is temporary in nature.

The few differences discussed here regarding these patterns of labour migration bring the issue of ethnic tensions and differences in Fiji to the forefront. More research is needed in this field and other questions such as the social and economic costs of labour migration, other labour migrant communities, as well as return migration for Fiji still need to be studied.

Earlier studies focusing on Indo-Fijians identified insecurity and fear of the future, economic and political, as key motives for emigration from Fiji. My study, which focuses instead on indigenous Fijians, finds that they are emigrating to other parts of the Pacific not because of insecurity at home, but in order to make the most of better economic and social opportunities elsewhere, and that they have every intention of returning to Fiji.

What is more remarkable is that the temporary nature of this skilled migration (clearly spelt out in the legal provisions of travel and temporary work and in the generous contracts) is further supported by the prevailing socioeconomic environments and the geographical proximity of those countries to Fiji. Those conditions have provided a perfect scenario for temporary migration of skilled indigenous labour from Fiji to fulfil their socioeconomic aspirations in a most cost-effective manner. Based on this study, it seems that the success and future of this trend of intra-regional migration in the Pacific rests largely on one crucial aspect of temporary labour migration: that it remains just that — temporary.

References

Belloni, S. 2004. 'Fiji on the Way to Full Recovery?' *Pacific Economic Bulletin*, 19, 2. pp. 1–18.

Chand, A. and Vijay Naidu. 1998. 'Legal Aspects of International Migration in Fiji.' In Patrick Brownlee (ed.), *Migration and Citizenship in the Asia-Pacific: Legal Issues, Working Paper* No. 5, University of Wollongong: Asia-Pacific Migration Research Network. pp. 15–24.

Chagas, Carlos. 2004. *What's Left to Cheer Brazil's Lula? Banks and Speculators.* http://www.brazil.com-brazil

Chetty, N. K. and S. Prasad. 1993. 'Fiji's Emigration: An Examination of Contemporary Trends and Issues.' *Demographic Report* No. 4. Suva: School of Social and Economic Development, University of the South Pacific.

Connell, J. 2003. Draft Report on the Study of Migration of Skilled Health Personnel in the Pacific (Phase I). World Health Organisation, Regional Office for the Western Pacific.

Cox, David and Mary Low. 1985. *Migration from the South Pacific: A Welfare Perspective.* Melbourne: Department of Social Studies, University of Melbourne.

Fiji Nursing Association. 2002. *Report of 45th Annual General Meeting*, Tanoa International Hotel, Nadi, March 23.

Gani, Azmat. 2000. 'Some Dimensions of Fiji's Recent Emigration.' *Pacific Economic Bulletin*, 15, 1. pp. 94–103.

Leweniqila, M., L. Camaivuna and F. Dokoni. 2000. 'Why the Nightingales are Flying Away.' *Nursing Research News*, Pioneer Issues: 1.

Mohanty, M. 2001. 'Contemporary Emigration from Fiji: Some trends and issues in the post-independence era.' In V. Naidu, E. Vasta and C. Hawksley (eds), *Current Trends in South Pacific Migration, Working Paper* No. 7, Asia-Pacific Migration Research Network, University of Wollongong. pp. 54–73.

Toh Thian Ser (ed.). 1998. *Megacities, Labour and Communications.* Singapore: Institute of Southeast Asian Studies.

United Nations. 1997. *International Migration and Development: The concise report.* New York: Population Division, United Nations Secretariat.

ENDNOTES

[1] Fiji Nursing Association 45th Annual General Meeting, Tanoa International Hotel, Nadi, March 23, 2002.

[2] Carlos Chagas, 2004, What's Left to Cheer Brazil's Lula? Banks and Speculators, http://www.brazil.com-brazil

[3] Toh Thian Ser (ed.), 1998, *Megacities, Labour and Communications,* Singapore: Institute of Southeast Asian Studies, pp. 67–102.

[4] *Ibid.*, p. 68.

Sugar and Garments

10. Fiji: Sugar and sweatshirts, migrants and remittances

Kate Hannan

There is general agreement that the Fiji economy is moving towards a particularly difficult period. It is recognised that the negative effects on Fiji's sugar and garment industries flowing from the promotion of free trade in our globalised world are resulting in an ever-more challenging economic and social environment that requires careful, fair, innovative and, above all, prompt and effective planning responses. WTO pressure on the EU to end agricultural subsidies and the end of the Multi-Fibre Arrangement (MFA) without its replacement by alternative measures that would serve to apportion quotas for clothing, footwear and textile markets in the USA have rebounded on the Fijian economy. Those who have been commenting on the worrying prognosis for Fiji's economy range from Savenaca Narube, the Governor of Fiji's Reserve Bank, to local media and an array of grassroots religious groups. They also include a wide range of academics, Australian and New Zealand politicians and representatives from aid organisations, including the ADB and Oxfam. All agree that Fiji's sugar industry faces economic hurdles that are set so high they might well end the industry's role as an important source of grassroots income and as a leading provider of the country's foreign exchange income. They also all recognise that the decline in employment opportunity and exchange earning capacity of Fiji's garment industry is likely to be permanent. [1]

In this chapter I will briefly profile the problems facing Fiji's sugar and garment industries before suggesting two possible scenarios for the future. In the first scenario, I concentrate on the employment and housing implications flowing from the likely flood of rural-to-urban migrants in the wake of the restructure of the sugar industry. I begin by noting the obvious point that the loans and general economic assistance being made available for the amelioration of the serious economic effects of changed EU quotas and price preferences must be carefully spent. I then argue that even in the case of agreed and well-designed restructuring initiatives that are promptly implemented (and to date there is little sign of this), it is unlikely that these monies will be distributed in a sufficiently egalitarian manner to offset the significant disruption that will come with the measures needed to make Fiji's sugar industry competitive in today's global marketplace. [2] What is likely to happen is that a significant number of sugar farmers and people employed in the industry will find that they have no option but to migrate to the cities, particularly the capital, Suva. They will be following the path taken by previous sugar farmers who felt they had little in the way of alternative options when their land leases were not renewed and, like these farmers, they will hope to find work in the informal economy where it is estimated that more than 60 per cent of Suva's residents are already employed. [3]

In my second scenario, I canvass the possibility of the foreign exchange now earned by the export of sugar and garments being replaced by funds remitted by Fijian workers employed overseas. This scenario is already unfolding. There is a large increase in remittances to Fiji from workers who have accessed overseas employment and this must be a cause of some optimism, particularly if remittance funds can be channelled successfully into areas that reach beyond consumption and the reproduction of a further generation of unskilled workers. Areas such as the funding of rural cooperatives or grassroots banks offering micro-financing show considerable promise. There are, however, also causes for concern in relation to remittances and I discuss a number of these, including a current worldwide push by international financial interests to regulate, formalise and profit from the funds workers send home to their families and communities. [4]

Sugar and garments

The difficult position that Fiji's sugar industry faces now that the EU will no longer pay a heavily subsidised price for a substantial proportion of the country's crop is underlined by a number of issues that are coming to the fore on a regular basis. Among these is the Fiji Government's action in taking out a loan from the ADB for no less than $F41 million (approximately $A33.7 million). This loan is for the stated purpose of 'helping to develop alternative livelihoods for rural dwellers at risk in the restructure of the sugar industry'. The loan will cover half the estimated cost of the alternative livelihoods project — almost $A67.4 million — and must be repaid over 25 years with an upfront five-year grace period. It seems that the future must now be mortgaged to pay for past neglect of an industry that has hidden behind, and been nourished by, first British and then EU trade preferences. The Fiji Government is also scheduled to directly provide $US8.7 million and the Fiji Development Bank $A11.7 million to the project to 'help develop alternative livelihoods' and this is in addition to a significant tranche of EU 'conscience money' and Fiji's usual and significant aid receipts from a number of sources, including Australia's $A30.5 million aid package for the year 2005–06 and a further $A33.8 million for 2006–07. [5]

In June 2000 when the Lomé Conventions were reconstituted as the Cotonou Agreement, the European Commission (EC) was already signalling its intention to alter, or at least to update, trade arrangements between itself and the African, Caribbean and Pacific (ACP) states. The EC used the Cotonou Agreement to clearly flag that changes in trade relations were to take place 'in conformity with

WTO rules' and to point out that updated trading arrangements would come into force no later than January 1, 2008. [6]

In spite of many commentators noting the obvious point that 'the relationship between the EU and the ACP has never been an equal one', the Cotonou Agreement has been presented as one that 'foresees the negotiation between September 2002 and December 2007 of economic partnership agreements (EPAs)'. These agreements are to cover the delicate terrain of being WTO-compatible and based on an apparently benevolent initiative that boosts asymmetrical reciprocity, which 'allows ACP regions to open their markets to the EU at a slower rate than the EU would open its market to the ACP'. [7] However, while this benevolence will obviously be appreciated, the EC is left in a position where it must take at least some responsibility for the harsh economic and social effects that will attend the forthcoming changes it has adopted in relation to the preferred status that has long been enjoyed by ACP banana and sugar producers selling into the EU market. The commission flagged that in the case of sugar, 'the real price offered to ACP Sugar Protocol producers will be substantially reduced under the EU's current proposals for CAP [Common Agricultural Policy] reform to begin in 2006', and it is in this context that commentators have noted:

i. that 'the EU's commitments under the Cotonou Agreement to ensure the continued viability of the Protocol industries will be difficult, if not impossible, to maintain in higher-cost countries following [this] reform'; [8] and
ii. that 'Article I of the EU-ACP Sugar Protocol provides that "the European Community undertakes for an *indefinite period* to purchase and import, at *guaranteed prices, specific quantities* of cane sugar, raw or white, which originate in the ACP States and which these States undertake to deliver"'. [9]

The latter point was interpreted as meaning that in strictly legal terms the EU was obliged to negotiate and agree to a guaranteed price for specific quantities of sugar with ACP Sugar Protocol countries such as Fiji. However, the unequal nature of the relationship between the EU and the ACP states has meant that the EC alone has decided what it will do. At one level, the EC has taken the view that the transitional assistance that is to be negotiated under the EPAs will atone for its withdrawal from 'a binding undertaking which was of indefinite duration' and at another level the EC is pressing the argument that the Common Organisation of the Market in Sugar (COMS), to which the Sugar Protocol is linked and on which it depends, 'can be amended'. Changes to the COMS can be made with matters such as WTO commitments in mind. Faced with this situation, ACP countries have been left with only a narrow range of realistic alternative options. [10]

One of the options open to the governments of ACP countries severely affected by the EC's change of approach is to draw public attention to what they see as the EC's breach of the principle of fairness. For example, Fiji's Minister for Foreign Affairs and External Trade, Kaliopate Tavola, complained to the EC that its intended removal of trade quotas and price subsidies did not take Fiji's situation (and the situation of the other affected ACP countries) 'into account in any way'. He added that the ending of quotas and price subsidies for Fijian sugar, which the EC had flagged, was 'completely at odds with EU development policy, the general objectives of the Doha Development Round of the WTO, and the pursuit of the UN Millennium Development Goals'.

Ministers and administrators representing other ACP countries have also noted what they depict as a 'cold-hearted' approach being taken by the EU and they too have questioned the legality of the EU's alteration of the Sugar Protocol. They have been keen to point out that 'the ACP has faithfully met its obligations and should reasonably expect the EU to respect its commitments enshrined in the Protocol in terms of the three guarantees of price, access and indefinite duration'. For their part, EC sources have noted that 'some ACP countries have used the economic rents associated with preferences to secure long-term efficiency gains by diversifying into new export sectors ... [while] for other countries ... preferences have resulted in resource allocations to uncompetitive sectors.' These are sectors that are uncompetitive in world market terms. The EC then argues that the removal of market access preferences and price subsidies will result in gains in the long-term. However, it is admitted that in the shorter term, 'any large-scale reallocation of production could undermine employment and foreign exchange earnings which would impose high adjustment costs'. In spite of significant funds being made available from a range of sources, including and particularly the EU, Fiji, and those who have been associated with the Fijian sugar industry, will have to pay 'high adjustment costs'. [11]

While the EC's assessment of the negative employment and foreign exchange effects of the end of their preferential arrangements on recipient ACP countries smacks of blaming the victim, it is the case that Fijian interests sat back and sheltered under the preferential umbrella and chose to take little or no account of the possibility of their future exposure to the full force of the global marketplace. This is a view that I expect underpinned a remark made by Australia's Foreign Minister, Alexander Downer, who argued that 'European Union practices have done Fiji's sugar industry enormous damage over the years.'[12]

Those who have profiled Fiji's sugar industry note that 'in and before the 1980s, Fiji was regarded internationally as an efficient producer and reliable supplier of high quality sugar'. This is no longer the case. Sugar was 'the single largest industry in the country during the 1970s' and, although its success in terms of the relative size of its economic contribution to national coffers has been reduced (particularly and most recently in the period since 1994), the industry still dominates the rural economy. A number of scholars estimate that it continues 'to provide employment directly or indirectly to about 51,000 people'. This would mean that more than '250,000 people, or 31% of the country's population, are directly reliant on the sugar industry'. There are said to be about 22,000 individuals (the Government's estimate is 21,000) who are sugar growers and a further 20,000 who are engaged as cane harvesters. They farm an average of only three to four hectares and raise less than 200 tonnes of cane per annum. The productivity of these small leased holdings has been falling for some time and the average net income of sugar farming households is recognised to already be below the poverty line. [13]

It is a generally agreed view that low productivity in Fiji's sugar industry as a whole 'stem[s] from the inability of the FSC [the Fiji Sugar Corporation, currently with a 67 per cent government-owned shareholding] over many years, to improve its efficiency and provide leadership to the industry'. The continuing need to contend with inefficient milling procedures, a decrepit sugar rail system, and tensions over the renewal of land leases are among the issues that have further exacerbated problems associated with the relatively small size of leaseholdings, low returns to farmers and the low level of investment. There is also an array of problems associated with Fiji Governments and authorities, which have consistently adopted a delayed, dithering and dispute-ridden approach to restructuring the industry. What has happened is that the end of EU preferences has left the industry with nowhere to go other than to effect a massive restructuring program. About 90 per cent of Fiji's raw sugar is exported to international markets, with the majority of this being taken up by the EU under terms established and agreed to under the ACP/EU Sugar Protocol. In March 2005 it was estimated that the EU was paying 529 euros per metric tonne for Fijian sugar. This amount is now scheduled to be reduced to approximately 329 euros per metric tonne in the next five years, a reduction of more than one-third. The price paid by the EU under the Sugar Protocol 'has been frozen since 1993/4 at more than three times the world price'. [14] The substantial (even catastrophic) price reduction for raw sugar exported to the EU that is looming must surely be recognised as the 'straw that will break the back' of an already ailing and beleaguered industry. [15]

At this point in my argument I think it is well worth adding a comment made by Isikeli Mataitoga, CEO of Fiji's Ministry of Foreign Affairs and External Trade. He recognised that, at least in the short term, Fiji can expect to 'still export its Sugar Protocol quota allocation of 163,600 tonnes but with decreasing price (initially a reduction of 25 per cent) to come into effect from 2006/2007 and a further 11 percent from 2007/2008'. This means that under present conditions and production costs, 'Fiji would simply be unable to supply the EU market on a commercial basis'. This is a view that is supported by Fiji's Sugar Cane Growers Council, whose leader, Jaganath Sami, has stated that the new European prices would mean that under the present conditions for sugar production and milling, 'by 2009, at least 65 per cent of cane farmers may not be viable'. He went on to note that 'the revenue of the farmers would be reduced by as much as 31 per cent under the new prices' and we can add that this is in the context where, as noted above, the average net income of sugar farmers is already considered to be below the poverty line. [16]

In spite of the advantageous price paid by the EU for a large proportion of Fiji's sugar exports (and in part as a consequence of the declining productivity of the sugar industry), between 1997 and 2001 Fiji's garment manufacture replaced sugar as the country's leading export earner. [17] Garment industry exports, however, will not be capable of replacing sugar exports now or in the future. Fiji-based garment manufacture is in decline. Like the sugar industry, the garment industry is occupying an increasingly untenable position in relation to the international marketplace. This situation is made clear when:

i. it is remembered that the garment industry is largely labour-intensive and that investment capital involved in the clothing, textile and footwear sector of the global economy has for the most part sought out the cheapest reliably available labour in the international marketplace; and
ii. it is pointed out that the average income for a Chinese clothing, footwear and textile worker engaged in the cut, make and trim production that has sustained the Fijian garment industry is 700-800 yuan a month or approximately $A114–130 a month. [18] The pay for a Fijian garment industry worker has hovered about $F80 a week (though quite often less, down to $F60) with 'illegal' overtime now being unusual. The Fijian wage would equal approximately $A225–280 a month. [19]

Descriptions of day-to-day working conditions in Fiji, including the attitude of managers towards workers, show that they are hardly better than in Chinese factories and the wages paid are considered to be below the poverty line in terms of the cost of living in urban centres. It is widely recognised that 'despite Fiji's relatively high labour costs, wages of garment factory workers are low compared to other industries'. However, they are much higher than the wages paid in China and Chinese workers (in China and those who have come to Fiji to work) are considered to be more highly skilled and more productive. They work longer hours and there is far less absenteeism among Chinese workers. [20]

Until January 1, 2005, Fiji could produce behind the shield of the MFA that had been operating in concert with various preference and protection arrangements provided by Australian manufacturers. The MFA that was in place in the global marketplace for three decades had run its course and in the absence of any further international agreement effectively offering preferential treatment for various geographically located sectors of the garment industry, a number of developing countries, including Fiji, found that their industries could not compete with the cheap labour offered by Chinese rural-to-urban migrant workers. While Fijian production has already found several niche markets (and this approach clearly offers a way forward for a number of manufacturers with an attendant reprieve for their workers), benefits derived from bilateral trading arrangements between Australia and Fiji cannot be expected to offset the advantages offered to manufacturers by the Chinese-based clothing, textile and footwear sector.

The South Pacific Regional Trade and Economic Cooperation Agreement (SPARTECA), in tandem with a number of other arrangements including those bearing the titles Import Credit Scheme (ICS), Tax-Free Factory Scheme (TFF) and SPARTECA–Textile, Clothing and Footwear scheme (S–TCF), has allowed Fiji's exports to enter Australia (and to a lesser extent New Zealand) duty-free. The finished garments exported under these arrangements have had to meet 50 per cent rules-of-origin requirements (later, in 2001, reduced to a minimum of 35 per cent). These arrangements allowed Fiji's garment industry to boom during the 1990s. [21] However, faced with the coup of May 2000, coupled with the end of the ICS in June the same year (a scheme that had 'given incentives for Australian companies to source raw materials from Asia, add value in Australia and then export to Fiji for offshore processing where the finished product could re-enter Australia under SPARTECA' [22]), and now battling the consequences of the end of the MFA, Fiji-based manufacturers are finding that their industry has been dealt first one blow and then another. Moreover, rules of origin advantages — even if now reconstructed in a streamlined, clear and well-organised fashion into a program that successfully succeeded the ICS — could obviously do nothing to reinstate the loss of Fiji's MFA-protected quota for garments to be sold into the US market. It is now too late for specially constructed Australian preferences to produce the outcome needed to ensure the continued health of Fiji's cut, make and trim garment industry. Nevertheless, Fiji's Foreign Minister found himself again pleading for a better export deal for his country. In spite of the already agreed extension of S–TCF advantages for a further seven years (until 2011), in September 2005 he requested that Australia further 'relax its current rules relating to market access to Australia for garments manufactured in Fiji'. This reduction in origin requirements would be from 35 per cent to 25 per cent. [23]

It is also worth noting that there is now concern among Fiji's garment manufacturers that if Australia signs a bilateral free trade agreement with China, they would be further disadvantaged. Fiji-based manufacturers are stating that if this happens the jobs of their remaining garment workers 'are likely to disappear overnight'. It is clear that their fear over this issue is doing its part in further eroding their confidence in their increasingly fluid and already fragile industry. [24]

The obvious and widely agreed view that Fiji's garment industry has made a significant contribution to the nation's economy must now be tempered by the observation that, in the protected form that it took, the industry was likely to fail to increase its productivity levels to a point where it would justify its relatively high wages and on-costs. It is now clear that the industry will no longer play its previous role in absorbing low-skilled workers and providing foreign exchange earnings. The best-case scenario is that, with government support and clear goals, the industry will be in a position to nurture a smaller, but internationally competitive garment industry that will survive without the benefit of preferences or subsidies. [25]

In a manner that mirrors criticism of the sugar industry's failure to restructure while protected by EU price and quota preferences, it has been pointed out that the Fiji-based garment industry 'illustrates the problems preferences can cause developing economies'. The industry and its workers became trapped in labour-intensive, 'low-skill and low-technology' cut, make and trim manufacture. Nevertheless, it will be sorely missed. The consequences of its demise will be 'immeasurable' and will have a particularly sad and serious impact 'on the tens of thousands of urban poor … who are inextricably linked to its continued existence'. Most estimates are that the industry continues to employ some 12,000 to 15,000 workers, mostly women and often Indo-Fijian women, whose incomes are estimated to affect as many as 80,000 people. [26]

When considering the low-wage, low-technology state of Fiji-based garment manufacture (a situation nurtured by MFA access to garment markets in the USA, and both nurtured and exacerbated by 'tied trade' arrangements with Australia), most commentators would agree with the observation that preferences 'represent bad trade and bad development policy approaches'. [27]

Scenario one: Migrants, settlements and the informal economy

In this first scenario I will outline what could happen if Fiji governments continue to be indecisive in the face of the significant economic problems that are on the horizon. They are also the problems that will come into view if the Government is unwilling and unable to ensure that the money offered for the purposes of restructuring the sugar industry and providing alternative avenues of employment for sugar farmers who are disadvantaged by the restructure fails to 'trickle-down'. With the sugar industry in decline and faced with, at best, a choice between significant restructure, the inclusion of new forms of production such as ethanol production, or closure, and a garment industry that is already well in decline, the Fiji Government and the people of Fiji obviously cannot afford anything other than prompt, decisive, effective and efficient action. [28]

In spite of the loan that has been approved by the ADB, a report published by the bank notes that 'accessible alternative occupations' for those who leave sugar leases that are no longer viable and who have been displaced by shrinking employment opportunities in sugar-related occupations are likely to be difficult to obtain. It is already clear that 'formal employment will not keep pace with population drift to urban areas'. This will mean that the rural-to-urban drift will accelerate the expansion of informal settlement in Suva and there will be an increased reliance on informal avenues for employment. [29] Already, anecdotal evidence suggests that the profile of the residents of the Suva-Nausori corridor has changed. It has been commonly agreed that residents in this corridor were once predominantly indigenous Fijians. Today, it is said that almost half are Indo-Fijians. The deleterious effect on the sugar industry of the end of a significant number of sugar-farm leases and the reduced productivity of the continuing leases, coupled with an attendant reduction in confidence in the industry, is a sensible and reasonable way to account for this change.

The problems associated with urbanisation in Pacific Island countries are already well documented. They are depicted as 'numerous and serious'. Lack of sufficient employment opportunities (particularly in the more secure and predictable formal sector) in peri-urban areas of spontaneous urban settlement and the downward pressure on wages in the formal and informal sectors created by competition for work, are already cause for concern among planners and academic commentators. They also note the obvious pressure on already hard-pressed services such as a reliable water supply (now often having to be accommodated in Suva's outer suburban areas by the use of a 44-gallon drum covered by a flap of plastic and left on the roadside to be filled from a water truck) and waste disposal (with a significant portion finding its way into waterways and lagoons). Indeed, the overall profile of urban poverty in Fiji is becoming a matter of acute concern. ADB policy-makers have estimated that for the period 2002–03 urban poverty in Fiji rose to the point where it included some 30 to 40 per cent of urban residents. [30] (Just a little more than five years earlier, in 1997, a Government/UNDP report found that in Fiji as a whole 25 per cent of people were living below the poverty line, with a further 25 per cent surviving just above this line). It has also been recognised that as many as 83 per cent of those in poverty are employed. They are the working poor, and research has shown that many of these working poor are already living in informal urban settlements. [31]

Urban commentators have been keen to point out that in the context of today's global economy, there are cities that gain and cities that lose. The cities that gain are obviously those favoured by substantial international investment. Some cities have become 'mega' or 'world' cities. They include New York, London and Shanghai and maybe even Sydney. They are cities that face outward, embracing the world marketplace. However, other cities have suffered as the manufacturing base they grew on has been shipped offshore. These cities include Detroit and Pittsburgh, Sheffield and Liverpool, Dresden and Leipzig. (In Australia they are rust-belt cities such as Geelong, Newcastle and Wollongong.) In order to again flourish, these cities have had to reinvent themselves. Dresden has wanted to become a new centre for micro-electronics in Germany, the English city of Liverpool has presented itself as a cultural centre and the Australian cities of Geelong, Newcastle and Wollongong have been keen to foster their image as university cities. [32] However, there are obviously other types of cities. They are not losing or in danger of losing their residents and they have not been left behind and forced to retool and reorient because the manufacturing base that gave rise to their very existence has moved offshore. These are developing-country cities that are growing due to rural push. And, in the case of Fiji, the likely outcome of a future considerable contraction in sugar production means that cities (particularly Suva) are likely to undergo substantial growth.[33]

The changing spatial form of cities is reflecting the dynamics of globalisation and it is clear that Fiji's cities have been and will continue to be affected by this dynamic. It is equally clear that it will be difficult for Suva to take advantage of advice that suggests that cities 'lower down the [global] system' will 'have to find niches in the global marketplace in order to survive'. This advice is not appropriate.[34] Finding a market outlet (or niche) is obviously a good idea, but the city will survive and grow even without this market chance. Though Fiji's second city of Lautoka can be twinned with the tourist entry town of Nadi to share the benefits that derive from tourism and so take advantage of a global market niche, Suva is not geographically well placed to take advantage of tourism. Suva is likely to survive as the country's administrative centre and grow as a warehouse for those whose incomes have benefited from protective sugar and garment markets and pricing arrangements, and who are now to be left without a regular, formal income.[35]

While a number of First-World urban commentators either ignore the type of developing-country city I have outlined above (doing no more than express concern over cities where the population rises, but employment opportunities are barely increasing or static), others are busily identifying interesting possibilities for cities such as Suva. This latter group of commentators argues that we should stop deploring the growth of informal settlements, squatter towns and even slums. They argue that we should value measures such as 'spontaneous housing'. They are keen to point out that there are benefits to be derived from 'self-help' housing and the growth in the informal economy that comes with significant levels of rural-to-urban drift. Indeed, this approach seems to be already having an effect. In their latest pronouncement on development in the Pacific region, those who set Australia's aid goals have been arguing that self-help and self-employment must be encouraged. They have noted the benefit that would be gained from 'removing regulatory barriers in the informal sector' and have even noted that measures such as moving street-traders on because 'local authorities decide to "clean up the town"' (and quite often it is because they lack formal permission and business licences) are not sensible initiatives in the context of very high and still rising rates of urban unemployment. [36]

In the West, the process of increased industrialisation and urban growth usually accommodated the growing number of urban residents' need for formal employment. The cities needed the workers, but this is an experience that is in stark contrast with that of most developing countries where there is insufficient formal employment to satisfy residents' needs. [37] Commentators who are arguing for reassessment of Third World informal self-help communities and their employment patterns recognise that the informal economy, where those who come to town might well find work, has its faults. These have been extensively debated. They know that 'the great mass of unskilled workers has encouraged the growth of "informal sectors" in every developing country' (reflecting a lack of investment in human capital) and they are well aware that these workers are subject to insecure employment and are not protected by minimum wage provisions. They also lack access to welfare services, and health and safety provisions in the workplace are often ignored. Nevertheless, there is no doubt that many poor urban households derive their living from the informal sector. They and their families depend on it. It is also clear that this sector represents concrete action by the poor to provide employment and to service their own and others' needs. [38]

Today a number of respected sources such as the ILO have not only recognised the importance and value of this sector, they have argued that it would derive considerable benefit from 'state intervention in the areas of credit, technical support and infrastructure'. In concert with this advice, a number of Fiji-based academics have noted that most participants in their country's informal sector depend on moneylenders and relatives to access finance. They estimate that these two sources account for 80 per cent of the finance used for investment in informal enterprises and that the interest charged by moneylenders is 'quite high'. They estimate that it averages 34 per cent per annum. Moreover, the Fiji Government has already recognised the need to support small, often family-run and often informal-sector enterprises and now has legislation in place to promote small and micro-enterprises. As well, aid donors are well aware of the benefits to be gained from offering micro-financing to these enterprises (for example, the EU has already established an EU/ACP Microfinance Framework Program). It therefore seems that the considerable body of grant and aid funds from a range of other sources that are to be used for the declared purpose of helping to 'develop alternative livelihoods for rural dwellers at risk in the restructure of the sugar industry' should be extended to those who are or who will come to live in Suva. It will be sensible, indeed necessary, to extend the stated intention of 'livelihood' projects aimed at encouraging sugar farmers 'to engage in off-farm livelihoods by promoting the development of small and micro-enterprises' to urban areas and particularly to what will be a fast-growing informal sector.[39]

A further option with regard to addressing the needs of recently arrived rural-to-urban migrants begins with the observation that while developing-country governments have constructed public housing in answer to the demands of the poor, it is clear that their capacity to meet this housing demand is often woefully inadequate. In many cases even maintaining any existing stock of public housing is neglected, which might even worsen the plight of the poor. It is then no wonder that in a manner that parallels their advice in relation to the benefits that would derive from supporting the informal economy, some commentators have concluded that public housing has proved to be too costly for many developing-country governments and that this means that self-help shelter is the best realistically available option. They also note that spontaneous self-help shelters have an advantage over public housing because they are likely to be improved and upgraded over time. And, in most cases, self-built communities give rise to the spontaneous development of local religious-centred communities (churches, temples and mosques) and informal shops. These matters are clearly evident when viewing Suva's dilapidated supply of public housing and its squatter settlements. The obvious conclusion is that government attention would be better directed towards providing support for settlement housing. It has been pointed out that developing-country governments could (and should) establish formal land lease arrangements that provide some security for self-help settlements (indeed, the Fiji Government has done this in the past) and that this innovation should be given preference ahead of continuing investment in what has often become substandard and inadequate public housing.

Many indigenous Fijian settlements in and around Fiji's main cities are based on informal arrangements with formally recognised indigenous landowning groups. However, with increasing numbers of Indo-Fijian families likely to come to town as rural-to-urban migrants, these arrangements will be forgone. These migrants do not usually have connections that would encourage formal indigenous-Fijian landowners to informally sublease land to them. This leaves them relying on the use of public land, and experience to date demonstrates that settlement then might often take place on land situated alongside suburban waterways or under high-voltage electricity cables. More appropriate areas set aside to be formally leased to self-help families would obviously be a very useful government innovation in this context.

Those commentators who are urging that informal settlement should be reassessed also have a further point to make. It amounts to a sober caution. They note that we (scholars, policy-makers and journalists resident in developed and developing countries) have too often viewed self-help housing through a middle-class/permanent urban resident lens. We have therefore seen squatter settlements only as a source of increased social problems, as eyesores, a nursery for crime and violence, and an environmental hazard. These settlements are seen as a blot on the urban landscape rather than attempts by the poor to cater for themselves. However, even with the best intentions, one of the problems that it will be difficult to fund is the need for essential services, such as clean water, electricity and sewerage for self-help settlements.[40] The latter situation is underlined in the case of Suva when it is remembered that there are squatter settlements that have been in existence for decades and that have had stable and continuous informal agreements with legally recognised landowners for this period of time and yet have not so far been able to raise the funds required to have electricity connected. The matter that all parties agree on is that ignoring the problems associated with informal urbanisation is most certainly ill-advised. [41]

Scenario two: Workers and remittances

Worker-remitted funds are already a well-established and recognised part of Fiji's economic landscape. However, today the quantity of remitted funds is substantially increased. This is a phenomenon that does not apply only to Fiji, or even only to the Pacific or the wider Asia–Pacific region. It is a worldwide occurrence and now respected and sober international institutions such as the ILO, the World Bank, the ADB, the Asia-Pacific Economic Cooperation (APEC) group and the IMF, together with a range of aid providers including the Australian Government and the EC, are paying attention to a situation that they now argue 'provides the most direct, immediate, and far-reaching benefit to overseas workers, their families, and their countries of origin'.

Overseas worker remittances to families and communities in Fiji have risen and risen again. By 2002 remittances from Fijian nationals living overseas had risen to an estimated $F232.4 million (approximately $A180 million). A year later, this figure was deemed to be $F243.4 million (approximately $A190 million) and, by the end of 2004, some sources estimated it was as high as $F317 million (approximately $A244 million). [42] It is clear that remittances are replacing sugar and garments to rest alongside Fiji's flourishing tourist trade as the country's main means of generating foreign exchange. It is then equally obvious that 'maximising the benefits from international migration is crucial'. Other Pacific Island countries have already had considerable success in this area. Residents have enjoyed increased consumption and the provision of services including education and health facilities. They have also had access to improved housing and there are reports of some small-scale investment, though it is also generally agreed that consistently successful formal schemes (rather than local ad hoc schemes) aimed at encouraging investment instead of consumption have yet to be implemented.

It is against the background of increased living standards for residents of other Pacific Island countries and a demonstrated willingness for unskilled or semi-skilled Fijians to seek overseas employment that Fiji's Prime Minister, Laisenia Qarase, has applied pressure on richer neighbouring countries, particularly Australia, to accept Fijian 'guest workers'. He argued that if the Australian Government was to demonstrate real concern over good governance and security in the region, it must offer policy initiatives based on the premise that 'you can only have good governance and security if the citizens of the country are living a reasonable standard of living.' He went on to say that 'once you take that away, then you have very fertile grounds for instability'. Nevertheless, Australia's Foreign Minister, Alexander Downer, and Treasurer, Peter Costello, insisted that guest workers were not consistent with Australia's culture. Their immediate reaction was to conclude that Australian labour shortages would be better met by extending the visas of working travellers (usually young backpackers). [43]

The extent of the improvement in a family's lifestyle on the basis of remittances received has proved to be hard to estimate, but it should not be underestimated. While it is a widely held view that remittance funds are used primarily to meet the consumption needs of recipient families, we also already know from anecdotal evidence that remittances have been used as a source of low-level, informal-sector investment and we would expect this to have the advantage of not being encumbered with the very high interest rates imposed by moneylenders. John Connell, who has done a great deal of work on the issue of remittances by Pacific Island workers, has (together with Richard Brown) also noted that a range of developing countries have already adopted formal measures aimed at encouraging migrants to become investors. Connell and Brown have cited Turkish measures giving migrants preferences in village development cooperatives, a scheme in Pakistan that allows migrants to import machinery at concessional rates and to invest in export-processing zones; and a Bangladeshi Government offer of incentives for investing remitted funds domestically. [44] These types of initiatives are becoming increasingly popular with developing-country governments and international policy advisors. There are many examples. It is currently being suggested to the Mexican Government that the role of micro-banks should be boosted in order to promote rural and peri-urban development using remittance monies. The argument used is a familiar one. It is that to date some 80-90 per cent of remittance monies are dedicated to consumption and the reproduction of workers. While there is evidence that remittance funds are also used for housing and community projects and for health care and educational opportunities, and it might well be the case that they reach further than merely reproducing usually unskilled migrant workers, the argument that remitted funds are used predominantly for day-to-day consumption is well suited to the push for a more productive domestic approach to the use of remittances. Those promoting Mexican micro-banks have further boosted their argument by recognising that many families in the home country lack efficient and safe ways to save as well as lacking credit opportunities. They also cite the case of a micro-bank having been spontaneously established by home country members of a transnational community. This Mexican community was not only locked out of usual financial services by the lack of formal financial credentials held by citizens, but by geography. It was two hours from the nearest city on an unpaved road. The community offered as an example consists of a municipality that has 16,000 inhabitants in 60 small towns where somewhere between 40 and 70 per cent of the population have emigrated seeking work. The populations of the towns are reliant on remittances as their main source of income.[45]

At the same time as discussions, conferences and debates in the international arena have been focusing on the issue of worker remittances, commentators within and outside Fiji continue to display a somewhat ambiguous approach to the considerable growth in the country's remittances. On one hand, they note that skilled migrants such as nurses and teachers (together with rugby players and soldiers) represent a loss of scarce human capital and, on the other hand, they note that 'remittances are one of the main sources of domestic spending and are driving growth in the economy'. However, these commentators pay too little attention to what is most likely to be a fast-growing number of unskilled migrant workers who will remit funds to families who might well have been reliant mainly on the informal sector for their income. Unless they add this group to their consideration of the overseas worker/remittance issue, they will be out of step with what is happening on the ground in terms of the current international market in labour-time. Having made this point, I should also note that the pressure to provide opportunities for not only skilled, but unskilled potential migrants has been reflected in Prime Minister Qarase's plea to Australia to accept unskilled guest workers from Fiji; in the reported 'success' of the Pacific Forum in an agreement sought with the EC to allow guest workers to enter the EU; and in Fiji Government concern that 'some order and accountability' be brought to bear on 'the overseas job rush'. It is known that 'a sizeable number work, some illegally, in Australia, New Zealand, and the United States'.[46]

It is quite clear that in spite of a degree of indecisiveness in terms of the approach of a number of commentators, 'Fiji is catching up fast on the world's latest lucrative exporting commodity: human labour'. However, a number of the pitfalls of this form of 'export' are already evident. Apart from those who are working overseas illegally, a number of Fijian workers remitting funds are newly employed in contract work in Kuwait or Iraq and this has led to some problems. In contrast with the 1,000 positions offered to Fijian men by the British Army,

American contractors have been recruiting workers at rates much lower than the cost of their home-country workers and this has allowed some people to suggest that the present contracting of relatively cheap Fijian workers amounts to 'a form of 21st-century black-birding'. [47]

Among the problems associated with the present growth in overseas workers' remittances is one that has the smell of corruption. The promise of overseas employment is offered in order to make quick and less-than-honest money. There are a number of reports of fees as high as $F250 to $F300 being paid to be considered for an overseas posting, usually in Kuwait or Iraq, while $F150 is a quite usual payment. There are reported to be as many as 20,000 paid-up applications for what is estimated to be a contract to supply a maximum of 2,000 workers. In the context of Fijian incomes, the application fee is considerable and is often borrowed. The Fiji Government initiated an investigation into the company concerned. [48] A further problem associated with the now much greater reliance Fiji's citizens have on overseas remittances for employment opportunity, domestic consumption and the generation of foreign exchange earnings is the vulnerability to global forces that this form of income represents. Fiji's sugar and garment industries have already demonstrated just how hazardous the international marketplace is. A possible and equally serious vulnerability would be an economic contraction affecting host countries. This would, as we saw in the 1997 Asian financial crisis, lead to migrant workers (legal and illegal) being summarily repatriated. Their temporary status would ensure that they were ineligible for severance payments; quite often migrant workers have not received the wages owing to them. In the period after the Asian financial crisis it was reported widely that some employers took advantage of the vulnerability of their workers. They intentionally delayed or avoided wage payments and dismissed employees unfairly. In some places, most notably in Malaysia and Indonesia, xenophobia was expressed and had a marked effect on the treatment of migrant workers. In times of economic contraction, it is likely that workers will be given little or no notice of the change in their circumstances. Migrant workers, and indeed resident garment workers in Fiji, have often been presented with no more than a chained gate and, at best, a rough sign. [49] And, as though the above concerns are not enough to consider, they by no means exhaust the problems countries and workers and their families might have to address in the course of depending on remittance incomes. For example, another global hazard that has appeared on the remittance agenda concerns the push by a number of well-established global financial institutions, and at least one regional grouping, APEC, to 'shape and formalise' (or more correctly, influence, regulate and, for private companies, derive further profit from) worker remittance payments.

In mid-2004, a symposium was held in Tokyo to discuss 'Shaping the Remittances Market by Shifting to Formal Systems'. APEC, the World Bank and the ADB sponsored this symposium. Their declared mission was to bring together 'key stakeholders to discuss opportunities and innovations in the cross-border remittance industry'. Their stated goal was to 'create market incentives for customers [workers remitting funds overseas] to shift from informal to formal financial systems'. The World Council of Credit Unions, a range of developing-country credit union providers, the Global Trade Association, Western Union (claiming its success and 'very strong business model') and those who favour 'ATM-based money transfers', and particularly 'Visa and MasterCard branded transfers', were uniformly keen to point to the problems associated with informal money transfer. They noted that when funds travelled home via friends and relatives the delivery time was often slow. They also noted the potential for loss and theft using informal transportation methods. They noted the potential for black-market transactions and money laundering and then cited the need to develop technologies, and delivery channels (with some suggesting not only ATMs, but pre-paid cards and use of the Internet) in order 'to harness' workers' remittances. In some cases, those presenting their 'research' to the symposium found it necessary to display a disclaimer stating that their company 'does and seeks to do business with companies covered in its research report [and] as a result, investors should be aware that the firm may have a conflict of interest that could affect the objectivity of the report'. The big business aspect of many of the presenters was displayed particularly clearly when Western Union boasted that it already had an 'unmatched global network' that included 5,600 locations in Citibank branches, 4,300 in Wal-Mart stores, 11,400 Fedex outlets, and no fewer than 30,000 outlets situated in McDonald's restaurants. Representatives from this same company also took time to lament that the market for global remittances was fragmented and immature. It offered scope for further development. [50]

The attitude of international financial institutions to shaping and 'enhancing the efficiency of overseas workers' remittances' is in considerable contrast with others who have focused principally on a range of social issues related to these remittances.

Included among the institutions commenting on and attempting to influence the ever-increasing flow of worker remittances is the IMF. Its focus, however, differs from the concerns expressed by big business and those outlined by academics, social commentators and NGOs, who are advising that funds be spent in a manner that provides long-term benefits for the recipient society. IMF administrators are concerned that 'the compensatory nature of remittances presents a moral hazard, or dependency syndrome' and that this might impede economic growth. They argue that developing country residents' participation in productive endeavours might be reduced and it is on the basis of this concern that they are urging developing-country governments 'to come up with policies that will induce migrants to invest productively'. [51]

Yet another group of researchers who have been drawn into the forum shaping and regulating international remittances (including a number employed by the ADB) argue that developing-country governments whose workers are employed overseas should upgrade the quality of preparatory education, provide special skills training, identify new overseas labour markets and negotiate with host governments for the proper accreditation of their workers. These researchers have also noted that sending workers overseas who then remit funds to their families and communities at home might go some way to 'compensate for the losses that a sending country might incur from brain drain or the skimming of its highly skilled workers'. [52] This is the view that is currently reflected in Australian government plans and pronouncements in relation to remittances and overseas workers from the Pacific region. Claiming an 'important new direction for the aid program', Australian Prime Minister, John Howard, has announced the establishment of a Australia-Pacific Technical College. Noting that 'currently, workplace competencies in the Pacific often fall short of [Australian] industry requirements', Howard said that 'the college concept is aimed at increasing the number of skilled Pacific Island graduates as well as the quality of their training'. A detailed design of the college was scheduled to be presented to the Pacific Islands Forum meeting held in October 2006. [53]

The Australian Government's skills-based approach to hosting overseas workers might well be comforting for Pacific Island governments when they consider the longer-term benefits of exporting their citizen workers. This is because it comes with the assurance that at least a portion of the human capital generated through this form of post-secondary education will be available for domestic purposes together with recognition of the obvious point that the wages (and therefore the expected remittances) of skilled workers are higher than those of unskilled and semi-skilled workers. However, it will not provide immediate employment and income for the workers who are already knocking at Australia's door. On the other hand, unless the workers of a sending country have access to skills acquisition (either by the relatively widespread provision of appropriate education through investment by aid providers or through the willingness and ability of domestic governments to harness income remittance monies for the purpose of educating workers), the present disadvantage in the international division of labour will be cemented ever more firmly into place.

Conclusion

The EC's decision to begin the withdrawal of its trade and pricing preferences for ACP sugar exports as early as 2006 has led to criticism even from within EU member states. For example, a British House of Commons report on fair trade and the EU's trade agreements with ACP countries, while not critical of the EC's reform of the sugar regime per se, gives voice to concern that due attention be paid to the implications of reform on ACP countries that rely on the EU market.

The authors of the Report were seeking reassurance that capacity outside the sugar sector would be built in affected countries. [54] If this production capacity is to be successfully built in Fiji then the funds borrowed by the Fiji Government from the ADB, together with the considerable flow of monies from a range of other sources, including from the EC, will have to be used wisely. These funds must not be used only to restructure the ailing sugar industry. They will need to be invested in projects that provide employment opportunities for grassroots sugar producers who lose confidence in their industry and find they have little option other than to seek work in Fiji's growing informal sector.

Employment opportunities and income for citizens and their families and communities and the nation's capacity to generate foreign exchange are areas where the loss of EU sugar trading and pricing preferences will be keenly felt, particularly when it is remembered that the problems associated with the sugar industry do not stand alone. Fiji's garment industry has declined. The free market-informed decision to end the MFA without provision for any form of global market regulation aimed at offsetting the disadvantage to be borne by garment-producing countries that cannot match the low wages paid to China's rural-to-urban migrant workers is the most immediate cause of the difficulties now faced by Fiji-based garment manufacturers. These are difficulties that have combined with but cannot be overcome by trading concessions granted to Fijian manufacturers by the Australian Government. Extending the S–TCF scheme and reductions in 'rules-of-origin' percentages for cut, make and trim garments returning to Australia will not compensate for the loss of US market quotas attached to the MFA.

In the argument I have presented above, I note that the Fiji Sugar Cane Growers' Council's leader, Jaganath Sami, projected that 'by 2009, at least 65 per cent of cane farmers may not be viable'. [55] This is a worst-case scenario. However, it is already clear that a significant number of cane growers whose families will no longer be in a position to live from the proceeds of their crops will move to town and it is equally clear that the quality of their lives will be impacted greatly by the policies adopted by their government. Not only will they require their share of the funds flowing into Fiji to offset the negative impact of the end of trade and price preferences for sugar, they will need to benefit from innovative polices adopted by their government with respect to the provision of housing and secure tenure of suitable land; the provision of basic services such as water, electricity and sewerage; promotion of the informal economy, including the possible licensing of informal trading enterprises such as roadside stalls and backyard mechanical repair shops; the provision of accessible grassroots saving opportunities and micro-credit facilities; and suitable investment in human capital, particularly in the training of workers.

The growth in remittances is a bright spot on Fiji's economic landscape. Remittances are being touted by international bodies such as the World Bank, the IMF, the ADB, the ILO and even APEC as a means of providing 'the most direct, immediate, and far-reaching benefit for overseas workers, their families, and their countries of origin'. The authors of such glowing endorsements then often go on to note that 'despite the social and other costs of migration, many families of overseas workers, particularly those in the low-income sectors, rely on remittances'. It is this reliance that has led to the current push to identify measures that would 'harness' inflowing funds as an investment resource. There would be considerable benefit to be derived from schemes intending to channel these funds into projects such as the establishment of grassroots credit cooperatives or micro-banks. However, there is another face to the current push to 'harness' remittance monies. It relates to what has been described enthusiastically as the 'generation of vibrant competition among banks, money transfer agencies, and other traditional remittance players … to serve as remittance conduits'. These banks, money transfer agencies and others are claiming for themselves the brief of facilitating the shift of remittance payments from informal to formal channels. They claim that their participation in 'the remittance market' will benefit those who work overseas and remit monies to their families in their home country. [56] However, there is room for some suspicion when it comes to assessing their claim to be promoting primarily altruistic motives. Western Union's 'vision' of ever-more McDonald's restaurant outlets for money transfers serves to underline the predominantly commercial, profit-driven nature of their endeavours.

References

Appana, Subhash. 2003. 'New Public Management and Public Enterprise Restructuring in Fiji.' *Fijian Studies: A Journal of Contemporary Fiji*, 1, 1. pp. 51–73.

Asian Development Bank. 2005. *Pacific Economic Outlook 2005*. (See particularly 'Fiji Islands', pp. 192–5.) Manila.

Asian Development Bank. 2005. *Enhancing the Efficiency of Overseas Workers' Remittances*. Technical Assistance Report. Manila.

AusAID. 2005. Summary of Australia's Overseas Aid Program 2005/6. Canberra.

AusAID. 2006. *Australian Aid: Promoting Growth and Stability, A White Paper on the Australian Government's Aid Program*. Canberra.

Australian Broadcasting Commission, Radio Australia, *Pacific Beat*, September 30, 2005, http://www.abc.net.au/ra/pacbeat/

Barr, Kevin. 2003. 'Wages Councils and Just Wages in Fiji.' *Fijian Studies: A Journal of Contemporary Fiji*, 1, 1. pp. 199–208.

Bezard, Gwenn (Celent Communications speaker). 2004. 'Global Money Transfers — Can New Technologies Bring More Competition?' *Shaping the Remittances Market by Shifting to Formal Systems*, APEC Symposium, Tokyo, June 3–4.

Chami, R., C. Fullenkamp and S. Jahjah, 2003 'Are Immigrant Remittance Flows a Source of Capital for Development?', *IMF Working Paper* 03/189, IMF, September

Commission of the European Communities. 2005. 'The Trade and Development Aspects of EPA Negotiations.' *Commission Staff Working Document*, November 9.

Commonwealth of Australia. 2006. *Pacific 2020: Challenges and Opportunities for Growth*. May.

Connell, John and Richard Brown. 2005. *Remittances in the Pacific: An Overview*. Asian Development Bank. March.

Cruz, Isabel. 2004. 'Rural Microbanks — Financial Services for Local Development.' *Shaping the Remittances Market by Shifting to Formal Systems*, APEC Symposium, Tokyo, June 3–4.

Department of Foreign Affairs and Trade. 2003. *Scoping Study: Future Directions for Fiji's Garment Industry*. Economic Analytical Unit. August.

Economic Association of Fiji. 2005. Published Panel Discussion: 'Sugar Reforms: Do We Have a Choice?' *Reserve Bank of Fiji Quarterly Review*, March. pp. 34–6.

European Commission. 'Bilateral Trade Relations: Africa, Caribbean, Pacific.' http://ec.europa.eu/comm/trade/issues/bilateral/regions/acp/index_en.htm

European Commission. 'EU-ACP Microfinance Framework Programme.' http://ec.europa.eu/comm/europeaid/projects/microfinance/index_en.htm

European Commission. 2004. *Pacific ACP-EC EPA Negotiations Joint Road Map*. EC: Directorate-General for Trade.September 15.

European Commission. 'The Cotonou Partnership Agreement.' http://europa.eu.int/comm/development/cotonou

Fiji Sugar Corporation. 2003. 'A Brief History of the Sugar Industry in Fiji.' Briefing notes prepared for the EU Commissioner for Development and Humanitarian Affairs, 2002, reproduced in *Fijian Studies: A Journal of Contemporary Fiji*, 1, 2. pp. 315–26.

Fiji Times, 'Sugar Prices to Fall by July 2006', January 7, 2005; 'More Dollars From Abroad', January 24, 2005; 'Stay Out of Politics, Army Told', September 30, 2005.

Gillson, Ian, Adrian Hewitt and Sheila Page. 2005. *Forthcoming Changes in the EU Banana/Sugar Markets: A Menu of Options for an Effective EU Transitional Package*. London: Overseas Development Institute.

Handelman, Howard. 2003. *The Challenge of Third World Development*, 3rd ed. New Jersey and London: Prentice Hall.

Hannan, Kate. 2005. 'China's Rural-to-Urban Labour Migration: Mobility, Exclusion and Opportunity.' International Convention of Asia Scholars (ICAS) 4 Conference, Shanghai, August 20–24.

Hannan, Kate. 2006. 'China's Trade Relations with the US and the EU: WTO Membership, Free Markets(?), Agricultural Subsidies and Clothing, Textile and Footwear Quotas.' *Copenhagen Business School Discussion Paper*, May.

Holland, Martin. 2002. *The European Union and the Third World*. Palgrave.

House of Commons International Development Committee. 2005. 'Fair Trade? The European Union's Trade Agreements with African, Caribbean and Pacific Countries.' *Sixth Report of Session 2004–05*. March 23, 2005.

Kingsbury, Damien, Joe Remenyi, John McKay and Janet Hunt. 2004. *Key Issues in Development*. New York: Palgrave Macmillan.

Murphy, Craig N. (ed.) 2003. *Egalitarian Politics in the Age of Globalization*. New York: Palgrave Macmillan.

Narayan, Paresh and Biman Prasad. 2003. 'Fiji's Sugar, Tourism and Garment Industries: A Survey of Performance, Problems and Potentials.' *Fijian Studies: A Journal of Contemporary Fiji*, 1, 1. pp. 3–27.

National Farmers Union. 2003. 'Dark Clouds on the Horizon.' *Fijian Studies: A Journal of Contemporary Fiji*, 1, 2. pp. 381–8.

Nielson, Poul (European Commission Commissioner for Development and Humanitarian Aid). 2002. Speech to the ACP-EU First Meeting on Negotiation of Economic Partnership Agreement, Brussels, September 27, 2002. (See also European Union Press Release, October 4, 2002, 'Commission Signs EUR 29 Million Aid Package with the Pacific Island Countries', http:/europa.eu.int/rapit/start/ggi/guesten.ksh?p_action.getxt=gr&doc=IP/02/1432/RA)

New Zealand Ministry of Foreign Affairs and Trade, Pacific Division, 2002. *Economic Update — Republic of the Fiji Islands*. October.

O'Brien, Robert and Marc Williams. 2004. *Global Political Economy: Evolution and Dynamics*. New York: Palgrave Macmillan.

Pacific Islands Forum. 2005. 'Urbanisation and the Pacific.' *Trends and Developments*, January.

Pacific Islands Report, 'ADB Outlook for Fiji Economy Grim', April 7, 2005; 'Fiji's Long, Risky Road to Kuwait', April 22, 2005; '3,000 Lose Jobs As Fiji Garment Factory Closes', April 26, 2005; and 'Fiji Gets $25 Million ADB Loan for Farmers', June 30, 2005.

Pareti, Samisoni. 2005. 'Human Labour — Lucrative Export — Fiji Rakes in $m From Overseas Jobs.' *Islands Business*, May.

Prasad, Satendra and Kevin Hince. 2001. *Industrial Relations in the South Pacific*. Suva: USP.

Prasad, Satendra. 2003. 'Energy Aspects of Fiji's Sugar Industry: A Case for More Efficient Electricity Generation from Bargasse.' *Fijian Studies: A Journal of Contemporary Fiji*, 1, 2. pp. 243–64.

Rao, Gyaneshwar, 2003. 'Lending Trends in the Sugar Cane Sector in Fiji.' *Fijian Studies: A Journal of Contemporary Fiji*, 1, 2. pp. 301–15.

Reddy, Mahendra. 2003. 'Farm Productivity, Efficiency and Profitability in Fiji's Sugar Industry.' *Fijian Studies: A Journal of Contemporary Fiji*, 1, 2. pp. 225–41.

Reddy, Mahendra, Vijay Naidu and Manoranjan Mohanty. 2003. 'The Urban Informal Sector in Fiji: Results From a Survey.' *Fijian Studies: A Journal of Contemporary Fiji*, 1, 1. pp. 127–54.

Reddy, Narendra. 2003. 'Survival Strategies for the Fiji Sugar Industry.' *Fijian Studies: A Journal of Contemporary Fiji*, 1, 1. pp. 265–85.

SBS-TV, *Dateline*, 'The Real Pacific Solution', June 15, 2005, transcript, *Dateline* Archives, http://news.sbs.com.au//dateline/index:php?

Secretariat of the African, Caribbean and Pacific Group of States, Press Release/Brussels: 'African, Caribbean and Pacific (ACP) countries express extreme dissatisfaction with EU sugar reform proposals and accompanying measures — Reform too fast, too deep, and too soon', June 22, 2005.

Schuurman, Frans (ed.) 2001. *Globalization and Development Studies: Challenges for the 21st century*. Sage.

Storey, Donovan. 2003. 'The Fiji Garment Industry.' OXFAM.

Sugar Commission of Fiji. 2003. 'Sugar Industry Strategic Plan.' *Fijian Studies: A Journal of Contemporary Fiji*, 1, 2. pp. 327–88.

Sydney Morning Herald, 'ALP Floats Single Pacific Market', September 30, 2005; *The Australian*, 'Howard Backs Jobs Over Trees', October 7, 2004, and 'PM's $4m Poll Deal With Union', October 7, 2005

Weekend Australian, 'Islander Jobs Push Attacked', October 1–2, 2005.

White, Michael. 2003. 'The Financial Viability of Fiji Sugar Corporation: An Assessment from the Corporation's Annual Financial Reports.' *Fijian Studies: A Journal of Contemporary Fiji*, 1, 2. pp. 286-300.

ENDNOTES

[1] A very useful account of the problems facing Fiji's sugar and garment (and tourist) industries is Narayan and Prasad, 2003, pp. 3-27. The end of the Multi-Fibre Arrangement has also ended the stable distribution of garment quotas to developing countries for imports to the EU and Canada.

[2] There is considerable evidence of government dithering and disagreement over reform of the sugar industry and there have long been 'allegations of corruption and mismanagement in the FSC [Fiji Sugar Corporation]'. See Narayan and Prasad, 2003, p. 19.

[3] Commentators and academics often agree that the percentage of people living from the informal economy who are resident in Suva is at least 60 per cent and many would argue that it is likely to be higher. Conversation with Professor Biman Prasad, USP.

[4] Those who represent the interests of international financial capital are now talking of a pressing need to 'shape the remittances market by shifting to formal systems'. It seems that while those whose interests are associated with global investment have been very successful in resisting the calls to regulate capital flow using measures such as the Tobin Tax, there is a considerable push to ensure that the flow of workers' funds in the form of remittances is subject to regulation and control. (Calls to regulate investor capital flows were particularly loud in the wake of the 1997 Asian financial crisis.) The Tobin Tax has been usefully profiled as a tax that 'would levy a charge on foreign exchange dealings. The idea is that the tax would discourage those people trading currencies just to make money, but would not deter foreign exchange transactions for purposes such as medium to long term investment, buying imports or tourism.' It has been noted that 'although there are technical objections to the Tobin Tax and other measures to slow [and regulate] the flow of capital, the primary obstacles are political'. See O'Brien and Williams, 2004, pp. 246 and 248-50. Apart from interests obviously associated with international capital (with companies such as Western Union and banks who favour ATM-facilitated remittances, there are also calls from such esteemed bodies as the World Bank, the ADB and even APEC to effect remittance controls. If these controls are implemented successfully (and this is by no means a foregone conclusion) the effects and the effectiveness of this form of financial regulation are unknown.

[5] See 'Fiji Gets $25 Million ADB Loan for Farmers', *Pacific Islands Report*, June 30, 2005; 'Summary of Australia's Overseas Aid Program 2005/6', AusAID, 2005; and 'Summary of Australia's Overseas Aid Program 2006-7', AusAID, 2006. See also Poul Nielson's (EC Commissioner for Development and Humanitarian Aid) speech to the ACP-EU First Meeting on Negotiation of Economic Partnership Agreement held in Brussels on September 27, 2002 and the EU press release dated October 4, 2002 titled 'Commission signs EURO 9 million aid package with the Pacific Island countries'. This speech is available on: http://europa.eu.int/rapit/start/ggi/guesten.ksh?p_action.gettxt=gt&doc=IP/02/1432/RA

[6] House of Commons International Development Committee, Sixth Report of Session 2004–05, titled 'Fair trade? The European Union's trade agreements with African, Caribbean and Pacific Countries', published March 23, 2005; the EC, 'The Cotonou Partnership Agreement', http://europa.eu.int/comm/development/cotonou/statistics/stat01

[7] Ibid., and Gillson et al., 2005, particularly p. 10. There has been (and still is) considerable confusion over the starting date for the reduction of benefits derived by ACP countries from the EC's Sugar Protocol. There are now 79 ACP countries. See Holland, 2002, particularly p. 113.

[8] Gillson et al., 2005, p. 4.

[9] Ibid., p. 9. Commentators who note that the protocol 'cannot be changed unilaterally' have also noted that 'it may be denounced by the EU, with respect to each ACP state and by each ACP state with respect to the EU, subject to two years' notice', ibid., p. 30. See also *Pacific ACP — EC EPA Negotiations Joint Road Map*, EC Directorate-General for Trade, Brussels, September 15, 2004.

[10] Gillson et al., 2005, p. 31.

[11] Ibid., p. 9.

[12] Alexander Downer's comment is as quoted in an editorial titled 'Stay Out of Politics, Army Told', *Fiji Times*, September 30, 2005.

[13] See Narayan and Prasad, 2003, p. 17; Reddy, Narendra, 2003, pp. 225–31; and Rao, 2003, pp. 301–14, particularly p. 304. See also White, 2003, pp. 287–300.

[14] Gillson et al., 2005, pp. 34–5.

[15] Narayan and Prasad, 2003, pp. 17–21; Narendra, Reddy, 2003, p. 266; and Fiji Sugar Corporation, 2003 pp. 315–26 (see particularly p. 316). It is worth pointing out that because sugar entering the EU under the preferential quota system is priced 'at levels similar to those paid to EU producers ... there is no price competition [within the EU] between preferential sugar imports and domestic [sugar beet] production. It is also worth noting that in 2003–04 the subsidy for exported excess EU white sugar was 511 per metric tonne. The extent of the above global market price paid by the EU is underlined when it is noted that when the EU re-exports sugar that is surplus to its own market it must supplement the average export cost in order to meet the price expectations of the international marketplace. See Gillson et al., 2005, pp. 31and 35–6. The March 2005 figures have been drawn from Economics Association of Fiji Panel Discussion, 2005.

[16] Isikeli Mataitoga's comment at the Economics Association of Fiji Panel Discussion, op. cit., pp. 35–6. See also 'Sugar Prices to Fall by July 2006', *Fiji Times*, July 1, 2005.

[17] Fiji's garment industry was nurtured in the wake of the 1987 coups. It was in 1987 that the Tax Free Factory scheme was introduced. This scheme allowed factories exporting more than 70 per cent of production to enjoy a tax holiday for 13 years. For most of the period of the scheme the tax holiday meant there was no customs duty on imported capital goods, no withholding tax on interest, dividends or payments abroad and when the final dividends to resident Fijian shareholders were taxed it was at 15 rather than 35 per cent. See Storey, 2003, p. 9.

[18] In China garment production is undertaken by rural-to-urban migrants who have been provided with little or anything in the way of services, housing, education and decent health and safety-based working conditions. Their pay is often withheld by their employers, usually for up to one year, and there are many reports of unpaid overtime being extracted from workers by using threats such as 'illegal' deductions from wages for refusing to work hours that are reported as often lasting from 7am to midnight. See Hannan, 2005 and 2006.

[19] See Storey, 2003, p. 26. It has been estimated that as much as 90 per cent of overtime done by Fijian garment workers was paid at 'the proper rate'. See DFAT, 2003, p. 32.

[20] See DFAT, 2003, pp. 8–9.

[21] While SPARTECA (signed at the 11th Pacific Islands Forum in July 1980) 'allowed garment manufacturers in Fiji preferential but non-reciprocal access to markets in Australia and New Zealand', throughout the 1990s (from 1991) it was an Import Credit Scheme (ICS) that provided particular benefit. See Storey, 2003, pp. 10–11. However, a number of commentators have voiced some criticism of this scheme. For example, Storey has pointed out that 'the ICS relationship proved very good for Australian fabric makers'. He has also approvingly cited an argument that notes that an agreement (i.e., SPARTECA) that nurtures 'a strong relationship between Fiji exports of garments to Australia and New Zealand and her imports of textile yarn from the same destinations ... implies that SPARTECA ... may not be, as claimed, a non-reciprocal trade arrangement'. See Storey, 2003, pp. 13–14. Nevertheless, there is no doubt that the ICS scheme provided considerable incentives to Australian companies who 'received import credits in return for exports of eligible TCF products; these credits could be [were] used to reduce the customs duty payable on eligible TCF imports ... Exports to Pacific Island Forum countries were eligible for credits despite the existence of SPARTECA'. See DFAT, 2003, p. 12. For its part, the Tax-Free Factory scheme, had given 'tax and duty concessions to companies exporting more than 95 per cent of their output. They are exempted from company tax for 13 years [beginning 1987] and import and licensing duties on capital goods and production materials.' The scheme also allowed for final dividends paid to Fijian resident shareholders to be taxed at 15 rather than the usual 35 per cent. As noted above, 'bilateral trade in TCF products between Australia and Fiji boomed in the 1990s but has fallen significantly as preferences have wound down'. See DFAT, 2003, pp. 3 and 11, and Storey, 2003, p. 9. For comment/explanation concerning the S–TCF scheme, see footnote 23 below.

[22] Storey, 2003, p. 11.

[23] The Australian Government began the S–TCF scheme in March 2001 with the express purpose of reducing the impact of the end of the ICS. 'The S–TCF scheme allows certain TCF goods manufactured in FICs [Forum Island Countries] but not meeting all the provisions of SPARTECA to enter Australia duty free in certain circumstances. In particular, excess local area content, or local content above 70 per cent, can be distributed to other imports with local area content below the required level, that is between 35 and 49 per cent.' As I have noted in the text above, this scheme has now been extended to the year 2011. See DFAT, 2003, p. 13. However, there seems to be a general agreement that this scheme 'has been ineffective, with many industry representatives, both in Fiji and Australia claiming it is overly

complicated and offers little incentive for Australia-Fiji TCF trade'. See Storey, 2003, p. 18. See also Radio Australia, *Pacific Beat*, September 30, 2005, http://www.abc.net.au/ra/pacbeat/stories/s

[24] See 'The Real Pacific Solution', *Dateline* Archives, June 15, 2005, http://news.sbs.com.au/dateline/index.php?

[25] DFAT, 2003, p. 1.

[26] Storey, 2003, p. 53. An estimate made in 2002 listed 18,000 people (80 per cent of them women) employed in Fiji's garment industry. However, when it is remembered that a further 3,000 workers lost their jobs when Ghim Li Garments in Lautoka was closed in April 2005, the current figure of 15,000 workers is likely to be too high. See DFAT, 2003, p. 3, and '3000 Lose Jobs as Fiji Garment Factory Closes', *Pacific Islands Report*, April 26, 2005.

[27] Quoted from Australian Bureau of Agricultural Resource Economics Report, 2002 cited in DFAT, 2003, p. 2.

[28] Narendra, Reddy, 2003, p. 269. See also DFAT, 2003, p. 16; and Economics Association of Fiji Panel Discussion, op. cit., p. 34. The most alarming reports estimate that 'the impact zone of the [sugar] industry collapsing would mean that approximately 250,000 people, who directly or indirectly depend on the sugar industry for their livelihood, would have nothing to sustain them'. Regardless of the figures they use, most commentators expect that rural and urban poverty will increase in the near future.

[29] *ADB Pacific Economic Outlook 2005*, p. 195, and Storey, 2003, p. 33.

[30] *ADB Pacific Economic Outlook 2005*. See section titled 'Fiji Islands', pp. 192–5, particularly p. 192.

[31] See Barr, 2003, pp. 199–200.

[32] In Australia, the administrators of the cities of Geelong, Newcastle and Wollongong have all been keen to emphasise the role of their resident universities when constructing their city's new image.

[33] Suva's population (or the population of other Fijian cities such as Lautoka or Ba) cannot be seen to have increased substantially due to employment offered in the garment industry; rather the garment industry has provided employment for existing residents and so the loss of jobs in this industry does not result in an outward population flow. It is more likely that workers will be driven from the formal to the informal sectors of the economy.

[34] Ton van Naerssen, 'Cities and the Globalization of Urban Development Policy', in Schuurman, 2001, pp. 177–95.

[35] It has been pointed out that if the issues surrounding the pressing need to restructure Fiji's sugar industry are not carefully addressed, the sugar towns of Labasa, Rakiraki, Tavua and Ba could become 'ghost towns'. Narayan and Prasad, 2003, p. 17.

[36] See 'Rapid Urbanization and the Politics of the Urban Poor', Handelman, 2003, pp. 174–98, and Pacific Islands Forum, 2005, pp. 14–17. Also see Biman Prasad, 'Economics Association of Fiji Panel Discussion', op. cit., p. 34, and Commonwealth of Australia, 2006, particularly pp. 5, 89 and 93.

[37] The same could be said for China's cities today where, in the wake of the end of the Multi-Fibre Arrangement, many of China's eastern seaboard cities are reporting a significant shortage of entry-level unskilled migrant workers.

[38] Kingsbury et al., 2004, p. 130.

[39] See Reddy, Naidu and Mohanty, 2003, p. 129. This group of particularly well-informed authors has noted that 'the debate over what comprises the formal and what [is] the informal sector, is still far from resolved'. Nevertheless, they have sensibly defined Fiji's urban informal employment sector as 'that part of the economy which is not part of the formal sector'. They go on to note that 'as such there is no official record of informal enterprises. Nor do such enterprises pay taxes'. They then give examples of informal enterprises: 'the road-side vendors, bottle sellers, back-yard mechanics and other crafts-men, domestic workers, hawkers and shoe shine boys. Included also are illegal activities like prostitution and drug peddling'. See also p. 131 and p. 146 and see 'EU-ACP Microfinance Framework Programme', http://ec.europa.eu/comm/europeaid/projects/acp/microfinance/index_en.htm, accessed on May 13, 2006.

[40] See Handelman, 2003, pp. 177–92. Also see Pacific Islands Forum, 2005. The authors of this paper cite 'numerous and serious' problems associated with urbanisation in Pacific Island countries and then attempt to put a brave face on matters by announcing that 'the concentration of large proportions of the population in urban areas is both a challenge and an opportunity for government … the opportunities of scale, scope and concentration presented could be seized upon, which would mean transport, health, education, sanitation and other services being provided'.

[41] See ibid. It is in line with this view that the Australian Government has recently been stressing the need to offer funding to assist Pacific Island governments, including the Fiji Government, to provide improved means of land administration and for the development of urban infrastructure ('from roads to solid waste management'). See Commonwealth of Australia, 2006 and *Australian Aid: Promoting Growth and Stability, A White Paper on the Australian Government's Overseas Aid Program*, Australian Government/AusAID, 2006.

[42] 'More Dollars From Abroad', *Fiji Times*, January 24, 2005. It has also been estimated that remittances from Fijian citizens living abroad have quadrupled since 1994. Radio Australia, *Country Profile*, http://www.radioaustralia.net.au/news/countries/FIJI_to.htm, accessed on September 30, 2005.

[43] See 'The Real Pacific Solution', op. cit., June 15, 2005; *Australian Aid: Promoting Growth and Stability*, and Commonwealth of Australia, 2006

[44] Connell and Brown, 2005, particularly p. 46.

[45] Ibid. and Cruz, 2004.

[46] It is argued that all Fijians who work overseas must be protected by their government. Samisoni Pareti, 'Human Labour — Lucrative Export — Fiji Rakes in $m From Overseas Jobs', *Islands Business*, May 2005. In a recent (April 2006) conversation with Roman Grynberg from the Pacific Islands Forum it was noted that the forum had been successful in an agreement with the EC that would allow Pacific Island workers to stay in EU countries for agreed periods and under agreed conditions.

[47] Ibid.

[48] See 'Fiji's Long, Risky Road to Kuwait', *Pacific Island Report*, April 22, 2005, and 'The Real Pacific Solution', *Dateline* Transcript, June 16, 2005, http://news.sbs.com.au/dateline/index.php?page=transcript&dte=2005-06-15&headlineid=

[49] Murphy, 2003, pp. 194–5.

[50] Bezard, 2004. It is also worth noting that in the case of the Philippines, where overseas workers and worker remittances are well established, research has shown that 'nine out of 10 [respondents] said they save in banks or through personal hoarding, with 70% maintaining bank accounts in the Philippines and 52% using an automated teller machine (ATM) for their payments or remittances'. See ADB Technical Assistance Report, 'Enhancing the Efficiency of Overseas Workers' Remittances', 2005, p. xiv.

[51] Chami, C. Fullenkamp and S. Jahjah, 2003, quoted in ADB Technical Assistance Report, op. cit., p. 9.

[52] Peter Stalker, 'Proceedings on the NOVIB Experts Meeting on Migration, Globalization and Development', held in the Netherlands, March 2003, cited in ADB Technical Assistance Report, op. cit., p. 9.

[53] *Australian Aid: Promoting Growth and Stability*, particularly p. 39

[54] House of Commons, International Development Committee Report, op. cit., particularly p. 23.

[55] *Fiji Times*, 'Sugar Prices to Fall by July 2006', January 7, 2005.

[56] ADB Technical Assistance Report, op. cit., pp. 1–2.

11. End of the Line? Globalisation and Fiji's Garment Industry

Donovan Storey

Introduction

The Fijian garment industry has had a short and often turbulent history. A product of the post-1987 coup strategy of export-led economic development coupled with key preferential trading arrangements, it experienced a dramatic early growth. The industry rapidly became a critical part of the economic structure of Fiji, often surpassing sugar as the number-one export sector. Immediately before the 2000 coup, about 105 factories were employing 18,000 to 20,000 workers and were exporting more than $F300 million in garments to Australia, the USA, Europe and New Zealand. This accounted for an estimated 28 per cent of local weekly waged employment (Keith-Reid 2001). Not only was the industry important in terms of providing employment to some of the estimated 17,000 annual new entrants into the labour market (new formal sector jobs typically average 2,000 annually), it was recognised as the largest employer of urban low-income earners in the country. From 1997 to 2001, garments replaced sugar as the country's leading export sector, accounting for an average 26 per cent of total exports (MoF and National Planning 2002: 15). It was even hoped that the Textiles, Clothing and Footwear (TCF) sector would reach $F1 billion in exports in 2005, that employment would reach 30,000, and that the industry would be in a position to move beyond its reliance on preferential trade agreements and its dependence on Australasia and the USA (FTIB 1999).

Despite the industry's rapid and impressive growth there has always been disquiet over the sustainability of the industry and the benefits of garment factory employment for employees, especially women. While the garment sector has proved to be a critical source of livelihood for low-income earners it has come in for sustained criticism over the years regarding poor labour conditions, low wages and exploitation of female labour (Harrington 2004: 496). Arguably these conditions have been accentuated by regional and global trade agreements, which essentially consign the garment sector in Fiji to a low-wage and low-skill role, thus perpetuating industry dependence and its workforce to 'working poverty'. The industry's economic bases have remained fragile and dependent on markets and buyers over which it has little control. Consequently the sector has struggled to mature in terms of becoming an efficient and sustainable industry. Reliance on preferential trade agreements, which gave rise to its rapid growth, has masked the garment sector's inability to add value to products and develop key markets outside the region. Some of these vulnerabilities have been exposed by the loss of quota access to the USA as a result of the expiry of the Multi-Fibre Arrangement (MFA) on January 1, 2005. Even government and some owners appear to be going cold on the sustainability of the industry, considering garments to be a 'stagnating' or even a 'dying' sector.

The garment industry's rise, particularly in the 1990s, was in many ways a case of 'dependent development' evolving on the back of preferential trading agreements, notably the South Pacific Regional Trade and Economic Cooperation Agreement (SPARTECA, 1980), the Import Credit Scheme (ICS) and the MFA. As a result, manufacturers have relied on a few key markets (notably Australia) for continued purchasing support and as a source of raw materials. Today this initially dominant role as a cut, make and trim industry has been all but eliminated by cheaper production sources in China and South-East Asia. As a result of the failure to move beyond this dependence on expiring trade agreements a number of factories closed during 2004–05. Recent estimates are that employment has dropped below 12,000, with an estimated 6,000–8,000 jobs lost in 2005 alone. In terms of economic impact, in the first few months of 2005 garments earnings were $A80.9 million below the 2004 figure, leading the ADB to forecast diminishing growth rates for the country as a whole (Radio New Zealand International, April 28, 2005). Production in the Fiji garment and footwear industry, measured in physical output, fell 55% between 2004 and 2005 (*Fiji Times* 2006).

Notwithstanding these challenges and criticisms, the garment industry has survived and continues to be critical for Fiji in economic growth, employment creation, foreign investment and skill development. While critics of the industry remain, particularly of its record on labour issues, no one would wish to see the sector disappear altogether. There are fewer than 12,000 people, mostly women, still employed in the garment industry and their incomes are critical for many urban poor households for which few fall-back positions exist (see Harrington 2004).

Regionalism and globalisation have played a significant role in shaping the Fijian garment industry. This chapter begins by examining the origins of the industry in terms of regional trade agreements, which have had a profound impact on the evolution of the sector and have, arguably, created an industry in Fiji without the skills and linkages that it needs to survive outside of those agreements. This chapter further depicts regional and global trade agreements as a response to global capitalism and a rapidly changing political economy of trade, which is neither predictable nor fixed. Nor is it always logical, often reflecting complex local responses to the flow of trade and its impact on domestic markets and labour, which are mediated and negotiated by states. Ironically, the challenge facing countries such as Fiji is not necessarily the inability to compete globally or regionally but their lack of power in renegotiating the trade agreements made by larger powers which seek to curtail and regulate the competitive impact of less-developed countries and their labour in the global marketplace. A problem which is then faced by states such as Fiji is how to have a greater impact on the governance of global capitalism and globalisation, which will lead to more opportunities for industries such as the garment industry (WCSDG 2005). However, the ability of Fiji to influence decisions made at a regional/global level is constrained by its small-state status as well as the small size and role of its factories in textile and garment production.

Nevertheless, players in the garment industry in Fiji are neither passive nor static in the face of these shifts and the debates that surround them. In the past five difficult years a number of factories have demonstrated an awareness of the changing nature of the trade and a degree of autonomy and agency in terms of repositioning themselves. Consequently an important aim of this paper is to trace these responses in order to demonstrate the range of strategies and decisions being made, the opportunities (or otherwise) for adaptation or regeneration, and what this tells us about globalisation (and more specifically global capitalism) in the region. Such an actor-network approach has been utilised to great effect in analysing the garment industry and globalisation in Turkey (Tokatli 2003) and Asia (Yeung 2000).

The local/regional/global origins of the Fijian garment industry

The garment industry in Fiji has had a number of local, global and regional spurs. In particular, it evolved within a unique political economy of growth and structural adjustment in Fiji and the region. The industry experienced rapid expansion after the coups of 1987 and the shift to foreign exchange earning policies. Its growth (in terms of income and employment) was also attributed to the gradual repositioning of the garment industries of Australia and New Zealand. The Fijian garment industry, then, was established to fill an important role following import-substitution policies and preceding the experience of wider globalisation (for example, through SPARTECA and the ICS).

The Tax-Free Factory/Tax-Free Zone scheme

The Tax-Free Factory (TFF) scheme of 1987 included incentives of a 13-year tax holiday, duty exemptions on capital goods and raw materials, and freedom to repatriate capital and profits (FTIB 1999: 85). Under the Tax-Free Factory/Tax-Free Zone (TFF/TFZ) scheme, companies exporting more than 70 per cent of their annual production were granted a corporate tax holiday for 13 years. Initially this was 95 per cent but was reduced. It also included a total waiver of licensing for import of capital goods and other production materials and exemption from customs duty on imported capital goods. In addition, there was no withholding of tax on interest, dividends and/or royalty payments paid abroad if they were not subjected to tax in the shareholders' country.

Furthermore, final dividends were taxed at a rate of 15 per cent when paid to resident shareholders compared with the then normal rate of 35 per cent. A further benefit for TFFs, together with the investment permits granted by the Fiji Trade and Investment Board and tax-free status, was the entitlement to import 'specialist labour' without passing the stringent tests of importing labour from other countries as provided for under the immigration laws (Narayan and Prasad 2003: 13).

Early growth was spectacular, with garment factories accounting for 78 of the 114 implemented TFF projects and 83.4 per cent of TFF employment between 1987 and 1990. Garment employment more than tripled from 3,000 to 10,000 in just four years (between 1988 and 1992) (Reserve Bank of Fiji 1993: 28). New Zealand (16 factories) was the leading source of early foreign ownership, followed by Australia (13) and Singapore (three) (TFF Sector Report n.d.: 2). The scheme came to be dominated by the burgeoning garment sector. In the period 1988–98, 57 per cent of all TFF investment was in the garment sector (Narayan 2001: 37) and garment employment became the dominant source of manufacturing jobs.

Table 1: Fiji's garment exports, 1986–2005 ($F million).

Year	Garment exports	As % of total exports	As % of GDP
1986	4.8	1.6	0.36
1987	8.8	2.2	0.66
1988	30.1	5.7	2.1
1989	97.3	14.8	6.24
1990	113.7	15.5	7.73
1991	131.1	19.7	7.14
1992	116.7	16.8	5.78
1993	128.7	17.5	5.92
1994	140.9	18.4	6.2
1995	185	21.4	6.62
1996	189.9	21.3	7.41
1997	200.1	22.9	7.7
1998	302.8	29.8	10.8
1999	322.1	31.6	11.4
2000	332.9	32.7	11.8
2001	313.9	30.8	11.1
2002	245.4	25.9	–
2003	252.7	26.8	–
2004	256.4	26.7	–
2005*	120	–	–

* provisional
Source: Data from Fiji Bureau of Statistics (various issues).

It was Australia, however, that came to dominate the industry. Export growth to Australia was spectacular through the 1990s as it moved from a quota to a tariff system and in 1991 Australia implemented the ICS, which gave incentives for Australian companies to source raw materials from Asia, add value in Australia and then export to Fiji for offshore processing where a finished product could re-enter Australia under SPARTECA. Under the scheme, Australian companies could claim a 'duty drawback' on imported Asian fabrics. Coupled with SPARTECA, the ICS offered further opportunity for the Australian garment industry to strengthen ties with the Fijian garment sector. Consequently, by the late 1990s, Fiji became a key supplier for major Australian brands such as Rip Curl, Country Road, Lee Jeans, Just Jeans, Hot Tuna, Voodoo Dolls and Wet Wet Wet. Indeed, the Fijian garment industry continues to be quite embedded in the production of recognisable global and regional brands. For example, brands identified through research in 2003 in Suva included Nike, Yakka, Target, Country Road, Adidas, David Jones, Lee Jeans, SirNormies and Ada.

Foreign ownership, particularly Australasian, has remained pronounced. In the late 1990s Cawthorne (2000) estimated that two-thirds of factories were foreign-owned, including 37 under Australian and New Zealand ownership. Nevertheless, one of the lesser-appreciated aspects of this growth was the number of Fijian-owned factories that were established (Gaunder 1990: 19). Certainly, local entrepreneurs saw great opportunity in the garment industry. They also played a key role in the early growth years of the 1990s and continue to be important today.

The Fijian garment industry: Dependent development

The preferential trade agreements that provided an important impetus to early growth proved a double-edged sword. SPARTECA and the ICS benefited manufacturing plants in Fiji, but also Australian businesses. Raw materials were more likely to be sourced from Australia, processed, then resold in Australia. Fiji's garment sector therefore developed a low-skill and low-technology cut, make and trim focus based essentially on a regional comparative advantage of low wages. Grynberg's (1997) study of 40 firms showed that 80 per cent were involved in cut, make and trim operations. There was little real reason then to invest in staff development or technology or to enter competitively into other markets. Throughout the SPARTECA regime, trade imbalances *increased* between Fiji and Australia/New Zealand. SPARTECA could be seen as having several weaknesses which held back the maturity of the industry, notably the rules-of-origin clauses; a lack of size which hampered competitiveness; a dearth of marketing and management skills; uncompetitive exchange rates; and supply constraints, especially the tied nature of raw material supply, which impeded flexibility and competitiveness (Rao 2002: 4). In a study critical of SPARTECA, Rao (2002: 23) concluded: 'There is a strong relationship between Fiji exports of garments to Australia and New Zealand and her imports of textile yarn from the same destinations. This finding implies that SPARTECA agreement [sic] may not be, as claimed, a non-reciprocal trade arrangement.'

As is the case with a number of smaller players in the global garment industry, Fijian factories became 'trapped in the role of manufacturing for others who collect[ed] the real rents' (Tokatli 2003: 1885). The 'real rents' are to be found in design, marketing, retailing and commercial and financial capital, not in industrial capital (Tokatli 2003: 1878). As such, and as is evidenced with a number of Fijian producers, the global garment industry is one of asymmetrical power dominated by commercial capital, leaving little room for autonomy or influence from small producers and manufacturers whose development and sustainability are therefore stunted for the benefit of powerful firms and states (Tokatli 2003: 1884).

While demand was strong and policies stable, the garment industry was able to flourish, albeit on an unequal footing. However, an underlying lack of competitiveness and autonomy was demonstrated, even during the boom times in the late 1980s and early 1990s, by Fiji's falling export trade to New Zealand. New Zealand had moved quickly into a trade liberalisation pattern in the late 1980s. Significant early New Zealand investment in the Fijian industry quickly declined. The reason was that Fiji, without preferential agreements (such as the ICS), remained unattractive to New Zealand investors even after the disestablishment of many of its own garment manufacturers. While New Zealand holds in place the derogation period for garment imports from Fiji until 2006, subject to the 25 per cent local content rule, investment has lagged. Of late, this has been mirrored in Australian patterns of investment.

Dependence on the Australian market became more pronounced as the industry grew. This included decisions on design, fabric sourcing and even marketing. At its peak, the Australian market absorbed more than 70 per cent of total Fijian exports in 1999 (Radio Australia, September 30, 2000). The ICS relationship proved very good for Australian fabric makers. In 1996, Fiji exported $F93 million in garments to Australia, but it *imported* textiles from Australia valued at $F65 million (Grynberg 1997: iii-iv). The main cost to Fiji was and is that it subsequently 'has had little propensity, or opportunity, for product development or growth into other export markets' (TCF Council and MoC 2003: 7). A further weakness is that it did not develop backward and forward supply and integration (for example, its own fabric making and dyeing capacity) (Gaunder 1990: 65). This is not, however, to deny the undoubted positive legacies: 'Over 13 years the industry developed rapidly and helped reduce the number of unemployed people. It served as a catalyst for the building, transport and food sectors. More families were able to afford education and better living conditions' (*Fiji Times*, March 13, 2001).

New initiatives: Breathing life or buying time?

Consequently, rather than a single cause, a combination of factors explains why the Fijian garment industry went into stagnation then steady decline: the political crisis of 2000; the end of a significant number of 13-year tax concessions; increasing competition from China and South-East Asia; the loss of the ICS (a clear consequence of single-market dependence) and the MFA; and reaction to impending trading agreement changes. Today the industry is being hollowed out, hampered by uncertainty, the loss to Asia of former customers and a cost structure that is uncompetitive by international garment sector standards. Given the lack of a single factor, this poses a range of potential challenges for policy-makers and those interested in the continued viability and health of the industry.

In response to this 'crisis', and the lobbying of Fiji's Prime Minister, Laisenia Qarase, there have been recent moves to breathe life back into SPARTECA, but little that is likely to create a more profitable and sustainable Fijian garment industry. In August 2003, Australian Prime Minister, John Howard, offered to conduct research on the garment industry in order to help its restructuring and he instructed his officials to 'prepare a package of substantial technical support to ease the industry's transition into the global market' (Fiji Government Online, August 16, 2003). This resulted in a 'scoping study' of the industry by the Australian Department of Foreign Affairs and Trade (DFAT) in which it stated that 'Australia feels some sense of responsibility for the industry's future' (DFAT 2003: 2). The same report also noted that 'a declining garment industry brings the prospect of adverse socio-economic impacts, including increased unemployment and growing poverty in the Suva area' (DFAT 2003: 6). The somewhat hurried passing of the Textile, Clothing and Footwear Investment Program Amendment Bill in late 2004 guaranteed Fiji's export agreement under SPARTECA for an additional seven years while Australia sought a 'structural adjustment' of Fiji's garment industry (*Pacific Magazine*, December 21, 2004). However, increasing the earnings through niche marketing of higher quality garments is hampered under SPARTECA, which allows access only to cheaper textiles for production. More recently, Prime Minister Qarase has also sought to diminish the rules-of-origin quota level, thus endorsing Fijian factories to re-export garments with even less local input.

Finally, some factories see hope in more 'local' markets. This includes tapping into Fiji's substantial tourism sector but also in the Pacific through PICTA, which came into force in April 2003. Through PICTA, 14 Pacific Island states have agreed to mutually remove tariffs and other barriers in order to free up trade in the region. The eventual aim is to move towards a regional free-trade area with the larger states (Fiji, PNG, Tonga and the FSM) eliminating trade barriers by 2010, with small island states and least developed countries having until 2012

(Oxfam 2003). Already several factories are placing more emphasis on building markets in Tahiti, Hawai'i and New Caledonia, though this trade remains small in scale.

The impact of shifting from regionalism to globalisation: three chronicles

In this section I outline the strategies being employed by various factories operating in different fields of regionalisation and globalisation. These range from 'local' companies, which engaged in exporting with the advent of tax-free zones and SPARTECA and which are now seeking to lessen offshore exposure, and those which have placed their success in the hands of regional, especially Australian, policies and which were established in response to SPARTECA and have developed strong links with Australasia, to factories that could be described as truly 'global' and have faced tremendous, perhaps insurmountable, challenges with the demise of the MFA and the rise of China in particular.

'Local companies'

Company C is based in Lautoka, on the western side of the main island of Viti Levu. Towards the end of the 1990s, Lautoka and nearby Nadi were very significant in terms of foreign-owned factories, but a number of these closed hurriedly during and after the political turmoil of 2000. Company C is going through difficult times. At its peak it employed 275 workers and manufactured for Rip Curl and Hot Tuna. Factory income averaged between $F30,000 and $40,000 a week. Some of these contracts continue, but most have been lost to factories in China. In particular, an earlier relationship with Rip Curl has been lost. Two of its factories closed in 2000, and today it occupies a second-storey location employing 30–40 workers for four or five days a week, depending on demand.

Finding new contacts is increasingly difficult. To offset this, the factory has opened its own outlet shops, to help tap into the local (tourist) market. The owner is currently putting faith in PICTA offering alternative markets and has already established markets for 'Hawaiian' or 'Bula' shirts in Tahiti (2,000–3,000 shirts a month) and the Cook Islands. The most consistent and high-value market is in surfwear. The company sees its comparative advantage remaining in terms of quick turnover (two weeks for most orders) and proximity for Australian and New Zealand buyers. As a small manufacturer, however, Company C feels that the cards are stacked against it in favour of the larger, mass-export factories to which policy and financial assistance are principally directed despite their low levels of value-adding. For example, 'export tours', which the Government had touted as helping create new markets, were seen as merely promoting 'the big politically connected Suva operations'. The new credit scheme with Australia (which replaced the ICS) was seen as 'worthless' and government assistance was 'nil' for local companies.

Company A has always been a family-owned enterprise. In the 1970s it was a shop, involved mainly in cutting and outwork, and employed seven or eight workers. In 1983, it evolved into a manufacturing factory. By 1986, the company was exporting to the USA and Europe. From 1989 to 1993, when it was a TFF, it shifted its focus to New Zealand. With greater competition into the New Zealand market making sales difficult, it then focused on Australia. Finally, with the demise of the ICS in 2000, the Australian market also dried up. At its peak, the company consisted of two factories, one for export production and the other for the local market. The export-only factory recently closed and operations were consolidated into the one factory. This effectively finished their knitwear trade: 'The coups were irrelevant compared with the loss of ICS.' The company owners essentially followed opportunities as they arose and to a great extent trade agreements dictated their markets and strategic planning.

Today 75 per cent of its output goes to the local market and the remainder is exported. Of the export markets that remain most are other Pacific Island countries, while two connections remain in New Zealand and just one in Australia. The factory is now moving into sports clothing and the owners estimate that the local market is now more lucrative than exports, particularly in terms of price per garment. Carlton Breweries, Mobil, schools, government departments and resorts are established buyers. They have the occasional 500- or 1,000-garment order from Australia and still have four years remaining on their TFF status. At its peak, the company employed more than 215 workers, but in 2003 the figure was only about 100. The owners estimated that their focus on the local market had saved at least 50 jobs, especially those of experienced staff, as cut, make and trim operations 'destroyed skilled people'.

In terms of Company A's relationship with overseas purchasers, price is everything. They have never been asked about working conditions, wages or been affected by compliance issues. On the question 'Do your buyers want value-added, more expensive garments, or cheaper ones?', the response was 'They want it all!' 'They basically quote the price in China to us, but we can't make that price. They want good stuff, for as cheap as possible.'

Company B originated from a tailoring business but in 1992 this long-time clothing store in central Suva was closed in favour of a tax-free-status company being formed with six employees. Though operations are controlled by an Indo-Fijian family, the company is 100 per cent Australian owned. High-quality materials are imported from the USA, Korea, and Taiwan and made into niche export products destined primarily for New Zealand and Australia. The factory has manufactured products for the Australian police and Australian Army and its labels include Mount, Traverse, Astral and Sienna and other outdoor brands.

It manufactures Polar Tec and Gore-Tex products and is moving towards small quantities of value-added garments. The factory employs about 140 workers and typically has enough business to operate 40-hour weeks. Labour is seen as the company's biggest expense and a key to profitability is to keep labour costs as close to the minimum wage as possible. However, to offset the loss of skilled staff, good workers are offered between 5 and 10 per cent more than the going rate. This is especially the case for skilled machinists. The future of the industry is seen as 'poor', especially in woven garments. The company has looked at relocating to China but does well enough through its own outlet shops in New Zealand and Australia, which are run from Fiji.

While engaging with the local and global market from very different starting points, these 'local' firms have struggled to find markets, are laying off staff and portray cut, make and trim operation days as numbered. Many of these operations have evolved from Indo-Fijian tailoring backgrounds and entered the export market through TFF status. They are now facing painful readjustments in trying to move towards more value-added markets — a move they feel is generally unsupported by trade policies. Some have gained success through selling locally and are emerging as exporters to other Pacific Island states. They see opportunities in PICTA, but are sceptical of ties to Australasia. By far, these factories are the greater number, and they span those that are experiencing modest growth to those who feel they are in terminal decline.

'Regional companies'

Company E is a large and well-established operation in Suva. It makes men's work shirts, business shirts and up-market ladies' wear. Some notable brands include King G and Yakka although most of its products are sold to wholesalers, which are also shareholders. Its biggest business at the moment is Australian demand for OH&S-compliant protective workwear. About 70–80 per cent of exports are bound for Australia, where the company also has its own distribution arm. This allows it some control over distribution. It also, through a partner, owns its own fabric mill, which avoids difficulties with raw material supply. The company currently employs 580 workers. Seventy per cent are women and 70 per cent are described as long-term employees, while a further 15 per cent have been with the factory for two to three years. The remainder are typically 'transient young people straight from their villages' who tend to move on regularly.

Company E strongly believes that to survive companies will have to find niche markets and add value to their products, but this will not be an easy transition and 'plenty of factories will be lost along the way'. It was remarked that anyone competing with China, or 'in their way … should just give up'. The comparative advantage that the Fijian garment industry retains after the expiry of the MFA is based on specialist and well-trained staff; short runs; the ability to adapt to specified styles; having English as the main language of communication; being close to Southern hemisphere markets; and having a fast turnaround time.

Consequently, Company E has invested significantly in technology. Even so, the industry was described as a 'bums on seats' one and labour costs were the key factor for profit margins and the reason for being in Fiji. It was argued that there was a 'ceiling on wages' and if you went over this you would be out of business: margins were described as 'generally tight … we sell and operate on minutes'. The company claimed to adhere strictly to the minimum wage. Still, there was an appreciation that the industry, at the bottom of the wage scale, had a responsibility to its workers. Company E had claimed some effort in improving its workers' lives apart from direct wage increases. Examples include the funding of a (sporadically open) nearby creche, health assessments for workers, an on-site health centre and a micro-finance and savings scheme, from which workers can draw money against their wages for emergencies. They feel that this policy has created a much better working environment, a more responsive workforce, and less potential for conflict with unions and buyers, which is 'good for business, after all'.

'Global companies'

Finally, there are those factories that have been integrated into the global economy in a quite different way. Many of these are Asian-owned and are exporting to the USA. The most spectacular (in terms of size) of these was Ghim Li. Ghim Li, which was Fiji's major exporter to the USA under the MFA, shut down factories in Ba, Lautoka, Nadi and Suva in April and May 2005 with the loss of 3,000 jobs, devastating communities in Lautoka and Nadi (*Pacific Magazine*, April 25, 2005). There were eight Ghim Li factories located in the west of Viti Levu employing about 4,000 workers at its peak. Ghim Li, a Singaporean-Malaysian company, is a truly global operation with 13 factories in Singapore, Malaysia, Indonesia, Brunei, China, Guatemala and formerly in Fiji. It produced for Wal-Mart, Sears, Warner Brothers and K-Mart. Its Fiji operations produced mainly for Wal-Mart in the USA.

Ghim Li Fiji owed its existence to the fact that it could utilise Fijian quota access to the US market as a 'quota-hopping' operation under the MFA. Its production was based on a high quantity of cheap products, which set it apart from other Fijian manufacturers as a truly 'globally competitive and focused' operation. It also operated a number of outsourcing factories in Fiji. Ghim Li was always a controversial enterprise, with its high use of female labour recruited from China, a protracted strike in 2003 over labour conditions and wages, and accusations of 'slavery' in terms of migrant labour housing and of being 'a sweatshop' in terms of the way it operated.

While the company gave regular assurances that its Fijian operation was profitable, it existed largely at a break-even level in terms of fulfilling quotas as part of much larger orders. Ghim Li Fiji certainly expanded significantly throughout the 1990s, including the purchasing in 2000 of at least two factories from manufacturers who were closing their operations down. However, there were always concerns about the ultimate sustainability of what many insiders saw as an 'opportunist' operation. In a matter of months after the end of the MFA, the company closed all its Fijian operations, perhaps giving the greatest indication of the limitations (some would say folly) of pursuing 'globally competitive' (i.e., low-wage) industrial operations in the Pacific.

The industry today and tomorrow: multiple futures

What do these factory examples indicate in terms of the industry, its present and its future? There are a number of common challenges but also a number of different futures. The 'heyday' of the cut, make and trim sector has passed, and today the more successful factories are seeking to add value, find niche markets (including within Pacific Island markets) and diversify products. While commenting on the Fijian garment industry at the 16th Australia Fiji Business Forum, Australian Minister for Foreign Affairs, Alexander Downer, stated, 'We must be realistic — increased competition means that reform is not a choice, it's a necessity. ... The choice is between having a textile [industry] that is competitive, or watching it disappear altogether' (*Pacific Islands Report*, September 1, 2003). But what should the nature of this comparative advantage be?

Despite noting the need for reform in order to add value, many industry representatives still 'sell' their role as a 'low-cost, flexible, short-run clothing and footwear manufacture' (TCF Council and MoC 2003: 3). Indeed, the industry promotes itself as playing the same 'strategic role' for the Australian TCF sector 'as Mexico and the Caribbean Basin do for the USA and Eastern Europe and Northern Africa do for Europe' (TCF Council and MoC 2003: 8). Dependence on Australia continues. There remain an estimated 50 garment factories exporting garments to Australia (*Daily Post*, September 8, 2003).

Today there is huge variation in the experiences of factories: some are on the brink of collapse while others are looking to the future with cautious confidence. With the loss of preferential trade agreements, and as a result of the shakedown of the past five years, it is a misnomer to talk of a single garment industry today. The garment sector is divisible by size, export orientation, target markets and comparative advantage, as well as positions in value chains. A number of factories had anticipated the effects of increased competition and upgraded their factories with equipment and staff training in order to be able to produce higher quality value-added products for niche markets. It is widely held that Asian exporters are either not interested in, or not geared for, providing higher quality garments in short time frames, especially for orders that are distinct from high-volume/standard-cut production lines. This was reiterated to me by industry representatives and factory managers who saw this as an opportunity (Interviews 2003). In addition, several larger operations (with consequences for the industry as a whole) have attempted to improve their relations with workers and even trade unions, seeing this again as a point of differentiation.

It is fair to surmise that these companies are the better-placed ones with regard to future prosperity. They are currently undergoing stress but surviving as they are embedded locally and globally. However, they are not necessarily typical of the industry as a whole. That they have found niche markets has a great deal to do with their unique and long-term links with wholesalers and their ability to develop markets purchasing high-quality, high-cost products. One such company even has subsidiaries in New Zealand and Australia. The exports of successful businesses such as this include suits, safety wear, business shirts and specialist clothing (such as Gore-Tex).

Who benefits from a competitive garment industry?

Labour issues, along with trade agreements, are a key factor in the sustainability and health of the garment industry in Fiji as well as its contribution to social and economic development. Garment manufacturing remains a highly labour-dependent process and labour costs are the most significant production factor (Dicken 2004: 331). Labour, working conditions, and particularly wages, are often contentious political issues worldwide in the garment sector. The 'sensitivity' of the industry is further compounded by the predominance of female labour in production. Dicken (2004: 332) estimates that 80 per cent of the global garment labour force is female. Often these workers have limited income and few other employment choices. Given the competitive price nature of the garment industry, this means that most employment is characterised by low wages and insecure employment.

The issue of wages and worker conditions is inseparable from that of where Fiji's garment factories want to position themselves in terms of the global garment value chain. Wages and labour issues have been perennial problems throughout the Fijian garment industry's short history and have really been seriously addressed only by a select few factories. Father Kevin Barr — a critic of Fijian development policy for a number of years — has lamented that, even during the growth years of the late 1990s, wages lagged behind the minimum wage for those living in urban areas, which was $A75 in 1999. At that time, garment workers' wages were as low as $A31 for 45 hours' work. Wages in the garment sector remain comparatively low by formal sector standards in Fiji. The experienced daily 'minimum' wage of $12.24 in 2002 fell significantly below the mean manufacturing wage of $14.93 in 2000, while mean wages across all sectors were $17.08 (RBF 2003: A42). As the Government wants wages to be related to productivity and profit, there remains a clear resistance to shifting to a higher-wage industry.

These issues are more pressing in terms of the garment industry because of the prevailing gender inequalities of income. Manufacturing had a worse gender/wage differential in 1997 than any other sector, with women's pay 63 per cent that of men's. Given that the garment sector employs about 12,000 women today, 'there is no doubt that the Fiji garment industry, with its rapid expansion of employment for women but very low wages, presents a substantial conundrum for people concerned with the economic position of women' (ILO/UNDP 1996: 16).

Table 2: The minimum wage: a liveable wage?

Year	Learner	Other
1991	$0.65	$0.85
1999	$1.05	$1.26
2002	$1.15	$1.36
2004	$1.21	$1.43

Note: A 'learner' is described as someone with less than six months' experience though factories are not legally bound to this definition.

While some have argued that Fiji's comparative advantage lies in its skilled and comparatively well-educated workforce, others still see the future health of the industry as being based on low wages. They consider that wage increases will be the final blow to the sector:

The cost of garments is not going up, but the price of making them is. In 1983 labour was 40c, it is now $1.15 — for someone with no experience! After five months this has to be $1.35. For good ones you need $1.70. Otherwise they are leaving the industry for shopkeeping jobs, etc., which pay more than $2. But basically these are school dropouts! (Factory owner interview 2003)

This has created a situation where garment employees can be accurately described as 'the working poor'. Eradicating poverty in Fiji, as Father Barr has noted, is not only a matter of creating employment. Wages are also a critical issue. A recent study has shown, based on 1996 figures, 'that 46.8 per cent of those who were in full-time employment earned wages below the poverty line. ... Of these 67.9 per cent were women.' Barr estimated that in 2002 the poverty line in urban areas was about $128–132 a week for a family with two or three children (Barr 2003: 200), while full-time garment wages averaged between $40–60 a week. Cawthorne (2000) has also estimated that approximately 80 per cent of employees are women earning wages that are below the poverty line. Even then, union organisers feel that the minimum wage is not met in many factories, a situation compounded by a lack of enforcement by the Ministry of Labour (Interviews 2003).

Responsibility for this 'working poverty' cannot be laid solely at the feet of the industry itself. Government policy and trade agreements have also played a role and perpetuated this situation. The Garment Industry Wages Council came into being in 1990 and set a wage level of between 65 cents and 85 cents an hour, well below other sectors, including manufacturing in general, and again, below the then poverty line. A critical factor in the profitability of the industry for owners has been in successive governments pursuing a 'competitive wage policy'. This has been done through regular devaluations of the dollar, baulking at the idea of a minimum wage, and restrictions on trade unions: 'Yet the policies may have done more to shape the structure of the industry than guarantee its expansion' (ILO/UNDP 1996: 17).

The losses to the industry resulting from a low-wage strategy might be higher than the immediate gains. Even in the early years of the push to exporting it was noted that the Fijian garment industry had no chance of competing with Asian countries and that it needed to move towards a quality, value-added, niche-marketing strategy (FWRM 1986). To break out of the dependence on preferential agreements and reliance on the Australian market, the TCF Council of Fiji has argued that the industry needs to create higher efficiency, productivity and quality: 'only by investing in human and managerial capital will the industry be able to create comparative advantage and keep pace with technological progress' (TCF Council and MoC 2003: 23).

However, the garment industry remains dependent on producing cheap, poor-quality garments that cannot possibly compete with garments made in Asian countries whose costs of labour and utilities are five to 10 times lower than Fiji's (TCF Council and MoC 2003: 23–4). Unfortunately, this vision, which is unrealistic and contrary to sustaining social development through employment, is how Australia and New Zealand see the garment sector, and these views are in many ways buttressed by the Fijian private sector and government.

The end of the line?

Globalisation, or more accurately global capitalism, poses a very difficult set of challenges to industry in small island states. The Fijian garment industry is essentially a creation of special access to the Australian, New Zealand and US markets under preferential trade arrangements. Now that these agreements have ended, or are coming to an end, the industry finds itself at a significant crossroads.

The challenge for the garment industry is in the erosion of preferences and a shift from a focus on production quantity to niche marketing and quality (MoF and National Planning 2002: 12). The way forward is to produce for niche markets, such as corporate suits and women's wear, and not in the volumes market occupied by China (MoF and National Planning 2002: 15). Perhaps the *greater* challenge is to establish trading agreements which allow this. As Nadvi (2003) has noted, 'Trade preferences such as the MFA quotas can be an important driver in promoting industrial development, but do not necessarily encourage moving up the value chain into functions with a higher value.'

Nadvi has further noted that the key to post-MFA survival will be in upgrading technology, enhancing linkages with the textile sector, reducing delivery times and improving product quality. One strategy for garment exporting countries which are being squeezed by the loss of preferential agreements and by low-cost competition, is to upgrade to higher value-added activities within the value chain. The downside of this is that a number of the least-skilled workers will lose their jobs, replaced by higher-skilled workers and more efficient technology. To date, the industry in Fiji has not developed along these lines. It has evolved essentially as a service industry to satisfy buyer and consumer preferences in countries seeking competitively priced garments. Key inputs, designs and even ownership were and are still external to Fiji's garment industry development. Change will not be easy and will depend on more than merely extending the relationships that have created a number of problems.

This challenge is taking place alongside rapidly shifting regional and global trading contexts. The Australasian markets continue to 'liberalise' and prefer to seek bilateral free trade arrangements with North American and Asian countries, not small island Pacific states. The emergence of Chinese production is also critical. It is simply not conceivable for Fiji to be competitive with what China, or any other low-cost Asian country, exports. Progressive government initiatives are critical to the survival of the garment sector. To date, government policies have effectively exacerbated the low-quality/low-wage cul-de-sac the industry finds itself in. A cheap-labour policy has not helped in the development of a quality-oriented, high-skilled, value-adding industry.

Though some within the Fijian industry have repositioned themselves, there remains doubt as to whether they can ever become truly competitive without preferences in the global economy. Likewise, other industry representatives see 'no way out except for government assistance', including efforts to secure greater trade access to the US market (*Daily Post*, June 18, 2001). Robert Read has argued that it is 'not surprising that many countries have sought or are seeking strategic refuge in regional trading agreements … with neighboring states' (Read 2004: 365) in response to globalisation. There are a number of innovations emerging, some more likely to be successful than others. In January 2002 the Fijian Government appointed US-based Sandler, Travis and Rosenberg (www.strtrade.com), a trade advisory service, to lobby on its behalf to negotiate preferential access for Fiji's garments into the US market. The firm had been contracted to pursue an African Growth and Opportunity Act (AGOA)-type agreement, which includes duty-free access to the USA for African garments.

The Fijian Government and the Fiji TCF Council hoped that such a deal would help exports to the USA reach $US400 million ($A539 million) (Fiji Government Online, February 1, 2002). However, the recourse to regionalism and regional agreements is, for large and small states, 'a political act advanced by social and political action, or corrective, towards a political goal' (Knutsen 2003: 227–8). AGOA, for example, which opens the doors for duty-free and quota-free access to the USA for garment manufacturers in Africa, stipulates conditions in the form of market-based economies, a development of political pluralism and the rule of law, the elimination of barriers to US trade and investment, the protection of intellectual property rights, combating corruption, poverty reduction, and policies against child labour and for health care and education, human rights and workers' rights. Clearly, AGOA is an example of political leverage through 'free' trade agreements.

This leverage can, however, work both ways. Throughout 2005, Prime Minister Qarase linked the future wellbeing of the garment industry to Fiji's commitment to good governance and to globalisation. Calling for Australia to be a 'good mate' and 'open the door' to more relaxed import rules, Qarase has publicly commented that the country will face increased danger of instability, social breakdown and higher crime rates if the industry were allowed to fail. Qarase further contended that globalisation was 'fatally flawed' if markets were closed off and Fiji might reassess its commitment to trade agreements if the end result was devastation of its economy (*Pacific Magazine*, May 14, 2005).

The garment industry in Fiji remains important. Any complete collapse would create a human and economic crisis. Though low even by local standards, garment wages are critical in supporting the urban poor. The garment industry still employs the majority of manufacturing labour, and a disproportionate number of workers are women of all racial groups. Government officials have inadequate policy responses on the question of alternative employment, seeing opportunities in the depressed rural sector. A further or full collapse of the industry would substantially increase poverty and would likely represent a threat to social and political stability. Substantial effort is needed to refocus the industry for a number of reasons.

The UN (UNDP 2003: 1) has argued that 'the expansion of trade guarantees neither immediate economic growth nor long term economic or human development'. Trade is a means to an end, not an end in itself. What are critical in transforming trade into development are the internal and external institutional and social conditions that allow companies and workers to reap the rewards of trade and give countries and industries a sense of security. It is essential that efforts be made in multiple areas which seek to develop progressive industry initiatives as well as more directly enhancing the lives of female factory workers. The potential of Fiji's garment industry in shifting into higher value chains and as a tool for poverty alleviation is dependent on the evolution of the industry *as well as* the enhancement of labour rights and rewards.

In conclusion, the future for Fijian garment manufacturers will most likely come from the following two directions: first, the ability of certain businesses to scale up into value-added products which allow greater control over quality and prices above that of the cost of labour; and secondly, trade agreements which allow and encourage the shift away from dependent low-waged industries in the Pacific. The challenge is for Pacific Island countries to develop high-quality niche products and for the region's more developed countries to develop trading policies which facilitate this shift. In contrast, an argument based solely on global comparative advantage is facile and offers little hope for any form of economic or human development through trade among Pacific Island countries. Somewhat inevitably, these experiences might lead to a growing reluctance to commit to further 'free' trade arrangements in the future.

Acknowledgements

I wish to acknowledge Oxfam New Zealand for the commissioning of some of this research in 2003–04. The Oxfam report that examined the garment industry and labour issues can be found at http://www.oxfam.org.nz. At the time of writing, \$F1 = \$A0.80.

References

Barr, Fr. K. J. 2003. 'Wages councils and just wages in Fiji.' *Fijian Studies,* 1 (1). pp. 199–208.

Cawthorne, P. 2000. 'Fiji's garment export industry: An economic and political analysis of its long-term viability.' *School of Economics and Political Science Working Paper* ECOP2000-3. University of Sydney.

Dicken, P. 2004. *Global Shift: Re-shaping the global economic map in the 21st Century*. London: Sage.

Department of Foreign Affairs and Trade. 2003. *Future Directions for Fiji's Garment Industry: Scoping study*. Economic Analytical Unit, August.

Fiji Government Online: http://fiji.gov.fj

Fiji Reserve Bank. 1993. 'The Tax Free Factory/Tax Free Zone scheme in Fiji.' *Pacific Economic Bulletin*. pp. 27–34.

Fiji Times. 2006. 'Fiji Garment Industry Takes 55 Percent Plunge'. 5 April.

Fiji Trade and Investment Board. 1999. *Fiji Product Directory 1999–2000*. Suva.

Fiji Women's Rights Movement. 1986. Submissions to the Garment Tribunal.

Gaunder, Radha K. 1990. *In-depth study of the garment industry in Fiji*. Report prepared for the Forum Secretariat, Suva.

Grynberg, Roman. 1997. *A survey of the Fiji garment export industry*. Economics Department, University of the South Pacific.

Harrington, C. 2004. '"Marriage" to capital: The fallback positions of Fiji's women garment workers.' *Development in Practice*, 14 (4). pp. 495–507.

ILO/UNDP. 1996. *Fiji: Towards equality and protection for women workers in the formal sector*. Suva: International Labour Organisation and the United Nations Development Program.

Keith-Reid, Robert. 2001. 'Uncertain Future for Fiji's Garment Industry.' *Pacific Magazine and Islands Business*, June.

Knutsen, H. M. 2003. 'Globalisation and the Garment Industry in Sri Lanka.' *Journal of Contemporary Asia*, 33 (2). pp. 225–50.

Ministry of Finance and National Planning. 2002. 'Rebuilding Confidence for Stability and Growth for a Peaceful, Prosperous Fiji.' *Strategic Development Plan 2003–2005*. Suva.

Nadvi, K. 2003. 'Cutting cloth to fit: Competing in global garment value chains.' *Insights*, June.

Narayan, P. 2001. 'Globalisation of the garment industry: Implications for Fiji's economy.' *Development Bulletin,* 55. pp. 36–8.

Narayan, P. and B. Prasad. 2003. 'Fiji's sugar, tourism and garment industries: A survey of performance, problems and potentials.' *Fijian Studies,* 1 (1). pp. 3–27.

Oxfam, 2003. *Pacific Islands Free Trade Agreements*. Oxfam Briefing Paper for the Pacific Islands Forum Leaders Meeting, August 2003.

Rao, G. 2002. 'Fiji exports to Australia and New Zealand under SPARTECA agreement.' *USPEC Working Paper* 5/2002. University of the South Pacific.

Read, R. 2004. 'The implications of increasing globalization and regionalism for the economic growth of small island states.' *World Development*, 32 (2). pp. 365–78.

Reserve Bank of Fiji. 2001–03. *Quarterly Reviews*.

Tax Free Factory Sector Report. n.d. The performance of the Tax Free Factory sector as at June 1990 and June 1991.

Textile, Clothing and Footwear Council of Fiji and Fiji Ministry of Commerce. 2003a. *Productivity Commission Inquiry into Australia's TCFL Industries Post 2005 Assistance*, March.

Textile, Clothing and Footwear Council of Fiji and Fiji Ministry of Commerce. 2003b. *Productivity Commission Inquiry into Australia's TCFL Industries Post 2005 Assistance.* Supplementary Submission, May.

Tokatli, N. 2003. 'Globalization and the changing clothing industry in Turkey.' *Environment and Planning A*, Vol. 35. pp. 1877–94.

UNDP. 2003. *Making Global Trade Work for People.* London: Earthscan.

World Commission on the Social Dimensions of Globalisation. 2005. 'A Fair Globalization: Creating opportunities for all.' *Globalizations,* 2 (2). pp. 241–9.

Yeung, H. W.-C. 2000. 'The dynamics of Asian business systems in a globalising era.' *Review of International Political Economy,* 7. pp. 399–432.

Corporate and State Governance in Mining and Forestry

12. Global Capital and Local Ownership in Solomon Islands' Forestry Industry

Tarcisius Tara Kabutaulaka

As humanity ventures further into the 21st century, we are constantly being reminded of how global forms and processes have reached even the most remote corners of the world. This is what, in contemporary mantra, is referred to as 'globalisation' — the term used to describe the increasing integration of global communities.

In the past decade there has been considerable inquiry into the origins, nature and impact of globalisation, and the threats and opportunities it offers. Even its most resolute critics would admit that the forms and processes that encompass globalisation have reached even the most isolated corners of the globe. Today, for example, it is not unthinkable that children in relatively remote places such as the Weather Coast of Guadalcanal in Solomon Islands have tasted Coca-Cola and can buy it from a village store, the same product that can be bought from a 7-Eleven shop at a street corner in New York. This interaction between the 'global' and the 'local' was dramatically illustrated in the 1980 film *The Gods Must Be Crazy*, in which Xi, a Kalahari Bushman, encounters technology for the first time in the form of a Coke bottle. He takes it back to his people and they use it for many tasks. But when they start fighting over it, he decides to return it to the gods, from whom he thinks it has come. In his quest to throw the bottle over the edge of the Earth, Xi encounters Western 'civilisation' and is fascinated and captured by it. In the process, Xi also influences Western perceptions about Kalahari Bushmen, their deep and complex knowledge of the bush, their ability to survive in it, and their innovative use of the Coke bottle.

Similarly, in many cases, the more local communities attempt to resist globalisation and 'throw its evils over the edge of the Earth', the more they engage with it. Understanding how the global and the local interact is vital for helping local communities formulate strategies to deal with and benefit from globalisation. This chapter uses natural-resource development to explore the interaction between global forces and local communities. It examines how local communities react to global forces, with a focus on the Pacific Islands and Melanesia, with particular reference to Solomon Islands' forestry industry.

Here, I assert that local communities are not simply passive victims of global forces. Rather, they actively interrogate, negotiate, strategise and engage with global forms and processes, and use them to meet local needs and demands. This assertion is based on the premise that Melanesian societies, rather than being the 'traditionalised', static and timeless entities that conventional anthropology sometimes presents them to be, are dynamic and engaging. I am not suggesting that there is an equal power relationship between the local and global. Of course, the power relationship is often tipped in favour of the global, but the local is not always simply a passive victim of globalisation.

Global capital and local resources

Transnational corporations driven largely by the desire to maximise profit are among the most aggressive agents of globalisation. They create and transfer capital, ideas, languages, cultures, values and ways of life across national, ethnic and linguistic boundaries. In the process, they integrate societies around the world into the cash economy, the backbone of the capitalist system, which pushes global forms and processes to remote parts of the globe.

This is vividly illustrated by the documentary film *Advertising Missionaries* (Aspire Films 1996), which shows how theatre is used to advertise and introduce Western goods to previously 'untouched' villages in the remote Highlands of PNG. Behind the Papua New Guinean actors are transnational corporations which own the products and ensure they reach anyone who has the potential to make and spend money. To acquire these products, people in isolated parts of the globe — like those in the Highlands of PNG — have to participate in the cash economy by allowing goods and capital from industrialised countries to flow into their communities. This is often facilitated by the export of Western media — including television programs and popular culture/music — that promote the 'large-scale transfer of meaning systems and symbolic forms' (see Hannerz 1997: 107) and in turn transform cultures and consumption habits. For many of these communities the only way that they could have access to the cash economy is to sell their labour and natural resources.

History is littered with stories of how cheap labour from developing countries has been used to support industries that are registered and based in developed countries, or owned by people who live in industrialised countries. It was, for example, the massive export of African, Asian and Pacific Islander labourers to the Americas, the Caribbean, Australia and other Pacific Islands such as Fiji, Samoa and Hawai'i in the 17th, 18th and 19th centuries that supported plantation industries vital for the production of capital that later became the force pushing contemporary global forms and processes. Horton and Horton (2005: 7) provide an insightful account of how African labour in the form of slaves 'played a profoundly important role in the making of the United States'. Similarly, it was labourers from the 'South Seas' — Solomon Islands, Vanuatu and PNG — who were used in the development of sugarcane plantations in Queensland, Australia (Moore et al. 1990). Indian labourers were shipped to Fiji and the Caribbean to work in the sugarcane plantations (Lal 2004; Mintz 1995).

Labour from developing countries continues to play an important role in the production and transfer of goods and capital. It is, for instance, common for businesses to take advantage of cheap labour in developing countries through outsourcing arrangements. In the USA, for example, it is widely known that the person who answers the phone at a call centre might be located in Bangalore, India. Similarly, most of the goods sold in Wal-Mart shops are produced in China, using cheap Chinese labour. Recently, the host of *The Tonight Show*, Jay Leno, commented that one of the few positions in the USA not yet outsourced was the country's Presidency. Such comments might be humorous, but they illustrate the significance of outsourcing in our contemporary world.

Much of the world's labour has been used for the extraction and development of natural resources such as oil, minerals, timber, fisheries and the cultivation of land for large-scale plantation agriculture. A significant percentage of the natural resources needed to sustain the capitalist market economy are located in Africa, Asia, the Caribbean and Oceania. In 2005, for example, the sub-Saharan countries of Africa exported about 1.5 million barrels of oil a day to the USA and Canada and 700,000 barrels a day to Europe to keep the industries of those places afloat and to sustain their mass-consumption societies (Kotch 2005: 56). On the other hand, much of the capital invested in the mining of oil from countries such as Nigeria, Angola, Gabon, Sudan, Chad and Congo is from American oil giants such as Chevron and Exxon Mobil. Similarly, most of the transnational companies that extract oil and mineral resources in South American countries such as Venezuela, Bolivia, Chile, Mexico and Peru originate from North America and Europe.

In the Pacific Islands it is Australian companies that dominate the mining industry in PNG, Solomon Islands and Fiji, while Japanese-, Korean- and Taiwanese-registered companies dominate the fisheries industry. Malaysian and Korean companies dominate the forestry industry. In PNG the recently established Gas to Queensland (GTQ) project at Kutubu is led by Chevron, the US petroleum giant (Tiensten 2001: http://www.pomcci.org.pg/hiri2001/Tiensten.doc, accessed on February 9, 2006). Large-scale oil palm, coconut and cocoa plantations were originally dominated by British companies such as Levers Brothers, but are increasingly being taken over by Australian and Asian companies.

This has led to many developing countries becoming economically dependent on foreign capital for the extraction and export of natural resources. Sub-Saharan countries such as Nigeria and Angola, for example, have become heavily dependent on oil exports to North America, Asia and Europe. In recent years, '[t]hree factors — rising global demand for oil, increasing deepwater reserves off West Africa, and threats to oil supplies from the Middle East — have pushed both North America (mainly the USA) and Asia (mainly China) to import more oil from sub-Saharan Africa' (Kotch 2005: 56).

Similarly, many Pacific Island countries, especially the relatively larger Melanesia countries, are economically dependent on natural resources. Development plans in these countries are tied to the availability and exploitation of natural resources. For many remote communities, natural-resource exploitation is often the only source of income generation. Hence, activities such as mining and logging are often accepted as the way forward in the development process, and communities close to these large-scale natural-resource development projects are greatly influenced by them. Discussions of globalisation and the Pacific Islands highlight the importance of transnational corporations in natural-resource development (Lockwood 2003; Firth 2000).

In the past two decades the flow of capital to developing countries for purposes of natural-resource development has been exacerbated by the push for economic liberalisation, which encourages — and in some cases forces — countries to not only open their markets but allow foreign investors to exploit their natural resources. This is pitched as a necessary part of the development process.

For Pacific Island countries, access to natural resources for large-scale commercial development is often complicated by the fact that land and inshore fisheries are communally owned. This communal ownership and control of resources is in many cases recognised and protected by law. In the Melanesian countries of PNG, Solomon Islands and Vanuatu, for example, this is recognised as 'customary' ownership. In Solomon Islands, more than 80 per cent of land is 'customarily' owned. This means that potential investors have to deal with not only the State and individual owners, but with entire communities before any natural-resource development initiative can take place. Anyone who has ever been associated with natural-resource development in the Pacific Islands would attest to the number of people and the multitude of interest groups that need to be consulted. Hence, while global capital is important, local communities, because of their ownership of land and inshore fisheries, can influence how their resources are exploited. This is not to suggest that they have, in the past, done so successfully. Rather, it is to say that given appropriate capacity they have the potential to influence the processes and outcomes.

In realising the potential power that they have, landowning communities often mobilise themselves primarily to maximise resource rent. How they mobilise themselves and the way they use resource rents have been the subjects of much discussion (see Hviding and Bayliss-Smith 2000; Turia 2003; Ernst 1999; Filer 1997; Foale 2000; Golub 2004).

In this discussion it is important to note that 'local communities' are not always a homogeneous entity, existing in harmony. Rather, they are often a dynamic group with members who have varying interests and degrees of exposure to the world. There are women, children, elders, those with formal education, government officials, aspiring big-men, con-artists, etc. In some cases, landowning communities reorganise themselves in order to deal successfully with corporate powers (see Ernst 1999; Fa'anunu unpublished; Filer 1998; Foale 2000; Gerritsen and Macintyre 1991; Golub 2004). Rather than simply watch global forces take over their societies, local communities (either collectively or as individuals) react to and come to terms with these global forces.

We often equate globalisation with the expansion of Western ideas, cultures, values, lifestyles, technology, people and capital. Increasingly for many Pacific Island countries, however, globalisation also involves the flow of people, ideas, cultures, values, technology and capital from Asia. It is, for example, Asian people, capital and markets that dominate the Solomon Islands forestry industry.

Solomon Islands forestry: A brief background

Commercial logging started in Solomon Islands in the 1920s. Bennett documents the story of the Vanikoro Kauri Timber Company (VKTC), an Australian-owned company, that harvested kauri timber (*Agathis macrophylla*) on Vanikoro Islands in the eastern Solomons from 1926 until 1964. During that period the company struggled to make a profit, and eventually closed its operations and left due to the high cost of production and transportation, and restrictions on access to potential markets (see Bennett 2000a).

Large-scale commercial logging is, however, a recent phenomenon. As Frazer (1997a: 45) notes, in the past three decades there have been two distinct regimes, 'each marked by differences in the ownership and location of the forests being harvested, the number and size of the companies engaged in export logging, and government management of the industry'. The first was from 1963 to the early 1980s, when most logging took place on government land, or customary land leased by government. During this period, under the Colonial Government's *Timber Ordinance*, it was the Government that had the responsibility for acquiring land and giving logging licences to companies interested in harvesting timber. At that time the British-registered company Levers Pacific Timber (a subsidiary of Levers Brothers) monopolised the timber industry, accounting for about 75 per cent of log production (Bennett 1998: 2).

The second period began in the early 1980s and continues today. This period is marked by a shift from government land to customary land and an influx in the number of foreign (especially Asian) companies with logging concessions. Between 1981 and 1983, for example, the number of foreign companies with logging licences increased fourfold (Frazer 1997a: 46). The beginning of this period coincided with an event that marked an important turning point in the history and development of the logging industry in Solomon Islands: in 1982, Levers Pacific Timbers' logging camp and equipment at Enoghae on New Georgia in the Western Province were destroyed by landowners opposed to the company's operations. This led to the subsequent establishment of the *North*

New Georgia Timber Corporation Act, which allowed customary landowners to set up logging companies (Tausinga 1989). The Enoghae incident demonstrated the displeasure of local landowners and their leaders with attempts by the Government to facilitate the allocation of logging rights on customary land to Levers. The *Forest and Timber Amendment Act (1977)* had recognised the customary landowners' rights to the forest and their ability (albeit via the cumbersome process of adjudicating claims to rights by the Area Council) to allocate these within the process. The *North New Georgia Act* enhanced this recognition of landowners' authority over land and forestry resources (Tausinga 1989).

Figure 1. Log production, export and estimated sustainable yield for natural forest (CBSI log export records; Forestry Review 1995; ADB 1998)

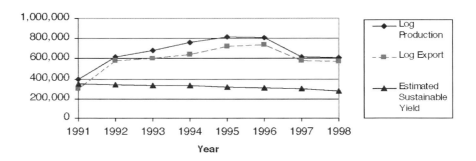

This period also coincided with the first Solomon Mamaloni Government's time in office. This was a government known for its pro-logging policies, which encouraged Asian companies to invest in the logging industry. The Mamaloni Government pushed for a shift away from a concentration on Western investors to 'looking north' towards Asia. The Government also wanted to encourage landowners' active participation in the industry (Bennett 2000; Frazer 1997).

This period was also characterised by a rapid increase in log production. In 1989 the volume of log production was about 300,000 cubic metres as compared with about 700,000 and 800,000 cubic metres in 1993 and 1996 respectively (see Figure 1). This rapid increase was due to an increase in the number of logging companies with logging concessions, a shift into customary land, the increasing demand for hardwood timber in international (particularly Asian) markets, an increase in the price of hardwood timber, and Solomon Islands' increasing economic dependence on log exports (Duncan 1994; Price Waterhouse 1995).

The rapid increase in log production led to harvests going beyond the estimated sustainable yield. In 1992, for instance, it was estimated that about 13 million cubic metres of commercial timber was harvestable using conventional logging methods. By the mid-1990s, production was way above the potential sustainable yield. Log production in 1994 and 1995, for example, was 735,000 and 826,000 cubic metres respectively. These figures were more than double the potential sustainable yield for those two years, of 294,896 and 275,710 cubic metres respectively (CBSI 1996). If these levels of log production continued, it was estimated that the logging industry would not be sustained for another decade (Montgomery 1995; Price Waterhouse 1995; Frazer 1997).

Predicting the depletion of forests is, however, not an exact science. In 2005, nearly a decade later, authorities were saying that forests would be depleted in 15 years if harvested at the current rate, which was higher than it was in 1997 (CBSI 2006).

Figure 2. Log volume to major export destinations 1994-1998 (Log export data from CBSI.)

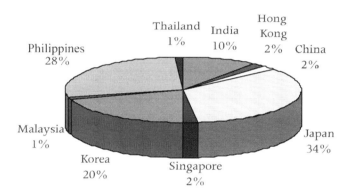

In 1997 there was a sudden decline in log production, due mainly to the Asian economic crisis and the collapse of Asian timber markets. This was especially serious because of Solomon Islands' dependence on the Asian log markets (see Figure 2). The ADB (1998: 54) estimated that the volume of log production in 1996 was 811,000 cubic metres while in 1997 it dropped to 637,000 cubic metres (see Figure 1).

Despite the decline in production, the Central Bank of Solomon Islands (CBSI) reported that in 1998 the volume of logs harvested from natural forests did not drop to the extent anticipated at the beginning of that year and was still well above the estimated sustainable level. For instance, while the volume of timber harvested from natural forests in 1998 was estimated to be about 640,000 cubic metres, the predicted sustainable yield was about 220,000 cubic metres. This was attributed mainly to the 20 per cent devaluation of the Solomon Islands dollar in December 1997, which 'positively impacted on exporters' balance sheets, government's preferential taxes for stockpile exports, and partial recovery in the market that raised the average price for Solomon Islands' logs from a trough of US$45 [$A60] per cubic [metre] to US$80 [$A108] per cubic [metre] towards the end of 1998' (CBSI 1999: 15).

By 2000, most of Solomon Islands' major industries were affected by the civil unrest, which started in late 1998 (see Fraenkel 2004; Moore 2005). The Solomon Islands Plantation Limited (SIPL) oil palm plantation stopped operations in June 1999. A year later, in mid-2000, the Gold Ridge mine on Central Guadalcanal also suspended operations after militants took over the mine site and threatened workers.

In the first year of the civil unrest, the forestry sector was not as severely affected as other sectors. The CBSI reported that this was because 'the Western and Isabel provinces are the major hosts to logging operations and therefore while logging on Guadalcanal ceased for some time, or [was] operating at below capacity, the overall output actually rose' (CBSI 2000: 16). In 1999, because log production data were not available, the CBSI used export shipment data to make estimations: about 624,000 cubic metres of logs were exported, up by 3 per cent on the previous year.

By March 2000, however, log production declined. This was attributed to the deteriorating security situation, which had by then affected other parts of the country, especially the high log production areas such as the Western and Choiseul Provinces. The Commissioner of Forests, Peter Sheehan, quoted in March 2000 a harvest rate of 550,000 cubic metres per annum (Sheehan 2000). This was well below the 624,000 cubic metres of the previous year, but still well above the expected sustainable harvest rate of 250,000 cubic metres per annum.

The claim that forests would be depleted in less than a decade if current logging practices were maintained was disputed by the Solomon Islands Forest Industries' Association (SIFIA). In January 1997, SIFIA showed a video documentary produced for the purpose of what Eric Kes, the then Executive Director of SIFIA, described as correcting 'widespread misconceptions about the Solomon Islands forest industry sector, which have often resulted in misinformed and emotion[al] criticism[s] of the industry and government, both locally and abroad' (*Solomon Star*, January 29, 1997). The underlying argument in the video was that while close to 80 per cent of Solomon Islands' land was covered by forests, only about 12 per cent was suitable for commercial logging operations. Kes stated that 'the often used stereotype of total forest destruction is simply untrue' (*Solomon Star*, January 29, 1997). In a printed document released by SIFIA along with the video, Kes argued that 'approximately 10 per cent have been previously logged, but are not, as often argued, completely destroyed, but will generally recover and can be re-harvested over the years'. The document also asserted that 80 per cent of Solomon Islands' natural forest would never be subject to large-scale commercial logging.

Apart from unsustainable log production, another issue that dominated discussions of the forestry industry was Solomon Islands' economic dependence on log exports. In 1990, logging contributed 34.5 per cent of the country's total exports. This increased to 54.9 per cent in 1993. In 1994, it contributed 56 per cent of the country's export earnings and 31 per cent of all government earnings (Montgomery 1995). In the 10 years between 1988 and 1998, timber made up a huge percentage of Solomon Islands' principal exports (see Figure 3). From 1992 to 1996, receipts from log exports increased dramatically and dominated total exports. The average value of timber exports in that period was $SI285.2 million per annum. In 1998, however, there was a dramatic decline in log export receipts: $SI196.3 million compared with $SI290.7 million in 1997 and an average of $SI285.2 million in the period from 1993 to 1996 (CBSI 1999: 25). The 1997 and 1998 declines were due to the fall in export prices and volume as a result of the continued adverse developments associated with the Asian financial crisis. Despite this decline, the value of log exports was still well above that of other commodities (CBSI 1999: 25–6; see Figure 3).

Figure 3: Export values of principal commodity groups (CBSI data on value of exports by commodity)

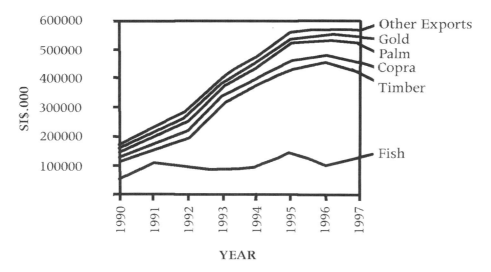

There was also concern that unsustainable harvest rates would cause severe economic and financial disruption when the commercially accessible forests were depleted. The ADB asserted that if timber production was reduced to meet the sustainable level by 2000, then, although it would involve some short-term disruption as government and the economy adjusted to lower levels of forest revenue, 'the forest resources would remain a source of revenue in perpetuity' (ADB 1998: 66). The bank presented three possible scenarios for managing the natural forest: i) continue at about the current harvest rates; ii) allow harvest rates to rise to a new maximum level potentially set by logical constraints on harvest operations; or iii) implement sustainable yield levels by 2000. The ADB proposed that the 'government should carefully consider the harvest level options, which are likely to actually fall within the range between scenarios 1 and 3' (ADB 1998: 66).

Because of the country's dependence on log exports, the negative developments of 1997 and 1998 had an impact on the rest of the economy, contributing to a decline of about 7 per cent of Solomon Islands' real GDP in 1998 compared with an estimated growth of 3 per cent in 1997. This had an adverse impact on the country's economy.

Further, despite increasing log exports, in the late 1990s actual revenue collected from log exports declined. The *Solomon Star* reported on April 4, 1996, that although the value of round log exports in 1995 increased by $SI16.7 million, the amount collected in export duties by the Government fell by $SI12.6 million. This signified weaknesses in Solomon Islands' tax system, which meant that the Government was unable to collect potential revenue. Price Waterhouse (1995) discussed the deficiencies of the tax system and highlighted the need for trained manpower and an improved administrative and monitoring system to enable the Government to capture much needed revenue. If that were not done the country was bound to lose enormous amounts of money through potential lost revenue.

Apart from the weaknesses of the tax collection mechanism, a substantial amount of potential revenue was also lost as a result of inefficient government policies. One such policy was the granting of duty remissions to log-exporting companies. This increased significantly in 1995 and 1996. As a result of these remissions, lost government revenue from 1995 to 1997 was $75 million (ADB 1998: 59). This is a dramatic increase, compared with about $34 million of potential revenue forgone in 1994 (Duncan 1994).

The duty remissions were given largely to landowner companies with the intention of assisting them to participate in the logging industry and encouraging them to invest in domestic processing. Most of these landowner companies have contractual agreements with foreign-registered companies because they do not have the financial capital or technology to extract and process logs on their own.

Price Waterhouse (1995) asserted that subcontractor agreements were either fixed at a rate per cubic metre of logs exported, irrespective of free-on-board (f.o.b.) value, or accepted a percentage share of the f.o.b. price, which is the price calculated without charge for delivery to the ship. Consequently, it was concluded that although most landowner companies received a share of the forgone tax revenue, 'the logging contractors are capturing up to 77 per cent of this' (Price Waterhouse 1995: 35) because of the structure of the contractor/landowner company agreements.

Further, logging companies evaded taxes because of a poor taxation system in the country. Dauvergne (1998–99: 8) discussed how structural defects in Solomon Islands' timber management policies enabled 'multinational investors to operate with remarkably poor harvesting and environmental standards, and make windfall profits'. Price Waterhouse (1995) reported that insufficient finance and lack of technical and human resources to monitor logging operations meant that it was difficult to implement the state's forestry policies, especially environmental rules. Further, there is evidence that companies used transfer pricing and made informal agreements (between buyers and producers) to ensure they benefited from the timber industry. By comparing Solomon Islands' import clearance records into Japan and the Republic of Korea with Solomon Islands' log exports for the first half of 1995, Price Waterhouse (1995) concluded that under-invoicing had reduced declared f.o.b. prices by at least $A108 per cubic metre after reasonable allowances for freight and insurance. FORTECH (1995c) compared log export volume and value from Solomon Islands with log import volume and value to Japan and the Republic of Korea, and found that while for 1994 export and import volumes essentially correlated, after providing allowances for freight and insurance, sales to Japan were under-invoiced by about $A46 per cubic metre and to Republic of Korea by $A43 per cubic metre. According to Price Waterhouse (1995), under-invoicing is a common method of minimising taxation payments and that 'to claim that under-invoicing does not exist in Solomon Islands would make this country unique among log exporting countries around the world'.

Economic surplus forgone from 1990 to 1997 as a result of transfer pricing was estimated to be about $481 million, compared with the $131 million lost through under-taxation. The Government's cumulative recurrent budget deficit for the same period was an estimated $295 million (ADB 1998: 71).

By the mid-1990s, there was widespread awareness of and concern (locally and internationally) over the issues confronting forestry developments in Solomon Islands. The Australian Government, for example, criticised the Mamaloni Government's policy on logging, and, to back its criticism, in 1996 it cut back aid to Solomon Islands and stopped funding the Timber Control Unit Project of the Forestry Division, set up to monitor the rate of logging. The EU also threatened to stop its funding of projects 'if the government failed to address forest management concerns' (*Solomon Star*, April 2, 1996). From 1998, however, AusAID revived its funding of government efforts to monitor and regulate the forestry industry, through the Solomon Islands Forest Management Project.

Because of the issues raised above, it was realised that the Government needed to develop policies that provided a coherent framework for developing the forestry sector. The ADB (1998: 76) suggested that, because of the cross-sectoral impact of these activities, developing forestry policy should be part of the broader public sector policy reform process. It also suggested that a subregional approach (through the Melanesian Spearhead Group) aimed at improving resource rent capture should be established. This suggestion was not taken up.

Because of widespread awareness of the problems associated with the logging industry, Francis Billy Hilly's National Coalition Partnership (NCP) Government, which came to power in mid-1993, attempted to introduce policies to reform the timber industry. In July 1993, for instance, the NCP Government announced plans for increased local processing and the phasing out of large-scale logging in favour of eco-forest logging. A Timber Control Unit was established within the Ministry of Forests to monitor timber production. The effort of the NCP Government was thwarted after its collapse in 1994. It was alleged that logging companies opposed to forestry reforms had a hand in its collapse (Bennett 2000: 340–4).

Another attempt to reform the forestry sector was the Bartholomew Ulufa'alu Government's introduction of the *Forestry Act 1999*, which, despite being tabled in Parliament, was never gazetted. The Ulufa'alu Government's initiatives, however, suffered a setback when Ulufa'alu was forced to resign as Prime Minister after the Malaita Eagle Force coup of June 5, 2000.

The collapse of the Asian economies and log markets gave the Government an opportunity to re-evaluate the industry. By late 1997 there was a drop in demand and price for Solomon Islands logs. The CBSI (1998: 26) reported that from 1992 to 1996, the period of the logging boom, the annual average export price had been more than $A160 per cubic metre. In 1997 and 1998, however, this fell dramatically to an average of $A140 and $A80 per cubic metre, respectively. These included prices for plantation logs (about $A86 per cubic metre), which are lower than for natural forest logs (CBSI 1998: 18).

The collapse in demand and price for logs caused a corresponding decline in log exports. In 1998 an estimated 604,000 cubic metres of round logs were exported compared with 650,124 cubic metres in 1997, and 811,000 cubic metres in 1996 (see Figure 1). The total value of shipments amounted to $A93 million in 1997, dropping from $A124 million in 1996. The value of log shipments in 1998 came to $A48.5 million, down by 47 per cent from the previous year, reflecting the subdued demand in Asia for much of the year (CBSI 1999: 15). However, as noted above, there was a rise in production in 1999 that corresponded with the improvement of Asian economies, especially log markets in Korea, Japan and the Philippines.

The Asian economic crisis and the collapse of log markets caused many logging companies to stockpile. At the end of 1997 the volume of log stockpiles reached 300,000 cubic metres and uncollected logs left in the jungles were estimated by the Ministry of Forestry, Environment and Conservation (MFEC) to number about one million cubic metres.

Logging and local communities

Drawing from the above story, let us now explore how the Solomon Islands forestry industry and the global forces associated with it interacted with local communities. In this exploration, it is important, as Lockwood notes in relation to the Pacific Islands more generally, to understand not only what motivates foreign interests, but what motivates local people 'as they encounter globalizing forces, and how their particular cultural lenses shape the ways they choose to interact with those forces' (Lockwood 2003: 10).

In most instances, what motivates many customary landowning communities to engage in logging (or any large-scale natural resource development) is the potential financial benefit that it brings. Those who allow logging on their land often do not have access to other forms of income generation, or other forms of income generation are too labour intensive, they do not have readily accessible markets, and have relatively low returns. Hence, for them it makes perfect sense to allow the extraction of timber in return for rent, even if that rent makes up for only a small percentage of the value of the log on the international market. Indeed, for many customary landowners the resource rents from logging constitute amounts of money that they would otherwise never have access to, or would never be able to make producing copra or cocoa, etc.

Hence, for people who struggle daily to find money to pay for basic needs such as clothes, kerosene, salt, sugar, soap and school fees, the decision to allow logging on their land is a rational one. It allows them to have access to and enjoy the goods and services that the global economy has to offer.

One of the reasons why policies aimed at reducing logging and anti-logging campaigns have often failed is because they have not offered alternative sources of income generation. Alfred Ghiro from Central Makira, for example, accused NGOs such as the Makira Conservation Foundation of trying to stop logging in his area without providing people with alternative sources of income generation (SIBC News, January 18, 2006). Because of people's desire for goods and services offered by the global market economy, environmental conservation by itself is insufficient. It is easy to sit in an air-conditioned office, enjoy all the trappings of the global market economy, and tell people who struggle daily to find money to pay for basic needs that they should not sell their forests.

In contemporary Solomon Islands societies the cash economy has become an important part of people's livelihood, and land, along with resources such as forests, often provides the only means to have access to it. This was, for example, aptly put by Enoch Sila from North Choiseul: '*Lan ia sapos hemi stap nating, bae iumi no garem selen long hem ia*' (If the land stays idle, we will have no money from it) (Personal conversation, April 14, 1998). Land is therefore important, not only in the traditional sense as a source of food and a place of residence and identity, but as a potential source of income.

Another interesting development has been how local societies transform in order to accommodate logging and the money that it brings. Logging companies search for landowners for purposes of negotiating timber rights, and for the legal and corporate structures they need. They often expect landowning entities to fit into those structures. This influences landowning entities and how they organise themselves. Fa'anunu (unpublished) discusses how in North New Georgia, the Christian Fellowship Church organises its members into '*blokos*' (blocks) as the social basis for planting and owning trees in forestry plantations. She explores whether this means changes in land tenure and, if so, how they work. Hviding (2000) discusses how the social changes associated with forestry in North New Georgia centre on the Christian Fellowship Church and the traditional *butu butu* (tribes), and how that has proven to produce positive outcomes in terms of the community's ability to provide social services — education and health — for its members.

In some cases landowning groups have formed themselves into 'companies' to resemble the corporate industries that they are dealing with. Consequently, from the mid-1980s, we have seen the establishment of 'local companies'. In 2005, for example, there were about 24 foreign companies, or contractors, working under contractual agreements with about 89 'local companies', or licence holders. The formation of local companies has important implications for how landowning entities organise themselves. First, the structured nature of companies creates hierarchies and immediately excludes certain people, especially women and youth, from the affairs of the community. It is often the case that big-men and those who are formally educated take on active roles, and in time dominate the affairs of the landowning group, or local company. This influences the way in which the community relates to the land and to each other.

These changes in social organisation surrounding land are not unique to Solomon Islands, or to the forestry industry, and do not necessarily mean that they are 'inauthentic', or 'unMelanesian'. Rather, they are interesting local reactions to the involvement of corporate powers in natural-resource development. Ernst (1999), Filer (1998) and Golub (2004) have discussed how mining triggered social changes and definitions of landowning groups in PNG.

In many cases, the demand for land and the injection of logging money often unwraps the complexities of local communities. As I said earlier, landowning communities are rarely homogeneous entities. They are made up of a dynamic group of people who have varying backgrounds, opinions and interests. Enoch Sila, a big-man of the Sarabani landowning group in North Choiseul, for example, said that his decision to sign a timber rights agreement was influenced not only by the Eagon Resources Development Company (SI) Ltd's promise that *'sapos iu givim kambani lan blong iu bae iu wanpala rich man'* (if you give your land to the company you will become a rich man), but because of pressure from other members of the landowning group. As Sila stated in March 1998:

… *olketa wantok blong mi tu … Olketa sei, ei, bos, ma olketa olo olo blong iumi olketa onim lan ia olketa olo pinis ia. Ma sampala kolsap dae. Taem olketa dae hu nao bae tekem seleni. Ating gud chanisi olketa stil laev. Mekem olketa olo olo blong iumi tekem lelebet seleni bipoa olketa dae. Den mi sei, Oh no! nomoa nao! Olketa se nomoa iumi go. So, mipala go saenim* (… it was my wantoks [relatives] who said, 'Hey boss, our elders who own the land are now very old. Some of them are about to die. If they die, who is going to take the money? It's good they are still alive so that they receive some money before they die.' I said, 'Oh, no! No!' But they said, 'Let's go.' So, we went and signed. (Interview, March 17, 1998)

This highlights the debates that go on within landowning groups and how decisions are made. In other cases decisions were made by a few who were able to exert control over the landowning company. In these instances, it often incites disharmony, as illustrated in the case of Lokuru on Rendova in the documentary film *Since the Company Came*. Much of the discontent within landowning groups often centres on the distribution of income, especially in cases where the big-man or those with formal education benefit more than women and the rest of the community.

Further, those who control the 'local companies' and the incomes accrued from royalty payments often become powerful individuals, creating new power dynamics within the community. We see the traditional big-man's position being challenged, very often by younger and formally educated individuals who are more knowledgeable about the world outside of the local communities. One could argue that there is nothing new in the emergence of new big-men who challenge existing ones. That is the nature of politics in many Melanesian societies. The difference, however, is that the power of the new big-men is derived from the existence of logging operations and their accumulation of wealth from it. It is, therefore, often not in their interest to see the logging companies go, or the wealth from logging distributed equitably among members of the landowning group.

Logging money could also create dependency and reduce economic productivity because the landowning community becomes so dependent on logging rent it simply sits and waits for the money. The local saying *'lif blong akwa nomoa tok'* (it is the leaf of the akwa tree that talks) implies that one does not have to work, but simply wait for money to come from logging rent — for money to fall from the trees.

Much of the discussion on forestry centres on the State, logging companies and the mismanagement of logging money. It is also true, however, that some of the money from logging is often used for traditional social obligations, or for individuals to establish themselves as big-men. Hence, from a capitalist point of view, such money has been misused because it is not invested. For the Solomon Islander, however, the money has been used to lubricate social relations and fulfil traditional obligations. This is an example of how global capital is used for local purposes. Of course, this was not always the case, and it is also true that income from logging is often misused.

Conclusions

What does the story of the Solomon Islands forestry industry tell us about the interaction between global capital and local communities? Are local communities simply victims of globalisation? What motivates local communities to participate in large-scale natural resource developments such as logging?

First, transnational corporations will continue to be important in the development of natural resources in developing countries such as Solomon Islands. This is something that some of us might detest, but the realities are such that it is unlikely that the role of transnational corporations will diminish. Many local communities even in remote parts of the world are already connected to the global network of resources, capital, production and markets.

This, however, does not mean that local communities are simply passive victims of global forces. Indeed, in many cases, as we have seen in the case of the Solomon Islands forestry industry, local communities have attempted to mobilise and strategise in order to maximise their benefits from globalisation. They have their own motives for getting involved, which might vary between as well as within communities.

Second, it is useful to note that the ability of local communities to benefit from their dealings with transnational corporations varies from community to community depending on that community's capacity to deal with global forces. It might, therefore, be unrealistic to shut off globalisation and throw its evil over the edge of the Earth. Rather, it might be more useful to build and strengthen the capacity of local communities to deal with global forces, forms and processes.

References

Asian Development Bank. 1998. 'Solomon Islands, 1997 Economic Report.' *Pacific Studies Series*. Manila: Asian Development Bank.

Aspire Films, 1996. *Advertising Missionaries*. Aspire Films and Ellipse Program. Produced by ABC Australia and France 3, RTSR in association with the Australian Film Finance Corporation and the Centre National de la Cinematographie. New York: First Run/Icarus Films.

AusAID. 1999. *Solomon Islands Forestry Management Project: Feasibility Study Report and Project Design Document*. Prepared for AusAID and Solomon Islands Government Rural Development Group. Canberra: AusAID.

Auty, Richard M. 1993. *Sustaining Development in Mineral Economies: The Resource Curse Thesis*. London and New York: Routledge.

Bennett, Judith A. 2000a. 'Grievous Mistake of the Vanikoro Concession: The Vanikoro Kauri Timber Company, Solomon Islands, 1926-1964.' *Environment and History*, 6. pp. 317–47.

Bennett, Judith A. 2000b. *Pacific Forest: A history of resource control and contest in Solomon Islands, c. 1800-1997*. Cambridge: The White Horse Press.

Central Bank of Solomon Islands. 1996. *CBSI Annual Report 1995*. Honiara.

Central Bank of Solomon Islands. 1998. *CBSI Annual Report 1997*. Honiara.

Central Bank of Solomon Islands. 1999. *CBSI Annual Report 1998*. Honiara.

Central Bank of Solomon Islands. 2000. *CBSI Annual Report 1999*. Honiara.

Diamond, Jared. 1999. *Guns, Germs, and Steel: The Fate of Human Societies*. New York: W. W. Norton and Company.

Dauvergne, Peter. 1998–99. 'Corporate Power in the Forests of the Solomon Islands.' *Pacific Affairs*, 71, 4. pp. 524–46.

Dauvergne, Peter. 2001. *Loggers and Degradation in the Asia-Pacific: Corporation and Environmental Management*. New York: Cambridge University Press.

de Gregorio, Jose. 2002. 'The Role of Foreign Direct Investment and Natural Resources in Economic Development.' *Central Bank of Chile, Working Papers*, No. 196, January 2003, http://www.bcentral.cl/Estudios/DTBC/doctrab.htm (accessed December 7, 2005).

Duncan, Ron. 1994. 'Melanesian Forestry Sector Study.' *International Development Issues*, No. 36. Canberra: AIDAB.

Ernst, Thomas. 1999. 'Land, Stories, and Resources: Discourse and Entification in Onabusulu Modernity.' *American Anthropologist*, 101, 1. pp. 88–97.

Fa'anunu, Kalisi. Unpublished. 'Christian Fellowship Church Reforestation: A Change in Customary Land Tenure in the Solomon Islands?'

Filer, Colin. 1997. 'Resource Rents.' In Illa Temu (ed.), *Papua New Guinea: A 20/20 Vision?*, Canberra: NCDS.

Filer, Colin. 1998. 'The Melanesian Way of Menacing the Mining Industry.' In L. Zimmer-Tamakoshi (ed.), *Modern Papua New Guinea*, Kirksville: Thomas Jefferson University Press.

Firth, Stewart. 2000. 'The Pacific Islands and the globalization agenda.' *The Contemporary Pacific*, 12, 1. pp. 178–92.

Foale, Simon and Martha MacIntyre. 1999. 'Dynamic and Flexible Aspects of Land and Marine Tenure at West Nggela: Implications for Marine Resource Management.' *Oceania*, 71, 1. pp. 30–45.

FORTECH. 1995. 'Report of Visit to Japan and Korea by TCUP Commercial Unit Manager and CBSI Foreign Exchange Manager, 26 March–8 April 1995 (by S. Mulholland and G. Simbe).' *Timber Control Unit Project Report*, No. 18. Canberra: AIDAB.

Fraenkel, Jon. 2004. *The Manipulation of Custom: From Uprising to Intervention in the Solomon Islands*. Wellington: Victoria University Press.

Frazer, Ian. 1997a. 'The Struggle for Control of Solomon Islands Forests.' *The Contemporary Pacific*, 9, 1. pp. 39–72.

Frazer, Ian. 1997b. 'Resource Extraction and the Post-colonial State in Solomon Islands.' In R. F. Watters and T. G. McGee (eds), *Asia Pacific: New Geographies of the Pacific Rim*, London: Routledge.

Gerritsen, Rolf and Martha MacIntyre. 1991. 'Dilemmas of Distribution: The Misima Gold Mine, Papua New Guinea.' In J. Connell and R. Howitt (eds), *Mining and Indigenous Peoples in Australasia,* Sydney: Sydney University Press. pp. 34–53.

Golub, Alex. 2004. 'Making the Ipili Feasible: Imagining Local and Global Actors at the Porgera Mine, Enga Province, Papua New Guinea.' PhD dissertation, University of Chicago.

Gosarevski, S., H. Hughes and S. Windybank. 2004. 'Is Papua New Guinea viable with customary land ownership?' *Pacific Economic Bulletin*, 19, 3. pp. 133–6.

Hannerz, Ulf. 1997. 'Scenarios for Peripheral Cultures.' In Anthony King (ed.), *Culture, Globalisation and the World System: Contemporary Conditions for the Representation of Identity*, Minneapolis: University of Minnesota Press. pp. 107–28.

Horton, James Oliver and Lois E. Horton. 2005. *Slavery and the Making of America*. New York: Oxford University Press.

Hviding, Edvard and Tim Bayliss-Smith. 2000. *Islands of Rainforest: Agroforestry, logging and eco-tourism in Solomon Islands*. UK: Ashgate Publishing.

Kotch, Nick. 2005. 'African Oil: Whose Bonanza?' *National Geographic Magazine — Africa: Whatever You Thought, Think Again*, Special Issue, September 2005. pp. 50–65.

Lal, Brij V. 2004. *Girmitiyas: The Origins of the Fiji Indians*. Lautoka: Fiji Institute of Applied Studies.

Lockwood, Victoria S. (ed.) 2003. *Globalisation and Culture Change in the Pacific Islands*. New Jersey: Prentice Hall.

Makim, Abigail. 2002. 'Globalisation, Community Development, and Melanesia: The North New Georgia Sustainable Social Forestry and Rural Development Project.' *SSGM Discussion Paper* 02/1. Canberra: ANU.

Montgomery, Phillip. 1995. 'Forestry in Solomon Islands.' *Pacific Economic Bulletin*, 10, 2. pp. 74–6.

Mintz, Sidney W. 1995. *Sweetness and Power: The Place of Sugar in Modern History*. New York: Penguin Books.

Moore, Clive. 2005. *Happy Isles in Crisis: The Historical Causes for a Failing State in Solomon Islands, 1998–2004*. Canberra: Asia Pacific Press.

Moore, Clive, Jacqueline Leckie and Doug Munro (eds) 1990. *Labour in the South Pacific*. Townsville: James Cook University.

Price Waterhouse. 1995. *Final Draft Report — Forestry Taxation and Domestic Processing Study*. Honiara: Ministry of Finance and Ministry of Forests, Environment and Conservation.

Ross, Michael L. 2001. *Timber Booms and Institutional Breakdown in Southeast Asia*. Cambridge: Cambridge University Press.

Sheehan, Peter. 2000. 'Solomon Islands economic and governance update on forests sector.' Paper presented to SICHE/ANU Solomon Islands Economic and Governance Update, Solomon Islands College of Higher Education, Honiara, March 16–17.

Solomon Star, November 14 and 17, 2005, January 29, 1997, April 2, 1996.

Tausinga, Job Duddley. 1989. 'Logging in North New Georgia Timber Corporation (NNGTC).' In Ron Crocombe et al. (eds), *Independence, Dependence, Interdependence: The First 10 years of Solomon Islands Independence*, Suva and Honiara: Institute of Pacific Studies with the University of the South Pacific, Honiara Centre and the Solomon Islands College of Higher Education. pp. 55–66.

Tiensten, Paul. 2001. 'Gas Commercialisation: Efforts to Secure PNG's Economic Future.' http://www.pomcci.org.pg/hiri2001/Tiensten.doc (accessed on February 9, 2006).

Turia, Ruth C. H. 2003. 'Efficient Management of Forest Resources.' In David Kavanamur, Charles Yala and Quinton Clements (eds), *Building a Nation in Papua New Guinea: Views of the Post-Independence Generation*, Canberra: Pandanus Books. pp. 183–97.

13. Mining, Social Change and Corporate Social Responsibility: Drawing lines in the Papua New Guinea mud

Glenn Banks

The Pacific Islands have been the focus of international academic and policy 'concern' in the past decade. Much of this has centred on the issue of governance, with examples such as PNG, Fiji and the Solomon Islands used to support arguments of state failures and a regional crisis of governance (see, for example, Larmour 1998; Hughes 2004). There is a tendency to see 'state failure' in these cases as an internal issue (that is, due to internal problems of governance), although this is obviously questioned by the prevalence of the problem across the region. Indeed it is surprising how little attention has been given to the ways in which external processes associated with globalisation contribute to these internal 'crises of governance'. Connected to the governance concern is a parallel policy discourse on the mismanagement of resource rents from natural resources, particularly forests and minerals. The inability to translate mineral resources into effective broader-based development and nation-building has fuelled regional resource conflicts, and necessitated regional interventions by external countries. There is evidence from elsewhere, however (see Ross 1999), that resource booms tend to undermine the very capacity for governance that economists frequently declare is needed for proper management of resource rents in the first place. Paradoxically, then, liberalisation of investment regimes and promotion of resource developments as tools for generating government revenue and economic growth are accompanied by calls for improved governance and management of resource rents despite these same rents being shown to actively undermine good governance itself.

Governance as a discourse has been touted widely by aid donors throughout the Pacific in recent years, and clearly links with broader concerns about globalisation. Receiving less attention in the region has been the parallel development of concepts of corporate governance. In contrast with broad definitions of governance along the lines of processes by which different elements in society mobilise power to influence policy and practice in the public spheres, corporate governance is concerned with more explicit themes of accountability and transparency within the private sector. In places and industries such as the PNG mining sector, the two discourses come together. Hence concerns over governance of the mining sector in PNG (in the context of the management of new or existing resource developments) occur alongside the formalisation of corporate governance mechanisms within the multinationals involved in the sector. Indeed one can argue that this 'corporate governance' has been implicated to a greater extent than formal 'state governance' in the development and implementation of 'good governance' within PNG. This is because within the publicly listed multinationals the links between discourse and practice are much more direct and are embedded within an institution with higher accountability and transparency requirements and standards. Thus the level of training in and implementation of 'governance' ideals for Papua New Guinean mining staff in all areas — from engineering and accountancy to the environmental fields — have a greater degree of professionalism and oversight, as well as more applied utility, than in the public sector. The old adage that something lived is better learnt than something taught is of relevance here.

There is now a significant literature on communities, sustainability, corporate social responsibility and extractive industries. Much of this looks at the ways in which corporations construct notions of 'sustainability' (Cowell et al. 1999; Humphreys 2000; Cesare and Maxwell 2003) and particular communities (Hamann 2004; Jenkins 2004; Cragg and Greenbaum 2002) that reflect their own identities and agendas. Another focus of this literature is case studies of the translation of corporate notions of sustainability and responsibility into practice around specific mining or oil complexes (see Wheeler et al. 2002; Kapelus 2002; Watts 2005). One of the assumptions here is that the driver of change is only ever a globally derived discourse of sustainability, and that the local expression of the corporation (the mining operation) must always adapt to this, a point with which I take issue below.

One area of note is environmental discourse and governance, and particularly the notion of sustainability. In this paper, I am interested to explore the ways in which the corporate discourse of sustainability has impacted on the relationships between miners and communities in PNG. Using the example of Placer Dome at the Porgera mine, the paper aims to highlight how changing corporate discourses can impact on the evolution of relationships between stakeholders at the mine. In large part this occurs through the reshaping of lines, particularly the metaphorical lines of responsibility that corporations draw around themselves. The paper emphasises that discourses (such as 'sustainability') within an industry such as mining have effects — and as such they have implications for the lives and development prospects of people within affected communities (see also Hilson and Murck 2000).

The chapter opens with a discussion, albeit brief and partial, of the impacts of large-scale mining on communities with a view to identifying the processes by which these effects occur. This highlights the role of local cultural and social forces and local agency in shaping the nature of these impacts. The motivation and progress of the adoption of a discourse of 'sustainability' by one mining corporation (Placer Dome) and its majority-owned and -operated (by the Porgera Joint Venture, or PJV) mine at Porgera forms the basis for the second section. The link with the impacts of the mine is in terms of the shifting corporate concern with and attribution of responsibility for such impacts and effects. The third section examines the implications of this for issues of mine closure, corporate responsibility and instituting 'sustainability' around mine operations. In the conclusion, I return to the theme of the power of global discourse to reshape our understandings of and relationships to the world. Despite scepticism about the green discourse of corporations, in the Porgera case it is clear that discourse can drive new socially focused cartographic practices, and these in turn can reshape relationships and lives.

Mining as the driver of change

Large-scale mining has dramatically changed the social landscape around these mine sites in PNG. The diversity and intensity of the effects are well documented, although much of this literature is fragmentary in temporal and geographic scope. This chapter is not the forum for the overdue comprehensive review of these effects. Instead the focus is on a number of the more significant effects identified and the processes that drive these trends within the community.

Elsewhere I have identified the economic relationship between the company and the adjacent population as a central driver of many of the impacts: the substantial flows of revenue into the communities (through compensation, wages, royalties and business contracts) are implicated in sparking many of the oft-cited negative 'impacts' of mining. Here we can include in-migration (see Banks 2003) and the exaggeration of economic inequalities (Banks 2005), shifting cultural horizons and frames of reference, and the rise of all the social pathologies (alcoholism, gambling, prostitution and violence) associated with mining. Some of these effects, particularly those related to 'culture' in all its manifestations, are certainly linked to the landscape transformations and environmental destruction that accompany large-scale mining. People lose land to the bulldozer, and, as Bougainvilleans quoted by Dove et al. (1974) in the early 1970s stated, 'For us to be landless is a nightmare that no dollar in the bank can allay.' Land is so intimately tied to social relationships and identity that loss of land ruptures social as well as environmental links. In this sense the bulldozer assaults the society as completely as it does the environment. And so does the snail. Macintyre and Foale's (2004) discussion of the introduction of the Giant African snail to Lihir again highlights the cultural frames within which mine-related impacts are constructed and argued. In this case, the introduction of snails (through timber for new housing on the island that was purchased with the increased cash that landowners now have as a result of the mine) is causing havoc within the local agricultural setting. Here the issue is that local arguments frame the problem less as an environmental one, and more one that is concerned fundamentally with the relationship between the landowners and the company — a social rather than environmental exercise. Environmental change becomes linked back into the world of relationships — in many cases the economic relationship, framed through the lens of compensation, between communities and the mining company.

Building on the direct environmental impacts, and indeed accentuating their cultural effects, are the revenue streams with which Porgerans are supposed to be compensated for the environmental impacts. Designed (in theory at least) to be used to rebuild lives and relationships, the cash instead often erodes these further. One of the central ways in which this occurs is the in-migration associated with mine developments in PNG. In many parts of the developing world, the issue of migration and mining is concerned with the relationships between imported mine employees and local populations (e.g., Indonesia, Africa). This was also the case on Bougainville (see Imbun 1995) and to an extent at Ok Tedi (Polier 1994). At Porgera, as well as Misima and Lihir, the issue is different. Here workforces comprise workers who 'commute' without their families, and relatively small numbers of expatriate workers mean that the in-migration is driven largely through networks of kinship and relationships. The migrants are predominantly from neighbouring groups and a large proportion have utilised their kinship networks to enter and stay at Porgera. This is borne out by the figures for migration into the Special Mining Lease at Porgera (the most contested ground at Porgera, where complete strangers — unattached migrants — would have no chance of establishing a house) that show that while the 'Porgeran' population within the Special Mining Lease grew by 11 per cent in the period 1995–99, the *'epo arene'* (loosely, 'visitor' or 'migrant') population grew by more than 250 per cent in the same period (Banks 2003). Importantly, the utilisation of individual kin networks by migrants to secure residence implicates Porgerans in this process, a fact that is acknowledged by community members with the caveat that they feel custom-bound to accommodate their incoming kin (see Banks 1999).

While the make-up of migrant groups and the pathways they utilise to become established might differ from other settings, the attractions are always the same: money, jobs, development and 'action'. Likewise the outcomes for the resident population tend to be the same regardless of the specific nature of the migrants. Here we can list the 'watering' down of benefits intended for landowners — cash, jobs, wages, health and education services, and housing — in the form of pressure on subsistence resources (water, agricultural land, the village environment), the straining of social relationships and a general rise in feelings of insecurity due to increasing numbers of 'faces we do not know', migrants who are not part of their existing social universe. This last effect forms part of the larger sense in which landowning 'communities' themselves become more complex: they shift from being relatively self-contained and known (by the people in them, at least) to being much more diverse and fragmented in terms of people and agendas, and residents experience a loss of control, direction and security in their lives.

The almost legendary short-term consumption focus of Papua New Guinean mining and petroleum landowners is in part a reflection of this insecurity. But in the case of Porgera, as Alex Golub (2003) has perceptively observed, it is also in a somewhat perverse way an attempt by Porgeran Ipili to 'become more like themselves than they ever were', to exaggerate elements of their own culture to an extreme, in the same way that we can refer to the broader developments at these mine sites as a form of 'hyper-development'. It is not a lack of development as usually conceived (benefits, cash and infrastructure) but a surfeit of these that drives many of the problematic aspects of the mines (Banks 2005). It is not the tools or technology of 'development', then, that are the problem, rather it is the cultural appropriation of these technologies by the Ipili that drives the outcomes we tend to recognise as the 'pathologies' of mining.

This untangling of lines of responsibility for the various effects is important, not for the attribution of 'blame' but for the modification or redirection of trajectories of change. The case I have put above has been deliberately a caricature and a reversal of the standard narrative of mining in PNG. But it is an important check in terms of discussions about the responsibilities of mining companies in PNG and elsewhere. Put simply, to attribute responsibility for problems of alcoholism, of a decline in the effectiveness of leadership, of increasing rates of domestic violence, or the myriad other indirect effects of mining developments to the mining company is to miss the agency and cultural inflections of the Ipili (and their neighbours, it must be said) in shaping the outcomes of the mining development. This has implications when we begin to think about the extent of control of the mining company over the processes and hence possible remedies: the line of maximal extent of responsibility, in other words. Drawing these lines is never a simple task and will itself always be a point of contestation. What is particularly interesting at Porgera is the way in which one of the parties, the mining company, has redrawn its view of where the line in the mud at Porgera is in terms of its responsibilities. It is to this redrawing in the past 15 years that the chapter now turns.

Entering the sustainability debate

The evolution of interest in the discourse of sustainability by the PJV, the mining company at Porgera, makes an interesting case study of the motives, means and outcomes of corporate attachment to sustainability. From the start of the operation, the company put resources into meeting and indeed exceeding the environmental expectations of its key stakeholders, the National Government and the local community at Porgera (although in the late 1980s these groups would not have known they were stakeholders as the word did not have the currency it has had subsequently). Hence, after some negotiations, the extensive Environmental Impact Assessment was accepted by the State, as was the subsequent Environmental Monitoring and Management Plan. The mine began construction in 1989 and production in late 1990.

An environmental management program was established, focusing on monitoring the effects of the mine's tailings and waste on the downstream environment. The environment team worked alongside, although not closely in tandem with, a community affairs group, focused primarily on two main issues. These were day-to-day community relations with the Porgeran community, and relocation and social development, concerned primarily with helping women adjust to the new housing and social problems created within the Special Mining Lease area and, to a lesser extent, elsewhere in the Porgera Valley and, to an even lesser extent, beyond. The community affairs focus was circumscribed geographically and reactive in the sense that its major concern was with managing the day-to-day issues and conflicts that arose between the company and the community. Likewise, the environment team maintained a strong focus on the compliance monitoring of water quality along the downstream river system as it was required to by the Environmental Monitoring and Management Plan and the Department of Environment and Conservation.

The relatively cosy calm of this situation was shaken in late 1995 when a documentary on Porgera aired on SBS Television in Australia to coincide with the release by the newly established Mineral Policy Institute (MPI) of a report entitled, *The Porgera File* (MPI 1995). The report and the documentary were based on an Honours thesis by Phil Shearman, a geographer at the University of Tasmania, who had conducted environmental fieldwork downstream from the mine (Shearman 1995). In the ensuing media scrum, Porgera was suddenly being compared poorly with Ok Tedi, where BHP had just settled the lawsuit brought by landowners downstream of the mine for an estimated cost of $500 million (see Kennedy 1996a, 1996b), and there were allegations that the mine tailings were killing people downstream. Initially there were said to be 133 such victims. Soon after, in March 1996, the operator and key shareholder in the PJV, Placer Dome Asia-Pacific (PDAP; itself a publicly listed, majority-owned subsidiary of Placer Dome), became embroiled in and embarrassed by a major tailings spill at the Maranduque mine in the Philippines.

Together these two events sparked the formalisation of a higher profile for environmental issues within the corporation. Driven largely by the PDAP Environment Manager at the time, PDAP became the first business unit of Placer Dome to adopt a more rigorous and transparent approach to reporting on environmental and social issues, putting out a corporate-wide first Sustainability Report in 1998, entitled *Towards Sustainability*, on events and progress in 1997

(PDAP 1998). A year later, Placer Dome published its own first annual *Sustainability Report* (Placer Dome 1999) and this was accompanied by operation-level sustainability reports in 1999 that were effectively reviews of sustainability related issues for the previous year (see, for example, PDAP 1999). These reports have now become increasingly sophisticated and glossy annual publications, and corporate-level reporting on sustainability has also continued. This high-level corporate adoption of the sustainability discourse has not of course occurred in isolation, and broader industry trends around sustainability have been watched and participated in by Placer Dome, including the Global Mining Initiative and the Mining, Minerals and Sustainable Development process.

In the Porgera case, the response at the mine level to the MPI document (although it was never publicly acknowledged as being in any way related to the MPI report) was the commissioning of a major report by the CSIRO (CSIRO 1996) into the downstream riverine effects of the mine. Flowing from the CSIRO report (which essentially cleared the company of any involvement in deaths, but charged it with an inadequate knowledge of the downstream environment) was the establishment of the Porgera Environment Advisory Komiti (PEAK). PEAK was originally tasked with being an external advisory and reference group to 'enhance the understanding of Porgera's environmental (physical and social) issues with external stakeholders, and to assist in improving PJV's environmental performance and public accountability in these areas' (PEAK Charter). Its primary original aim was to provide an oversight function in terms of the implementation of the recommendations of the CSIRO report.

PEAK membership was originally intended to comprise a group of NGOs, PNG government departments (Mining, and Environment and Conservation), landowners and mining company representatives, along with technical advisers that each member could nominate. Due more to logistical and representational difficulties than intent, the landowners, who were to be from the middle and lower Strickland, never made it to the PEAK table. PEAK has maintained a relatively high profile on the riverine issues and, despite a turnover of personnel (some in controversial circumstances), has developed at least some credibility and been an important element in reducing external criticism of the Porgera project.

PEAK has never had a strong mandate for or presence at the mine site itself (although recent discussions within PEAK over its future might change this). Indeed it can be argued more broadly that adoption of the rhetoric of sustainability at the mine site had little influence on the structures and practices of the PJV towards the Porgeran community for at least five years. Recently though, this has changed, and two related events have led to the adoption of new approaches and structures aligned much more closely to the rhetoric and the concept of sustainability. The failure of negotiations over access to land within the Special Mining Lease in 2000-2001 (the Yakatabari negotiations detailed in Golub 2005) and the subsequent rethinking of the mine design and waste dump strategies had implications for the ways in which longer-term community issues were approached. Essentially, communities which it was anticipated would be relocated as part of the development of the new waste dump were not moved, and this led to some re-evaluation of the future of these communities. Directly following this process, but apparently independent of it, was the initiation of a mine closure planning process within the company. This led to the publication in December 2002 of the Porgera Mine Closure Consultation document (PJV 2002) that canvassed a range of social and economic issues in the context of the gradual wind-down and closure of the mine, scheduled for 2014.

At the same time, in 2002, a position was created to head up a Social Closure and Sustainability section, working under the environment team, but also working closely with community affairs staff. In 2003, sustainability formally entered the structure of the PJV, with the creation of a 'Sustainability Manager', who effectively dealt with environmental and corporate communication issues, and with the 'sustainable development' section. In 2004, after a major internal corporate-led review, there were significant changes to the relationship between those units dealing with community and environmental issues. A new senior management position of Sustainability Manager was created with oversight of the Environment, Community Relations and Sustainable Development departments. This structure clearly reflects broader corporate concerns with the various strands of sustainability, even if these concerns were not the overriding rationale behind the restructure.

These new structures of engagement are clearly couched within the rhetoric of sustainability. From their limited origins as a response to external criticism of the handling of environmental issues, evolving corporate notions of sustainability have become entrenched in the rhetoric, structures and practices of the PJV. Shifts have clearly occurred in the discourse of the corporation and the company that it manages, and the internal structure of the company has been reshaped to reflect this. The focus on mine closure issues has given the concept of sustainability 'teeth' or traction within the company and in its dealings with the community.

In large part this has been reactive and in response to corporate problems and issues, but it has also been driven by key 'change individuals' within the corporate management, and has occurred in the context of the rapidly developing global discourse on sustainability (Cowell et al. 1999; Hilson and Murck 2000; MMSD 2002). It should also be noted that while the reactive nature of mines to community concerns is a typical marker of an early operation, the more mature operation (and more established relationships) facilitates planning within a less reactive 'sustainability' framework. In other words, the mine is more proactive in terms of its social and environmental planning (and hence better fits notions of best practice) in part at least because it is not as preoccupied with as many day-to-day issues and crises. In the final section of the paper, the effects of this corporate realignment towards sustainability in terms of notions of boundaries and responsibilities are outlined.

Drawing lines

Mining operations are constantly drawing lines of all kinds. Perhaps the most influential are the precisely surveyed lines that define the mining leases. These can be viewed as expansive at Porgera, with a number of new additional leases being mapped out in the past decade as the waste dumps from the mine have extended in different directions. These lines are critical, as they define a line in terms of the knowledge that companies have of the communities on either side (with generally much better knowledge of the individuals and relationships of those inside), and mark an abrupt economic schism between ground eligible for royalties and other economic benefits and land which is not. Rather than existing as the sole cadastral markers on the landscape, though, these lease boundaries intersect with the genealogically grounded lines of landownership around the mine sites (for in-depth anthropological accounts of the basis for these genealogical lines at Porgera see the PhD dissertations of Jacka (2003) and Golub (2005). Biersack (1999) and Jackson and Banks (2002) provide accessible introductions, while Jorgenson (1997) provides a more general statement on the issue). Many of these socially derived boundaries are natural features (ridges, rivers, etc.), in contrast with the systematically and precisely surveyed straight lines of mining leases.

A third set of lines, and the ones of most interest in the current context, are those of corporate responsibility: what is the extent, geographically and in terms of sectors and issues, of corporate responsibility in social terms at Porgera? Where geographically and socially do the boundaries of corporate responsibility extend? This is really a question of which communities the mining companies are responsible for, and to (and often these are two different groups). At Porgera at least this question is closely linked with the previous section. In the initial stages of the mine development, the mining company's most immediate concern was the relationship with the landowners of the Special Mining Lease area, a tightly circumscribed geographic and social group (the role of migrants within this geographic area was problematic and the source of much early concern from the company, see Robinson (1991, 1994)). Other lease landowners were certainly important, and those along the Hides power line became critical for a short time until their leases were negotiated, but the Special Mining Lease landowners had assumed a position of dominance on the mine's corporate radar, as indeed they had on the local, and the national, horizon.

Even within these leases, though, the areas of corporate responsibility were tightly prescribed and certainly not all-embracing. Two examples should serve to illustrate the point. First, the company assumed no responsibility for the maintenance of the new, permanent-material houses that had been constructed for relocated families within and around the mining leases. This was clearly stated in the Relocation Agreement signed between the company and the Special Mining Lease community in 1988, and has been tightly adhered to in the face of increasing demands for assistance as the houses have aged and deteriorated in the past 15 years. Second, the company never assumed any role in terms of the division or use of monies within landowning groups within the Special Mining Lease or the other leases. Thus, once the agents of the extended family group who were the recognised 'landowners' of a particular parcel of land eligible for compensation had been identified, and once a list of recipients had been submitted by the group to the lands office of the company, the cash (in the overwhelming majority of cases, it was cash) was simply handed over to the listed beneficiaries. There were few attempts made to either ensure the cash was appropriately distributed (according to notions of 'tradition' or 'equity') among all the eligible recipients, or to intervene in terms of the uses to which the cash was put. This was not an oversight, mischievous or deliberate, by the company — any such attempt in either area would have been outside the legal scope of the company, would have been strenuously resisted by landowners and would have attracted allegations of paternalism by Porgerans and observers.

Subsequently a number of factors have extended this relatively small geographic horizon of corporate interest and responsibility. The first, referred to above, has been the increase in the number and extent of leases associated with the mine. While this essentially incorporated more people into the immediate group of interest to the mining company, there have been changes in the nature of the relationship between the company and these communities, which are discussed below. A second actor in the extension of the boundaries of corporate responsibility at Porgera, and subsequently elsewhere in PNG, was the introduction of the Infrastructure Tax Credit Scheme (ITCS or often just TCS) in 1992. Under the TCS, the company could spend a small proportion of its annual gross revenue — between 0.75 per cent and 1.25 per cent — on community infrastructure within the province in return for a credit against its tax assessment from the National Government. This scheme had its origins in management concerns at Porgera with the return of tax revenue from the mine to the province. Given the exposure of the mine to disruption along the extended road linkage through Enga Province, the TCS was seen as a way of spreading the corporation's responsibilities (in a limited way) beyond just the Porgera Valley. The boundary of the company's attention, albeit a partial view with at least one eye kept on the bottom-line, extended dramatically with the TCS.

A third set of influences in reshaping the boundaries of corporate social responsibility have been events such as media controversy about downstream pollution in the mid-1990s. Where the direct financial interests of the company or its image have been threatened or compromised by actors outside its own notion of its existing boundaries of responsibility, then the boundaries have widened. Hence, in the wake of the downstream riverine pollution controversy, much more attention was paid to the broadly defined developmental needs of the communities along the Laigaip and Strickland River systems, and these villages received water tanks, bridges, compensation and health patrol visits (see PEAK web site for details of some of these). Likewise, the disintegration of public order in Southern Highlands Province in 2002, along with the felling of numerous pylons along the transmission line from the Hides gas plant to the mine, brought an intensive period of company interventions in terms of support for the restoration of law and order and much broader-based development efforts within a community that had previously been marginal to the mine. The deterioration of law and order and the physical road along the Highlands Highway also saw the commitment of much greater funds by the PJV and other resource companies to this area, some of which took the form of an additional TCS.

Finally, and most significantly in terms of the current argument, the refinement and increasing traction of notions of sustainability within the corporation have significantly reshaped the geographic and metaphoric boundaries of corporate responsibility at Porgera. The scope of 'community' at Porgera has been broadened by the corporate focus on sustainability. This was shown by the production of a Porgera Mine Closure Consultation Document at the end of 2002, in which it was clear that while the Special Mining Lease communities presented one geographic group in terms of mine closure, the social and economic issues faced ran significantly wider — into, for example, areas of local governance and economic development across the district and beyond (PJV 2002). The *Closure Consultation Document* was an attempt to map out those areas and those parties with responsibility for addressing different community issues, making the point that the mining company was rarely the sole party with responsibilities or influence in the area (and the other parties included various arms of the State and the community itself): indeed, in many areas the potential contribution of the company beyond mine closure was limited. Partnerships with NGOs were seen as a potential way of extending influence beyond this point, although few NGOs were tempted by the prospect of multinational mining houses as partners (though at least one major long-term NGO partner has been secured at Porgera).

In terms of social responsibility, there are signs that the PJV has sought to extend its influence over some of the more destructive community processes, albeit in limited ways. One example is the writing into new relocation and compensation agreements of alternatives to permanent-material houses and cash payouts. Two such schemes included assistance with real estate investments, and the use of trust funds to ensure the value of relocation packages were maintained until at least the end of the mine life. The first of these has been popular among the latest round of relocated parties, although a number of 'cultural influences' have also started to impact on the success of these schemes.

Interestingly, the effect of sustainability as a discourse on such boundaries is now the subject of increasing institutional interest among multinationals. An industry-led Global Reporting Initiative recently brought out a report on the issue of where the boundaries of responsibility lie when it comes to the reporting of progress towards sustainability (GRI 2005). In this report, the issue of control and influence is central: that is, over what subsidiaries does the corporation extend control and influence in terms of reporting its compliance with sustainability targets and guidelines? Much the same debate occurs at Porgera over the responsibility of the company for 'leaving behind a better future'. The key emphasis from the company perspective is to identify those areas and issues where they are able to influence or control processes and events in a way that can translate into tangible positive outcomes. The trust funds and NGO partnerships mentioned above are viewed in this light. Obviously, such long-term planning is far removed from the reactive nature of early PJV community affairs at Porgera. To be clear, then, the lines of corporate concern and responsibility at Porgera have been continually redrawn in an expansive way by the corporation and other parties with influence over it, and have recently been heavily influenced by the discourse of sustainability, a key element of current global corporate rhetoric and governance.

Conclusions

The increasing emphasis on notions of sustainability, especially in the context of mine closure, and social responsibility at the global level has led to discussion within corporations, national governments and international institutions about the limits of responsibility for, and their ability to mitigate, negative social effects within communities. This has occurred at the same time as transparency and social responsibility have become central to notions of corporate governance among multinationals in developing countries. The boundaries of corporate social responsibility and the limits for reporting of progress towards sustainability are increasingly being institutionalised through global regimes and standards. In this paper, some of these limits have been outlined in the context of the Porgera mine. External factors, global trends and key personnel have all been important in reshaping boundaries of corporate influence and responsibility at Porgera in the past decade. There is a tendency to see global capital as static once it becomes established at particular locations. Instead, as we have seen, there is a constant dialectic between local and global discourses that the company must traverse and negotiate. And there is certainly not a unidirectional, global-to-local set of processes operating: events at one or two sites have had a profound influence on the higher level discourse within the corporation and this in turn feeds back to local operations.

The basic tension between drawing a line at the mine gate and behaving responsibly within it with no interest or involvement in the outside community except as it impinges on the mine operation, and becoming engaged with the myriad and complex social processes that occur within the community, is one that is constantly being negotiated by corporations in development contexts. Leaning too far one way can attract charges of corporate imperialism (or at least paternalism), while in the other direction lies irresponsibility, danger and immorality (companies that do not know about human rights violations within their sphere of influence would certainly deserve this label).

All lines in PNG are drawn in mud — the murky (in the sense of ambiguous and/or flexible) rules of community inclusion and exclusion, occasionally shifting (and sometimes less than obvious) mining lease boundaries and gradually expanding and encompassing responsibilities accepted by the mining company at Porgera. Initiated in part in response to the attacks on its environmental record, the discourse of sustainability at the corporate level has fed back into the creation of new structures and policies within the company. These map out new, expansive boundaries of social responsibility at Porgera. Despite the fact that it occurs within a discursive world dominated by global sustainability concerns, the current corporate cadastral trend at the Porgera mine site is still a largely pragmatic one, targeting those areas where some degree of control over process is possible and results are tangible. This makes for safer public relations and sustainability reporting, and hence is too easily labelled as a more sophisticated form of corporate green-washing, but it might also represent the real limits of corporate power in these highly dynamic and complex social environments.

References

Ballard, C. and G. Banks. 2003. 'Resource Wars: Mining and Anthropology.' *Annual Review of Anthropology,* 32. pp. 287–313.

Banks, G. 1999. 'Gardens and Wantoks.' In C. Filer (ed.), *Dilemmas of Development: The Social and Economic Impact of the Porgera gold mine 1989-1994,* Canberra and Port Moresby: Asia-Pacific Press (*Pacific Policy Paper,* 34), Resource Management in Asia Pacific Project, and National Research Institute (*Special Publication,* 24). pp. 160–90.

Banks, G. 2003. '"Faces we do not know": Mining and migration in the Melanesian context.' Unpublished paper presented at the *Mining Frontiers: Social conflicts, property relations and cultural change in emerging boom regions* workshop, Halle/Saale, Germany, June 18, 2003.

Banks, G. 2005. 'Globalization, poverty, and hyperdevelopment in Papua New Guinea's mining sector.' *Focaal, European Journal of Anthropology*, 46. pp. 128–43.

Biersack, A. 1999. 'Porgera — Whence and Whither?' In C. Filer (ed.), *Dilemmas of Development: The Social and Economic Impact of the Porgera Gold Mine, 1989-1994,* Canberra and Port Moresby:Asia Pacific Press and National Research Institute. pp. 260–79.

Cesare, P. and P. Maxwell. 2003. 'Mine closure legislation in Indonesia: The role of mineral industry involvement.' *Natural Resources Forum*, 27. pp. 42–52.

CSIRO. 1996. *Review of Riverine Impacts: Porgera Joint Venture*. Canberra: CSIRO Environmental Projects Office.

Cowell, S., W. Wehrmeyer, P. Argust and G. Robertson. 1999. 'Sustainability and the primary extraction industries: Theories and practice.' *Resources Policy*, 25. pp. 277–86.

Cragg, W. and A. Greenbaum. 2002. 'Reasoning about responsibilities: Mining company managers on what stakeholders are owed.' *Journal of Business Ethics*, 39. pp. 319–35.

Dove, J., T. Miriung and M. Togolo. 1974. 'Mining bitterness.' In P. Sack (ed.), *Problem of Choice: Land in Papua New Guinea's Future*, Canberra and Port Moresby: ANU Press and Robert Brown and Associates. pp. 181–9.

Filer, C. 1990. 'The Bougainville rebellion, the mining industry and the process of social disintegration in Papua New Guinea.' *Canberra Anthropology*, 13 (1). pp. 1–39.

Global Reporting Initiative. 2005. *GRI Boundary Protocol*. GRI. (Available online at http://www.globalreporting.org/guidelines/protocols/boundaries.asp

Golub, Alex. 2003. 'Migration, gold-mining and reconfigurations of kinship and ethnic relations in highlands Papua New Guinea. Cultural authenticity, novelty and cultural change.' Unpublished paper presented at the Mining Frontiers workshop, Max Planck Institute for Social Anthropology, Halle, Germany, June 18, 2003.

Golub, A. 2005. 'Making the Ipili feasible: Imagining local and global actors at the Porgera gold mine, Enga Province, Papua New Guinea.' Unpublished PhD dissertation, Department of Anthropology, University of Chicago.

Hamann, R. 2004. 'Corporate social responsibility, partnerships and institutional change: The case of mining companies in South Africa.' *Natural Resources Forum*, 28. pp. 278–90.

Hilson, G. and B. Murck. 2000. 'Sustainable development in the mining industry: Clarifying the corporate perspective.' *Resources Policy*, 26. pp. 227–38.

Hughes, H. 2004. 'Can Papua New Guinea come back from the brink?' *Issue Analysis* No. 49. Sydney: The Centre for Independent Studies. (Available online at http://www.cis.org.au/)

Humphreys, D. 1999. 'A business perspective on community relations in mining.' *Resources Policy*, 26. pp. 127–31.

Imbun B. Y. 1995. 'Enga social life and identity in a Papua New Guinea mining town.' *Oceania*, 66. pp. 51–61.

Jacka, J. 2003. 'God, gold and the ground: Place-based political ecology in the New Guinea borderlands.' Unpublished PhD dissertation, Department of Anthropology, University of Oregon.

Jackson, R. and G. Banks. 2002. *In Search of the Serpent's Skin: The History of the Porgera Gold Project*. Port Moresby: Placer Niugini Ltd.

Jorgenson, D. 1997. 'Who and what is a landowner? Mythology and marking the ground in a Papua New Guinea mining project.' *Anthropological Forum*, 7 (4). pp. 599–627.

Jenkins, H. 2004. 'Corporate social responsibility and the mining industry: Conflicts and constructs.' *Corporate Social Responsibility and Environmental Management*, 11. pp. 23–34.

Kapelus, P. 2002. 'Mining, corporate social responsibility and "the community": The case of Rio Tinto, Richards Bay and the Mbonambi.' *Journal of Business Ethics*, 39. pp. 275–96.

Kennedy, D. 1996a. 'Ok Tedi all over again: Placer and the Porgera Gold Mine.' *Multinational Monitor* (March). pp. 22–4.

Kennedy, D. 1996b. 'Porgera: Arsenic and Gold.' *Mining Monitor*, 1 (2). pp. 7–8.

Larmour, P. (ed.) 1998. 'Governance and reform in the South Pacific.' *National Centre for Development Studies, Pacific Policy Paper* 23. Canberra: ANU.

Macintyre, M. and S. Foale. 2004. 'Global Imperatives and local desires: Competing economic and environmental interests in Melanesian communities.' In V. Lockwood (ed.), *Globalization and Culture Change in the Pacific Islands*, Upper Saddle River, New Jersey: Pearson Prentice Hall. pp. 149–64.

Mineral Policy Institute. 1995. *The Porgera File: Adding to Australia's Legacy of Destruction*. Sydney: Mineral Policy Institute.

Mining, Minerals and Sustainable Development Project. 2002. *Breaking New Ground: The Report of the Mining, Minerals and Sustainable Development Project*. London: Earthscan.

Placer Dome Asia Pacific. 1998. *Towards Sustainability*. Sydney: Placer Dome Asia Pacific.

Placer Dome Asia Pacific. 1999. *Porgera Mine: 1998 Sustainability Report*. Sydney: Placer Dome Asia Pacific.

Placer Dome Incorporated. 1999. *Sustainability Report*. Vancouver: PDI.

Polier N. 1994. 'A view from the "cyanide room": Politics and culture in a mining town in Papua New Guinea.' *Identities,* 1. pp. 63–84.

Porgera Joint Venture. 2002. *Porgera Mine Closure Consultation Document*. Porgera: PJV.

Robinson, F. 1991. 'Anthropology and the Porgera gold mine.' Paper presented at New Perspectives on the Papua New Guinea Highlands: An Interdisciplinary Conference on the Duna, Huli, and Ipili Peoples, RSPAS, ANU, Canberra, August 16–18.

Robinson, F. 1994. 'Squatters and outsiders.' Paper presented at *Second Business Development and Community Affairs Conference*, Port Moresby, PNG Chamber of Mining and Petroleum, March 15.

Ross, M. 1999. 'The political economy of the resource curse.' *World Politics,* 51 (2). pp. 297–322.

Shearman, P. 1995. 'The Environmental and Social Impact of the Porgera Gold Mine on the Strickland River System.' Unpublished BSc. (Hons) thesis, Department of Geography and Environmental Studies, University of Tasmania, Hobart.

Shearman, P. 2001. 'Giving away another river: An analysis of the impacts of the Porgera Mine on the Strickland River system.' In B. Imbun and P. A. McGavin (eds), *Mining in Papua New Guinea: Analysis & Policy Implications*, Waigani, N.C.D.: University of Papua New Guinea Press. pp. 173–90.

Watts, M. 2005. 'Righteous oil? Human rights, the oil complex and corporate social responsibility.' *Annual Review of Environment and Resources*, 30. pp. 373–407.

Wheeler, D., H. Fabig and R. Boele. 2002. 'Paradoxes and dilemmas for stakeholder responsive firms in the extractive sector: Lessons from the case of Shell and the Ogoni.' *Journal of Business Ethics*, 39. pp. 297–318.

14. The 'Resource Curse' and Governance: A Papua New Guinean perspective

Mel Togolo

In discussing what has become known as 'the resource curse' one is confronted with two predominant views about the impacts of mineral and petroleum extraction on a national economy.

The conventional wisdom is that mineral resource developments can add value to the economy of a mineral-rich country. The principal effects of such developments are that they provide revenue to a host government through taxation and royalty payments, and they generate income and wealth for individuals and companies through the many financial transactions involved in the development process. In some sense this is certainly true for PNG, as the economy has always been buoyed by the mineral and petroleum sector. Thus, in a general sense, the traditional view maintains that 'mining plays an important role in the development process by converting mineral resources into a form of capital that contributes to a nation's output' (Davis et al. 2002: 6).

The other view, which has emerged in the past 20 years, is that it has a negative impact on the economy as it harms the traditional sources of exports and weakens the manufacturing base.[1] This view is based principally on studies carried out on several mineral-dependent economies,[2] particularly in the developing world. In some of these countries economic growth during this period has been negative. Those who subscribe to the view that resource development is a curse maintain that resource extraction has not contributed to sustainable increases in socioeconomic development in countries with rich mineral resources. At the extreme end, the argument is made that mining activity in poor countries will lead 'inexorably and inevitably to poor outcomes and growth' (Roe et al. 2004: 6). Such a situation would confirm the 'resource curse' view and might lead us to conclude that there should not be any mining, particularly in developing countries. A related issue that has contributed to the development of this view is the suggestion that resource development causes 'violence and civil wars' within countries (Shultz 2004: 34), leads to foreign intervention to protect multinational interests, and foreign intervention in internal affairs, or leads to 'social disintegration' within communities (Filer 1990: 88).

While poor economic performance has undoubtedly been the experience in some situations, recent empirical case studies have shown that while this might be true in some countries it is not the case in others (Roe, et al. 2004; DiJohn 2002). The obvious question is: why is this so?

In discussing this question, I shall draw on the two case studies of the Porgera and Ok Tedi mines, which operate in the highlands of PNG, and will examine their contributions to the benefit streams that accrue to governments, in particular, and, to a lesser extent, landowners and communities.

In the context of PNG, direct benefits of mining and petroleum are significant indeed. In the past decade, this sector represented more than 70 per cent of total PNG exports, more than 30 per cent of total government revenues and contributed about 25 per cent of GDP. In 2004 alone, the combined mineral and petroleum sector made up more than 73 per cent of total merchandise exports. That means for every kina of export revenue, 73 toea came from this sector. The mineral sector itself accounted for more than 53 per cent of total exports in 2004. From 1989 to 2004, the Porgera mine produced more than 13 million ounces of gold, worth more than K8.5 billion in export value. In 2004 the gold and silver from Porgera made up 16.4 per cent of the total exports from PNG. These contributions are matched by public revenue benefits. In 2004, the National Government received K170.4 million in taxes and duties from Porgera and, since production started in 1989, it has received more than K1.1 billion in taxes (corporate and income) and customs duties.

With respect to mineral royalties, which in the case of Porgera are granted directly to provincial and local institutions, since 1989, Porgera landowners and the Enga Provincial Government have received K157 million. This went to the Provincial Government (50 per cent), Porgera Development Authority (5 per cent), Special Mining Lease landowners (15 per cent), Children's Trust Fund (10 per cent), Porgera Landowners' Association (12 per cent) and Young Adults (8 per cent). Between 1989 and 2004, Porgera spent more than K51 million on employee education. Porgera also spent more than K10 million to sponsor more than 500 students (non-employees) to schools, colleges and universities during the period 1989-2004.

The case of the Ok Tedi mine paints a similar picture. During the period 1982-2004 the National Government received almost K1.4 billion from the Ok Tedi Mining Lease (OTML) in taxes and duties (corporate and income tax, customs duties). From 1982 to 2004, OTML paid K238 million in royalties and K246 million in dividends and spent more than K44 million on employee education and training.

What I have described above supports the traditional view that mineral deposits are assets and part of a country's natural capital. The argument continues that the more capital and natural wealth a country possesses and extracts in a sustainable manner, the richer and better off it will be. The extraction or capital conversion of a country's natural assets keeps the economy buoyant and provides the necessary public and private revenue to support services and further socioeconomic advancement.

In PNG, this sector is responsible for more than 70 per cent of the value of merchandise exports. Mining is the means through which dormant mineral wealth in the ground can be translated into public goods such as schools and hospitals and productive assets such as roads, bridges and ports. Further, the sector produces enhanced human capital in the form of new skills that in turn can facilitate economic development in other sectors of the economy. Therefore mineral development is crucial to the development of a country like PNG. Mineral resources are part of the nation's realisable capital and the revenues from them can and are being used in the improvement of other types of capital, including physical, human, knowledge and institutional forms. So, according to the traditional view, mining, like other economic activities, plays an important role in the development process and can convert 'a mineral resource in the ground into sustainable improvements in people's lives' (Togolo 1999: 597).

How then should we understand the critical view of mining that has emerged in the past 20 years, which argues that there is no positive correlation between resource extraction and economic development? Some studies have suggested that countries where mining is important have not progressed as rapidly as countries where there is no mining. They would argue that this would be true for PNG and might well extend the argument to suggest that there should be no mineral development because it has a negative impact on economic development.

The 'resource curse'

This view is articulated in the term 'Dutch disease' or the 'resource curse'. In brief, this view says that during a resource boom wages rise as the sector competes for scarce skilled labour and draws resources away from other sectors. As well, it is contended that an increase in mineral exports brings about the appreciation of the local currency, which in turn makes it difficult for agricultural exports and the manufacturing sector to compete internationally. When the mineral boom is over the country's traditional sources of exports could well have been destroyed, unable to be sustained in a high exchange rate environment.

Certainly from its macro-economic performance this seems to be true for PNG. Using the year 2000 as a base, the real exchange rate (PNGK/$US) was generally high during the period between 1980 and 1998 (Roe, et al. 2004: 55). Apart from the influence of the mining industry on the local currency, PNG's own 'Hard Kina' policy before 1994 was thought to be a sound macro-economic tool of stabilisation. In fact, it was highly distortive and, in the context of this discussion, was responsible for inflaming the 'resource curse'. It was a disincentive to the agricultural and manufacturing sectors by making them less competitive in the global market. At the same time, it increased the domestic cost of the mining industry. Foreign reserves fell to almost zero and the country was forced to float the currency in October 1994. This policy change is bearing fruit, though slowly. From 1995 to 2004, during the period of massive currency devaluation, GDP growth remained erratic and there were three consecutive years of negative growth from 2000 to 2002, a period in which mineral prices were depressed and oil prices were reasonable.

Additionally, the resource curse view might argue, in the context of PNG, that resource extraction (mineral, oil and gas) creates a handout mentality among a few wealthy rent-seeking landowners, who might have no idea about sustainability, creating expectations that are well beyond the reach of ordinary villagers. Rent-seeking behaviour encourages 'unearned' income to be wasted on consumption rather than investment and can become an excuse for poor governance (Shultz 2004: 37).

Let us look, however, at what has happened in the past and more recently to countries with large mineral resources. Many countries, such as Britain and Germany, took advantage of their mineral endowments and used them to build their productive industrial base for long-term economic growth. The USA, Australia, Canada, South Africa, Botswana, Indonesia and Chile are examples of countries that have done well by converting revenues from the development of their mineral and petroleum resources into further economic development. Conversely, there are countries such as Zambia, Sierra Leone and PNG, which have not done so well with wealth from minerals and other resources. It is my belief that the assertion that mineral extraction is responsible for negative impacts on the national economy is overly simplistic and ignores other contributing socioeconomic factors and governance challenges. If developing countries such as PNG are struggling to minimise poverty, discouraging mining where it promotes the goals of poverty reduction and long-term growth is counterproductive, economically irresponsible and clearly not sensible.

What are the reasons why mineral extraction (or for that matter any resource development) is able to promote economic development in some countries and not in others? Why does it work, for example, in Botswana but not in Zambia? What are the factors that have allowed some countries to maximise benefits from their mineral endowments and prevent the resource curse while others have not maximised the benefits? What should governments in these countries do to avoid the woes of the resource curse?

It is important to note here that the resource curse is not something unique to mineral-rich developing countries. Writing about why some countries are so rich and some are so poor, Landes (1999: 171–3) points out that from the age of discovery to the 18th century, Spain, probably at that time the wealthiest country in all of Christendom, used its money from its newly discovered territories on luxury and war and did not invest for the future. In other words, it became poor because it spent all its money ('unearned income') on non-productive ventures, the result of bad decisions.

In this sense, the question should not be whether mineral extraction is good or bad for economic development or even whether it is a result of an enclave development detached from the rest of the economy. The real question should be: do such countries have development policies and institutional frameworks that are capable of maximising the benefits for human development from mining and petroleum? And are such policies consistent, predictable and enduring? How and where should they invest the revenues for long-term broad-based economic development? How can such policies ensure that the benefits are used to build sustainable and durable productive capacity for real economic growth and poverty alleviation? Do leaders have the discipline to ensure that economic management and governance are entrenched in order to deliver sustainable development? Do they have the institutional integrity to support policy frameworks for sustainable development?

All of these questions are related. I think these are the real policy questions in relation to resource development, be that in mineral extraction, agriculture or manufacturing. How do they impact on the questions of public policy?

In a major study by Oxford Policy Management (Roe et al. 2004: 41) which studied 33 mineral-dependent countries — countries in which mineral production constitutes more than 40 per cent of total exports and contributes 10 per cent or more of the GDP — it was concluded that the difference between 'better' and 'poorer' performing countries was essentially to do with the quality of governance and the quality of macro-economic management. Clearly the determining factors were the 'capacity and efficiency of governance and institutions and how these are impacted by the presence of large scale mining'. This study pointed out that the so-called resource curse can be avoided and that 'there is no inevitability about it'.

I would argue that from the perspective of PNG, over many years, it has clearly been a combination of macro-economic management, sociopolitical institutions and governance structures that have contributed to poor performance. As an economic activity, mineral extraction has provided the country with huge opportunities to improve the performance of its economy and governance institutions, yet in many instances this opportunity has been squandered. The mineral sector should be considered a bonus (Auty 1993: 257) to facilitate opportunities for diversification of the economy.

Koyama (2005), writing about the externalities of oil production in the Southern Highlands of PNG, has shown that the poor development outcomes in that province are due largely to poor public policy choices, lack of governance, rent-seeking behaviour, corruption and, might I add, 'the culture of the big-man'. The opportunities provided by oil revenues could not be maximised under such conditions. Koyama did not argue that there should not be any investment in petroleum development but rather prescribed a number of 'antidotes' to cure what he described as the 'PNG disease' (2005: 22). The main thrust of his argument accords quite neatly with the commonality that exists between the traditional view and the new view. Neither view disputes the fact that mineral deposits can create human, physical and technological capital and bring about economic growth. Mineral resources provide a country such as PNG with opportunities for economic growth and human development but they have to be accompanied and protected by institutional integrity and governance provisions, which are accepted and supported by both the community and the leadership.

In a paper I delivered in December 2004 at the Eighth Papua New Guinea Mining and Petroleum Investment Conference, I argued that 'macro-economic stability is not sustainable without effective structural reforms and institutional integrity' and further noted 'that stability has to be grounded on institutions that improve the performance and productivity of the economy'. These include the institutions of decision-making, institutions of planning and central coordination, institutions of public policy and institutions of law and order. I noted that if there was going to be any success, such 'institutions have to be open, consistent and predictable, transparent and accountable'. Institutional integrity and durability is a prerequisite to disciplining a fiscal regime and improving the performance of public expenditure.

Addressing governance issues and implementing institutional reforms that would capture the benefits of mineral development can help to avoid the resource curse. PNG has attempted some corrective measures in this area. In the past it tried to establish governance structures to deal with mineral revenues through the Mineral Revenue Stabilisation Fund.

The Mineral Revenue Stabilisation Fund (MRSF)

The MRSF was designed as a fiscal tool to support prudent macro-economic management in an economy dominated by a few large resource projects, whose profitability was linked to cyclical world commodity prices (Auty 1993: 211). The legislation came into force in 1974. The rationale was to provide procedures for smoothing the flow of mine tax revenues to government. The MRSF set a basis for budget integrity and governance.

The statutory provisions of the act established rigid fiscal discipline. But even before the forced closure of Bougainville Copper in 1989, there were moves to amend and relax the provisions of the act. When the MRSF Act was revised in 1987, the Government was given greater discretion in making withdrawals from the fund. From the late 1970s and early 1980s, PNG adopted an expansionary monetary policy in anticipation of future revenues from its vast mineral resources and, as Parsons and Vincent (1991) showed, withdrawals from the MRSF increased significantly from 1980 to 1990. Little attention was paid to providing 'processes and policy settings so that the revenue collected from mining is spent' to build infrastructure and other productive capacity projects to ensure macro-economic sustainability (Parsons and Vincent 1991: 33). Needless to say, expenditure was highest in conspicuous consumption and in supporting the public service infrastructure in the period from 1980 to 1990. It is indeed a sad indictment of Papua New Guinea's governance that the act was diluted (amended) to allow ministerial and management discretion in the use of the MRSF, which supports the view that 'unearned' income of rentier states avoids reciprocal obligations between government and civil society (taxpayers) (DiJohn 2002: 3).

Institutional reforms

In the past 10 years, PNG has undertaken vigorous institutional reforms in the public and financial sectors, which could assist in capturing the benefits of mining and petroleum revenues. When Sir Mekere Morauta was Prime Minister, one of the amendments to the *Public Finances Management Act* was to restrict the use of budget surpluses to the repayment of public debt. This amendment ensures that 90 per cent of any budget surplus is used to repay public debt. It would seem that the current Treasurer, Bart Philemon, is utilising this provision.

During the past several years, macro-economic stability has been sustained, inflation has come under control, the currency has stabilised, foreign exchange controls are gradually being liberalised and public debt is declining. The economy is quite buoyant, but remains fragile as it continues to be a commodity-based economy susceptible to volatility caused by external and internal factors.

In the past decade, in the mineral and petroleum sectors, several reforms have taken place in order to address issues relating to community benefits.

Development forum

After the first-generation agreements of Bougainville Copper Limited and Ok Tedi Mining Limited, an initiative that changed the landscape of stakeholder relationships in mineral development and which was later extended to petroleum projects was the creation of what is known as the Development Forum. In 1988, the PNG Cabinet endorsed the creation of the Development Forum as part of the 'approval process' for large mining development. The requirement to convene a Development Forum has subsequently been included within the *Mining Act 1992* and the *Oil and Gas Act*. This is an established process in which the landowners in a mining or petroleum area, provincial governments and the National Government discuss their respective responsibilities and obligations in relation to a project to be developed and the associated benefits accruing to each group before the approval for development is given to the developer.

These discussions lead to the creation of a set of interlocutory Memoranda of Agreements (MOAs) outlining respective responsibilities and obligations. In many respects they articulate how the benefits are to be distributed between the various interest groups. Before 1992 these MOAs were part of public policy. With the review and amendment of the *Mining Act* in 1992, MOAs are now entrenched in law and have become a requisite for all major mineral and petroleum projects. In the early MOAs the developer was not a signatory, but was normally consulted and asked to brief the parties on the content of the 'Proposal for Development'. There were often misunderstandings by many leaders at that time that the developer was a signatory to these agreements, however, at that time the only agreement for which the developer was a signatory was the Mining Development Contract. In mineral developments since 1995, the developers have become signatories to the MOAs and have become an integral part of the benefits management process.

In its role as a mechanism to involve landowners and provincial governments in the process of resource development, the Development Forum has allowed discussions and decision-making processes to be more transparent as well as clearly qualifying and identifying benefits and accountabilities.

Tax Credit Scheme (TCS)

Invariably, mining operations take place in isolated and rugged regions where there are few or no existing government services. The geography of the mineral projects poses significant problems of inaccessibility for the Government and communities. Clearly, such conditions make it difficult for communities to be served adequately by government agencies, particularly when such agencies have weak administrative and technical capacities, even in the major population centres.

It has always been a concern to developers that mining revenues to the Government might not directly benefit the local communities in mining areas. In addition, isolated regions tend not to attract the kind of skills and expertise required to plan and implement infrastructure projects under difficult conditions. The recognition by mining companies that pre-existing conditions of poor development in isolated communities need to be urgently addressed led to discussions about industry involvement in assisting with key infrastructure development. In addition, such an approach would assist in providing social stability in a mining area, and a social licence for future development for a mining company.

In the early 1990s Placer Niugini Limited (now Placer Dome Niugini Limited) proposed a framework of tax rebates for infrastructure development that would be undertaken by developers on behalf of the Government.[3] It was agreed in 1992 that up to 0.75 per cent of the gross taxable income from a mining project would be used for approved infrastructure projects such as schools, roads and bridges and this expenditure would be deducted from tax to be paid by the project. To my knowledge, it does not happen in any other mining jurisdiction in the world, where 'a portion of the nation's share of benefits from mining projects has been handed back to the companies to fund local development' (Jackson 2005: 7). The process involves the landowners, provincial government and the developer agreeing to the types of project to be built and submitting the proposals to a committee of national departments (National Planning and Rural Development, Department of Mining or Department of Petroleum and the Internal Revenue Commission) for approval. In 2004, Porgera mine spent more than K70 million on TCS projects and Ok Tedi mine K19.25 million.

Mineral Resources Authority (MRA)

A recent reform that has great potential for good governance is the creation of the MRA. The Mineral Resources Bill has been approved by the National Executive Council and will soon be passed by the Parliament. Essentially this bill will convert the Department of Mining into a statutory authority, making it financially autonomous, giving it flexibility to recruit expertise and making it easier for it to engage short-term consultants in order to improve its performance. The aim is to make the MRA more effective in serving the industry through promotion and better regulation with the long-term objective of continued sustainable mineral-related revenue for the national budget. The board of the MRA is made up of government officials and private sector representatives in almost equal numbers. Obviously it will mean that the authority is going to be run more like a business entity than a government department.

Conclusion

To conclude, I would like to emphasise again that the differences in development outcomes between the 'poorer' and the 'better' performing mineral-rich countries lie in their quality of governance and the quality of their macro-economic management and how these are related to a mineral- and petroleum-extraction activity. It is not mining nor is it petroleum activity as such that is responsible for poor economic performance. Mining companies cannot do the work of a sovereign government. They can only assist and facilitate.

PNG has been criticised for not doing as well as it should. That's now a bit of history. I hope that I have shown how PNG is trying to improve its governance performance in utilising the opportunities created by mining and petroleum revenues. Major efforts have been made in public and financial sector reforms, which are likely to have a positive impact in managing the benefits from mining.

References

Auty, Richard M. 1993. *Sustainable Development in Mineral Economies: The resource curse thesis.* London: Routledge.

Davis, A. Graham and John E. Tilton. 2002. *Should Developing Countries Renounce Mining? A perspective on the debate. A study for the International Council for Mining and Metals.* http://www.icmm.com/uploads/62TiltonDavisfinalversion.pdf

DiJohn, Jonathan. 2002. 'Mineral Abundance and Violent Political Conflict: A Critical Assessment of the Rentier State Model.' Crisis States Programme Working Paper Series No. 1. London: Development Studies Institute, LSE.

Filer, C. 1990. 'The Bougainville Rebellion, the Mining Industry and the Process of Social Disintegration in Papua New Guinea.' In R. J. May and Matthew Spriggs (eds), *The Bougainville Crisis*, Bathurst: Crawford House Press. pp. 112–40.

Jackson, R. 2005. 'The Challenge of Sustaining Mining Benefits.' *Mining and Environmental Management.* London: Mining Communications Limited. pp. 6–9.

Koyama, Samuel K. 2005. 'Black gold or excrement of the devil? The externalities of oil production in Papua New Guinea.' *Pacific Economic Bulletin*, 20, 1.

Landes, David. 1999. *The Wealth and Poverty of Nations.* London: Abacus.

Parsons, David and David Vincent. 1991. 'High Stakes: Mineral and Petroleum Development in Papua New Guinea.' Institute of National Affairs Discussion Paper No. 49. Port Moresby, Papua New Guinea.

Roe, Alan et al. 2004. 'Using resource endowments to foster sustainable development: How to enhance the economic contribution of the mining and metal sector.' Oxford Policy Management Draft Report. London.

Shultz, Jim. 2004. *Follow the Money: A Guide to Monitoring the Budgets and Oil and Gas Revenues. A Report for the Open Society Institute.* New York.

Togolo, M. 1999. 'Mining and sustainability — Placer Niugini Limited.' In PACRIM '99, Proceedings of International Congress on Earth Science, Exploration and Mining Around the Pacific Rim. Bali, Indonesia.

Togolo, M. 2004. 'Private Sector View of the Economy and the Investment Initiatives.' Paper delivered at the Eighth Papua New Guinea Mining and Petroleum Investment Conference, Sydney, December 6–7.

ENDNOTES

[1] It could be argued that this was due to bad policy, which discouraged the development of competitive manufacturing and agricultural sectors. In the 1970s and 1980s many resource-rich countries, including mineral-dependent developing countries, pursued policies of import substitution supported by various forms of government subsidies, particularly at the period of surging nationalism.

[2] A mineral economy is one in which mineral production makes up more than 40 per cent of total exports and more than 10 per cent of GDP, according to World Bank definition.

[3] In about 1990, on my regular visits to Porgera gold mine in my capacity as the first General Manager of the Mineral Resources Development Company Limited (a member of the Porgera Joint Venture), I was once asked by Vic Botts, the then Managing Director of Placer Niugini Limited, if I thought there were ways the Bougainville crisis might have been avoided. Among other things, I told him that one of the things the North Solomons Provincial Government demanded in the negotiations during the review of the Bougainville Copper Agreement was to allow Bougainville Copper Limited to build selected and prescribed infrastructure in the province and have those costs deducted from its corporate tax. In this way the mining company would have been seen as contributing directly to the development of provincial infrastructure and, hence, be more acceptable to the community. I told him that senior Bougainville Copper Limited officials in private conversations were quite comfortable with the concept, but the National Government refused to listen to this suggestion at that time. I believe this discussion was the genesis of the Tax Credit Scheme, an initiative of Placer Dome, which became effective in 1992 and is now well accepted by all stakeholders.

Tradition, Culture and Politics

15. Keynote Address — Governance in Fiji: The interplay between indigenous tradition, culture and politics

Ratu Joni Madraiwiwi

Commentators and observers alike have long decried the ethnic nature of politics in Fiji. It is seen as an obstacle to the creation of a more unified and cohesive society. Those concerns are well taken, however, the forces of history cast a long shadow over the present. For indigenous Fijians there is a constant struggle between embracing other communities and maintaining a distinct and separate identity. There is ambivalence about compromise. It is feared something is indelibly lost in that process. Fijian unity as an ideal is extolled and valued because it is perceived as the only way Fijians believe they can protect their 'Fijianness'. The reality is far more complex. But it provides a reassuring sanctuary against the challenges they face both individually and collectively.

British colonial rule in 1874 created the legacy we have today. The first Governor, Sir Arthur Gordon, established the Fijian Administration. It introduced a separate system of indirect rule by the British through the Fijian chiefs over their Fijian subjects. Having served as Governor of Mauritius, Gordon had no qualms about importing Indian indentured labour to plant cane for sugar production in order to finance the running of the nascent colony. The first labourers arrived in 1879 and the scheme continued until 1916, when it was ended, owing to widespread protests by Mohandas Gandhi among others.

The separation of Fijians from other ethnic communities was maintained until the abolition of the Native Regulations in 1967. They regulated the lives of Fijians in the villages and restricted their movement to and from the urban centres. From 1894 to 1963, the *Bose Levu Vakaturaga* or Great Council of Chiefs nominated Fijian members to the Legislative Council. Only Fijians of chiefly rank occupied the positions of *Roko Tui*, or chief administrative official, of the 14 provinces of Fiji. In 1947 the first non-Fijian chief was appointed as *Roko Tui Tailevu*. In this decade, education began to be made available more widely. The return of Fijian soldiers from the Solomons campaign in World War II, and participation in the Malaya campaign against the Communists in the 1950s, broadened horizons beyond their villages as well. Only in 1963 were Fijians given the right to directly elect members to the Legislative Council.

With the arrival of the indentured labourers, the Fijian chiefs, while wary of these newcomers, were initially quiescent. However, as more of them chose to stay permanently and their numbers grew, coupled with the declining Fijian population as the result of measles and other epidemics, perceptions and responses changed. The Fijian chiefs became quite hostile to Indo-Fijian interests and concerns. There was little chance of the two communities making common cause against the Colonial Administration. When the Indo-Fijian population exceeded that of the Fijians in the mid-1930s, that merely stoked Fijian fears further. Moreover, they had differing attitudes towards the British rulers. Indo-Fijians had suffered greatly under indenture, whereas the Fijian experience of the British was largely benign if highly regulated.

In establishing the Fijian Administration, Sir Arthur Gordon further wished to preserve and protect Fijian society, as he saw it, in its natural state. Progress should move at a pace Fijians could absorb without harming their way of life. This approach suited the Fijian chiefs because it reinforced their status. The communal nature of their social organisation, and the overarching structure of the Fijian Administration, instilled in Fijians a clannish perspective. While there were undercurrents, and notable figures such as Apolosi R. Nawai who challenged the status quo, the Fijian chiefs presented a united front to the Colonial Administration. Their interests were asserted as uniform and inseparable. Consensus among Fijians papered over the misgivings and dissent which some might have had. A strong sense of cohesion and reluctance to question, for fear of being set apart, kept Fijians together. It was no surprise that, with the autonomy given the colony in the decade before independence, Fijian leaders established a political party to protect and advance Fijian interests. Other communities were welcome to join as allied associations, but the emphasis was never in doubt.

Until his death in 1958, Ratu Sir Lala Sukuna was the seminal influence and voice on matters regarding the Fijian people. Sukuna had the right bloodlines. He was the best-educated Fijian in his time. Sukuna was a war hero. He was mannered in the way the English loved. The British Colonial Administration found him useful as an interlocutor for the Fijian people. Sukuna himself was not averse to manipulating the British Colonial Administration to protect what he regarded as Fijian prerogatives: retention of the traditional system by preserving the Fijian way of life in the villages. Democracy was envisaged as a destination a long way off. In the interim, Sukuna, together with others of like mind and chiefly background, would play guide. The paramountcy of Fijian interests reflected in the protection of land, customs and culture was the central tenet of this vision. The priorities set by Sukuna would be pursued by his political heirs; Ratu (later) Sir Kamisese Mara was groomed by Sukuna to succeed him.

It is generally thought that the British were acquiescent in the political developments leading to eventual independence in 1970. Far from it. They were very concerned with how matters transpired. From the late 1950s, Whitehall had hoped that multi-ethnic politics would gradually emerge. They underestimated the strength of Fijian feeling in the *Bose Levu Vakaturaga* and among elected Fijian Legislative Council Members. Neither would countenance a single electoral roll and open seats. Seats in the Legislative Council for the first general elections in 1966 for self-government were allocated on ethnic lines. This pattern was to persist after independence. Although we now have open seats under the 1997 Constitution, ethnically based seats still constitute the majority in the elected House of Representatives. Neither of the two significant political parties advocates any change and reform in the current electoral arrangements. If anything, the governing Fijian party has indicated that there should be more Fijian representation based on population changes.

Self-government and independence were determined by a relatively small group of people. In the case of the Fijian people, they trusted their leaders, and particularly the prominent chiefs of the time, including Mara, to make the right decisions. Many accepted those developments only because of their leaders. The assumption was that they as a community would always wield political power. Their leaders understood full well this outcome was premised on Fijian unity. It was believed, somewhat arrogantly, that this was almost immutable. Fijians themselves were superficially familiar with the process of elections and of having a law-making body of their representatives. However, it was a quantum leap to imagine that governments of a Fijian complexion could be removed. The possibility existed only in their worst nightmares. It was also easily manipulated by opportunist elements to foment political unrest. A mix of those factors occurred in 1987. What little understanding there was of the democratic process was overwhelmed by nationalist sentiment.

Fijian leaders from Ratu Sir Kamisese Mara to Rabuka to Qarase have largely encouraged ethnic Fijians to be united. Dr Timoci Bavadra has been the exception. He believed in a multicultural and multi-ethnic country. His colleagues for their part saw Fijians as forming the centre around which other communities would cohere. What is the basis for this unity? It is in a sense a circling of the wagons, of drawing the *laager* together. This is the rationale. There are only 400,000 Fijians on this planet. Who will protect them if they cannot stand together? No one. They will be divided and all that they hold sacrosanct will be forfeit: their land, their culture and traditions, their language, their very soul. Only if Fijians held political power as an ethnic group could their rights and interests be secure. These perceptions continue to be held by a significant number of Fijians. They resonate more than any current constitutional safeguards. These beliefs are continually reinforced by their chiefs, non-traditional leaders and the clergy, and are endorsed in discourse among ordinary Fijians.

Fijians have a strong sense of identity. They pride themselves on knowing who they are and where they come from. Urbanisation has eroded these sentiments only slightly. In recent times it has become tinged with some sense of bewilderment and confusion. The emergence of disparate interests and discordant voices appears very troubling. There is no shortage of speculation about the possible causes. It is attributed to indiscipline, disloyalty, defiance of authority, arrogance and opportunism. It is easy to forget that these islands were a collection of warring and contending *vanua* or chiefdoms before cession in 1874. The British imposed a unity on the country that had never existed before. Our sense of nationhood dates back only to that time. In this more open environment, some divisions are re-emerging. That need not be feared but should be considered in a historical context. In May 2000, the provinces which were largely the centres of unrest were Naitasiri, Northern Tailevu and parts of Macuata and Cakaudrove. Much of the unrest concerned perceptions of marginalisation and underdevelopment. These divisions appear to be a consequence of social change whether caused by urbanisation, rising levels of education, the rural-urban divide or the emergence of interests based on economic groupings.

Much has been said about the Fijian traditional system and the regard Fijians have for their chiefs. There is a lot said and written about the authority exercised by those leaders. When one peers beneath the surface, there have been profound changes and more are in store. Fijians among themselves tend to adopt a more ambivalent view, which they will not necessarily share openly. It generates a sense of disloyalty to be looking askance at their own. However, there is increasing recognition that any leader, be they chief or commoner, needs to have some education and means, because that is the measure by which success and standing are reckoned in contemporary society. It is no longer sufficient just to have the right bloodlines. It is an issue of credibility. The focus on inter-ethnic relations has often disguised the erosion of chiefly authority and the more questioning attitude of Fijians. These developments are being played out even as national issues are debated and considered. This is most evident in the media and in the attitudes of young urbanised Fijians, who seem more taken with globalised youth culture. The result has been the rise of more populist Fijian leaders having less inclination to compromise sectarian interests.

The period of leadership of Ratu Sir Kamisese Mara and Ratu Sir Penaia Ganilau covered the first 30 years of independence. It was common to see this as the continuation of chiefly leadership. In a sense it was an illusion. For while these two towering figures dwelt at the apex, the pyramid was actually made up of far more educated Fijians of non-chiefly rank. This was not what Sukuna envisaged, for he wished to preserve the role of the chiefs. The broadening of educational opportunities, and the inability of chiefly families to exploit and make use of their initial advantages, have altered the balance decisively. The process occurred gradually but inexorably. Bavadra, Rabuka, Chaudhry and now Qarase demonstrate that political power has passed to career politicians. Chiefs wishing to participate in politics must do so on equal terms with others. There is no prior right of leadership and to that extent democratic norms have taken root.

Most problematic have been Fijian attitudes to the rule of law. I have said elsewhere that the concept is little understood by Fijians. They see their rights as indigenous people as existing outside and above the law. Those attitudes incline them to break the law whenever they feel their rights are under threat. That in itself is a dangerous assumption because it allows whoever is strongest to make the rules. It was the rule of the club that Ratu Cakobau and other high chiefs surrendered to Queen Victoria in return for the rule of law and civilisation. One cannot have it both ways. To that end, Fijian leaders need to be open and direct with their people. They cannot be seen to be encouraging them to break the law when it suits them, and enforcing the law when it comes to expiring tenancies and leases. Fijians themselves need to be more questioning of those who would invoke indigenous rights as a rallying cry for disaffection and defiance of authority whenever it suits. While their fears and insecurities might be real, too often they are open to manipulation and exploitation.

It is interesting to chart the movement of moderate Fijian opinion since the first coup in May 1987. It generated a strong sense of nationalist feeling among ordinary Fijians from across the social spectrum. Post-1987 the concept of indigenous rights has been asserted with increasing confidence. Before that, it was trumpeted only by ardent nationalists. Yet to those who were taken by surprise by the outpouring of sentiment following that first coup, those concepts lie close to the surface. They always have. Part of the problem is that we do not listen intently enough to each other. The attempted coup of 2000 encouraged and justified the present government's initiatives to further advantage Fijians. The blueprint prescribing ambitious incentives for narrowing the margin between Fijians and others in a number of fields, and the *Qoliqoli* Bill, which extends proprietary rights to traditional owners of fisheries, were presented as palliatives to help assuage nationalist sentiment. While the blueprint broadened affirmative action extant since independence, no previous government had felt confident enough to legislate fishing rights. It had been mooted since the earliest days of independence and raised in the *Bose Levu Vakaturaga* continually since the late 19th century. It was a telling reflection of the movement of moderate Fijian opinion to the right because there appeared to be widespread support for it among Fijians.

The upheavals of May 2000 were far more divisive and traumatic than the coups in 1987. No longer was there consensus in the Fijian community. Certain Indo-Fijians were subjected to acts of violence and thuggery the likes of which one hopes never to witness again. Reconciliation and forgiveness have been vexed questions ever since. Fijians have drawn on their customs and traditions as well as their Christian heritage to initiate the process. One does not doubt the sincerity of the gesture. Neither does one question the need for some kind of healing that allows the nation to bind up its wounds. However, if reconciliation is to be meaningful, cathartic and all embracing, it has to be in a language everyone can speak: an engagement in which all can be involved. Anything less would be demeaning and diminishing. Unless all are part of the process, it is difficult to see how the nation can come to terms with its past hurts and pain.

As we move into the future, the issues of national identity and language remain unresolved. Because it is considered a sensitive issue, it is not discussed widely by either our leaders or the country at large. We are a multicultural and multi-religious nation. There is as yet no consensus on how we deal with these concerns. I am comfortable with the teaching of Fijian and Hindustani in school, however, our character ought to be shaped by the region of which we are part, and the spirit of the indigenous people who first inhabited our islands. I do not say that out of chauvinism, more out of a sense of trying to find an appropriate point around which we can rally. Why should that be the choice? The indigenous people are the host culture, they own most of the land and they are half the population. But most importantly, we are a Pacific people. Is identity important in a globalised world where there are seemingly no borders? Yes. It will remain so if only because people will increasingly need to take comfort and find assurance in the familiar.

Those thoughts require greater discussion and reflection, however, they would probably be given short shrift if mooted by Fijian politicians. Given their experiences, their upbringing and their mind-set, most find it genuinely difficult to conceive of all the ethnic communities collectively in terms of 'us'. The discourse is always 'us' and 'them', particularly in relation to Indo-Fijians. So, were any of them, with few exceptions, to make such proposals, the other communities would simply regard that as Fijian racism. Although Fijians tend to be more open-minded in relation to political choices within their own community, their Fijian political parties approach national issues in ethnic terms. Considering broader alternatives is not an option when one's perspectives are reinforced by others at every turn. There is a very real fear of leaving the fold to embrace multi-ethnic perspectives. Such straitjacket perspectives do not augur well for the future of multi-ethnic politics.

Religion reinforces these attitudes. The Methodist Church is totally Fijianised. It preaches a theology that makes little or no attempt to bridge the ethnic divide. A Fijian gloss has been put on the Christian message that provides justification for political developments since 1987. The newer Christian churches, which have their roots in American evangelical Christianity, have complemented the role of the Methodist Church in promoting an exclusionary approach which distinguishes between those within the fold and those outside. Such certainties leave little room for interfaith or any dialogue and merely widen our differences. In this context, the concept of a Christian state is not a new theme in our history. It has, however, gathered strength in recent years from the position of the Methodist Church and the stance of the newer denominations. To put this issue in perspective, the Methodist elders are more concerned with form than substance. Any such initiative, however well intended, would be divisive and dangerous. It is unacceptable in principle and would, in any case, be open to abuse.

Relations with the Indo-Fijian community remain a vexed issue. While interpersonal relations are generally good, members of both communities retain a guarded wariness about each other. Politicians reflect these emotions from time to time. Fijian politicians continue to remain distrustful of their Indo-Fijian counterparts. Part of the problem is that it is doubtful whether any Fijian leader has made any real and genuine effort to engage with and understand Indo-Fijians in all their complexity. The same can be said in reverse. Ratu Sir Kamisese Mara did try but it was coloured by his private reservations that were shaped by his upbringing. He nursed a real sense of hurt and anger at the defeat of his Alliance Party in April 1987. It mattered not that it was a small number of Fijians voting for the opposition which caused the result, or that he had been misled by close Indo-Fijian confidants who had little support or credibility in their own community. Such deep-rooted emotions can be overcome only by sustained and meaningful dialogue and engagement.

Colonial rule, entrenchment of Fijian chiefly structures and the Indo-Fijian presence resulted in the evolution of communal politics grounded in notions of Fijian identity. In the transition to independence and subsequently, there was little recognition or understanding by Fijians of the full implications of democracy. The commitments made by Fijian decision makers, in political settlements with other communities, were not necessarily shared by their people. The coups of 1987 and upheavals of 2000 appear to have borne that proposition out. Fijian leaders will need to consult more closely with the Fijian community to ensure they are conversant and comfortable with what is mooted. But they also owe it to the country to develop a vision that is inclusive and truly multicultural in character. It has to be more than a motley group of communities that merely accept a role secondary to the assertion of indigenous interests; rather, it has to be a genuine partnership where all feel they have the opportunity and the space to play a meaningful part in the deliberations about how the nation is governed. We owe that to our children, and to generations as yet unborn, so that the future is not a mere repetition of our past.

References

Macnaught, T. J. 1982. *The Fijian Colonial Experience: A study of the neotraditional order under British colonial rule prior to World War II*. Canberra: The Australian National University.

Mara, Ratu Sir K. K. T. 1997. *The Pacific Way: A Memoir*. Honolulu: University of Hawai'i Press.

Norton, R. 2002. 'Accommodating Indigenous Privilege: Britain's Dilemma in decolonising Fiji.' *Journal of Pacific History*, 37, 2. pp. 133–56.

Routledge, D. 1980. *Matanitu: The struggle for power in early Fiji*. Suva: Institute of Pacific Studies, USP.

Scarr, D. 1980. *Ratu Sukuna: Soldier, Statesman, Man of Two Worlds*. London: Macmillan Education Limited.

Sukuna, Ratu Sir J. L. V. 1983. *Fiji: The Three-legged Stool. Selected Writings of Ratu Sir Lala Sukuna*. Edited by D. Scarr. London: Macmillan Education.

16. The State of the State in Fiji: Some failings in the periphery

Vijay Naidu

The State in Fiji has sought to exert control and manage an increasingly difficult external and internal environment and has consequently undergone a transformation that has affected its capacities to mediate change and reproduce Fijian society and economy. On the one hand, there are powerful forces of globalisation that the State has limited control over, and, on the other hand, within the country, there are fissiparous tendencies that have changed the nature of society and state. Fiji's membership of the World Trade Organisation (WTO) requires compliance with rules based on a neo-liberal notion of free trade which means the loss of preferential access to a number of markets for its exports. This has consequences for the economy and employment in an increasingly restive local context where class and ethnic dynamics in politics test the capacity of the State to mediate and resolve these tendencies. The State has become ever more ethnicised, raising serious issues about its effectiveness and its legitimacy.

Several contradictory trends have been evident. With globalisation there has been a degree of 'denationalisation' (Ould-Mey 1999) of the State, but the State has acted fiercely in the interest of an emergent indigenous 'middle class', which has allied itself with the established chiefly oligarchy. While subscribing however reluctantly to market principles, competition and the 'level playing field' at the level of rhetoric and with respect to international and regional trade, the State has been an instrument of the hegemonic bloc in implementing affirmative-action policies that secure its economic position as well as provide it with legitimacy in the eyes of indigenous Fijians. The latter policies in line with the objectives of ethno-nationalists have led to the ever-increasing alienation of non-ethnic Fijian citizens who have hitherto been dominant in the mainstream economy and in the professions. The ethnicised Fijian State is not a 'weak state'. It is robust and resilient but it does have several failings: its inability to create a 'nation' out of Fiji's culturally diverse citizens; diminished capacity to nurture and enforce law and order; reduced capacity to generate 'investor confidence'; inability to resolve the outstanding land tenure problem that is jeopardising the sugar industry, in particular, and commercial agriculture in general; reduced capacity to provide social services; poor to bad governance and a lack of proactive measures to provide an enabling environment for civil society.

For good or ill, in the past two decades dominant forces in the global politico-economic system have significantly transformed the nature of global society and the place of nation-states within it. In this chapter, the experience

of Fiji will be examined. As a small island developing state, it is exposed to
changes at the global level in a much more dramatic way than larger states.
However, the conditions in which Fijians find themselves have also to do with
the internal dynamics of their society and the workings of their state. The
post-colonial transformation of Fiji has intensified contradictions within society
and state and in the complex web of relationships between them. These in turn
seriously compromise the country's capacity to meet the challenges of the
changing global economic and political environment. As the topic is large and
complex, this chapter will limit itself to some of the more significant
characteristics of the State in Fiji and its relationship with wider society,
'nationally' and internationally. It identifies a number of significant parameters
to assess the 'state' of the State, followed by a more detailed discussion of each
of these and concluding with a prognosis of what the immediate future might
hold for Fiji.

Without privileging any of these dimensions but emphasising their
interconnections, they include: a) the nature of the State; b) intensification of
market-led development; c) increasing social inequality and poverty; and d) the
changing global politico-economic environment. The discussion of these
dimensions provides a backdrop for a commentary on what are perceived as
'some failings' of the peripheral state in Fiji. But first a story.

A post-1987 coup story

In one of the early consultations/workshops organised in Nadi by what became
the Citizens Constitutional Forum (CCF) in 1993, the colourful and eloquent
brother-in-law of former Prime Minister Ratu Sir Kamisese Mara and a claimant
of the paramount chiefly title of Rewa and the confederacy of Burebasaga,[1] the
late Ratu Mosese Varasikite Tuisawau, remarked on the peculiar nature of the
Fijian republic.[2] He pointed to the absence of people's sovereignty in the republic
as the decision to cease connections with the Crown was made by Lieutenant
Colonel (later self-promoted to Brigadier General) Rabuka and his Taukei advisers.
He noted that the Fijian flag remained the same, with the Union Jack in its top
lefthand corner. He observed that Fijian money, including the latest $20 notes,
had the Queen's head on them and not that of the President of the Republic. He
went on to openly accuse his brother-in-law of complicity in the May 1987 coup:
'I have nothing to fear as I am guilty of nothing, only guilty people run from
their own shadow,' he said. He saw Rabuka as an instrument of the chiefly
establishment and its allies to maintain themselves in power.

I begin with this story to highlight the continuing contradictions of the Fijian
republic's outward symbols and to provide my point of entry into my
characterisation of the Fijian State as a 'schizophrenic state' deeply imbued with
racialism, unable to pursue nation-building and the national interest but faced
with very real challenges that emanate from wider society and its linkages with

the still broader world economy. The victory of the Dr Timoci Bavadra-led Fiji Labour Party and National Federation Party Coalition over the governing Alliance Party, which had ruled the country since 1970, reflected an erosion of the ethnic politics of the post-colonial era. Socioeconomic processes had led to greater social inequality and poverty as well as a growing perception that those who were in economically and politically powerful positions were enriching themselves at the expense of the broad masses of Fiji's people. There were two types of response to these changes: one that saw them through ethnic lenses, which triggered an ethno-nationalist response; and the other that understood them as creating cleavages between 'the haves and the have-nots' in Fijian society. Peripheral capitalism generated vertical and horizontal asymmetries. The hegemonic bloc with the chiefly establishment at its heart had relied on ethnic divisions to maintain its hold on the State, and this strategy was now being threatened by class-based politics.

The nature of the Fijian State

The post-colonial State in Fiji inherited from its colonial progenitor its territorial boundaries, its institutional ensemble and above all its class, ethnic, gender and regional nature. The latter reflected the ownership and control of land and capital and the racial system of power and privilege of the colonial social order. Ideologically, this was represented by the notion of the paramountcy of Fijian interests and its protection by chiefs and Europeans. The established hierarchy had been challenged and even severely tested at various times in the 96 years of colonialism but, through a process of selective coercion, ethnic and religious appeal and cooptation, it survived intact. Resistance and rebellion had come initially from ethnic Fijians outside the Christianised eastern and central regions incorporated in the system of 'indirect rule' (Durutalo 1986; Routledge 1985) and, from the second decade of the 20th century onwards, emanating from these regions but extending Fiji-wide as indigenous Fijians sought through the *Viti Kabani* to exert greater control over the mercantilist colonial trading system and their lives. At the economic and later the political level, Indian and Indo-Fijian workers and farmers periodically challenged the dominant order, reinforcing their position as the 'Other' and the hegemonic alliance of dominant Europeans and eastern chiefs (Gillion 1977; Durutalo 1986). In the post-colonial period, the composition of the hegemonic bloc changed with eastern chiefs and Europeans accommodating some commoner Fijians, general voter elements and Indo-Fijian capitalists (Sutherland 1992). Needless to say, state power was and is wielded by men and manifests the patriarchal character of Fijian society.

On three occasions, in 1959, 1987 and 2000, the hegemonic bloc was severely tested and elements within it resorted to open violence. The first happened during a strike by oil and general workers when ethnic Fijian, Indo-Fijian and mixed-race workers sought higher wages. They rioted, attacking European property and people after the police had tear-gassed and baton-charged them. The second event followed the victory of the coalition of National Federation (NFP) and Fiji Labour (FLP) Parties against the Alliance Party in 1987. These two events featured the working people of Fiji acting as a 'class for itself' in an effort to change the balance of power. The ruling class in Fiji has been most mindful of such unity of purpose and has successfully resorted to the use of ethnicity to keep workers divided. The Alliance Party adopted a 'strategy of facing both ways, uttering multi-racial mumbo-jumbo to the electorate at large, particularly to the Indo-Fijian audience, while reiterating the paramountcy of Fijian interest to an indigenous audience' (Durutalo 1986: 31).

Ironically, the failure to deal with the substantial economic disadvantage faced by ethnic Fijians as a consequence of policies of 'separate development' resulted in Butadroka and his Fijian Nationalist Party (FNP) outbidding the 'multiracial' Alliance Party and contributing to its defeat a decade earlier in 1977.[3] A 'palace coup' by the Governor-General and his European advisers ensured the return to power of the defeated Alliance Party.[4]

In 1999, the two–year–old 'new' Constitution's electoral system, divisions among ethnic Fijian political parties and bad governance by the Soqosoqo ni Vakavulewa ni Taukei (SVT) Government resulted in the landslide victory of the Peoples Coalition.[5] This constituted a significant challenge to the hegemonic bloc which was further rattled by the choice of an Indo-Fijian militant trade unionist as Prime Minister. As in 1987, elements of the defeated dominant ethnic Fijian party immediately set about intriguing to shorten the life of the Government, but there appeared to be a wider acceptance of the Government as it was backed by the President, the last surviving paramount chief of the eastern triumvirate.[6] The putsch and coup of 2000 was the expression of a complex combination of narrow ethno-nationalism, fragmentation and power plays in the eastern chiefly component of the hegemonic bloc, opportunistic manoeuvring by an aspirant class of ethnic Fijians, attempts to secure their financial interests by Indo-Fijian and 'other' businessmen previously patronised by the State, disorder created by disaffected youth, and the failure of the Labour-led coalition to effectively deal with its opponents.[7]

In the past five years, society and state in Fiji have become further divided and fragmented. Routledge, in the epilogue of his book *Matanitu*, wrote that '[p]olitical leadership has been in the hands of the great chiefs, but when Ratu Mara leaves the prime ministership, it is unlikely that a single person will again combine high traditional status with high political office' (1985: 221). However, his observation that chiefly tradition will be a cohesive force, 'giving life and strength to Fijian society in the multicultural complexities of the contemporary state, and the region beyond' appears to have been overly optimistic. Chiefly hegemony has been jeopardised with the divisions between and within confederacies, the vying for power among 'younger' chiefs, widespread disputes over succession to chiefly titles, and the machinations of 'middle-class' ethnic Fijians who have used affirmative action policies to acquire wealth, power and influence for themselves (see Ratuva 2000, 2002; Tuimaleali'ifano 2000; Fraenkel 2000; Fry 2000; Lal 2003). Non-ethnic Fijian owners of capital remain influential but recognise the uncertainties that arise from the fragmentation among ethnic Fijian elements of the ruling class. There has been a continuing flight of capital from Fiji since 1987.

State institutions and ethnicity

Separate development of the 'races' in Fiji was a keystone of colonial policy. Indirect rule was backed by a Department of Native Affairs, renamed the Department of Fijian Affairs in the 1960s. A Native (now Fijian) Affairs Board was at the apex of the separate administration and worked in tandem with the Great Council of Chiefs, provincial and *tikina* councils. The intention was to 'preserve the traditional Fijian socio-economic order with its emphasis on communal values, reciprocal exchange and obligations of commoners to their chiefs. … The effect, as opposed to the intention, was to place Fijians at a disadvantage in the face of changes that were inevitable as capitalism with its emphasis on individuality rather than communality penetrated the social order more completely' (Routledge 1985: 218–19). Ethnic Fijians were ruled and represented by their chiefs. They did not vote until 1963, just seven years before the country's independence. The Native Land Trust Board and related Native Commission had and has purview over land reservations, leaseholds and rent collection and distribution as well as responsibility for the adjudication of disputes over chiefly titles and landownership. Although indigenous landowning groups owned more than 83 per cent of the land, they had little to do with the negotiation of rent and how the proceeds from the leasing of their land were apportioned. The Fijian military evolved over time as largely an exclusively ethnic Fijian institution to underwrite chiefly power.

The late Rev. Paula Niukula, a former President of the Methodist Church to which most ethnic Fijians belong, described how there were close interconnections between the *vanua* (or community), the *lotu* (Christianity) and the *matanitu* (the Government/the State). In the perception of indigenous Fijians, these entities overlap and are mutually reinforcing.

These exclusive ethnic Fijian institutions in the State (including state-funded schools) and the Methodist Church embody 'Fijian interests' that seek to maintain ethnic Fijian solidarity and paramountcy.[8] The presence of Indo-Fijians provides a significant force in manufacturing institutional and ethnic solidarity. In wider society, the Methodist Church has played a critical role in the maintenance of chiefly hegemony, ethnic Fijian identity and in-group/out-group divisions.[9] The church is a strong advocate of making Fiji a 'Christian' state and was behind the 'Sunday Sabbath' decree in 1987. Generally, these institutions operate on the basis that they exist to protect and promote the special place of the *I-Taukei*[10] in the country. They constitute in many ways the institutional basis of ethno-nationalism as denoted by the precept '*noqu vanua, noqu Kalou*' (my land, my God).[11] This narrow nationalism has severely undermined the emergence of a broader nationalism incorporating all ethnicities in the country.

The presence of these 'state within the state' institutions also generates several issues. At the level of local government there is the obvious matter of duplication. There are rural advisory boards and town councils which also have the remit of local-level decision-making and the provision of services. Although the presence of a separate Fijian administration has been questioned, it remains intact to this day. Attempts to reform what has been perceived as a system of top-down administration and patronage inimical to ethnic Fijian progress have thus far been unsuccessful. The Native Land Trust Board's leadership sought to end leasing agricultural land under the *Agricultural Landlord and Tenant Act* and has seriously undermined agricultural production. In the post-1987 period, the military expanded to more than 6,000 and its budget increased from $F12–13 million to more than $F50 million. The desecration and burning of temples, mosques and Catholic churches can be attributed to overzealous Methodists.

Besides requiring scarce state funds, some of these institutions also make direct demands on ethnic Fijian resources. Levies have been imposed on ordinary ethnic Fijians to raise funds for provincial projects. Such funds, supplemented by subventions from the State and from private banks, have been used to purchase equity in investments in provincial companies, Fijian Holdings Limited and in urban real estate. According to Ratuva (2000), these forms of 'communal capitalism' favour chiefs and their families as well as elements of the 'emergent middle class' rather than rank-and-file Fijians, who see little or no benefit from their 'investments'. Much the same can be said of the periodic fundraising efforts of the Methodist Church with the use of the funds unquestioningly left to the top echelons of the church.

As a result of these *vakavanua* and *vaka misonari* demands, ethnic Fijians find that they have limited capital for individual enterprise. This is reinforced by the lack of collateral to borrow from private banks and the competition from those who are better established in the marketplace. Invariably these include non-indigenous Fijian individuals and businesses.

State functions

Fiji, like other post-colonial states, has coercive, ideological, political and economic dimensions. The State's law and order role is supposed to guarantee property rights and individual safety, the settlement of civil disputes and the enforcement of contracts. Antecedent customary laws and practices are recognised by the State. The rule of law facilitates economic activities, as do fiscal and monetary policies adopted by the State. Money supply, the value of currency, exchange rates with foreign currency, import and export duties, tariffs and taxation regimes are the prerogative of the State. The State in Fiji has been an initiator of private-sector development. The origins of the Fiji Trade and Investment Board lie in the Commercial Investment Committee established in the 1970s. Incentives for business, the promotion of human resource development, and infrastructural development have been part of this facilitation process. When private investment has not been forthcoming, the State has become directly involved in capitalist enterprise. This is evident in the sugar and airline sectors as well as in the network of parastatals that were established to operate telecommunications, ports, airports and the provision of services. Besides state capitalism, the State has become a significant source of finance through entities such as the Fiji National Provident Fund, the Reserve Bank and the Development Bank. The State also acts as the arbiter in disputes between labour and capital.

Thus the State has a pivotal role in the development process. While privatisation and deregulation are modifying its multiple and complex interventions, the centrality of the State in Fiji is beyond doubt. What is in doubt, however, is its continuing effectiveness in promoting the wellbeing of all citizens and its effectiveness in meeting contemporary challenges. State capacity in this regard is reflected by state power-holders and the bureaucracy.

State personnel

At the highest levels of the post-colonial State, ethnic Fijians, usually of chiefly rank, took over from British officials. In governments between 1970 and 2004, cabinets comprised between 70 and 90 per cent ethnic Fijians (Fraenkel 2004: 14). Many of these individuals graduated from the Public Service into politics. On the two occasions when there was a more ethnically proportional representation at this level, in 1987 and in 1999, with Indo-Fijians in cabinet at 50 per cent and 33.3 per cent respectively, campaigns of destabilisation were initiated by ethnic Fijians displaced from political leadership.[12]

In the State bureaucracy, from near parity between ethnic Fijians and Indo-Fijians in the early 1980s, the number of Indo-Fijian public servants has declined. 'By 2000 ... ethnic Fijians accounted for 62% of civil service jobs, and were particularly over-represented in the senior ranks (91% of permanent secretaries, 86% of Deputy Secretaries, 82% of chief administrative officers)' (Fraenkel 2004). The 1990 Constitution stipulated the reservation of the positions of President, Prime Minister, certain other ministerships, the positions of military commander and police commissioner as well as no less than 50 per cent of all public service positions for ethnic Fijians and Rotumans. In post-coup Fiji, political loyalty, ethnicity, provincialism and cronyism became the primary criteria for appointments and promotions in the Public Service and the police force rather than merit. There has been a militarisation of the Public Service as senior military personnel have secured positions at the level as commissioners of divisions and as district officers. For a period after the second 1987 coup, the judiciary was also compromised by doubtful appointments.

With the politicisation and ethnicisation of state personnel combined with affirmative action policies and hate speeches by the ruling Soqosoqo Duavata ni Lewenivanua (SDL) Party politicians, the perception of non-ethnic Fijian citizens is that the 'Government and its apparatuses' do not serve their interests. State rituals such as Fiji Day, Reconciliation Week and Ratu Sukuna Day have been primarily ethnic Fijian events.

Besides the initiatives to placate and even reward ethnic Fijian agitators after the 2000 coup, the Qarase Government introduced a Ministry of National Reconciliation to promote harmony among ethnic Fijians first and then inter-ethnic tolerance with Indo-Fijians and other minorities. Needless to say, for the latter the hollowness of the appeals for forgiveness and moving on were clearly evident in the very concrete steps being taken by state power-holders to divert state resources primarily to ethnic Fijians who were responsible for Fiji's troubles. Herein lies a fundamental contradiction of the State: is it a state that acts in the national interest which has to be an amalgam of the interests of all classes and ethnicities, or will it work in the interest of the politically dominant ethnic group?

The quality of public services, including the provision of utilities such as water, has been declining. Standards of health and educational services have dropped as have police services. On an annual basis, the Auditor-General's Office reports on a litany of inefficient uses of public funds, of tendering processes that are less than transparent, of outright misappropriation of funds and open abuse of office. Very few of these cases are investigated and fewer still lead to prosecution. In this context, it is noteworthy that where the Government or powerful individuals in the Public Service wish to take punitive measures against a public servant for 'political purposes', the Public Service rule books are fully utilised. The very public action against the military commander recently for overspending is a case in point.

This case reveals divisions and tensions between departments and sections of the State apparatus itself. Some of the tensions relate to resourcing issues and the power of the Ministry of Finance to override other sections. The antagonism between the military commander and the Government relates to the Promotion of Reconciliation, Tolerance and Unity Bill. While the Commissioner of Police also expressed his opposition to the bill and was asked to not make public statements about it, the military commander refused to accept directives from the Minister of Home Affairs on this matter and firmly asserted his right to speak directly to the President of the country. The commander, who survived the mutiny in November 2000, is single-minded about ensuring that all those who broke the law in the putsch, hostage-taking, riots, killings and mutiny are brought to justice. The Government, which came to power on the back of these manifestations of the breakdown of law and order, sees them as a reflection of indigenous Fijian political uprising. The bill has some support among ethnic Fijians and the Methodist Church, however, other ethnic Fijians have joined nearly all other citizens to oppose the bill.

From the mid-1980s powerful core countries of the world politico-economic system generated the idea that the State should not be involved in business and that the private sector must be given primacy in generating growth. Market-centred economic growth has become the dominant development paradigm in the 1990s. In Fiji, the period of relatively authoritarian rule from 1987 to 1992 also allowed the intensification of market-based reforms begun in the mid-1980s.

Intensification of market-led development

To counter the severe economic downturn after the coups, the widespread loss of jobs and the more than 30 per cent devaluation of the Fijian dollar, efforts at restructuring the economy by instituting 'painful reforms' were undertaken. These included a stronger emphasis on private sector-led export-oriented manufacturing, promotion of tourism investment, corporatisation, tax reform and labour market reform. Import substitution and tariff protection approaches that centred on the domestic market and building 'local industries' were displaced by giving freer rein to market forces to make local industries more competitive and export orientated. The periodic advice of the IMF was taken seriously and production for exports became the 'centrepiece of the new strategy'. Measures were introduced such as 13-year tax-free incentives and subsidised infrastructure to promote tax-free zones and tax-free factories. 'Within a year manufacturing was emerging as a substantial contributor to export earnings, especially in the garment sector. More than 11,000 jobs were eventually created and by the end of 1991, tax free factories were selling goods overseas worth about $200 million. It was one of the most dramatic structural changes in the Fiji economy' (Mara 1997: 217).

Firm political commitment to facilitate tourism development and to provide incentives for investment in this sector saw significant new investment in Denarau Island near Nadi of up to $300 million by EIE, a Japanese company. Several other resort investments were under way on outer islands.

State-owned enterprises were subjected to market-based principles such as improved efficiency, profitability and accountability to customers. Post and Telecommunications, Ika Corporation, the Fiji Pine Commission and the National

Marketing Authority were corporatised. Corporatisation and privatisation have continued into the post-2000 period. FINTEL, a profitable state-owned enterprise, was sold by the SVT Government to obtain funds to cover the financially insolvent National Bank. The Fiji Electricity Authority has been split into three separate companies.

Taxation reforms have included the simplification of the tax regime, raising the tax threshold, reducing tax for the highest- and lowest-income categories and, most importantly, the introduction of the Value Added Tax (VAT). The latter began at 10 per cent with promises that the price of goods and services would not rise as tariffs would be brought down by a similar percentage. Opposition to the imposition of this regressive tax was countered by the provision of a $7 million poverty alleviation fund that would see increased spending on the poor. Once the VAT came into force, prices increased and a majority of the poor did not benefit from the poverty alleviation fund, which dried up after three years. While VAT expanded the tax base beyond the 20 per cent who used to pay the pay-as-you-earn tax and the company tax, it burdened sections of the community least able to cope with increased costs of basic foodstuffs. VAT was further increased to 12.5 per cent.

Labour market reforms included the disciplining of the labour movement — an end to the check-off system for the payment of union membership fees, government scrutiny of elections of union office-bearers and voting for industrial action. Unions were no longer exempt from damages caused by disputes and members could withhold their contributions if they disagreed with the actions of the union leadership. Measures were instituted to restrict individuals from being in the executive of more than one union. In taking these measures, the State acted to reduce the bargaining power of unions generally and encouraged a movement away from broad-based multi-sector unions to enterprise-based unions. The earlier tripartite forum of government, employers' and workers' representatives was replaced by a new forum, the National Economic Summit (NES). State power-holders maintained that the meetings of the NES allowed wider consultation, beyond unionised workers, to non-unionised workers, farmers and rural dwellers, employers and social welfare groups.

The State and affirmative action

Ethnic Fijians as a general rule have been resource rich and cash poor. Their participation in the mainstream economy was previously mediated by chiefs and the Colonial Administration. Efforts at reforming the Fijian Administration and the nurturing of entrepreneurship have been limited. Despite several projects and programs during the post-colonial period, there are very few ethnic Fijian businesses or businesspeople. Post-coup governments have redoubled their efforts to address this disadvantage. In this regard, the State contributes to the higher-status lifestyles of state power-holders and facilitates the accumulation of wealth by them and their associates in wider society.

The Ratu Mara-led interim government (1988–91) adopted a nine-point plan in addition to the existing provisions for ethnic Fijian education, rural development, cooperatives and village development to foster equity and savings. Fijian Holdings Limited (FHL) was loaned $20 million to buy shares in established successful companies. FHL was formed in 1984 by Fijian provinces as an investment company. With the additional funds, FHL equity in large near-monopoly companies, such as Standard Concrete and Carlton Brewery, increased significantly with improved returns on investment. Two classes of shares existed in FHL, an A class and a B class. The former were sold to selected ethnic Fijians, who could borrow investment funds from the Fiji Development Bank, and the latter category were held by provinces. FHL has been embroiled in controversy as it is seen as a vehicle for a group of elite ethnic Fijians to acquire wealth on the back of other Fijians (see Ratuva 2000). Subsequently, the SVT Government decided to make the FHL loan into an outright grant.

Ethnic Fijians also received support in investing in the Unit Trust of Fiji. Individuals and provinces constituted 58 per cent of unit-holders by the end of 1991. The Fiji Development Bank maintained its role in assisting ethnic Fijians in business. 'For three years from 1989 loans amounting to $45.4 million were approved for 3,532 Fijians' (Mara 1997: 221). The bank's Emicol store project to build commercial acumen among selected ethnic Fijians was instituted at this stage.

From 1991 to 1999, these affirmative-action programs were continued and expanded. The SVT Government purchased a sizeable track of farm land from the Chairman of the Fiji Development Bank and FHL for the inflated price of $7 million on which to train ethnic Fijian youth in commercial farming. Rabuka had appointed Vasanti Makarava as the CEO of the National Bank of Fiji and he saw his task as supporting ethnic Fijians and Rotumans seeking loans. Unsecured and poorly documented loans were provided and some bank employees systematically siphoned off funds for themselves, while others arranged kickbacks. The bank became insolvent with a loss of $220 million. The defaulting borrowers could be listed in a Fijian 'Who's Who'!

After the appointment of the 'caretaker' government led by Qarase, a 'blueprint' for Fijian development was endorsed by the Great Council of Chiefs. A further $20 million was allocated to this end. Provision was made for a separate building for the chiefs and a permanent secretariat; $3 million was allocated to FHL. The caretaker government converted itself into the SDL Party, successfully contesting the 2001 general election. Before the elections, a generous and highly irregular distribution of a range of tools for ethnic Fijian and Rotuman development was made. These ranged from gardening forks to boats, brush-cutters to computers and bicycles. Many of these items were purchased at highly inflated prices from hardware stores, including those owned by Indo-Fijians. Since then an 'agricultural scam' has been uncovered involving the sum of $30 million.

Affirmative action continued with the SDL regime's adoption of a '50/50 by 2020' plan to increase ethnic Fijian participation in the mainstream economy. It is apparent that the primary beneficiaries of grants and soft loans have been a relatively small group of ethnic Fijians who have become shareholders either directly or indirectly in established companies. Especially favoured are individuals and their families who have A-class shares in FHL. 'Communal capitalism' has enriched some chiefs and an aspirant middle class, but has not changed the situation of most ethnic Fijians. Indeed, income distribution has remained highly unequal. Political instability and the constitutional impasse, reduced investor confidence, mismanagement of public funds, inappropriate policies and ineffective policy implementation have resulted in economic stagnation and lack of employment opportunities. A good 20 per cent of land formerly under sugar cane is no longer cultivated. Farming families have become squatters in and near urban centres. Politicians and the Native Land Trust Board continue to squabble over appropriate legislation to govern land leases as farming becomes an increasingly unattractive livelihood for younger people.

Increasing social inequality and poverty

Rural livelihoods have ceased to be a drawcard for some time in Fiji, however, urban formal-sector jobs have not been increasing at a rate to absorb the 17,000 school-leavers each year. Only 1,500 to 2,000 jobs are available annually for them. The presence of large numbers of unemployed puts downward pressure on wage levels, especially for unskilled and semi-skilled labour. It is little wonder that the Fiji Poverty Report found that 86 per cent of Fiji's poor (based on out-of-date surveys) were the working poor. Income distribution is skewed heavily in favour of business, the professions and the salaried. Agricultural, garment factory, construction and transport workers, clerical and retail employees, security guards and even police personnel constitute more than 40 per cent of the poor in Fiji. Destitutes include deserted women with children, street children, urban unemployed youth, dependent elderly, the disabled and the chronically sick.

As in other Third World countries, Fiji has experienced a boom in the informal sector. Activities range from the legal to the illegal: backyard workshops, home-based craft work, tailoring, food preparation, roadside stalls, barbecue stands, hawking of wares, passenger transport services, shoe shining, grass cutting, bottle collecting, the growing, processing and selling of drugs, bootlegging and prostitution. Central and local government regulations have not facilitated these people's entrepreneurial activities.

As social inequality has increased and the sense of community has diminished during a generation, the State's capacity to resolve law and order problems has been seriously challenged. The extra-legal overthrow of duly elected governments and the immunity given to those responsible appear to have emboldened others to bend and break the law. There is an ethnic dimension to the law and order problem. It is evident that there is 'structural violence' against young people and ethnic Fijian youths react to it by externalising their sense of deprivation. Their victims have been largely Indo-Fijians. The latter tend to internalise their feelings of inadequacy and frustration. This is reflected in higher levels of psychosomatic illnesses and suicides. With opportunities of employment severely limited and, for those in employment, wage levels too low for decent living, relatively large numbers of Fijians have sought opportunities abroad.

The changing global politico-economic environment

At the political level, the collapse of the Soviet Union has provided almost infinite scope for private wealth accumulation on a world scale. There has been a rampant push to open markets for capital, goods and services by corporations backed by powerful G7 states. The Soviet collapse has also reduced the strategic significance of small island states in the South Pacific and their bargaining power. Always open and 'export-import' orientated, Pacific Island states have relied heavily on tariff charges as the major source of public revenue. Fiji, with a relatively large private sector, also had the luxury of extracting funds through income and company taxes. The thrust towards free trade is compelling Fiji and other Pacific states to rapidly reduce tariffs. Fiji became a founding member of the WTO and is a signatory of regional free trade agreements such as PICTA and PACER. With other Pacific ACP member countries, Fiji is negotiating an Economic Partnership Agreement (EPA) with officials of the EU.

In the short to intermediate term, there are few prospects for Fiji to make substantial gains from these free trade agreements. Indeed, with the erosion and loss of preferential market access to the EU, Australia, New Zealand, the USA, Japan and Malaysia, the Fijian economy is likely to continue in a downward spiral. It is intriguing, therefore, that Fiji joined the WTO so early in the piece. Professor Jane Kelsey, in her article 'World Trade and Small Nations in the South Pacific Region' (2005), which provides many insights into the accession process and the unrealistic demands on small vulnerable economies, quotes a senior Fijian state official explaining the country's WTO membership:

> The question of why Fiji joined the WTO has been raised many times. The answer, put simply, is that Fiji has no choice. While the rules of the game are not always fair and the playing field is not always level, we must make efforts to become part of the process that influences and addresses both advantages and shortcomings of the current strategy of globalisation. It is important to recognise that behind every challenge,

> there is an opportunity. Adopting a head-in-the-sand response to globalisation will not permit us to avoid its impacts but means missing out on the opportunities it offers ... Never before has open trade with the international community done so much to lift the living standards and increase opportunities; yet never before has the persistence of poverty and exclusion been so glaring in most of our societies. (Fiji's Permanent Secretary for Foreign Affairs and Trade cited in Kelsey 2005: 258)

The impending curtailment of multilateral and bilateral non-reciprocal trade agreements spells a major disaster for Fiji. Under the Cotonou Agreement between the ACP group of countries and the EU, the high price paid for Fijian sugar, in the order of two to four times world market price since the early 1970s, will be phased out. Australia, Brazil and Thailand have formally lodged a joint complaint with the WTO against the EU for its differential treatment of ACP countries.

Two industries on which a very large number of people depend for their livelihoods are beginning to unravel. As Stewart Firth points out,

> A second preferential trade regime that originated in the 1970s expired in 2005. This is the Multi Fibre Arrangement (MFA), which gave Fiji an export quota for garments exported to the USA. Within a few months of the end of the MFA a major garment manufacturer in the Fijian town of Lautoka closed with the loss of 3,000 jobs, and, as a consequence, the Fiji government revised its growth predictions for the economy sharply downwards, from the 3.8% achieved in 2004 to 1.5% in 2005 and 0.7% in 2006. Fiji's Prime Minister Laisenia Qarase saw 'a chill wind blowing from the direction of the World Trade Organisation. The unrealistic policies of the WTO have created a crisis in our garment industry, which provides employment for many Fiji people. Because the US must conform to WTO rules we no longer have assured entry into that market for our garments ... If this is globalisation, then it is fatally flawed. It is making a mockery of our efforts to reach national standards of governance we have set for ourselves and which the international community expects of us.' If Fiji lacked export markets, Qarase said, 'we will face an increased danger of instability, social breakdown and higher crime rates'. (Firth, pers. comm. 2006)

The people of Fiji have not waited for state power-holders to extract Fiji from its impending difficulties. They have sought opportunities for employment in the 'globalising world'. Ironically, employment opportunities have been generated by the 'war on terror' of the US and its allies. I have been informed by a former British soldier that there are a couple of thousand ethnic Fijians in the British Army. There are also several hundred employed by private security agencies in Kuwait and Iraq. Other 'migrant workers' include Fijians who provide care-giving services in the US mainland and who work in the health sector in Australia and New Zealand. There are smaller numbers employed in Micronesian health services. In addition, Fiji continues to provide peacekeeping soldiers and police to the UN, with contingents in East Timor and the Middle East. Remittances from labour migrants have been increasing, with the Reserve Bank of Fiji estimating figures in access of $300 million each year. Opportunities for employment overseas, however dangerous, will become attractive as employment prospects within Fiji remain stagnant and even decline.

Conclusion

The Fijian State has ethnic, class, regional and gender dimensions. During the post-colonial period, the hegemonic bloc led by ethnic Fijian chiefs has shown increasing signs of disintegration as there is intense rivalry for power among a younger generation of the aristocracy. State personnel represent predominantly one ethnic category and appear to be committed to the 'paramountcy of Fijian interests' which entails ethnic Fijian political primacy and affirmative action designed to enrich a minority of indigenous people. This means that the State's ability to pursue the 'national interest' is seriously compromised.

With the moves to comply with WTO rules, the State's capacity to generate revenue will be seriously affected as the Fijian economy undergoes shifts away from the sugar and garment industries. It is likely that in the immediate future inequality and poverty will be further aggravated as unemployment escalates. Given the tendency of the State and political leaders to give primacy to ethnic explanations, it is possible that the predicated social unrest and political instability will yet again take ethnic dimensions.

Most Fijians understand very well the current predicament and what the foreseeable future holds for them in the country and have sought employment opportunities abroad. Remittances, with tourism, might save the day for Fiji but the general prognosis for a vibrant multi-ethnic country is not favourable and will require a profound change in the approach of state power-holders and their allies.

References

Ali, A. 1980. *Plantation to Politics*. Suva: University of the South Pacific.

Amuwo, K. 2002. *Globalisation, NEPAD and the Governance Question in Africa*. www.codesria.org/Archives/Past%20events/ programme_for_the_governance_ins.htm

Asian Development Bank. 1995. *Governance: Sound Development Management*. Manila.

Burns, A. 1960. *Fiji*. London: HMSO.

Dauvergne, P. (ed.) 1998. *Weak and Strong States in Asia — Pacific Societies*. Canberra: Allen & Unwin and ANU.

Doornbos, M. 2001. 'Good Governance: The Rise and Decline of a Policy Metaphor.' *Journal of Development Studies*, 37, 6. pp. 93–108.

Durutalo, S. 1986. 'The Paramountcy of Fijian Interest and the Politicisation of Ethnicity. South Pacific Forum', Working Paper No. 6. Suva: USP Sociological Society.

Firth, S. 2000. 'The Pacific Islands and the Globalisation Agenda.' *The Contemporary Pacific*, 12, 1.

Firth, S. 2005. 'The Impact of Globalisation on the Pacific Islands.' Paper presented at Second South-East Asia and the Pacific Subregional Tripartite Forum on Decent Work, ILO, Melbourne, April 5–8.

Fraenkel, J. 2000. 'The Clash of Dynasties and the Rise of Demagogues; Fiji's Tauri Vakaukauwa of May 2000.' *Journal of Pacific History*, 35, 3. pp. 298–308.

Fraenkel, J. 2004. 'Regulating Bipolar Divisions; A Case Study of Ethnic Structure, Public Sector Inequality and Electoral Engineering in Fiji'. Suva: PIAS-DG, University of the South Pacific.

Fry, G. 2000. 'Political Legitimacy and the Post-colonial State in the Pacific: Reflections on Some Common Threads in the Fiji and Solomon Islands Coups.' *Pacifica Review*, 12, 3. pp. 298–304.

Ghai, Y. 1983. 'Constitutional Issues in the Transition to Independence.' In R. Crocombe and A. Ali (eds), *Foreign Forces in Pacific Politics*, Suva: University of the South Pacific.

Gillion, K.L. 1977. *The Fiji Indians: Challenge to European Dominance, 1920-1946*. Canberra: Australian National University Press.

Gravelle, K. 2001. *Good Governance in the South Pacific*. Suva: University of the South Pacific.

Grynberg, R., D. Munro and M. White. 2002. *Crisis: The Collapse of the National Bank of Fiji*. Adelaide: Crawford House.

Kelsey, J. 2005. 'World Trade and Small Nations in the South Pacific Region.' *The Kansas Journal of Law & Public Policy*, XVII, 11. pp. 247–306.

Lal, B. 1983. 'The 1982 Fiji National Election and its Aftermath.' *USP Sociological Society Newsletter* No. 5 (July).

Lal, B. 2003. 'Heartbreak Islands: Reflections on Fiji in Transition'. *Asia Pacific Viewpoint*, 44, 3. pp. 335-50.

Lemke, T. 2000. 'Foucault, Governmentality, and Critique.' Paper presented at the Rethinking Marxism Conference, University of Amherst, September. pp. 1–17.

Lemke, T. '"The Birth of Bio-Politics" — Michel Foucault's lecture at the College de France on Neo-Liberal Governmentality.' Mimeo.

Mara, R. K. 1997. *The Pacific Way*. Honolulu: University of Hawai'i Press.

Migdal, J. 2001. *State in Society: Studying How States and Societies Transform and Constitute One Another*. Cambridge: Cambridge University Press.

Naidu, V. 1988. 'State, Class and Politics in the South Pacific.' Unpublished D.Phil thesis, University of Sussex, Falmer.

Naidu, V. 2000a. 'Democracy and Governance in the South Pacific.' In E. Vasta (ed.), *Citizenship, Community and Democracy*, London and New York: Macmillan and St Martin's Press. pp. 45–68.

Naidu, V. 2000b. 'The Oxymoron of Security Forces in Island States.' *Island Security Perceptions and Priorities* Island Security Conference, Centre for Asia-Pacific Security Studies, Honolulu, Hawai'i.

Naidu, V. and R. Reddy. 2002. *Na ghar ke, na ghat ke: ALTA and expiring land leases: Fijian farmers' perceptions of their future*. Wollongong: Ford Foundation in association with Asia Pacific Migration Research Network, University of Wollongong.

Nation, J. 1978. 'Customs of Respect: The Traditional Basis of Fijian Communal Politics.' *Development Studies Centre Monograph* No. 14. Canberra: The Australian National University.

Naidu, V. 2003. 'Governance, Ethnicity and the State in Fiji: A Case of Diminishing Legitimacy.' Development Research Symposium, University of the South Pacific, Suva.

Norton, R. 1977. *Race and Politics in Fiji*. St Lucia: University of Queensland Press.

Niukula, P. n.d. *The Three Pillars*. Suva: Christian Writing Project.

Ould-Mey, M. 1999. 'The New Global Command Economy.' *Environment and Planning D: Society and Space*. 17, 2. pp. 155-180.

Premdass, R. 2001. 'Ethno-Racial Divisions and Governance: The Problem of Institutional Reform and Adaptation.' Paper for United Nations Research Institute for Social Development Conference on Racism and Public Policy, September, Durban, South Africa.

Powles, C. G. 1980. 'Law, Decision-Making and Legal Services in the Pacific Island States.' In R. T. Shand (ed.), *Island States of the Pacific and Indian Ocean: Anatomy of Development*, Canberra.

Qalo, R. 1982. *Divided We Stand*. Suva: Institute of Pacific Studies.

Routledge, D. 1985. *Matanitu: The struggle for power in early Fiji*. Suva: University of the South Pacific.

Ratuva, S. 2000. 'Addressing Inequality? Economic Affirmative Action and Communal Capitalism in Post-Coup Fiji.' In A. H. Akram-Lodhi (ed.), *Confronting Fiji Futures,* Canberra: Asia Pacific Press. pp. 226–48.

Ratuva, S. 2002. 'Anatomizing the Vanua Complex: Intra-Communal Land Disputes and Implications on the Fijian Community.' Paper presented at South Pacific Land Tenure Conflicts Symposium, University of the South Pacific, Suva.

Reddy, M., B. C. Prasad, S. Kumar and V. Naidu. 2001. 'The 2002 Fiji National Budget: A Nation in Search of Economic Growth and Stability.' *Working Paper* No. 01/1. Suva: Centre for Development Studies, SSED, University of the South Pacific.

Reddy, M., V. Naidu and M. Manoranjan. 2002. 'Economic Cost of Human Capital Loss from Fiji: Implications for Sustainable Development.' Fifth International Conference of the Asia Pacific Migration Research Network, Naviti Resort, Fiji.

Sharpham, J. 2000. *Rabuka of Fiji: The authorised biography of Major-General Sitiveni Rabuka*. Rockhampton: Central Queensland University Press.

Simpson, S. 2003. 'Perceptions of Civil Society in Fiji.' Paper presented at the Commonwealth South Pacific Regional Consultation: Maximising Civil Society's Contribution to Democracy and Development, Auckland.

Sutherland, W. 1992. *Beyond the Politics of Race: An Alternative History of Fiji to 1992*. Political and Social Change Monograph no. 15. Canberra: Australian National University.

Tuimaleal'ifano, M. 2000. 'Veiqati Vaka Viti and the Fiji Islands Elections in 1999.' *Journal of Pacific History*, 35, 3. pp. 253–67.

Turner, M. and D. Hulme. 1997. *Governance, Administration and Development: Making the State work*. London: Macmillan.

ENDNOTES

[1] Before British colonial rule, contemporary Fiji was known as Viti and was divided into more than 40 polities, which formed wider alliances with each other. The latter, known as 'confederacies', waxed and waned over time depending on a range of factors. Some of these took proto-state forms. Warfare appeared to be endemic between 'tribal' groups. The late 19th century saw the emergence of three sizeable confederacies, conceived as '*matanitu*' (government and state). These were Kubuna, which was led by Ratu Seru Cakobau, proclaimed by the settlers as Tui Viti (King of Fiji), Burebasaga and Tovata, which was united under the rulership of the Tongan aristocrat Ma'afu, who previously had ambitions to conquer the archipelago. None of these 'confederacies' had Fiji-wide control and the people of parts of the interior of the larger islands remained autonomous. It took a war of pacification by the British to subjugate them (Derrick 1946; Durutalo 1986).

² The Queen, venerated as 'Tui Viti' (the highest chief in the hierarchy of chieftainship), in her statement during the Vancouver Commonwealth Heads of Governments meeting, responded to the Taukei Movement and Rabuka's declaration of the republic, 'Her Majesty is sad to think that the ending of the Fijian allegiance to the Crown should have been brought about without the people of Fiji being given an opportunity to express their opinion in the proposal' (cited in Sharpham 2000: 136).

³ Sakeasi Butadroka, the ethno-nationalist leader, used the slogan 'Fiji for the Fijians', first coined by a white member of the colonial legislature in 1946. Following in the footsteps of Idi Amin of Uganda, he called for the repatriation of all 'Indians' to India. Surprisingly, it was known that there was some collaboration between the National Federation Party, led and supported by Indo-Fijians and the FNP (Premdass 1978).

⁴ The NFP had seen itself as an opposition-in-perpetuity party, unprepared to form government. The party took three days to decide who would lead it as Prime Minister. The Governor-General used a clause in the 1970 Constitution that gave him authority to appoint as Prime Minister the person who appeared to have the most support in Parliament. The Alliance leader, Ratu Mara, was to lose a vote of confidence, three months later; returning as Prime Minister after the second election of 1977 when the Alliance was returned by an overwhelming majority, thanks to major divisions within the NFP.

⁵ This included, among other things, the collapse of the National Bank of Fiji with the loss of more than $F220 million in unsecured loans to prominent individuals and businesses.

⁶ Ratu Sir Kamisese Mara's support for Mahendra Chaudhry as Prime Minister extended to persuading demurring Fijian Association Party (FAP) Members of Parliament. He was perceived to have carried out a behind-the-scenes campaign for FAP against the ruling Rabuka-led SVT (see Lal 1998: 21, for beginnings of the schism between Ratu Mara and Rabuka). The President's action in swearing in Chaudhry as Prime Minister redeemed him in the eyes of many FLP and NFP supporters who had regarded him as the person behind the first 1987 coup.

⁷ Prime Minister Mahendra Chaudhry's personal style; his slamming the door shut in further negotiating power sharing with the SVT; his marginalisation of his political ally, Apisai Tora; his government's naive policies relating to a Land Commission; meddling with affirmative action policies for ethnic Fijians; differential compensation for Indo-Fijian farmers ($F28,000) and support for ethnic Fijian landowners taking up sugarcane farming ($10,000); and apparent manipulation of chiefs as well as his alienation of the media: all these contributed to widening opposition.

⁸ The notion of 'paramountcy of Fijian interest' is said to emanate from the fact that chiefs unconditionally ceded the country to the British Monarch, Queen Victoria, and to the claim that on Fiji's political independence, sovereignty was returned to them. It has various meanings, which range from the recognition of indigenous Fijian interests in decision-making and at the symbolic level to ethnic supremacy extending to the Parliament and government comprising entirely ethnic Fijians.

⁹ The Methodist Church in rural Fijian districts has long preached against the idol-worshipping heathen 'Indians' (Radio NZ interview with Poseci Bune, October 24, 2005).

¹⁰ Owners of the land.

¹¹ Durutalo (1986) had pointed to the nexus between 'ratuism, religion and rugby' in cementing ethnic solidarity and the leadership of chiefs.

¹² Three factors have contributed to elements of ethnic Fijian political leadership resorting to destabilisation (apart from the well-publicised 'Indian-dominated government'): i) the absence of well paying jobs outside the Public Service for defeated politicians; ii) the significant difference between the salary and perks of office of a minister and a backbencher; iii) the personal ambitions of individuals concerned. For instance, Rabuka had applied unsuccessfully for three jobs outside the military before his mission to overthrow Dr Bavadra's Government and become the country's military 'strongman' (Sharpham 2000).

17. Power Sharing in Fiji and New Caledonia [1]

Jon Fraenkel

Fiji and New Caledonia adopted mandatory power-sharing institutions in an effort to mitigate conflict in the late 1990s. Both are bipolar polities, where politics has revolved around the conflicting objectives of substantial indigenous and migrant or migrant-descended groups. Both experienced severe conflict during the 1980s, culminating in a military coup in Fiji in 1987 and more than 50 people killed in New Caledonia in the 1980s. Both countries subsequently settled on compacts aimed at resolving those conflicts (the 1997 Constitution in Fiji and the 1988 Matignon and 1998 Noumea Accords in New Caledonia). Whereas Fiji witnessed a second coup only a year after the first elections under the new system and protracted controversies before the law courts over the multi-party cabinet laws, New Caledonia achieved some degree of accommodation between former antagonists, with representatives of the Kanak and settler parties sharing power in a multi-party executive. This paper examines the Fijian and New Caledonian institutions and the two countries' differing experience with multi-party cabinets, drawing also on the international literature examining power-sharing arrangements.

Internationally, mandatory power-sharing institutions do not have a particularly strong track record. The notorious collapses of power sharing in Cyprus in the early 1960s and Northern Ireland in the early 1970s suggest that such arrangements are regularly fraught with difficulties. Lebanon's 1943–75 National Pact proved more successful, but the associated institutionalisation of confessional politics left internal rigidities that were vulnerable to regional destabilisation and themselves became an issue of dissension in the run-up to the civil warfare of the post-1975 period (Seaver 2000, Kliot 1987). South Africa had some success with power-sharing devices, but these were employed as a transitional measure during the shift away from apartheid and were abandoned in 1996 (Koelble and Reynolds 1996, Lijphart, 1998). Elsewhere in Africa, particularly in post-civil warfare contexts, power-sharing arrangements have often proved fleeting and unsustainable arrangements that quickly come unstuck (Spears 2002; 2000, Akinyele 2000). Switzerland's Federal Council provides an often-cited positive model, but here power sharing is informal although reinforced by federal autonomy and direct democracy. No law prohibits majority rule in the Federal Council. Reliance on some of the northern European models also attracts criticism (Barry 1975a; 1975b) and suspicion lingers that these might not be viable in less prosperous and more deeply divided countries — such as Guyana, Iraq or Bosnia

— where ministers from distinct communities are under greater popular pressure to play to a communal gallery.

Nevertheless, power sharing remains a continuing focus of attention, despite all evidence of difficulties. The alternatives of hegemony of one group over the other, or the mutual destruction of contending forces, are sufficiently unpalatable to encourage external mediators and in-country reformers to persevere in seeking out appropriate and workable power-sharing arrangements. Lebanon's post-civil war 1989 Ta'if Accord restored many of the 1943-75 National Pact arrangements, although with parity replacing the earlier 6:5 bias in favour of Christian representation and with a shift in power from the Maronite President to the Sunni Prime Minister (Hudson 1997, Nasrallah 1999). Northern Ireland's 1998 Good Friday Agreement also involved a renewed effort to establish Republican/Loyalist executive power sharing (O'Leary 1999, McGarry 1998). [2] Methods have repeatedly been sought in post-Dayton Bosnia to bring together in government Serbs, Croats and Muslims, to combine Sunni, Shi'ite and Kurdish leaders in Iraq or the Pashtun, Tajiks, Uzbeks and others in Afghanistan. The collapse of power-sharing arrangements, where this has occurred, might owe its origins to the severity or intractability of conflict, to regional destabilisation, to the forces unleashed or strengthened by the associated empowerment of communal elites or to the absence of simultaneous civil society-based peace-building initiatives; but this might also arise due to bad timing or quick-fix approaches, the absence of involvement of key players or failures to popularly embed arrangements through referenda or elections or, last but not least, to the poor design of the institutions themselves.

One regularly preferred mix of power-sharing institutions is Arend Lijphart's (2004; 2002; 1991a; 1991b) 'consociational' model, involving usage of list proportional representation, mandatory power sharing, group autonomy and minority (or mutual) vetoes. List proportional representation has the inclusive impact of bringing the political representatives of ethnic groups into Parliament roughly in proportion to their shares in the population, while mandatory power sharing is to ensure some form of cooperation between elected leaders in government. Vetoes and autonomy, perhaps including federal arrangements, are further devices aimed at ensuring that majority groups do not simply lord it over minorities. Majoritarian institutions, such as Westminster democracy or presidentialism, are rejected as 'winner-takes-all' models that offer little to ethnically divided societies.

Lijphart prefers ethnicity-blind, or self-determination-based, power-sharing arrangements of the type adopted in South Africa to the kinds of ethnic predetermination witnessed in Lebanon's 1943-75 ratio of 6:5 between Christian and Muslim parliamentarians, or the 7:3 ratio between Greek and Turkish Cypriot ministers embodied in the 1960 Cyprus Constitution. South Africa's 1993

Constitution provided that all parties with more than 5 per cent of seats in the National Assembly would secure cabinet portfolios and all parties with more than 20 per cent of seats would obtain a vice-presidency.[3] In practice, that provision ensured that although Nelson Mandela's African National Congress easily won the 1994 elections, it did not control *all* the positions in the new government. F. W. de Klerk's National Party gained six and Chief Mangosuthu Buthelezi's Inkatha Freedom Party acquired three of the 27 cabinet portfolios after the 1994 elections (Reynolds 1995).[4] Yet the South African power-sharing provisions did not imply a permanent allocation of positions to either party. Had the 1994 arrangements been retained, future elections might have led to the allocation of portfolios and vice-presidencies to different political parties, empowering other ethnic or interest groups.

Fiji and New Caledonia adopted Lijphart's favoured South African-style non-ethnically predetermined power-sharing arrangements in the late 1990s. In Fiji, all parties with eight or more seats in the 71-member Parliament secured legal rights to enter cabinet. In New Caledonia, all parties with six or more seats in the 52-member Congress were entitled to participate in the Executive. Fiji combined these arrangements with a majoritarian electoral system (the 'alternative vote') and a substantial number of communal constituencies (23 of the 71 seats were reserved for ethnic Fijians, 19 for Indo-Fijians and only 25 were 'open' or 'common roll' constituencies[5]). New Caledonia, despite its neglect in the international literature on power-sharing and consociational democracy,[6] more faithfully reflects the Lijphartian model. It has used a list proportional representation system since the early 1950s, Kanaks have a substantial degree of autonomy in the Northern and Loyalty Islands Provinces, there is a proportionally elected multi-party cabinet, and there is an indirect minority veto. Part of the reason for the greater success of power sharing in New Caledonia than in Fiji, I argue in this paper, had to do with the design and drafting of the new multi-party cabinet laws, although there were also other reasons why cooperation was more likely to succeed under the 1988 Matignon agreement and the 1998 Noumea Accord than under Fiji's 1997 Constitution that are worth reviewing briefly.

Fiji's coups and constitutional crises (in 1977, 1987 and 2000) each came in the wake of electoral victories by predominantly Indo-Fijian-backed political parties and each centred on resurrecting 'indigenous paramountcy', whereas New Caledonia's principal conflict has been between those who back independence and those who want to remain part of the French Republic. Consequently, the French Government was intimately involved in negotiations for the Matignon and Noumea Accords, and was influenced by UN pressures towards 'decolonisation' (de Fontenay 2001). In Fiji, retention of the status quo, coupled perhaps only with a few cosmetic changes, seemed a more plausible strategy during the mid-1990s deliberations than it did in New Caledonia, particularly given the likely electoral repercussions of the growing numerical advantage of ethnic Fijians. The mid-1990s constitutional review at first seemed likely to make few alterations to the racially discriminatory 1990 Constitution. Fijian Prime Minister Sitiveni Rabuka's efforts to win support for the 1997 Constitution within his Soqosoqo ni Vakavulewa ni Taukei (SVT) Party were couched in terms of the likelihood of Fijian retention of the premiership coupled with concessions of only the deputy premiership and cabinet representation to Indo-Fijians. In contrast, reversion to the style of politics of the 1950s and 1960s (i.e., liberal multi-ethnic Kanak-backed territorial government with little real autonomy from France) never seemed a realistic option in New Caledonia after the conflict of the 1980s. Once the peace process seemed to be paying political dividends, even changes in government in metropolitan France did not derail continuing efforts to strengthen cooperation around the implementation of the Noumea Accord.

Potential benefits associated with the 'buy in' to the accords differed in New Caledonia and Fiji. Under the Matignon and Noumea Accords, heavy metropolitan subsidies and rebalancing (*rééquilibrage*) in favour of Kanak communities in the north and in the Loyalty Islands offered a pay-off associated with the peace process, and fostered patronage systems that enticed veteran pro-independence leaders to break away and form alliances with loyalist leaders and created tensions within the independence movement itself (Chappell 1999a, Connell 2003). By contrast, the 1997 Fijian Constitution offered few tangible benefits, aside from re-entry into the Commonwealth. The accommodation between Rabuka and Indo-Fijian Opposition Leader, Jai Ram Reddy, provided little in the way of immediate advantages for the Indo-Fijians, particularly given the absence of any associated deal on the issue of the expiry of sugarcane farming leases under the 1976 *Agricultural Landlord and Tenants Act*. Indian overseas migration continued through the 1990s, and intensified difficulties faced Reddy's National Federation Party (NFP), which secured only 32 per cent of the Indian vote at the 1999 polls and consequently obtained not a single seat in Parliament. Mahendra Chaudhry's Fiji Labour Party (FLP) campaigned at the 1999 polls on the slogan 'the constitution won't put food in your mouths', and, once in office, offered a range of measures aimed at assisting poorer citizens of both communities, including the abolition of VAT on basic food items. With time, the FLP's Fijian allies in the People's Coalition might have cemented indigenous support behind the Government, but after the first year in office the signs were not promising. All three Fijian parties had splintered; while their leaders remained in cabinet, many rank-and-file members joined opposition efforts to destabilise the Government. None of the Fijian cabinet ministers in the Chaudhry Government proved able to secure election, drawing on indigenous Fijian votes, at the 2001 election. [7]

Finally, New Caledonia had a history of mandatory power sharing, from 1976 to 1979 and briefly again under the 1988 Pons Statute, as well as informally (i.e., through non-mandatory methods), in successive pro-autonomy administrations run by the Union Calédonienne (UC), which was able to secure Melanesian and liberal European support for most of the postwar period until the 1970s. By contrast in Fiji, Ratu Sir Kamisese Mara's Alliance Party was never able to surpass the 25 per cent share of the Indian vote it received in 1972. From the 1987 coup onwards, mainly Indian-backed parties could count on no more than 2 or 3 per cent of the nationwide Fijian vote and mainly Fijian-identified parties gained less than 1 per cent of the Indian vote. Some degree of power sharing had been achieved in the 'membership system' of 1964-67, in which representatives of the three major communities, Ratu Mara, A. D. Patel and Sir John Falvey, had shared portfolios with colonial officials (Norton 2004: 165; 2002: 147, Lal 1992: 191). But, crucially, this was before independence in 1970. Prime Minister Ratu Mara proposed a Government of National Unity in 1980, although controversially so since this was on the basis of the weakened representation secured by the NFP at the September 1977 polls. Equal representation between antagonistic parties had been mooted after the 1987 coup in the Deuba Accord, before this was derailed by a further coup in September of that year. Power sharing was a realistic, and much debated, possibility in mid-1990s Fiji, but it would have been necessary to overcome a long history of much more rigid ethnic compartmentalisation than prevailed in postwar New Caledonia.

The making and unmaking of Fiji's multi-party cabinet laws

Fiji's 1997 Constitution was intended to put an end to a decade of inter-ethnic discord after the military coup in 1987, which dislodged a largely Indo-Fijian-backed government. The post-coup administration put in place an interim constitution in 1990, which reserved the presidency and the premiership for indigenous Fijians and reverted to an entirely communally-based electoral system with seats unevenly distributed in favour of ethnic Fijians (who obtained 37 seats as against 27 for Indo-Fijians in a 70-member Parliament, despite the two populations being roughly equal in number at that time). In the mid-1990s, Rabuka's Government appointed a Constitutional Review Commission (CRC) to advise on amendments to Fiji's fundamental laws. The CRC engaged in extensive consultation, in Fiji and abroad, including a visit to South Africa to assess the merits of the power-sharing arrangements adopted in that country. That visit occurred in 1996, just as South Africa was about to abandon its transitional multi-party cabinet laws. The CRC concluded that mandatory power sharing was fraught with difficulties.[8] It advised instead retention of the Westminster model, with the institutional encouragement of multi-ethnic government to be provided instead by the adoption of the alternative vote system. Instead of the post-election coalitions facilitated by mandatory power-sharing laws, the alternative vote, it was hoped, would encourage robust pre-election coalitions arising from deals over party preferences.[9]

The Joint Parliamentary Select Committee that gathered to deliberate on the CRC report departed from some of the CRC's recommendations. In particular, it announced an intention to 'go further' in the direction of encouraging multi-ethnic government by embracing a power-sharing deal (Parliament of Fiji 1997: 17). At first, all parties with more than 4 per cent of the seats in the House were to be invited by the Prime Minister to join cabinet. That threshold was later raised by Parliament to 10 per cent, and included in Section 99 of the 1997 Constitution. Subsection 99(5) of the 1997 Constitution specified that

> In establishing the Cabinet, the Prime Minister must invite all parties whose membership in the House of Representatives comprises at least 10% of the total membership of the House to be represented in proportion to their numbers in the House.

The section covering appointments to the 32-member Senate — which was to include 14 members appointed by the Great Council of Chiefs, nine appointed by the Prime Minister, eight by the Leader of the Opposition and one by the Council of Rotuma — also entailed a multi-party distribution of members nominated by the Leader of the Opposition.

> [T]he Leader of the Opposition must ensure that the 8 persons proposed for appointment comprise such number of nominees of those parties as is proportionate to the size of the membership of those parties in the House of Representatives (Constitution of Fiji 1997, 64(2)).

As the courts later pointed out, insufficient attention was directed towards reconciling these new government formation rules with the underlying bedrock of Westminster democracy. The result was a hybrid Westminster system with superimposed multi-party cabinet provisions governing formation of cabinet and the Senate. Prime Ministers still needed to 'command a majority' on the floor of the House, but also to appoint ministers in accordance with Section 99. The formulas required for determining cabinet allocations and the distribution of nominees by the Leader of the Opposition in the Senate were not entirely clear, there was no ceiling on cabinet membership, there were no controls (aside from 'consultation' initiated by the Prime Minister) granted to participating parties as to which MPs might be selected and there were no rules governing the conduct of cabinets (or preventing government by single-party caucus reducing cabinet to a mere talking shop). The poorly drafted section covering Senate appointments specified a proportional distribution only of opposition nominees, but not those nominated by the Prime Minister (and potentially entailed a double dip for the Prime Minister's party, which might, in theory, have been entitled to secure some of the Leader of the Opposition's nominees as well as all of those of the Prime Minister). These arrangements proved a source of continuing litigation after the 1999 and 2001 elections.

Outcomes of the 1999 election

After the 1999 elections, the FLP emerged with an absolute majority (37 of 71 seats). It had a formal coalition with two smaller, Fijian-backed parties (the Fijian Association Party [FAP], with 11 seats, and the Party of National Unity [PANU], with four seats — see Table 1). It also had entered some informal arrangements with the Fijian Veitokani ni Lewenivanua ni Vakarisito (VLV, with three seats) about the exchange of preference votes (cf. Fraenkel 2001). After the election, FLP leader, Chaudhry, unexpectedly and controversially became Prime Minister, the first time an Indo-Fijian leader had ever assumed that position. Given the coup that had occurred in the aftermath of the FLP's previous victory in 1987, FLP coalition-building was inevitably sensitive to the broader security situation, rather than being narrowly constrained by the multi-party cabinet laws. Although the VLV held only three seats, its MPs included family members of the ethnic Fijian President, Ratu Mara, whose influence was critical for the survival of the new government. Two of these VLV MPs, including Mara's daughter, were granted cabinet positions, along with three FAP MPs and two PANU MPs. According to the Constitution, neither the VLV nor PANU was entitled to ministerial portfolios (and therefore these allocations were legally part of the Prime Minister's party entitlements). The political imperative of creating a broadly based coalition government, with a good number of ethnic Fijian ministers, took precedence over the formal power-sharing requirements.

Table 1: Composition of the Fijian Parliament, eligibility of parties under the 10 per cent rule and the make-up of cabinet as of June 11, 1999

	Parliamentary seats		Cabinet positions	
	No.	%	No.	%
Qualifying parties:				
FLP	37	52.1	11	61.1
FAP	11	15.5	3	16.7
SVT	8	11.3	0	0
Non-qualifying parties:				
PANU	4	5.6	2	11.1
VLV	3	4.2	2	11.1
UGP	2	2.8	0	0
NVTLP	1	1.4	0	0
Independents	5	7	0	0
Total	71	100	18	100

Source: Parliamentary seats from Fiji Elections Office, 'Elections '99; results by the Count', Suva, 1999; cabinet portfolios from the 'Statement of Agreed Facts and Issues in Supreme Court of Fiji, Miscellaneous Case No. 1 of 1999 between the President of the Republic of the Fiji Islands and 1. Inoke Kubuabola (Leader of the Opposition), 2. Mahendra Pal Chaudhry, Prime Minister, Government of the Fiji Islands and Leader of the Fiji Labour Party and 3. Adi Kuini Speed, Leader of the Fijian Association Party (cited as The President of the Republic of the Fiji islands v. Kubuabola & others, Misc. 1/1999, September 3, 1999).
Notes: Seats include adjustment for June 11, 1999, revocation of election of NVTLP candidate for Tailevu North/Ovalau in favour of the FAP. FLP = Fiji Labour Party; FAP = Fijian Association Party; SVT = Soqosoqo

ni Vakavulewa ni Taukei; PANU = Party of National Unity; VLV = Veitokani ni Lewenivanua Vakarisito; UGP = United Generals Party; NVTLP = Nationalist Vanua Lavo Tako Party.

Nevertheless, the new government remained precarious. The FLP had been party to the negotiations over the 1997 Constitution, but the key players had been the SVT and NFP, both of which had experienced heavy defeat at the polls. The SVT remained the largest indigenous party in terms of its share of the Fijian vote (38 per cent), but usage of the new alternative vote system had left it with only eight seats (as compared with the 18 it might have received under the former first-past-the-post system). Nevertheless, with eight seats, the SVT just reached the 10 per cent threshold for inclusion in cabinet. As constitutionally required, Chaudhry issued a lawful invitation to the SVT to join the cabinet. The SVT accepted, but insisted that party leader, Sitiveni Rabuka, become Deputy Prime Minister, that the SVT secure a total of four cabinet positions and three of the Prime Minister's Senate nominees, and that all SVT diplomatic appointees, as well and those appointed to statutory and state-owned boards, complete their terms of appointment.[10] The Prime Minister responded by rejecting these conditions. In the newspapers, the SVT announced a decision to lead the opposition and Rabuka resigned the leadership to become instead the Chair of the Great Council of Chiefs. Accordingly, a cabinet was formed that excluded the SVT, as shown in Table 1. New SVT leader, Ratu Inoke Kubuabola, was sworn in by the President as Leader of the Opposition. Only in July, with Supreme Court hearings looming over the allocation of positions in the Senate,[11] did the SVT lodge a protest against 'the decision of the Prime Minister to exclude the SVT from Cabinet'.[12]

The conditions in the SVT letter were deliberately severe.[13] Based on the 18-member cabinet eventually put together by Prime Minister Chaudhry, the SVT would have been entitled to no more than two or three cabinet positions.[14] According to Fiji's Supreme Court, '[T]hese were clearly conditions which the Prime Minister, acting reasonably, was not bound to accept. The Constitution does not provide for an acceptance qualified in this way. In the circumstances, what purported to be a conditional acceptance amounted to a declining of the invitation.'[15]

For this reason, the court upheld the constitutionality of the People's Coalition cabinet. Whatever the legal position, from the standpoint of rendering effective the new multi-party cabinet provisions or embedding support for the new Constitution among Fijian leaders, that decision, as well as the absence of negotiations on the issue of including SVT leaders in the new cabinet, was problematic. The SVT leaders were left in opposition, and quickly became involved in efforts to galvanise indigenous Fijian disquiet and unite Fijian parties, including backbenchers from among the FLP's coalition allies, against the Government. The consequent political climate, although it varied in intensity during the FLP's year in office, had much to do with the putsch that occurred on May 19, 2000 (cf. Fraenkel 2000).

Outcomes of the 2001 polls

Although that putsch was ultimately defeated, the FLP-led 1999-2000 government was never restored. Instead, an all-Fijian interim government assumed office. In the wake of a landmark Court of Appeal decision in March 2001 restoring the Constitution (the *Chandrika Prasad* case), fresh elections were held in August 2001. This time, a newly formed Fijian party, the Soqosoqo ni Duavata ni Lewenivanua (SDL), gained the largest number of seats, and party leader, Qarase, became Prime Minister. This was a truer test for the multi-party cabinet laws, since — as we saw — the post-1999 cabinet had been influenced more by security concerns than legal constraints. This was also closer to the type of situation envisaged by the drafters of the Constitution. With a growing majority in the population, the indigenous Fijians had been expected in the mid-1990s to be likely to secure the premiership, and the power-sharing provisions had been aimed principally at ensuring that they would do so in cooperation with Indo-Fijian political leaders. But the coup had polarised Fiji along ethnic lines, and annihilated much of the goodwill that had accompanied the negotiations on the 1997 Constitution. The 2001 elections were fought as a 'winner–takes-all' affair, with the SDL's principal campaign strategy being an appeal to indigenous Fijians to keep the FLP from returning to office. In the wake of the elections, multi-party cabinet provisions were to receive their sternest test.

That the SDL did not have an absolute majority after the 2001 polls also influenced the multi-party cabinet negotiations. The SDL had 32 seats, while the FLP had 27 seats (see Table 2).[16] No other party crossed the 10 per cent threshold. To form a durable majority government, Qarase obtained the support of the Conservative Alliance–Matanitu Vanua (CAMV, six seats), and formed a government with the backing of 41 of the 71 members. As constitutionally required, the new Prime Minister wrote to Chaudhry on the day of his appointment extending an invitation to participate in cabinet, but also pointing out that the two parties had 'diametrically opposed' policies and that there existed insufficient basis for a workable partnership. His letter stated that in the contemporary political context, Section 99(5) of the Constitution was 'unrealistic and unworkable', and made clear that government would be based on SDL policy.[17]

Chaudhry's response, also on September 10, accepted the invitation to join cabinet, although the FLP leader demanded representation in cabinet in accordance with the Korolevu Declaration, a pact that had been signed between political parties shortly before the 1999 polls. This had suggested a slightly modified interpretation of the constitutional power-sharing provisions such that the proportional entitlement of parties that crossed the 10 per cent threshold would be calculated not on the basis of their membership of the entire House (71 seats), but rather specified that 'membership of the cabinet should be in proportion to the number of seats held in parliament *by those parties participating in the cabinet*' [18] (in this case, 32 SDL + 27 FLP = 49). The Korolevu Declaration had also specified that 'cabinet decision making in Government should be on a consensus seeking basis especially with regard to key issues and policies'. [19] No such requirement had been included in the 1997 Constitution.

Hoping to follow the familiar 1999 sequence of events, in a further letter, Prime Minister Qarase stated that he was no longer obliged to include Labour in cabinet since Chaudhry had not accepted the 'basic condition' that the cabinet be based on SDL policies. Qarase also rejected the Korolevu Declaration, describing this as an agreement into which the SDL had not entered as a signatory. He highlighted public statements in the press by Chaudhry emphasising differences between SDL and FLP policy and pointed out that a workable coalition had already been forged with independents and smaller parties which had 'accepted the SDL manifesto as the central policy guidance of Cabinet':

> As your party has not accepted the same condition, I can only assume that you are unwilling to make a commitment at the outset, which would best promote the object of a stable and workable government which, in turn, would best assure the effective promotion of national unity. In all the above circumstances, I regret to say that the conditions of your acceptance of my invitation are unacceptable, as they will not contribute to a stable and workable Cabinet, so essential to the promotion of national unity in Fiji. [20]

On September 18, 2001, the Prime Minister wrote to the President advising the appointment of SDL and CAMV members and independents. Qarase gave two ministerial portfolios to the CAMV, one to a floor-crossing member of the NLUP and another to an independent (see Table 2). As is invariably the case with modern Fijian-led cabinets, portfolios were distributed carefully not solely along party lines, but to ensure some balance between indigenous political leaders from the major Fijian provinces and confederacies. [21]

Table 2: Composition of Fijian Parliament, eligibility of parties under the 10 per cent rule and make-up of cabinet as of September 26, 2001

	Membership of House		Cabinet positions	
	No.	%	No.	%
Qualifying parties:				
SDL	32	45.1	16	80
FLP	27	38	0	0
Non-qualifying parties:				
CAMV	6	8.5	2	10
NLUP	2	2.8	1	5
UGP	1	1.5	0	0
NFP	1	1.5	0	0
Independents	2	2.8	1	5
Total	71	100	20	100

Source: Opinion of the Supreme Court in the Matter of Section 123 of the Constitution Amendment Act 1997 and in the Matter of a Reference by the President for an Opinion in Questions as to the effect of Section 99 of the Constitution, Miscellaneous Case No. 1 of 2003, Judgment, July 9, 2004, pp. 4–5.
Notes: SDL = Soqosoqo ni Duavata ni Lewenivanua; CAMV = Conservative Alliance–Matanitu Vanua; for other designations, see Table 1.

In the wake of the formation of the new government, Fiji's Chief Justice lamented that 'the letter and spirit of the Constitution under the section pertaining to the formation of a Cabinet based on the constitutional concept of a multiparty government would appear to have been overlooked' (*PINA News Online* 14 September, 2001). Qarase and Chaudhry wrote to the President, Ratu Josefa Iloilo, urging, respectively, acceptance and rejection of the constitutionality of the newly sworn-in cabinet (*Fiji Daily Post* 21 September 2001). Unlike in the wake of the 1999 polls, the President did not refer the matter directly to the Supreme Court. Instead, the controversy over the constitutionality of the post-2001 poll cabinet, which was to dominate the political agenda for the next three years, was first brought by the FLP before the High Court in Lautoka, in western Viti Levu, which then requested advice from the higher courts. There followed a succession of judgments, in the Court of Appeal and then twice in the Supreme Court, each pitting government lawyers against those representing the FLP.

2002 Court of Appeal judgment

In the first of these judgments, the Court of Appeal found 'no basis at all for allowing the Prime Minister to impose any conditions on the invitations he must make', refusing to be swayed by any 'potential difficulties, real or imaginary, of a Cabinet constituted in accordance with that provision':

> The obligation placed on the Prime Minister is clear and precise. There is no ambiguity. There is no necessity for reading in any words. Any practical difficulties that may arise in the working of a multiparty cabinet

cannot affect the clear meaning of the words. The 1999 Supreme Court
Opinion makes it clear that a prime object of the Constitution is to
promote the sharing of power. A construction that would allow the Prime
Minister to impose a condition requiring a qualified party to agree to
conform to the policies of the Prime Minister is contrary to the Opinion
of the Supreme Court. We therefore hold that [the Constitution] obliges
a Prime Minister to invite, in unconditional terms, parties which have
10% or more of the membership of the House to be represented in the
Cabinet in accordance with that provision. This means the invitation to
be represented in the Cabinet may have to be issued across political lines.[22]

Nevertheless, the court found that Qarase's 'invitation was unconditional' and therefore in accordance with the Constitution. It was in the wake of Chaudhry's acceptance letter that 'the Prime Minister breached a constitutional duty' and, the court found, he remained in breach of those duties. On 24 April 2002, the High Court gave effect to the Court of Appeal's ruling, and required the Prime Minister to advise the President to appoint to cabinet 'such number of parliamentary members of the Fiji Labour Party as is in proportion to their numbers in the House of Representatives'.[23] The Government appealed, resulting in a fresh case heard before Fiji's Supreme Court.

2003 Supreme Court judgment

The Supreme Court upheld the decision of the Court of Appeal, agreeing that the requirement that the Prime Minister issue invitations to entitled parties was unambiguous, that Qarase's letter of invitation on September 10, 2001, had been unconditional and that the SDL leader had breached the Constitution in not subsequently appointing FLP ministers. It found that 'an invitation issued with a prognosis that the functioning of the Cabinet will be difficult or close to unworkable does not thereby cease to be an invitation'.[24] Nevertheless, the 2003 Supreme Court judgment sought to meet the Prime Minister's concerns regarding the potential unworkability of a multi-party cabinet. Although power sharing implied that rival parties might take into cabinet deliberations their 'own policies and agendas',

> [i]f they do so however, they do so subject to the requirements of collective responsibility and confidentiality which are recognised in the Constitution as aids to effective government. This may mean a more difficult Cabinet to manage than a Cabinet whose members belong to the same party or a coalition that has worked out some consensus before its formation. But this is the kind of Cabinet that is envisaged by the Constitution and it cannot be rejected as unworkable in principle because of that difficulty.[25]

And there the court's involvement in the deliberations surrounding cabinet formation might have ended were it not for the fact that the 2003 Supreme Court judgment sowed the seeds of further litigation in the course of one effort to allay fears, expressed by the Government's lawyers, that the Prime Minister's party might have only a minority within cabinet:

> [W]hen, as has occurred, there are only two parties which have more than 10% of the membership of the House, the Prime Minister can ensure that the majority party has a majority in the Cabinet ... It may also be noted that as long as the Prime Minister's party has a majority of the total of parliamentary seats held by that party and all other eligible parties it will have an entitlement to a majority of positions in Cabinet. For assuming each eligible party accepts the invitation for representation in the Cabinet its entitlement to representation will be measured by the *proportion of the number of parliamentary seats it holds to the total number of parliamentary seats held by the Government or Coalition party and all eligible parties*. On that basis, in the present case, the Prime Minister's party has an entitlement to a majority position in Cabinet. [26]

The penultimate sentence specified a proportional distribution of cabinet entitlements relative to the total of *eligible parties* (as in the New Caledonian, 1998 Northern Irish and 1994–96 South African rules [27]), rather than relative to the membership of the House as a whole. According to the first interpretation, the FLP might have gained 47 per cent of cabinet positions (28/60). According to the second, it might secure 39 per cent (28/71). [28] The FLP's submissions had urged a court verdict in line with the January 1999 Korolevu Declaration. But the 2001 Court of Appeal judgment and the 2003 Supreme Court judgment rejected this FLP argument on the grounds that 'the Korolevu declaration was a document prepared by the leaders of certain political parties in January 1999 to which the SDL never assented'. [29] Despite this, neither the Court of Appeal in 2002 nor the 2003 Supreme Court judgment specified precisely how cabinet entitlements should be calculated or what number of cabinet positions the FLP could expect to receive.

With the Supreme Court case concluded, Prime Minister Qarase announced his intention to form a 36-member cabinet, with the FLP to be granted 14 positions (38 per cent) and 'the balance of 22 is the Prime Minister's share'. [30] Qarase rejected the option of calling fresh elections, anticipating that these would produce a result similar to those in 2001, therefore entailing a repeat of the multi-party cabinet controversies. To retain his coalition government (and therefore his majority on the floor of the House), the Prime Minister construed it necessary to retain the services of his existing 22 ministers. [31] That cabinet, as we saw earlier, had been carefully assembled to ensure a balance between the provinces, as well as between parliamentary coalition partners. Any ministerial reshuffles to accommodate the court's ruling would have been likely to destroy that balance, and the wounded pride of those who lost their portfolios would have been likely to have political repercussions. As a result, Qarase might lose the confidence of the House. The FLP would have been unlikely to step in to back the Government in a confidence vote. Only by expanding the cabinet to 36 members could the governing coalition be retained intact while ensuring that the FLP was constitutionally included. The FLP was to be offered a host of token ministries, with minimal responsibilities (*Daily Post* 7 August 2003).

In response, Chaudhry criticised the proposed 36-member cabinet as a costly and oversized burden on the taxpayer. The FLP leader also disputed the Prime Minister's authority to choose which FLP members might take up portfolios and demanded 17 (47 per cent) rather than 14 (39 per cent) positions in a 36-member cabinet (*Daily Post* 27 July, 2003; 7 August 2003). The FLP refused, as requested by Qarase, to submit names for consideration until the issue of cabinet entitlements had been settled legally, and soon launched yet another High Court case on this matter. Chaudhry wrote to Qarase, making clear reference to the 2003 Supreme Court's implied inclusion of the Prime Minister's party in any calculation of entitlements in cabinet:

> I have carefully considered your formula restricting Labour to 38 per cent for Cabinet seats. May I point out that applying the same formula to your own party would restrict it to a maximum of 16 ministers in a Cabinet of 36, based on the fact that the Soqosoqo Duavata ni Lewenivanua Party holds 45 per cent of the 71 seats in the House. You will agree that 45 per cent of 36 comes to 16 but you have 19 SDL ministers in your present Cabinet of 22 and you intend to retain the same number in the extended Cabinet of 36, that is three more than your entitlement using your own formula (*Daily Post* 11 August 2003).

By agreement between the two parties and with the assent of the President, this issue of numerical cabinet entitlements was referred back to the Supreme Court for further deliberation.

By 2003, Talanoa talks aimed at bringing together the two main party leaders had failed, and the FLP was publicly justifying its decision to pursue the issue of multi-party cabinet entitlements as intended primarily to clarify for the future ambiguous sections in the law, rather than as likely to lead to an accommodation in government. Senior FLP leaders acknowledged that a genuine partnership in cabinet between the SDL and FLP was unlikely, given the extent of bitterness and rancour between senior leaders. No compromises were offered publicly by either party leader, for example, to exchange raw numerical cabinet entitlements for favoured portfolios or concessions on policy issues which were significant to one or other of the two communities. Chaudhry explicitly emphasised that the proper application of the court ruling required the Prime Minister to dismantle the coalition that gave him a majority in the House: '[Y]our argument to retain your ineligible coalition partners and an independent minister in addition to a full complement of your own party ministers in order to retain and maintain your position as PM and the confidence of the House runs counter to the court's judgement' (*Fiji Times* 2 August 2003).

For the FLP, the multi-party cabinet court controversies were to become, ever more explicitly, a method of breaking up the governing coalition and casting perpetually into doubt the legitimacy of the Government due to its breach of the letter, as well as the spirit, of the 1997 Constitution. International opinion was also rallied in defence of this cause, although politicians schooled in the majoritarian traditions of Australia and New Zealand were not greatly sympathetic to Chaudhry's pleas. For the SDL-led Government, repeated court cases kept ethnic polarisation at the forefront of Fiji's politics and emphasised the need for 'Fijian unity' in the face of a threatened return of Chaudhry and his colleagues into government. Inter-ethnic polarisation, and the need to placate Fijian discontent had, after all, been the principal justification for the emergence of the SDL in the wake of the 2000 coup. [32] To justify holding to its uncompromising stance on the multi-party cabinet issue, senior SDL leaders pointed to the precedent of Rabuka's SVT which, it was thought, had sown the seeds of its own demise by opting for a more conciliatory stance towards Indo-Fijians. [33] Instead of fostering compromise, the power-sharing provisions in the Constitution had become the principal focus of inter-ethnic antagonism, serving to sustain and entrench the polarisation of 1999-2000. Compromise seemed unnecessary over an issue that was, repeatedly, being settled by recourse to the law courts.

The 2004 Supreme Court judgment

In its 2004 judgment, the Supreme Court acknowledged that its 2003 interpretation of the proportional entitlements of parties in cabinet had not been 'the product of detailed submissions and close scrutiny of earlier precedent involved in the present reference'. [34] Now required to rule expressly on numerical cabinet entitlements, the court found that the Prime Minister's own party, as well as other qualifying parties, was constrained by the provisions regarding cabinet entitlements. It rejected the interpretation, based on a literal reading of s. 99(5) in isolation, which implied that the Prime Minister was obliged to issue an invitation only to *other* parties which crossed the 10 per cent seat threshold and which identified proportional entitlements based on the membership of the House as a whole. It did so because later subsections implied that the party of the Prime Minister was also bound by the proportionality provisions, rather than being the recipient of all residual places after allocations to those parties entitled to mandatory representation. [35] It made reference also to the section of the Constitution governing Senate appointments where proportionality is established by reference to the total only of the qualifying parties, not the total membership of the House. [36]

Yet, as in the case of the 2003 judgment, the majority opinion of the Supreme Court recognised conflicting elements in the 1997 Constitution, and, controversially, sought an interpretation enabling consistency with its majoritarian aspect. On this issue, the court was divided. The majority opinion noted that agreeing to the FLP submission 'entails the possibility of a Cabinet dominated numerically by parties hostile to the Government, with the consequence that the Cabinet (or government) would not have the confidence of the House'. [37] Whereas the majority's interpretation of proportional party entitlements implied an inflexible constraint on the Prime Minister's freedom of action, room for manoeuvre was restored by a new interpretation of the scope for independent or non-party affiliated Senate members into cabinet:

> Cabinet [need not] be composed only of members of qualifying parties. [This allows] for the appointment of Independents or Senate members, provided they do not belong to any of the parties represented in the House of Representatives. But whether the Cabinet is composed only of members of qualifying parties or includes non-party appointments, the relationship between the number of seats held by the Government and qualifying non-government parties must remain the same. [38]

In other words, the SDL Government might appoint to cabinet as many non-party MPs or Senators as it deemed fit, needing to retain only the 32/28 or 1.14 ratio of SDL to FLP cabinet ministers. The reasoning here was aimed explicitly at strengthening the position of the governing party:

> Given that some constituencies may be represented by Independents and that persons of standing and experience may be appointed to the Senate who are not necessarily members of a political party, there is no apparent constitutional purpose to be served by precluding the Prime Minister from appointing a person or persons in those categories into the Cabinet in appropriate circumstances. Such appointments could involve co-operative arrangements with the governing party. [39]

The minority opinion, lodged by Justice Thomas Gault, strongly criticised this aspect of the majority judgment as unnecessary to resolve the matters under dispute and inconsistent with Section 99 of the Constitution. [40] Justice Gault suggested that the majority's interpretation implied unwarranted unfairness to smaller political parties, and an unjustified bias in favour of independents and Senate members. For Gault, independents should have been treated in the same way as parties that failed to secure the 10 per cent threshold (i.e., that they might obtain portfolios only as part of the Prime Minister's or other qualifying parties' entitlements).

After the 2004 judgment, Qarase offered the FLP 14 seats in a 30-member cabinet (preserving the court's required 1.14 ratio), specifying a list of minor portfolios and the names of FLP members for inclusion, but making clear his government's intention to exercise the right to appoint additional independents and non-party Senators (*Fiji Sun* 23 July 2004). Even before the Supreme Court's decision, the FLP had issued a further writ challenging the Government's right to choose which FLP members might be included in cabinet (*Fiji Sun* 18 March 2004). But the protracted 2001–04 sequence of court controversies was over. Public opinion was tiring of the multi-party cabinet controversies, and newspaper editorials repeatedly berated both senior party leaders for their intransigence. The FLP recognised its efforts to use the courts to undermine the governing coalition were likely to prove fruitless. A new election was looming in 2006, and the 2004 Supreme Court decision had given the Prime Minister considerable scope to retain his majority in cabinet. In November 2004, Chaudhry formally rejected the Prime Minister's invitation to join the cabinet and became Leader of the Opposition.

The 2004 Supreme Court decision ended a period of protracted controversy about the multi-party cabinet, which had endured for more than half the government's five-year term in office. In compliance with the 2004 Supreme Court judgment, a Prime Minister could henceforth pack the cabinet with sympathetic independents and senators, and so diminish the portfolios held by rival parties. The strategic repercussions of operating under this new ruling are peculiar. Since encouraging more allied independents to stand for Parliament would potentially diminish a Prime Minister's own party entitlements under the 10 per cent rule, the incentive exists to appoint a good number of non-elected Senators to cabinet (as we saw above, the Prime Minister appoints nine of the 32 Senators). The only constraint is that the Prime Minister's own party has to retain its House of Representatives proportions to other entitled parties. Fiji's multi-party cabinet laws had deliberately discriminated against smaller parties (those obtaining less than 10 per cent of the membership of the House). Now its application based on legal precedent potentially discriminated against larger parties as well, but in favour of the Prime Minister's own nominees to the Senate. Whichever way, the 2004 judgment undermined the objectives of power sharing in Fiji, even if this was a response to ambiguities left in the 1997 Constitution and poor legal drafting.

Unravelling majoritarian rule in New Caledonia

As in Fiji, New Caledonia's power-sharing rules were part of a broader compact between political leaders from the two major communities, entailing a host of concessions and compromises. The 1998 Noumea Accord put back the scheduled vote on independence for 15-20 years, established a program for a phased devolution of powers to the territorial Congress and a Senate for Kanak chiefs, as well as providing for a government 'elected by the Congress on a proportional basis'.[41] The *Organic Law* of March 19, 1999, and the 1999 Standing Orders (or 'Interior Rules') of the New Caledonia Congress put this provision into practice by specifying that all 'elected groups' with more than six seats in Congress were entitled to positions in cabinet.[42] Under the new arrangements, Congress established the size of the Executive, but was constrained to choose between five and 11 ministers. Qualifying groups with more than six seats, which could consist of combinations of allied parties, put up lists of candidates for inclusion in cabinet. Ministers were then selected from these qualifying groups 'by proportional representation following the rule of the highest average'.[43] Only after the executive was formed were the ministers required to elect a President and Vice-President and the Executive was charged with conducting decision-making in a 'collegial' fashion.[44] Like Fiji, New Caledonia experienced considerable litigation on the cabinet entitlements issue, although in New Caledonia legal battles and political controversies also centred on the election of the President and Vice-President, portfolio distribution and the nature of cabinet decision-making.

The 1999 elections

At the first elections after the introduction of the Noumea Accord in May 1999, the main settler-backed party, the Rassemblement pour la Calédonie dans la République (RPCR), won 24 of the 54 congress seats. The RPCR secured a majority by allying itself with a breakaway Kanak group, the Fédération des Comités de Coordination des Indépendantistes (FCCI, four members). The FCCI had controversially called for a 'mutation' among New Caledonia's political leaders and claimed that the mainstream Kanak coalition, the Front de Libération Nationale Kanak et Socialiste (FLNKS), had 'fulfilled its historic mission' (Chappell 1999b, *Radio Australia* 7 June 1999). They were heralded by Jacques Lafleur, RPCR leader, as a 'party of peace', but condemned by the larger Kanak-backed parties (*Radio Australia* 11 May 1999).[45] The National Front, with four seats, also backed the RPCR-FCCI slate. The RPCR's Jean Lèques became President, while the FCCI's Leopold Jorédie became Vice-President. Of the pro-independence parties, the FLNKS won 12 seats in Congress, while the Parti de Libération Kanak (PALIKA), standing separately, obtained a further six seats. The other mainly settler-backed party, Didier Leroux's Alliance pour la Calédonie, gained three seats, failing to reach the threshold for cabinet representation.

Table 3: Congress slates and cabinet portfolios after the 1999 polls in New Caledonia

	Congress slates		Cabinet posts	
	No.	%	No.	%
Qualifying groups:				
RPCR (24) – FCCI (4) – FN (4)	32	60.4	7	63.6
FLNKS (12) – PALIKA (5) – LKS (1)[1]	18	34	4	36.4
Non-qualifying parties:				
Alliance pour la Calédonie[2]	3	5.7	0	0
Total[1]	53	100	11	100

Source: Les Nouvelles-Calédoniennes, May 29, 1999.
Notes: For party abbreviations, see text. LKS = Libération Kanak Socialiste.
[1] Charly Pidjot of FLNKS did not vote, as a result of which the total is 53 rather than 54.
[2] The Alliance in fact submitted three blank ballots.

In accordance with the new multi-party cabinet rules, Congress decided on an 11-member executive. With 32 of the 54 seats, the RPCR-FCCI obtained seven ministerial portfolios, while FLNKS-PALIKA obtained four positions in cabinet (see Table 3). Initial controversy surrounded the Vice-Presidency, with FLNKS leaders arguing that the position should have gone to the pro-independence groups, rather than to the FCCI. The majority RPCR-FCCI coalition also took the major portfolios, such as economics, labour and education, with the FLNKS receiving health, culture, equipment, and youth and sports. FLNKS leader, Rock Wamytan, protested that the Government was 'drifting away from the spirit and the letter of the Noumea Accord' (Chappell 2000, *PINA News online* 1 October 1999). In its first year participating in cabinet, the FLNKS repeatedly took cases before the Administrative Tribunal complaining of a lack of 'collegiality' in the conduct of the Executive (Chappell 2000; 2001, Connell 2003). The RPCR leaders insisted on 'majority rule' in executive decision-making, and retained control of all congressional commissions (Chappell 2001, Bastogi 2003, Maclellan 1999, Connell 2003).

On his re-election as Mayor of Noumea in 2001, Jean Lèques resigned the Presidency, an act that automatically led to the fall of his government. A new government was elected by Congress on April 3, 2001. The RPCR's Pierre Frogier was elected President, but now PALIKA's Déwé Gorodé, a Kanak activist and writer, was appointed as Vice-President, thus meeting one of the major FLNKS objections to the Lèques Government. The RPCR again had seven ministers, FLNKS three and Union Calédonienne (UC) one, an allocation that entailed no change in the portfolios allocated to the pro-independence groups (*Les Nouvelles-Calédoniennes* 4 April 2001). The FCCI challenged the outcome, protesting that it, rather than the FLNKS, was entitled to the 11th cabinet portfolio. During the executive election of 3 April 2001, the RPCR-FCCI and

FLNKS had been tied in the contest for the final executive position. The President of Congress employed the rule benefiting the more aged candidate, with the result that the FLNKS' M. Manuohalalo was elected (*Oceania Flash* 26 September 2001). After a reference by the FCCI, the Council of State reversed the previous decision, applying instead rules that favoured the group which secured the largest number of votes. As a result, the FCCI gained the seat. Wamytan resigned from the Government in protest, but PALIKA's Gorodé remained in cabinet (*Oceania Flash* 7 November 2001). Although controversies over the implementation of the Noumea Accord and 'collegiality' in cabinet continued, frictions within the FLNKS were becoming increasingly prominent.

Two decisions under the first Frogier Government also confirmed the scope and limitations for the minority in cabinet to exercise an indirect veto over policy, the first of which involved a decision taken under the previous government. On December 21, 2000, then President Lèques had appointed a new Director of the Central Territorial Hospital, publishing the decision in the *Official Journal of New Caledonia*. The 1999 *Organic Law*, however, required a countersignature by the Minister of Health, FLNKS' Manuohalalo, who refused on the grounds that proper procedure had not been respected. President Lèques referred the matter to the Administrative Tribunal, which in turn asked for the advice of the Council of State. On July 27, 2001, the Council of State ruled that the minister's refusal rendered the decision invalid, an outcome interpreted by French legal specialist Jean Yves Faberon (2002), as intended to reinforce the Noumea Accord's provisions for 'collegiality' in cabinet.

More importantly, the other article in the 1999 *Organic Law* that entailed an indirect minority veto provides that if a party participating in the Government collectively resigns, the result is that the entire government falls and needs to be re-elected by Congress.[46] In October 2002, cabinet offices were moved to a new building. The three FLNKS ministers refused to shift, protesting that the building was designed as an 'annex' to the powerful RCPR-dominated Southern Province headquarters. Describing this as a further example of lack of 'collegiality' in decision-making, UC leader, Gerald Cortot, and all members of the UC list beneath him, collectively resigned from the Executive causing the Government to fall on November 13, 2002 (*Oceania Flash* 14 November 2002, Chappell 2003). Before the new government was elected, Congress endorsed the RPCR's proposal that the Executive be restricted to 10 members (rather than 11), in the face of UC protests (*Oceania Flash* 22 November 2002). Outcomes were similar to 1999 and 2001: the RPCR-FCCI won seven, the FLNKS secured two and the UC a single cabinet portfolio. The Administrative Tribunal rejected UC's appeal against the reduction in cabinet size from 11 to 10.[47] Frogier was re-elected President on November 28, 2002, with Gorodé again as Vice-President. The pro-independence parties boycotted cabinet meetings in late 2002 (*Pacific Islands Report* 20 December 2002).

Outcomes of the 2004 polls

The 2004 election proved a watershed in New Caledonian politics. It ended an era of government by the RPCR and resulted in multiple political parties securing representation in Congress. It also threatened to produce an impasse. The newly formed Avenir Ensemble and the Rassemblement–UMP (the renamed RPCR[48]) were tied on 16 seats each, and the FLNKS and UC counted together also had 16 seats. No party had an absolute majority in Congress and no alliance of parties initially proved able to agree on a new President. One result was that the institutions established under the 1998 Noumea Accords were subjected to a severe test. Eventually, the outcome was consensus, at least between the mainly settler-backed political parties on the election of the newly formed Avenir Ensemble's Marie-Noëlle Thémereau as President. Avenir Ensemble and the pro-independence parties agreed on the re-election to the Vice-Presidency of PALIKA's Gorodé. The new government proclaimed for itself the goal of achieving a more effective style of power sharing than its predecessors.

In the wake of the polls, Congress decided to establish an 11-member executive. Owing to the distribution of Congress seats, the expected entitlement of parties to ministerial portfolios would have given the Rassemblement–UMP and Avenir Ensemble four portfolios each (*Les Nouvelles-Calédoniennes* 2 June 2004). However, one of the new Rassemblement–UMP Congress members, Suzie Vigouroux, marked the ballot 'Frogier' rather than voting for the Rassemblement–UMP–FCCI list. This rendered her vote invalid and lost the Rassemblement–UMP a crucial vote. Without the Vigouroux vote, the RPCR was entitled to only three cabinet posts. Consequently, Thémereau won the initial election for the Presidency, with Gorodé as Vice-President. Several hours later, however, the resignation of the Rassemblement–UMP, using the same provision as that used in November 2002 by the UC, brought about the fall of the new government (*Les Nouvelles Calédoniennes* 11 June 2004). As a result of the ensuing legal battles, the Rassemblement–UMP regained the Vigouroux vote. The Administrative Court also advised that the President had to be elected by an absolute majority of six of the 11 cabinet members (rather than a simple majority).[49] Avenir Ensemble and the Rassemblement–UMP were now tied on four votes each, while UC and Uni-FLNKS again abstained from the presidential election. The possibility of fresh general elections, called by the French High Commissioner, loomed if the impasse was not resolved. Eventually, a compromise was reached. Thémereau received all eight Avenir Ensemble and Rassemblement–UMP votes and was re-elected as President (Bastogi 2004). Gorodé was also re-elected, drawing on the three pro-independence party votes and four Avenir Ensemble votes and two of the votes from the Rassemblement–UMP.

Table 4: Congress slates and cabinet portfolios in New Caledonia as of June 24, 2004

	Congress slates		Cabinet posts	
	No.	%	No.	%
Qualifying groups:				
AE (16) – FN (4) – LKS (1)	21	38.9	4	36.4
R-UMP (16) – FCCI (1)	17	31.5	4	36.4
Uni–FLNKS	9	16.7	2	18.2
UC	7	13	1	9.1
Total	54	100	11	100

Notes: Elections to the New Caledonian Executive are by secret ballot, and the lists are not released publicly. Nevertheless, references to the size of Congress slates make it possible to calculate combined lists. For abbreviations, see Table 3 and text.

In the new cabinet, portfolios were allocated without the friction witnessed during the presidential election. Gorodé retained the culture portfolio, but also took responsibility for women's affairs and citizenship; UC's Cortot received transport, infrastructure and energy; and PALIKA's Charles Washetine acquired responsibility for teaching and research. Avenir Ensemble's Didier Leroux gained the economy and communications portfolio and the Rassemblement–UMP's Frogier took charge of foreign affairs and trade. President Thémereau described the allocation of ministerial portfolios as being accomplished in 'an entirely collegial fashion, with perfect agreement and without difficulty', while Frogier talked of a 'balanced division' (*Les Nouvelles-Calédoniennes* 3 July 2004). In some respects, the mainly Kanak-backed parties acquired greater influence in the new government. For example, PALIKA and UC persuaded the Government to strengthen the responsibilities of the Kanak customary Senate, rather than dealing with customary matters through a separate ministerial post. Compromises were also reached with the Rassemblement–UMP, not only on the presidential election issue but with regard to a new meeting of the signatories to the Noumea Accord. Such a meeting had not occurred since June 2003. At first, the Rassemblement–UMP insisted that only those who had signed the accord be represented at the negotiations (i.e., RPCR and FLNKS), pointing out that some Avenir Ensemble leaders (such as Leroux) had voted against the Noumea Accord. Eventually, a compromise was reached by which other parties could be included as part of the RPCR and FLNKS 'historic' delegations.

Verdicts differ on the likely future direction of cooperation under the Noumea Accord, and whether elite conciliation might galvanise Kanak rebellion (Chanter 2006, Crocombe 2001: 424, Chappell 1999b), what emphasis to place on grassroots reconciliation efforts as compared with top-level constitutional arrangements (Maclellan 2005a), or whether the Noumea Accord is merely a delaying tactic designed to ultimately avoid independence (Connell 2003). Although early signs might be promising (Chappell 2005, Maclellan 2005b, Angleviel 2003), the potential exists for deadlock if parties representing the different communities fail to cooperate in the Executive. Whichever way, New Caledonia's experiment with a multi-party cabinet proved considerably more successful than that in Fiji. Even if future political directions are uncertain, there is little sign that the design of New Caledonia's laws governing cabinet composition places any significant impediments in the path of cooperation between the pro-independence and settler-backed parties.

Lessons with regards to power-sharing institutions

Fiji's power-sharing provisions are internationally peculiar. Combining a Westminster-style constitutional framework with a multi-party cabinet proved incongruous; the result was a majoritarian electoral system shorn of the often claimed virtues of such systems coupled with a proportional cabinet formation system without its usual associated merits of fairly and equitably representing the major ethnic communities or other interest groups. Historically, most cabinet power-sharing arrangements have been adopted together with proportional representation systems, as in New Caledonia, Northern Ireland and Switzerland. Proportionality in parliament ensures a reasonably representative election of competing ethnic or interest groups, which are then brought, also proportionally, into government. Majoritarian systems, for better or worse, make likely party seat shares that differ from vote shares. A small favourable nationwide swing in votes results in a big swing in seats to the victorious party. Coalition governments are less likely to be necessary, leaving governing parties free to implement their manifestos undisturbed by compromises with allied parties (hence, the often-heard 'stable government' argument). In the context of a proportionality rule as regards cabinet formation, it will frequently be the case that the Prime Minister's party's majority in Parliament is not dependent on, or even assisted by, parties which the power-sharing provisions bring into cabinet. Conversely, minority parties brought into cabinet are less likely to have their position reinforced by a real strength on the floor of Parliament. Their role in cabinet is more likely under such systems to be solely a function of legal constraints and consequently considerably weaker. Difficulties might arise with power-sharing institutions under either arrangement, but they are much more likely with majoritarian electoral systems.

Specific features in the design of Fiji's power-sharing institutions imparted additional tensions to the process of government formation. Under the 1997 Constitution, governments are potentially formed twice. Initially, the onus is on a potential Prime Minister to persuade the President that he or she can command the support of a majority in the House.[50] Where a coalition is required, this is likely to be accompanied by inter-party agreements regarding the distribution of ministerial portfolios. Once appointed, the Prime Minister must reform his or her government in accordance with the 10 per cent entitlement provision, often incorporating parties from the opposite end of the political spectrum. After the 1999 elections, this posed no great difficulty since i) the FLP held an absolute majority in the House of Representatives, ii) the FLP had a pre-election alliance with the FAP, and iii) the SVT was ruled to have forfeited its entitlement to cabinet participation owing to conditions placed on acceptance. After the 2001 polls, it posed a major difficulty because the coalition forged on the floor of the House (SDL plus CAMV) differed from that required to comply with the multi-party cabinet provisions of the 1997 constitution (SDL plus FLP). In other circumstances, potential Prime Ministers might anticipate the impending constraints of the 10 per cent rule, and form a cabinet accordingly. But a party leader urging claims to the premiership straight after an election is more likely to be able to elicit support from like-minded allies than adversaries. A party from the opposite end of the political spectrum, particularly if it has a substantial representation in Parliament, is more likely to field alternative candidates for the premiership than to anticipate, and acquiesce in the acceptance of, a junior position in a power-sharing cabinet.

The potential alternative arrangement, as used in neighbouring New Caledonia, entails the formation of a multi-party cabinet *before* the selection of the Prime Minister or President and Vice-President of the Territorial Assembly. As we have seen, first, Congress decides how many ministers will make up the government (somewhere between five and 11: i.e., unlike Fiji, there is a ceiling on membership avoiding over-inflation of cabinet size to accommodate dual coalitions). Second, all groups with more than six seats gain the right to participate proportionally in cabinet, and present lists for inclusion, which can include people not elected to Congress. Groups thus, more reasonably than in Fiji, select their own favoured representatives for cabinet inclusion, rather than leaving this to the discretion of a President/Prime Minister who might belong to a rival political party. New Caledonia's rules are also fairer to smaller parties, since they can combine with bigger parties to enhance the allied group's cabinet entitlement and, in this way, potentially negotiate portfolios of their own. Only after the composition of the Executive has been determined are the President and Vice-President selected, although the President retains freedom to determine the allocation of portfolios among ministers.

The Northern Ireland Good Friday arrangements follow a similar principle, but in these a formula is also used to calculate a proportional distribution of ministries. The First Minister and Deputy are elected by 'parallel consent', i.e., they require Unionist and Nationalist majorities. After this, 'the posts of ministers will be allocated to parties on the basis of the d'Hont system by reference to the number of seats each party has in the assembly'. [51]

Oddly, the functioning of Fiji's power-sharing institutions depended ultimately on politicians following Westminster-style conventions regarding cabinet government despite the changed context. Years of Westminster government had fostered well-established routines regarding the nature of ministerial responsibilities, and, particularly for ethnic Fijians, acquisition of cabinet or other top-level government positions frequently entailed prestigious status that could be deployed simultaneously to acquire standing in the customary order. For example, after becoming President in December 1987, Ratu Sir Penaia Ganilau was able to use his new position to acquire the *Tui Cakau* title, covering the province of Cakaudrove and the Tovata confederacy, although this reverted to the descendants of his predecessor after his death. Similarly, the position of Ro Teimumu Kepa as a minister in the Qarase Government enhanced her claim to the powerful *Roko Tui Dreketi* title after the death of the former titleholder.

Chaudhry's short-lived administration was less convention-bound in this respect, and the affairs of the 1999-2000 government were anyway mostly run through a behind-the-scenes FLP caucus, rather than through cabinet (Field, Baba and Nabobo-Baba 2005). [52] In this sense, Fiji's multi-party cabinet controversy during 2001–04 was blown out of proportion by the reaction of the SDL Government. Nothing in the 1997 Constitution specified the functions of cabinet, or its numbers or how often it was to meet or even the salaries and perks of ministers. Compliance with the letter of the law was therefore not particularly onerous, and the post-2001 Fijian Government could reasonably straightforwardly have embraced FLP participation in cabinet without making significant concessions in terms of policy. Even if cabinet had continued to play a central role in policy formulation, the Prime Minister was constitutionally free to resolve any internal differences by a vote on the floor of the House.

New Caledonia's arrangements are more flexible than those in Fiji. The Noumea Accord sets out only the principle of a multi-party cabinet; the Government must be 'elected by the Congress on a proportional basis'. How that is done is left up to the Congress. The Administrative Tribunal functions largely in an advisory capacity, although the Council of State's decisions have the force of law. There are mandatory aspects of the New Caledonian institutions, but there is also a recognition that not everything can be set down in law and that, ultimately, the success of the Noumea Accord system rests on voluntary cooperation between former adversaries. Even the most elaborate power-sharing rules are vulnerable to strategic manipulation and do not guarantee cooperation between deeply divided political parties. Where power-sharing institutions have proved effective, cooperation has depended on a *prior* consensus among political elites, rather than representing an institutionally driven outcome that would have worked effectively irrespective of whether or not elites were oriented towards compromise.

For example, the temporary success of power sharing in South Africa did not owe its origin primarily to ingenious and well-crafted legislation. Rather, F. W.

De Klerk's National Party and the African National Congress perceived gains to be obtained from sharing power; the former because this implied ministerial responsibilities that it would be unlikely to otherwise secure in the wake of the 1994 polls, the latter because this offered to enhance domestic and international legitimacy, and therefore stability, during the transition from apartheid. As Vincent Maphai (1999: 97) concludes,

> Consociationalism was not the cause of tolerance, but the result. Power-sharing was the mechanism adopted to give expression to parties' prior readiness to eschew racially exclusive politics in the interest of mutually beneficial outcomes ... Consociationalism is designed to minimize conflict in 'deeply divided' societies. Yet it would appear that such societies would not adopt consociational measures in the first place until levels of hostility have diminished substantially. [53]

In 1990s Northern Ireland, it was the ending of the unionist veto and the recognition that the alternative to power sharing was greater involvement of the southern Irish State in the affairs of the North that exerted pressure on Loyalist parties to sign up to the Good Friday Agreement (McGarry 1998: 854, 858, 866, 869). Both sides henceforth had an interest in making the arrangements operate effectively, even if continuing intransigence stalled the restoration of the Northern Irish Executive. Conversely, in 1970s Northern Ireland and 1960s Cyprus, the dominant groups (Protestants and Greeks respectively) saw little benefit associated with defending power-sharing institutions, whereas minority groups (Catholics and Turks respectively) sought to extend and entrench the legal protections (Palley 1978:17). In both cases, intransigence was encouraged by the links of majorities and minorities with neighbouring powers. Multi-party cabinet rules might serve to set in place meaningful parameters, which with time become accepted principles encouraging cooperation (as in Switzerland), but the bare legal bones of mandatory arrangements are unlikely, in themselves, to transcend top-level political conflict or to bring antagonistic elites into cooperative arrangements.

There were numerous reasons for the greater success of power sharing in New Caledonia than in Fiji. Fiji's divisions were in many ways sharper, and the incentives for accommodation by the indigenous elite were less than those confronting the RPCR leadership. Violent resistance by Kanaks in the 1980s destabilised the French Pacific territory, and political realignments threatened to fracture the precarious unity of the settler parties, which, after all, had emerged only in the late 1970s as Kanak opinion hardened around the independence issue.[54] Time also played its part in building consensus around the new compact, which took a decade to move from the Matignon to the Noumea Accord. Whereas in 1988 the majority of voters in the predominantly non-Kanak south of the Grande Terre had opposed the Matignon Accord, in the Noumea Accord referendum a decade later 63 per cent of those in the Southern Province voted 'yes' (Chappell 1989:154; 1999b:434-5). Fiji's 1997 Constitution was much more of an elite deal struck between the leaders of political parties: one which came unstuck in large part because its key architects were subsequently defeated at the polls (indicating their failure to win popular support for the new alliance by demonstrating policy advantages of cooperation). Nevertheless, Fiji's Constitution survived, due to its restoration by the law courts in March 2001. What did not survive unaltered, again because of the decision (and Westminster-based proclivities) of the court, were the multi-party power-sharing provisions, which were so diluted as to permit a reversion to majoritarian cabinet formation. In this paper, my argument has been that one part of the reason for the failure of power sharing in Fiji had to do with institutional design, even if other factors also made cooperation in multi-party cabinets much more difficult to achieve in Fiji than in New Caledonia.

References

Akinyele, R. T. 2000, 'Power-sharing and Conflict Management in Africa: Nigeria, Sudan and Rwanda', *Africa Development*, XXV, 3–4: pp. 209–33.

Angleviel, F. 2003, '"The Bet on Intelligence": Politics in New Caledonia, 1998–2002', State, Society and Governance in Melanesia Discussion Paper, 2003/4. Canberra, The Australian National University.

Barry, B. 1975a, 'Political Accommodation and Consociational Democracy', *British Journal of Political Science*, 5: pp. 477–505.

Barry, B. 1975b, 'The Consociational Model and its Dangers', *European Journal of Political Research*, 3: 393–412.

Bastogi, M. 2004, 'Le Gouvernement de la Nouvelle-Calédonie Issu des Elections du 9 Mai 2004', *Revue Juridique Politique et Économique de Nouvelle Calédonie*, 4, 2: pp. 14–19.

Bastogi, M. 2003, 'Le Gouvernement de la Nouvelle-Calédonie à l'épreuve de la durée', *Revue Juridique Politique et Économique de Nouvelle Calédonie*, 1, 1: pp. 30–6

Cama, N. 2005, 'Stop, Take Stock, Move On', *Daily Post*, 5 March.

Chanter, A. 2006, 'Party Fragmentation and the New Political Logic in New Caledonia', in R. Rich et al., *Political Parties in the Pacific*, Pandanus Books: p. 21

Chappell, D. 2005, 'New Caledonia', *The Contemporary Pacific*, 17, 2: pp. 435–48;

Chappell, D. 2003, 'New Caledonia', *The Contemporary Pacific*, 15, 2: p. 452.

Chappell, D. 2001, 'New Caledonia', *The Contemporary Pacific*, 13, 2: p. 542

Chappell, D. 2000, 'New Caledonia', *The Contemporary Pacific*, 12, 2: p. 515-520.

Chappell, D. 1999a, 'The Noumea Accord; Decolonization without Independence in New Caledonia', *Pacific Affairs*, 72, 3: pp. 373-391.

Chappell, D. 1999b, 'New Caledonia', *The Contemporary Pacific*, 11, 2: p. 416.

Chappell, D. 1989, 'New Caledonia', *The Contemporary Pacific*, 2, 2: p. 154.

Connell, J. 2003, 'New Caledonia: An Infinite Pause in Decolonisation?' *The Round Table*, 368: pp. 127–8.

Connell, J. 1987, *New Caledonia or Kanaky? The Political History of a French Colony*, National Centre for Development Studies, Canberra: The Australian National University.

Crocombe, R. 2001, *The South Pacific*, Suva: University of the South Pacific.

de Fontenay, P. 2001, 'New Caledonia: Problems and Promises — A Survey', *Pacific Economic Bulletin* 16, 2: pp. 15–26.

Dornay, M. 1984, *Politics in New Caledonia*, Sydney University Press.

Faberon, J. V. 2002, 'Nouvelle-Calédonie: Les Difficultés d'un Gouvernement Constitué à la Représentation Proportionelle', *Actualité Juridique, Droit Administratif* 58, 2: pp. 113 – 117.

Field, M., Baba, T. and U. Nabobo-Baba, 2005, *Speight of Violence: Inside Fiji's 2000 Coup*, Canberra: Pandanus Books;

Fraenkel, J. 2003. 'Electoral Engineering and the Politicisation of Ethnic Frictions in Fiji', in S. Bastian, S. and R. Luckham (eds), *Can Democracy be Designed? The Politics of Institutional Choice in Conflict-Torn Societies*, IDS, Sussex: Zed Books Ltd: pp. 220–52.

Fraenkel, J. 2001, 'The Alternative Vote System in Fiji: Electoral Engineering or Ballot-Rigging?' *Journal of Commonwealth and Comparative Politics*, 39, 2: pp. 1–31.

Fraenkel, J. 2000, 'The Clash of Dynasties and the Rise of Demagogues: Fiji's *Tauri Vakaukauwa* of May 2000', *Journal of Pacific History* 35: pp. 295-308.

Hudson, M. 1997, 'Trying Again: Power-Sharing in Post-Civil War Lebanon', *International Negotiation*, 2: pp. 103–22.

Kettley, C., J. Sullivan and J. Fyfe, 2001. 'Resolving Self-Determination Disputes Through Complex Power-Sharing Arrangements', Workshop February 9–10, 2001, Pembroke College, University of Cambridge, University of Cambridge and Carnegie Corporation of New York, p. 14n. Retrieved 10 October 2006 from http://www.intstudies.cam.ac.uk/centre/cps/

Kliot, N. 1987, 'The Collapse of the Lebanese State', *Middle Eastern Studies* 23: pp. 54–74.

Koelble, T. and A. Reynolds, 1996, 'Power-sharing Democracy in the New South Africa', *Politics and Society*, 24, 3: pp. 221–36.

Lal, B. 1992. *Broken Waves: A History of the Fiji Islands in the Twentieth Century*, University of Hawai'i Press:

Lijphart, A. 2004, 'Constitutional Design for Divided Societies', *Journal of Democracy*, 15, 2: pp. 96–109.

Lijphart, A. 2002, 'The Wave of Power-Sharing Democracy', in A. Reynolds (ed.), *The Architecture of Democracy: Constitutional Design, Conflict Management, and Democracy,* Oxford and New York: Oxford University Press.

Lijphart, A. 1991a, 'The Power Sharing Approach', in J. Montville (ed.), *Conflict and Peacemaking in Multiethnic Societies* Lexington, Massachusetts: Lexington Press;

Lijphart, A. 1991b, 'Constitutional Choices for New Democracies', *Journal of Democracy* 15: pp. 2.

Lijphart, A. 1998, 'South African Democracy: Majoritarian or Consociational?', *Democratization* 5: pp. 4

Maclellan, N. 2005a, 'Conflict and Reconciliation in New Caledonia: Building the Mwâ Kâ', State, Society and Governance in Melanesia Discussion Paper, 2005/1. Canberra, The Australian National University.

Maclellan, N. 2005b, 'From Eloi to Europe: Interactions with the Ballot Box in New Caledonia', *Commonwealth & Comparative Politics*, 43, 3: pp. 394–417.

Maclellan, N. 1999, 'The Noumea Accord and Decolonisation in New Caledonia', *Journal of Pacific History*, 34, 3: pp. 245–52

Maphai, V. T 1999, 'The New South Africa: A Season for Power-sharing', in L. Diamond and Marc F. Plattner (eds), *Democratization in Africa*, Baltimore: John Hopkins Press.

McGarry, J. 1998, 'Political Settlements in Northern Ireland and South Africa', *Political Studies* XLVI: pp. 853–70.

Nasrallah, F. 1999, 'Lebanon: The Two Republics', in D. MacIver, 1998, (ed.), *The Politics of Multinational States*, Basingstoke: Macmillan.

Norton, R. 2004, 'Seldom a Transition with such Aplomb: From Confrontation to Conciliation on Fiji's Path to Independence', *Journal of Pacific History*, 39, 2: pp. 163–84.

Norton, R. 2002. 'Accommodating Indigenous Privilege; Britain's Dilemma in Decolonising Fiji', *Journal of Pacific History*, 37, 2: pp. 133–56

O'Leary, B. 1999, 'The Nature of the British-Irish Agreement', *New Left Review* 233: pp. 66–96.

O'Leary, B., B. Grofman and J. Elklit, 2005, 'Divisor Methods for Sequential Portfolio Allocation in Multi-Party Executive Bodies: Evidence from Northern Ireland and Denmark', *American Journal of Political Science*, 49, 1: pp. 198–211.

Palley, C. 1978, *Constitutional Law and Minorities*, London: Minority Rights Group.

Parliament of Fiji 1997, '*Report of the Joint Parliamentary Select Committee on the Report of the Fiji Constitutional Review Commission*',Parliamentary PaperNo 17. of 1997, S. G1

Reynolds, A. 1999, *Electoral Systems and Democratization in Southern Africa*, Oxford University Press.

Reynolds, A. 1995, 'Constitutional Engineering in Southern Africa', *Journal of Democracy* 6, 1: pp. 90.

Seaver, B. M. 2000, 'Regional sources of Power-Sharing Failure: The Case of Lebanon', *Political Science Quarterly* 115: pp. 247-71.

Spears, I. S. 2002, 'Africa: The Limits of Power-Sharing', *Journal of Democracy* 13, 3: pp. 123-36.

Spears, I. S. 2000, 'Understanding Inclusive Peace Agreements in Africa: The Problems of Sharing Power', *Third World Quarterly*, 21, 1: pp. 105–18.

ENDNOTES

[1] I am indebted to Marion Bastogi, of the University of New Caledonia, for assistance in assembling materials on cabinet formation in New Caledonia.

[2] Good Friday Agreement, http://www.nio.gov.uk/agreement.pdf

[3] *Constitution of the Republic of South Africa*, c. 200 of 1993, s. 88(1)–(3), as amended by *Act 14* of 1994, s. 2. For the rules governing Deputy Presidents, see *Constitution of the Republic of South Africa, Act 200 of 1993*, s. 84(1).

[4] The National Party had 20.4 per cent of the vote, and the IFF 10.5 per cent.

[5] Each voter had two votes; one in his or her own communal constituency and another in one of the open constituencies.

[6] The Carnegie Project on 'Complex Power-Sharing and Self-Determination' excludes New Caledonia on the questionable grounds that 'the settlement established by the 1998 Noumea Accords does not in essence qualify as a complex power-sharing arrangement. The Noumea Accords instead provide for the gradual devolution of powers from Paris to New Caledonia over 15 years, and grants the territory's Congress loi du pays, or local autonomy. The case of New Caledonia is therefore exempt from this study on several grounds: there is a lack of international involvement, the arrangement is essentially one of autonomy, and in the longer term it appears that the dispute will be settled wholly in favour of the Kanaks' (see Kettley and Fyfe 2001). In fact, there is considerable international involvement, not only from metropolitan France, but by virtue of the inclusion of New Caledonia on the UN Decolonisation list, and it is far from universally accepted, at least among the French loyalists, that the Noumea Accord will result in eventual independence. The project also includes Bougainville, where the peace agreement was influenced by the one in New Caledonia and similarly puts off the independence issue for a later referendum.

7 The only exception, Poseci Bune, abandoned his Fijian communal seat, joined the Fiji Labour Party and stood successfully in the 70 per cent Indo-Fijian Labasa open constituency.

8 South Africa was a poor model for Fiji. The issues were entirely different. Power sharing in Fiji was not merely a potential transitional arrangement, as it was in South Africa.

9 On the strengths and weaknesses of the new voting system (not covered in this paper), see Fraenkel (2003; 2001).

10 Supreme Court of Fiji, Miscellaneous Case No. 1 of 1999 between the President of the Republic of the Fiji Islands and 1. Inoke Kubuabola (leader of the Opposition), 2. Mahendra Pal Chaudhry, Prime Minister, Government of the Fiji Islands and Leader of the Fiji Labour Party and 3. Adi Kuini Speed, Leader of the Fijian Association Party (cited as *The President of the Republic of the Fiji islands v. Kubuabola & ors*, Misc. 1/1999, September 3, 1999).

11 Leader of the Opposition, Inoke Kubuabola, initially claimed the right to nominate all eight opposition senators, but the FLP and the FAP claimed entitlement to nominate candidates for inclusion among the opposition senators (according to the provisions of s. 64[2] cited above). The court resolved the dispute by rejecting the claim that the Prime Minister's party was entitled to nominate opposition senators, yet it allowed the FAP, despite being in the governing coalition, to share in the nominees of the Leader of the Opposition.

12 See 'Statement of Agreed Facts and Issues', appended to 1999 Supreme Court Judgment.

13 The author of the SVT letter, Jone Dakuvula, the party's then Election Campaign Consultant, later became a prominent civil society activist urging power sharing in Fiji. He was to regret these conditions placed on cabinet entry, and to regard this episode as a major failure to secure a viable multi-ethnic government in Fiji. The conditions were recommended by MPs Jim Ah Koy and Sam Speight, who had themselves declined to be selected for cabinet positions. There was no objection from the other SVT MPs (Jone Dakuvula, personal communications, July 2004, November 2005).

14 The figure chosen, two or three, depends on which interpretation of Section 99(5) is chosen, as will later become apparent.

15 Supreme Court of Fiji, Miscellaneous Case No. 1 of 1999, Original Jurisdiction, p. 22.

16 This was raised to 28 seats after the Court of Disputed returns overturned the result for Nadi Open, resulting in a recount. As a result, the solitary NFP MP lost his seat to a Labour MP.

17 Qarase to Chaudhry, September 10, 2001.

18 'Korolevu Declaration', *Parliamentary Paper* 15/99, S. 2. (b) — emphasis added.

19 'Korolevu Declaration', (2) (b); (4) (a).

20 Qarase to Chaudhry, September 12, 2001.

21 For an indication of the importance of such balanced provincial allocations in indigenous Fijian politics, see Cama (2005).

22 Court of Appeal, Chaudhry v. Qarase, President & Attorney-General, Civil Action No. 282 of 2001, Misc 1/2001, February 15, 2002: p. 14.

23 High Court of Fiji at Lautoka, April 24, 2002.

24 Qarase, President & Attorney-General v. Chaudhry, Civil Appeal No. CBV 0004 of 2002S, Judgment, July 18, 2003, S117.

25 Qarase et al. v. Chaudhry, 2003,S111.

26 Qarase et al. v. Chaudhry, 2003, S142 — emphasis added.

27 No mention of these cases was made in any of the Court of Appeal or Supreme Court judgments.

28 As we saw above, the FLP's membership of the House had risen from 27 to 28 seats after a recount gave them the Nadi Open seat.

29 2003 Supreme Court judgment S21; 2002 Court of Appeal judgment, p. 16.

30 Qarase to Chaudhry, August 11, 2003, cited in *Daily Post*, August 18, 2003, full letter reproduced in *Sunday Post*, July 27, 2003; see also 'Prime Minister, Laisenia Qarase's Statement on the Inclusion of the Fiji Labour Party in a Multi-Party Cabinet', in *Fiji's Business Magazine*, September 2003.

31 The number of SDL ministers in cabinet had risen from 20 straight after the election to 22 by the time of the 2003 Supreme Court case.

32 That this was having some impact was suggested by the liquidation of the Party of National Unity (PANU), the last-surviving Fijian party that had been allied to the FLP as part of the People's Coalition (although this party was later re-registered in the run-up to the 2006 polls). Tomasi Vakatora, the indi-

genous Fijian member of the CRC, publicly denounced the multi-party cabinet provisions in the Constitution on numerous occasions, pointing out that these had not been part of the *Reeves Report*.

[33] See Josaia Dani, SDL General Secretary, letter, *Daily Post* 3 August 2003.

[34] Opinion of the Supreme Court in the Matter of Section 123 of the Constitution Amendment Act 1997 and in the Matter of a Reference by the President for an Opinion in Questions as to the effect of Section 99 of the Constitution, Miscellaneous Case No. 1 of 2003, Judgment, July 9, 2004 (hereafter 2004 Supreme Court judgment), Section 24.

[35] The three sections of the 1997 Constitution (1997 Constitution, 99[6], [7] and [8]) strongly imply that the Prime Minister's party is also to receive proportional entitlements to cabinet portfolios.

[36] Reference was made to the March 15, 2002, Supreme Court judgment on the issue of Senate appointments, which had expressly interpreted the earlier 1999 judgment as entailing a calculation, in the case of two parties, 'in accordance with the proportion the size of their respective memberships in the house bore to one another' (i.e., *rather than* to the total membership of the House), Supreme Court of Fiji, 'In the Matter of section 123 of the Constitutional Amendment Act 1997', Opinion of the Supreme Court, March 15, 2002: p. 10.

[37] 2004 Supreme Court judgment, S97, p. 37.

[38] Ibid., S114.

[39] Ibid., S117, p. 42.

[40] 'Opinion of Gault JSC', appended to 2004 Supreme Court judgment, S17, p. 5.

[41] For further details regarding the Noumea Accord, see Maclellan (1999; 2005)

[42] *Loi Organique Modifiée No. 99–209 du 19 Mars 1999 Relative à la Nouvelle Calédonie* (henceforth 1999 Loi Organique); *Deliberation No. 009 Modifiée du 13 Juillet 1999 Portant Reglement Interieur du Congres de la Nouvelle-Calédonie* (henceforth 1999 Interior Rules).

[43] 1999 Loi Organique, Art. 79, 109, Art. 110; 1999 Interior Rules, Art. 11.

[44] 'New Caledonia's Executive will become a collegial Government, elected by and answerable to Congress' (Noumea Accord, S. 2.3, see also 1999 Loi Organique, Art. 128).

[45] The FCCI lost three of its four Congress seats at the next election in 2004, and some senior members were convicted on corruption charges.

[46] 1999 Loi Organique, Art. 121.

[47] Tribunal Administratif de Nouvelle-Calédonie, No. 02-0792, Séance du Novembre 26, 2002; Lecture du Novembre 27, 2002.

[48] Before the 2004 elections, theRPCR changed its name to Rassemblement–UMP, in line with new centre-right alliances in mainland France, which brought together the Rassemblement pour la République (RPR), Union pour la Démocratie Française (UDF) and Liberal Democrats, under the banner of the Union pour un Mouvement Populaire (UMP).

[49] Tribunal Administratif de la Nouvelle-Calédonie, Avis No. 05 04 du Juin 22, 2004.

[50] The President offers the premiership to the 'member of the House of Representatives who, in the President's opinion, can form a government that has the confidence of the house' (1997 Constitution s. 98).

[51] Good Friday Agreement [15], [16], 5. (d), (i); see also (O'Leary, Grofman and Elklit 2005)

[52] Ema Tagicakibau, FAP, personal communication, August 2005.

[53] see also the discussion in Reynolds (1999: 118–20)

[54] For accounts of the schisms among the settler parties in the pre-1970s era, see Dornay (1984) and Connell (1987).

18. More Than 20 Years of Political Stability in Samoa under the Human Rights Protection Party

Asofou So'o

Except for a short time in 1982 and during the time of the Coalition Government in 1986–87, the Human Rights Protection Party (HRPP) has run Samoa since 1982. Among the attributes of HRPP rule in that time has been its ability to maintain political stability in the country. This chapter argues that a combination of factors contributed to political stability during the period of HRPP rule from 1982 to the present (2006) and that the HRPP has been successful in managing these factors to its political advantage. They include the distinct manner in which the country's constitution has made possible a blending of indigenous and introduced democratic institutions and practices: HRPP leadership style, HRPP consolidation strategies, HRPP policies, the relatively small size of the national population, and the ability of the HRPP to bring the Public Service into its political orbit, among others.

The Constitution

The Constitution of the independent state of Samoa blends selected elements of Samoa's indigenous sociopolitical system with those of liberal democracy. The end result is a compromise of the two systems that so far has been satisfactory enough to prevent any drastic social and political upheavals in the country. For example, the inclusion of elements of Samoan custom and tradition in the Constitution has allowed the continuation of institutions and practices with which Samoans are comfortable as they form part of the Samoans' world on a day-to-day basis. As long as Samoans feel that they are part of the system, they want to abide by it and uphold it. Moreover, the value system associated with custom and tradition has helped prevent situations of potential conflict from erupting. The inclusion of democratic institutions and practices in the constitution, on the other hand, has served two purposes. First, it provides the processes for the operation of democracy and, secondly, as long as those processes are adhered to, they become a mechanism for absorbing and diffusing potential conflict.

When the Constitution was drafted in 1960, a conscious decision was made to accommodate holders of the four highest-ranking *matai* (chiefly) titles, *tama-a-'āiga* (So'o 1996: 130). In that way the traditional respect for these titles was continued. Those four titles include Mālietoa, Tupua Tamasese, Matā'afa and Tuimaleali'ifano. Holders of the Mālietoa and the Tupua Tamasese titles became Joint Head of State for life (Constitution Art. 17). Matā'afa Fiamë Faumuinā Mulinu'ū II became the first Prime Minister of Samoa and Tuimaleali'ifano Suatipatipa was appointed the Council of Deputies, which effectively was Deputy Head of State.

There have been three situations during the HRPP rule that could have led to political instability. In each situation, however, a combination of democratic processes and the traditional respect for the Head of State, who also holds one of the four *tama-a-'āiga* titles, prevented an eruption into open conflict. The first was in May 1982, when the HRPP lost the prime ministership and with it the government when its leader, Va'ai Kolone, lost his seat in an election petition. The loss of Kolone's seat brought to 23 each the number of seats held by the HRPP and the opposition parliamentary faction under Tupuola Efi. Instead of awaiting the result of the by-election to be held in late 1982, inviting the next in rank in the HRPP to take over from Kolone, or asking the HRPP to elect a replacement, the Head of State invited Efi to form a government. The result of the keenly awaited by-election gave the HRPP the one-seat majority it desperately needed to regain the government. By that time, the HRPP had elected Tofilau Eti Alesana to be its next leader (*Samoa Times* [*ST*], October 11, 1982). Instead of accepting Efi's offer of four ministerial posts in a coalition government under him as Prime Minister, the HRPP put pressure on the Head of State to convene the next session of Parliament in which Efi's budget was defeated (*ST*, December 10, 1982). The result was to bring the HRPP back to power with Alesana as Prime Minister.

The second situation came immediately after the 1985 general elections, when the HRPP had an outright majority, winning 32 of the 47 seats in Parliament. Before the 1985 general elections, the party had decided not to make a decision on its next leader until after the general elections. On February 26, 1985, the HRPP met to decide its next leader (*Pacific Islands Monthly* [*PIM*], April 1985: 7). Although four candidates were put forward, it came down to a choice between Alesana and Kolone. Although Alesana won, it was clear that Kolone had strong support in the parliamentary party. Fallout from the decision included three resignations immediately after the meeting. Le Tagaloa and his wife, 'Ai'ono Fanaafi, who had been elected to Parliament for the first time, announced they were leaving the party. According to Tagaloa, he was unhappy with the manner in which cabinet in the previous government treated caucus (*ST*, March 15, 1985). Tagaloa had been one of the candidates for the HRPP leadership. About the same time, Kolone also announced his resignation. He claimed that the HRPP had walked away from its founding principles and that he might never have another chance to be Prime Minister (*ST*, March 8, 1985).

Rumours abounded that the HRPP was breaking up and that Kolone's supporters would follow his example (*ST*, March 22, 1985). By the time of the ministerial elections, however, Alesana was elected unopposed after Kolone had turned down his nomination for the prime ministership by an MP of the Epi faction (*Western Samoa Hansard* 1985, Vol. I: 2–3). It was not until late 1985 that rumours of a defection from the HRPP became a reality. By the time of the last session of Parliament in that year, 11 HRPP MPs had defected to form a coalition government with Efi's 15 supporters. Alesana's budget for 1986 was defeated in parliament by the combined force of Kolone and Efi supporters and Kolone and Efi became Prime Minister and Deputy Prime Minister, respectively.

The third situation arose in the 1990s during protest marches organised by the traditional representatives of *Tumua* and *Pule* and *'Äiga* (*TPA*) against the Government. *TPA* encapsulates the totality of indigenous sociopolitical structures and their associated practices and processes, and value system. The origin of these protests can be traced to the introduction of the 10 per cent Value Added Goods and Services Tax (VAGST) on January 1, 1994. A misunderstanding between the government and the Price Control Board resulted in the enforcement of the new price order on the day the VAGST became effective (*Observer*, March 1, 1994), resulting in a 40 per cent increase in the cost of living (*Observer*, February 11, 1994). Protest marches continued intermittently until mid-1995. The two objectives of the protest marches were the abolition of the VAGST and the changing of the Government (*Observer*, March 1, 1994). The high and end point of the protest marches was when a petition allegedly signed by 133,354 supporters was submitted to the Head of State. On receiving the petition, the Head of State told the delegation that the Executive Council would meet to discuss it (*Observer*, March 12, 1995). On March 11, a special 14-member committee was appointed by the Government, with terms of reference that included investigation of the validity of the signatures in the petition (*Observer*, May 12, June 6, 1995). Its report, presented to the Government in mid-August 1995, invalidated the *TPA* petition. The report claimed the petition was illegal because any petition was supposed to be presented to Parliament.

In what ways have the incorporation of custom, tradition and democracy into the country's constitution prevented these three situations from erupting into public disorder and lawlessness, and what role did the HRPP play in them? I will try to answer these questions with reference to the three situations described above. The fact that Samoa had three prime ministers in 1982 suggests instances of potential political instability given the difficulty to govern under those circumstances. For a prime minister to lose his seat in an election petition that simultaneously resulted in a change of government shocked the HRPP and the country. There were rumours that Alesana, who succeeded Kolone to the HRPP leadership and the prime ministership, had instigated the election petition that brought down his party leader (Ale 1990: 13). Some political observers reasoned that such political engineering was necessary to provide an opening for Alesana to wrest the party leadership from Kolone. It was unfortunate, therefore, that Kolone became the pawn on Alesana's political chessboard, but such was the nature of politics. Thus there was potential instability in the HRPP organisation although this would surface only in the leadership meeting after the results of the next general elections were known.

The appointment by the Head of State of Efi to form a government immediately after Kolone had lost his seat and the prime ministership in 1982 received sharp public criticism. Some critics expressed their distaste for what the Head of State had done, suspecting that he, a *tama-a-'āiga*, had always preferred Efi as Prime Minister as he was the son of a former *tama-a-'āiga*. Why else would he appoint Efi to form a government when he did not have a mandate to govern the country? He had neither the support of the majority of Members of Parliament nor had he been elected by Parliament under the relevant constitutional provisions (*ST*, September 24, 1982). Nevertheless, despite these criticisms, no one was prepared to go further than publicising their views in the local newspapers or speaking their minds in Parliament. The choice of Efi to succeed Kolone was that of the Head of State, who was also a *tama-a-'āiga*. Traditional respect for the Head of State's ranking in the Samoan chiefly hierarchy and the accepted legitimacy of his position as Head of State, given the fact he was also a *tama-a-'āiga*, helped prevent any further protest beyond public criticism in the media.

In the two situations described above, there was always the opportunity for resort to democratic processes. Kolone lost and regained his parliamentary seat having followed the due processes of democracy and the law. It was an election petition that brought down Kolone and it was a by-election that brought him back to Parliament. Whether there was any truth in the rumours that Alesana had engineered Kolone's fall, the fact remains that Alesana was later elected by his peers to lead their political party. Alesana's later election to the Prime Ministership was done by Parliament after the defeat in Parliament of Efi's budget. Thus, although there was the potential for political instability in the early years of HRPP rule, respect for the Head of State, the legitimacy of his constitutional role and ranking in the chiefly system, and adherence to the due processes of law and democracy prevented serious political instability. As HRPP rule became more entrenched, it had to deal with a potential conflict situation of a different kind. This happened in 1985.

The results of the general elections on February 22, 1985, gave the HRPP 32 of the 47 seats in Parliament. It was a keenly contested election. For the first time since independence all the seats in Parliament were contested. The HRPP had decided before the general elections that it would wait until after the results were known before it chose its next leader. Although Kolone and the other leadership candidates and their respective supporters were disappointed, the democratic principle of majority decision won out in the end. Alesana, who had the HRPP's majority vote, formed the government. However, when Kolone and his 11 supporters eventually left the HRPP to form a coalition government with Efi's supporters, despite Alesana's unwillingness to step down from the prime ministership, the democratic process of succession to the prime ministership as decided by Parliament again won out, thereby avoiding open conflict, which could have led to political instability.

The *TPA* protest marches of the 1990s were perhaps the most sensitive political situation in post-independence Samoa and could easily have led to political instability. Initiated by the *Tumua* political centres on Upolu Island, the organisers of the demonstration met with and obtained the support of the six *Pule* political centres on Savai'i Island as well as the traditional political district of Aiga-i-le-Tai. As one spokesman of the movement pointed out, the six *Pule* 'didn't have any sense of hesitation'; they had 'been waiting for *Tumua* to make the move' (*Observer*, February 11, 1994)). In an article that explained the developments which led to the formation of the *Tumua* and *Pule* demonstration, the *Observer* referred to *Tumua* and *Pule* as the 'traditional arbitrators over national crises' (ibid.). Another article in the same edition called on *Tumua* and *Pule* to save the country from the current crisis. In a press release on February 24, 1994, the *TPA* stated that the two objectives of its planned demonstration were the abolition of the VAGST and the changing of the government (*Observer*, March 1, 1994). In a speech on national television on February 27, 1994, the prime minister responded to the second objective by stipulating the various constitutional ways in which a government could be changed.[1] He was driving home the point that by their planned protest march, *Tumua* and *Pule* could not force an immediate change of government (*Observer*, March 1, 1994). An editorial had alluded to the possibility that the Head of State would most likely

> declare a state of emergency exists if the protest march against the high cost of living goes ahead on 2 March as planned. He is empowered under the Constitution to do this. But only if he is satisfied 'acting in his discretion after consultation with Cabinet' that the 'economic life of Western Samoa' is threatened by an 'internal disturbance'. (*Observer*, February 23, 1994)

The protest march went ahead as planned on March 2, 1994; close to 20,000 people participated. About half of them were *matai* (*Observer*, March 3, 1994). The demonstrators marched for about five miles from Vaimoso, a village on the western outskirts of the national capital Apia, towards the main government building in the centre of Apia to deliver their petition to the prime minister and his cabinet. *Tumua* and *Pule* designated the Leader of the Opposition, Tui Ātua Tupua Tamasese 'Efi, to be their spokesman and officially deliver their petition to the Government. Alesana responded that the Head of State had agreed to an

Executive Council meeting on March 4 in an effort to solve the matter. Furthermore, the government was planning a further reduction in prices of items on the Price Order (*Observer*, March 3, 1994). Insisting that the VAGST be abolished, *Tumua* and *Pule* refused to disband until that objective was realised, and began a two-week camp in front of the government building. Responding to the prime minister's reply to their petition, 'Efi said: 'If you cannot see what is happening, then you must be blind. And if you cannot hear the people's moaning, then you must be deaf' (ibid.).

In an announcement on national radio 2AP, the Prime Minister said that after a decision of the Executive Council on March 4, the VAGST would remain unchanged. Instead, duties on all basic commodities would be reduced. The details would be announced officially in Parliament when it met on March 15 (*Observer*, March 6, 1994). With the government prepared to compromise, a solution to the demonstrators' demands seemed imminent. The *TPA* leadership then sent a second delegation to the Head of State asking him to hold a referendum to ascertain the public's views on how the cost of living was affecting them (*Observer*, March 9, 1994). When Parliament convened on March 15, 1994, the Minister of Finance, in his 1993–94 budget, announced the 32 basic commodities on which tax would be reduced. The tax reduction ranged from total abolition to a 50 per cent reduction (*Observer*, March 16, 1994). On announcement of the tax reductions, the demonstrators, who had stayed on the government premises since March 2, decided to disband. However, the *TPA* leadership decided to keep up the pressure to have the VAGST abolished on all goods.

Another *TPA* delegation was sent to the Head of State in August 1994 asking him to abolish the VAGST and to acknowledge the Chief Auditor's report, in which, among other things, the Chief Auditor 'gave detailed instances of wide-scale corruption and implicated a number of ministers and government officials' (*Observer*, January 13, 1995).[2] The Head of State asked the delegation to give him a written petition and an indication of the number of people who supported it (*Observer*, September 13, 1994). A signed petition was presented on March 11, 1995, by a *TPA* delegation, immediately after another public march in which about 30,000 people participated. A total of 133,354 people were claimed to have signed the petition. Of these, 122,954 were Samoans residing in Western Samoa while the other 10,400 were Samoans residing in Wellington, New Zealand. People in the latter group 'were concerned that the remittances they were sending over for their families' upkeep here were being subject to the 10% tax when the funds had already been taxed in New Zealand' (*Observer*, March 10, 1995). On receiving the petition, the Head of State told the delegation that the Executive Council would meet to discuss it (*Observer*, March, 12, 1995). On March 11, a special 14-member committee was appointed by the government, with terms of reference that included investigation of the validity of the signatures in the petition (*Observer*, May 12, June 6, 1995). Its report, presented to the Government in mid-August 1995, invalidated the *TPA* petition. The report claimed that the petition was illegal because any petition was supposed to be presented to Parliament. Of the 12 *matai* who signed the petition, one had not officially registered his title with the Land and Titles Court. Of the alleged signatures in the petition, 122,179 had not personally signed their names. The president of *TPA*, Fa'amatuäinu, 'said that even babies and children who cannot read or write were included in the petition as their parents can sign for them as they are the ones taking care of them and [feeding] them' (*Samoa Bulletin*, September 22, 1995). Furthermore, the issues of the VAGST and the Chief Auditor's report had all been debated and passed in Parliament (*Savali*, September 15, 1995; *Observer*, September 27, 1995).

In its June 24, 1994, edition, the *Observer* noted that the Police Department was probing whether there were seditious intentions behind the *TPA* national protest on March 2, 1994. The government pressed ahead with sedition charges against *TPA* President, Mailei, and one of its executive members, To'alepai Toesulusulu Si'ueva, despite persistent pressure from the local and international media and Amnesty International to have the charges dropped (*Observer*, March 15, June 28, 1995). Mailei was charged under the *Criminal Act* with two counts of speaking seditious words and two of publishing seditious libel. Si'ueva was charged with two counts of speaking seditious words and one of publishing seditious libel. The charges originated from events leading up to the March 2 protest march. In court, Magistrate Lussick dismissed all seven charges 'when the prosecution failed to produce any evidence' (*Observer*, June 30, 1995). The magistrate's decision contrasted with the Police Commissioner's earlier remarks that 'the charges were valid and would not be withdrawn by the police' (*Observer*, March 31, 1995). After this court decision, the two men planned to sue the Government for one million tala 'for the unconstitutional way in which we were both charged [with] sedition' (*Observer*, August 4, 1995).

Reflecting upon the sedition case, the leader of the opposition SNDP, in an article in the *Observer* (June 30, 1995) said: 'It was an attempt to portray the *Tumua* and *Pule* movement as a real threat to law and order. The objective was to discourage the local council of churches and those who are supporting or sympathetic from a more public demonstration of support for the *Tumua* and *Pule* movement. Additionally it was intended to distract attention from the acute economic problems and corruption raised in the Auditor's report. The tight government control on TV and radio, combined with the fact that the constituency is relatively uninformed, ensure impact and effectiveness of the message, i.e., that the *Tumua* and *Pule* movement is a threat to law and order.'

From a democratic perspective, there were important political gains arising from the *TPA* demonstrations and the sedition charges that resulted from them. One of them was well depicted in an *Observer* (June 28, 1995) editorial on the day the sedition charges were heard in court: 'For this hearing will set a standard by which future court cases of this kind will be judged … It will serve as a powerful indicator to the nation of the amount of freedom we can really expect to have in the future.' In other words, the sedition charges were the ultimate test of the individual rights provisions in the Constitution. The *TPA* legal victory was significant particularly in a situation where one political party had a large majority in Parliament, such that its power and political influence could appear to be unlimited. Yet against such power, and within a modern political system that coexists with an indigenous one, the indigenous system is now the last resort for checking that power.

The publicity generated by these developments was another milestone in educating the voting public and creating an awareness among them of the political importance of government policies. The demonstrations in February 1965 and mid-1981 were by wage and salary earners. This section of the public, in 1994, comprised only 13 per cent of the national population. The *TPA* was a 'national' protest movement, as everyone was affected by the VAGST. Ironically, the Public Service Association (PSA) did not join the protest as an organisation, although its members were not prevented from joining as individuals. The introduction of the VAGST had reduced income taxes substantially. Some 19,000 people were exempted from income tax because their salaries were below T100 a week (*Observer*, June 9, 1995). For the purpose of this argument, the manner in which the Head of State dealt with the *TPA* petition — having it referred to the Executive Council, which is a constitutional body comprising the Head of State and cabinet — demonstrated again the value of abiding by the democratic process. It helped cooled off the anger of the protesters and at the same brought about decisions on several issues the protesters had raised.

Political leadership

The late Tofilau Eti Alesana, the HRPP leader and Prime Minister from April 1982 until his retirement in 1998 because of ill health, is credited with his party's political success in the polls because of his astute leadership skills. The following party political events under his leadership testify to this claim. After the defection of 11 HRPP MPs in 1985 to form a coalition government with Efi's opposition supporters — thereby defeating the HRPP Government's 1986 budget — the HRPP came up with a party-pledge system to keep HRPP MPs bound to the party. MPs who had signed their consent to the pledge system would be fined T50,000 if they left the party. Since then, no one has left the party. In the 1988 general elections, the HRPP desperately needed one more HRPP supporter in order to win government back from the coalition. After the results were known, Alesana managed to convince one of the MPs who contested the elections under the coalition ticket to switch party allegiance on the eve of the prime ministerial elections in Parliament. Alesana and his party successfully wrested the reins of power from the Coalition Government and the MP who defected from the opposition camp was chosen as a minister in the new cabinet.

In government, Alesana passed two important pieces of legislation. The *Parliamentary Under-Secretary's Act 1988* gave Parliament the power to appoint parliamentary undersecretaries. Nine such appointments were made, thus guaranteeing political rewards for another nine HRPP caucus members for their support of the prime minister's party. The prime minister and the eight ministers in his cabinet were each given a parliamentary undersecretary. After securing a two-thirds majority in Parliament to amend the Constitution in 1991 after the general elections, Alesana passed a constitutional amendment to increase from eight to 12 the number of ministers in cabinet, each of whom was entitled to a parliamentary undersecretary. With 13 ministers in cabinet including the prime minister and 13 parliamentary undersecretaries, the HRPP already had the guaranteed support of 26 MPs. In a Parliament of 49 seats, the HRPP would already have the support of the majority. Political experience has been that the issue of appointments to cabinet would make or break parliamentary support. Alesana consistently argued that the defection of the 11 HRPP MPs to form the coalition government had arisen out of unhappiness with his selection of HRPP MPs to be in his cabinet. Four of those who defected became ministers in the coalition cabinet, under Kolone as Prime Minister.

There have been times in the past when the Government found it hard to work with the Public Service. One example was the PSA strike, which lasted for three months in 1981. The Government was powerless to control the public servants. Arguably, this strike helped put the HRPP in government in the general elections the next year. Mindful of these recent events, the HRPP passed the *Special Posts Act 1990*. It transferred from the Public Service Commission (PSC) to cabinet the right to appoint heads of government ministries and corporations on a two-year contract basis. It was a subtle way of obtaining HRPP support from among the senior public servants and holders of corporate positions and through them the political support of lower-ranked employees.

When Alesana sensed that his party would probably lose the 1991 general elections because it had not been able to do enough in terms of improving the condition of roads, he introduced universal suffrage in the 1991 elections after a positive vote in a referendum that was conducted on the issue in the previous year. At the time, only the *matai* (chiefs) had the right to vote in parliamentary elections. The HRPP was ushered back into power, winning 32 of Parliament's 47 seats (So'o and Fraenkel 2005).

Alesana's leadership style had been severely criticised by the opposition party and the public generally. In the early 1990s when the report of the Controller and Chief Auditor was tabled in Parliament, it pointed to possible corruption in high places. It created embarrassment for the Government. As a consequence of the political debate arising from this report, the HRPP Government passed a constitutional amendment which limited the term of the Controller and Chief Auditor to a contract of three years, in line with heads of other government corporations whose appointments were made under the *Special Post Act 1990*. At the time, the appointment of the Controller and Chief Auditor was a constitutional one for a term of 60 years, which was basically for life (Constitution Art. 97.3). The new amendment gave the Government the power to not renew the contract of a Controller and Chief Auditor after three years. The controversial Controller and Chief Auditor, whose report to Parliament created much animosity between the Government and the opposition and some sections of the community, was given the right to apply for his old job under the new conditions. He chose not to apply.

In the late 1990s, while Alesana was Prime Minister, the leader of the parliamentary opposition, Tupua Tamasese 'Efi, lodged a petition with the Supreme Court complaining that his party had been prevented from having air time on television and the government-controlled radio station, thereby preventing the public from knowing about its views. When Alesana passed away in 1999, his successor, Tuila'epa Sa'ilele Malielegaoi, took over the leadership and therefore became the main defender of Tamasese 'Efi's complaint in the court. The court ruled in favour of 'Efi. Yet despite the controversial nature of the two cases already described and the negative media publicity they generated, they did not seem to affect the political status of the HRPP as it was brought back to power in the 1996 general elections, having won 27 of the 49 seats in Parliament. Despite these controversial issues under Alesana's leadership, he and the HRPP clearly retained the voting public's support.

The political success of Alesana's party can also be explained by projects it was able to complete throughout its time in office. The electrification program in the 1980s took electricity to about 90 per cent of homes. The country's first national television station was opened in 1993. The National University of Samoa was opened to its foundation class in 1984 and has since developed into a fully fledged university with five faculties, an Institute of Samoan Studies and the appointment of its first three professors in 2004. There has been intensive work on water infrastructure and access roads for plantation agriculture. The old-age pension, though meagre by overseas standards, has not only given T100 a month to those who are 65 years and over, it has made that section of the population feel important. The establishment of the Ministry of Women's Affairs on the eve of the introduction of universal suffrage recognised the contribution of women to the development of the country. It was also a gesture that earned for the HRPP the respect and political support of women throughout the country, who in turn contributed to the electoral success of the HRPP in the polls in the general elections the next year.

Equally important, if not the most important variable, in the HRPP's ability to create and maintain political stability in Samoa is the local culture, which is generally referred to as *fa'a Samoa* (the Samoan way). An editorial in the most-read local newspaper, *The Samoa Observer* (September 2, 2005), tried to describe the contribution of Samoan culture to political stability:

Fa'a Samoa prevents political upheavals

Though Samoa, Tonga and Fiji have a lot of cultural similarities, Samoa's social structure has always been less stratified than its neighbours. Power and prestige in Tonga is exclusive to its royal family and the King's nobles. The rest of the population are deemed to be 'commoners', locked in an age-old role of servitude. Fiji's chiefly system is similar, in which one is born a *Ratu* or *Adi*. On the other hand, rank and status in Samoa have always been owed to personal merit and achievement. Title accession is largely the prerogative of the *aiga*, family. While chiefly titleholders have authority, real power remains with the family. Power broking, many would argue, has been the domain of silver-tongued orators who are always on the lookout to elevate their *ali'i*'s status, thus their own. Often when Tongans speak of their King, Samoans respond: 'In Samoa everyone is a king (and queen).' This is based on *fa'a Samoa*'s emphasis on *matai* titles and genealogy. It is a culture that embraces interpersonal relations. Every Samoan has access to any number of *matai* titles and all titles are interconnected through lineage. Dig deep enough and one will find every Samoan is related, many times, in many ways.

Furthermore, Samoa, unlike Tonga and Fiji, has never had any form of central government. It always existed as fiercely independent states, which in modern times have been termed districts. The states were a cluster of relatively autonomous villages: *Fa'alenu'u*, village polity, being the embryonic fabric of *fa'a Samoa*. Though there are paramount titles particular to each district, many times the titleholder is powerful only as far as his ability to gain the full support of his district villages and form allegiances with other districts. Will Samoans one day reject the *tama-a-'āiga* as some observers ask? As long as Samoa practises its culture and holds dear its intricate familial connections, it will never happen.

Nafanua

Set to wage war on Lea'ea i Sasa'e district, which had been enslaving her people, the war goddess Nafanua was advised by her mother, Tilafaiga, 'A pa'ia le pa i Fualaga, sua le tuli aua le Ali'ioaiga' (When you reach the pa at Fualaga, stop the killing in respect to the Ali'ioaiga — this is in reference to Siali'itu, who resided at Faia'ai village, some accounts say, and was a brother of Tilafaiga). It was said to be one of the bloodiest wars in Samoa but Nafanua's clubs were never wielded beyond Fualaga. Even in times of war, Samoa's family connections are upheld.

It is personal respect among Samoans because of family connections, among other considerations, that makes Samoans think twice before involving themselves in activities that could contribute to or result in political upheaval. As one doctor who has served in the national hospital for 56 years has recalled of a planned strike by the doctors in the past because of salary issues: 'The strike was averted when the Head of State, His Highness Malietoa Tanumafili II, intervened. He came to the hospital, sat down with the doctors and asked for the strike to be called off. What can the doctors do, this was the Head of State? Out of respect, no strike took place' (*The Samoa Observer*, September 6, 2005). The HRPP succeeded in preventing open conflict by appealing to and taking advantage of those cultural elements.

Conclusion

Political stability has been a feature of the HRPP regime, which began in 1982, when it first became the government, until the present. Several factors have contributed to this state of affairs. The existence of a still vibrant indigenous sociopolitical system alongside Samoa's introduced liberal democratic system adopted before independence in 1962 means that Samoans will always revert to their indigenous political system in difficult political situations as the only means by which to check political dominance and what is perceived by the public as abuse of power. Powerless to check the political dominance of the HRPP regime since it first took office in early 1982, the indigenous sociopolitical institutions of *Tumua* and *Pule* and *'Äiga* organised a series of protest marches against the government in the early 1990s. However, tactful political leadership in a highly sensitive situation in which the *TPA* protest marches played a determining role averted the possibility of serious violent confrontation between HRPP and anti-HRPP protesters.

Because *fa'a Samoa* creates obligations between relatives in a country where almost everyone is related, it has the effect of dampening the potential for instability. For example, even though some voters might have been unhappy with the way the HRPP had been running the country, they would not be prepared to have those political sentiments translated into voting out the sitting HRPP MP in their respective constituencies if the MP was a relative of theirs. Respect for others, especially for those of traditional rank, also discourages extremism and instability.

Samoa has been unusually successful, compared with Fiji and Tonga, at blending the modern parliamentary system of representation with cultural tradition. Since 1962, when Samoa became independent, there have not been any major amendments to its constitution. Nor have there been any constitutional crises in Samoa like those that resulted in the Fiji coups of 1987 and 2000, or the continuing constitutional problems of Tonga. Any constitutional amendments in Samoa have been relatively minor and have been achieved through constitutional, democratic and legal means.

Finally, HRPP's twofold political strategy of formulating and implementing policies that have helped keep it united, and changing the rules through legislation introduced in Parliament during its period in office, have contributed to the party's electoral success. This success, in turn, has led ultimately to the maintenance of political stability in Samoa.

References

Ale, L. I. 1990. 'The development of political parties in Western Samoa.' Unpublished essay in the author's possession.

Observer: February 11, 1994; March 1, 1994; March 3, 1994; March 6, 1994; March 9, 1994; March 16, 1994; July 15, 1994; September 13, 1994; January 13, 1995; March 10, 1995; March 12, 1995; March 15, 1995; March 31, 1995; May 12, 1995; June 6, 1995; June 9, 1995; June 28, 1995; June 30, 1995; August 4, 1995; September 2, 2005; September 6, 2005.

Pacific Islands Monthly, April 1985.

Samoa Bulletin, September 22, 1995.

Samoa Times: October 11, 1982; September 24, 1982; December 10, 1982; March 8, 1985; March 15, 1985; March 22, 1985.

Savali, September 15, 1995; September 27, 1995.

So'o, A. 1996. '*O le fuata ma lona lou*: Indigenous institutions and democracy in Western Samoa.' PhD thesis, The Australian National University.

So'o, A. and J. Fraenkel. 2005. 'The Role of Ballot Chiefs (Matai Pälota) and Political Parties in Samoa's Shift to Universal Suffrage.' *Commonwealth and Comparative Politics*, 43, 3 (November). pp. 333–61.

The Constitution of the Independent State of Samoa, 1962.

Western Samoa Hansard, Vol. I, 1985.

ENDNOTES

[1] These included a vote during the general elections, a vote of no-confidence against the Government in Parliament, the resignation of the Prime Minister or his absence from the country without having first consulted the Head of State (*Observer*, March 1, 1994).

[2] A government-appointed commission of inquiry, which was set up 'to look into allegations in the report to allow those implicated the chance to defend themselves', 'downplayed the report and exonerated most of those implicated in it' (*Observer*, July 15, 1994; January 13, 1995). Substantial sections of the Chief Auditor's report had been published in the *Observer* (July 15, 22, 1994).

19. *Matai* Titles and Modern Corruption in Samoa: Costs, expectations and consequences for families and society

A. Morgan Tuimaleali'ifano

On a bright October Saturday morning in 2005, I could make out his outline in front of the R. C. Manubhai hardware store in Raiwaqa, Suva. Desmond Dutta was a Fiji-born Samoan who had left Fiji almost 20 years ago. His father was an Indo-Fijian and his mother a Samoan of Chinese ancestry. We first met in Fiji in the mid-1980s while I was doing fieldwork in Fiji's minority communities. Proud of his Samoan heritage, Dutta frequently discussed with me his desire to retrace his mother's family.[1] These topics were the focus of our regular Friday afternoon discussions at the Suva market where he earned a living selling the popular cumquat fruit juice. Soon after Fiji's two coups in 1987, Dutta made good his word and left Fiji for Samoa.

When he returned to Fiji, he appeared fragile, ageing prematurely, his body bent and face drawn with signs of affliction by diabetes. But now he was looking forward to returning to Samoa again. 'Our side of the *'aiga* has just won a major court case over the [Manuleleua] family title. It took us six years to fight this case, and lots of money went into it. Boy, I took a lot of hammering. But, the title has finally returned to the right side of the family.'

'What do you mean by hammering?' I asked.

'During the court case, the other family parties called me by all sorts of names. *Fai mai o a'u o le Fiki. Ga lau lo'u Igikia. Fai mai o a'u o le Saiga oga o le kiga o le Saiga. Fai mai o a'u o le Fiki ua sau fia pule i le aiga*. [They called me an Igikia (Indian), a Saiga (Chinese) because my mother is Chinese and they said that I was a Fijian who was coming to take over the family.] It was very painful. But you know what our fa'a Samoa is like, eh? That is part of our culture. One minute we're stabbing each other and the next we're crying and making the loku [church] to forgive each other. And we forget everything that was thrown at each [other] until the next court case. Oh, I tell you, our fa'a Samoa, it's funny, eh?' We both laughed knowingly and then parted. Dutta had not only retraced his roots but was revelling in the consequences of that knowledge.

Modern Samoa is a nation that is a product of all the forces of globalisation. The legacy of the wave emanating from the west 3,000 to 3,500 years ago is apparent in the way the island nation is governed largely through family and village titles. As ancestral names, titles are passed down in families and are ceremonially conferred on chosen individuals who then represent the family in public life. Without a title, an individual has no right to speak in family and village councils. A title secures membership and rights within a family to land and common village property. Conferral ceremonies can range from elaborate gift exchanges for high titles to tea parties for minor ones. The normal practice is for the family to consult the village council on a date for their candidate's installation in a *saofa'iga* (an installation ceremony) and thereupon, formal admission into the village council. Titles are also significant because, as the sole decision-makers in the village, councillors collectively control about 80 per cent of the land. [2] From the West, the second wave, beginning in 1492 and finally reaching Samoa in the 19th century, introduced the apparatus of a modern state. When titles are disputed, virtually every development effort under the state apparatus is threatened, including land rights, homes and livelihoods. There is little incentive to develop. Under the laws of the first wave of colonisers, when families could not agree, war decided the disputes, but wars had a habit of lingering. These forms of conflict resolution and settlement were inefficient and disruptive to second-wave settlers and eventually led to colonial takeover.

When Germany took over in 1900, the German Administration effectively circumvented local conflicts by establishing a Land and Titles Commission (later a court) to arbitrate disputes. It did not stop the conflicts, but it stopped the wars. The Germans managed to successfully channel local disputes through the court system. Since independence in 1962, title disputes have become so numerous that resolution of conflict can take years. And this is what I would like to consider. In Samoa, as elsewhere in the Pacific, the problem of resource ownership such as land is tied inextricably to family titles. In Fiji, the land issue is tied to leases controlled by the Native Land Trust Board, and the relationship between it and the landowner and tenants. In Samoa, when families are locked into a title succession dispute as they often are, production invariably is restricted. [3]

How are these titles appointed and their titleholders installed, and what are the consequences for the social and state apparatus? What is the place of cash in the title-installation process? Is cash, much of it generated in the global economy beyond Samoa's shores, corrupting that process? More broadly, in what ways is Samoan tradition adapting to and being corrupted by the forces of globalisation?

My case study is the Samoan village of Salelologa, on the island of Savai'i, fabled home of Hawaiki. In early 2001, my mother's 64-year-old cousin and holder of the Luamanuvae title, Kirika Fiso, approached me with his wish to install new family titleholders, including one of my mother's children. Appointed in 1970 as a co-titleholder, Fiso had outlived many of his peers, and had held the senior elder position in the Sa Luamanuvae clan of the Li'aga branch for some time.

Though many appointments had been made, many titleholders chose to live outside the village. The title Luamanuvae was one of two titular titles of Salelologa village. [4] Like many of his generation, Fiso had moved between subsistence and the cash economy having been a clerical officer with various merchandising companies and government departments. He had also served in managerial positions with the Congregational Christian Church in Samoa and overseas and with the Seventh-Day Adventists. In inviting us to assume the title, he made it clear that he could not guarantee another opportunity during this lifetime. When he finished his story, I thanked him and accepted the offer, and told him that it was largely out of respect for the memory of my mother's longstanding desire to honour her ancestors. During her lifetime, her children were all young and more immediate needs assumed higher priority.

Fiso had an ulterior motive, which he hinted at but which I did not comprehend fully until after the installation. In the mid-1980s, Salelologa, Tafua and Fa'ala, located along the south-eastern coast of Savai'i, entered into an agreement with a Swedish environmental NGO in which the villages were to be paid several thousand dollars in aid not to develop or log their land for at least 50 years, and to use the forest only for customary uses, e.g. the occasional harvesting of timber for local needs and of plants for medicines. The arrangement worked well with regular payments and minimal pressure on the land. But after most of the money had been paid, in 1999, the Salelologa Council was induced by the Tofilau Eti Alesana-led HRPP government to sell 1,162 hectares of its conserved rainforest land for a politically motivated township scheme. The council saw nothing wrong with selling the land it had already agreed and been paid to preserve. [5] In early 2002, the government paid $4 million to Salelologa. Instead of using some of this money to repay the Swedish NGO for violating the agreement, the village council was instead incensed at the NGO for not paying the final 10 per cent instalment of the money due! [6] After the $4 million was paid, another faction of the Salelologa Council, led by Pauli Elisara, petitioned the Supreme Court, claiming that they should have been paid $45 million based on 'unfair evaluation' by the government valuer. [7] This case continues with many senior *matai* creating new titleholders in a bid to cash in on the likelihood of more handouts.

My family's acceptance of the title implied expenses for the ceremonial gifting. The next question for the installation was costs: Fiso said the total outlay would be $35,000. In order to defray the costs, there would be six to seven titleholders, thus reducing the individual outlay to about $5,000 a person.

Who gave what and where did it come from?

On the evening before the title installation, the extended family and their candidates met to take stock of their contributions. Immediately, a problem arose. Two of the seven expected candidates failed to attend and that meant the five candidates had to come up with an additional $2,000 to meet the $35,000 outlay. This was clearly impossible with less than 12 hours left before installation. Who were the five candidates and what were their contributions?

1. Tovia, son of late Luamanuvae Lokeni and Poufitu; 40 years old; a gas stove manufacturing company employee in Mangere, South Auckland, New Zealand: $5,000, seven cartons of mackerels and 11 large fine mats.
2. Mokeni (Morgan), son of Ta'alefili, the granddaughter of Luamanuvae Pae'e; 47; university lecturer, Fiji: $3,500, two cartons of chickens and six fine mats.
3. Tofu, son of Tia'itupe Luamanuvae Tofu and Leatigaga Fa'aafu of Lauli'i village, 'Upolu; 34; Apia-based employee (after the installation, he and his young family migrated to live in Salelologa in February 2002): $3,000, five *'ie toga*, seven cartons of mackerels and five large fine mats.
4. Punivalu, son of Luamanuvae Pule; 43; a village farmer from Fatusi, Savai'i: $3,000, 10 large fine mats.
5. Keli, grandson of Luamanuvae Tofu; 64; casual worker for the Electricity Power Corporation and the only candidate who was a permanent resident of Salelologa. He donated $1,000 consisting of $300 cash and $700 worth of groceries, five cartons of mackerels and five large fine mats. He had also undertaken extensive repairs to the family house in which the installation ceremony was conducted.

At the meeting, an elderly female family member, Mateai, attended and contributed $280. Mateai and her son, Fonoia, lived one kilometre away and were gifted $20 for the bus fare and were driven home. The total amount collected was $15,780, 19 cartons of mackerels [8] and two cartons of chicken. [9] Although the 38 fine mats were considered a small number, they were all high-grade mats, as attested by those present. The immediate problem was the cash. Though short by $20,000, it covered the cash payments and fine mats for religious ministers, the speech-maker, clan heads, and lesser titleholders in attendance at the 'ava ceremony, who received less than at previous installations.

Where did this cash come from?

It was considered bad taste to seek details of sources of income from the other four co-titleholders, and this paper is limited to my own sources. In Suva, my wife and I took the view, one common to many, that since I was the recipient, we should take the initiative and provide at least half the cash. As we did not have spare cash, we raised funds by selling *umu* packs, organising cake drives, and making monthly cash deductions from salary and allowances. Our Suva *umu* packs were sold for $20 each (two *luau*, one *taro*, one bowl of raw fish, one No. 12 chicken, and a bowl of fruit salad). Our dollar target was $4,000, with the expectation that my siblings would make up the $1,000 balance. Despite our ambitious plans, our efforts raised the modest sum of $700, barely enough for one return airfare. In the end, the bulk of the money came from two sisters and a brother living in the USA, [10] two of whom were awaiting Green Cards from the Department of Immigration and Naturalization Services. What were their sources of livelihood? My oldest sister worked as a primary schoolteacher and the other worked at a pharmaceutical plant and was studying part-time. My 39-year-old brother had only recently begun working as a part-time primary schoolteacher after being an unpaid volunteer for almost 10 years. They contributed $3,000. The only one who could travel from the USA, my oldest sister, attended the installation at her own expense and bought more food. In addition to her airfare, she paid $1,000 for hotel accommodation and a rental car, and another $100 contribution to the first Sunday *to'ona'i*, a lunch following the installation. In addition, my three siblings contributed to other installations. One thousand tala ($1,000) was given to another sister's husband whose uncle was installed in Satupa'itea, [11] $2,000 for a New Zealand-based brother, a recipient of two titles, [12] and $2,000 for a Samoan-based brother for taking a title from Iva village. [13] At the last moment, more titles were on offer for cash, and for another $1,000, my oldest sister was persuaded to take one from the same village. [14] The total amount for installations came to $8,500 (about $A4,000), in addition to about $100 customary contributions for each new titleholder for the Sunday lunches. Almost all of this money was derived from the modest wages of primary schoolteachers and factory workers.

The installation ceremony and the political agenda

At installation ceremonies, there are two main events. After the introduction and exchange of pleasantries and collection of *'ava* stems from the assembled *matais*, the first major item is the *fa'atau* — the selection of the speech-maker through an open contest among the orators. The second is the *lauga* — the act of making the speech, during which reference is made to the genealogy of the title and the title is situated within existing village and district hierarchies. When strong and powerful speakers take the stage, the contest is the most thrilling part of the ceremony, with seasoned orators eager to display their political wares. The contest provides a window of opportunity for newly installed titleholders to witness first hand the power structure and those behind it. The higher the title, the higher the rewards are likely to be.

Salelologa, like most other villages, operates under a dual system of authority exercised by titular family heads and orator clan heads, in oppositional relationship to each other. While the two titular titles stand at the apex of the hierarchy, their power is largely ceremonial. Effective power is wielded by two bands of orators, the *falefia* and *falesalafai*, numbering seven clans. [15] In the speech contest, everyone waited expectantly for the customary rivalry between the two groups. Pipi Lavilavi, the head of the Pipi clan and leader of the *falefia* on that day, initiated the contest. He began by acknowledging clan heads and stated firmly and clearly his wish to speak on behalf of their band, and each clan head of the *falefia* conceded their right in favour of him. Pipi then turned to the three clan heads of the *falesalafai* and repeated his wish. The head of the Seumanu clan, Seumanu Tupea, responded on their behalf and obtained Pipi's concurrence to allow their band to negotiate a consensus. After about 30 minutes of protracted negotiations with the *falefasalafi*, Seumanu obtained their vote to represent them against the *falefia*. Seumanu then turned to Pipi and thus began a two-way contest.

For the next 45 minutes, the two clan heads dug deep into their political repertoire of emotional blackmail and vanity, to outmanoeuvre the other. Both stood their ground and there was considerable entertainment value as they parleyed and toyed with each other's apparent foibles. Those new to the contest feared physical violence.[16] In the contest, the two men showed no sign of yielding and eventually Pipi resorted to higher authority. In front of a captive audience, he told Seumanu that their absent leader, Matamua (Pua'atoga), on account of ill health, had appointed him as his representative. Pipi explained that before the installation, the *falefia* had assembled at Matamua's residence and waited for the *falesalafai*. When the latter failed to attend this preliminary meeting, Matamua extended his blessing and anointed Pipi as spokesperson. As proof, Pipi lifted Matamua's flywhisk as the badge of office. Seumanu at this point became visibly angry and reaffirmed his allegiance to Matamua as leader and, in regretful tones, turned to his *falesalafai* colleagues and asked them to accept Pipi as their spokesman. Pipi returned the compliments and proceeded with his speech, first acknowledging the assembled dignatories, then outlining the procedure for *'ava* distribution and enunciating the family genealogy. Before he could continue with the genealogy, he was stopped by the head of the Muagututi'a clan, Muagututi'a Ami, who politely interjected and asked Pipi to skip this aspect, and beckoned him to go straight to the blessing of the titleholders and distribution of *'ava*. Pipi concurred and, as he concluded his speech, the master of the *'ava* ceremony, from the back of the house, began the chant and enunciated each titleholder's *'ava* cup title. It began with the new titleholders followed by the clan heads according to a predetermined order of precedence, with the older peers first.

As the clan heads received their *'ava* cup, each took the opportunity to give words of advice to the new titleholders. In wishing them well, they also emphasised the importance of commitment to family, the village council (by implication, its constituent women, and non-titled men and women elements), the church and the government, in that order. They spoke of the customary relationship between the orator groups and the titular clans as represented by senior holders of Muagututi'a and Luamanuvae titles. Others emphasised the courtesies expected of us as younger and newer titleholders towards older and more senior titleholders. Others were more blunt in their expectations as graphically illustrated by the head of Fiu Loimata II, representing the Fiu clan. A former member of parliament and a forceful speaker, his advice was a stinging reminder of the paradoxical relationship between titular and orator chiefs. Pointing to senior Luamanuvae and Muagututi'a titleholders sitting at the opposite end of the house, Fiu spelt out to us the relationship in dollar terms. He said, *'E uma le ola o kama la ia makou. O le lakou masagi a fekaui ma I makou i le makeki, e ke'i a ua fai mai, ku'u aku le selau kala I lau koga. Pe o'o i se isi kaeao, fagu fagu mai, kago mai I lau afe kala lea e ku'u I lau kaga'*. (The lives of those men [pointing to senior Luamanuvae and Muagututi'a] end with us. They make it their habit, whenever we meet, to give us money. They will say to us, 'Here, take this $200 and put it in your pocket.' Or early one morning, they would wake us up and say, 'Here, take this $1,000 and put it in your pocket.')[17]

In other words, it was his view that the orators' role was to support and speak on behalf of titular titleholders and it was the role of the titular titleholder to pay the orators, which in Fiu's terms was best done not by fine mats and pigs but in cash.

The gifting

Although I had been to other title installation ceremonies, the Salelologa ceremony was different. The one-way gifting without immediate return was of serious concern. Moreover, nothing had prepared me for what was to happen that day. I would not have believed the shameless public demands if I had not seen them myself. After the speech and drinking of *'ava*, the assembly of clan heads moved to the open space outside for refreshments and in anticipation of receiving customary gifts. The sponsors also moved outside ready to distribute what had been planned the night before. As they received their gifts of cash and fine mats, some orators shamelessly demanded more and publicly stated, *'Fa'aatoa mai le fia … tala o la'u lafo'* (Give me some more dollars to make up the rest of my entitlement.) One threatened to recommend deregistering the newly installed titleholders. When our party, the sponsoring party, tried to appease them, some begrudgingly sat down only after being promised more cash.

Pipi Lavilavi, the speaker at the ceremony, as expected, got the lion's share. But having receiving $1,000 in cash plus the largest and choicest fine mats, he then made an extraordinary plea on behalf of the 70-year-old sickly and absent Matamua Pua'atoga. In the lead-up to the gifting, it was expected that whatever gifts the speaker received would be shared with the absent orator. Instead, Pipi demanded a similar donation be given on the basis that the absent orator was sickly and might not live to see another installation. In other words, so it seemed, we were asked, on behalf of the village, to provide a parting gift. The stunned sponsors took a full minute to recover and renegotiate amid muffled terse epithets.

Seeds of corruption

These gifting events have a life of their own and have significant consequences. As remembered events, they are transmitted and re-lived at the next crisis such as a title installation or funeral. If the payback is not matched or bettered, the sponsoring family is stigmatised. The consequences are transmitted to a future generation of *matai* titleholders and their families. As opportunity arises, they will demand no less than what was demanded of them as their 'just due'.

When expectations of titleholders and families are not matched by return gifts, conflict is apt to spiral into other arenas, including places of employment, churches and schools as part of loyalty to family and village. Customary gifts derived from a subsistence economy are less likely, these days, to satisfy the needs of a family and clan structure accustomed to cash and remittances. While there is always money, there are not enough fine mats, pigs and foodstuffs. [18] When food was gifted instead of cash, tropical climatic conditions required efficient redistribution. But when cash infiltrates gifting whether in the form of remittances or otherwise, redistribution it not required and gifting is taken out of the public into the private and individualised arena. As reciprocal exchanges increasingly take the form of cash payments, they enter a world of capitalism never intended for this type of family-oriented activity. In the past, installations encouraged family gatherings and redistribution of gifts. The cash installation in Salelologa did not elicit redistribution of any sort among the candidates and their families. They dispersed knowing they had debts to return to and there was little else to discuss or take home to celebrate. It seemed, at least for those remaining behind, that the focus was on payback at the next life crisis.

References

Laura, P. 2002. Family DVDs of *Saofa'is* in Foua, Salelologa, Samoa. Copy with author.

Methodist Board of Trustees. 1985. *Ole Tusi Fa'alupega o Samoa Atoa*. Compiled by the Tusi Fa'alupega Committee. Apia: Methodist Printing Press.

O'Meara, T. 1987. 'Customary Individualism.' In R. G. Crocombe (ed.), *Land Tenure in the Pacific*, Suva: Institute of Pacific Studies, USP.

Tuimaleali'ifano, A. M. 2006. *O Tama a 'Aiga: The Politics of Succession to Samoa's Paramount Titles*. Suva: USP.

Tuimaleali'ifano, M. 1990. *Samoans in Fiji: Migration, Identity and Communication*. Institute of Pacific Studies, Fiji, Tonga and Western Samoa Extension Centres, USP, Star Printery.

Whistler, W. A. 2002. *The Samoan Rainforest, A Guide to the Vegetation of the Samoan Archipelago*. Honolulu, Hawai'i: Isle Botanica.

ENDNOTES

[1] His mother, Mali Dutta, is a descendant of the Manuleleua family clan, titular orator of Vaimoso village. See A. M. Tuimaleali'ifano, 1990, *Samoans in Fiji*, pp. 45–6.

[2] The balance comprises 16 per cent government land and 4 per cent freehold. This control, it has been argued, is more theoretical than actual, and much Samoan land is de facto under individual tenure.

[3] A. M. Tuimaleali'ifano, in press, O Tama a ' iga: The Politics of Succession to Samoa's Paramount Titles, USP.

[4] The other was Muagututi'a. See Board of Trustees of the Methodist Church in Samoa, 1985, *O le Tusi Fa'alupega o Samoa Atoa*, Malua Printing Press, pp. 142–5. The Sa Luamanuvae clan is split in two branches, Pouseilala and Li'aga, each with sub-branches.

[5] The late Prime Minister, Tofilau Eti Alesana, had earlier represented Fa'asaleleaga No. 1 in which Salelologa was included under his tenure of the Luamanuvae title. His Luamanuvae connection was to the Pouseilala branch.

[6] See W. Arthur Whistler, 2002, *The Samoan Rainforest, A Guide to the Vegetation of the Samoan Archipelago*, Honolulu: Isle Botanica, pp. 150–1. Similar compromises are also appearing in Fa'ala.

[7] 'Salelologa wants $45m', *Samoa Observer*, December 12, 2002.

[8] A carton of mackerel retailed at $71 and a carton of chicken for $81.

[9] In addition to the Luamanuvae title, the Le Atigaga title was also on offer for $400–500.

[10] Pinelo Laura (45), Suatipatipa Tuimaleali'ifano (39) and Vaivase Maualaivao (37).

[11] Falani and Vaosa Asiata for the Gasu title.

[12] Wellington Fiso for Le Atigaga in Salelologa and Fiso in Vaito'omuli, Palauli.

[13] Lilomaiava Rev. Nerony Fiapia Tuimaleali'ifano for the Tofilau title in Iva village.

[14] Laura was conferred as the Tagaloasa orator title at the same ceremony in Iva.

[15] *Falefia* aka *To'afia* and comprises the titles Taotua (represented by Ioane), Pipi (represented by Lavilavi), Matamua (unidentified), and Fonoia (absent). *Falesalafai* comprises Seumanu (represented by Tupea), Pauli (represented by Afele) and Fiu (represented by Loimata II). See Board of Trustees of the Methodist Church in Samoa, 1985, *O le Tusi Fa'alupega o Samoa Atoa*, Malua Printing Press, p. 142.

[16] I was later informed of earlier contests between Seumanu Tupea and Matamua Pua'atoga, the head of the Matamua clan and highest-ranking orator. At an earlier contest, the rivalry over the speech led to physical blows. The two elders rolled about the centre of the house hurling abuse at each. It ended as both quickly ran out of breath. No one lifted a finger to stop them. Scores were settled for the time being until the next round of *saofa'i*.

[17] From DVDs of the ceremony.

[18] I am grateful for Dr William Clarke's interest in and pertinent comments on this paper on October 28, 2005.

Media, Civil Society and Democracy

20. Keynote Address — Keeping the Information Flow Open: A key condition for good government in Micronesia

Father Francis X. Hezel

The crusade for good governance

Good governance has become a catchphrase today. It is commonly seen as the standard by which nations are measured in the balance, the axle on which any nation's wheel turns. It is as if the whole planet has used its collective force to mount a global campaign for good governance. Development banks, lending institutions and international organisations, not to mention large donor countries, have earmarked good governance as the essential condition for granting foreign aid. However many oilfields or gold mines a country might possess, without good governance it is consigned to a status of mediocrity or worse.

Just what is good governance? Even if a suitable technical definition could be found, good governance is probably best defined by what happens in its absence. Without good governance, public services are substandard and little is done to arrest further deterioration. Businessmen find that the most effective way to get things done is by making under-the-table deals with government officials. Cronyism abounds, with a small group of individuals seemingly holding unlimited power over resources. Meanwhile, of course, government leaders make frequent calls to their overseas banks and invest in real estate abroad, which they would never have been able to afford on their salaries alone. Laws are understood to apply to 'others', not to those who make them or enforce them. But the 'others', quick to follow the precedent their leaders establish, find no reason why they should be trammelled by laws that are not enforced. As foreign investors lose confidence in the country's ability to guarantee legal protection and social order, they pull their money out, fuelling a downward economic spiral.

Good governance, then, touches every aspect of a nation's life. Without it a country can count on nothing — not international aid, not foreign investment, not a strong economic system, not good schools and hospitals, not civil order.

As the theory goes

Good governance is not simply an accident of history or culture, today's theory holds. In what amounts to a thorough reversal of the position Western countries took a century or more ago, the present day theory rejects the old notion that certain cultures are naturally capable of governing themselves, while others are inherently unable to do so. Of course, this belief was often drawn on to legitimate the Western colonialism rampant at the time. Today, however, the reigning theory of good governance, rooted in our contemporary understanding of democracy, is that public pressure is what keeps the government in check and makes it responsible and responsive to its citizens.

Unless people know what the government is doing, there will never be any public accountability. Hence, the government is obliged to lift the veil that conceals its inner workings so that citizens can peek in, if they care to, and find out what is happening in government. To the extent that the government removes the barricades at the door, throws open its windows, and provides information to its citizens, it can be said to practice transparency — another catchword of our day.

The supposition is that, even if few individuals will take the trouble to acquire such information on their own, a small group of professional snoops are prepared to do the necessary legwork and to present the information in an understandable form to the rest of society. This is why the media plays such an important role in a modern society. It has the resources and interest, despite the delays and rebuffs from officials, to convey to the rest of us what's going on in government. The media not only offers the means to convey this information to the public — at least in most societies — but it also represents a group of dedicated information-seekers who will doggedly pursue officials who don't return their calls and keep knocking on doors that are slow to open.

The theory, then, is that good governance depends heavily on a steady flow of reliable information on government workings to the public, most of this coming through the media. If the media functions as it should, people will act on this information and vote corrupt or ineffective leaders out of office and replace them with a better lot. This, of course, supposes that people have the power and the will to do so. It supposes that the country enjoys a political system in which the people have their hands on the controls in some way: through free elections, open challenges to the administration, a fair court system, and laws that really work.

In other words, the conditions for good governance come down to just a couple of basic requirements. The first is a functioning political system that offers people real choices over who their leaders are and how they will be governed. The second is a good flow of reliable information from the government to the people, without which they would never be able to make an informed judgment on the performance of their leaders. Given these two conditions, any nation should be able to achieve good governance, whatever its cultural milieu.

The machinery of government

Micronesian nations, like most other Pacific Island states, have been quick to adopt the machinery of a modern political system. They have legislatures and chief executives at the helm of their governments, supported by an administrative bureaucracy and the body of law that is generally required of a government today. Top public officials are chosen through elections run in accordance with international standards. Most of these nations have public auditors whose role is to examine financial statements and flag dubious expenses. These governments have incorporated into their political systems the checks and balances that are meant to ensure responsible leadership. Even beyond this, if the ADB or another international institution should insist on new legislation deemed necessary to encourage investment, more often than not it is promptly enacted.

The premise on which foreign consultancies sponsored by international financial institutions seem to operate is that once the apparatus for good government is in place, the rest will take care of itself. But this does not seem to be the case. Underneath these trappings of a government system lies a set of down-home attitudes very different from what Westerners might expect. The way of conducting business, informed as it is by attitudes stemming from a small island society, might even pose a greater threat to what is called good governance than wanton corruption or deliberate abuse of the system.

One of the best known symbols of justice shows a blindfolded woman holding scales to indicate that the justice system, and the government of which it is a part, is not a respecter of personal status or other individual characteristics. But how can this sort of impartiality be expected in an island society in which interpersonal dealings were always conducted with an eye to the status of each party? Any public official is bound to be dealing on an almost daily basis with high-titled persons, close relatives, and individuals to whom favours are owed or expected. In a small society in which there is virtually no such creature as a faceless citizen, an even-handed justice system can be an elusive ideal.

Reciprocity is the norm in small societies everywhere. Favours are given and received, with a sense of indebtedness incurred by the recipient. It is incumbent on any modern state to enact legislation that attempts to draw boundaries beyond which a government official may not go in paying back favours. But making this legislation effective is another matter altogether. A public official indebted to his brother-in-law or uncle might not be able to hire him for fear of violating the norms against nepotism, but there are other ways in which he can and will use his government position to take care of such persons.

Even with the apparatus of government in place, the process of good governance can be subverted in countless ways. For instance, some of the state courts in the FSM, although adequately staffed, are reluctant to preside over critical land disputes in their jurisdiction because of the emotional intensity of the issue among the contesting parties. These cases are put off until tempers subside, often delaying the court appearance for years. If there is any truth to the old adage that 'justice delayed is justice denied', the dispensation of justice in these states is seriously imperiled. Similarly, public auditors can produce audits of government bureaus, flagging questionable expenses as they should, but their work is in vain unless there is follow up in the Attorney-General's Office or by the Public Prosecutor. Elections are regarded as a necessary instrument to allow competent office-bearers to emerge. Yet, if the island populace casts its vote simply on the basis of ethnic or kin affiliation, the purpose of elections will be unrealised. The modern political apparatus is a necessary but not a sufficient condition for good governance.

What foreigners can do to help

People will grow into their governance systems in time, we are told. There is certainly a good measure of truth to this claim, as the history of the new Micronesian governments shows. Undeniable progress has been made in the past 20 years as island people have adjusted to the new forms and norms of their governments. True, the response from Micronesian leadership to the demands of international financial institutions and foreign governments for better governance has been querulous at times, and now and then even strident. Voices in the local governments will lash out at US infringement on the sovereignty of the island nations and construe proposed reforms as yet further instances of neo-colonialism at work. The truth is, however, that a great number of Micronesians understand full well the need to make their political machinery more effective, just as they subscribe to many of the reforms that are proposed by international organisations. For various reasons, political and cultural, local people might not wish to voice their sentiments, although they will silently applaud when others take up the standard.

One of the most important functions that foreigners can serve in Micronesia today is to articulate positions that many local people might embrace but are unwilling to endorse publicly. International financial institutions such as the ADB are in an especially favourable position to promote such reforms under the aegis of good governance and the investment opportunities and economic benefits that might result. Such institutions might serve as convenient scapegoats for government reforms that are already endorsed by the silent majority, providing they are not overly sensitive to criticism from their clients. Beyond this, these institutions could assume a pivotal role in nation-building if they better appreciated the need for continuing support for reform-minded elements in the local governments. This could entail a radical departure from the normal way in which the ADB and other such institutions assist developing Pacific nations. It would probably mean fewer short-term consultancies and more long-term colleagues residing in situ to assist with the inevitable political battles that reforms will provoke. I have made the point elsewhere that foreigners can do more than impart managerial expertise; they can build political will, a task at least equally important. Finally, the timing for the reforms should be informed by the real but unarticulated need that local people might feel for a particular change. This means that more of the initiative for a program ought to come from the Islanders than from the bank.

There remains much that foreigners and foreign institutions cannot do, of course, but this is a given in the Pacific today. If outsiders in partnership with Pacific nations can act as a catalyst for reforms and an excuse for mobilisation, much of the burden of public education will fall to local people. They will bear the responsibility for educating their own leaders and alerting fellow citizens that their best interests cannot be well served unless their modern political structures are utilised as intended. Their reaction to government reforms, reflecting as it does subtle changes in the attitude of Islanders, can be a useful gauge for the proper timing of these reforms.

Yet people can carry out this task only if they are aware of what is happening in government. This, then, brings us to the second and perhaps even more important condition of good government: public access to information.

Knowledge as a valued commodity

Some years ago a congressman, who was smarting at the accusation that FSM Congress fund were being misused, presented me with an interesting challenge. He asked me to check on his own special projects money for the past five years to verify that the money had been spent legitimately. I immediately sent out an older American with time on his hands who had volunteered his help to obtain the information we needed. Armed with a list of projects funded, he spent a month or more visiting offices and talking to officials. When he returned to report on what he had accomplished, he was frustrated and seemed beaten. The government officials he visited weren't rude to him, but they were clearly reluctant to release the information he needed for our little study. 'Why do you want to know this?' was the most common response he encountered. The long delays and the endless chase from one office to another were as effective as if windows had been slammed shut. In the end, we had to abandon our project, to the dismay of the congressman and myself. We had been defeated by the unwillingness of government functionaries to release the information we needed.

There is probably no one in Micronesia who has not had an experience like this. Sometimes we are told that the computer is down. Often we might be told to wait until the office supervisor returns so that he can authorise the release of the information we need. To protest that what we seek is 'public information' will be of little avail. In practice, public information is a rare commodity in Micronesia today. Even when there is nothing to hide, people seem reluctant to share information. This often confounds Westerners, for the same Islanders who are so generous with food and material things can be astonishingly reserved with knowledge.

Some of the reluctance to release what Westerners see as public information can be traced to traditional cultural attitudes. The Pacific stance towards passing on knowledge has always been guarded. This is especially true of certain types of knowledge — such as local medicine, navigational chants, genealogies and even favourite fishing spots — for they are seen as the valued possession of those in the know. This type of knowledge can be parlayed into personal prestige. This might explain why many government officials who are in command of a database of any sort are reluctant to share the information they possess with those who could use it for their own work. It might also help explain why bureaucrats who have attended a conference abroad so often return to their office and resume their work without breathing a word of what they learned to anyone else in their department. The specialised knowledge they have acquired at such conferences and workshops is quietly added to their fund of personal expertise, enhancing their value and making them irreplaceable in their job.

Even a little knowledge is a dangerous thing

Knowledge is not just a valued possession; it can be dangerous. In my experience, Islanders are very slow to say anything, even in personal conversation, that might reflect badly on a third party. A large part of this reluctance is owing to the fact that personal relationships are easily damaged in a small island community. Understandably, no one wants to say anything negative that could get back to the person and create ill will. It's one thing to do that sort of thing in a large American city, but quite another to risk this enmity in a small society where day-to-day encounters with others are almost guaranteed.

The problem is compounded in an age in which new channels of communication carry messages instantaneously to large numbers of people. If certain information were to fall into the wrong hands, it could be used to mount a public attack on a government official. Even if no malice was intended, the information could be misinterpreted by those who gained access to it and reflect badly on the government. Worse still, its release could be traced back to the one who surrendered the information, with damaging effects for this individual and his job. I'm sure that this was why my colleague, who went from office to office seeking information on congressional funds, was met so often by the question: 'Why do you need this information?'

Micronesians are no less eager than the rest of us to protect their national reputation. When I went public with my article on the 'Chuuk Problem' many people wrote in to object, some of them quite angrily, to what they considered an assault on the reputation of Chuuk. 'Why would anyone want to hang out their dirty laundry in public?' one of them asked. I could protest that the laundry was already on the line before I got there, or that the purpose of the article was not to vilify Chuuk, and certainly not to smear the reputation of any individuals, but simply to get people thinking and talking about how they could best deal with what were undeniably their problems. Yet, these people were simply reflecting a strong Islander gut reaction to public criticism. while I was the typical Westerner in my insistence that such public criticism was the best way to ensure better performance by public officials.

I have to admit that the reluctance to criticise openly is one of the many qualities that I find endearing in the Pacific. I regard the desire to spare the feelings of others as admirable. (Well, I should, because I myself have profited from this forgivingness many times over.) The issue is not whether the attitude is good or not — that is taken for granted — but at what point it must give way to another, more demanding approach in a modern government system. How do we get a government to work properly if everyone is forgiven everything and not a word of criticism is ever heard in public?

Enter the media

The establishment of the media with its roving band of news hawks has made government officials all the more wary of releasing information to the public. While most island governments appreciate the need to issue press releases on newsworthy events, they are much more reluctant to offer the unedited facts to newspapers and other media outlets for fear that they will put an unfavourable spin on the information. Pacific Island governments, in their desire to control the release of information, do not easily embrace the idea of others gleaning what they can to present their own interpretation of events. One Marshallese congressman recently complained: 'Some people access government information and distort the truth to mislead people.' He added that, while he believed in transparency in government, 'something needs to be done to safeguard information so that not just anyone can access it'.

The position he is reflecting is a common one in Micronesian government circles: the danger of twisting information so as to misrepresent the government is serious enough to justify withholding such information altogether. A striking but by no means isolated example of this occurred two years ago after the conclusion of the FSM Constitutional Convention. In its zeal to ensure a perfectly balanced, objective presentation of the proposed constitutional amendments, the FSM Government submitted the script of a video program to one committee after another to be screened for errors or any hint of bias. When the committees had scrupulously examined the material and finally okayed it for release two days before the referendum on the proposed amendments, it was too late to air it. The program might have passed the close scrutiny of the committees as sufficiently sanitised and harmless to all concerned, but it never reached the people it was supposed to educate.

The media comes under still more suspicion because of its insatiable appetite for news, even news that is not fit to print. It's often regarded as a stray dog that will devour any scrap of information with gusto, only to leave a smelly pile of manure on your backyard lawn afterwards. There is a shared understanding in Micronesia that some things, even things that are known by everyone, should not be discussed publicly. The paternity of an important public official, for instance, or his sexual preferences or past indiscretions might be generally acknowledged, even though it is tacitly understood that they are not to be mentioned. Some of the champions of a very free press, however, are seen as challenging this pact by their assertion: 'If it's news, then the people have a right to hear about it, even in a public forum.' It's hard not to credit criticism of the public media today when we look at the way in which invasion of privacy has rolled back the private lives of government leaders in other parts of the world. Even so, we must come to terms with the question: are we better off with the media, for all its excesses, than without it?

Perhaps we have no choice in the matter. The media, which is assuming an ever-larger role in even the off-the-beaten-path parts of the world, seems to be an essential component of society today and an indispensable condition of good governance. Whatever might have happened in the past, today the flow of information from the government to the people takes place through the media: television, radio, newspapers and, increasingly, through the Internet. The media, then, is the means through which people in modern societies find out what their government is up to.

The media as a watchdog

Building an effective media system to relay information to the public is a serious need, one that must be addressed but is not going to be easily resolved. Even apart from the gaping holes in the media umbrella in a country such as the FSM, there is the additional problem of presenting to a linguistically diverse population the workings of a national government that is beyond their field of vision because it operates at a level or two above the local politics people are most familiar with. The public in any state might be aware of what the state government is doing, especially if the state legislature's sessions are broadcast in the local language, but their knowledge of the Congress of FSM is likely to be scant.

Admittedly, public interest in the National Government surged in 2004 when the FSM Congress introduced several measures, one of them the infamous 'Amnesty Bill', that were construed as bald attempts to protect its own interest. This happens from time to time when word of controversial bills gets out to the public. But Congress, like most other government institutions, would prefer to conduct its business far from the public eye. When an enterprising local man set up his video camera in the congressional chambers to record a session some years ago, a policeman was ordered to position himself in front of it to block shooting. The attitude of the Congress might be exemplified by a statement that one of its members once made: 'My people elected me because they trust me. They're willing to let me make the judgments on what's good and bad for them. They don't have to know what goes on in the sessions.'

If the media is supposed to be the watchdog of the nation, it might still be a toothless puppy in some Pacific nations. The construction of an effective media system will take time and more resources than any single institution has at its disposal, but we can at least begin to change the cultural attitudes that block the flow of information. We can hold these attitudes up to the light and let the public see them for what they are: a remnant from an earlier day that can no longer be maintained because they impede the workings of a modern government system. That puppy will eventually grow to a full-sized dog, but we might want to ensure that the dog doesn't remain leashed in the garage.

Conclusion

Some Micronesians profess to yearn for former times, before the arrival of the mass media, when the traditional attitudes towards information ruled and villagers knew just how to approach their leaders about their reaction to decisions. They know, however, that this will never happen because our societies are pointed forward rather than backward. The world demands conformity to certain standards of governance, and so do our own people. This is part of the price of nationhood in today's world, just as it is the effect of decades of exposure of Micronesians to new and higher political expectations. Deep in their hearts, Islanders recognise that life in splendid cultural isolation from the rest of the planet is a chimera.

Good governance requires more than adoption of the proper political institutions, notwithstanding the exclusive emphasis placed on this by some reform movements. Good governance, as it is universally understood today, demands accountability of government to the people it serves. This depends on those conduits of information that we call the media, but it in turn depends on a reliable information flow from the government, which allows everyone an X-ray view of what government is doing. The current position taken by government on dispensing information is understandable, particularly in view of traditional Pacific attitudes to the possession of information, but it is counterproductive in a modern government. Without information flow between the government and the people it serves, there can be no government of and for the people.

References

Goodenough, Ward H. 2002. *Under Heaven's Brow: Pre-Christian Religious Tradition in Chuuk*. Philadelphia: American Philosophical Society.

Hezel, Francis X. 1998. 'Why Don't Our Government Offices Work?' *Micronesian Counselor,* 22.

Hezel, Francis X. 2002. 'Settling Dispute.' *Micronesian Counselor,* 39.

Hezel, Francis X. 2003. 'Power or Partnership? Making the New Compact Work.' *Micronesian Counselor,* 45.

Hezel, Francis X. 2004. 'The "Chuuk Problem": At the Foot of the Political Pyramid.' *Micronesian Counselor,* 50.

Hezel, Francis X. 2005. 'Peeking into the Public Process.' *Micronesian Counselor,* 54.

Larmour, Peter. 2005. *Foreign Flowers: Institutional Transfer and Good Governance in the Pacific Islands*. Honolulu: University of Hawai'i Press.

Metzgar, Eric H. 1991. 'Traditional Education in Micronesia.' PhD dissertation, UCLA, Los Angeles.

21. Governance, Globalisation and the PNG Media: A survival dilemma

Joe R. Kanekane

This chapter attempts to examine how the PNG media has promoted good governance. It also examines some of the global developments imposed in the country and how these have been embraced. But the bulk of this paper will look at some of the hurdles faced by the PNG media in attempting to better disseminate governance issues. Some recommendations are offered to solve this dilemma.

Background

The demise of the reputable weekly newspaper the *Independent* in May 2003 heralded a reality check for the other forms of media seeking to survive in the tough and depressed PNG economy. Despite significant economic reforms by the People's Democratic Movement (PDM) Government headed by Sir Mekere Morauta, their fruits were marginal. Media organisations confronted the truth; the operating environment appeared to be tough. Costs were high and radical interventions were needed.

The *Independent*, one of the pillars of investigative journalism in PNG as well as an advocate of good governance and transparency, was shelved after 23 years. During those years, it unravelled some of the country's worst corruption scandals, from the Tos Barnett inquiry into the forestry sector, to the controversial purchase of the Cairns Conservatory, and the Defence Force Retirement Fund's purchase of the Vanimo Motel. The *Independent*'s demise was a blow, at least to the checks and balances in the PNG media, and particularly to coverage of issues in detail. While other media concentrated on day-to-day issues, this publication was meticulous, conservative and thorough, giving decision-makers insights into debates. Anna Solomon (2005), former editor-in-chief of the Word Publishing Group, recalled the *Independent*'s coverage of Bougainville crises, where, despite threats of legal suits and confrontation, the paper pressed on printing stories about atrocities allegedly committed by PNG Defence Force soldiers. The real reason for the end of the *Independent* was that its parent company, Word Publishing, was hit with cash crises. It had to make drastic decisions. Despite staff reductions and folding the popular *Weekend Sports* and the *Saturday Independent*, with its controversial Australian turf guide, the paper was not able to sustain itself.

The introduction of *The National* in 1993 had taken its toll; media competition in the country was becoming tough. The media market in the country was small and daily newspapers such as the *Post-Courier* and *The National* had to embark on aggressive marketing strategies. The printing of regional newspapers, featuring news and developments in regions beyond Port Moresby, proved too costly. The *Independent* had opened regional bureaus in Mt Hagen, Lae, Rabaul, Madang and Bougainville in an attempt to improve its circulation.

FM and community radio stations have mushroomed, offering specific programs for their listeners and with restricted frequencies. The cost of doing media business in PNG has been high with little return. Yet, with a very low literacy rate in PNG, the media business has continued to excel in its fundamental role of educating and informing the masses — although at a price. On a global scale, the PNG media had come of age, embracing global developments of free markets and capitalism.

The PNG media today

There is no doubt that the privileges enjoyed by the media organisations in PNG are considerable when compared with the restrictions and gags on media freedom many other countries face, some as close as its Polynesian neighbour, the Kingdom of Tonga. Media establishments are numerous, giving the public the opportunity to choose from a wide range of information sources to satisfy their needs. PNG is dynamic in technology and the pace of changes and reporting styles are akin to those of the Western media. But, as in all developing nations, much of PNG's population is rural based and there comes the key question: are these people informed and knowledgeable about governance issues? And are they contributing to make the country truly vibrant and robust?

H. C. Brookfield's (1972) observation remains true despite the advent of technology, access and education levels of Papua New Guineans. He claimed that towns and cities in Melanesian countries were 'poorly informed'. He went further to claim that word-of-mouth was a pivotal link between those who have access to information and those who don't. Oseah Philemon, editor-in-chief of the PNG *Post-Courier*, says the country lacks a 'comprehensive and elaborative communication plan' where everyone is abreast of rapid changes. Speaking during the popular gun summit in Goroka in 2005, he was sceptical about the fundamental role of the media. Philemon admitted that access to the media was restricted despite the technological advances apparent in the country. He said, 'Newspapers were available only in towns; radio was listened to by those who could afford it, while TV was a luxury to many Papua New Guineans.' This dichotomy reflects contrasting scenarios in rural and urban settings. For advocates of good governance, this is not helpful as it falls short of reaching the country-wide audience, concentrating instead on the very few that can either read or have access to electronic media. The issues put forward are known only in one sector of the community while the rest miss out.

An example is the campaign against HIV/AIDS. In November 2004, the chairman of the Special Parliamentary Committee on HIV/AIDS, Dr Banare Bun, launched the fourth phase of the HIV/AIDS campaign targeting the stigmatisation of people living with HIV/AIDS. The objective was to ensure that those living with HIV/AIDS were accepted as members of the community. This effort was the result of a survey in 2004 in which 30 per cent of 2,000 people from the four regions of PNG who were interviewed were unsure about treating sufferers as fellow citizens. This is an interesting revelation because the HIV/AIDS publicity campaign had been prominent in all the main forms of the PNG media.

I have attempted to present these two cases as a prelude to my paper assessing whether the PNG media plays its fundamental role, which is to educate and inform the masses. In a diverse country such as PNG, the proper role of the media is often questioned. Does it have an obligation to inform the masses, should it be a partner in development or should it just concentrate on making a profit? Too often people don't necessarily understand the challenges faced by the media industry as it endeavours to sustain itself. It is true that PNG has media freedom, but along with that freedom comes responsibility. Former Prime Minister Sir William Skate's statement in Parliament on July 6, 2005, is a good example of the responsibility of journalists to get things right. The media had once again erroneously reported that former Deputy Prime Minister Mao Zeming was Skate's deputy. 'The media should check facts before reporting,' Skate said. The PNG media has operationalised a process where it goes ahead to report and then allows the aggrieved parties to defend themselves. David Robie has argued that the PNG media has not allowed itself sufficient scrutiny to be able to claim objectivity: 'The media now needs to subject itself to the same rigorous scrutiny that it applies to the nation's institutions for it to make a greater contribution to democracy.' While members of parliament have the privilege of explaining misconstrued facts on the floor of Parliament, the public have the unenviable task of pestering the media to seek redress, after publication.

Then there is the issue of sources and their credibility. When faced with a looming deadline, reporters sometimes invent a source to lend support to their story. Daniel Kapi (2002), former political adviser to Sir Michael Somare, queried how journalists got their information. According to Kapi, naming a source was often wishful thinking on the part of the reporter. Kapi, a long-time Pangu Pati stalwart, was also instrumental in the late 1980s in the deportation of respected ABC correspondent Sean Dorney. Mark Felt (2005) suggests that the use of two sources, as is the standard in the USA, is absolutely necessary so that journalists are not manipulated by a single source. Felt admitted to being the CIA source for the two journalists who broke the 'Watergate' scandal, which led to the demise of President Richard Nixon.

Unfortunately PNG cannot be compared with the rest of the world because it has a very short history of independence. The sad trend has been its inability to keep experienced journalists. Many have moved to greener pastures while the young and inexperienced are attempting to make a mark in mainstream journalism. A huge vacuum then opens up and the treatment of news is more superficial than it ought to be. Moreover there is no journalists' union that can fight for the rights of journalists, so that they can be encouraged to remain in the mainstream. In essence, journalists are at the mercy of their employers, and are in some circumstances disadvantaged. Despite constant efforts to reactivate the union, support and commitment from the journalists have been abysmal. Meetings have taken place, suggestions made, interim executives appointed, and membership drives attempted, but all to no avail.

The PNG media has to fight for its survival and then squeeze in governance issues when it sees them as relevant, although there are no policies, criteria or obligations specifically to cover governance issues. Media organisations are aroused mainly through community commitment and paid messages.

Governance and the PNG media

During the 2001 Media Freedom Day celebrations at the Divine Word University, then resident ABC correspondent, Richard Dinnen, outlined the difficulties faced by the PNG media in reporting to the masses. He admitted that the PNG rural populace did not have enough positive news reported and there was a huge bias towards news from Port Moresby. He urged journalists to probe further into the rural areas and write about positive developments. Dinnen touched on the media's role in a country such as PNG and how it mirrors the changes and developments in places like Port Moresby.

War against corruption

When the PNG Media Council launched its 'War Against Corruption', I was elected Chairman of the Editors' Task Force, a group comprising senior PNG journalists. This group came directly under the auspices of the PNG Media Council, whose role was to provide direction and advice. One of our primary roles was to screen each and every file, piece of information and document that came before us. We met once every month and went through the files. While the awareness aroused by the campaign was appreciated, the response was poor outside Port Moresby.

I remember a file coming from Misima Island, where the author wanted our help to solve a domestic matter, something along the lines of an affair turned sour. Another file from Wewak wanted us to do a character check on an unfair selection of a candidate to a public service position. Another file from Port Moresby perceived us as a kind of Ombudsman and requested that we investigate a nepotistic practice within the organisation the author was working for. A village councillor in the Southern Highlands attempted to convey to us the failure of the provincial government to pay councillors' allowances, which, he claimed, amounted to something like a thousand kina.

We received a lot of files but then we had several difficulties.

First of all, we had to gather enough reporters to work on the stories systematically. The idea was to pass the information to everyone so that they could work on the stories separately. Those who were on my team were senior reporters with specific responsibilities and had to juggle their primary responsibility with this new role. We ran into a few hurdles. I was the chief political reporter and news director of the *Independent* and had to ensure that my own newsroom was fully functional while chairing this committee. Ruth Waram, another key member of our group, was business editor of the *Post-Courier* while Michael Asagoni was chief political reporter with the National Broadcasting Commission (NBC). Titi Gabi was chief of staff of EMTV. It was a big ask, blending the two roles. I was lucky as I worked for a weekly and the timing was okay. The others were committed and enthusiastic but just did not have enough time to work together with us; however, they were all ready and willing to help.

Secondly, most of the stories were merely allegations and lacked substance and facts for us to pursue. The authors also did not want to be identified and we could not deliberate on what was there.

Thirdly, the public expected us to write their stories the way they sent them to us. They were, I presume, desperate to have their grievances heard and seek redress, and many felt that we facilitated that role; however, they wanted results the moment the stories came out.

Fourthly, we weren't able to keep reporters when they were offered jobs elsewhere. Our key group became smaller as I succumbed to the closure of the *Independent* and took up a civil service job, while Waram joined the corporate circles and Robert Palme resigned from the *Post-Courier*. Jane Nuia also left and so did Collin Taimbari. Our core team was reduced and I could not do anything more than leave mainstream journalism. However, some of the stories that were run were effective. A director of a semi-government body resigned, while Parliament debated a number of issues including the PNG Raggianna Account in the Cayman Islands and many others. There were also changes in some government departments and awareness that the task force wasn't going to play around. Unfortunately, most of the impact of the stories was within Port Moresby and only one or two changes were made in the provinces.

As to whether this was successful, I could not say, but I don't think people really understood exactly what we were advocating. However, the 2002 election saw three-quarters of the sitting MPs lose their seats. Again, without concrete evidence, I cannot say whether the war against corruption had an impact, but it was obvious to me that those who really understood what we were pushing were urbanites. Many others were cynical about our modus operandi, because it was disjointed. I had phone calls from people saying that they wanted immediate action, and they wanted to know why some issues were taking longer than others to achieve results. Some people were not prepared to accept our role, nor did they appreciate exactly what we had set out to do. Former national editor Yehiura Hriewazi pointed out to me that our role was not to be the juror and the judge; it was merely to report and it was up to the authorities to take the next step. But the effort by the PNG media was a relief for those who did not otherwise have access to appropriate avenues to express their grievances.

Daily coverage of governance-related issues

Former *Wantok* editor Yakam Kelo commented on the dilemma his staff endured trying to simplify some issues. According to Kelo, often the generic messages are hard to dissect and, while attempting to simplify them, the gist of a story is lost.

Titi Gabi of PNGFM, on the other hand, is pressured by time restrictions and news and information is edited accordingly. As news director of one of PNG's most popular radio stations, her challenge is to ensure that the news is tight. News items on the Tok Pisin and English stations are carefully selected on their merits. Gabi is the only experienced journalist on the station and has young reporters who have just finished school. She says she often has to explain stories, verify them and put them into perspective before they go to air.

Dorah Masueng, news manager of the NBC, says there is no special treatment given to governance issues. She credits the Government with allowing the network to carry out its role without fear or favour. However, special programs promoted by UNICEF or the YWCA are prepaid. The airing of specific issues on governance would have to be paid for even if they were intended to address the community at large and contributed to a better PNG.

The law and justice sector also has to pay for its members to speak on FM radio stations. While issues of law and justice are critical to the progress of the nation, even promoting positive news about this sector's achievements has to paid for.

Daniel Korimbao, *The National's* night editor, says that while there is no specific emphasis on a particular area, governance issues are given prominence. He adds that *The National* has worked on its rural-reach strategy with its circulation manager travelling up and down the Highlands Highway opening outlets to sell the paper. These revelations prove that governance issues, in spite of their significance, don't receive special treatment. The onus again is on the anti-corruption agencies to produce their own media campaigns and often huge amounts of money are required to achieve this.

Global issues and the PNG media

Global issues are ever present in the PNG media. Because of the freedom of expression provisions in the Constitution, the reporter plays a crucial role, one more robust than in many other countries.

Section 51 of the Constitution guarantees freedom of information and the profession of journalism embraces that pillar; however, foreign cultural imperialism is well and truly apparent in the country. The BBC and the ABC are accessible on the FM band. Pay TV offers CNN as well as a number of channels in French, Bahasa and Korean.

EMTV relays shows such as *McLeod's Daughters*, *Blue Heelers*, *Who Wants To Be A Millionaire?*, *Survivor*, *The Apprentice* and a couple of outdated programs. On top of that it relays the US Open, State of Origin rugby league matches and one-day cricket matches. Because of the costs of pay TV, viewers have no choice but to view these programs. Before the introduction of EMTV, rugby league was the game of choice, however, today on the streets of PNG, little kids play cricket.

Kevin Pamba (2005), in his *Note Book* column, concurs with this scenario adding that, 'The news of the world that is reproduced daily by the PNG Media comes from major Western news syndicates. These reports carry a Western spin or bias in the language chosen.'

The international media has become so persuasive and pervasive that it erodes national cultures and traditional values. Papua New Guineans resent this and have attempted to call for changes. Urban Papua New Guineans are well versed in developments in globalisation, privatisation and corruption. The advocates of globalisation are the overseas agencies. The World Bank's user-pays policy, privatisation and land reforms have all been met with increased resistance. The PNG media, although meant to report fairly and accurately, has been under a lot of scrutiny. Its reporting style has been subject to compromise, often contrary to the spirit of its intent.

In March 2005, *The National* ran a series of articles against the controversial Enhanced Cooperation Package (ECP), particularly the presence of Australian police. Several front-page articles appeared without by-lines, and, in subsequent weeks, conveniently, stories attributed to 'a source' started appearing. As the weeks unfolded and the debate on the ECP grew, it became apparent that the 'source' was linked to the police union. At that time, *The National* did not attempt fairness by reporting the positive developments of the ECP presence.

In April 2004, the *Post-Courier* featured an article about looming ethnic warfare between the Kimis of Okapa and Mt Hagen landowners, over a lost shoe. As a result, there were disruptions to businesses, roadblocks and millions of kina were lost including supplies to the giant Porgera mine in Enga Province.

Hundreds of commuters were stranded in Goroka and Lae as police in Mt Hagen mediated in the crisis. Western Highlands Provincial Police Commander, Winnie Heano, commented later that the *Post-Courier* report was wrong. He stated that the second-hand information the reporter had obtained had been taken out of context, resulting in the mayhem. Fortunately, no lives were lost, however, the businesses in the Simbu, Western, Enga and Eastern Highlands provinces incurred significant losses.

On Sunday July 17, 2005, during the 6 pm news, Government Chief Secretary, Joshua Kalinoe, accused EMTV's John Eggins of being irresponsible. A week earlier Eggins had insinuated in his 'Sunday Commentary' that the Chief Secretary had recommended a candidate for the vacant Attorney-General's position. Kalinoe said the media, like public offices, should play a responsible role because of its power.

Former Chief Ombudsman Charles Maino (1995) had raised concerns about the power of the media and its need to be responsible. He stated that freedom of the press was not a privilege but a responsibility that required all involved in the mass media to be independent, impartial, honest and fair in all methods of reporting.

These are examples of subjectivity in reporting. The ECP was geared towards assisting the country and improving governance. One component of the package involved the presence of Australian police on the streets of Port Moresby and, for a while, crime seemed to have declined. Moreover, more crimes were reported to police than previously, a reflection of the confidence the public had in the Australian police.

The third example shows the power of television. Eggins, a respected commentator, attempted to query the delay on the appointment of a permanent Attorney-General. But the way his comments were perceived took them out of their original context and they were rebutted in the wrong spirit. In spite of the significance of the issue, resentment from the top levels of government was ominous.

But it shows that television is used well and can bring home the desired messages. The PNG media does not have criteria to consult when choosing stories and operates on the basis that, in the editor's judgment, people need to know certain information and certain issues are significant. Global governance issues might be well received in other nations, but the PNG media prides itself on freedom of information and, in practice and in the context of commercial reality, that notion often means giving less prominence to global governance issues than to cases of rape, murder or a mass prison breakout.

Critical analysis of the PNG media's role towards governance

The PNG media is keen to assist in governance issues but has to face some stark realities for its own survival. I want to now dwell on some key issues that might have some effect on the dissemination of governance issues.

a. Journalists

Journalists are low paid despite being well educated. An average cadet reporter is paid between K150-K200 a week and he/she has to survive in a place like Port Moresby, with skyrocketing rental costs and high day-to-day expenses. Compare that with other professionals such as lawyers, doctors and accountants. Journalists' salaries are in no way comparable. There is therefore a high turnover of journalists joining the private sector and newsrooms are filled with mainly young reporters. Family demands have seen experienced reporters leaving the mainstream media for well-paid government jobs, leaving huge gaps of experience and aptitude in the reporting of governance issues. The absence of a journalist union aggravates the situation because employers can hire and fire at will.

Various concerns have been raised about why journalists are quick to cover press conferences organised by certain ministers. I recall a press conference I attended on Christmas Eve 2003 by a government backbencher. The backbencher, who was also the parliamentary leader of a political party, was merely welcoming a new MP into his camp, but the number of reporters present was comparable with the Prime Minister's monthly press conferences. After the press conference, I noticed the MP beckoning my colleagues to follow him to his office. I tagged along and, there in his office, he handed out bundles of K50 notes.

b. Media organisations

Media organisations are pressed to make money. Advertising rates have increased significantly and so have other costs, such as talkback, which were once free. Today for one hour's talk on HIV/AIDS, corruption or the environment, there is a fixed charge of between K3,000–5,000. It seems that making money is more important than promoting governance for a better PNG. Since their corporatisation, media organisations such as the NBC have been urged to make money, despite its mandate to inform Papua New Guineans. The ratio of news to advertisements is 60:40. Peter Aitsi, President of the PNG Media Council, admitted at the 2005 Media Freedom Day at the University of PNG that the media had obligations to its shareholders. Addressing students during the celebration, he said the media was a service provider and shareholders expected some form of return for their investment.

c. The public's perception

The consumer focuses on what concerns him most. He will attend to his own parochial needs rather than worry about issues such as governance. If the issues propagated are linked to him/her, time is set aside to deal with this. Other than that, people get carried away doing their own thing. Take the sales of newspapers during the State of Origin rugby series, when rural provinces have significant sales, compared with ordinary days.

d. Access to media

Rural areas have limited access to media services. Mike Jeliffe, Missionary Aviation Fellowship's (MAF) director of operations, says scores of people greet his planes during their trips to rural areas. To them, access to the world in information terms is through the MAF. Few communities have electricity for television or radio and the literacy rates are very low.

e. Government information

The PNG Government has attempted to reach the population through some of its initiatives. They include the *City Sivarai*, which is produced by the Department of Information and Communication, and government talkback radio. The former is printed at the Government Printing Office and distributed through the main government offices and inserted into the *Post-Courier*, *The National* and *Wantok*. It is written in English, Tok Pisin and Motu.

Government talkback radio is coordinated by the Information and Communication Office in conjunction with the NBC. According to the Acting Secretary for Information and Communication, a lot of departments have expressed interest in using the *Sivarai*. However, with limited space, it cannot accommodate everyone's interests, and, in any case, it concentrates on the Government's positive achievements at the expense of educating and informing its readers. Ward (2000) describes this practice eloquently: governments everywhere have learned the art of 'packaging the news', of steering journalists towards covering the news stories they want and in the form they want, and the PNG Government is no different.

f. Use of paid advertisements for governance issues

As well as the government media, the use of paid advertisements is a regular option. The British High Commission has a weekly one-hour program on FM100 which features people such as the Public Prosecutor, Chronox Manek, speaking on a multitude of governance issues. Inserts into newspapers are paid for and even the use of coloured advertisements is a regular feature, in this case by PNG's Transparency International.

g. Locally driven agendas

There are no local, indigenous movements opposing corruption that can be supported by the PNG media, which must therefore work out exactly how it can dissect global issues and present them to the public. The media could easily promote how to be a responsible Papua New Guinean. It could also push issues about being a successful Papua New Guinean. So far, environmental groups such as Eco Forestry Forum have pushed for stringent control of logging practices, which are a global and local issue. The media does not endeavour to encourage home-grown issues; it plays a stereotyped role, opting to present news and information and not worrying about its effects, even if it exacerbates a situation.

h. Coordinated campaigns

The PNG media, if it was really serious, should address issues in a coordinated fashion. That means structuring carefully how each message is to be presented. At the moment, it takes on any issue as long as there is funding. There is no regard to whether readers are aware of the relevance particular information has for them. Former chief of staff of the PNG Defence Force, Colonel Leo Nuia, writing in the *Post-Courier* on July 29, 2005, accused the Gun Control Committee of wasting its time: 'I have decided to write to the Guns Control Committee because I do not believe all the publicity so far has been balanced. It seems that the campaign against guns has been stage-managed and views to the contrary [have] been ignored and played down.'

i. Taking for granted the reader's ability to understand

I believe one of the professional cardinal sins committed by journalists in PNG is to assume that everyone understands and interprets information as they do. This notion has been the subject of a lot of debate with the media claiming that it is up to readers to understand, and that they try to simplify the information wherever possible.

j. The media's adaptation of foreign issues

Finally I believe that the PNG media prides itself on being on par with the rest of the world. It attempts to relay, print and use syndicated pieces of news all in the context of giving the consumer the cutting edge in whatever service it provides. Global issues such as children's rights, poverty, gender equity and even governance were quickly embraced by the media organizations; however, there was no attempt to relate this to the common people. Take the issue of poverty: the World Bank had stated that PNG was on a poverty line, yet Papua New Guineans vehemently refused to accept that.

Sarah Garap (2003), a prominent Highlands woman, reported that no Papua New Guinean had ever died of starvation and or because of a lack of access to services, because of the presence of *wantoks*. According to Garap, the global definition of poverty had no bearing on the local folk and its constant use in the media was insulting and derogatory to Papua New Guineans. Shelley Launa (2005), a community development worker, is sceptical about women's rights in the country. She believes that in a male-dominated society, men will embrace and accept the efforts of women only if they coexist with the menfolk.

Conclusion

The media has no obligation to publicise any specific issue and addresses each issue when it arises. Media companies want to make money, often at the expense of good governance, despite giving rebates like free coverage up to a certain point. In other words, the media's prime mandate is to make money and survive.

Reporters are well trained yet underpaid, and there is often a lack in the depth of their experience. Former Prime Minister Sir Julius Chan (1995) concludes succinctly: 'It would be better to have experienced senior journalists assigned to write [about] important subjects, rather than young journalists who often have no sense of history and appear to have been assigned to a task simply because they are on duty and there is an assignment.' And, even if issues are presented, most Papua New Guineans don't grasp the essence of the issues that are being reported.

Morris Dogimai, chairperson of the Wakawa Theatre, and his team visited 436 villages between Oro and Central Provinces and were astounded to find that people still weren't attuned to the mass awareness programs promulgated by the National AIDS Council. This stark reality shows that outside observers are mistaken if they think that the PNG media has adequately addressed key issues facing the country. Because of a lack of a coherent, precise and simple message, the bulk of the populace remain marginalised.

While the media has shown that it can cover global and governance issues, it neglects its potential to be a responsible partner in PNG's development. As Chan says, 'Perhaps if it was seen less as a product, a commodity, a source of ratings and income, and more as the lifeblood of democracy and freedom, more as the people's right to know the truth, then we would have a better source of news in the world today.'

Recommendations

1. Review the role of PNG media organisations in relation to their performance and ascertain if the media has too much freedom. Establish a committee to re-examine whether it has been consistent with its perceived role and whether the Independent Media Standards Commission has implemented its aims.
2. Strengthen the Office of Information in PNG with improved facilities and funding and use provincial governments to open information offices. Officers

should be employed by this department but attached to the respective provincial governments. The office could also pour more resources into the NBC and consider having its own television station.
3. Use the Army for patrols to remote areas, with members of the infantry to be engaged in the dissemination of information as part of their civic responsibility. This can be done twice a year and good governance can be promoted and marketed.
4. The school curriculum needs to promote and reinforce patriotic values. Traditional governance principles should be adapted, reinforced and made an integral part of the curriculum in each of the 19 provinces. This will enable students to relate to their own values and then embrace national governance issues.
5. Establish and strengthen the Journalists' Union so that it can fight for the rights of journalists, ensuring that journalists have better conditions, are content with their jobs and perform well. Currently they work long hours, are underpaid and are prone to bribery, intimidation and lack of interest.
6. Establish an Independent Centre for Journalism that can support good governance and fight corruption. It can be linked with other international bodies such as the Australian Centre for Independent Journalism and the Philippines Centre for Independent Journalism.
7. Build the capacity of PNG journalists. They need to spend time with overseas-based governance organisations and undertake training, particularly with regard to issues of good governance.

References

Media

'Cheezed Off, UPNG', *Post-Courier*, 'Viewpoint', 25 July, 2005.

Dogimai, Morris, 'HIV awareness not reaching majority', *Post-Courier*, August 10, 2005.

Felt, Mark, 'Deep Throat sparks media debate', *Post-Courier*, June 3, 2005.

Garap, Sarah, at the Enga Maseamana meeting, Wabag, November 2003.

Honimae, Johnson, ABC, *Pacific Beat*, Thursday July 7, 2005.

Nuia, Leo, 'Law and Order — Illegal Guns', *Post-Courier*, July 29, 2005.

Pamba, Kevin, 'The Ripple effects of Western Bias', *The National*, July 27, 2005.

Solomon, Anna, at the Reporting Law and Order conference, Vunapope Conference Centre, Rabaul, May 8, 2005.

'The Insider, Part II, Waigani', *Post-Courier*, July 27, 2005.

Scholarly

Aitsi, Peter John. 2005. Address at the 2005 Media Freedom Day, University of Papua New Guinea, May 1.

Brookfield, H. C. 1972. *Colonialism, Development and Independence: The Case of Melanesian Islands in the South Pacific*. Cambridge: Cambridge University Press.

Chan, Julius. 1995. 'Serving truth with development news.' *Pacific Journalism Review*, 2, 1.

Kanekane, Joe. 2003. 'Challenges in Reporting Corruption in Newspapers.' In David Kavanamur, Charles Yala and Quinton Clements (eds), *Building a Nation in Papua New Guinea: Views of the post-independence generation*, Canberra: Pandanus Books.

Maino, Charles. 1995. 'People, News and Government.' *Pacific Journalism Review*, 2, 1.

Molloy, Ivan (ed.) 2004. *Eye of the Cyclone: Issues in Pacific security*. Maroochydore, Qld: Sunshine Coast University College.

Pearson, Mark. 2001. 'Journalists are different from their audiences.' *Pacific Area Newspaper Publishers' Association Bulletin*, 209. p. 26.

United Nations Research Institute for Social Development. 1995. *States of Disarray: The social effects of globalization*. An UNRISD report for the World Summit for Social Development. Geneva, Switzerland.

Ward, Ian. 2000. 'A genuinely free press?' *Pacific Journalism Review*, 6, 1. pp. 13–14.

Stiglitz, Joseph. 2002. *Globalization and its Discontents*. New York and London: W. W. Norton.

Conversations

Daniel Kapi, telephone interview, October 2002

Daniel Korimbao, telephone interview, July 2005

Shelley Launa, Community Justice Liaison Unit, June 2005

22. Democracy in Papua New Guinea: Challenges from a rights-based approach

Orovu Sepoe

PNG has encountered numerous challenges to its youthful and fledging democracy since independence in 1975. Against the background of critical issues facing the country, this chapter sets out to provide the rationale for and explore the importance of adopting a rights-based approach to strengthening democracy in PNG. The discussion also attempts to identify the opportunities offered by the rights-based approach for building a viable and meaningful democracy. Major legislative reforms and initiatives in institutional strengthening undertaken in PNG, in particular the Limited Preferential Voting system (LPV) and the *Organic Law on the Integrity of Political Parties and Candidates* (OLIPPAC), can serve as the means for strengthening democracy. A rights-based approach, applied through the LPV and the OLIPPAC, will establish a firm foundation for a bottom-up approach to building democracy. The rights-based approach needs to be considered as an alternative framework for strengthening and deepening democracy, and, more specifically, to ensure 'the people' become the focus of political practice in PNG.

The democratic system of governance, in its Western, liberal and representative form, is the model sought and promoted by the international community but its realisation has been problematic for many countries outside the West. In PNG, its introduction has been quite recent and the challenges emerging from this adoption process remain immensely difficult for a culturally heterogeneous society and historically autonomous clan- or tribal-based political entities.

In contemporary PNG political life, the peaceful and fair conduct of elections, an important hallmark of democratic government, remains an ideal. This paper suggests one pathway towards the realisation of this principle. It focuses specifically on two related aspects of electoral politics that have a tremendous bearing on democratic practice in PNG: the role of political parties as mechanisms of democracy and how voting behaviour, especially in the choice of political leadership, impacts on the quality of democracy.

There are two sections to this paper. The first section presents an overview and highlights some of the critical issues that continually threaten and weaken the functioning of a healthy democracy in PNG. The second section introduces the rights-based approach and the analytical framework that informs this discussion, and then proceeds to present the empirical reasons that necessitate a rights-based approach for strengthening democracy in PNG. The central argument in this discussion will be that a rights-based approach is critical for democracy. Applied through the OLIPPAC and the LPV system, it *could* help strengthen democracy in PNG. The critical question is how? In addressing this issue, the discussion will identify opportunities for strengthening democracy in PNG offered by the rights-based approach.

The political context in PNG: Challenges and critical issues

Symptoms of political decay are evident in PNG and these pose real risks for a healthy democracy (Gelu 2003). Endemic corruption, a general lack of government accountability to the people, the weak capacity of the State to deliver basic services, law and order, and a host of other governance issues endanger the effective functioning of institutions and the processes of democracy. The existence of a weak party system also poses formidable challenges for democracy. Party weakness results in political instability. There is also a lack of accountability where political party policies are displayed merely for voter enticement during elections rather than as a serious agenda for voters to base their decisions on, and much less for nation-building and promoting the common good. The weakness of PNG's party system results in threats of votes of no confidence in the Government, the frequency of which poses a major threat to political stability. Political instability turns the attention of government away from fulfilling its democratic mandate of serving the society and meeting its needs.

Election promises do not seem to bear fruit once political parties assume office. The result is poor delivery of services for a majority of the population. The political parties that form government in PNG have no concern for accountability to the people and no real basis for providing the linkage between government and society. Therefore, it is unreasonable for political parties in PNG to claim any affinity with the populace. The democratic role of political parties is often compromised as a result of their preoccupation with power games.

Poor political leadership is evident in widespread corruption, and mismanagement continues to impact negatively on democracy in PNG. Poor political leadership effectively means that the wellbeing and interests of people are not central to the thinking and conduct of elected leaders. People are deprived of basic security and suffer from many other forms of injustice. A dismal record of low indices of human development for PNG is illustrative of this point.

Weak state institutions are another established feature in PNG. Given the weak capacity of the State to deliver services for a majority of its citizens, the democratic link between citizens' aspirations and the activities of government agencies and elected representatives is effectively severed. This imposes serious constraints on the State's authority over society.

Violence has become common in PNG elections, especially in the Highlands, seriously compromising the possibility of free and fair voting. Harassment, intimidation and bribery are common during elections and leave little room for a healthy electoral contest. Violence, actual or potential, has resulted in disenfranchisement for many citizens.

The acceptance and institutionalisation of democracy at the formal legal level has yet to be matched with the internalisation of human rights and the principles, norms and values of democracy in the national conscience. This is evident in the way Papua New Guineans today grapple with the notion of citizenship, which links individuals directly to the State but also poses difficulties for their traditional and familial relationships. This tension is evident in the electoral process in a number of ways: for instance, where voters prefer to choose *wantok* or *haus lain* candidates and the prevalence of *haus lain* or bloc voting rather than one person, one vote.

Given the context of political life outlined above, it is imperative for PNG to embrace human rights in the electoral process. The next section attempts to analyse why and how rights are essential to the process of building and sustaining democracy in PNG.

A rights-based approach to democracy

At the outset, it is important to highlight that democracy is an issue of degree, not something that you either have or do not have. In addition, the values and principles intrinsic to democracy have to be acknowledged. These principles include 'popular control over public decision making and decision makers; and equality between citizens in the exercise of that control' (IDEA 2005). The democratic quality of a government is determined by taking these values seriously in political practice. These issues are explored through the context of electoral politics in PNG.

Rights-based approach: A developmental perspective

> A rights-based approach deliberately and explicitly focuses on people achieving the minimum conditions for living with dignity. It does so by exposing the root causes of vulnerability and marginalisation and expanding the range of responses. *It empowers people to claim and exercise their rights and fulfil their responsibilities.* A rights-based approach recognizes poor, displaced, and war-affected people as having inherent rights essential to livelihood security, rights that are validated by international laws. (CARE 2001, in Uvin 2004)

The above definition of a rights-based approach to development has important lessons for political life and in particular democratic governance. Addressing the root causes of vulnerability is a central concern in a rights-based approach

(Uvin 2004: 135). This requires identifying the systemic and structural causes of vulnerability preventing people from meaningful participation and exercising free choice in voting for people who will represent their interests. A rights-based democracy means, in effect, recognising democracy as people-centred and as a representative, participatory and developmental process.

Analytical framework

The human rights community recognises two broad categories of rights (Uvin 2004; Heywood 2004): civil and political rights and economic, social and cultural rights. In relation to civil and political rights, the important questions that must inform the discussion as well as the practice of democracy include:

- Are civil and political rights guaranteed equally for all?
- How effective and equal is the protection of the freedom of movement, expression, association and assembly?
- How secure is the freedom for all to practise their own religion, language or culture?
- How free from harassment are individuals and groups working to improve human rights? (IDEA 2005)

Economic, social and cultural rights encompass a range of special rights such as women's rights, children's rights and minority rights. This category accommodates the interests and needs of the vulnerable or marginalised, and they are given special consideration to overcome their relative disadvantage. The central purpose of a democratic system of government ought to be to serve the people and, in particular, how they can be empowered to participate in and benefit from processes of government.

Empirical reasons for a rights-based approach

Highlighted below are some observations that demonstrate the general disregard for rights in electoral politics and also provide a strong premise for a rights-based approach.

Does PNG enjoy free and fair elections? The highly competitive and volatile nature of elections in PNG is recognised widely by political commentators. Electoral contests are usually characterised by large numbers of competing candidates, averaging more than 20 candidates per electorate in 1997 and 2002 (May 2002; Okole and Kavanamur 2002). The 1992 national election signalled the beginning of violent elections in the Highlands. In his account of the Chimbu election in 1992, Bill Standish raised the first alarm relating to the harmful and destructive move 'towards gunpoint democracy'. By 2002, 'gunpoint democracy' was well and truly established in electoral politics in the Highlands. Another commentator's account of the 2002 election in Simbu reaffirms this point: 'Many people were not able to cast a vote. They were deprived of their rights as citizens by the use of guns, money and pigs throughout Chimbu and the rest of the Highlands region' (Dika 2003: 46). Lakane and Gibbs (2003: 109–13) also noted the widespread abuse of rights in the case of elections in Enga:

> With so much at stake, voting becomes a matter of survival. Specific events of the 2002 election in Enga included hijacking of ballot boxes, the fire-bombing of ballot papers, shooting and killing …
>
> The experience of the 2002 elections shows a political culture developing in Enga which is neither just nor democratic. It is a culture of violence and intimidation, with links to traditional means of waging war and establishing alliances, but with new kinds of tribalism and a new type of leader who has access to guns and the ability to open or obstruct access to money and resources. The stakes are high with large discretionary 'electoral development funds' available to Members of Parliament and access by governors to Provincial Government funds. Elections are a form of investment, with successful candidates rewarding their supporters and disregarding others …
>
> Counting the cost of the last election, in money, soured relationships, and lives lost, people say that elections as experienced in 2002 are just not worth the trouble. For them, particularly the have-nots, it is not a question of money and miracles, but of poverty and a feeling of powerlessness.

Is political leadership determined through the exercise of democratic choice? To some extent, voters in PNG do exercise democratic choice in choosing their leaders. This is evidenced by the high turnover of MPs in all elections since 1977. In every election, two-thirds of sitting MPs have been voted out of office. However, in cases where guns, violence and intimidation are involved, as in most of the Highlands provinces, the choice of leadership is not democratic. Leadership choice is also gender-biased and discriminatory. The following testimony of a male voter's preference of leader is a stark revelation of gender discrimination: 'As much as I may want to vote for a woman candidate, the community and the tribe will despise or reject me, and even abandon me so I have to follow the way the community or tribe operates.' One observer gave the following account: 'During the 2002 national election in Enga, two women contested; one for the regional seat and the other for Wabag Open electorate. Most male candidates came out in public forums and said: "Women cannot climb a pandanus tree".' This metaphor means several things: women are not supposed to stand for election; women cannot win elections; and women cannot participate in politics and decision-making.

The Organic Law and LPV system: Opportunities for democracy in PNG

The *Organic Law on the Integrity of Political Parties and Candidates* and the LPV system are the two most notable political reforms that PNG has undertaken to improve its governance since 2001. Current problems encountered in relation to the effective implementation of both have much to do with not taking rights seriously in PNG. Thus, it is crucial for rights to be considered as integral to the OLIPPAC and the LPV system. The overall lack of concern for principles, values and norms in the political life of the country ought to be a cause for concern. A similar point has been made by Louise Baker in her conceptualisation of 'integrity', where she argues that the OLIPPAC tends to emphasise the operational aspects of political party organisation and structure rather than the 'honesty' and 'uprightness' of the behaviour of key actors (Baker 2005: 213). Baker argues: 'The [OLIPPAC] has not been able to encourage all MPs to take initiatives to address public interests above and beyond their own, more limited interests' (2005: 114). A positive national consciousness and attitude reflecting respect for human rights can go a long way towards strengthening and sustaining democracy. While these are significant political reforms, their effectiveness is not fully realised because power dynamics take precedence over citizenship rights and respect for democratic norms and principles. Political parties need to play a leading role in strengthening democracy.

The democratic role of political parties

Several related issues must be considered as crucial to the democratic role of political parties: Are the rights of citizens promoted? Are people participating in political parties? How can rights become integral to the functioning of political parties? To what extent are political parties accountable for their election manifestos or policy platforms?

Fragmented, fluid and lacking any sort of discipline and popular membership, political parties tend to be more interested in power games than in fostering and promoting democratic governance. The obvious lack of commitment to party policies raises serious doubts about the democratic role of political parties. It raises questions about how political parties can be made accountable to popular demands and aspirations, and how they demonstrate their ability to address the diverse and varied interests and priorities of the people. In this respect, the OLIPPAC has to ensure that voters claim their right to hold political parties accountable for their stated policies. This requires the implementation agency of the OLIPPAC to be adequately resourced to carry out public awareness about reform and make it accessible for voters to obtain information on the policies of registered political parties.

The elite-dominated and urban-based political parties' poor or non-existent linkage with society calls into question their democratic role. Encouraging grassroots membership is crucial for deepening democracy. The inclusion of a provision for a minimum of 500 members in the 1995 amendment to the OLIPPAC is a step in this direction, although much remains to be done in terms of ensuring that this provision is enforced well in advance of future elections. To be more gender inclusive, the OLIPPAC needs further amendment. Although Section 62 of the OLIPPAC provides financial incentives to political parties to endorse women candidates, this is insufficient. This needs to be complemented with the provision of a quota system for the endorsement of women by every registered political party.

Limited Preferential Voting system

Compared with the first-past-the-post system, the LPV system is arguably more democratic for PNG because it allows three choices for a voter. In an electorate with a large number of candidates, it also ensures that an MP is elected to office with more than 50 per cent of the votes from his/her electorate.

Under the first-past-the-post system in the 2002 national election, women in the Highlands generally did not vote. Their right to vote as individuals was blatantly abused and denied them. There was absolutely no freedom of choice, no freedom of expression and no freedom of movement in the Highlands. The election atmosphere was anarchic and the rule of law was non-existent in most parts of the Highlands during the election. Yet the MPs in power in the current Parliament and their supporters have not been held accountable for their illegal activities and inappropriate behaviour during the 2002 election, which clearly infringed the rights of voters, especially women. Even under the LPV system, women did not vote in the by-election held in the Anglimp South Wahgi open electorate. Instead, individuals appointed by contesting candidates marked the ballot paper for others, especially women. How can we ensure that women, indeed all voters, exercise their right to vote? A provision needs to be included in the *LPV Act* to effectively nullify the counting of votes for candidates who engage in bribery, intimidation and violence during an election. All candidates, and 'warlords' in particular, ought to be made accountable for their actions. In addition, separate polling booths for male and female voters should be provided to allow independent voting. In this way, the principles of secret and free voting, as well as more choice for voters, can be exercised effectively.

All the measures suggested above could help strengthen democracy in PNG.

Conclusion

Many Papua New Guineans are deprived of their basic rights during elections. Ironically, political leaders in PNG often go to great lengths to defend their own rights in the courts, especially for alleged involvement in corruption and misconduct. Yet they often infringe and abuse the rights of ordinary citizens in their quest to enter Parliament. Such political practice bears little resemblance to the democratic principles espoused in the PNG Constitution.

Although PNG is formally recognised as a Westminster parliamentary democracy, some of the underlying values and principles of this form of democracy have yet to take firm roots, especially in electoral politics. There are several critical issues, in particular a weak party system, group-voting behaviour and a harmful leadership culture, which require immediate attention if this country is to experience free and fair elections.

The central aim of this discussion was to offer an alternative approach to strengthening democracy. From a rights-based approach, some practical ways of achieving a people-centred, participatory and more representative democracy were suggested. Ultimately, a rights-based approach will require being sensitive to local power dynamics and political struggles. A rights-based democracy recognises the inevitably political nature of this approach. Through political struggle rights-based democracy is attainable (Uvin 2004).

There is a need for political parties to 'think human rights' in their operation. In this respect accountability is crucial. People's participation is crucial to realising the democratic role of political parties. The LPV system has to be premised on human rights claims to ensure the free and fair choice of competing candidates by voters. Ultimately, a rights-based approach would enable people to boldly claim their right to government services and political power.

References

Baker, Louise. 2005. 'Political integrity laws in Papua New Guinea and the search for stability.' *Pacific Economic Bulletin,* 20, 1 (May).

Democracy Assessment: The basics of the International IDEA Assessment Framework. 2005.

Dika, Elijah. 2003. 'The 2002 National Election in Chimbu Province.' *Catalyst: Social Pastoral Journal for Melanesia*, 33, 1.

Gelu, Alphonse. 2003. 'Political Decay in Papua New Guinea: The conduct of the 2002 National Election.' *Catalyst: Social Pastoral Journal for Melanesia*, 33, 1.

Gibbs, Philip. 2005. 'LPV and the Wabag Open By-Election.' Unpublished manuscript.

Grimshaw, Patricia, Katie Holmes and Marilyn Lake. 2001. *Women's Rights and Human Rights: International historical perspectives*. Basingstoke: Palgrave.

Heywood, Andrew. 2004. *Political Theory: An Introduction*. Third edition. New York: Palgrave Macmillan.

Kanaparo, Peter. 2003. 'Democracy in Flames: Behaviours and Actions in the Heart of Wabag Town.' *Catalyst: Social Pastoral Journal for Melanesia,* 33, 2.

Kaupa, William Gari. 2003. 'PNG Culture and Politics: Election in the Gumine District 2002.' *Catalyst: Social Pastoral Journal for Melanesia,* 33, 1.

Lakane, J. and P. Gibbs. 2003. 'Haves and Have-Nots: The 2002 Elections in the Enga Province of PNG.' *Catalyst: Social Pastoral Journal for Melanesia,* 33, 2.

May, R. J. and R. Anere. 2002. *Maintaining Democracy: The 1997 Elections in Papua New Guinea.* Department of Political Science, UPNG.

Okole, Henry and David Kavanamur. 2002. 'Gender & Governance in Papua New Guinea.' Unpublished manuscript.

Standish, Bill. 2003. 'Papua New Guinea's Most Turbulent Election.' *Catalyst: Social Pastoral Journal for Melanesia,* 33, 2.

Standish, Bill. 1996. 'Elections in Simbu: Towards Gunpoint Democracy?' In Yaw Saffu (ed.), *The 1992 PNG Elections: Change and Continuity in Electoral Politics,* Canberra: The Australian National University.

Uvin, Peter. 2004. *Human Rights and Development.* Bloomfield, CT: Kumarian Press.

23. Governance and Livelihood Realities in Solomon Islands

Morgan Wairiu

The three institutions of Solomon Islands life are traditional governance (custom), the Church and the State. In the past century, the first two have been strong, the third weak (Brown 2003). Despite this, the condition of traditional governance and the Church are sometimes not noticed by the outside world, which concentrates instead on the State. Modern governance systems have displaced traditional governance. Modern governance is perceived by people to be alienating and disempowering (Wairiu et al. 2003). It is characterised as alienating people from their family or tribe, land and culture. Participation in decision-making and reciprocity are inherent characteristics of traditional governance. To Solomon Islanders, governance is about livelihood, that is, working together to meet people's basic needs. Under the modern governance system, the most vulnerable groups in society — women, youth and people living in isolated areas — are often ignored. It is vital for peace and national security that the current recovery plans made possible through the Regional Assistance Mission to Solomon Islands (RAMSI) are put into practice, to reach and make a difference to the bulk of the people in the villages. This chapter presents communities' perspectives on governance, key governance issues and the need to strengthen leadership and promote good governance to enable people to actively participate in governance and livelihood activities.

Community perspective on governance

Most rural communities have difficulty defining governance. For most, aspects of governance were described as service delivery and working together to meet people's daily basic needs (including food security, shelter, health, traditional education, security and personal safety, self-reliance, peace, spiritual growth and cultural heritage).

Traditional structures of governance were organised around tribes and/or the family. Each unit of the structure provided the necessary power for the functioning of the system in order to accommodate the different needs and interests of all the people bound to the system. Leaders earned their position and respect among their people. People knew who their leaders were and why they commanded leadership and looked only to that one person as leader. Peace and security within and between communities was a priority of the traditional leadership system. Men dominated the leadership and governance domain while women dominated the traditional welfare domain. Traditional governance systems sustained communities for ages, but they have been displaced by modern governance systems.

Under the state, modern governance is perceived by people to be alienating and disempowering (Wairiu et. al., 2003). It is characterized as alienating people from their family or tribe, land, and culture. The modern governance system is said to 'represent the voices of the people', but in practice this has not been the case. The majority do not understand the structure and functions of the modern governance system and people do not actively participate in it. Modern governance is seen among communities as something that exists at a distance, at provincial headquarters and in the capital, Honiara. Links between community-level governance bodies and those at the provincial and national level are weak or non-existent. This creates the environment for natural resource exploitation by individuals because there is no effective leadership to safeguard people and their resources.

Governance issues at the community and national level

At the community level, key governance issues include concern over the erosion of traditional governance structures and authority; confusion over the complex interplay between systems; lack of participation in decision-making; lack of proper development policies on issues affecting village life; and poor service delivery. Addressing these issues has become critical to the future stability of Solomon Islands. Village youth, who believe their views are not being heard by decision-makers and who are marginalised by modern governance processes, were instrumental in initiating and perpetuating the recent conflict. Roughan (2000) stresses that this issue cannot be ignored as 41 per cent of the country's population is under 15 years of age.

At the national level, poor leadership, corruption, inadequate service delivery and lack of participation in decision-making processes are major governance issues. Some of these issues have existed since colonial times. The modern governance system has long been considered a threat to traditional governance structures and authority and there is much dissatisfaction over heavy-handed, top-down approaches. Because of this top-down approach, village people tend to see their role as the 'receivers' of nationalism rather than the 'builders' of a nation-state (Wairiu et al. 2003). The government has become the creator and producer of services, while people see themselves simply as consumers. The recent ethnic tension that ravaged the country's economy is only one example of people's longstanding dissatisfaction with governance arrangements, service delivery and resource allocation.

Governance and civil society

Civil society organisations have become increasingly vocal on issues of corruption and 'bad governance'. After the ethnic tension and the arrival of RAMSI, civil society organisations gained momentum and seem determined to bring about a new political order. This is evident through the establishment of the Civil Society Network. A number of local NGOs are now active in promoting leadership and good governance, addressing issues at village, provincial and national levels. These organisations include the Solomon Islands Development Trust, Solomon Islands Christian Association, the Civil Society Network, National Council of Women, Voice Belong Mere Solomon, Environmental Concerns Action Network of Solomon Islands and the Winds of Change Movement. International NGOs such as Conservation International, Worldwide Fund for Nature, the Nature Conservancy and Greenpeace are also promoting good governance through the sustainable use of natural resources and environmental protection and management.

In 2003, the UNDP initiated a pilot project in Isabel Province to build management capacity at the provincial level. This project builds on the unique 'tripartite system' of governance in Isabel Province, which comprises the joint leadership of chiefs, the Church and provincial government. The Rural Development Volunteers Association (RDVA), under the Ministry of Provincial Government and Rural Development, operates the '*Pipol Fastaem Network*' (People First Network), a robust email system that facilitates communication between people in remote locations. This innovative technology enables Islanders spread across thousands of kilometres to access electronic mail and communicate with one another using a central computer, short-wave radio and solar power. The network seeks to promote equitable and sustainable rural development and peace building through improved information-sharing and awareness-building between people in isolated communities. The RDVA plans to establish 29 stations throughout the country; 17 were operational in early 2006.

Churches throughout Solomon Islands continue to play their part in promoting good governance, although this is restricted primarily to messages from the pulpit. Some clergy are moving beyond the church building and 'going public' about governance, development and social justice issues. For instance, a bishop from the Church of Melanesia recently published a report listing 10 priority issues that need to be addressed by RAMSI, including corruption, land disputes and education. The country's five mainstream churches (Catholic, Anglican, United Church, South Seas Evangelical and Seventh-Day Adventist) formed the Solomon Islands Christian Association. This network has become outspoken on governance issues and is constantly reminding government to be transparent, accountable and responsible in its decision-making.

Women's groups, through their national body, the National Council of Women, are also making their voices and choices heard. Women constitute approximately half of the total population of Solomon Islands (Solomon Islands Government 2000); more than 80 per cent live in villages and are engaged in subsistence agriculture. Women historically played numerous and important roles in traditional governance, including their involvement as decision-makers, mothers, nurses, providers of food and income, community leaders and educators — all of which are necessary for sustainable livelihoods and good social relations. Liloqula (2002) notes that these roles were widely recognised and highly valued within the traditional governance system, giving women status and prominence in their families and communities. Today, women's contributions are often overlooked resulting in the vast under-utilisation of women's potential to contribute to good governance.

Leadership

Links between community-level or traditional governance bodies and those of the provincial and national governments are weak or non-existent. This weak linkage and confusion over the interface between traditional and modern governance systems creates weakness in leadership and exploitation of the country's natural resources at the expense of people's livelihoods. At present, there is a leadership vacuum at all levels, from community to government. People are confused and nobody is giving direction. The leadership crisis has taken form at different levels and in different manifestations and has reached a level where, if it not addressed now, it will remain a major obstacle to Solomon Islands' prosperous future.

Governance, livelihood realities and challenges

Governance and livelihoods are interrelated because peace, security and the opportunity to participate in decision-making are important issues and part of people's livelihood. The majority of Solomon Islanders derive their livelihoods from their own land, sea and labour resources. For centuries, this has provided them with food, water, shelter, medicine, recreation and other benefits. People's livelihoods are underpinned by the tribal ownership of land, which enables all members of a customary landholding group to access resources for subsistence and income-earning purposes. More than 90 per cent of Solomon Islands land is tribally owned (owned by a whole tribe) through 'customary land tenure'. Most landowning groups or tribal members live in rural villages, which comprised 86 per cent (352,600) of the total population of 410,000 in 2000 (Solomon Islands Government 2000). The population of Solomon Islands is now considerably higher.

Although the subsistence sector has directly supported people's livelihoods, it has never been a development priority for colonial and post-colonial governments and donors. Past interventions have concentrated on the cash economy. Women still dominate the subsistence economy for family survival while men are in the domain of leadership and governance. In the past three decades, women have slowly moved into the cash economy as income opportunities became accessible in some areas. Their involvement in cash cropping adds an extra workload to their existing social commitments to family, community, school, church and women's group activities. Pollard et al. (2004) estimated that there were about 3,000 community women's groups, approximately 10 national women's organisations and 10 indigenous women's associations operating throughout Solomon Islands. The women's groups have established networks at the national level that are reaching rural communities and touching the heart of the key providers of rural livelihoods, the women. It is, however, evident that the network is unrecognised, under-utilised and under-resourced. As women directly support the livelihood of their family, it is important that such women's networks are well resourced and strengthened to ensure continuous support for improvement and sustenance of people's livelihoods. Current governance systems and structures should accommodate women to participate equally in governing the country.

There has been a gradual shift from the subsistence to the cash economy over many years, however, there are limited opportunities in the villages to earn cash to meet basic needs. Prices are low for major commodities such as copra and cocoa and there is a lack of reliable and affordable transport to markets. There is no information on alternative sources of income for villagers and few marketing arrangements for selling the produce they grow. Given this reality, their best option is for men to go to urban centres such as Honiara seeking paid work, while others resort to destructive resource-extraction activities such as logging or over-harvesting of coastal marine resources. The solutions lie in providing a way of gaining cash income for those who are ambitious for their children and themselves, who are prepared to work and who wish to use the two resources that they have — their land and their family labour. This will require leadership and vision, which is lacking in the country. There is a leadership vacuum at all levels and a lack of sound management strategies for resource use. People are making uninformed decisions about their resources, which compromise the future of their natural resource base and their children. Past interventions by government and donor partners have not adequately addressed these problems. The arrival of extractive and destructive industries such as logging exacerbated the problem.

In some communities income-generating activities such as cash cropping, logging, fishing, marketing of garden produce and small business enterprises are having some beneficial results. They bring cash income to rural villages, employment, slow migration to towns and enable people to meet basic needs such as paying for kerosene, soap and school fees. The increase in income is good but people are not investing their modest income to support their livelihood because governance structures are weak, and government services such as police to maintain order, are absent. As a result, greater cash incomes have brought more social problems. These include: 1) increased consumption of imported processed food (rice, noodles, tinned fish/meat, tea and flour-based items); 2) consumption of alcohol and drugs; 3) gambling (*kura*); and 4) the introduction of entertainment equipment such as videos and modern dance music. All these are leading to a growth in non-communicable diseases (diabetes and infant malnutrition) and criminal activities, causing disharmony among communities. Home-brewed alcohol, locally known as *kwaso,* and drugs such as marijuana are readily available in many rural communities. Meanwhile, population pressure on the land has led to short fallows, land degradation and poor crop yields.

One of the major governance and livelihood challenges is landownership and use. To most people, land is much more than a provider of the basics of life such as food, water and shelter. It is part of the people's life. Land problems lie at the heart of the country's current problems and the recent ethnic tension. Roughan (2003) argues that land problems have come about because of the way people in Solomon Islands view land. The outside world sees land as a resource base, a commodity, something that is bought and sold. Land is something that can be used to make a profit. Solomon Islanders, on the other hand, understand it as part of their life and not as a commodity, not something that can be bought and sold. Since current leaders are associated with wealth and power, some use land as though it does not belong to the tribe but to the individual. Roughan (2003) pointed out that to address land problems a strong and well-funded program of educating people about how the wider world works was critical. The customary land situation has to be sorted out and a common understanding and workable mechanism need to be established to make land available for development in a way that provides equitable benefits for all parties. Otherwise, endless conflicts will ensue and pose threats to a peaceful and prosperous future. Solomon Islanders need assistance in this area.

Associated with land is the use of the country's natural resources. The desire to improve living standards drives current economic development, which in most cases involves uncontrolled conversion of natural resources in the country into wealth. Timber and fish remain the country's two greatest natural resources. The timber harvest (mainly round-log production) has been beyond sustainable levels for years, reaching a peak of one million cubic metres in 2004. The same is increasingly true for the fish harvest, with illegal fishing by overseas vessels going on and the country incapable of doing anything to stop it. RAMSI can provide some help in these areas. The dependence on the subsistence production system to support a rapidly growing population makes the environment particularly important to the wellbeing of Solomon Islanders. The current trend creates the potential for significant livelihood impacts from the extractive industries which form the bulk of national exports.

Another challenge is whether Solomon Islands has received a fair return from its natural resources exploited in the 28 years since independence. As Suri and

Rarawa (2004) state, it is essential that we refer to the country's balance sheet to see how much of the country's resources have been harvested and how much the country and resource owners have received in return. At present, government and community attitudes towards reliance on socially, economically and environmentally destructive resource extraction have not changed, even after the ethnic tension and the intervention of RAMSI. There is no evidence of changed thinking about the country's economic base, and RAMSI seems to accept the present basis of the national economy.

The need for good governance and livelihood interventions

RAMSI's program is in areas of: 1) law and justice, 2) the machinery of government and 3) economic governance. Its objectives are to: 1) contribute to a safer and more secure Solomon Islands, 2) help the Solomon Islands Government to better serve its people, and 3) contribute to a prosperous Solomon Islands (RAMSI 2005). The program strongly promotes good governance and livelihoods. In promoting good governance, RAMSI is concerned more with the State and less with civil society, but it is important that RAMSI is also engaged with civil society, particularly communities, in its effort to promote good governance. Past interventions have failed because they attempted to change people's attitudes towards increasing incomes to improve their livelihoods. It is important that interventions to address livelihoods are not top-down but are carried out in partnership with the people.

Leadership, landownership, and equal participation and partnership as well as nation-building must be the cornerstones of livelihood interventions. Interventions must aim to benefit the most vulnerable groups in Solomon Islands society — women, youth and people living in isolated areas — and build on the strengths of the subsistence system. It is vital for peace and national security that the current recovery plans reach and make a difference to the bulk of the people in the villages. It will be a lost opportunity to rebuild Solomon Islands if RAMSI simply creates an enabling environment and assumes that people will pick things up from there. Poor leadership in the past 28 years has plunged the country into deep problems and the Solomon Islands certainly requires some assistance to move forward.

References

Brown, T. 2003. *Ten ways Australia and New Zealand can help Solomon Islands.* Auki, Malaita Province: Church of Melanesia (Anglican).

Liloqula, R. 2002. 'Women and youth.' *Solomon Islands National Assessment for World Summit on Sustainable Development.* Honiara, Solomon Islands.

Pollard, A. A., K. R. Maemouri, E. Iramu and C. Watoto. 2004. 'Gender, Social and Cultural Issues in Rural Livelihoods.' *Solomon Islands Rural Livelihoods and Broad Based Growth Strategy (Draft)*. Canberra: AusAID.

RAMSI. 2005. *Regional Assistance Mission to Solomon Islands Performance Framework* (August). Honiara, Solomon Islands.

Roughan, J. 2000. 'A second look at the ethnic crisis in Solomons. The village: Metaphor for Solomon Islands women.' *Proceedings of Experts Group Meeting on the Post-Conflict Situation in Solomon Islands*. Brisbane, Australia.

Roughan, J. 2003. *Land is the Issue*. Umi Nao Network.

Solomon Islands Government. 2000. *1999 Solomon Islands Population and Housing Census Report*. Honiara.

Suri, G. and D. Rarawa. 2004. 'Economic Development and Environment Management for Sustainability under Solomon Islands Context.' *Proceedings of the National Conference on Balancing Economic Development and Environment with Sustainability*, ECANSI/EASI Honiara, Solomon Islands.

Wairiu M., S. Tabo and J. Hasiau. 2003. 'Assessing community perspectives on governance in Solomon Islands.' *RETA: Assessing community perspectives on governance in Pacific Region, A report for Asian Development Bank*.

List of Contributors

Glenn Banks is in the School of Geography, Geology and Environmental Science, University of Auckland and has worked on mining issues in Melanesia since 1988. His PhD (1997) from the Australian National University was on the relationship between the Porgera gold mine and the surrounding local community in the highlands of Papua New Guinea. His publications include *The Ok Tedi Settlement: Issues, Outcomes and Implications* (edited with Chris Ballard) Canberra, 1997, and *In Search of the Serpent's Skin: The Story of the Porgera Gold Project* (with Richard Jackson), Port Moresby, 2002.

John Connell is Professor of Geography in the School of Geosciences, University of Sydney. He has published numerous articles and books on the Pacific including *New Caledonia or Kanaky? The Political History of a French Colony*, Canberra, 1987, *Papua New Guinea: the Struggle for Development*, London, 1997, *Urbanisation in the Island Pacific. Towards Sustainable Development* (with John Lea), London, 2002. His latest book, written with Eric Waddell, is *Environment, Development and Change in Rural Asia-Pacific*, London, 2006.

Jon Fraenkel is a Senior Research Fellow in Governance at the Pacific Institute of Advanced Studies in Development and Governance at the University of the South Pacific. His research focuses on contemporary Pacific politics, electoral systems and the economic history of Oceania. He has published widely on these subjects and is the author of *The Manipulation of Custom: From Uprising to Intervention in the SolomonIslands*, Wellington and Canberra, 2004. He has recently co-edited a volume on Fiji's 2006 elections, to be published in 2007 by Asia-Pacific Press.

Kate Hannan is an Associate Professor in Politics in the School of History and Politics, University of Wollongong. She taught previously at the University of the South Pacific, and her research focuses on contemporary political and social change in China as well as the politics of small island states in the Pacific. She is the author of *Industrial Change in China: Economic Restructuring and Conflicting Interests*, London, 1998, and co-edited the governance issue of *Fijian Studies: A Journal of Contemporary Fiji*, 2, 2, November 2004. Her current research focuses on the garment industry in China in a project funded by the Australian Research Council.

Father Fran Hezel is a Jesuit priest and historian who has lived in the Federated States of Micronesia since 1963, and is Executive Director of the Micronesian Seminar in Pohnpei, a Jesuit-run, non-profit, non-governmental organization that has been engaged in Micronesian social, cultural and developmental issues for over thirty years. The Micronesian Seminar is a vehicle for community education in Micronesia serving Palau, the Federated States of Micronesia and the Marshalls as well as Guam and the Northern Marianas. Father Hezel has published more prolifically on Micronesian history and current issues than anyone, and is internationally recognized as a leading historical and social expert on Micronesia.

Elise Huffer is Acting Director and Associate Professor of the Pacific Studies Program of the Pacific Institute of Advanced Studies in Development and Governance at the University of the South Pacific. She coordinates the Pacific Studies Postgraduate Program and oversees the Institute of Pacific Studies Publications. She joined the University of the South Pacific in 1997 after running her own consultancy in New Caledonia from 1992 to 1996. Her main interest lies in contemporary governance with a particular focus on cultural and gender issues, including Pacific political thought.

Tarcisius Tara Kabutaulaka is a Research Fellow in the Pacific Islands Development Program at the East-West Center, Honolulu. Born at Haimarao on the weather coast of Guadalcanal, he is an expert on Solomon Islands politics, the Solomons logging industry, and the place of Solomon Islands in regional affairs. His most recent publications include 'Australian Foreign Policy and the RAMSI Intervention in Solomon Islands', *The Contemporary Pacific*, 17: 2, 2005, and he is the co-editor of *Intervention and State-Building in the Pacific: the Legitimacy of 'Co-operative Intervention'*, Manchester University Press (forthcoming).

Joe R. Kanekane is a journalist and author from Ialibu in the Southern Highlands Province of Papua New Guinea. He works as the Media Adviser with Papua New Guinea's Department of National Planning and Rural Development. He was formerly chief political reporter of the *Independent* newspaper and news director of the Word Publishing Company. A journalism trainer, he was a member of the PNG Media Council and Chairman of the Editorial Task Force on Reporting Corruption.

Helen Lee is a Senior Lecturer in Anthropology in the School of Social Sciences at La Trobe University. Since the 1980s her research has focused on the people of Tonga, both in their home islands in the South Pacific and in the diaspora. Her publications include *Becoming Tongan: an ethnography of childhood*, Honolulu, 1996 (as Helen Morton) and *Tongans overseas: between two shores*, Honolulu, 2003. Currently she is conducting research on second generation Tongan transnationalism in a project funded by the Australian Research Council.

Nic Maclellan and **Peter Mares** contributed their chapter in this book in their capacity as research fellows at the Institute for Social Research at Swinburne University of Technology in Melbourne. It draws on the 'Pacific Labour and Australian Horticulture' project, which was funded through the Australian Research Council Industry Linkage scheme (see http://www.sisr.net/cag/projects/pacific.htm) As part of the research, Peter also travelled to Canada with funding from the Canadian government's Faculty Research Program. **Nic Maclellan** works as Senior Policy Adviser for the Pacific with Oxfam International. He has worked as a journalist, researcher and community development worker in the Pacific islands and travelled extensively throughout the region for more than 20 years. He is the co-author of three books on the region: *La France dans le Pacifique - de Bougainville à Moruroa*, Paris, 1992; *After Moruroa - France in the South Pacific*, New York and Melbourne, 1998; and *Kirisimasi*, Suva, 1999. **Peter Mares** is a journalist and writer with a particular interest in migration issues. He currently hosts the weekly discussion program 'The National Interest' on ABC Radio National.

Ratu Joni Madraiwiwi is the Vice President of the Republic of the Fiji Islands and carries the chiefly title Roko Tui Bau, one of the highest titles of the Kubuna confederacy. Educated in law at Adelaide and McGill universities, he became a judge of Fiji's High Court in 1997, only to resign in protest at the unconstitutional events of 2000. He is well-known for his strong advocacy of constitutionalism, moderation, tolerance and the protection of human rights, and he plays an important conciliatory role in Fiji's public life.

Manoranjan Mohanty is a Senior Lecturer at the Centre for Development Studies, the University of the South Pacific, Suva, Fiji, and was previously in the Political Geography Division, School of International Studies, Jawaharlal Nehru University, New Delhi. A development geographer with many publications to his name, he is especially interested in urbanisation, migration, NGOs, civil society, geopolitics, population and sustainable development in the Third World, especially in the Pacific Islands region.

Vijay Naidu was born in Fiji and educated there and in the United Kingdom. He is Professor and Director of the Development Studies program at the Pacific Institute of Advanced Studies in Development and Governance at the University of the South Pacific, and was Professor and Director of Development Studies at Victoria University of Wellington from 2003 to 2007. He has written on aid, migration, ethnicity, higher education, electoral politics, land tenure, the state, development and poverty, and taken an active role in the civil society movement in Fiji over many years. He has recently served a term as co-chair of Aotearoa New Zealand International Development Network (DEVNET).

John Rapley is a Senior Lecturer in the Department of Government, University of the West Indies, Mona, Jamaica, and visiting lecturer at the *Centre de Recherches et d'Études sur l'Amérique latine et les Caraïbes, Institut d'Études Politiques*, Aix-en-Provence, France. His research focuses on development and the state in an age of globalization, and the new medievalism in the developing world. Among many other publications, he is the author of *Globalization and Inequality: Neoliberalism's Downward Spiral*, Boulder, 2004, and *Understanding Development: Theory and Practice in the Third World*, 2nd edn, Boulder, 2002.

Avelina Rokoduru teaches in the Division of History, School of Social Sciences, University of the South Pacific. She undertook research in the Marshall Islands for the chapter in this volume as part of her development studies thesis, for which she gained her MA with distinction in 2006. Her research interests include regionalism, women's issues, contemporary labour migration, identity and human rights.

Orovu Sepoe is a Senior Lecturer in Political Science in the School of Humanities and Social Sciences, University of Papua New Guinea. She was educated in Papua New Guinea and the United Kingdom and holds a PhD from the University of Manchester. Her teaching and research interests encompass issues of governance, gender and development. She is the author of *Organic Law on the Integrity of Political Parties and Candidates: A Tool for Political Stability*, SSGM Working Paper, 2005/4, ANU.

Claire Slatter is a Fiji citizen, and a graduate of the University of the South Pacific, the Australian National University, and Massey University (PhD). She taught political studies in the Department of History and Politics at the University of the South Pacific for 17 years. She has a background in the nuclear free and independent Pacific movement, the women's movement, trade unionism and journalism, and is a founding member of the Citizens' Constitutional Forum in Fiji. She is also a founding member of the third world feminist network, Development Alternatives with Women for a New Era (DAWN), and was its general coordinator from 1997-2004.

Asofou So'o is the Director of the Institute of Samoan Studies at the National University of Samoa. He has written widely on Samoan politics, the Samoan electoral system and governance in Samoa, and is a co-editor of *Governance in Samoa: pulega i Samoa*, Suva and Canberra, 2000. His most recent article - on the shift by Samoa to universal suffrage - appeared as a co-authored study in the *Journal of Commonwealth and Comparative Politics*, 43, 3, Nov. 2005.

Donovan Storey is a Senior Lecturer in Development Studies at Massey University. His research interests lie in Pacific Island development but especially urban issues facing the region. Before his move to Massey University Donovan taught at the University of the South Pacific's Suva campus. Among his many publications is *Urban Governance in Pacific Island Countries: Advancing an Overdue Agenda*, SSGM Discussion Paper 2005/7, ANU.

Mel Togolo is PNG Country Manager of Nautilus Minerals Niugini Limited, which is conducting seabed exploration for gold, copper, silver and zinc. He has postgraduate degrees in economics and geography, and during the 1980s worked for the North Solomons Provincial Government. He is a foundation member of the Papua New Guinea chapter of Transparency International. Over the years he has played a leading role in Papua New Guinea's business life, and is well known as an expert on the impact of mining on development in Papua New Guinea and other developing countries.

Morgan Tuimaleali'ifano is a Senior Lecturer in History in the School of Social Sciences, University of the South Pacific. In his youth he took the unprecedented step of declining the Tama'aiga Tuimaleali'ifano title, one of the four highest titles in Samoa, in favour of an academic career, and has since become an authority on the chiefly system in Samoa, Tonga and Fiji. His research focuses on title disputes in Fiji and western Polynesia, Pacific migration and resettlement and his latest book is *O Tama A 'Aiga: The Politics of Succession to Samoa's Paramount Titles*, Suva, 2006.

Morgan Wairiu is Executive Director of Environmental Concerns Action Network of Solomon Islands (ECANSI), and coordinates projects in forest advocacy, good governance and resource management in selected communities in Solomon Islands. His PhD is from Ohio State University and he was formerly Permanent Secretary of the Ministry of Agriculture and Livestock in Solomon Islands. He has 17 years experience in project management and planning, research and development.

Index

ACP (Africa, Caribbean, Pacific) group of states, 28, 140, 190-3, 199, 206, 309-10
ADB (Asian Development Bank) 2, 27, 28, 30, 36, 41-42, 60, 123, 139, 141, 147, 189, 190, 197, 201, 207, 244-50, 378
aid 2, 14, 27, 36, 41, 60-61, 74-76, 79, 87-88, 95, 96, 122, 132, 159, 189, 190, 199, 201, 206, 212, 249, 259, 365, 375
Alesana, Tofilau Eti 350-3, 356-8, 365, 371
American Samoa 2, 66, 138
Australia 3, 28, 32, 66, 67, 72, 73, 78, 81, 86-90, 91, 110, 127-32, 137-71, 190, 392, 397
   aid policy 87-89, 131-2, 199, 206
   immigration policy 87-90, 131-2, 139, 140
   mining and other commercial interests 241, 259-74, 189-215, 217-20, 228, 231, 231, 240-41, 249, 264, 309-11
   seasonal work programs 137-71, 202-3, 206

Barr, Father Kevin 29-31, 171, 299-30
Bavadra, Timoci 291, 292, 299
Bougainville 67, 71, 113, 261-2, 280, 281, 285, 385-6

Canada 3, 67, 81, 112, 114, 137
   Seasonal Agricultural Workers' Program 88, 140, 151-7, 161, 163
Chaudhry, Mahendra 292, 315, 323-7, 330-1, 333
citizenship 53, 73, 93-94, 401, 404
Cook Islands 3, 41, 66, 68, 72, 73, 75, 76, 78, 81, 82, 84, 87, 90, 92, 138, 142, 173, 224
   migration 71, 72, 73, 75, 76, 78, 82, 84, 138
   remittances 72, 73, 75, 76, 142
corruption 6, 17, 204, 212, 233, 279, 348, 354-7, 370, 377, 385, 388-91, 393, 395, 397, 400, 405, 410, 411
Cotonou Agreement 28, 32, 34, 140, 190-91, 310
crime 17-19, 43, 62, 66, 201, 233, 310, 392, 414
Crocombe, Ron 34, 42, 48-50, 52, 53
cultural identity 3, 43-55, 93, 94, 121, 126-7, 252, 260, 261, 289-296, 301

development 7, 9, 14, 20, 23-42, 43-55, 59-106, 107-20, 122, 124, 132, 137-171, 192-202, 217-236, 239-85, 291-2, 298, 303, 305-7, 385-98, 401-3, 409-16

economic policy 1, 2, 4, 7-21, 23-42
   Chilean example 10-12
   global context 7-21
   neo-liberalism 2, 12-16, 297;
   resistance to, 23-37
   new medievalism 18-20
   state retreat 16-20
ECREA (Ecumenical Centre for Research, Education and Advocacy), 29-31, 171
education 42, 59-73, 78, 79, 81, 95, 109, 112, 137, 138, 145, 147, 162, 164, 174, 181, 201, 202, 206, 222, 233, 242, 252, 253, 262, 276, 289, 292, 304, 379, 386, 409, 411
'Efi, Tupua Tamasese, 353, 358
EPA (Economic Partnership Agreement) with EU 28, 32, 140, 212, 309

Fiji 1, 3, 4, 5, 14, 29, 34-36, 41-42, 47, 48, 52, 61-64, 67-69, 71, 75, 79, 81-87, 89-91, 107-20, 122, 137, 138, 141-5, 147, 149, 154, 158, 160, 161, 173-86, 189-215, 217-36, 240-1, 263, 289-348, 359-61, 363, 364, 366
   affirmative action 306-8
   church groups 29-30
   civil service 303-5
   Constitution 5, 300, 317-48
   Constitutional Review Commission 320-2
   corruption 204, 212
   coups 1987 and 2000 14, 29, 48, 52, 67, 71, 82, 112, 143, 195, 293-4, 295, 298-300, 304, 305, 317, 319, 321, 323, 325, 331, 361, 363
   cultural identity 289-96, 301

development 107-18
elections 317-48
ethnic nature of politics 289-96
garment industry 4, 5, 117, 189-215, 217-36; end of Multi Fibre Arrangement 2005 5, 189, 212, 214, 218, 310
governance 289-348
history 5, 111-12, 289-96, 299-300, 314
Indo-Fijian emigration 67, 71, 114, 320
labour migration 4, 67-68, 69, 71, 81-85, 89-90, 107-18, 112, 141, 143-5, 173-86, 309-11
market-led development 305-6
military, peacekeeping and security work 67-68, 113-14, 137, 143-5, 203-4, 309-11
national identity 294
NGOs 29, 34-35
political parties 317-48
poverty 61-62, 308-9
power sharing 317-48
reconciliation 52, 293-4, 304
religion 294-5
remittances 4, 68, 75, 112-13, 115-16, 142-3, 190, 201-6, 311
role of the military 303-4
rule of law 233, 293, 303
skill loss 82-83, 85, 112, 141, 143, 203
student mobility 114
sugar industry 4, 117, 189-215, 310
the state 297-315
trade unions 29
traditional leadership 289-96, 301-2
urbanisation 4, 61-62, 189-90, 197-201, 292
fisheries 74, 116, 156, 241-2, 293, 413-4
FLP (Fiji Labour Party), see Fiji, political parties
forestry 1, 5, 239-57, 259, 365, 385, 395, 414-5
free trade 1, 2, 4, 47, 297, 309

French Pacific 3, 7, 86, 95
see New Caledonia
FSM (Federated States of Micronesia) 1, 3, 41-2, 53, 68, 145, 173, 223, 337, 379, 381-2

Ganilau, Ratu Sir Penaia, 292-3, 341
garment industry, see Fiji
globalisation 1-6, 15, 23-27, 29, 31, 37, 43, 49-50, 70, 93-94, 107-18, 189-236, 239-57, 289-315, 375-84, 385-98, 409-16
see migration
governance 2-3, 5, 6, 25, 49, 66, 96, 202, 233, 259-74, 275-85, 289-348, 375-83, 385-98, 399-407, 409-16
'good governance' 1, 2, 6, 29, 34, 44, 45, 46, 49, 202, 233, 259-60, 283, 375-84, 385-6, 396-7, 409, 411-2, 415
weak states 96, 297, 400, 409, 412

Guam 2, 92, 95, 145, 173

Halapua, Sitiveni 52-53
Hawai'i 70, 90
health services 60, 61, 63, 69, 70, 79, 83, 112, 145, 146, 201, 202, 233, 252, 262, 304, 409

IMF (International Monetary Fund) 2, 13, 14, 24, 41, 201, 205, 208, 305

Kelsey, Jane 31-32, 41-42, 141-2, 309-10
Kiribati 3, 63, 64, 69-75, 82, 86, 87, 95, 137-8, 142, 146, 155, 161
Fijian workers 173-86
population 63, 64
labour migration and remittances 69-75, 137, 142, 146, 155

labour migration see migration
Lijphart, Arend 317-19
LPV (Limited Preferential Voting) system, 399-400, 404-6

Mamaloni, Solomon 248, 253
Mara, Ratu Sir Kamisese 47, 290-92, 295, 315
Marshall Islands 3, 4, 67, 68, 81, 82, 114, 145, 173-86, 381
  Fijian workers 173-86
media 1, 6, 28, 34, 36, 107, 189, 240, 375-83, 385-98
MFA (Multi Fibre Arrangement) 189, 194-6, 207, 218, 223-4, 226-8, 232, 310
Micronesia 6, 60, 61, 65, 68, 72, 73, 91, 138, 173, 375-84
migration 1, 3, 4, 59-186, 201, 208, 220, 262-2, 320, 413
  diasporic communities 93-94, 121-135, 138
  Global Commission on International Migration 108-10
  health professionals 81-3, 89, 91, 92, 95, 114, 178-82, 311
  labour migration 1, 3, 4, 53, 59-186, 309-11
  new opportunities for women 76-77
  overstayers 81, 90
  proposed seasonal or guest workers scheme 4, 85, 86, 88, 89, 90, 96, 132, 137-71, 202-3
  refugees 89
  return migration 82, 84-85, 109
  second generation islanders born overseas 72-73, 75, 77-78, 84, 121-35
  skill loss 81, 91-92, 109, 138, 141, 203
  skilled migrants 69, 72, 73, 81-86, 91-92, 95-96, 112, 137, 141, 203
  social impacts 144-6, 158-9
  see urbanisation
mining 5, 60, 69, 86, 142, 241-2, 259-85
  environmental impacts 261-7
  social impacts 261-2
MIRAB model 4, 72-80, 92, 121-2, 128, 131, 147
Molisa, Grace 35
mortality 63

Narube, Savenaca 143, 170, 189
natural resources 5, 75, 239-285, 409-16
  see mining, forestry, fisheries industry
  sustainability 260, 263-70
  'resource curse' 5, 275-85
Nauru 3, 69, 85, 88-89, 140
New Caledonia 2-3, 5, 86, 224, 317-48
  elections 317-48
  Matignon and Noumea Accords 317, 319, 320, 333-8, 341-2, 346
  nickel mining 86
  power sharing 317-48
New Zealand 3, 27, 28, 33, 41-43, 66-72, 75, 78, 81, 83, 85-91, 93, 109, 110, 112, 114, 115, 122, 130, 131, 137-141, 148-9, 155, 156, 158, 160, 162, 203, 213, 217-231, 309, 311, 354, 366-7
  immigration policy 86-87, 140, 148-9, 155, 156
NFP (National Federation Party), see Fiji, political parties
NGOs (non-governmental organisations) 23-42, 141, 156, 159, 162, 164, 170, 182, 205, 251, 265, 269, 270, 365, 411
Niue 3, 66-67, 76, 78, 84, 87, 138, 142
Northern Marianas 2, 71

ODA (official development assistance), see aid

PACER (Pacific Agreement on Closer Economic Relations) 28, 31, 32, 42, 47, 140-1, 148-9, 170, 309
Pacific Islands Forum and Secretariat 2, 4, 27-29, 31-33, 43-55, 86, 132, 139, 149, 160, 162, 164, 206
See Pacific Plan
Pacific Plan 4, 32-34, 43-55, 86, 132, 139, 173
Pacific Way 47-48, 50, 54
Palau 3, 67, 68, 81, 145
PANG (Pacific Network on Globalisation) 31-2
Papua New Guinea 1, 3, 5, 6, 30, 61-64, 65, 66, 71, 74, 84, 86, 89, 240-1, 259-85, 385-98, 399-407
  corruption 6, 279, 385, 388-91, 393, 395, 397, 400, 405

crime 62
Development Forum 281-2
governance 259-85, 385-98
HIV/AIDS 387, 393
media 385-98
mining 5, 241, 259-85
opposition to economic restructuring 30
Organic Law on the Integrity of Political Parties and Candidates 399-400, 404-5
poverty 61-63
rights-based approach to democracy 399-407
royalties 276
urbanisation 61-63, 66, 84
violence 62
PICTA (Pacific Island Countries Trade Agreement) 27-28, 31, 32, 53, 140, 170, 223-226, 309
Pitcairn 66, 91
Porgera Joint Venture, 261, 263-6, 269-70
poverty 4, 5, 20, 29, 36, 43, 60-63, 65, 66, 85, 91, 96, 110, 117, 125, 139, 193, 194, 197, 214, 217, 223, 230-1, 233-4, 278, 279, 298, 299, 306, 308-11, 395-6, 403
power sharing 317-48

Qarase, Laisenia 160, 202, 223, 233, 291, 293, 304, 307, 310, 325-30, 333, 341

Rabuka, Sitiveni 291-2, 298, 307, 320, 324
RAMSI (Regional Assistance Mission to Solomon Islands), see Solomon Islands
remittances 3, 4, 59-80, 83, 86-88, 92-96, 107-20, 121-35, 138-43, 147-9, 152, 158, 161, 162, 164, 180-2, 190, 201-6, 208, 212, 215, 311, 354, 370
   investment of remittances 73-76, 78, 79, 147
   second generation remittances 77, 121-35, 147
Rokotuivuna, Amelia 23, 35, 37

Samoa 1, 3, 5-6, 28, 34, 41, 63, 66-7, 69, 70-75, 81, 82, 84, 86, 91-94, 110, 115, 137, 138, 142, 145, 240, 349-71
   Constitution 349-61
   corruption 354-7, 370
   fa'a Samoa 5, 359-360, 363
   Human Rights Protection Party 349-61
   labour migration 4, 66, 69, 70-75, 81, 82, 84, 86, 91-93
   leadership 349-61
   matai titles 349-71
   remittances 72-75, 92-93, 142, 354
   second generation Samoans in New Zealand 72, 75, 354
   TPA protests 1990s 351, 353-6, 360
SDL (*Soqosoqo Duavata ni Lewenivanua*), see Fiji, political parties
security 32-33, 45, 46, 47, 54, 202, 246, 323, 325, 400, 409, 412, 415
Solomon Islands 1, 3, 5, 6, 19, 41, 63, 64, 67, 71, 84, 113, 157, 164, 173, 239-57, 259, 285, 289, 409-16
   churches 411
   communication 411
   corruption 410, 411
   fisheries 414
   forestry 5, 239-57, 414-5
   governance 409-16
   impact of civil unrest 246
   land ownership 409-14
   mining 241
   Regional Assistance Mission to Solomon Islands 6, 173, 409-16
   royalty payments 253
   women 411-13
Somare, Sir Michael, 42, 387
SPARTECA (South Pacific Regional Trade and Economic Cooperation Agreement), 195, 213, 218-9, 221-4
suicide 69, 145, 309
Sukuna, Ratu Sir Lala 290-92
Sutherland, William 51-52
SVT (*Soqosoqo ni Vakavulewa ni Taukei*), see Fiji, political parties

Tokelau 66, 72, 87
Tonga 1, 3, 4, 28-30, 41, 63, 64, 66-79, 81, 82, 84, 86, 87, 90-93, 95, 110-11, 115, 121-35, 137, 138, 142, 145, 147, 160, 223, 314, 359, 360, 361, 386
    civil service strike 2005 30, 130
    democracy movement 29, 30
    labour migration 4, 66, 70, 71, 79, 81, 82, 84, 86, 91-92, 110-11, 121-35, 137
    remittances 4, 68, 72-75, 79, 110-11, 121-35, 142
    tourism 47, 60, 69, 74, 81, 95, 116, 122, 138, 142, 143, 198, 212, 223, 305, 311
Tuvalu 3, 64, 66, 69, 70-73, 75, 85-87, 95, 137-8, 142, 146, 155, 161

Ulufa'alu, Bartholomew 254
unemployment 43, 60-63, 65, 66, 85, 91, 96, 112, 121, 132, 138, 139, 143, 149, 152, 164, 199, 222, 223, 308, 311
UN Millennium Development Goals 52, 83, 192
United States of America 2-3, 7, 41, 66, 68, 72, 81, 82, 85, 86-87, 90-92, 112, 114, 115, 121, 126, 131, 137, 138, 143, 162, 176, 189, 196, 203, 217, 218, 225, 227, 233, 240-1, 309, 310
University of the South Pacific 28, 31, 35, 36, 42, 46, 178
urbanisation 4, 16, 61-66, 70, 72, 84, 93, 96, 137, 144, 145, 189-90, 196-202, 207, 214, 292, 308, 413
    peri-urban settlements 61-62, 65, 66, 197, 200-2, 308
Urwin, Greg 148, 160

Vanuatu 3, 28, 30, 41, 42, 62-63, 64, 65, 84, 157, 173, 240, 242
    Blacksands settlement (Port Vila) 62, 65, 66

Wallis and Futuna 3, 138, 142
World Bank 2, 13, 24, 27, 30, 41, 60, 139, 147, 201, 204, 208, 212, 391, 395
World Social Forum 23, 26
WTO (World Trade Organisation) 2, 24-31, 85, 107, 189, 191, 192, 297, 309-11

Made in the USA
Lexington, KY
05 December 2011